Tech-Economic Dynamics and Regional Growth Strategies

Jean Vasile Andrei
https://orcid.org/0000-0002-8332-6537
National Institute for Economic Research "Costin C. Kiriţescu", Romania

Ioan Sebastian Brumă
https://orcid.org/0000-0002-0549-5474
"Gheorghe Zane" Institute for Economic and Social Research, Romania

Jonel Subić
https://orcid.org/0000-0003-1342-1325
Institute of Agricultural Economics, Serbia

Dumitru Nancu
https://orcid.org/0000-0002-3278-0297
Ovidius University of Constanta, Romania

Mile Vasić
https://orcid.org/0000-0002-5637-9289
SRH University Berlin, Germany

IGI Global
Scientific Publishing
Publishing Tomorrow's Research Today

Vice President of Editorial Melissa Wagner
Director of Acquisitions Mikaela Felty
Director of Book Development Jocelynn Hessler
Production Manager Mike Brehm
Cover Design Jose Rosado

Published in the United States of America by
IGI Global Scientific Publishing
701 East Chocolate Avenue
Hershey, PA, 17033, USA
Tel: 717-533-8845 | Fax: 717-533-7115
Website: https://www.igi-global.com E-mail: cust@igi-global.com

Library of Congress Cataloging-in-Publication Data

LCCN: 2025022539 (CIP Data Pending)
ISBN13: 979-8-3373-2898-0
Isbn13Softcover: 9798337328997
EISBN13: 9798337329000

British Cataloguing in Publication Data
A Cataloguing in Publication record for this book is available from the British Library.

Editorial Advisory Board

Table of Contents

Detailed Table of Contents

In global circumstances of climate change and disturbed water cycles, maintaining yield stabilization and further support to food security require implementation of irrigation systems. Frequent irrigation and increase in fresh water scarcity are opposing sides in many areas. Therefore, active adjustment of agriculture, mainly crop production, to climate change issues strongly relies on technical-technological progress. Strivings to approach the Agriculture 4.0 or even 5.0 concept, while to fortify the resilience of agri-food production in a long run, generally asks the appliance of fully automated irrigation systems linking the water supply and crop needs in specific moment. Performed research provide deep insight in economic justification of investment in mentioned systems done by one regionally recognized agricultural company in Serbia. According to derived results for applied static and dynamic methods for economic assessment of investment efficiency, established irrigation system could be assumed as good business alternative in securing the company incomes.

The integration of Serbian companies into global agro-industrial chains, particularly in the raspberry sector, has brought significant changes in business operations and distribution. Prior to 2014, Serbian companies such as Yugent Food and Frucom Food were dependent on intermediaries, leading to price fluctuations and uncertainty in product placement. However, following the acquisition by Roger Descours Group,

and municipalities that have leveraged innovative financial instruments to fund circular economy projects such as sustainable packaging, renewable materials, waste-to-energy technologies, and product-as-a-service business models. The paper also identifies challenges such as inconsistent sustainability metrics, greenwashing risks, and the need for stronger collaboration between financial institutions, governments, and innovators.

The chapter investigates how digital technologies transform the worldwide dairy industry by analyzing their effects on productivity levels, environmental sustainability and rural economic growth. The chapter examines IoT sensors and artificial intelligence used for herd health monitoring, blockchain technology for supply chain traceability and advanced data analytics to explain how these technologies will enable precision farming, optimize resource allocation, and improve animal welfare. The analysis recognizes the wider social and structural effects, which include changes in labor needs and requirements for new skills and ongoing digital inclusion problems in rural areas. The chapter examines policy frameworks that appear necessary for achieving sustainable digital adoption that benefits all stakeholders. The analysis positions digital transformation as a complex socio-economic phenomenon rather than viewing technology as a universal solution, thereby providing strategic guidance for dairy industry stakeholders who aim to sustain innovation while ensuring inclusivity and resilience.

The current chapter examines the European sustainable rural development policies based on multifunctional farming and farm entrepreneurship linked to diversification. When it comes to sustainable development policies,multifunctional farming and farm entrepreneurship engaged in diversification are part of the agenda as well.

Furthermore, the views, experiences and expectations of rural residents involved in the aforementioned field are of particular importance for evaluating the effectiveness of the European rural development policies drawn in this study. Empirically, a qualitative approach has been employed utilising semi-structured interviews with sixteen farmers and rural residents to detect their opinions on the European funded programmes wherein they are involved and to assess the effectiveness of European rural development policies. The study revealed, among others, that European support policies are vital despite any existing obstacles indicated that European programmes contribute to changing the way agriculture is produced and lead to sustainability.

Serbia has high-quality natural, social and human resources for the development of rural tourism. The problem of rural tourism is that supply is located in rural areas and demand is located in city centers. Role of marketing is to connect supply and demand. Until now demand for rural tourism is mostly come from domestic market, but the interest of tourists come from a broad. The promotion of rural tourism, as an additional activity on agricultural farms, is important in many ways. Primarily for the purpose of increasing tourist traffic, but also the development of agrarian entrepreneurship, increasing the income of agricultural farms, as well as stopping process of depopulation rural areas in the Serbia. Nowadays exsist many maketing tools how to communcate opposite sides of market – supply and demand. In order to develop promotion in rural tourism, adequate investments are also needed. The aim of the paper is to analyze the current forms of promotion of rural tourism, as well as to present development opportunities in this important segment of the marketing mix.

This chapter looks at Serbian rural development in the context of the digital economy, covering a variety of socioeconomic initiatives aimed at rural communities and defined by rural policy. Therefore, this chapter's goal is to examine Serbian rural growth in the digital economy from two perspectives: (1) the application of digital marketing and (2) the deployment of precision agriculture technologies. For businesses looking to achieve sustainable success in Serbia's dynamic agro-product trade, digital marketing is an essential component. The authors also examine examples of rural areas in Serbia that have successfully implemented modern digital technologies, with the aim of establishing a framework for effective transformation and modernization in this domain. The research findings may contribute to the advancement of rural areas in Serbia, specifically through the application of digital marketing strategies and the adoption of precision agriculture systems.

The research objective is carbon farming, here encompassing sustainable soil management practices for soil organic carbon sequestration and/or soil GHG emissions reduction in croplands and grasslands, and business model that generates farmers reward for climate change mitigation outcomes and co-benefits for environment and society. After reviewing the main issues of carbon farming and its role in climate change mitigation policy, the authors analyzed pedoclimatic conditions, land use dynamics and management, carbon content in agricultural soils, and farm structure in main agricultural regions of Serbia-Vojvodina and Central Serbia. The research results, together with findings on carbon farming mechanisms, allow the authors to consider the region-specific combination of carbon farming practices and business models relevant to Serbian agriculture on the path to EU membership, as well as the main barriers to their adoption. Further research should include engaging stakeholders in testing identified carbon farming solutions to ensure fine-tuned policy design.

A complex universe, with a rich history and traditions passed down from one generation to another, with a unique rhythm of life, the Romanian rural environment is a vast space, with a specific cultural, economic and cultural identity, covering 85% of Romania's surface and hosting 9645.9 thousand inhabitants (44.2% of the total population). Beyond the main challenges, as depopulation and aging of the population, the lack of qualified labour, poor infrastructure, difficult access to financing, lack of support, lack of know-how, competition from large companies, rural area hides a significant development potential, which is based on rich natural and cultural resources, authentic traditions and a close connection with nature. In this context, the chapter addresses the Romanian entrepreneurship landscape and a responsible business model, and its aim is to contribute to current empirical research through a real-life experience.

The success of a business in today's world depends on acquiring and developing the necessary digital knowledge and skills. More than ever, entrepreneurship relies on advancements in digital technologies, particularly in areas such as digital marketing, the effective use of communication and collaboration tools, financial management applications, and access to online platforms that offer various courses to enhance entrepreneurial skills. According to official data (Eurostat, Micro & small businesses, 2024), the European Union had 32.3 million enterprises in 2022, employing 160.1 million people. Of these, micro and small enterprises accounted for 77.5 million employees, representing almost half of the total workforce in enterprises. Considering the importance of digitalization in modern business, this paper analyzes the Digital Intensity Index (DII), which measures the use of 12 different digital technologies by companies, with a particular focus on small and medium-sized enterprises.

This chapter explores the theoretical bases for transition economics, focusing on market reform models like liberalization, privatization, and stabilization. It compares shock therapy and gradualism and highlights the role that institutional change and governance can play in determining the outcomes for reform efforts. The chapter also discusses criticism against orthodox reform paradigms as well as introducing emerging frameworks that incorporate dimensions of equity, sustainability, and local development.

Preface

The twenty-first century economy is defined by intertwined forces: digitalization, decarbonization, and demographic transition. These processes do not operate in isolation; they reinforce or constrain one another through complex feedbacks. Regions that understand and manage these interactions can build adaptive, knowledge-based systems capable of sustained and inclusive growth. Those that fail to do so risk stagnation, dependency, and divergence. Policy frameworks such as the European Green Deal and CAP reforms promise sustainability, but implementation depends on local capacity, governance, and participation. Within this complex reality, the chapters collected in this edited volume provide empirical evidence, critical insights, and pragmatic visions in field of tech-economic dynamics and regional growth strategies.

The volume Tech-Economic Dynamics and Regional Growth Strategies addresses one of the central challenges of our time: how technology, economic structure, and spatial policy interact to shape patterns of regional development. As global economies undergo accelerating digital transformation and ecological transition, the traditional boundaries between innovation, production, and territorial governance have become increasingly porous. The book tries to respond to this complexity by integrating theoretical reflection with empirical investigation, offering a multidisciplinary view of how technological change can be converted into balanced and sustainable regional growth.

CHAPTER OVERVIEW

The first chapter, *Evaluation of Investments in Automated Systems for Irrigation of Agricultural Areas*, initiates this dialogue by placing technology at the core of agricultural adaptation to climate change. It demonstrates, through rigorous economic assessment, that automation in irrigation is not merely a technological luxury but an economic necessity in regions affected by unpredictable rainfall and water scarcity. The findings underscore a principle that resonates throughout the book:

sustainability and profitability are no longer opposing goals but two dimensions of the same rational strategy.

The second chapter, *The Impact of Agro-Industrial Enterprise Integration on the Competitiveness of the Serbian Raspberry Market*, turns attention to the social and economic transformations within globalized agri-food chains. Through the case of Serbia's raspberry industry, the authors reveal how foreign investment and vertical integration can stabilize markets while simultaneously generating new forms of dependency. This duality—stability through integration and vulnerability through concentration—captures the essence of many transitional economies navigating global capitalism.

The third chapter, *Redefining Food Sovereignty: The Strategic Role of Local Food Systems and Short Food Supply Chains*, shifts the analytical focus from global markets to local autonomy. It presents food sovereignty not as a nostalgic retreat to the past, but as a structured, policy-supported alternative capable of restoring balance between producers, consumers, and ecosystems. Local Food Systems and Short Food Supply Chains are portrayed as instruments for community empowerment, but also as frameworks that demand deliberate governance and equitable access to thrive.

The fourth chapter, *Bridging Green Innovation and Finance: Circular Economy Transitions by Green Financial Instruments*, introduces the economic architecture necessary to sustain environmental transformation. By examining green bonds, ESG frameworks, and sustainability-linked loans, it demonstrates that financial innovation is indispensable for operationalizing ecological innovation. The discussion reveals the tension between genuine sustainability and the growing risk of "greenwashing," urging a more rigorous alignment between financial instruments and measurable environmental outcomes.

The fifth chapter, *Digital Transformation in the Dairy Sector: A Multidisciplinary Approach to Rural Economic Growth*, explores digitalization as a driver of systemic change. The integration of AI, IoT sensors, and blockchain technologies in dairy production is analyzed not only for its efficiency gains but for its wider social implications—changes in labor structures, knowledge demands, and inclusivity. Digitalization, the authors argue, is a process that can either democratize opportunity or deepen inequality, depending on the surrounding policy environment.

The sixth chapter, *EU Policies for Sustainable Rural Development: Emphasizing Multifunctional Farming and Farm Entrepreneurship*, provides a policy-level reflection on European rural strategies. Drawing from qualitative data gathered through interviews with farmers, it concludes that EU programs play a decisive role in stimulating diversification, innovation, and sustainability. Yet, their effectiveness is mediated by local administrative capacity and the entrepreneurial culture of rural residents—factors that remain uneven across the Union's periphery.

The seventh chapter, *Importance of Promotion for Development of Rural Tourism and Agricultural Entrepreneurship in the Republic of Serbia*, brings to light the underexplored potential of rural tourism as a form of economic revitalization. Marketing and promotion are presented as bridges between rural supply and urban demand, with clear implications for income diversification and demographic stability. The analysis calls for professionalized communication strategies and investments that treat tourism not as a seasonal supplement but as a long-term development tool.

In Chapter Eight, *Rural Development of Serbia in the Era of the Digital Economy*, the digital transition is examined through the dual lenses of marketing and precision agriculture. The authors show how rural enterprises can harness data and connectivity to improve competitiveness and sustainability, but they also stress the necessity of institutional support and training to ensure that digital transformation does not exacerbate rural inequalities.

Chapter Nine, *Prospects for Carbon Farming in Serbian Agriculture*, situates agriculture within the global climate agenda. It identifies carbon farming as both a mitigation strategy and a potential economic opportunity for Serbian farmers. Through the analysis of soil carbon dynamics and land-use structures, the chapter envisions new business models where ecological stewardship is financially rewarded—aligning national agriculture with European Green Deal objectives.

Chapter Ten, *Romanian Rural Entrepreneurship: From Challenges and Opportunities to Sustainable Business Models*, expands the geographic and conceptual scope by focusing on the Romanian countryside. It presents a nuanced portrait of rural entrepreneurship caught between structural challenges—aging populations, weak infrastructure, limited financing—and latent potential rooted in cultural and natural capital. The chapter argues for the creation of locally adapted business models that valorize authenticity, tradition, and community cohesion as assets for sustainable development.

Chapter Eleven, *The Importance of Digital Knowledge for a Successful Entrepreneurial Venture*, turns the discussion toward human capital. Drawing on EU data, it demonstrates that digital literacy is now a fundamental determinant of entrepreneurial success. The chapter emphasizes that investment in skills and digital education is not ancillary but central to the competitiveness of micro and small enterprises in modern economies.

Chapter Twelve, *Transition Economics and Market Reforms*, provides theoretical grounding for understanding systemic economic change. It revisits the major reform paradigms—shock therapy and gradualism—while highlighting that institutional robustness and governance quality, rather than speed of liberalization, are the key determinants of sustainable transition outcomes. This reflection links the micro-level analyses of previous chapters with broader macroeconomic processes.

The volume ends with Chapter thirteen, *A Participatory Vision of Local Producers Regarding the Future Development of Specific Activities*, which re-centers the human element in the development process. Based on participatory research with local producers in northeastern Romania, the chapter highlights the importance of collective visioning, social capital, and institutional involvement in shaping the trajectory of local markets. Development, it suggests, is most resilient when communities articulate and co-own the processes that affect them.

This volume is intended for researchers, policymakers, and practitioners seeking to understand and shape the evolving relationship between technology and regional development. By integrating theory with case-based analysis, it provides conceptual clarity and practical guidance for designing strategies that link innovation with inclusive growth.

Jean Vasile Andrei

National Institute for Economic Research "Costin C. Kiriţescu", Romania & Petroleum-Gas University of Ploiesti, Romania

Ioan Sebastian Brumă

"Gh. Zane" Institute for Economic and Social Research, Romania

Jonel Subić

Institute of Agricultural Economics, Belgrade, RS Serbia

Dumitru Nancu

Ovidius University of Constanta, Romania

Mile Vasić

SRH University Berlin, Germany

Acknowledgment

The editors gratefully acknowledge the invaluable contributions of all those knowledge, effort, and dedication made this volume, "Techno-Economic Dynamics and Regional Growth Strategies", possible. Their collaboration, ideas, and continued support provided the intellectual and practical support that allowed this book to take shape and contribute to ongoing discussions in the field.

We extend our sincere gratitude to IGI Global Scientific Publishing for offering the opportunity to publish this edited volume and for the consistent support provided throughout the process. Our special appreciation goes to Ms. Amelia Bucher for her direct involvement, professionalism, and commitment in guiding the book through the publishing process.

The editors also wish to thank all those who contributed, directly or indirectly, to the realization of this work. Their constructive feedback, thoughtful reviews, insightful comments, and continuous support in promoting and guiding the project were invaluable to the success of Techno-Economic Dynamics and Regional Growth Strategies, without their dedication and collaboration, the completion of this book would not have been possible.

Chapter 1
Evaluation of Investments in Automated Systems for Irrigation of Agricultural Areas

Marko Janez Jelocnik
https://orcid.org/0000-0003-4875-1789
Institute of Agricultural Economics, Belgrade, Serbia

Jonel Vasa Subić
https://orcid.org/0000-0003-1342-1325
Institute of Agricultural Economics, Belgrade, Serbia

ABSTRACT

In global circumstances of climate change and disturbed water cycles, maintaining yield stabilization and further support to food security require implementation of irrigation systems. Frequent irrigation and increase in fresh water scarcity are opposing sides in many areas. Therefore, active adjustment of agriculture, mainly crop production, to climate change issues strongly relies on technical-technological progress. Strivings to approach the Agriculture 4.0 or even 5.0 concept, while to fortify the resilience of agri-food production in a long run, generally asks the appliance of fully automated irrigation systems linking the water supply and crop needs in specific moment. Performed research provide deep insight in economic justification of investment in mentioned systems done by one regionally recognized agricultural company in Serbia. According to derived results for applied static and dynamic methods for economic assessment of investment efficiency, established irrigation system could be assumed as good business alternative in securing the company incomes.

DOI: 10.4018/979-8-3373-2898-0.ch001

INTRODUCTION

Water is a prerequisite for life. It's one of the major constituents of all living organisms, as it usually involves around 70% of their overall mass. So, it is definitely indispensable for humans, and other living things existence (Del Giudice et al., 2009; Kilic, 2020). In nature, it could be found in 3 physical forms (liquid, gas, and solid), while all of them are useful in several ways to human population. Today, water covers almost ¾ of the Earth, mainly contained in oceans. It could exist as salty and fresh water, or surface and groundwater (Okafor, 2011; Chakraborty, 2021). The fresh water is the most necessary, while less than 3% of overall volume of water worldwide is fresh, or suitable enough for drink or irrigation. Basically, the most part of fresh water is captured in form of ice at higher altitudes, or less than one per mile is available within the lakes and rivers (Jackson et al., 2001).

Sustainability of agricultural production, both plant growing or animal breeding, or even aquaculture deeply depends on availability of sufficient volume of fresh water (Rockström et al., 2009; Banaduc et al., 2022). Agriculture is the major freshwater consumer among the sectors of global economy. Some estimation shows that it consumes around 70% of total sum of freshwater withdrawals (mostly for irrigation), or even more including food processing industry (Kay et al., 2022; Egbo et al., 2023).

During the rhetorical linking agriculture and water, usually the first thought is irrigation. Irrigation could be seen as man-controlled water supply to the plant, mainly performed in agriculture. Basically, it is water support to crop production, as it represents the substitution or supplement to precipitation in areas with disturbed rainfall patterns or insufficient water availability in local natural surroundings. It technically secures expected crop growth and yielding, pairing the plant requirements for water with controlled volume of water portions in predefined time schedule (Osman, 2013; Jeločnik et al., 2016; Naorem et al., 2023).

Currently, there are two actual issues that are affecting the formal shaping of the future of agriculture, primarily segment of crop production. No matter to established system of plant production (dry farming or under the irrigation), or implemented type of irrigation at the farm, yields stability is endangered by intensified processes of climate change (mainly its negative side), as well as general trend of spreading the profound scarcity of available fresh water worldwide. What this mean in practice?

Firstly, water cycling in nature has continuity, predefined patterns and dynamics set through the ultra-long period. It determines the water movement schemes within the all Earth zones (including atmosphere too). Mainly affected by climate changes, there comes to certain disturbances (micro-interruptions or certain level of delay in process' sequencing) in water cycles that have global influence on nature. Agriculture and other economy sectors, or entire ecosystems and human society are intensively pressed by opposite weather extremes, in previous time usually with increase in occurrence of catastrophic accidents. From huge floods and mega storms (including hurricanic winds, hail storms, heavy rains, etc.), to intensive drying of territories with generally fertile soil (including droughts, frequent heat waves, etc.), or introducing and expansion of desertification process even in unexpected locations worldwide. At the end, agri-food sector has already suffered harmful impact of climate change (Ledger, Milner, 2015; Woodward et al., 2016; Zubović et al., 2018; Jeločnik et al., 2019; Whitt, 2022; El Moll, 2023).

On the other side, there is emerging issue of fresh water scarcity. Significant growth in world population, intensive urbanization, as well as industrial and society progress have been requiring more and more fresh water for many activities. In many macro or micro regions, local authorities make the selection of activities giving them seasonal or constant priority in fresh water consumption (for communal use, mainly for drinking, for agro-food production, processing industry, etc.). Mentioned prioritization is so difficult process, as all underlined activities are necessary in daily routine of certain local community. Besides, in many territories, striving for rapid economic development at all costs leads to pollution of water streams or lakes, or underground water basins. Share of food processing industry (mainly dairy and meat industry) and agriculture (use of agrochemicals) in that process is significant. In same time, intensive agriculture (frequent and abundant irrigation) initiates depletion of natural water reservoirs, as happened in some zones within the corn belt in USA (Malmqvist, Rundle, 2002; Baron et al., 2002; Subic, Jelocnik, 2013; Arsić et al., 2018; Evett et al., 2020; Gleick, Cooley, 2021; Mishra, 2023).

There is need for brief run through the irrigation and its historical correspondence with agriculture and food supply. As it is known, water availability is essential for implementation of irrigation. From ancient times to couple centuries ago (agriculture 1.0), plant production was mainly based on dry farming, while irrigation was applied in hinterland or basins of huge rivers. It considers just plain seasonal river flooding or digging a water channels through the cultivated area for water spreading and its further manual or natural withdrawal. In next step, „green revolution" (agriculture 2.0) brings to agriculture several things, among all, mechanization of performed activities, appliance of agrochemicals, or development of irrigation concept and implementation of few irrigation systems usually powered by machine (different pumps). In this period, irrigation starts to spread more intensively worldwide, while farmers were facing with plentiful fresh water sources. Water was very often used inefficiently. As was mentioned, irrigation has been exercised for centuries during the ruling of several old civilizations, but just with rapid growth of human population there come to quick enlargement of irrigated areas and acceleration in development of irrigation systems (XX and XXI centuries could be considered as period when irrigation was generally ranked as the major water consumer). For example, immediately after II WW the irrigated areas were doubled, while they did the same until the end of last century (Pinstrup Andersen, Hazell, 1985; Ameen, Raza, 2017; Angelakis et al., 2020; Valipour et al., 2020).

During the end of XX century, use of irrigation has been faced few issues, as are negative environmental footprint, water scarcity, awareness of climate change, etc. Agriculture at that time required shift to 2nd green revolution, while entering the agriculture 3.0 was primarily based on scientific progress. Introduction of nanotechnologies, development of new water conservation practices, discovering new materials and initiation of real step forward in automation and IT sector enables launching of precise agriculture. It provides optimization of irrigation processes towards available volume of fresh water and plants requirements (emergence of drip, micro-irrigation, or subsurface irrigation systems), increase in mobility of irrigation systems, combined use of various fertilizers and pesticides within the irrigation process, etc. (Sojka et al., 2002; Pandey et al., 2022).

At the beginning of XXI century, agriculture has been involved into the digital revolution (agriculture 4.0). It strives to pair the modern information technology with common practices in agriculture, mainly by the use of IoT, different sensors, drones and upgraded robotics, GPS technology, various high-resolution images, real-time and big data, AI, etc. The main intention was to support overall farming sustainability by the use of sophisticated technologies, that will lead to costs reduction or their elimination, stabilization of yields, optimized use of available inputs, upgrade in livestock and waste management, increase food safety, or after all improvement of farms' competitiveness at the markets. Integrating agriculture 4.0 and irrigation, i.e. involvement of smart digital technologies in more efficient use of water. Irrigation has been mainly supported by the knowledge and data-based decision-making systems, that collect, select, and analyze various data linked to soil, weather, or plant conditions, while involving renewables for irrigation process powering (Sima et al., 2020; Silva et al., 2020; Monteleone et al., 2020; Jeločnik et al., 2024; Petrović et al., 2024). As smooth advancement, there is in short time launched agriculture 5.0 as a process that gives more space to artificial intelligence, cobots and cobit platform, improved biotechnological systems, etc., basically trying to substitute human labor in core production processes or implement human centered activity (intensive collaboration between machines and humans). According to this, from irrigation systems are expected to be highly independent in exercising activities, quite efficient and economic, and resilient to climate change (predictable towards weather conditions), (Saiz Rubio, Rovira Mas, 2020; Singh, Sobti, 2022; Toth et al., 2023; Holzinger et al., 2024; Dmitrović et al., 2024).

At the end, observed globally, just some parts of the world (mainly developed countries) are ready for agriculture 4.0 or 5.0. Others (majority of developing countries) are currently missing preconditions for their implementation, while trying for the start to implement the concept of agriculture 3.0, preparing themselves slightly for digital world. In general, average farm in Serbia nowadays has to strive to overmaster the automation and optimization of agriculture (including the irrigation activity), and in later steps to join the digital league.

In that context, water scarcity and changed rainfall patterns in many regions, define irrigation as necessity, but in same time limit its use in some, up today, commonly used forms. Today's progress in science and technology offers the more or less successful solutions for approaching the fresh water and its efficient distribution to the plant. Desalination as one of solutions, at least for now is not the optimal one. It is still expensive process, formally complex, require further organization of water transport, while it is inaccessible to wider group of consumers (Karagiannis, Soldatos, 2008; Ziolkowska, 2015).

Consequently, the solution to the problem could be sought in acceptance of the concept of climate-smart agriculture (CSA), which sustainably ensures an increase in productivity and adaptability to climate change, contributing to the achievement of goals of food security and sustainable development of agriculture and rural communities. In accordance with this concept, like in several countries worldwide, the agrarian policy in Serbia is adapted to the principles of the green economy and UN's SDG goals, while it is directed towards alternatives that ensure: decrease in lagging behind of technological development to competing countries; effective coping of the sector of agriculture with the effects of climate change; increase in efficiency and competitiveness of production and stabilizing the incomes of agricultural producers; achieving economic, ecological and social goals of sustainable development, where the multifunctional agriculture and rural development have a specific role (Jeločnik, Subić, 2022; Subić et al., 2024). As a part of mentioned, there are implemented smart irrigation systems fine-tuned to optimal water feed of specific plants and local water supply conditions (Subić et al., 2017a; Subic et al., 2017b; Bojago, Abrham, 2023; Ala'F et al., 2025).

There have to be underlined some main facts related to irrigation at global or national scale. Observed worldwide, totally irrigated areas are generally small (up to 20% of available arable land complex), while they are usually covered by technically simple or obsolete irrigation systems (Jeločnik et al., 2022). Meanwhile, according to last agricultural census (SORS, 2024), less than 10% of utilized agricultural land (UAL) is irrigated in Serbia (268,868 ha of totally available 3,239,373 ha of UAL). More closely, within the total number of registered agricultural holdings (508,325) during the season 2022/2023. around 27.5% of them (139,789 farms) have been used irrigation systems, i.e. effectively applied agrotechnical measure of irrigation.

LITERATURE REVIEW

Investments are the core of any business development and further society progress. They make the world go around (Sachs, Reid, 2006; Stiglitz, Greenwald, 2014; Zhan, Santos Paulino, 2021). In line to necessity for human existence, dealing with living organisms, and certain specificities of agriculture subsectors and individual lines, investment process in agriculture is usually very complex, demanding, and subject of various risks (Subić, 2010; Deininger, 2011; Mogues et al., 2015; Komarek et al., 2020).

From the aspect of investing, there is impossible to underline the production line or investment object in agriculture that it is the most challenging for investor, as any of them has its own specificities. Anyway, investment in irrigation system belongs to the group of demanding investments, as it interlinks crops with several elements and processes into the one whole.

Considering the existential need of food for human population, there occurs logic doubt, i.e. does any agricultural subsector or agriculture at all has to be profitable for farmer or society. So, there is smoldering conflict between economy and human existence. Similarly, if some production line is not profitable, does it have to be subsidized by state support. In same time, investment is the locomotive of initiating some activity. It is usually financed by internal or/and external capital. Knowing that, mentioned doubt could be skipped to justification if the available or borrowed capital has been used properly, while does investment have to be financially supported if it is not economically justified but it brings huge social benefit to wider population.

In initial stages, irrigation system implementation could be usually observed as investment object, that requires certain level of investment for its functioning. Technically, from any irrigation system, no matter to its complexity and technological novelty, it is expected to boost the level of gained crop yields, as well as to secure farm sustainability and food security of local community. It is hard do decide, what makes them justified to be financed? Easiness in handling and level of ergonomic, system mobility and autonomy of work, deepness of ecological footprint, initial price or costs of maintaining and appliance, effectiveness in applying related to spent water, type of used system or level of innovation it brings, etc.

Whichever system is in producers focus, it requires economic (investment) analysis as a basis for making the adequate farmers' or agro-enterprise decision. Similar consideration towards investment also has policymaker, as in accordance to derived parameters of investment analysis there should be chosen proper support measure or level of its intensity, or way how it will be implemented, etc. Mentioned is done with the goal to officially popularize irrigation in certain form, or like agrotechnical measure at all as it represents a trustful instrument in accomplishing food security.

Both, producer and local community has to be aware what the overall investment include, just implementation and further exploitation of irrigation system, or previous infrastructural equipping of the production area too (electrification, water supply, ICT elements, etc.). Missing or weak condition of infrastructural elements is basically demotivating for farmers towards irrigation system establishment, as building and implementation of these elements are so expensive, while they could have multipurpose role in local community. Thus, there has to be wider consensus who is in charged for implementation of certain elements and in which level.

There are several researches that used some methods of investment analysis in order to perceive if planed implementation of irrigation system is economically justified, or under what conditions.

Ağızan and Bayramoğlu (2021) try to determine the irrigation methods or systems in which the investment is cost effective the most in condition of Turkey (sprinkler or drip irrigation systems, as well as center-pivot or linear irrigation system). According to gained values for Internal Rate of Return (IRR), Net Present Value (NPV) and payback period, they found that the most preferred alternative could be linear irrigation system. Similarly, You and associates (2014) investigates the social and economic relevance of investment in infrastructural contents important for wider community (investment in several dams) and later investment in two irrigation alternatives in Kenya (several dam-based and small-scale irrigation systems). They found that all mentioned possibilities are in the most cases economically viable for the local users. Almost the same research is done in Indonesia (Nasution et al., 2018), that proves the economic justification to invest in irrigation facility (dam) that will be use in rice growing region faced with water scarcity especially in dry part of year.

Srivastava and associates (2003) analyses the investment in drip irrigation systems that becomes so popular in India (primarily vegetable production), as a substitution of previously dominating surface irrigation. By the use of certain software package for the observing and comparing several production and economic factors applied in many crop lines, they conclude that there is no suitable solution that fits to all production circumstances, but there could be set some threshold values while marking the lines where the skip from one to another irrigation system may be justified at different crops.

In situation of increasing water scarcity in Australia, farmers are forced to be more efficient in water use for irrigation. There are developed suitable software (WaterWorks) as a support for decision making (Khan et al., 2010) in selecting the appropriate investment in water-saving irrigation systems that fits to available soil, climate and grown crops. Other researches reconsiders investment in supplemental irrigation (Paoletti, Shortridge, 2020) usually exercised in humid regions of USA, where the farmers are mainly turned to rainfed farming. Investment in such these systems could be reconsidered as a part of risk management (yields protection), particularly in years with low rainfalls. Meanwhile, Sharma and Irmak (2020), examines behave of investment in variable or fixed rate irrigation combined with fixed or variable rate fertigation in corn growing in the production conditions of the corn belt area of USA.

It is not always the water scarcity the main irrigation task. In era of energy shortage, electricity costs occurred in irrigation rapidly increased in previous decades. Mentioned make space for wider investment in use of renewables (mainly photovoltaics) for powering the irrigation systems (Carrêlo et al., 2020). Plenty of sunny days in Mediterranean region shows that investment in both low-power or large-power photovoltaics irrigation systems could be a rational solution for local farmers. Similar conclusions are made in case of Serbian vegetable production in protected or open filed. Performed researches have been shown that investment in irrigation systems powered by solar and wind energy could boosts the farm sustainability, while initially be economically justified (Jeločnik, Subić, 2021; Jeločnik et al., 2023).

USED METHODOLOGICAL FRAMEWORK

There are several research objectives provided by the research, such are: Underlining the global and local needs for practicing the irrigation in crop production, towards the current state of climate change and water availability facts; Explaining the main requirements for implementation of contemporary irrigation systems, in line to appliance of the Agriculture 2.0 to even 5.0 concepts; Exposing the main benefits and constraints related to irrigation exercising at the farm level; and Performing the investment analysis in the form of case study, i.e. implementation of modern, hi-tech irrigation system, that has to encourage all local farmers to reconsider the investment into the irrigation system.

Core of used methods are focused to economic assessment of made decision to invest in modern highly automated irrigation system. Primary data used in analysis were collected through the in-depth interviews with managing staff employed in agricultural company that plans implementation of irrigation system during the 2024. Besides, proving the initial data and verification of derived results are consulted with professionals active within the sector of automation and hydro-melioration, as well as available literature sources and datasets. Data used in analysis have been related to production year 2023/24. Gained data and results have been presented in proper tables, while all values are in EUR.

Like in some previous research, economic analysis was based on appliance of standard static and dynamic methods for investment effectiveness assessment (Total Output-Total Input Ratio (TOTIR), Net Profit Margin (NPM), Accounting Rate of

Return (ARR), or Simple Payback Period (SPP), as well as Net Present Value (NPV), Internal Rate of Return (IRR), and Dynamic Payback Period (DPP)), (Subić et al., 2013; Jeločnik, Subić, 2020; Subić et al., 2021; Jeločnik et al., 2022; Jeločnik et al., 2023). Over the all, in order to explain current necessity for the irrigation and state of its use at global and national level, after intensive literature search, there will be also used some other methods common in social sciences, as are desk research, deduction, analysis and synthesis, etc.

RESULTS WITH DISCUSSION

In focus of the performed research are agriculture enterprise, active in crop production, mainly grains and industrial crops. Enterprise is located in the north part of Serbia, while it has available huge production capacities (land complex that involves several large parcels adequate for fully mechanized land cultivation), together with appropriate mechanization, labor and production facilities. Crop production is mainly organized under the system of dry farming.

In last several years, production is significantly affected by climate change, primarily in disturbed rainfall patterns and severe drought during the vegetative season. In order to advance production results, i.e. to stabilize and increase gained yields and incomes, while expecting even the more unfavorable weather conditions in close future, enterprise management have been made decision to establish fully automated irrigation system at larger part of production areas (slightly over 9,000 ha, or exactly 9,239 ha). Before the system implementation, there is done investment analysis, as support to correctness of expressed business venture.

Planed investment involves three segments. Firstly, there are need for building facilities and establishment infrastructural elements required as precondition for irrigation system exploitation, such are pump-stations, lying of pipeline network, weirs, displacement and forming of field-protection belts and field roads, building the crossings for mechanization over the set channel network, establishment of sub-stations in field and economic yard, and wiring with 10 kV wires-network. Secondly, it is required purchase and installation of equipment for pump-stations, pipelines and armature, irrigation machines, machine equipment for weirs managing, system for remote control and managing of pump-stations and irrigation system, and equipping with telecommunication elements, especially creation of fully automated command center. Thirdly, there are planed other costs required for system establishment as are certain permits and certificates, creation of project documentation, as well as some reservations for unexpected costs.

More closely, automatization of the planed system assumes quick reaction towards the system break downs, while it has to provide timely and correct transfer of information to any element of the irrigation system. In same time, system generally does not consider engagement of the human labor, or pump system, pipelines, sprinklers and other equipment has to be remotely driven (for the purpose of system surveillance and remote managing there is planed command communication center for centralized running). Communication between the system elements will be enabled by the GPRS or radio-relay links. Interconnecting with local weather station and different soil and air sensors will allow well-timed and precise water portions through the basic or supplementary irrigation, highly adjusted to current and upcoming water needs of grown crops.

Overall investment (Table 1.) will engage almost 90 million EUR. According to structure of overall investment, the most will be invested into the facilities, equipment and mechanization, over the 70%. Establishment and running the irrigation system requires certain volume of Permanent Working Capital (PWC), while in this case it takes roughly over the 15% of total investment.

Table 1. Structure of the overall investment (in EUR)

No.	Description	Overall investment	Share in overall investment (in %)
I	**Fixed assets**	**74,508,005.50**	**83.33**
1.	Facilities	27,662,051.00	30.94
2.	Equipment and mechanization	37,127,519.00	41.53
3.	Other	9,718,435.50	10.87
II	**Permanent Working Capital**	**14,901,601.10**	**16.67**
Total (I+II)		**89,409,606.60**	**100.00**

Source: IAE, 2024.

Major part of the fixed assets will be financed by external capital (credit issued by commercial bank), while smaller part of fixed assets and whole PWC (over the ¼ of overall investment) will be covered by companies' capital (Table 2.). Used credit line is burdened by annual interest of 3% (usual interest rate at the national capital market used for infrastructural investments), repayment period is 10 years, while grace period is 2 years. Credit repayment will be done by equal annuities (semiannually).

Table 2. Structure of the sources of financing (in EUR)

No.	Description	Overall investment	Share in overall investment (in %)
I	**Own capital**	**24,620,036.60**	**27.54**
1.	Fixed assets	9,718,435.50	10.87
2.	Permanent Working Capital	14,901,601.10	16.67
II	**External capital**	**64,789,570.00**	**72.46**
1.	Fixed assets	64,789,570.00	72.46
Total (I+II)		**89,409,606.60**	**100.00**

Source: IAE, 2024.

Exploitation of realized investment will initiate creation of incomes on annual basis. Income will be contained in selling of gained crops at the local market. Simplification of investment analysis assumes constant yields and crops prices during the observed period (10 years), i.e. income is unified in each observed year. Besides, its assumed that company exercise well-established crop-rotation, in line to irrigation use (Table 3.). It has to be underlined that state subsidies as a part of investment or annual production incomes are not considered. Wherever it is possible, double cropping has been established, mainly combination of grains and certain vegetables growing or fodder crops.

Investment exploitation, i.e. irrigation process in vegetable growing is followed by certain costs (Table 4.), so investment object use generates several costs grouped into the material costs and intangible costs, while during the observed period material costs are usually around 7.5 times higher than intangible costs. Within the group of material costs, costs of energy and other material costs are dominating, while within the sum of overall intangible costs depreciation and maintaining costs are dominating. Depreciation is mainly linked to facilities (expected period of use is 40 years) and equipment and mechanization (expected period of use is 10 years). Maintaining mainly considers trimming the systems elements in order to work without delay and system downtime. From third year there come to repaying of costs of interest for used credit line, that gradually decrease up to the end of observed period. In compare to initial year in last year the costs of interests are 20 times lower.

Table 3. Forming of total incomes (in EUR)

No.	Crop	UM	Years		
			I-X		
			Price per UM	Volume in UM	Total
0	1	2	3	4	5=3x4
1.	Mercantile corn	T	174.00	9,427.71	1,640,420.94
2.	Alfalfa	T	189.40	35,540.91	6,731,448.81
3.	Mercantile wheat	T	191.00	8,669.88	1,655,946.62
4.	Seed wheat	T	210.00	1,244.07	261,255.48
5.	Winter barley	T	171.00	2,100.00	359,099.75
6.	Rye for haylage	T	42.50	2,602.32	110,598.53
7.	Seed corn	T	1,100.00	526.33	578,963.47
8.	Soybean	T	500.00	4,599.73	2,299,864.27
9.	Seed soybean	T	575.00	492.75	283,329.33
10.	Soybean - second crop	T	499.40	355.97	177,771.90
11.	Silage corn	T	45.00	22,633.18	1,018,493.04
12.	Silage corn – second crop	T	45.00	3,403.14	153,141.38
13.	Sunflower	T	380.00	721.36	274,117.80
14.	Rapeseed	T	450.00	695.22	312,848.36
15.	Sweet corn	T	115.00	2,617.18	300,975.44
16.	Peas	T	246.00	1,330.25	327,241.43
17.	Fodder peas	T	55.00	341.82	18,800.31
18.	Peas – second crop	T	246.00	8,728.78	2,147,278.95
19.	Industrial hemp	T	650.00	2,513.01	1,633,455.20
20.	Lavender	T	5,000.00	9.24	46,195.00
21.	Potatoes	T	130.00	723.72	94,083.82
Total					**20,425,329.83**

Source: IAE, 2024.

In line to formed Income statement (Table 5.), there could be seen that investment exploitation is financially liquid in any year of observed period, i.e. it generates net profit to the company. Oscillations in gained net profit are mainly the results of change in the value of paid interest to used credit from commercial bank. In order to exercise static and dynamic investment analysis, previously has to be set the economic flow of the investment exploitation (Table 6.). Generated net cash flow also confirms liquidity of investment use. There could be seen significant level of salvage value left in tenth year of investment use.

Table 4. Structure of overall costs (in EUR)

no.	Description	Years									
		I	II	III	IV	V	VI	VII	VIII	IX	X
I	**Material costs**	**1,372,905.77**	**1,372,905.77**	**1,372,905.77**	**1,372,905.77**	**1,372,905.77**	**1,372,905.77**	**1,372,905.77**	**1,372,905.77**	**1,372,905.77**	**1,372,905.77**
1.	Direct material (seed and agro-chemicals)	102,456.12	102,456.12	102,456.12	102,456.12	102,456.12	102,456.12	102,456.12	102,456.12	102,456.12	102,456.12
2.	Energy and fuel	620,681.90	620,681.90	620,681.90	620,681.90	620,681.90	620,681.90	620,681.90	620,681.90	620,681.90	620,681.90
3.	Other material costs	649,767.75	649,767.75	649,767.75	649,767.75	649,767.75	649,767.75	649,767.75	649,767.75	649,767.75	649,767.75
II	**Intangible costs**	**8,189,370.53**	**8,189,370.53**	**10,192,232.23**	**9,958,986.00**	**9,718,689.90**	**9,471,130.85**	**9,216,089.33**	**8,953,339.18**	**8,682,647.40**	**8,403,773.97**
1.	Depreciation	3,950,486.69	3,950,486.69	3,950,486.69	3,950,486.69	3,950,486.69	3,950,486.69	3,950,486.69	3,950,486.69	3,950,486.69	3,950,486.69
2.	Maintaining	3,540,970.62	3,540,970.62	3,540,970.62	3,540,970.62	3,540,970.62	3,540,970.62	3,540,970.62	3,540,970.62	3,540,970.62	3,540,970.62
3.	Insurance	511,133.74	511,133.74	511,133.74	511,133.74	511,133.74	511,133.74	511,133.74	511,133.74	511,133.74	511,133.74
4.	Labor	108,559.17	108,559.17	108,559.17	108,559.17	108,559.17	108,559.17	108,559.17	108,559.17	108,559.17	108,559.17
5.	Interest (credit line)	0.00	0.00	2,002,861.70	1,769,615.47	1,529,319.37	1,281,760.32	1,026,718.80	763,968.65	493,276.88	214,403.44
6.	Other intangible costs	78,220.32	78,220.32	78,220.32	78,220.32	78,220.32	78,220.32	78,220.32	78,220.32	78,220.32	78,220.32
Total (I+II)		**9,562,276.30**	**9,562,276.30**	**11,565,138.00**	**11,331,891.77**	**11,091,595.67**	**10,844,036.62**	**10,588,995.10**	**10,326,244.95**	**10,055,553.17**	**9,776,679.74**

Source: IAE, 2024.

Table 5. Income statement

no.	Description	Years									
		I	II	III	IV	V	VI	VII	VIII	IX	X
I	**Total incomes**	**20,425,329.83**	**20,425,329.83**	**20,425,329.83**	**20,425,329.83**	**20,425,329.83**	**20,425,329.83**	**20,425,329.83**	**20,425,329.83**	**20,425,329.83**	**20,425,329.83**
1.	Selling incomes	20,425,329.83	20,425,329.83	20,425,329.83	20,425,329.83	20,425,329.83	20,425,329.83	20,425,329.83	20,425,329.83	20,425,329.83	20,425,329.83
II	**Total expenditures**	**9,562,276.30**	**9,562,276.30**	**11,565,138.00**	**11,331,891.77**	**11,091,595.67**	**10,844,036.62**	**10,588,995.10**	**10,326,244.95**	**10,055,553.17**	**9,776,679.74**
1.	Business expenditures	9,562,276.30	9,562,276.30	9,562,276.30	9,562,276.30	9,562,276.30	9,562,276.30	9,562,276.30	9,562,276.30	9,562,276.30	9,562,276.30
1.1.	Material costs	1,372,905.77	1,372,905.77	1,372,905.77	1,372,905.77	1,372,905.77	1,372,905.77	1,372,905.77	1,372,905.77	1,372,905.77	1,372,905.77
1.2.	Intangible costs without depreciation and interest (used credit)	4,238,883.84	4,238,883.84	4,238,883.84	4,238,883.84	4,238,883.84	4,238,883.84	4,238,883.84	4,238,883.84	4,238,883.84	4,238,883.84
1.3.	Depreciation	3,950,486.69	3,950,486.69	3,950,486.69	3,950,486.69	3,950,486.69	3,950,486.69	3,950,486.69	3,950,486.69	3,950,486.69	3,950,486.69
2.	Financial expenditures	0.00	0.00	2,002,861.70	1,769,615.47	1,529,319.37	1,281,760.32	1,026,718.80	763,968.65	493,276.88	214,403.44
2.1.	Interest (used credit)	0.00	0.00	2,002,861.70	1,769,615.47	1,529,319.37	1,281,760.32	1,026,718.80	763,968.65	493,276.88	214,403.44
III	**Gross profit (I-II)**	**10,863,053.54**	**10,863,053.54**	**8,860,191.84**	**9,093,438.07**	**9,333,734.17**	**9,581,293.21**	**9,836,334.74**	**10,099,084.89**	**10,369,776.66**	**10,648,650.09**
IV	**Tax income (20%)**	2,172,610.71	2,172,610.71	1,772,038.37	1,818,687.61	1,866,746.83	1,916,258.64	1,967,266.95	2,019,816.98	2,073,955.33	2,129,730.02
V	**Net profit (III-IV)**	**8,690,442.83**	**8,690,442.83**	**7,088,153.47**	**7,274,750.45**	**7,466,987.33**	**7,665,034.57**	**7,869,067.79**	**8,079,267.91**	**8,295,821.33**	**8,518,920.07**

Source: IAE, 2024.

Table 6. Economic flow

no.	Description	Zero moment	Years									
			I	II	III	IV	V	VI	VII	VIII	IX	X
I	**Total incomes**	**0,00**	**20,425,329.83**	**20,425,329.83**	**20,425,329.83**	**20,425,329.83**	**20,425,329.83**	**20,425,329.83**	**20,425,329.83**	**20,425,329.83**	**20,425,329.83**	**51,911,819.06**
1.	Selling incomes	0,00	20,425,329.83	20,425,329.83	20,425,329.83	20,425,329.83	20,425,329.83	20,425,329.83	20,425,329.83	20,425,329.83	20,425,329.83	20,425,329.83
2.	Salvage value	0,00	0.00	0.00	0.00	0.00	0.00	0.00	0.00	0.00	0.00	31,486,489.23
	2.1. Fixed assets	0,00										16,584,888.13
	2.2. PWC	0,00										14,901,601.10
II	**Total expenditure**	**89,409,606.60**	**7,784,400.32**	**7,784,400.32**	**7,383,827.98**	**7,430,477.22**	**7,478,536.44**	**7,528,048.25**	**7,579,056.56**	**7,631,606.59**	**7,685,744.94**	**7,741,519.63**
3.	Investment value	89,409,606.60										
	3.1. In fixed assets	74,508,005.50										
	3.2. In PWC	14,901,601.10										
4.	Costs without depreciation and interest	0,00	5,611,789.61	5,611,789.61	5,611,789.61	5,611,789.61	5,611,789.61	5,611,789.61	5,611,789.61	5,611,789.61	5,611,789.61	5,611,789.61
5.	Tax income	0.00	2,172,610.71	2,172,610.71	1,772,038.37	1,818,687.61	1,866,746.83	1,916,258.54	1,967,266.95	2,019,816.98	2,073,955.33	2,129,730.02
III	**Net cash flow (I-II)**	**-89,409,606.60**	**12,640,929.52**	**12,640,929.52**	**13,041,501.86**	**12,994,852.61**	**12,946,793.39**	**12,897,281.58**	**12,846,273.28**	**12,793,723.25**	**12,739,584.89**	**44,170,299.43**

Source: IAE, 2024.

Static Assessment of the Investment

Static methods do not consider time value of money. They assess the investment through a single short period, mainly predefined year where is assumed that investment is running in full capacity (Poggensee, Poggensee, 2021; Jelocnik et al., 2022; Zatrochova, Katrencik, 2023). In this case tenth year of system functioning is considered as representative, while indicators gained in that year are used for evaluation of investment successfulness. Related the available static methods, next have been used: Total Output-Total Input Ratio (TOTIR), Net Profit Margin (NPM), Accounting Rate of Return (ARR), or Simple Payback Period (SPP).

Total Output-Total Input Ratio (TOTIR)

In all years of loan repayment (observed period), including the representative one, Total Output-Total Input Ratio (TOTIR) is over the one (Table 7.), pointing out that overall incomes are greater than total expenditures, while there could be considered that the investment is economical.

Table 7. Total Output-Total Input Ratio (TOTIR = TI / TE > 1, in EUR)

Years	TI (Total incomes – products selling)	TE (Total expenditures)	TOTIR
0	1	2	3 = 1/2
I	20,425,329.83	9,562,276.30	2.14
II	20,425,329.83	9,562,276.30	2.14
III	20,425,329.83	11,565,138.00	1.77
IV	20,425,329.83	11,331,891.77	1.80
V	20,425,329.83	11,091,595.67	1.84
VI	20,425,329.83	10,844,036.62	1.88
VII	20,425,329.83	10,588,995.10	1.93
VIII	20,425,329.83	10,326,244.95	1.98
IX	20,425,329.83	10,055,553.17	2.03
X*	20,425,329.83	9,776,679.74	2.09

*Representative year (exploitation in full capacity)
Source: IAE, 2024.

Net Profit Margin (NPM) and Accounting Rate of Return (ARR)

Over the entire observed period (not just in representative year), Net Profit Margin (NPM) and Accounting Rate of Return (ARR) are over than pre-agreed interest rate that has to be payed to commercial bank for investment financing (3%), or even over the generally assumed interest rate (i) valid at local capital market for similar, but lower value investment (5%). Accordingly, it can be considered that the investment is accumulative and profitable, meaning that during the project exploitation all costs will be covered, while certain level of "earnings" will be made (Table 8. and Table 9.). Related to slight oscillations in Net Profit (NP), there comes to similar shifts in the values of NPM and ARR, while they are still several times above the predefined interest rate.

Table 8. Net Profit Margin (NPM = NP / TI x 100 > i, in EUR)

Years	NP (Net Profit)	TI (Total incomes – products selling)	NPM
I	8,690,442.83	20,425,329.83	42.55
II	8,690,442.83	20,425,329.83	42.55
III	7,088,153.47	20,425,329.83	34.70
IV	7,274,750.45	20,425,329.83	35.62
V	7,466,987.33	20,425,329.83	36.56
VI	7,665,034.57	20,425,329.83	37.53
VII	7,869,067.79	20,425,329.83	38.53
VIII	8,079,267.91	20,425,329.83	39.56
IX	8,295,821.33	20,425,329.83	40.62
X*	8,518,920.07	20,425,329.83	41.71

*Representative year (exploitation in full capacity)
Source: IAE, 2024.

Table 9. Accounting Rate of Return (ARR = NP / Iv x 100 > i, in EUR)

Years	NP (Net Profit)	Iv (Overall value of investment)	ARR
I	8,690,442.83	89,409,606.60	9.72
II	8,690,442.83	89,409,606.60	9.72
III	7,088,153.47	89,409,606.60	7.93
IV	7,274,750.45	89,409,606.60	8.14

continued on following page

Table 9. Continued

Years	NP (Net Profit)	Iv (Overall value of investment)	ARR
V	7,466,987.33	89,409,606.60	8.35
VI	7,665,034.57	89,409,606.60	8.57
VII	7,869,067.79	89,409,606.60	8.80
VIII	8,079,267.91	89,409,606.60	9.04
IX	8,295,821.33	89,409,606.60	9.28
X*	8,518,920.07	89,409,606.60	9.53

*Representative year (exploitation in full capacity)
Source: IAE, 2024.

Simple Payback Period (SPP)

Table 10. Simple Payback Period (T < t, in EUR)

Years	Net Cash Flow from Economic Flow	Cumulative Net Cash Flow
0	-89,409,606.60	-89,409,606.60
I	12,640,929.52	-76,768,677.08
II	12,640,929.52	-64,127,747.57
III	13,041,501.86	-51,086,245.71
IV	12,994,852.61	-38,091,393.10
V	12,946,793.39	-25,144,599.71
VI	12,897,281.58	-12,247,318.13
VII	12,846,273.28	-
VIII	12,793,723.25	-
IX	12,739,584.89	-
X	44,170,299.43	-

Source: IAE, 2024.

In line to the gained value for the Simple Payback Period (SPP), (Table 10.), investment will be repaid in 6,95 years, or 6 years and 11.44 months. By this indicator, investment could be seen as economically effective, how by investment exploiting there will be covered its entire initial value much before the moment of commercial credit expiration (10 years).

Dynamic Assessment of the Investment

Dynamic methods strictly consider the time value of the money. They respect the fact that current value of the money is not the same in near or far future, facilitating the investor to decide what to do with the money. It has to be underlined that investment is certain act of money saving, as individual is renouncing the current spending in favor to some future moment. Mainly, these methods give more objective assessment of investments as they are valuing entire period of their lifespan, or at least the period which is engaging the external capital. In line to available dynamic methods, next have been used: Internal Rate of Return (IRR), Net Present Value (NPV), and Dynamic Payback Period (DPP), (Ye et al., 2000; Cicea et al., 2008; Subić, Kuzman, 2016; Liu et al., 2019; Subić et al., 2025).

Net Present Value (NPV) and Internal Rate of Return (IRR)

During the ten years of investment exploitation, i.e. period of the loan repayment, investor could expect total increase in profit (i.e. Net Present Value), calculated by the discount rate ($i = 5\%$) to the initial moment of investment exploitation ($n = 0$), for 28,937,692.42 EUR. In same time period, the investment could be considered profitable, as investment's Internal Rate of Return is higher than the paid interest rate for the used loan ($10.34\% > 3\%$), or than the discount/weighted rate ($10.34\% > 5\%$). So, both indicators support the premise that the planned investment is economically justified (Table 11.).

Dynamic Payback Period (DPP)

According to obtained value for the Dynamic Payback Period (DPP), (Table 12.), investment will be repaid in 8,78 years, or 8 years and 9.34 months. Like in case of SPP, investment could be assumed economically effective, as by investment appliance in business activities of the company, initial value of investment will be covered almost one and a half year before the official expiration of used commercial credit (10 years).

Table 11. NPV and IRR (in EUR)

No	Description	Zero moment	Years										*Cumulative*
			I	**II**	**III**	**IV**	**V**	**VI**	**VII**	**VIII**	**IX**	**X**	
0	1	2	3	4	5	6	7	8	9	10	11	12	13
1.	Net cash flow from economic flow (columns 3 to 12)	-89,409,606.60	12,640,929.52	12,640,929.52	13,041,501.86	12,994,852.61	12,946,793.39	12,897,281.58	12,846,273.28	12,793,723.25	12,739,584.89	44,170,299.43	***159,712,169.31***
2.	Discount rate (%)	5.00	5.00	5.00	5.00	5.00	5.00	5.00	5.00	5.00	5.00	5.00	-
3.	Discount factor $(1+i)^{-n}$ or $1/(1+i)^{n}$, where i = discount rate; n = years	1.0000	0.9524	0.9070	0.8638	0.8227	0.7835	0.7462	0.7107	0.6768	0.6446	0.6139	-
4.	Current value of Net cash flow (columns 3 to 12)	-89,409,606.60	12,038,980.49	11,465,695.71	11,265,739.64	10,690,897.40	10,144,151.39	9,624,150.09	9,129,606.58	8,659,295.48	8,212,050.01	27,116,732.23	***118,347,299.02***
5.	**NPV**	**28,937,692.42**											
6.	**Relative NPV [(columns 2 to 12) / |column 2|] > i**	**0.32**											
7.	**IRR (IRR > i)**	**10.34%**											

Source: IAE, 2024.

Table 12. Dynamic Payback Period (T < t, in EUR)

Years	Current value of the Net Cash Flow from Economic Flow	Cumulative Net Cash Flow
0	-89,409,606.60	-89,409,606.60
I	12,038,980.49	-77,370,626.11
II	11,465,695.71	-65,904,930.40
III	11,265,739.64	-54,639,190.76
IV	10,690,897.40	-43,948,293.36
V	10,144,151.39	-33,804,141.97
VI	9,624,150.09	-24,179,991.88
VII	9,129,606.58	-15,050,385.30
VIII	8,659,295.48	-6,391,089.82
IX	8,212,050.01	-
X	27,116,732.23	-

Source: IAE, 2024.

Assessment in Conditions of Risk and Uncertainty

One more aspect that has to be considered in investment testing is its economic behave toward the exploitation in the condition of risk and uncertainty (Table 13. and Table 14.). According to this, two indicators have been developed Break-even Point and Safety Margin:

- Observing the Break-even Point, during the period of loan repayment, there could be allowed the fall in production volume for up to 21.80%.
- Observing the value for Safety Margin, during the period of loan repayment, the volume of overall production has not fallen below the 78.20%.

Table 13. Break-even Point and Safety Margin (in EUR, in %)

No.	Description	Years
		I-X
1.	Incomes (I)	20,425,329.83
2.	Variable costs (VC)	1,481,464.94
3.	Fixed costs (FC)	4,130,324.67
4.	Marginal result (MR = I-VC)	18,943,864.89

continued on following page

Table 13. Continued

No.	Description	Years
		I-X
5.	Break-even point - relative (BEPr = (FC/MR) x 100), in %	21.80
6.	Break-even point - value (BEPv = (I x BEPr) / 100), in EUR	4,453,327.99
7.	Safety Margin (Sm = ((1 - (BEPv / I)) x 100), in %	78.20

Source: IAE, 2024.

Table 14. Variable and Fixed Costs (in EUR)

No.	Description	Years
		I-X
1.	Variable costs (VC = MC + L)	1,481,464.94
2.	Material costs (MC)	1,372,905.77
3.	Labor (L)	108,559.17
No.	**Description**	**Years**
		I-X
1.	Fixed costs (FC = ITC - L)	4,130,324.67
2.	Intangible costs (ITC) without depreciation and interest	4,238,883.84
3.	Labor (L)	108,559.17

Source: IAE, 2024.

CONCLUSION AND RECOMMENDATIONS

In current agriculture, in general, there is no market oriented, or even sustainable crop production without the continuous or supplemental use of irrigation. Globally used systems of irrigation vary a lot, in sense of grown crop, used type, size of watered area, system capacity or its complexity (from primitive home-made to very sophisticated systems). There are several factors that have been affected the growth of the need for irrigation appliance. Whether they are containing the economic, social or environmental reason, they are linked with human's wellbeing and survival.

On global level, areas under irrigation have slow but stable upward trend, mainly influenced by growth of areas in Asia, Africa, and South America. Contrary to that, in several water-stressed regions, where the irrigation is traditionally practiced there come to slight decrease in irrigation areas, or skipping to irrigation systems suitable for water-saving production concept. In recent time, in line to intensification of climate changes and fresh water scarcity, together with rise in producer's or policymaker's awareness about stronger manifestation of mentioned production risks in agriculture worldwide, from science is required to develop standalone, automated, precise and water effective irrigation systems. So, smart farming starts with its presence in irrigation practice too. From the concept agriculture 3.0 to agriculture 5.0, irrigation systems were gradually changed into the systems that could independently track the production circumstances, and in accordance to them make timely and adequate decisions towards the water appliance in volume that perfectly match the crop needs, and among the all fresh water availability.

Basic economy logic imposes the need to analyze the effects of any investment prior to its implementation. Performed research has been assessed the economic effectiveness of investment in automated systems for irrigation that have to be installed at the agricultural area of 9,239 ha in northern parts of Serbia. In line to results derived from appliance of investment analysis (static and dynamic methods) there could be concluded that investment implementation and later exploitation is economically justified. More precisely, values for applied static methods TOTIR (2.09), NPM (41.71%), ARR (9.53%), or SPP (6 years and 11.44 months), as well as values for applied dynamic methods NPV (28,937,692.42 EUR), IRR (10.34%), or DPP (8 years and 9.34 months), recommend the investment as highly acceptable for agricultural company (potential investor). Furthermore, there could be expected from investment high reliability towards its functioning in the condition of risk and uncertainty, as the values for Break-even Point (21.80%) and Safety Margin (78.20%), additionally assures investor that irrigation system establishment is good business venture.

Developed case study brings certain recommendations to all stakeholders involved in crop production. Firstly, crop producers have to be aware that in current production circumstances (mainly drought intensification and disturbances in rainfall patterns) irrigation practicing is no more the competitive advantage, but the general precondition for sustainable business of the farm or company. So, they have to be encouraged, while externally supported to shift their production from dry farming agriculture to crop production under irrigation. Secondly, in line to overall wellbeing of all population from certain local community or entire country (mainly related to necessity to maintain the food security and prevent potential water scarcity, rebalancing the water appliance to comunal use or agriculture), policy makers and local authorities have to subsidize more pronounced implementation of irrigation systems (primarily advanced forms). Thirdly, contemporary scientific-research and industrial sector have to provide additional efforts in further development of irrigation systems in order to boost the overall sustainability, as well as the costs and water use effectiveness. At the end, any individual is obliged to behave in accordance to

UN's SDGs accomplishment, where the terms water and food could be directly linked to almost all of them.

Further research steps could be turned to evaluation of different modalities of previously observed investment (according to the change in size of irrigated agricultural area or predefined crop rotation, introduction of different level of subsidies, or change in the structure of external and internal assets used for investment financing, etc.). Similarly, there could be assessed the investment in observed irrigation system after some of elements and process solutions are additionally advanced.

ACKNOWLEDGMENT

The research study was supported by the Ministry of Science, Technological Development and Innovation of the Republic of Serbia (Grant no. 451-03-136/2025-03/200009 from 4.2.2025.)

REFERENCES

Ağızan, S., & Bayramoğlu, Z. (2021). Comparative investment analysis of agricultural irrigation systems. *Tekirdag Ziraat Fakültesi Dergisi, 18*(2), 222–233. DOI: 10.33462/jotaf.745548

Ala'F, K., Alqammaz, A., Khasawneh, A., Abualigah, L., Darabkh, K., & Zinonos, Z. (2025). An environmental remote sensing and prediction model for an IoT smart irrigation system based on an enhanced wind-driven optimization algorithm. *Computers & Electrical Engineering, 122*, 109889. DOI: 10.1016/j.compeleceng.2024.109889

Ameen, A., & Raza, S. (2017). Green revolution: A review. *International Journal of Advances in Scientific Research, 3*(12), 129–137. DOI: 10.7439/ijasr.v3i12.4410

Angelakis, A., Zaccaria, D., Krasilnikoff, J., Salgot, M., Bazza, M., Roccaro, P., Jimenez, B., Kumar, A., Yinghua, W., Baba, A., Harrison, J., Jimenez, A., & Fereres, E. (2020). Irrigation of world agricultural lands: Evolution through the millennia. *Water (Basel), 12*(5), 1285. DOI: 10.3390/w12051285

Arsić, S., Bulatović, M., Rakin, M., Jeločnik, M., & Subić, J. (2018). Economic and Ecological Profitability of the Use of Whey in Dairy and Food Industry. *Large Animal Review, 24*(3), 99–105.

Banaduc, D., Simic, V., Cianfaglione, K., Barinova, S., Afanasyev, S., Oktener, A., McCall, G., Simic, S., & Curtean Banaduc, A. (2022). Freshwater as a sustainable resource and generator of secondary resources in the 21st century: Stressors, threats, risks, management and protection strategies, and conservation approaches. *International Journal of Environmental Research and Public Health, 19*(24), 16570. DOI: 10.3390/ijerph192416570 PMID: 36554449

Baron, J., Poff, N., Angermeier, P., Dahm, C., Gleick, P., Hairston, N.Jr, Jackson, R., Johnson, C., Richter, B., & Steinman, A. (2002). Meeting ecological and societal needs for freshwater. *Ecological Applications, 12*(5), 1247–1260. DOI: 10.1890/1051-0761(2002)012[1247:MEASNF]2.0.CO;2

Bojago, E., & Abrham, Y. (2023). Small-scale irrigation (SSI) farming as a climate-smart agriculture (CSA) practice and its influence on livelihood improvement in Offa District, Southern Ethiopia. *Journal of Agriculture and Food Research, 12*, 100534. DOI: 10.1016/j.jafr.2023.100534

Carrêlo, I., Almeida, R., Narvarte, L., Martinez Moreno, F., & Carrasco, L. (2020). Comparative analysis of the economic feasibility of five large-power photovoltaic irrigation systems in the Mediterranean region. *Renewable Energy, 145*, 2671–2682. DOI: 10.1016/j.renene.2019.08.030

Chakraborty, S. (2021). *Water: Its properties, distribution, and significance*. Riverine Ecology Volume 1: Eco-functionality of the Physical Environment of Rivers, Springer, Cham, Germany, DOI: 10.1007/978-3-030-53897-2_2

Cicea, C., Subić, J., & Cvijanović, D. (2008). Beyond agriculture and rural development: investments, efficiency, econometrics. Institute of Agricultural Economics, Belgrade, Serbia.

Deininger, K. (2011). Challenges posed by the new wave of farmland investment. *The Journal of Peasant Studies, 38*(2), 217–247. DOI: 10.1080/03066150.2011.559007

Del Giudice, E., Elia, V., & Tedeschi, A. (2009). The role of water in the living organisms. *Neural Network World, 19*(4), 355–360.

Dmitrović, V., Petrović, M., & Jakovljević, N. (2024). Smart Agriculture, Data and AI in in the Context of Cobit 2019: Analysis of Potential and Risks. *Western Balkan Journal of Agricultural Economics and Rural Development, 6*(2), 83–196. DOI: 10.5937/WBJAE2402183D

Egbo, O., Ezeaku, H., Okolo, V., Anisiuba, C., Ibe, G., Okeke, O., & Igwe, P. (2023). Enhancing agricultural and industrial productivity through freshwater withdrawals and management: Implications for the BRICS countries. *Environment, Development and Sustainability, 25*(4), 3771–3799. DOI: 10.1007/s10668-022-02202-z

El Moll, A. (2023). Water resources and climate change: Regional, national and international perspective. In Prasad, M., & Smol, M. (Eds.), *Sustainable and circular management of resources and waste towards a green deal* (pp. 309–336). Elsevier., DOI: 10.1016/B978-0-323-95278-1.00010-3

Evett, S., Colaizzi, P., Lamm, F., O'Shaughnessy, S., Heeren, D., Trout, T., Kranz, W., & Lin, X. (2020). Past, present, and future of irrigation on the US Great Plains. *Transactions of the ASABE, 63*(3), 703–729. DOI: 10.13031/trans.13620

Gleick, P., & Cooley, H. (2021). Freshwater scarcity. *Annual Review of Environment and Resources, 46*(1), 319–348. DOI: 10.1146/annurev-environ-012220-101319

Holzinger, A., Fister, I., Kaul, H., & Asseng, S. (2024). Human-centered AI in smart farming: Toward agriculture 5.0. *IEEE Access : Practical Innovations, Open Solutions, 12*, 62199–62214. DOI: 10.1109/ACCESS.2024.3395532

IAE. (2024). *Collected dataset related to investment in fully automated irrigation system*. Internal documentation, Institute of Agricultural Economics, Belgrade, Serbia.

Jackson, R., Carpenter, S., Dahm, C., McKnight, D., Naiman, R., Postel, S., & Running, S. (2001). Water in a changing world. *Ecological Applications, 11*(4), 1027–1045. DOI: 10.1890/1051-0761(2001)011[1027:WIACW]2.0.CO;2

Jeločnik, M., Nastić, L., & Kuzman, B. (2023). *Improving the vegetable growing by the use of new technologies.* In: Andrei, J., Mateoc Sirb, N., Feher, A. (eds.) I International Conference TENDEV 2023 - Challenges and strategies for sustainable development facing the climate change (eds.), Peter Lang GmbH, Berlin, Germany, pp. 123-144.

Jeločnik, M., Puška, A., Nedeljković, M., Božanić, D., & Subić, J. (2024). Possibility of renewable energy solutions usage in rural areas of Western Balkans: Fuzzy-rough approach. *Rural Sustainability Research, 51*(346), 1–19. DOI: 10.2478/plua-2024-0001

Jeločnik, M., & Subić, J. (2020). Evaluation of economic efficiency of investments in organic production at the family farms. In Platania, (Eds.), *Course for trainers: Organic farming, eco-market and their capitalization through the entrepreneurial initiative* (pp. 261–300). Alexandru Ioan Cuza University.

Jeločnik, M., & Subić, J. (2021). *Economic effects of the wind-turbine and solar panels application in vegetables' production at the family farms.* In: Atanov, I. (edt.) IX International scientific-practical conference: Innovative aspects of the development service and tourism, Stavropol State Agrarian University, Stavropol, Russian Federation, pp. 61-75.

Jeločnik, M., & Subić, J. (2022). *Irrigation costs management at the family farms.* In: X International scientific-practical conference: Innovative aspects of the development service and tourism. Faculty of Social and Cultural Service and Tourism, Stavropol state agrarian university, Stavropol, Russian Federation, pp. 116-128.

Jeločnik, M., Subić, J., & Zdravković, A. (2022). Economic effects of investment in irrigation systems implementation at the small family farms. *Ekonomika Poljoprivrede, 69*(3), 793–817. DOI: 10.5937/ekoPolj2203793J

Jeločnik, M., Subić, J., Zubović, J., & Zdravković, A. (2016). Ekonomski aspekti primene obnovljivih izvora energije u procesu navodnjavanja u povrtarstvu. *Ecologica, 23*(83), 473–479.

Jeločnik, M., Zubović, J., & Zdravković, A. (2019). Estimating impact of weather factors on wheat yields by using panel model approach: The case of Serbia. *Agricultural Water Management, 221*, 493–501. DOI: 10.1016/j.agwat.2019.05.015

Karagiannis, I., & Soldatos, P. (2008). Water desalination cost literature: Review and assessment. *Desalination, 223*(1-3), 448–456. DOI: 10.1016/j.desal.2007.02.071

Kay, M., Bunning, S., Burke, J., Boerger, V., Bojic, D., Bosc, P., Clark, M., Dale, D., England, M., Hoogeveen, J., Koo Oshima, S., Mejias Moreno, P., Muchoney, D., Nachtergaele, F., Olivera Sanchez, C., Salman, M., Schlingloff, S., Unver, O., Vargas, R., . . . Ziadat, F. (2022). *The state of the world's land and water resources for food and agriculture 2021. Systems at breaking point*. Report, Food and Agriculture Organization of EU (FAO), Rome, Italy, DOI: 10.4060/cb9910en

Khan, S., Mushtaq, S., & Chen, C. (2010). A decision support tool for irrigation infrastructure investments. *Irrigation and Drainage, 59*(4), 404–418. DOI: 10.1002/ird.501

Kilic, Z. (2020). The importance of water and conscious use of water. *International Journal of Hydrology, 4*(5), 239–241. DOI: 10.15406/ijh.2020.04.00250

Komarek, A., De Pinto, A., & Smith, V. (2020). A review of types of risks in agriculture: What we know and what we need to know. *Agricultural Systems, 178*, 102738. DOI: 10.1016/j.agsy.2019.102738

Ledger, M., & Milner, A. (2015). Extreme events in running waters. *Freshwater Biology, 60*(12), 2455–2460. DOI: 10.1111/fwb.12673

Liu, D., Li, G., Hu, N., & Ma, Z. (2019). Application of real options on the decision-making of mining investment projects using the system dynamics method. *IEEE Access : Practical Innovations, Open Solutions, 7*, 46785–46795. DOI: 10.1109/ACCESS.2019.2909128

Malmqvist, B., & Rundle, S. (2002). Threats to the running water ecosystems of the world. *Environmental Conservation, 29*(2), 134–153. DOI: 10.1017/S0376892902000097

Mishra, R. (2023). Fresh water availability and its global challenge. *British Journal of Multidisciplinary and Advanced Studies, 4*(3), 1–78. DOI: 10.37745/bjmas.2022.0208

Mogues, T., Fan, S., & Benin, S. (2015). Public investments in and for agriculture. *European Journal of Development Research, 27*(3), 337–352. DOI: 10.1057/ejdr.2015.40

Monteleone, S., Moraes, E., Tondato de Faria, B., Aquino, P.Junior, Maia, R., Neto, A. T., & Toscano, A. (2020). Exploring the adoption of precision agriculture for irrigation in the context of agriculture 4.0: The key role of internet of things. *Sensors (Basel), 20*(24), 7091. DOI: 10.3390/s20247091 PMID: 33322252

Naorem, A., Jayaraman, S., Dang, Y., Dalal, R., Sinha, N., Rao, C., & Patra, A. (2023). Soil constraints in an arid environment: Challenges, prospects, and implications. *Agronomy (Basel), 13*(1), 220. DOI: 10.3390/agronomy13010220

Nasution, M., Rahmad, D., & Rusyanto, R. (2018). Financial and Economic Analysis Irrigation Area Development Bajayu–Serdang Bedagai. *SPECTA Journal of Technology, 2*(1), 53–62. DOI: 10.35718/specta.v2i1.95

Okafor, N. (2011). *Environmental Microbiology of Aquatic and Waste Systems.* Springer., DOI: 10.1007/978-94-007-1460-1

Osman, K. (2013). *Soils: Principles, properties and management.* Springer., DOI: 10.1007/978-94-007-5663-2

Pandey, N., Kamboj, N., Sharma, A., & Kumar, A. (2022). An overview of recent advancements in the irrigation, fertilization, and technological revolutions of agriculture. In Bahukhandi, K., Kamboj, N., & Kamboj, V. (Eds.), *Environmental Pollution and Natural Resource Management* (pp. 167–184). Springer., DOI: 10.1007/978-3-031-05335-1_11

Paoletti, J., & Shortridge, J. (2020). Improved representation of uncertainty in farm-level financial cost-benefit analyses of supplemental irrigation in humid regions. *Agricultural Water Management, 239*, 106245. DOI: 10.1016/j.agwat.2020.106245

Petrović, M., Marina, I., & Jeločnik, M. (2024). The significance and role of using innovative technologies in modern agricultural production. [JRISS]. *Journal of Research and Innovation for Sustainable Society, 6*(2), 289–303. DOI: 10.33727/JRISS.2024.2.32:289-303

Pinstrup Andersen, P., & Hazell, P. (1985). The impact of the Green Revolution and prospects for the future. *Food Reviews International, 1*(1), 1–25. DOI: 10.1080/87559128509540765

Poggensee, K., & Poggensee, J. (2021). Static investment calculation methods. In *Investment Valuation and Appraisal: Theory and Practice* (pp. 31–84). Springer., DOI: 10.1007/978-3-030-62440-8_2

Rockström, J., Falkenmark, M., Karlberg, L., Hoff, H., Rost, S., & Gerten, D. (2009). Future water availability for global food production: The potential of green water for increasing resilience to global change. *Water Resources Research*, *45*(7), 1–16. DOI: 10.1029/2007WR006767

Sachs, J., & Reid, W. (2006). Investments toward sustainable development. *Science*, *312*(5776), 1002–1002. DOI: 10.1126/science.1124822 PMID: 16709769

Saiz Rubio, V., & Rovira Mas, F. (2020). From smart farming towards agriculture 5.0: A review on crop data management. *Agronomy (Basel)*, *10*(2), 207. DOI: 10.3390/agronomy10020207

Sharma, V., & Irmak, S. (2020). Economic comparisons of variable rate irrigation and fertigation with fixed (uniform) rate irrigation and fertigation and pre-plant fertilizer management for maize in three soils. *Agricultural Water Management*, *240*, 106307. DOI: 10.1016/j.agwat.2020.106307

Silva, A., Silva, B., Souza, C., Azevedo, B., Bassoi, L., Vasconcelos, D., Bonfi, G., Juarez, J., dos Santos, A., & Carneiro, F. (2020). Irrigation in the age of agriculture 4.0: Management, monitoring and precision. *Revista Ciência Agronômica*, *51*(5), e20207695. DOI: 10.5935/1806-6690.20200090

Sima, V., Gheorghe, I., Subić, J., & Nancu, D. (2020). Influences of the industry 4.0 revolution on the human capital development and consumer behavior: A systematic review. *Sustainability (Basel)*, *12*(10), 4035. DOI: 10.3390/su12104035

Singh, D., & Sobti, R. (2022). Long-range real-time monitoring strategy for Precision Irrigation in urban and rural farming in society 5.0. *Computers & Industrial Engineering*, *167*, 107997. DOI: 10.1016/j.cie.2022.107997

Sojka, R., Bjorneberg, D., & Entry, J. (2002). *Irrigation: An historical perspective*. In: Lal R. (edt.) Encyclopedia of soil science, pp. 745-749, CRC Press Boca Raton, USA.

SORS. (2024). *Census of Agriculture 2023*. SORS, Belgrade, Serbia, retrieved at: Brosura KON - 16 april.cdr (stat.gov.rs)

Srivastava, R., Verma, H., Mohanty, S., & Pattnaik, S. (2003). Investment decision model for drip irrigation system. *Irrigation Science*, *22*(2), 79–85. DOI: 10.1007/s00271-003-0072-8

Stiglitz, J., & Greenwald, B. (2014). *Creating a learning society: A new approach to growth, development, and social progress*. Columbia University Press., DOI: 10.7312/stig15214

Subić, J. (2010). *Specificities of investment process in agriculture (Specifičnosti procesa investiranja u poljoprivredi).* Institute of Agricultural Economics, Beograd, Serbia.

Subic, J., & Jelocnik, M. (2013). Economic and environmental aspects of controlled vegetable production within the region of Danube basin. In Andrei, J., Turek, A., Subic, J., & Dusmanescu, D. (Eds.), *Sustainable Technologies, Policies, and Constraints in the Green Economy* (pp. 39–62). IGI Global., DOI: 10.4018/978-1-4666-4098-6.ch003

Subić, J., Jeločnik, M., & Petrović, M. (2025). *Economic assessment of investments in rural infrastructure in hilly-mountain areas.* In: Subic et al. (eds.) V International Scientific Conference “Sustainable agriculture and rural development”. Institute of Agricultural Economics, Belgrade, Serbia, pp. 301-316.

Subić, J., Jeločnik, M., & Potrebić, V. (2021). Economic justification of innovative subsurface capillary irrigation system appliance in vegetable production in protected areas (Ekonomska opravdanost primene inovativnog podpovršinskog kapilarnog navodnjavanja u plasteničkoj proizvodnji povrća). In *Kljajic, N. (edt.) Techno and agro-economic analysis toward pros and cons of wider application of innovative way of subsurface capillary irrigation in the sector of agriculture (Tehno i agro-ekonomska analiza prednosti i nedostataka šire primene inovativnog načina podpovršinskog kapilarnog navodnjavanja u poljoprivrednom sektoru), Institute of agricultural economics* (pp. 117–144). Serbia.

Subić, J., Jovanović, M., Despotović, Ž., & Jeločnik, M. (2017a). Possibilities of Applying Robotic Systems and Smart Sensor Networks in Integrated Agricultural Apple Production. In *Advances in Robot Design and Intelligent Control* (pp. 269–281). Springer., DOI: 10.1007/978-3-319-49058-8_30

Subic, J., Kljajic, N., & Jelocnik, M. (2017b). *Renewable energy and irrigation in the function of sustainable development of agriculture: Economic aspects (Obnovljivi izvori energije i navodnjavanje u funkciji održivog razvoja poljoprivrede: Ekonomski aspekti).* Institute of Agricultural Economics, Belgrade, Serbia.

Subić, J., & Kuzman, B. (2016). Guide and model for business plan development at the farms (Uputstvo i model za izradu biznis plana na poljoprivrednim gazdinstvima). In Subic, (Eds.), *Advancement of financial knowledge and recording at farms in the Republic of Serbia (Unapređenje finansijskih znanja i evidencije na poljoprivrednim gazdinstvima u Republici Srbiji), Institute of Agricultural Economics.* Serbia.

Subić, J., Nastić, L., & Potrebić, V. (2013). Economic effects of the thermal water use in vegetable production on the territory of Central Danube Region. *Economics of Agriculture, 60*(4), 745–757.

Subić, J., Vasiljević, Z., Rodić, A. (2024). *Razvoj inovativnih rešenja u oblasti pametnog korišćenja zemljišta u poljoprivredi u cilju smanjenja emisije gasova u atmosferu sa efektom staklene bašte primenom obnovljivih izvora energije i naprednih informacionih tehnologija – Ocena ekonomske efektivnosti investicije.* Interna dokumentacija, Institut za ekonomiku poljoprivrede (IEP), Beograd, Srbija.

Toth, A., Nagy, L., Kennedy, R., Bohus, B., Abonyi, J., & Ruppert, T. (2023). The human-centric Industry 5.0 collaboration architecture. *MethodsX, 11*, 102260. DOI: 10.1016/j.mex.2023.102260 PMID: 37388166

Valipour, M., Krasilnikof, J., Yannopoulos, S., Kumar, R., Deng, J., Roccaro, P., Mays, L., Grismer, M., & Angelakis, A. (2020). The evolution of agricultural drainage from the earliest times to the present. *Sustainability (Basel), 12*(1), 416. DOI: 10.3390/su12010416

Whitt, C. (2022). From flooded fields to a vanished lake: The politics of broken water cycles in the Bolivian Altiplano. *Geoforum, 131*, 243–251. DOI: 10.1016/j.geoforum.2018.03.009

Woodward, G., Bonada, N., Brown, L., Death, R., Durance, I., Gray, C., Hladyz, S., Ledger, M., Milner, A., Ormerod, S., Thompson, R., Pawar, S. (2016). The effects of climatic fluctuations and extreme events on running water ecosystems. *Philosophical Transactions of the Royal Society B: Biological Sciences*, 371(1694):20150274, DOI: 10.1098/rstb.2015.0274

Ye, S., & Tiong, R. (2000). NPV-at-risk method in infrastructure project investment evaluation. *Journal of Construction Engineering and Management, 126*(3), 227–233. DOI: 10.1061/(ASCE)0733-9364(2000)126:3(227)

You, L., Xie, H., Wood Sichra, U., Guo, Z., & Wang, L. (2014). Irrigation potential and investment return in Kenya. *Food Policy, 47*, 34–45. DOI: 10.1016/j.foodpol.2014.04.006

Zatrochova, M., & Katrencik, I. (2023). Investment evaluation methods for business performance. In Kryvinska, N., Greguš, M., & Fedushko, S. (Eds.), *Developments in Information and Knowledge Management Systems for Business Applications: Studies in Systems, Decision and Control* (pp. 211–244). Springer., DOI: 10.1007/978-3-031-27506-7_9

Zhan, J., & Santos Paulino, A. (2021). Investing in the Sustainable Development Goals: Mobilization, channeling, and impact. *Journal of International Business Policy*, *4*(1), 166–184. DOI: 10.1057/s42214-020-00093-3

Ziolkowska, J. (2015). Is desalination affordable? Regional cost and price analysis. *Water Resources Management*, *29*(5), 1385–1397. DOI: 10.1007/s11269-014-0901-y

Zubović, J., Jeločnik, M., Zdravković, A., Subić, J., & Radovanović, S. (2018). Using spatial and seasonal panel model to determine impact of climatic factors on maize yields in Serbia. *Romanian Biotechnological Letters*, *23*(2), 13383–13393.

ADDITIONAL READING

Arshad, A. (2012). Net present value is better than internal rate of return. *Interdisciplinary Journal of Contemporary Research in Business*, *4*(8), 211–219.

Carey, J., & Zilberman, D. (2002). A model of investment under uncertainty: Modern irrigation technology and emerging markets in water. *American Journal of Agricultural Economics*, *84*(1), 171–183. DOI: 10.1111/1467-8276.00251

El Mezouari, A., El Fazziki, A., & Sadgal, M. (2022). Smart irrigation system. *IFAC-PapersOnLine*, *55*(10), 3298–3303. DOI: 10.1016/j.ifacol.2022.10.125

García, L., Parra, L., Jimenez, J., Lloret, J., & Lorenz, P. (2020). IoT-based smart irrigation systems: An overview on the recent trends on sensors and IoT systems for irrigation in precision agriculture. *Sensors (Basel)*, *20*(4), 1042. DOI: 10.3390/s20041042 PMID: 32075172

Gittinger, J. (1972). *Economic analysis of agricultural projects*. Johns Hopkins University Press.

Gutiérrez, J., Villa Medina, J., Nieto Garibay, A., & Porta Gándara, M. (2013). Automated irrigation system using a wireless sensor network and GPRS module. *IEEE Transactions on Instrumentation and Measurement*, *63*(1), 166–176. DOI: 10.1109/TIM.2013.2276487

Khan, S., Tariq, R., Yuanlai, C., & Blackwell, J. (2006). Can irrigation be sustainable? *Agricultural Water Management*, *80*(1-3), 87–99. DOI: 10.1016/j.agwat.2005.07.006

Lefley, F. (1996). The payback method of investment appraisal: A review and synthesis. *International Journal of Production Economics*, *44*(3), 207–224. DOI: 10.1016/0925-5273(96)00022-9

McDermid, S., Nocco, M., Lawston Parker, P., Keune, J., Pokhrel, Y., Jain, M., Jagermeyr, J., Brocca, L., Massari, C., Jones, A., Vahmani, P., Thiery, W., Yao, Y., Bell, A., Chen, L., Dorigo, W., Hanasaki, N., Jasechko, S., Lo, M., & Yokohata, T. (2023). Irrigation in the Earth system. *Nature Reviews. Earth & Environment*, *4*(7), 435–453. DOI: 10.1038/s43017-023-00438-5

Obaideen, K., Yousef, B., AlMallahi, M., Tan, Y., Mahmoud, M., Jaber, H., & Ramadan, M. (2022). An overview of smart irrigation systems using IoT. *Energy Nexus*, *7*, 100124. DOI: 10.1016/j.nexus.2022.100124

Ragab, M., Badreldeen, M., Sedhom, A., & Mamdouh, W. (2022). IOT based smart irrigation system. *International Journal of Industry and Sustainable Development*, *3*(1), 76–86. DOI: 10.21608/ijisd.2022.148007.1021

Tace, Y., Tabaa, M., Elfilali, S., Leghris, C., Bensag, H., & Renault, E. (2022). Smart irrigation system based on IoT and machine learning. *Energy Reports*, *8*, 1025–1036. DOI: 10.1016/j.egyr.2022.07.088

Tozer, P. (2009). Uncertainty and investment in precision agriculture: Is it worth the money? *Agricultural Systems*, *100*(1-3), 80–87. DOI: 10.1016/j.agsy.2009.02.001

Turral, H., Svendsen, M., & Faures, J. (2010). Investing in irrigation: Reviewing the past and looking to the future. *Agricultural Water Management*, *97*(4), 551–560. DOI: 10.1016/j.agwat.2009.07.012

Vij, A., Vijendra, S., Jain, A., Bajaj, S., Bassi, A., & Sharma, A. (2020). IoT and machine learning approaches for automation of farm irrigation system. *Procedia Computer Science*, *167*, 1250–1257. DOI: 10.1016/j.procs.2020.03.440

KEY TERMS AND DEFINITIONS

Automation: represents the process of appliance of progressive technology, equipment, software, or even robotics. It could be considered as specifically developed system in any sector of economy that are performing tasks or whole procedures with minimal or without human interference, while ensuring gained outputs in much effective and efficient way.

Decision making: represents the process in selecting the best possible among available alternatives. Process is generally based on collecting, filtering and knowledge-based assessment of accessible datasets and information, that will derive the most appropriate solution toward the observed and analyzed issues.

Investment analysis: considers mechanism that support deeper economic observation of planed investment, in order to assess economic justification of individual investment implementation, or to select the most optimal among the group of disposed investment alternatives. Investment analysis assists the investor to better understand or perceive investment benefits and shortcomings, trying to compare investor's expectations and investment's performances upon the final decision and its implementation.

Investments in agriculture: as a concept of economic philosophy, investment usually represents any transfer of money, i.e. purchase, advancement or enlargement of capital goods in order to move current consumption to production of consumer goods and services in long run, expecting the economic prosperity for investor in future period. In agriculture it mainly considers acquisition or upgrading of production and processing facilities, land, livestock, plantations, machinery, tools and equipment, etc.

Irrigation: process of artificial introduction of water to agricultural land, most often with the goal to achieve for plants optimal soil moisture conditions in crop production, i.e. it provides compensation of required amount of water for optimal growth and development of plants in conditions of insufficient rainfalls or their unfavorable distribution during the growing season, while all with the purpose to obtain stable and high, but above all, economically justified yields.

Chapter 2

The Impact of Agro-Industrial Enterprise Integration on the Competitiveness of the Serbian Raspberry Market

Katica Radosavljevic
https://orcid.org/0000-0002-5609-8399
Institute of Agricultural Economics, Belgrade, Serbia

Natasa Kljajic
Institute of Agricultural Economics, Belgrade, Serbia

ABSTRACT

The integration of Serbian companies into global agro-industrial chains, particularly in the raspberry sector, has brought significant changes in business operations and distribution. Prior to 2014, Serbian companies such as Yugent Food and Frucom Food were dependent on intermediaries, leading to price fluctuations and uncertainty in product placement. However, following the acquisition by Roger Descours Group, raspberries were directly marketed, resulting in more stable prices and better conditions for producers. While the benefits of integration are evident, such as business stability and increased revenues, challenges have emerged, such as increased dependency on a single major buyer, France. This paper analyzes the advantages and disadvantages of this model, as well as potential development directions for the sector, including market diversification and the development of processed products.

DOI: 10.4018/979-8-3373-2898-0.ch002

INTRODUCTION

Raspberry (Rubus idaeus) is one of the most sought-after and widely consumed fruit species worldwide. It holds significant importance in human nutrition, not only due to its high nutritional value but also because of its health benefits and unique bioactive properties. Raspberries are rich in essential vitamins, particularly vitamin C, which is crucial for the proper functioning of the immune system, collagen synthesis, and the protection of cells from oxidative stress. Additionally, they provide a substantial amount of minerals, such as manganese, potassium, and magnesium, all of which contribute to maintaining healthy bodily functions. One of the key nutrients in raspberries is dietary fiber, which plays a significant role in digestive health, promotes satiety, and helps regulate blood sugar levels (Kljajić et al., 2017). The antioxidants found in raspberries, including flavonoids and anthocyanins, are potent compounds that protect the body against oxidative damage, thereby reducing the risk of chronic diseases such as heart disease, diabetes, and certain cancers (Zdravković et al., 2024).

Over time, the raspberry has transitioned from a wild forest plant to a major agricultural commodity, widely cultivated across various climates and regions. Beyond Serbia, the global raspberry market has expanded rapidly in recent decades, with countries such as Poland, Chile, and Mexico also emerging as key players. Understanding Serbia's role requires situating it within this broader international context of rising demand, changing trade patterns, and increasing competition.

Native to Europe and certain regions of Asia, the precise moment of its initial domestication is not definitively known; however, historical records suggest that raspberry cultivation began as early as the 16th century (Jennings, 1988). Over the centuries, selective breeding and advancements in horticultural practices have contributed to the development of high-yielding and disease-resistant cultivars, facilitating its expansion into a commercially important crop in both temperate and subtropical climates (Dale et al., 2013).

Today, raspberry holds a prominent place in human nutrition, valued not only for its distinct sensory characteristics but also for its health-promoting properties. It is rich in vitamins—particularly vitamin C—minerals, dietary fiber, and antioxidants, which contribute to immune system support, blood pressure regulation, and anti-inflammatory effects that help reduce symptoms of conditions such as arthritis (Beekwilder et al., 2005; Mullen et al., 2002). Additionally, raspberries contain ellagic acid, a phytochemical compound associated with a reduced risk of certain types of cancer (Daniel et al., 1989). Their high fiber content and low caloric value promote satiety, making them beneficial in weight management strategies (Slavin, 2005).

Although often consumed fresh, raspberries are also widely processed into jams, juices, purées, and various desserts. With approximately 85% water content, they are considered highly hydrating, playing an essential role in maintaining the body's fluid balance (USDA, 2022). Raspberries are typically consumed fresh, but they are also widely processed into jams, juices, purees, and various desserts, making them a versatile product in the food industry. The processing of raspberries into value-added products has significantly increased their economic importance, particularly in countries with favorable growing conditions. This versatility extends beyond fresh fruit consumption and provides a broader market reach, including the global export market, which has seen a sharp increase in demand for processed raspberry products. Beyond their nutritional and health-promoting qualities, raspberries are also considered a functional food, which has led to their integration into various dietary and health-conscious markets. The growing interest in organic and sustainably produced raspberries aligns with the increasing global demand for healthy, environmentally-friendly food options. The inclusion of raspberries in nutraceuticals and dietary supplements is also on the rise, driven by their high levels of antioxidants and other bioactive compounds (Popović et al., 2003).

As the demand for raspberries continues to rise, especially in developed markets such as Europe and North America, it is essential for raspberry-producing countries to implement strategic measures to maintain a sustainable supply of high-quality fruit. This includes improving cultivation practices, investing in processing technologies, and ensuring that the raspberry sector remains competitive in a globalized market. By focusing on sustainability, innovation, and market diversification, the raspberry industry can continue to thrive and meet the growing global demand for this nutrient-dense fruit.

In order to meet these evolving demands, raspberry-producing countries must adopt a multi-dimensional approach that integrates environmental sustainability, socio-economic resilience, and technological progress. Improving cultivation practices involves transitioning from traditional, input-intensive methods to more sustainable agricultural systems. This includes the adoption of integrated pest management (IPM), organic and regenerative farming techniques, soil fertility enhancement through composting and crop rotation, as well as the application of precision agriculture tools that optimize resource use. These approaches not only enhance productivity and fruit quality, but also contribute to the long-term ecological health of raspberry-growing regions, which is critical under the pressures of climate change.

Investment in modern post-harvest and processing technologies is equally crucial. Cold chain infrastructure, rapid freezing systems, and hygienic packaging lines are necessary to preserve the nutritional value, taste, and texture of raspberries destined for distant export markets. Furthermore, the development of secondary raspberry-based products—such as purées, concentrates, functional beverages, and nutraceuticals—can significantly increase the added value of raw fruit, opening new revenue streams and reducing post-harvest losses. Such vertical integration can also stimulate rural employment and support the growth of small and medium-sized agro-enterprises, particularly in regions with limited economic diversification. In addition to improving production and processing efficiency, competitiveness on the global market requires a proactive approach to branding, certification, and market positioning. Consumers in premium markets increasingly demand traceable, ethically sourced, and environmentally friendly food products. Therefore, the establishment of quality standards, certifications such as GlobalG.A.P., organic labeling, and fair-trade compliance can enhance the credibility and attractiveness of exported raspberries. This is particularly relevant for countries that aspire to build a national brand around their raspberries, emphasizing unique varietal traits, traditional cultivation knowledge, and pristine environmental conditions.

Horizontal and vertical cooperation and integration within the food supply chain play a crucial role in the efficiency of marketing channels in both domestic and international markets. In food production, integration establishes a new systemic framework. Market diversification is another key pillar of resilience. While Europe and North America represent mature and high-value markets, they are also highly competitive and sensitive to price fluctuations. Exploring new and emerging markets—such as East and Southeast Asia, the Gulf Cooperation Council (GCC) countries, and parts of Sub-Saharan Africa—can reduce dependency on traditional buyers and buffer the sector against regional trade disruptions. In parallel, e-commerce platforms and direct-to-consumer models are gaining relevance in fresh fruit marketing and should be considered in long-term export strategies. Comparable experiences can also be observed in transition economies of Central and Eastern Europe. For instance, in Poland and Hungary, foreign direct investment in the agri-food sector during the 1990s and early 2000s contributed to modernization of production facilities, improvement of food processing standards, and integration of local producers into European export chains. These cases demonstrate how FDI in agriculture and related industries can simultaneously enhance export competitiveness and accelerate structural transformation of the sector (Dries et al., 2004). Serbia is one of the leading global producers and exporters of raspberries, ranking consistently among the top three countries alongside Poland and Chile. While Poland dominates European markets with large volumes of fresh and processed raspberries, and Chile supplies off-season markets in Europe and the USA, Serbia specializes in high-quality production, particularly for processing industries, which gives it a competitive niche despite smaller overall production volumes. This positioning allows Serbia to maintain a strong presence in global trade and benefit from seasonal complementarities with its competitors (Radosavljevic, 2024).

This research examines key economic changes in Serbian frozen raspberry exports over the past decade, with a particular focus on the impact of horizontal and vertical integration on export competitiveness. Data clearly indicate that integration has led to a significant increase in exports and prices, yet it has also heightened dependence on a limited number of buyers.

Understanding the changes in Serbian raspberry exports over the past decade requires a combination of different research methods and data sources. This study goes beyond mere numbers—it seeks to tell the story of how market relationships have evolved, how domestic companies have become part of international supply chains, and what this transformation has meant for Serbian exporters.

Finally, government policy and international cooperation play a vital role in enabling the conditions necessary for sustainable sectoral development. This includes providing subsidies or co-financing schemes for climate-resilient infrastructure, supporting agricultural research and extension services, and ensuring that smallholder farmers have access to credit, training, and market information. Partnerships between public institutions, private investors, academia, and civil society can foster an inclusive and innovation-driven environment where the raspberry sector evolves in a balanced and forward-looking manner.

Raspberry cultivation in Serbia dates back to the 18th century, initially taking the form of wild fruits growing spontaneously in forested and inaccessible areas. However, its commercial cultivation began in the early 20th century, marking a turning point in the country's horticultural development.

Since the early 2000s, Serbia has emerged as one of the world's leading producers of raspberries, particularly recognized for the high quality of its fruit (Cvijanović et al., 2017). The expansion of raspberry production has largely been driven by the adoption of modern agricultural technologies, including irrigation systems, anti-hail protection, and plant protection products. Moreover, the implementation of ecological and sustainable farming practices has enabled Serbian producers to obtain certifications that meet the standards of demanding international markets. Over time, specific regions within Serbia have distinguished themselves due to their favorable microclimatic and soil conditions, particularly areas such as Arilje, Požega, Valjevo, and Raška. These regions have become synonymous with high-quality raspberry production and have played a key role in shaping Serbia's reputation on the global market (Cvijanović et al., 2017). In parallel, there has been a growing interest in organic raspberries, with an increasing number of small-scale farms and plantations obtaining ecological certifications. These developments reflect both global consumer trends and Serbia's strategic orientation towards high-value, environmentally sustainable agricultural products.

Today, raspberry is considered one of the most profitable fruit species in Serbia. However, achieving profitability requires the alignment of numerous production factors. These include the appropriate selection of raspberry varieties, optimal cultivation technologies, adequate infrastructure, sufficient labor availability, and well-developed processing capacities (Sredojević et al., 2013). The integration of these elements is essential for ensuring sustainable competitiveness and long-term growth in the raspberry sector.

Major export destinations include countries such as Germany, France, and the United Kingdom, as well as Russia and the United States (Kljajić, 2012; Kalanović-Bulatović et al., 2015; Milić et al., 2017; Wróblewska et al., 2019). Since the early 2000s, Serbia has been strengthening its export position through intensified production and increased export volumes. By 2009, the country had become the world's largest raspberry exporter, shipping 63,300 tonnes valued at approximately USD 200 million (STIPS, 2010). During 2010, over 90% of total production was exported, primarily to European Union countries—a trend that persisted until 2020 (FAO, 2021). Between 2011 and 2019, raspberry exports continued to develop, albeit accompanied by the emergence of notable challenges in terms of market organisation. For instance, in 2014, Serbia exported 73,253 tonnes of frozen raspberries worth EUR 117.9 million. A record-breaking year followed in 2019, with exports reaching 114,000 tonnes, valued at more than EUR 200 million (RZS, 2020). These results positioned Serbia as one of the global leaders in raspberry exports, particularly within the frozen raspberry segment. This success was achieved despite considerable limitations in infrastructure and procurement networks, owing to favourable agroecological conditions and a high number of small-scale individual producers located predominantly in western Serbia. According to Vapa-Tankosić et al. (2023), the European Union represents a key market for the export of Serbian agricultural products, accounting for more than half of the sector's total exports. The main drivers of export growth and job creation include the modernisation of agricultural production, improvement of operational efficiency, strengthening of competitiveness, and the acceleration of structural reforms in the sector.

However, despite robust export performance in certain years, the overall export trajectory has exhibited considerable volatility due to market fluctuations, climate variability, and structural constraints. Market pressures, climate change, low value-added processing, and fragmented production systems have posed significant challenges to the long-term competitiveness of Serbia's raspberry sector. The year 2020, marked by the COVID-19 pandemic, was particularly demanding, yet exports remained strong, with over 107,000 tonnes exported, valued at EUR 258.9 million (ITC, 2021). In 2021, export volumes remained similar to the previous year. In contrast, 2022 witnessed a notable decline in export quantities. According to data from the Ministry of Finance of the Republic of Serbia, only 68,752 tonnes were exported, though the total export value rose to EUR 378.98 million. This reflected rising global prices, but also a reduced supply due to adverse weather conditions and a decrease in cultivated areas. In 2023, the downward trend continued, with 57,612 tonnes exported at a total value of approximately EUR 237 million. In 2024, a slight recovery was recorded, with export quantities rising to 72,289 tonnes; however, the total value remained relatively low at EUR 278.2 million. These fluctuations point to underlying structural weaknesses in the sector, particularly related to the lack of producer organisation, dependence on intermediaries, and insufficient investment in processing infrastructure. in the global trade environment, quality alone is not sufficient. It is essential to identify the right markets, ensure stable prices, and establish long-term relationships with buyers. Horizontal and vertical cooperation and integration within the food supply chain play a crucial role in the efficiency of marketing channels, both in domestic and international markets.

For years, Serbian raspberries have been sold across Europe through an extensive network of intermediaries and traders who dictated prices and terms. Producers did their best but lacked full control over where and at what price their raspberries would be sold. However, a significant shift occurred in 2014 when the French company Roger Descours Group acquired the domestic exporters Frucom Food and Yugent Food, later merging Yugent Food with Frucom Food in 2019. This integration was not merely a financial transaction but a pivotal moment that reshaped the geographical structure of exports and the way Serbian raspberries reached their buyers.

This study examines the effects of horizontal and vertical integration on market structures, competitiveness, and marketing channels, using the acquisition of Yugent Food doo and Frucom Food doo by the multinational corporation Roger Descours Group as a case study. The main research objectives of the study can be formulated as follows:

1. To analyze how the integration of Yugent Food and Frucom Food influenced the quantity and value of Serbian raspberry exports.
2. To examine changes in market structure—who are the new key buyers of Serbian raspberries after the integration?
3. To compare prices before and after the integration and determine whether producers benefited from the increase in export value.
4. To analyze the advantages and challenges of eliminating intermediaries in raspberry trade.

Research Hypotheses:

Hypothesis One:: The integration of domestic firms into the Roger Descours Group led to an increase in export volume and more stable prices.
Hypothesis Two: After the integration, Serbian raspberry exports became more dependent on a few key markets, particularly France.
Hypothesis Three: The removal of intermediaries enabled better-controlled export prices but did not provide equal benefits to all participants in the supply chain.

Hypothesis Four: New export models improved the bargaining power of Serbian exporters but simultaneously reduced market flexibility.

The academic and practical significance of this research lies in its contribution to understanding market consolidation processes and their effects on economic conditions in exporting countries. Examining the business policies of multinational corporations and analyzing integration within the agro-industrial context provide broader insights into key market dominance strategies and their impact on the balance of power between local and international actors.

In addition to its theoretical and empirical contributions, this study offers practical value for policymakers, entrepreneurs, and other stakeholders in the agro-industrial sector. Understanding the dynamics of integration can aid in formulating strategies that enable a competitive yet sustainable market environment where domestic producers can achieve long-term stability and growth. Within the framework of rural development and agricultural policies, the findings of this research may serve as a foundation for further discussions on measures to support local producers and enhance export competitiveness.

BACKGROUND

Foreign direct investment (FDI) can have a direct impact on the export growth of the host country, particularly when subsidiaries of multinational corporations export all or part of their production abroad. This effect is described by the theoretical model of vertically integrated multinational corporations proposed by Helpman, in which companies fragment production processes and locate different stages of production according to the relative factor costs in various locations. An illustrative example of this strategy in agriculture is the investment of companies from the Persian Gulf countries in agricultural production in African states to vertically integrate their supply chains. Such intra-firm trade directly stimulates the host country's exports. Cotula (2009) note that agricultural investments from Gulf countries in Africa are often aimed at securing food supplies through vertical integration of supply chains, with significant implications for host countries' export dynamics.

Greater technological disparities between the host country and the investor country imply a lower capacity for local firms to absorb knowledge, thereby limiting the positive effects of FDI in such cases. Borensztein, De Gregorio, and Lee (1998) argue that the impact of FDI on economic growth is conditional on the host country's absorptive capacity, particularly its level of human capital, and that large technological gaps may reduce potential spillovers. From a theoretical standpoint, the role of the host country's economic development in realizing the potential benefits of FDI yields contradictory conclusions. The impact of FDI depends on the specific characteristics of the country under empirical analysis. Kokko (2003) stress that the benefits of FDI are not automatic and largely depend on host-country conditions such as market structure, institutional framework, and level of development.

There is a methodological shortcoming in the existing literature, as sector-specific characteristics are often overlooked when analyzing the effects of FDI (Radovanović et al., 2024). Entire economies or broadly defined sectors are often analyzed, which can lead to aggregation bias and inaccurate empirical results. One way to overcome this issue is to focus the analysis on individual sectors (Ganzorig & Nachin, 2006). Empirical research on the impact of foreign direct investment (FDI) on exports, at both macro and micro levels, has yielded mixed results, though the majority support the complementarity hypothesis. Greenaway, Sousa, and Wakelin (2004) confirm that multinational activity tends to complement rather than replace domestic firms' exports. At the macro level, Zhang and Song (2001) demonstrate that inward FDI has significantly contributed to China's export expansion. On the micro side, Bin and Jiangyong (2009) show that FDI enhances firm-level export upgrading, especially through processing trade.. Existing studies primarily focus on one or a few countries, either at the macro or micro level, considering the entire economy or broadly defined sectors (such as the manufacturing industry). This approach limits the generalizability of findings and, when analyzing entire economies, carries the risk of aggregation bias by simultaneously examining heterogeneous sectors with different conditions, types of FDI, and export values. Lipsey and Sjöholm (2005) emphasize that aggregation across diverse sectors and countries can obscure the true relationship between FDI and host-country outcomes.

Competition increasingly manifests between integrated systems rather than between independent agribusiness entities. As Gereffi, Humphrey, and Sturgeon (2005) explain, global value chain governance illustrates how vertical and horizontal integration reshape bargaining dynamics and redistribute value across supply chains. Marketing is becoming a key factor in the expanding vertical and horizontal cooperation between producers and trading organizations. According to Porter (2008), the restructuring of market forces through integration directly affects competition intensity and the strategic positioning of firms. Enterprises in the agro-industrial sector are characterized by an inherent necessity for integration, which is particularly evident in the raspberry sector. The benefits of integration in marketing channels include reduced operational costs, improved supply chain efficiency, and enhanced bargaining power in international trade. Hobbs (2021) emphasizes that integrated food supply chains demonstrate greater resilience to shocks, such as those experienced during the COVID-19 pandemic, but may also concentrate risks for smaller producers.

Foreign company investments in Serbia's agro-industrial sector have been common in recent years. Dries et al. (2009) show that in Central and Eastern Europe, vertical coordination in dairy supply chains similarly improved efficiency but increased pressure on smallholders. Foreign firms have taken over key domestic players in the grain, dairy, and meat industries to ensure stable supplies for the European market. Serbia is not the only country that has undergone the process of agro-industrial integration into foreign supply chains. Reardon and Timmer (2014) note that such agri-food transformations are part of broader structural shifts in developing and transition economies, with significant food security implications. For instance, in Hungary, the dairy industry has come under the control of major European processors, while in Poland, the meat sector has experienced similar changes. Findings suggest that although integration brings stability and new opportunities, it also reduces the number of independent exporters and increases dependence on a limited number of buyers. Kojima (1975) emphasizes that only foreign direct investments (FDI) in sectors where the investing country lacks a comparative advantage lead to a complementary relationship between FDI and trade. Understanding the impact of integration on raspberry export competitiveness can contribute to the development of better future strategies, both for individual firms and the entire sector.

In addition to Helpman's model, theories of market power and supply chain governance (e.g., Porter's Competitive Advantage, Transaction Cost Economics, and Global Value Chain approaches) provide useful perspectives for analyzing integration. These frameworks highlight how consolidation reshapes bargaining dynamics, influences value distribution, and creates long-term dependencies in agri-food systems. Beyond Serbia, similar experiences of agro-industrial integration have been recorded in Poland and Hungary. In Poland, the inflow of FDI into the berry sector contributed to the modernization of cold storage facilities and export chains, but at the same time increased dependence on large buyers from Western Europe. In Hungary, agro-industrial investments boosted export growth but also exerted stronger pressures on small producers due to stricter standards and higher market concentration. These comparisons further highlight the advantages and risks of FDI in the agriculture of Central and Eastern European countries. Clapp (2021) underlines that rising corporate concentration in global agri-food systems intensifies dependency risks and redistributes decision-making power away from local producers. OECD (2025) analyzes on FDI in agriculture confirm that foreign investments can significantly contribute to the modernization of the sector, but at the same time carry the risk of market concentration and weakening of the position of small producers.

To better understand how horizontal and vertical integration have influenced the competitiveness of Serbian raspberries, it is essential to consider the broader picture—how these processes unfold in the agro-industry, their impact on supply chains, and how foreign investors shape the domestic market (Cantó Calvo, 2022; Fatimah, et al., 2020).

RESULTS AND DISCUSSION

This casev study examines the effects of horizontal and vertical integration on market structures, competitiveness, and marketing channels, using the acquisition of Yugent Food doo and Frucom Food doo by the multinational corporation Roger Descours Group. The objective of this research is to analyze how changes in the business model have affected the competitive position of these companies, their export performance, and the redistribution of added value within the agro-industrial supply chain. A key aspect of the study is the impact of eliminating intermediaries in the export chain and shifting margin control to the multinational investor. This approach will evaluate how the shortening of marketing channels has influenced the competitiveness of local producers, export prices, and the profitability of the sector.

The findigs aims to indicate whether Serbian exporters are now in a stronger market position or have become overly reliant on a single major buyer. Frucom Food operates as a subsidiary of Roger Descours Group in Serbia, ensuring seamless access to foreign markets, as evidenced by the fact that 99% of its production is exported. A key advantage for Yugent Food, another subsidiary, is that Roger Descours Group already operates in raspberry-producing countries, facilitating market expansion and supply chain integration. Since the acquisition of Yugent Food and Frucom Food, Roger Descours Group has shortened the marketing channel by eliminating intermediaries, thereby capturing the margin previously retained by Yugent and Frucom. As a result, both firms have become more competitive by reducing operational costs. Frucom Food originated from Yugent and Frucom, both of which were initially suppliers to Roger Descours Group, operating through the broker firm Viva Fruit. To ensure market stability and procurement security, the three companies decided to merge.

Frucom Food Doo is one of the most prosperous businesses in Serbia as a result of the Roger Descours Group's backward connection and vertical integration of marketing channels with the cold storage facility. The business consistently strives to be a dependable manufacturer and exporter of frozen raspberries, guaranteeing adherence to supplier and client specifications while promoting mutual success. A push strategy for raspberry items appears to be a pertinent strategic approach, considering that sales are controlled by an inventory-based system.

The centralized management structure is located within Frucom Food doo, and since 2015, there have been significant operational shifts, including the relocation of fruit processing facilities and part of the workforce from Yugent Food doo to

Frucom Food doo. Since 2019, when Yugent Food doo became a business unit of Frucom Food doo, the number of employees has remained unchanged. The horizontal integration of Frucom Food doo with Yugent Food doo has been a key factor in achieving business success, particularly due to the reduction in operational costs following a decline in raspberry prices. Increased bargaining power, which Frucom Food doo has gained through horizontal integration, gives them a competitive market advantage; however, Yugent Food doo is not threatened by this integration because it still has direct access to international markets. At the regional level, competition includes 320 cold storage facilities as well as businesses and cooperatives that purchase fruit and wild berries for their own distribution and processing industry businesses.

Within the food manufacturing and supply chain, Frucom Food doo adheres to an integrated management system, maintaining high standards of quality and certification. The company has upgraded its equipment and consistently invests in personnel development, positioning itself for potential expansion in international markets. Its dedication to upholding international quality standards, such as IFS Food and IBRC certifications for the US and Japanese markets, strengthens its position as a key player in the market. The benefits of Frucom Food's business operations compared to those of Yugent and Frucom will be examined through the following business performance characteristics (Table 1).

Table 1. Business Characteristics of Yugent doo, Frucom doo, and Frucom Food doo

Yugent doo **Frucom doo**	**Frucom Food doo**
Serbian capital	French capital
For short-term Serbian loans, the interest rate for fruit purchase is 5.2-8% annually.	For short-term French loans, the interest rate for fruit purchase is 1.6% annually.
For long-term Serbian loans for fruit purchase, the interest rate is 7-10% annually.	For long-term French loans for fruit purchase, the interest rate is 3.5% annually.
Standards: HACCP, ISO 9001	Standards: HACCP, ISO 9001, BRC, IFS
One set of personal protective equipment (PPE)	Two sets of personal protective equipment (PPE)
Minimum employee insurance	Life insurance for employees
Working conditions in accordance with the regulations of the Republic of Serbia	Working conditions in accordance with the regulations of the Republic of Serbia and EU
Lack of own working capital (everything is financed through loans)	Own working capital
Lack of cooperation with other suppliers of deep-frozen fruit	Cooperation with other suppliers of deep-frozen fruit, increased export and business expansion
Lack of direct distribution of synthetic fertilizers and pesticides	Direct distribution of synthetic fertilizers and pesticides

continued on following page

Table 1. Continued

Yugent doo Frucom doo	Frucom Food doo
Uncertain product placement	Secure product placement
Lack of staff development	Staff development

Source: Author's own representation based on internal data from Yugent doo, Frucom doo and Frucom Food doo.

A comparative analysis of the performance of a cold storage facility owned by Serbian capital and one owned by French capital highlights the advantages of foreign investments in fostering a productive and competitive agro-industrial sector in the Republic of Serbia. Horizontal and vertical collaboration and integration within the food supply chain play a crucial role in the efficiency of marketing channels in both domestic and international markets.

Each year, thousands of tons of Serbian raspberries are transported from cold storage facilities across the country to major European and global markets. Once a symbol of small agricultural households, this fruit is now an integral part of a complex global trade and distribution system (Figure 1).

Figure 1. Raspberry Export Volumes, Total Export Value in EUR, and Average Price in EUR/kg from Serbia (2012–2023)

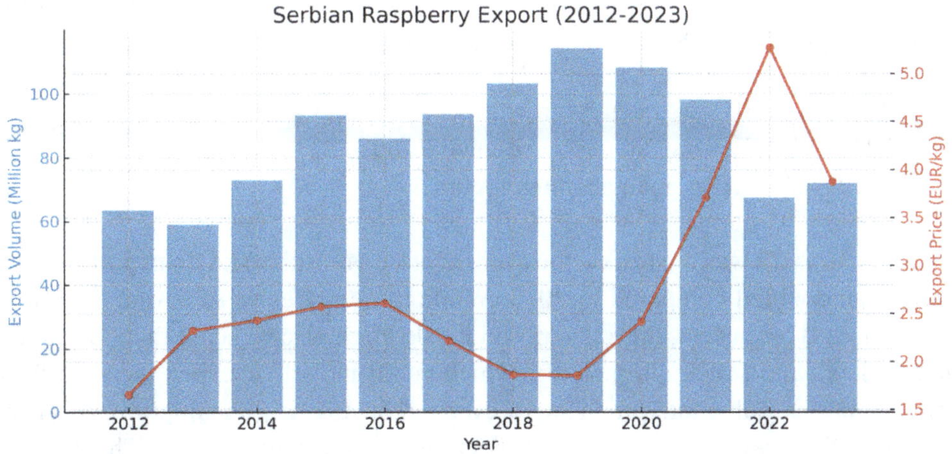

Source: Ministry of Finance of the Republic of Serbia, database on raspberry export, available at: https://www.carina.rs/ (accessed: 28 September 2024).

Before significant changes in the industry, Serbian raspberries had a stable market. The annual export in 2012 and 2013 averaged around 61 million kg, with the total export value being approximately 120 million euros per year. During this period, the market was characterized by stable, yet relatively low prices, averaging 1.99 EUR/kg (Figure 1). Serbian exporters were dependent on intermediaries, traders, and large importing networks, which often dictated the terms of sale. Producers operated at full capacity, but profits were limited, as value was added in the later stages of the production chain, most often in importing countries.

The year 2014 marked the first significant changes and the beginning of growth and development. That year, raspberry exports surged to 72.8 million kg, with the average price reaching 2.42 EUR/kg, recording the first substantial increase in the export price structure. This trend was not accidental, as it coincided with the acquisition of key Serbian exporters Frucom Food and Yugent Food by the French company Roger Descours Group. This move fundamentally changed the raspberry trade. Intermediaries were no longer needed – raspberries were directly sold in the markets, prices became more stable, and Serbian exporters gained greater bargaining power.

From 2015 to 2019, raspberry exports from Serbia reached record levels and showed stable growth. Annual quantities grew above 90 million kg, reaching a record 114 million kg in 2019. The price per kilogram stabilized in the range of 2.2–2.6 EUR, while the total export value grew, reaching 211 million euros in 2019. This was the period when Serbian raspberries were expanding into new markets, yet still susceptible to fluctuations in supply and demand. The onset of the 2020 pandemic brought a new reality, disrupting global supply chains, increasing transport costs, and driving up demand for healthy, frozen products. During this chaotic period, Serbian raspberries experienced a sharp price increase:

- **2020:** 2.41 EUR/kg, steady growth.
- **2021:** 3.70 EUR/kg, an unprecedented jump.
- **2022:** 5.27 EUR/kg, an absolute record.

The year 2022 was the peak – the average price of raspberries on export markets more than doubled compared to 2013. While these prices were advantageous for exporters and producers, they also posed a risk. High prices meant that consumers and traders would seek alternatives, which could include cheaper varieties from other countries, substitute products, or even a reduction in consumption. After the peak in 2022, there was a slight stabilization in the following year. The price of raspberries decreased to 3.87 EUR/kg, still a high level but far from the record values of the previous year. At the same time, export volumes did not return to the levels of 2019. This may indicate a global market adjustment, but also the emergence of competition from other countries offering more competitive prices.

The export of Serbian raspberries has gone through dramatic changes:

- **2012–2013:** Stable exports, low prices, dependence on intermediaries.
- **2014–2019:** Rapid export and price growth, market stabilization.
- **2020–2022:** Record prices, huge demand, but the risk of over-reliance on a few buyers.
- **2023:** Price stabilization, uncertainty about the future direction of exports.

Before integration, Serbia primarily exported raspberries to France, Germany, Belgium, the Netherlands, and Poland. France was a significant buyer, but in limited quantities. Looking at the last decade of Serbian raspberry exports, we observe a clear narrative of transformation and a shift from a fragmented market full of intermediaries to a centralized system dominated by a single large buyer. This change did not happen overnight but was the result of the integration of domestic companies into the global trade chain brought about by Roger Descours Group.

Before becoming part of a large multinational company, Yugent Food and Frucom Food had a similar business model. Raspberry procurement was carried out through local cold storage facilities, followed by processing and selling to European buyers. After the acquisition of domestic companies by Roger Descours Group, France became a key player in the Serbian raspberry market. France imported 3.08 million kg of raspberries from Serbia during 2012 and 2013, prior to the integration. After the integration (2014–2023), imports to France increased to 19.96 million kg, representing a growth of 548%. In addition, entirely new markets emerged, such as Canada, which became a significant buyer, importing 4.34 million kg, and the United States, with nearly 1 million kg of Serbian raspberries. Furthermore, the share of exports to Belgium increased by 126%, and Bosnia and Herzegovina became a new export market. France became the dominant buyer of Serbian raspberries after integration, while new markets such as Canada and the USA were opened. The benefits of integration include increased exports and higher revenues for producers. The price increase brought higher profits for exporters and established new markets like Canada and the USA.

The downside is that high prices may reduce demand, and the creation of greater dependence on a few key buyers may destabilize production due to market fluctuations. Competitiveness in exports has increased, and Serbian raspberries now reach end buyers directly, without intermediaries, meaning exporters achieve better prices and higher revenues. Prices have become more stable, as there are no longer large fluctuations in raspberry values, since market flows now rely on stable contracts with major buyers, but the flexibility and diversification once characteristic of the sector have diminished. Price-setting mechanisms are increasingly influenced by centralized purchasing departments abroad, reducing the autonomy of Serbian firms and producers. Furthermore, large exporting firms have established rigorous quality standards and purchasing protocols, forcing small producers to comply or risk market exclusion. While these changes have led to increased purchase prices and more streamlined logistics, the power asymmetry between producers and buyers has intensified, marginalizing smaller actors who cannot meet the technical or volume requirements set by leading buyers.

The concentration of power among multinational entities also limits competition. In the past, dissatisfied producers could seek alternative buyers or informal market arrangements. Today, many of the largest buyers are part of the same integrated network, leaving limited options for negotiation or dispute resolution. This shift underscores the urgent need for policy interventions and targeted investments to empower small and medium-sized producers through education, technological modernization, and organizational support.

However, these aggregate figures mask uneven effects: small-scale farmers often faced reduced flexibility and greater vulnerability to buyer concentration. Price increases improved short-term incomes, but production risks (climate shocks, rising input costs) continued to undermine long-term sustainability for many households. The role of digital technologies in the raspberry sector is becoming increasingly significant. The application of precision agriculture (sensors for moisture and nutrients, drones for monitoring crop health), as well as blockchain systems for export traceability, enables greater transparency and quality control. As the World Bank (2021) points out, digital agriculture, including precision tools, blockchain for traceability and remote sensing, is a key enabler to increase productivity and sustainability in agribusiness.

Remote sensing through satellite imagery and GIS is used to assess yields and respond in a timely manner to climate change. In addition, EU and national programs (e.g., IPARD funds) are already financing digital innovation projects in fruit growing, which can facilitate the integration of small producers into modern value chains. According to the European Commission (2023), digitization in agriculture becomes a strategic priority within the Common Agricultural Policy of the EU, which further encourages the introduction of innovative technologies among small producers.

SOLUTIONS AND RECOMMENDATIONS

The story of Serbian raspberries is a tale of hard work, tradition, and resourcefulness of producers who have spent decades building the image of one of the highest-quality fruit products on the global market. However, alongside quality, the way raspberries are exported, to whom they are sold, and under what conditions has shaped the fate of this sector. Strengthen producer cooperatives and clusters, provide credit access, and ensure better representation of smallholders in negotiations. Policymakers should incentivize sustainable farming (water management, reduced pesticide use) to align competitiveness with environmental goals. Before Serbian raspberries reach their final consumer, they go through several stages:

1. **Producers:** Farmers who cultivate raspberries and sell them to buyers.
2. **Cold storage facilities and processors:** Store and process the raspberries for export.
3. **Exporters:** Organize sales in international markets.
4. **Major buyers and distributors:** Set prices and supply retail chains.
5. **Final consumers:** Purchase raspberries in retail outlets worldwide (Radosavljevic, 2008).

The integration of domestic companies into global agro-industrial supply chains was not merely an ownership change but brought about a new business model, a new distribution strategy, and a shift in the market position of Serbian raspberries.

Before integration (2012–2013), Yugent Food and Frucom Food operated as separate entities, exporting raspberries through a network of intermediaries. Their influence on market prices was limited, and the export destinations were more diverse but less stable. After the integration (2014–2023), Roger Descours Group took control of distribution, eliminated intermediaries, and directly marketed Serbian raspberries to France and other key markets. As a result, export prices increased, but there was also a growing dependence on a smaller number of buyers. Higher profits for exporters have been achieved by eliminating intermediaries, with a portion of the profit remaining in the companies that directly market the product. More stable prices have resulted from fewer price fluctuations, as negotiations are now conducted directly with end buyers. The increased negotiating power of Serbian exporters due to the integration has led to greater stability in operations because contracts are now long-term, and raspberry sales have become more predictable. The market expansion to Canada and the USA means that Serbian raspberries have the potential to become a global brand.

An in-depth analysis of Serbia's raspberry export performance reveals that the country has successfully maintained its leading global position in the export of this fruit, particularly in the frozen raspberry segment. Despite such achievements, Serbia's export success remains heavily influenced by a wide range of external factors, including volatile international market prices, fluctuating global demand, and increasingly unpredictable climatic conditions. These vulnerabilities highlight the fragility and, in many cases, unsustainability of the current model in the absence of comprehensive and long-term structural reforms within the domestic raspberry sector (Vapa-Tankosić et al., 2023; FAO, 2021).

A negative consequence is the reduced flexibility of Serbian companies, as they no longer have the ability to freely choose who and under what conditions they sell their raspberries. Exporters once had the option to select markets; now they depend on the strategy of a single large buyer. Serbian exports could be jeopardized if France's import policy changes, as there is a significant dependency on its market. Smaller exporters are losing market share because large chains have taken over key operations, leading to reduced competition in exports. The competitiveness of Serbian raspberries can be maintained by diversifying markets and reducing dependence on France, expanding distribution to Asia and the Middle East. Government should adopt targeted export diversification strategies (Asia, Middle East, North America) and promote domestic value-added processing (jams, concentrates, nutraceuticals). Digital transformation can represent a key strategy for increasing the competitiveness of the Serbian raspberry sector. It is recommended: (a) greater participation of the state in financing digital infrastructure in agriculture, (b) education of producers in the use of digital tools, and (c) inclusion of small producers in pilot projects based on blockchain traceability and precision agriculture. These measures strengthen the sector's resilience and reduce dependence on a limited number of customers.

Precision agriculture tools, such as sensors, drones, and satellite imaging, can help farmers monitor their crops in real time, optimise irrigation, and apply fertilizers and pesticides more efficiently. This can lead to cost savings, higher yields, and a reduction in environmental impact. Additionally, digital platforms can help producers better manage their supply chains by providing real-time data on market prices, weather conditions, and demand patterns. A wider view of economic integration in agriculture should be taken into consideration, including the role of digitalization, the application of new supply chain tracking technologies, and opportunities for production diversification to enhance market resilience to fluctuations in international trade (Kljajić et al., 2024). This would allow them to make informed decisions, plan their production cycles more effectively, and minimise post-harvest losses.

The introduction of blockchain technology could also play a pivotal role in improving the transparency and traceability of raspberry exports. With increasing demand from international markets for certified, high-quality products, blockchain could provide a secure and transparent system for tracking the entire journey of raspberries from farm to final consumer. This would not only enhance consumer confidence but also allow Serbian producers to meet the stringent food safety and quality standards required by premium markets, such as the European Union and the United States (Vapa-Tankosić et al., 2023).

Investing in modern processing facilities will allow Serbia to diversify its raspberry products, adding value to raw materials and reducing dependence on low-margin bulk exports. The development of processing capacity could enable the production of a wide range of value-added products, including organic raspberries, jams, purees, freeze-dried raspberries, and nutraceuticals. These products command higher prices in international markets and can help Serbian producers access premium market segments that prioritise health, sustainability, and quality.

Moreover, it is essential for the Serbian government to provide incentives and create a favourable investment climate for both domestic and foreign investors. This could include offering tax incentives, providing subsidies for the construction of processing facilities, and supporting training programs for workers in the processing industry. By promoting investment in processing capacity, Serbia can increase the value-added content of its raspberry exports, stabilise the sector, and reduce its dependence on raw product exports.

Serbian raspberries are not just a commodity—they are part of national identity, a symbol of hard work, and a source of income for thousands of families. Integration into global value chains has offered stability but at the cost of flexibility and autonomy. To secure a competitive future, Serbia must embrace a holistic strategy that combines digital transformation, value-added production, market diversification, climate adaptation, and cluster development. Only through such coordinated efforts can the country preserve its leadership in raspberry exports while maximizing economic, social, and environmental gains for its rural communities.

According to Manić et al. (2019), the current state of Serbia's raspberry production sector is characterised by a high degree of fragmentation and a lack of institutional support, whereby producers are largely left to negotiate on their own with buyers and suppliers. The insufficient development of market institutions and regulatory mechanisms has resulted in significant systemic deficiencies, undermining the stability and long-term sustainability of the raspberry value chain. This has generated persistent dissatisfaction among producers, often manifested through recurring annual cycles of unrest, including farmer protests, contentious negotiations with government representatives, mutual accusations between producers, buyers and processors, and the implementation of only temporary, short-term solutions.

Through this analysis, the study aims to determine whether Serbian exporters are now in a stronger market position or have become overly reliant on a single major buyer. However, after the integration of domestic companies into the Roger Descours Group, Serbian raspberries are now sold directly to large buyers, which has led to significant changes. Until 2014, domestic companies like Yugent Food and Frucom Food were among the leading exporters but operated within a system that made them dependent on intermediaries. These intermediaries often had the final say in price formation, and producers had to accept what the market dictated. However, the arrival of Roger Descours Group changed the rules of the game.

This was not just an acquisition of companies but a turning point in which domestic exporters became part of the global distribution chain, with all the advantages and challenges this entails. By eliminating intermediaries, producers and exporters are securing better prices per kilogram. Higher export prices have been achieved because producers are receiving better prices for their products than before the integration. The loss of export competition is also evident as smaller exporters like Frucom DOO lose part of their market share. Therefore, it is crucial not only to track the numbers but also to make informed decisions to ensure that this sector continues to grow in the future.

One of the primary challenges facing the sector lies in the inadequate level of organisation among primary producers. The absence of strong producer associations and cooperatives limits the ability of small-scale growers to collectively negotiate better contract terms, stabilize prices, and exert influence on market trends. Without institutionalised collective action, producers often operate in isolation, facing difficulties in accessing relevant market information, technologies, and credit facilities. This situation not only weakens their market position but also hampers the development of a resilient and adaptive production system (Manić et al., 2019).

Furthermore, the lack of vertical integration across the raspberry value chain remains a major obstacle to value creation and competitiveness. Most of the value added is captured by intermediaries and foreign buyers, while Serbian producers and processors receive a disproportionately small share of final product revenues. Integrating production, processing, distribution, and export into cohesive and coordinated frameworks could significantly increase operational efficiency, reduce post-harvest losses, and improve profitability throughout the entire chain (Sredojević et al., 2013).

The post-transition period of the Serbian economy has clearly demonstrated the urgent need to adapt to new market dynamics and institutional frameworks. Unlike in more developed economies where coordinated agricultural policy and producer organisations play a key role in market regulation, the Serbian raspberry sector remains underorganised and exposed to fluctuations driven by both internal inefficiencies and external shocks. As a result, the bargaining position of individual producers remains weak, while the lack of contractual certainty and price transparency perpetuates instability in the sector. These structural weaknesses have been further exacerbated by limited access to credit, a lack of collective action mechanisms, and an underdeveloped system for risk management. Moreover, asymmetric power relations between smallholders and dominant intermediaries in the purchasing and processing segments create an uneven distribution of value added across the supply chain. This, in turn, has discouraged investment and innovation at the farm level, contributing to stagnation in productivity and competitiveness.

In conclusion, while Serbia has managed to preserve its status as a major global raspberry exporter, the sector's long-term sustainability and competitiveness depend on addressing core structural issues. Organisational reform, vertical integration, product diversification, and investments in advanced processing capacities must be treated as strategic priorities to ensure that Serbian raspberries not only remain globally relevant but also evolve into a model of resilience and innovation in agri-food export development. Based on the analysis of theoretical models and market data, it can be concluded that integration brought numerous benefits to Serbian raspberry exports: more efficient supply chains, more stable prices, and greater control over placement, with direct access to key European buyers.

However, there are also certain risks: greater dependence on smaller groups of buyers (e.g., France), reduced flexibility for domestic exporters, and fewer opportunities for smaller exporters to compete in the market. Policies supporting domestic farmers, such as fostering producer clusters, improving production standards, and diversifying export markets, can play a key role in maintaining sector competitiveness. While Serbia has maintained its position as a leading global exporter of raspberries, challenges arising from fragmentation in the raspberry sector have highlighted the need for comprehensive and systemic reforms. This includes addressing issues related to producer organisation, vertical integration, product diversification, and investment in processing infrastructure.

Furthermore, strengthening institutions such as producer organisations, export promotion agencies, and quality assurance bodies is essential for improving market access and ensuring compliance with international standards. By working closely with international partners, the government can help Serbian producers meet the increasingly stringent requirements of global markets and establish long-term trade agreements with key export destinations. To address these systemic challenges, a coordinated and multi-stakeholder approach is essential. Key actors in the raspberry value chain – including producers, aggregators, processors, and state institutions – must assume proactive roles within their respective domains to initiate and implement necessary reforms. These reforms should aim to improve governance mechanisms, establish fair and transparent pricing systems, promote contract farming models, and foster the development of strong producer organisations capable of negotiating better market conditions. Only through a comprehensive and collaborative effort will it be possible to overcome the limitations of the current system and create a more resilient, competitive, and equitable raspberry sector. The development of institutional infrastructure, coupled with targeted policy incentives and support for knowledge transfer, represents a strategic imperative for ensuring the long-term viability of one of Serbia's most important export-oriented agricultural sectors.

FUTURE RESEARCH DIRECTIONS

To improve the overall governance of the sector, Serbia should implement a sectoral development strategy based on four pillars: (1) strengthening producer organizations and clusters; (2) fostering innovation and digitalization; (3) attracting investment in value-added processing; and (4) expanding into new markets.

The establishment of a national raspberry board or interbranch organization, modeled on successful European examples, could facilitate public-private dialogue and promote coordinated export strategies. Investments in farmer cooperatives, digital traceability systems, and quality control mechanisms can help bridge the gap between smallholders and global markets, improving overall competitiveness and resilience.

Moreover, Serbia must reduce its overreliance on the export of unprocessed raspberries and focus on value addition through agro-industrial development. The production of raspberry-based products—such as organic juices, jams, concentrates, and freeze-dried formats—not only enhances product value but also creates opportunities for local employment, rural development, and export diversification.

This transformation requires strategic support for domestic processing capacities, especially through foreign direct investment (FDI), public-private partnerships, and innovation-driven clusters. The development of specialized fruit-processing zones with cold-chain infrastructure, food safety laboratories, and R&D centers could significantly raise the sector's productivity and product differentiation. Furthermore, branding initiatives and the protection of geographical indications (GIs) could elevate Serbia's position in high-value niche markets.

In light of these changes, digitalization of the agricultural value chain presents a unique opportunity to improve the transparency, traceability, and efficiency of raspberry production. By adopting smart farming tools, blockchain-based logistics platforms, and digital quality control, producers and exporters can ensure compliance with international standards, improve yields, and better align supply with global demand. The integration of digital platforms can also strengthen farmer–buyer relations, facilitate direct sales, and provide early access to market data, thus reducing reliance on intermediaries. climate-resilient farming practices must be urgently developed and disseminated through national extension services and academic-industry partnerships. The anticipated impact of climate change on temperature variability, rainfall distribution, and pest incidence could drastically affect future raspberry yields unless adaptive technologies—such as mulching systems, anti-hail nets, and precision irrigation—are systematically introduced. Serbia's higher education and research institutions have a role to play in developing and disseminating best practices. Universities can collaborate with industry partners to conduct applied research in post-harvest handling, processing optimization, and sustainable packaging. Capacity-building programs, including vocational training and agricultural entrepreneurship workshops, can equip farmers and rural youth with the skills needed to participate in higher segments of the value chain. Additionally, public funding programs, co-financed by EU pre-accession funds or development banks, should be directed toward innovation in sustainable agriculture and food processing. Incentives for energy-efficient machinery, eco-friendly packaging, and waste reduction practices could position Serbia as a model for green and inclusive growth in the agri-food sector.

It is equally important to explore and expand into emerging export markets such as the Middle East, East Asia, and North America, which show growing interest in premium and organic fruit products. By establishing trade promotion offices abroad, participating in international fairs, and negotiating bilateral trade agreements, Serbia could diversify its export portfolio and reduce dependency on the European Union market.

In Serbia, the cultivation of raspberries (Rubus idaeus) transcends the boundaries of agriculture—it represents a deep-rooted element of national identity, tradition, and economic survival. This fruit has become emblematic of perseverance, intergenerational agricultural heritage, and a vital source of income for tens of thousands of smallholder farmers, particularly in Western Serbia, where favorable agroecological conditions have supported its development for decades. Over time, Serbian raspberries have become synonymous with high quality and exceptional taste, earning global recognition. However, despite the global success of this export-oriented commodity, the journey from small rural farms to international supermarket shelves has been characterized by systemic inefficiencies, market volatility, and structural vulnerabilities (Radosavljević, 2016).

Historically, the raspberry value chain in Serbia was dominated by a fragmented network of intermediaries, which led to limited transparency and price unpredictability. Producers often lacked bargaining power and were subject to fluctuating market conditions, with little control over the terms of sale or the final value captured by the product. The absence of vertically integrated systems or strong producer organizations contributed to a supply chain in which small farmers bore disproportionate risks while reaping minimal financial benefits. During this period, Serbian exporters could independently select target markets and negotiate contracts with diverse international partners, allowing for a degree of flexibility and adaptability that helped navigate shifts in global demand.

One of the most pressing issues identified in the analysis is the lack of organisation among raspberry producers. Many smallholders operate independently, with limited access to market information, technology, and financial resources. This not only weakens their negotiating position in the market but also limits the sector's ability to leverage economies of scale. A strategic shift towards clusterization – the establishment of geographical clusters of producers, processors, and other stakeholders – could significantly enhance the collective competitiveness of Serbia's raspberry sector.

Clusters can enable producers to share resources, reduce costs, and improve product quality through the pooling of technological and human capital. By forming producer organisations or cooperatives, raspberry growers would be better positioned to collectively negotiate for higher prices, access better infrastructure, and secure long-term supply contracts. These organisations could also facilitate the exchange of best practices, ensuring that growers adopt modern agricultural practices and sustainable farming techniques. Furthermore, clusters can help integrate the raspberry production process, creating a more efficient value chain that reduces fragmentation and improves market access for small producers. Lessons from the Serbian case extend to other developing countries undergoing agro-industrial integration. The balance between stability and dependency, as well as the socio-economic resilience of rural communities, are issues common to many export-oriented agri-food systems.

A well-organised raspberry cluster could also provide a platform for collaboration with research institutions, universities, and extension services, ensuring that producers have access to the latest knowledge and innovations. This would help drive productivity improvements and enhance the resilience of the sector to market and climate shocks. Additionally, clusters can facilitate the development of shared services, such as cold storage facilities, packaging services, and distribution networks, which can help reduce costs and improve the efficiency of the entire supply chain (Sredojević et al., 2013).

However, a significant strategic shift occurred with the increasing integration of Serbian raspberry exporters into global agri-food networks, particularly with the rise of long-term supply contracts involving multinational corporations. France, for example, has emerged as the largest single destination for Serbian raspberries, accounting for more than 50% of total exports in recent years. While this development has brought greater market security, stability of sales channels, and improved price reliability, it has also introduced new challenges related to dependency and centralization of decision-making outside Serbian borders (Radosavljević, 2024). Exporters, now operating under the umbrella of multinational procurement systems, have gained stability and access to larger markets.

Looking ahead, Serbia's future competitiveness in the raspberry market will depend on its ability to transform from a supplier of raw agricultural commodities into a knowledge-based, export-oriented agro-industrial economy. Such transformation is possible only through a synergistic approach that includes international cooperation, investment incentives, rural innovation, and strong institutional frameworks. If Serbia successfully transitions to a vertically integrated, climate-resilient, and digitally enabled raspberry sector, it could serve as a replicable model for other high-value agricultural industries across the Western Balkans.

CONCLUSION

For years, domestic producers have faced numerous challenges, from price fluctuations and dependence on intermediaries to unstable markets. Companies operated independently, often with limited capacities and weak negotiating power. Raspberries were in demand, but the benefits of exports typically ended up in the hands of traders and intermediaries, while producers received only a fraction of the product's total value.

The change occurred in 2014 when domestic companies entered the vertical integration system through acquisition by the Roger Descours Group. Following the acquisition of domestic firms Yugent Food and Frucom Food by Roger Descours Group, the export process became more direct, allowing raspberries to reach buyers without unnecessary intermediaries. In practice, this led to a reduction in distribution costs, as direct exporters assumed a greater role in the supply chain. Additionally, price stability increased, as prices were no longer subject to intermediary speculation. However, market flexibility decreased, as domestic producers became dependent on a single large distribution system.

The most significant change occurred in how raspberries were exported and marketed. Before integration, France was already a major buyer, importing around 3 million kilograms of Serbian raspberries annually. After the acquisition, this number surged to 19.96 million kilograms, a 548% increase. The number of markets decreased, as Belgium, Germany, and Poland had been significant buyers, but now most exports are directed to France.

The export price rose from an average of €1.99/kg before 2014 to €2.88/kg, representing an increase of 44.9%. Previously, traders controlled the prices and resold raspberries to larger importers. However, after eliminating intermediaries, Serbian companies now work directly with end buyers, stabilizing prices but reducing flexibility in market selection. On the one hand, this meant security in sales as Serbian producers no longer had to worry about seasonal price fluctuations. On the other hand, they became highly dependent on one large buyer—France.

The future of Serbian raspberries will depend on the domestic sector's ability to adapt to global trends while recognizing its strengths—quality, tradition, and market recognition. The key to success will lie in smart development policies, further integration with new markets, and strengthening the Serbian raspberry brand as a premium product.

In conclusion, after the acquisition of Yugent Food and Frucom Food by Roger Descours Group, export volume and value increased. France became the dominant export market. The average export price significantly increased after 2015, reaching a peak of €5.09/kg in 2022. The removal of intermediaries and direct control over prices increased export profitability. Horizontal and vertical cooperation and integration within the food supply chain play a crucial role in the efficiency of marketing channels in both domestic and international markets.

In addition to strengthening vertical linkages, Serbia must prioritise product diversification as a core strategic objective. The heavy reliance on the export of bulk frozen raspberries makes the sector highly sensitive to global price shocks and market saturation. By investing in product innovation – including the development of value-added goods such as organic raspberries, freeze-dried raspberries, raspberry concentrates, purees, jams, and nutraceuticals – Serbian exporters could access premium segments and reduce vulnerability to commodity price fluctuations. Such diversification would also enable alignment with evolving consumer preferences in high-income markets, particularly those emphasizing health, traceability, and sustainability.

Investment in processing infrastructure and technological modernisation is another critical area. The current level of processing capacity is insufficient to absorb fluctuations in fresh raspberry supply, leading to inefficiencies and reduced export competitiveness. Developing modern facilities for sorting, freezing, packaging, and transforming raspberries into high-value products would enhance the quality and consistency of Serbian exports. Additionally, establishing quality certification systems (e.g., GlobalG.A.P., organic, HACCP) would allow producers to meet stringent international standards and unlock new market opportunities.

Finally, a robust national strategy for export development should include targeted state support for producer integration, innovation incentives, capacity-building programs, and facilitation of public-private partnerships. Without such interventions, Serbia risks losing its competitive edge in the face of rising international competition, especially from countries like Poland, Chile, and Mexico, which have made significant strides in modernising their horticultural sectors.

Foreign investments can bring significant advancements in infrastructure, technology, and logistics, but it is crucial to ensure that local producers are not excluded from decision-making processes and the distribution of economic value. To ensure the long-term sustainability of the sector and improve its competitiveness, it is crucial to adopt strategies such as clusterization, digitalization, and attracting investment in processing capacities. These strategies can serve as the cornerstone for modernising the raspberry sector, improving productivity, and creating a more resilient value chain capable of responding to both global market trends and internal challenges.

The process of digital transformation is rapidly reshaping the global agricultural landscape, offering new opportunities for improving efficiency, transparency, and market access. Digitalization is a critical component for increasing the competitiveness of Serbia's raspberry sector, as it can streamline production processes, improve traceability, and enhance market intelligence. By implementing digital technologies, such as precision farming, big data analytics, and blockchain, producers can optimise their operations and improve the quality and consistency of their products.

In addition, digital marketing platforms could provide Serbian raspberry producers with direct access to international buyers, bypassing intermediaries and enhancing their market access. E-commerce platforms dedicated to agricultural products could help Serbian producers reach global markets, particularly in regions with growing demand for high-quality fruits. Digital marketing tools, including social media and targeted advertising, could also help promote the unique qualities of Serbian raspberries, thereby increasing brand recognition and demand.

A significant portion of Serbia's raspberry exports consists of frozen raspberries, which limits the value-added potential of the sector. The heavy reliance on the export of bulk raw products exposes the sector to price fluctuations and makes it more vulnerable to competition from other countries with lower production costs. To improve the sustainability and profitability of the sector, it is essential to attract investment in processing infrastructure.

Attracting foreign direct investment (FDI) in processing infrastructure is crucial for transforming the sector. FDI can bring much-needed capital, technological expertise, and managerial know-how, which can help modernise processing plants, improve product quality, and expand capacity. Additionally, partnerships with multinational food companies could provide access to global distribution networks, enhancing Serbia's ability to penetrate high-demand markets such as the European Union, the United States, and Japan.

Sustaining the growth and global relevance of the raspberry industry requires coordinated efforts across the entire value chain. From the field to the final consumer, each stage must be guided by principles of sustainability, technological advancement, and strategic foresight. Countries that recognize and invest in these priorities will be better positioned to lead the next generation of raspberry production and export, securing long-term benefits for both rural communities and national economies.

In summary, Serbia's raspberry sector has significant potential to remain a leading global exporter. However, this potential can only be realised through the implementation of strategic reforms that address the core challenges facing the sector. Clusterization, digitalization, and investment in processing capacity are the key strategies that can enhance the competitiveness of Serbia's raspberry production and increase its global market share. By fostering cooperation, modernising production processes, and diversifying products, Serbia can strengthen its position as a major player in the global raspberry market while ensuring the long-term sustainability of its agricultural sector.

For the strategies of clusterization, digitalization, and investment in processing to succeed, there must be strong support from both the government and private sector. The Serbian government can play a pivotal role in creating a regulatory environment that encourages investment, innovation, and market-oriented reforms. This includes the introduction of policies that support infrastructure development, the creation of favourable tax regimes for producers and processors, and the provision of subsidies for research and development in agriculture.

ACKNOWLEDGMENT

Paper is a part of research financed by the MSTDI RS, agreed in decision no. 451-03-136/2025-03/200009 from 4.2.2025.

REFERENCES

Beekwilder, J., Hall, R. D., & de Vos, C. H. R. (2005). Identification and dietary relevance of antioxidants from raspberry. *BioFactors (Oxford, England)*, *23*(4), 197–205. DOI: 10.1002/biof.5520230404

Bin, X., & Jiangyong, L. U. (2009). Foreign direct investment, processing trade, and the sophistication of China's exports. *China Economic Review*, *20*(3), 425–439. DOI: 10.1016/j.chieco.2009.01.004

Borensztein, E., De Gregorio, J., & Lee, J. W. (1998). How does foreign direct investment affect economic growth? *Journal of International Economics*, *45*(1), 115–135. DOI: 10.1016/S0022-1996(97)00033-0

Cantó Calvo, V. M. (2022). *Development of a circular economy evaluation model for hotels* (Doctoral dissertation, Universitat Politècnica de València).

Clapp, J. (2021). The problem with growing corporate concentration and power in the global food system. *Nature Food*, *2*(6), 404–408. DOI: 10.1038/s43016-021-00297-7

Cotula, L. (2009). *Land grab or development opportunity?: agricultural investment and international land deals in Africa*. Iied.

Cvijanović, D., Ignjatijević, S., & Vapa Tankosić, J. (2017). Raspberry trade as a strategic export potential of the Republic of Serbia. *Competitiveness of Agro-Food and Environmental Economy*, 74–85.

Dale, A., Tzanetakis, I. E., & Walsh, C. S. (2013). Raspberry. In Badenes, M. L., & Byrne, D. H. (Eds.), *Fruit Breeding* (pp. 233–251). Springer.

Daniel, E. M., Krupnick, A. S., Heur, Y. H., Blinzler, J. A., Nims, R. W., & Stoner, G. D. (1989). Extraction, stability, and quantitation of ellagic acid in various fruits and nuts. *Journal of Food Composition and Analysis*, *2*(4), 338–349. DOI: 10.1016/0889-1575(89)90005-7

Dries, L., Germenji, E., Noev, N., & Swinnen, J. F. (2009). Farmers, vertical coordination, and the restructuring of dairy supply chains in Central and Eastern Europe. *World Development*, *37*(11), 1742–1758. DOI: 10.1016/j.worlddev.2008.08.029

Dries, L., Reardon, T., & Swinnen, J. F. (2004). The rapid rise of supermarkets in Central and Eastern Europe: Implications for the agrifood sector and rural development. *Development Policy Review*, *22*(5), 525–556. DOI: 10.1111/j.1467-7679.2004.00264.x

European Commission. (2023). *Digitalisation. Agriculture and Rural Development.* https://agriculture.ec.europa.eu/overview-vision-agriculture-food/digitalisation_en

FAO. (2021). *FAOSTAT – Raspberry Production and Export Data.* https://www.fao.org/faostat/en

Fatimah, Y. A., Govindan, K., Murniningsih, R., & Setiawan, A. (2020). Industry 4.0 based sustainable circular economy approach for smart waste management system to achieve sustainable development goals: A case study of Indonesia. *Journal of Cleaner Production*, *269*, 122263. DOI: 10.1016/j.jclepro.2020.122263

Ganzorig, B., & Nachin, D. (2006). Trends in international investment flows: Foreign direct investment in Mongolia. *Journal of International Logistics and Trade*, *4*(2), 107–120. DOI: 10.24006/jilt.2006.4.2.107

Gereffi, G., Humphrey, J., & Sturgeon, T. (2005). The governance of global value chains. *Review of International Political Economy*, *12*(1), 78–104. DOI: 10.1080/09692290500049805

Greenaway, D., Sousa, N., & Wakelin, K. (2004). Do domestic firms learn to export from multinationals? *European Journal of Political Economy*, *20*(4), 1027–1043. DOI: 10.1016/j.ejpoleco.2003.12.006

Helpman, E. (1984). A simple theory of international trade with multinational corporations. *Journal of Political Economy*, *92*(3), 451–471. DOI: 10.1086/261236

Hobbs, J. E. (2021). Food supply chain resilience and the COVID-19 pandemic: What have we learned?. *Canadian Journal of Agricultural Economics/Revue canadienne d'agroeconomie, 69*(2), 189-196.

ITC – International Trade Centre. (2021). *Trade Map – Serbia Raspberry Export Statistics* https://www.trademap.org/tradestatistics.aspx

Jennings, D. L. (1988). *Raspberries and Blackberries: Their Breeding, Diseases and Growth.* Academic Press.

Kalanović-Bulatović, B., Dimitrijević, B., Milić, D., & Milovančević, Z. (2015). Organization and costs of repurchasing, transportation, warehousing and storage of raspberry fruit. *Ekonomika Poljoprivrede*, *62*(4), 1017–1030. DOI: 10.5937/ekoPolj1504017K

Kljajić, N. (2012). *Ekonomska efikasnost investicija u različitim uslovima proizvodnje maline* (Doktorska disertacija, Univerzitet u Novom Sadu, Poljoprivredni fakultet).

Kljajić, N., Paraušić, V., & Kostić, Z. (2024). Economic aspects of digitalization in Serbian agriculture: Perceptions of farm managers. *Ekonomika Poljoprivrede*, *71*(3), 943–956. DOI: 10.59267/ekoPolj2403943K

Kljajić, N., Subić, J., & Sredojević, Z. (2017). Profitability of raspberry production on holdings in the territory of Arilje. *Ekonomika Poljoprivrede*, *64*(1), 57–69. DOI: 10.5937/ekoPolj1701057K

Kojima, K. (1975). International trade and foreign investment: Substitutes or complements. *Hitotsubashi Journal of Economics*, *16*(1), 1–12.

Kokko, A. (2003). *The economics of foreign direct investment incentives* (No. 3775). CEPR Discussion Papers.

Lipsey, R. E., & Sjöholm, F. (2005). The impact of inward FDI on host countries: why such different answers?. *Does foreign direct investment promote development*, 23-43.

Manić, E., & Janković, I. (2019). Održivost u sektoru malinarstva: primer Srbije. *Ekonomski vidici, 24*(1–2), 79–92.

Milić, D., Sredojević, Z., & Lukač-Bulatović, M. (2017). Sustainability organizational-economic model of value chain organic raspberry. *Journal on Processing and Energy in Agriculture*, *21*(3), 163–167. DOI: 10.5937/JPEA1703163M

Ministry of Finance of the Republic of Serbia. *Database on Raspberry Export*. Available at: https://www.carina.rs/

Mullen, W., McGinn, J., Lean, M. E. J., MacLean, M. R., Gardner, P., Duthie, G. G., & Crozier, A. (2002). Ellagitannins, flavonoids, and other phenolics in red raspberries and their contribution to antioxidant capacity and vasorelaxation properties. *Journal of Agricultural and Food Chemistry*, *50*(18), 5191–5196. DOI: 10.1021/jf020140n

OECD. (2025). *Agricultural Outlook 2025-2034*. https://www.oecd.org/en/publications/oecd-fao-agricultural-outlook-2025-2034_601276cd-en.html

Popović, V. Ž., Kalanović, B., & Živković, V. R. (2003). Malina u proizvodnji i izvozu poljoprivrede Srbije. *Ekonomika Poljoprivrede*, *50*(3), 267–275.

Porter, M. E. (2008). The five competitive forces that shape strategy. *Harvard Business Review*, *86*(1), 78.

Radosavljević, K. (2008). Market chain of fruit production in Serbia – Case study of raspberry and sour cherry. *Economic Annals, 177*(177), 103–121. DOI: 10.2298/EKA0877103R

Radosavljević, K. (2016). Enhancing agri-competitiveness – A cost-benefit analysis of raspberry production on a family farm. *The Economics of Enterprise, 7–8*(7-8), 492–498. DOI: 10.5937/ekopre1608492R

Radosavljević, K. (2024). The path of the Republic of Serbia into the global raspberry marketing channel. *The Economics of Enterprise, 7–8*(7-8), 379–386. DOI: 10.5937/EKOPRE2408379R

Radovanović, J., Radosavljević, K., & Pătârlăgeanu Simona, R. (2024). Analysis of the role of FDI in the economic growth and environmental protection with particular reference to certain economic sectors in Serbia. *International Review, Faculty of Business Economics and Entrepreneurship, 3–4/2024*, 22–32.

Reardon, T., & Timmer, C. P. (2014). Five inter-linked transformations in the Asian agrifood economy: Food security implications. *Global Food Security, 3*(2), 108–117. DOI: 10.1016/j.gfs.2014.02.001

Republic Statistical Office (RZS). (2020). *Statistical Yearbook of the Republic of Serbia*. Belgrade, Serbia: Republic Statistical Office.

Slavin, J. L. (2005). Dietary fiber and body weight. *Nutrition (Burbank, Los Angeles County, Calif.), 21*(3), 411–418. DOI: 10.1016/j.nut.2004.08.018

Sredojević, Z., Kljajić, N., & Popović, N. (2013). *Investing in raspberry as an opportunity of sustainable development of rural areas of western Serbia. Buletinul Revista categoria B+ CNCSIS, Seria Stiinte Economice, Petrol-Gaze din Ploiesti, 1/201, II.* LXV.

STIPS – Agricultural Market Information System of Serbia. (2010). *Izveštaj o izvozu voća* [*Report on fruit exports*]. Ministry of Agriculture, Forestry and Water Management of the Republic of Serbia.

USDA – U.S. Department of Agriculture. (2022). *FoodData Central: Raspberries, raw*. https://fdc.nal.usda.gov/

Vapa Tankosić, J., Ignjatijević, S., Lekić, N., Kljajić, N., Ivaniš, M., Andžić, S., & Ristić, D. (2023). The role of environmental attitudes and risk for adoption in respect to the farmers' participation in the agri-environmental practices. *Agriculture, 13*(12), 2248. DOI: 10.3390/agriculture13122248

World Bank. (2021). *Digital agriculture: Tools, policies and perspectives*. World Bank., DOI: 10.1596/978-1-4648-1658-4

Wróblewska, W., Pawlak, J., & Paszko, D. (2019). Economic aspects in the raspberry production on the example of farms from Poland, Serbia and Ukraine. *Journal of Horticultural Research, 27*(2), 71–80. DOI: 10.2478/johr-2019-0019

Zdravković, M., Grekulović, V., Štrbac, N., Zdravković, B., Gorgievski, M., Marković, M., & Marković, M. (2024). Malina i kupina gajene u Srbiji sa aspekta Zelene agende [Raspberries and blackberries grown in Serbia from the perspective of the Green Agenda]. *Ecologica, 31*(114), 137–143. DOI: 10.18485/ecologica.2024.31.114.3

Zhang, K. H., & Song, S. (2001). Promoting exports: The role of inward FDI in China. *China Economic Review, 11*(4), 385–396. DOI: 10.1016/S1043-951X(01)00033-5

ADDITIONAL READING

Chen, C., Sheng, Y., & Findlay, C. (2013). Export Spillovers of FDI on C hina's Domestic Firms. *Review of International Economics, 21*(5), 841–856. DOI: 10.1111/roie.12074

Hersleth, S. A., Kubberød, E., & Gonera, A. (2022). The farm-based entrepreneur's marketing mix: A case study from the local food sector. *Journal of Research in Marketing and Entrepreneurship, 24*(1), 176–194. DOI: 10.1108/JRME-12-2020-0166

Peano, C., Girgenti, V., Baudino, C., & Giuggioli, N. R. (2017). Blueberry supply chain in Italy: Management, innovation and sustainability. *Sustainability (Basel), 9*(2), 261. DOI: 10.3390/su9020261

Penson, B. J., Capps, O., & Rosson, C. P. (2002). *Introduction to agricultural economics* (3rd ed.). Pearson, Prentice Hall.

Stojanović, Ž., & Radosavljević, K. (2013). Food chain, agricultural competitiveness and industrial policy: A case study of the Serbian raspberry production and export. *Ekonomika preduzeća, 61*(3-4), 174-182.

Vermeir, I., & Verbeke, W. (2006). Sustainable food consumption: Exploring the consumer "attitude–behavioral intention" gap. *Journal of Agricultural & Environmental Ethics, 19*(2), 169–194. DOI: 10.1007/s10806-005-5485-3

Zeriti, A., Robson, M. J., Spyropoulou, S., & Leonidou, C. N. (2014). Sustainable export marketing strategy fit and performance. *Journal of International Marketing, 22*(4), 44–66. DOI: 10.1509/jim.14.0063

Zhang, X. (2010, August). Study on the effects of FDI in Chinese forestry on foreign trade of forest products. In *2010 International Conference on Management and Service Science* (pp. 1-4). IEEE DOI: 10.1109/ICMSS.2010.5576944

KEY TERMS AND DEFINITIONS

Export Dependency: Reliance on foreign markets for the majority of sales, which can create stability but also risk if demand shifts.

Export Stabilization: Maintaining consistent export levels through predictable pricing, contracts, or diversified markets.

Global Agro-Industrial Chains: Networks spanning countries that involve production, processing, and distribution of agricultural goods, enabling access to global markets.

Intermediaries: Middlemen connecting producers with buyers, facilitating market access but potentially reducing control over pricing.

Market Diversification: Expanding sales across multiple regions or customer segments to reduce reliance on a single market and increase resilience.

Negotiating Power: The ability to influence terms and outcomes of commercial agreements or transactions.

Processed Products: Agricultural goods that have been transformed or value-added, such as juices, jams, or packaged products.

Product Placement: Strategic positioning of products in the market to maximize visibility and accessibility to consumers.

Supply Chain Management: Coordination of production, processing, and distribution activities to ensure efficiency and timely delivery.

Vertical Integration: A business strategy where a company controls multiple stages of its supply chain to improve efficiency, reduce costs, or secure supply.

Chapter 3
Redefining Food Sovereignty:
The Strategic Role of Local Food Systems and Short Food Supply Chains

Tanasa Lucian
https://orcid.org/0000-0002-6127-0958
"Gheorghe Zane" Institute for Economic and Social Research, Romania

Sebastian Dobo
"Gheorghe Zane" Institute for Economic and Social Research, Romania

Ioan Sebastian Brumă
https://orcid.org/0000-0002-0549-5474
"Gheorghe Zane" Institute for Economic and Social Research, Romania

ABSTRACT

A synergistic relationship between Local Food Systems (LFSs) and Short Food Supply Chains (SFSCs) provides the essential framework for realizing food sovereignty. This conceptual review analyzes this framework as a vital alternative to the unsustainable trajectory of conventional agri-food systems. While the merits are clear—including local economic stimulation, enhanced social cohesion, and ecological integrity—the viability of these systems is constrained by structural barriers, affordability concerns, and fragmented governance that can paradoxically deepen inequities. Consequently, for LFSs and SFSCs to mature into genuine instruments of food justice, their development cannot be passive. It demands intentional governance and supportive policies underpinned by a foundational commitment to equitable access.

DOI: 10.4018/979-8-3373-2898-0.ch003

1. INTRODUCTION

Local agri-food systems play a crucial role in ensuring food security by providing direct access to fresh, high-quality produce while strengthening local economies and community bonds. These systems enhance resilience by reducing dependence on conventional global supply chains, thereby mitigating risks from external shocks such as economic crises, pandemics, and climate change. Furthermore, by championing local producers and cultural heritage, they cultivate an environment ripe for sustainable business innovation and contribute to robust rural economies that align effectively with regional development strategies (Tanasă, 2024a).

Recent societal upheavals, including economic crises, pandemics, and armed conflicts, have underscored global uncertainties and intensified focus on the sustainability of agri-food systems. Conventional systems are increasingly viewed as inadequately designed for long-term sustainability and resilience, compelling food value chains to implement new measures to bolster these aspects (McGarraghy et al., 2022). The societal demand for sustainable, safe, and high-quality food necessitates a fundamental shift in how food is produced, distributed, valorized, and consumed (Bilska, Piecek, & Kołożyn-Krajewska, 2018).

In response, the local food movement arose in the early 21st century, propelled by a shift in consumer values. Key drivers included a greater focus on nutrition and health, concerns for environmental sustainability, the desire to support local communities, and an increasing preference for strengthening local socio-economic systems by purchasing locally-sourced agricultural products (Mesić et al., 2020; Meyerding et al., 2019; Reich et al., 2018). This fundamental change in eating and buying habits stems from a combination of factors: the pursuit of public health objectives, a commitment to ecological stewardship by reducing conventional agriculture's carbon footprint, and a conscious effort to bolster community resilience through support for small-scale producers and processors.

Locavorism, an offshoot of localism, is a food movement that promotes consuming locally sourced, seasonal foods to enhance sustainability, support local communities and economies, and mitigate the environmental impact of extensive agrifood transportation. This burgeoning ideology holds increasing significance for marketers and consumer researchers (Reich et al., 2018). With its foundations in food sovereignty, local food systems, and SFSCs, locavorism prioritizes direct connections between producers or processors and end consumers, which are crucial for building trust and enabling food traceability. Research confirms its benefits, including smaller carbon footprints and the safeguarding of local biodiversity. However, challenges like restricted availability, the constraints of seasonality, and higher prices can impede its widespread adoption and accessibility (Feagan, 2007; Sims, 2009).

This paper explores the concepts of food sovereignty, Local Food Systems (LFSs), and Short Food Supply Chains (SFSCs) as strategic frameworks for this necessary transformation. It argues that these concepts are intricately linked, forming a powerful synergy for developing sustainable, resilient, and equitable agri-food systems.

2. METHODOLOGY

This paper employs a conceptual analysis methodology, grounded in a comprehensive review of specialized scientific literature. The research process involved a systematic search of academic databases, including Scopus, Web of Science, and Google Scholar, to identify relevant peer-reviewed journal articles, books, conference proceedings, and key policy documents. The search strategy utilized a combination of primary keywords: "food sovereignty," "local food systems" (LFS), "short food supply chains" (SFSCs), "proximity," "food governance," "sustainability," and "resilience."

The selection criteria prioritized sources that provided definitions, empirical evidence, or theoretical discussions on the interrelationships between these core concepts. The collected literature was then subjected to a thematic analysis to synthesize the primary benefits, challenges, and framework conditions associated with LFS and SFSCs. The objective of this approach was not to conduct a meta-analysis of quantitative data, but rather to construct a coherent and nuanced conceptual framework that defines, differentiates, and integrates the strategic roles of food sovereignty, LFS, and SFSCs in the development of sustainable and equitable agri-food systems.

Figure 1. Design Thinking Framework for Building Resilient Food Systems

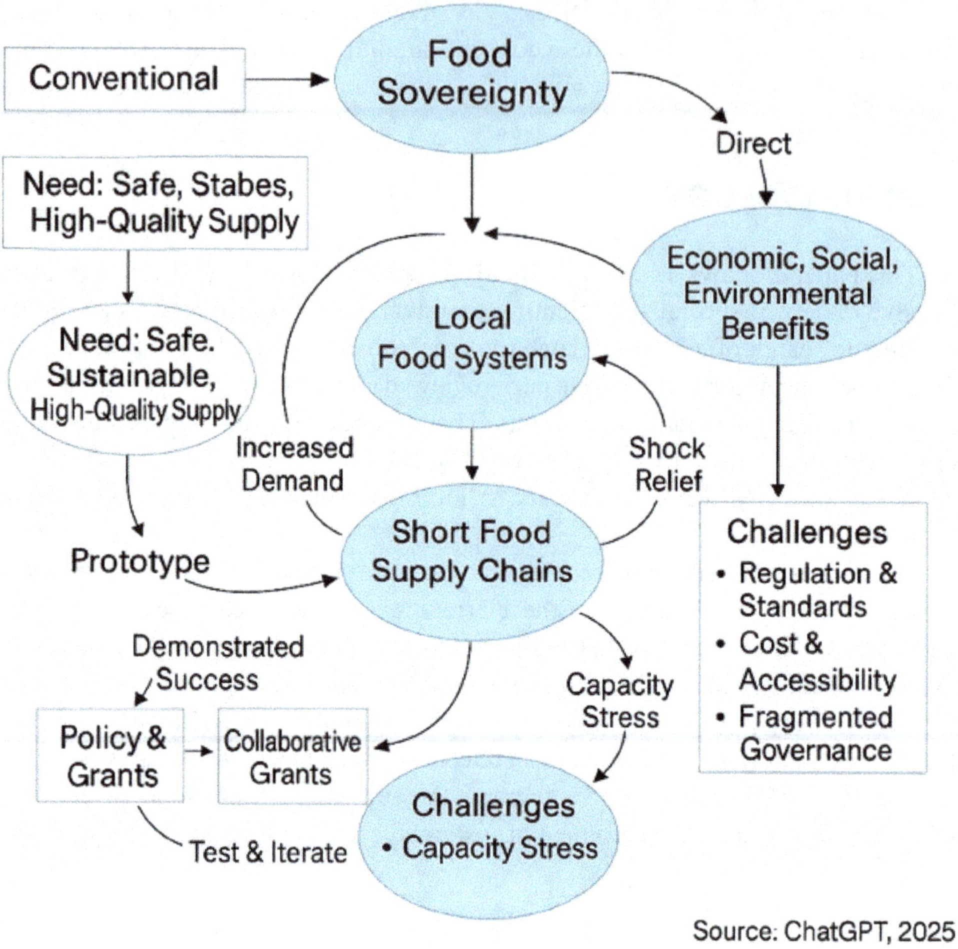

Source: Own computations based on ChatGPT software

3. CONCEPTUAL FRAMEWORKS: FOOD SOVEREIGNTY, LFSs, AND SFSCs

3.1. Food Sovereignty

Ensuring community autonomy over food production, distribution, and consumption hinges on the sovereignty of local agri-food systems, a concept with profound effects on food security, sustainability, and local economic growth. Food sovereignty is formally defined by the Declaration of Nyéléni (2007) as "the right of peoples to healthy and culturally appropriate food produced through ecologically sound and sustainable methods, and their right to define their own food and agriculture systems." This framework grants local communities the right to shape their own agri-food policies, thereby encouraging sustainable methods and diminishing dependence on global supply chains (Patel, 2009). By bolstering alternative models like SFSCs and championing local production, this approach actively contributes to preserving biodiversity, safeguarding soil health, and curtailing environmental damage (Altieri & Toledo, 2011).

3.2. Local Food Systems (LFSs)

A Local Food System (LFS) is an integrated, place-based network of interconnected processes including production, processing, distribution, consumption, and food waste management, all operating within a defined geographical region. Frequently recognized as territorial systems (Scaramuzzi et al., 2021, Felici and Mazzocchi, 2022), LFSs are designed to enhance the economic, social, environmental, and nutritional well-being of a community (Gillespie and Smith, 2008; Feenstra, 1997). They foster close cooperative relationships and shared values among local actors (Lund, 2012; Lutz et al., 2017; Sanz-Cañada et al., 2023) and are founded on local gastronomic identity and intangible cultural heritage (Bessière, 1998; Lee, 2023). Core objectives involve advancing sustainable agricultural practices, strengthening localized supply chains (Berti and Mulligan, 2016), and guaranteeing equitable access for all residents to fresh, nutrient-rich food. These systems actively promote traditional or innovative agri-food products and typically employ distribution models aligned with SFSCs (Kneafsey et al., 2013; Alessandrini, 2024b). Local Food Systems (LFSs) function primarily as distribution networks fostering direct relationships between producers and consumers, thereby playing a vital role in promoting sustainability, strengthening local economies, and increasing the resilience of local producers and processors. The local market, as defined in specialized literature, consists of a network of Short Food Supply Chains (SFSCs). These chains significantly shorten the distance between production and consumption, which in turn helps to lessen environmental impact (Renting et al., 2003). Such a market model inherently supports small-scale agriculture, conserves biodiversity through the cultivation of traditional crop varieties, and delivers agri-food products that are fresher and less processed than those found in extended distribution chains (Feenstra, 1997). Furthermore, research demonstrates that the transparency of local markets concerning product origin and production techniques builds consumer trust, stimulating demand for authentic, seasonal, and superior-quality foods (Marsden et al., 2000). Therefore, beyond fostering rural development and the circular economy, the local market critically contributes to enhanced food security and public health by presenting a robust alternative to industrialized food supply systems.

Figure 2. Literature Network Analysis of Key Foundational Texts on LFSs and SFSCs

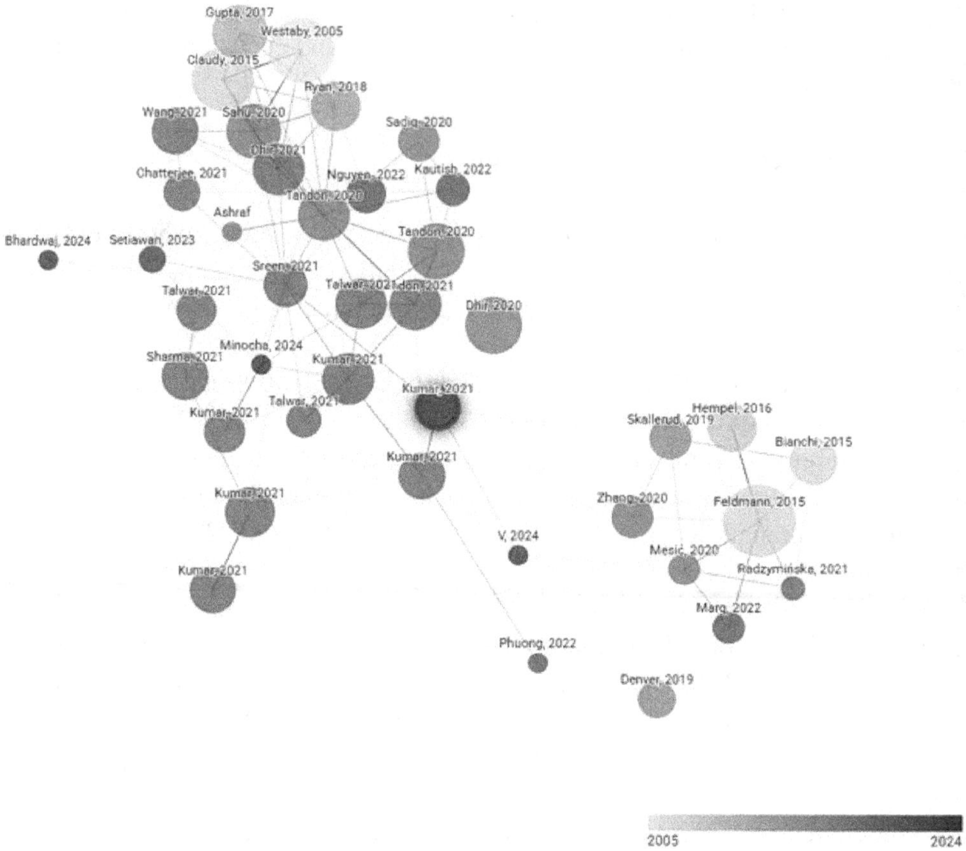

Source: Generated by the author in June 2025, using the Connected Papers visualization tool.

3.3. Short Food Supply Chains (SFSCs)

Over the past decade, LFSs and SFSCs have become increasingly prominent topics (Chiffoleau and Dourian, 2020), reflecting a broader community movement towards adopting sustainable and practices. Such initiatives align with major policies like the European "Farm to Fork" Strategy. EU Regulation No. 1305/2013 defines an SFSC as "a supply chain involving a limited number of economic operators, committed to cooperation, local economic development, and close geographical and social relationships between producers, processors, and consumers" (Canfora, 2016).

SFSCs are increasingly vital to local agri-food systems, primarily by minimizing intermediaries and forging direct connections between local producers and consumers. They offer a personalized alternative to industrial food systems, drastically reducing producer-consumer distances—often to face-to-face interactions—and improving information exchange (Csordás et al., 2022). The nature of these interactions is understood through three modes: 1) direct "face-to-face" contact; 2) spatial proximity; and 3) spatially extended supply chains, where consumers receive detailed information on food origin (Marsden et al., 2000; Renting et al., 2003; Aubry & Kebir, 2013; Kneafsey et al., 2013). Building on this, Malak-Rawlikowska et al. (2019) further proposed defining SFSCs based on three critical dimensions of proximity: Geographical proximity (food miles), Social proximity (direct relationships fostering trust), and Organizational proximity (the number of intermediaries). Furthermore, local food systems and short food supply chains have both the potential and the obligation to enhance recognition of women's contributions and promote gender equality (UNIDO, 2020). A consensus among authors underscores the societal advantages of SFSCs. Nevertheless, aspects related to health and governance remain insufficiently explored, and the economic and environmental advantages of SFSCs exhibit considerable variability (Chiffoleau and Dourian, 2020).

Short Food Supply Chains (SFSCs) - systems like farmers' markets, CSAs, AMAPs, GAS, SoLaWi, and REKO schemes (Lyson, 2004; Aiello et al., 2017) built on transparency, seasonality, and trust - rely on direct producer-consumer connections. These connections, which bypass traditional intermediaries (Hinrichs, 2003), are made possible by geographical proximity. This physical closeness between producers, consumers, and distribution hubs is foundational to SFSCs and broader Local Food Systems (LFSs) (Feenstra, 1997), as it reduces "food miles" (Paxton, 1994) and their associated emissions while fostering direct relationships.

Figure 3. Literature Network Analysis of Contemporary and Emerging Research on SFSCs

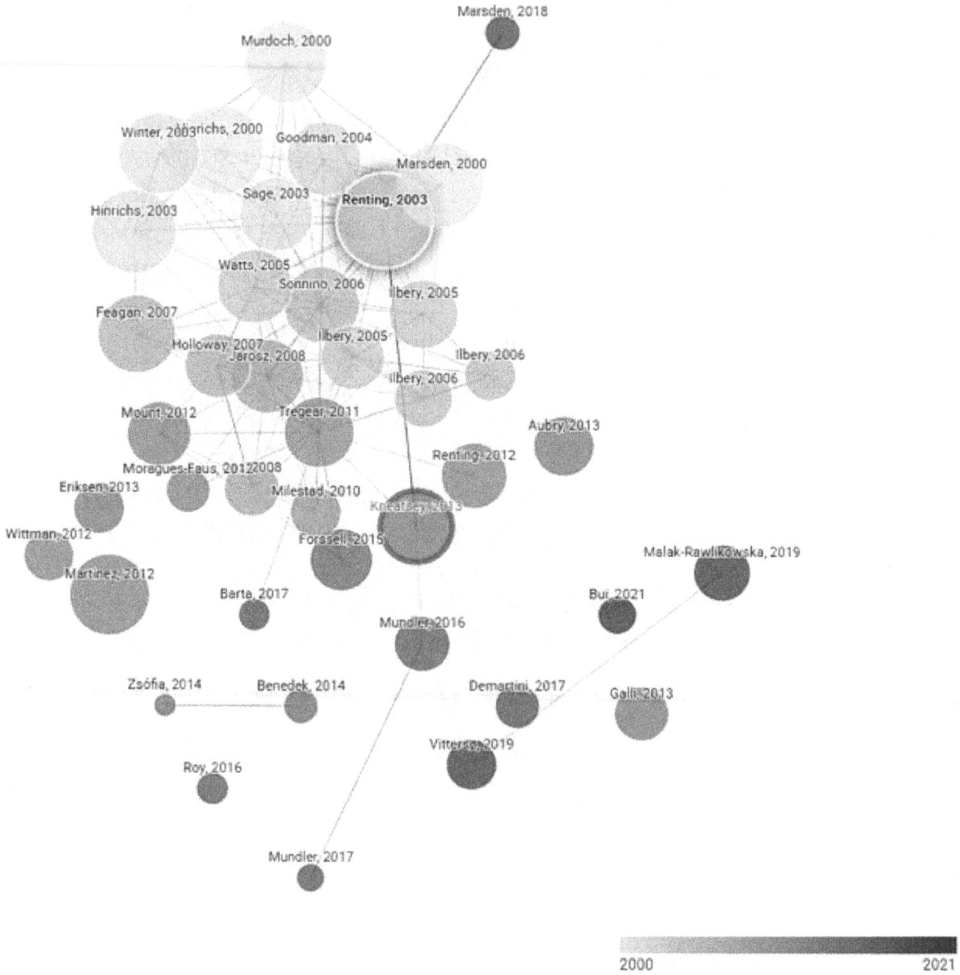

Source: Generated by the author in June 2025, using the Connected Papers visualization tool.

3.4. The Synergy of Concepts

Food sovereignty, the local market, and short supply chains are directly and interdependently connected. The concepts of food sovereignty, LFS, and SFSCs are intricately linked, forming a powerful synergy for developing sustainable, resilient, and equitable agri-food systems. Food sovereignty—which the Declaration of Nyéléni (2007) defines as "the right of peoples to healthy and culturally appropriate food produced through ecologically sound and sustainable methods, and their right to define their own food and agriculture systems"—relies fundamentally on establishing and strengthening LFS. These LFS, encompassing all actors and activities from production to consumption within a specific geographical area, create the necessary context for SFSCs to operate effectively. By reducing geographical and relational distances, SFSCs enhance transparency, foster trust, and promote economic viability for local farmers, while concurrently mitigating the environmental impacts associated with conventional, long-distance supply chains. This synergistic interaction cultivates a more decentralized, diversified, and ecologically sound agri-food system, better equipped to withstand external shocks, bolster community well-being, and contribute to long-term sustainability and equity. Local food systems are characterized as territorial frameworks that connect and integrate local stakeholders within the agri-food production, processing, and distribution sectors through collaborative efforts and shared values. Their foundation lies in local gastronomic identity, the promotion of healthy eating, and the championing of high-quality agri-food products (often voluntarily certified), coupled with innovative distribution models such as Short Food Supply Chains (SFSCs) (Sanz-Cañada et al., 2023).

Figure 4. The Role of Local Food Systems in Achieving Food Sovereignty

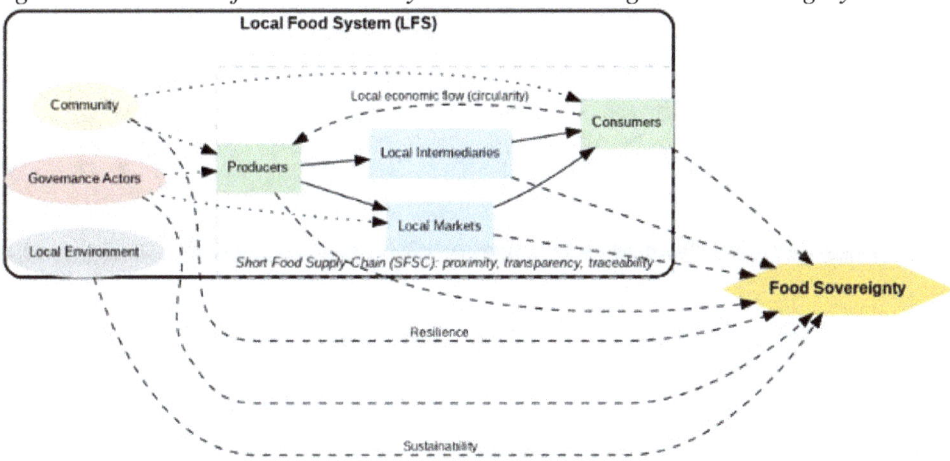

Source: Own computations based on ChatGPT software

4. THE CENTRALITY OF PROXIMITY AND THE LOCAL MARKET

4.1. The Multidimensional Role of Geographical Proximity

Geographical proximity is a defining feature of Local Food Systems (LFS), fundamentally shaping their structure, functionality, and overall impact (Mundler, 2022). This physical closeness between producers and consumers facilitates direct interactions, reduces transportation distances, and enhances food freshness and traceability (Ilbery and Maye, 2005). Such proximity enables shorter supply chains, thereby decreasing reliance on complex global logistics networks and mitigating environmental externalities, notably greenhouse gas emissions from long-haul transportation (Aubry and Kebir, 2013).

Figure 5. The Virtuous Cycle of Proximity in Local Food Systems

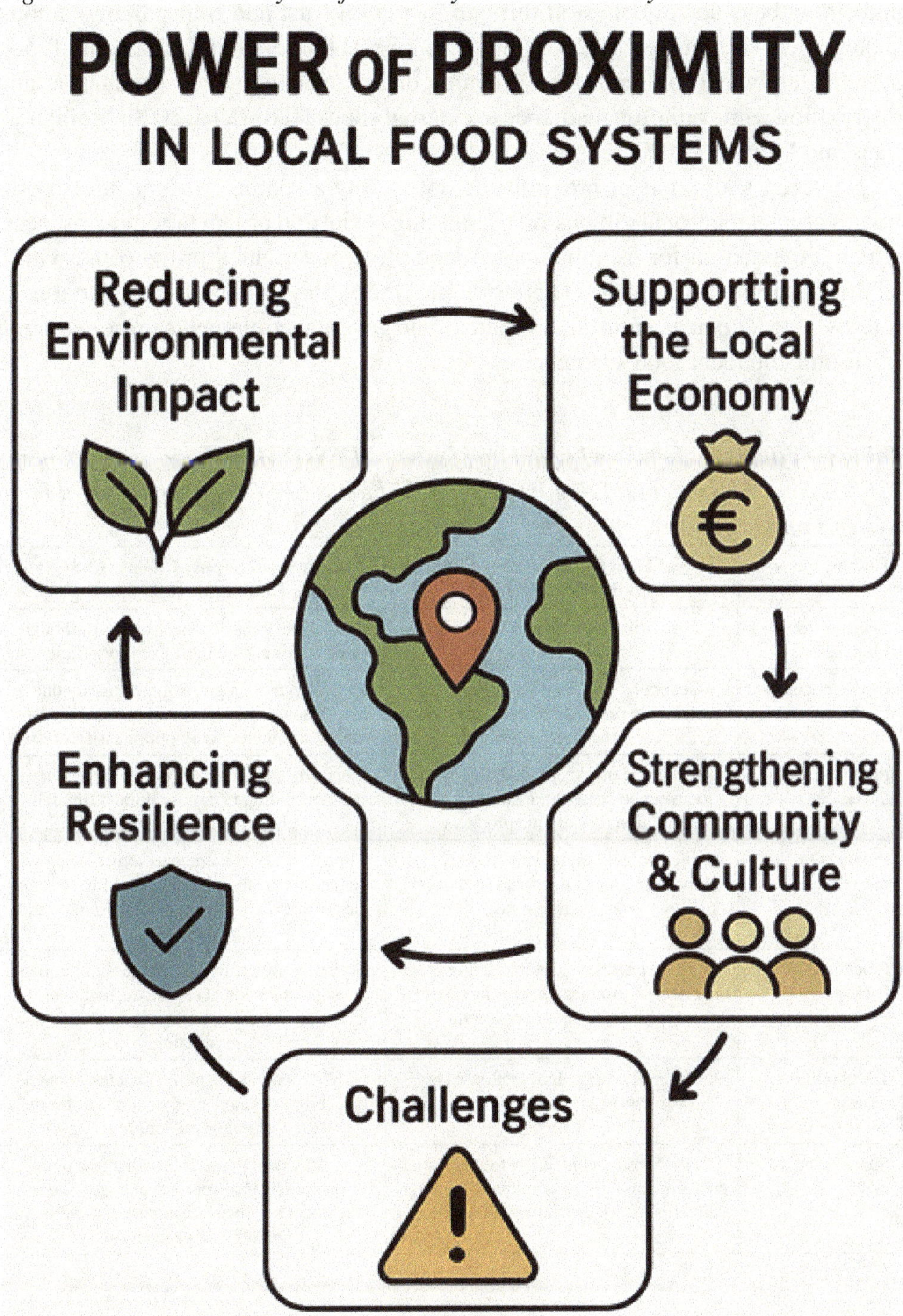

Source: Own computations based on ChatGPT software

Moreover, local proximity fosters the development of place-based food cultures and strengthens social cohesion through increased trust and transparency among stakeholders (Renting et al., 2003). It also supports the re-territorialization of food systems, allowing communities to regain control over their food production and distribution while building resilience to external shocks (Hinrichs, 2000; Moragues-Faus and Morgan, 2015).

However, geographical proximity is not merely a spatial concept; it also embodies crucial relational dimensions, including social and organizational closeness, which are essential for establishing collaborative governance frameworks within LFS (Kneafsey et al., 2013). Therefore, proximity plays a multidimensional role, intertwining logistical, cultural, ecological, and governance elements in the evolution of sustainable local food systems.

Table 1. Differences between Local Food Systems (LFSs) / Short Food Supply Chains (SFSCs) on one hand, and Long Food Supply Chains (LFSCs) / Conventional Food Systems on the other

Feature	Local Food Systems (LFS) / Short Supply Chains (SFSCs)	Long Food Supply Chains (LFSC) / Conventional Systems
Transport & Logistics	Primarily minimal and localized.	Extensive, long-distance transport, though often continuously optimized for efficiency.
Environmental Footprint	Generally, very low, resulting from sustainable production, processing, and local transport practices.	Typically, more significant, primarily due to long-distance transport and extended supply chains, despite ongoing optimization efforts.
Product Focus & Diversity	Emphasis on exceptional diversity, focusing on seasonal, local, and often traditional or unique products.	Focus on standardized, universal products, often leading to a more limited (though globally consistent) range.
Product Quality & Freshness	Typically, very high, with an emphasis on peak freshness due to short harvest-to-consumer times.	Can be variable (average to sometimes lower on certain freshness aspects), with a strong prioritization of shelf-life, consistency, and profitability.
Processing & Packaging	Minimal processing, emphasizing fresh and natural products; packaging is often simple, reusable, or eco-friendly.	Often involves extensive processing; utilizes sophisticated packaging designed for extended shelf-life, transport durability, and marketing.
Traceability & Transparency	Generally, very high, facilitated by direct relationships and shorter supply chains.	Often moderate or more complex, though traceability is increasingly addressed through technological solutions.
Social Impact	Strengthens local identity, fosters social cohesion, and builds community through direct producer-consumer connections.	May lead to the externalization or 'outsourcing' of social challenges and a disconnect between consumers and the social realities of production.

continued on following page

Table 1. Continued

Feature	Local Food Systems (LFS) / Short Supply Chains (SFSCs)	Long Food Supply Chains (LFSC) / Conventional Systems
Economic Focus/ Primary Goal	Prioritizes product quality, system durability (sustainability), support for local producers, and fostering local economic benefits.	Primarily focuses on operational efficiency, economies of scale, and maximizing overall profitability.
Market Access & Scale	Market access may be geographically limited but holds strong local advantages and can serve niche demands effectively.	Extensive market access and operates on a large, often national or international, scale.
Innovation & Technology	Innovation is often moderate, sometimes emphasizing traditional methods, but increasingly incorporates appropriate technologies for local scale (e.g., online platforms, small-scale processing).	High adoption of advanced technology across production, processing, logistics, and retail to enhance efficiency and consistency.
System Resilience & Autonomy	Can achieve high resilience and local autonomy through diversification, strong community ties, and reinforcement of local identity.	May exhibit lower local autonomy and can be vulnerable to widespread disruptions due to centralization, long supply lines, and dependence on fewer, larger actors.
Support Mechanisms & Governance	Often relies heavily on community engagement, grassroots initiatives, and supportive local/regional policies.	Typically supported by established corporate structures and national/international policies; sustainability efforts may be channeled through Corporate Social Responsibility (CSR) programs.

Source: Own computations.

4.2. The Local Market as a Nodal Point

Geographical proximity serves as a foundational pillar in the structuring of LFSs and SFSCs, constituting the foundation of LFS (Feenstra, 1997). By reducing the distance that food travels from farm to fork, proximity minimizes transportation-related emissions—the concept of "food miles" (Paxton, 1994)—and facilitates direct relationships among stakeholders. This spatial closeness enables the operation of SFSC systems that eliminate traditional intermediaries (e.g., wholesalers, global distributors) and directly connect producers with consumers (Hinrichs, 2003).

Within this framework, local markets function as nodal points where geographical proximity and SFSCs converge. These markets—whether physical (e.g., farmers' markets or mobile markets) or digital (e.g., regional online platforms or digital food hubs)—embed food transactions within social and cultural contexts. Such markets amplify the impact of LFS by circulating money within the community; indeed, many studies show that one unit of currency spent locally can generate three to four times more economic value than if spent in supermarkets (Kneafsey et al., 2008).

4.3. Core Characteristics of the Local Agri-food Market

The local agri-food market functions as a tangible or digital platform where regional producers directly sell their goods to consumers or intermediaries. This encompasses various venues, including establishments run by local producers and processors (such as butchers, bakers, and pastry shops), specialty food shops, farmers' markets, food fairs and events, agricultural associations and cooperatives, and mobile vendors like food trucks or vending machines. Research underscores that direct engagement between local producers and end consumers—with few, if any, intermediaries (at most one)—is a hallmark of Local Agri-Food Systems (LFS). This direct connection promotes enhanced transparency, efficient traceability, and greater accountability among all supply chain participants, from farm to fork. The crucial role of local markets in bolstering the sustainability and resilience of these systems is increasingly recognized by entrepreneurs, researchers, and local policymakers. Literature reveals the myriad benefits associated with these markets across economic, social, environmental, cultural, health, and governance spheres (Tanasă, 2024b).

1. **Origin of Products:** The origin of agri-food products in the local market is a critical characteristic fundamental to their freshness, authenticity, and traceability. These products typically originate from farms, individual households, or agricultural cooperatives within a defined region or an adjacent geographical area. This proximity minimizes the time between harvest and consumption, thereby helping to preserve the food's nutritional integrity and natural flavor. Furthermore, geographical closeness often encourages the adoption of sustainable agricultural practices, frequently rooted in traditional or organic methods, thus reducing the reliance on preservatives and chemical treatments typically required for long-distance transportation.
2. **Agri-food Diversity:** The diversity of agri-food products in the local market is a crucial indicator of the area's natural resource richness and its culinary traditions. This encompasses a variety of fresh products, including seasonal fruits and vegetables cultivated with minimal reliance on pesticides and chemical fertilizers, resulting in an authentic flavor and enhanced nutritional value. Dairy products, including artisanal cheeses, yogurts, and fresh milk, are sourced from animals raised in natural conditions and typically fed local fodder. Meat and meat products, including traditional sausages and pastrami, are produced following local recipes transmitted through generations, thereby maintaining the region's culinary distinctiveness.
3. **Quality and Freshness:** The local agri-food industry is distinguished by its emphasis on quality and freshness, which provides a notable advantage over products offered in large retail chains. The reduced physical distance between

farmers and consumers facilitates the swift market entry of food post-harvest or processing, thereby helping to maintain its inherent flavor, texture, and essential nutritional attributes. By circumventing long distribution chains and intermediaries, the local market offers not only fresher products but also clear traceability of origin, instilling greater consumer trust in what they purchase and consume. This freshness is evident not only in the improved flavor of the food but also in the health benefits, as less processed items ingested soon after harvesting better retain their vitamins, minerals, and natural enzymes.

4. **Sustainability:** The concept of sustainability serves as a crucial foundation for the local agri-food market, yielding beneficial effects for both the regional economy and the ecological landscape. By endorsing local producers, consumers play a pivotal role in advancing rural communities, invigorating the regional economy, and promoting traditional agricultural practices that prioritize biodiversity and the preservation of soil integrity. Moreover, sourcing products locally markedly diminishes the need for extensive transportation, leading to a substantial reduction in greenhouse gas emissions and fossil fuel consumption.
5. **Direct Producer-Consumer Relationship:** The direct connection between producer and consumer stands as a fundamental element of the local agri-food market, as it cultivates trust, transparency, and authenticity. In contrast to supermarket acquisitions, where the provenance and caliber of items may be challenging to ascertain, local markets provide consumers the opportunity to engage directly with farmers and producers, gaining insights into cultivation techniques, animal husbandry, food processing, and agricultural methodologies. This transparent dialogue instills in customers a sense of assurance regarding the freshness, natural quality, and ethical sourcing of the products they acquire.

4.4. Comparative Frameworks: Distinguishing Food System Models

Building on the foundational understanding of Local Food Systems (LFSs) and Short Food Supply Chains (SFSCs) established in previous sections, this part of the paper provides a comparative overview of their key characteristics, distinguishing them from conventional, long food supply chains (LFSCs). This comparison illuminates the unique operational models and inherent advantages these localized systems offer within the broader food landscape.

1. **Direct and Streamlined Agri-food Supply Chains:** LFS actively champion Short Food Supply Chains (SFSCs), which effectively minimize the distance between food producers and consumers. This approach significantly reduces the environmental footprint and yields extensive benefits across economic, social,

cultural, and health dimensions. SFSCs are typified by various direct-to-consumer channels, including local producer markets, mobile markets, food-related events and fairs (such as brunch gatherings), producer-owned shops, specialty grocery stores, open farm days, farm-gate sales or roadside sales, food trucks, and online platforms managed directly by producers. These diverse channels are fundamental to the growth of LFS, ensuring consumers have direct access to fresh and high-quality food.

2. **Modern Logistics and Collaborative Models:** A focus on innovative distribution is evident through the establishment of food hubs and cooperative supermarkets, which aim to enhance the sustainable delivery of local produce. Additionally, LFS support responsible public procurement by encouraging the integration of locally sourced and processed foods into public institutions, such as school cafeterias.
3. **Inclusive and Decentralized Governance:** LFS foster a governance structure that is inclusive, participatory, and decentralized, actively involving local stakeholders in collective decision-making processes. Producers, processors, and consumers are recognized as crucial voices within the community. In contrast to the typically top-down governance seen in conventional food systems (CFS), LFS promote multi-actor democratic models that prioritize collaboration and shared accountability.
4. **Connecting Urban and Rural Areas through Resource Management:** LFS prioritize the efficient management of local resources, aligning with circular economy principles, while also minimizing the environmental impact associated with food system resource flows. SFSCs are pivotal in this framework by enabling the efficient distribution of food between rural production and urban consumption, ensuring a more direct and sustainable food supply chain.

Table 2. Comparative matrix between Local Food Systems (LFSs), and Conventional/ Long Food Supply Chains (LFSCs)

Characteristics	Short Supply Chains (SFSCs)	Local Agri-food Systems (LASs)	Conventional/Global Chains (LFSCs)
Number of intermediaries	0-1	0-2, with focus on direct relationships	3+
Transparency	High	High, with emphasis on local origins	Low
Flexibility	Rapid adaptation to shocks/resilient	High adaptability, quick response to local needs	Vulnerability to disruptions

continued on following page

Table 2. Continued

Characteristics	Short Supply Chains (SFSCs)	Local Agri-food Systems (LASs)	Conventional/Global Chains (LFSCs)
Transportation costs	Generally low (depending on LAS type)	Minimal, local transport	High
Social impact	Support for local communities	Strengthening local identity and social cohesion	Outsourcing of social challenges
Product quality	High	Very high	Average or sometimes low, prioritizing profitability
Product diversity	High, with local emphasis	Exceptional, focusing on seasonal/ local products	Standardized, emphasizing universal products (limited range)
Seasonality	High	Very high	Moderate
Processing and packaging	Minimal, emphasizing fresh produce (eco-friendly packaging)	Minimal, emphasizing fresh/natural products (eco-friendly packaging)	Extensive, focusing on processed goods and sophisticated packaging for shelf-life extension
Economies of scale	Low	Limited, but with local advantages	High
Ecological impact	Reduced, due to minimal transport	Very low, due to sustainable production/processing/transport practices	Significant, due to long-distance transport, though continuously optimized
Innovation level	High (LAS recognized as innovative solutions in the food ecosystem)	Moderate – traditional character	High, aligned with technological progress across domains
Community integration	High, via direct producer-consumer interactions	High, through local identity reinforcement	Low, due to centralization
Support policies	Requires local policy support	Requires political and community support	Corporate/political support (often involving CSR activities)
Product lifecycle	Focus on durability and quality	Focus on durability, quality, and local products	Focus on efficiency and profitability

Source: Own computations.

- **LFSs vs. Conventional Systems (LFSCs):** A key distinction between Local Food Systems and Long Food Supply Chains lies in their core objectives. Unlike LFSC, which prioritize the most profitable products within large retail chains as part of a mass-market economy, LFS seek a balance between diversification and specialization to support local economies and enhance community resilience. LFS promote innovative models such as food hubs and cooperative supermarkets and support responsible public procurement.

They also encourage inclusive, participatory, and decentralized governance models, engaging local actors in collective decision-making, which contrasts with the top-down approach of conventional food systems.

- **Distinguishing Between SFSCs and Local Markets:** From a geographical standpoint, SFSCs and the local market differ but complement one another. SFSCs are primarily defined by a reduced number of intermediaries and a focus on social and organizational proximity, with an emphasis on reducing "food miles" rather than adhering to a strict radius (Bazzani and Canavari, 2017; Jarzębowski et al., 2020; Renkema and Hilletofth, 2022). The local market, conversely, is more strictly defined by its geographical scope (e.g., a radius of less than 50-100 km), reinforcing territorial identity. While the local market inherently incorporates SFSCs, its structure is more expansive, often integrating additional territorially bounded distribution mechanisms like regional gastronomic events or cooperative supermarkets. The principal distinction resides in their orientation: while the local market is rigorously delineated by geographic boundaries, SFSCs emphasize a reduction in intermediaries and the cultivation of relational proximity.

5. THE MULTIDIMENSIONAL BENEFITS OF LFSs AND SFSCs

Short Food Supply Chains (SFSCs) serve as pivotal instruments in the reconfiguration and revitalization of local agri-food markets. By minimizing the number of intermediaries and enhancing producers' access to end consumers, SFSCs contribute to a more equitable distribution of income, reduction in intermediation costs, and the activation of local economic circuits. Beyond their economic utility, SFSCs generate social value by fostering transparent, trust-based relationships between producers and consumers, thereby reinforcing community cohesion and solidarity-based economies. Moreover, these chains advance environmental protection goals by reducing food miles and encouraging localized, seasonal production. On a cultural level, they support the preservation and reinterpretation of regional gastronomic traditions, the promotion of territorial identity, and the valorization of traditional culinary knowledge. In doing so, SFSCs enhance the competitiveness of local agriculture and bolster the resilience of regional food systems against external shocks. Recent empirical research underscores the multifunctionality of SFSCs - not only as vectors of sustainability - but as catalysts for rural development, employment generation, and social innovation within the agri-food sector (Barry, 2012; Mundler & Laughrea, 2016; Chiffoleau & Dourian, 2020; Wronka-Pośpiech, 2024).

The integrated model of Local Food Systems (LFS) and Short Food Supply Chains (SFSCs) generates numerous, well-documented benefits across several key domains. These systems are recognized not only for their economic and environmental advantages but also for their profound social and cultural contributions.

5.1. Reducing Environmental Impact

By emphasizing seasonal and regional production and shortening the transportation distance between producers and consumers, LFSs reduce carbon emissions and energy consumption (the "food miles" concept) (Paxton, 1994). This approach diminishes reliance on fossil fuel-dependent global supply chains (Renting et al., 2003; Kneafsey et al., 2013). By endorsing local producers, consumers play a pivotal role in promoting traditional agricultural practices that prioritize biodiversity and soil preservation. In contrast to global supply chains, local markets and shorter supply chains champion a consumption model that prioritizes seasonal, fresh, and high-quality products, which mitigates food waste. However, some researchers highlight that the ecological efficiency of SFSCs can be contingent on operational scales, as suboptimal transportation of limited product quantities may sometimes offset the benefits of shorter distances (Majewski et al., 2020).

Short Food Supply Chains (SFSCs) constitute a transformative model significantly contributing to both environmental sustainability and food security at local and regional levels. While commonly assumed to reduce carbon emissions, energy use, and food waste by minimizing the physical distance between production and consumption—thus aligning with broader circular economy and agroecological goals—empirical research introduces a crucial nuance. Majewski et al. (2020), leveraging Life Cycle Assessment (LCA) data from 428 food chains across six EU countries, found that highly optimized long food supply chains can, in certain instances, demonstrate greater eco-efficiency than some SFSCs in terms of GHG emissions, fossil fuel consumption, and pollution per kilogram of food. These findings underscore that sustainability in food systems hinges not solely on geographical distance, but equally on logistical design, infrastructure efficiency, and modal choices.

Nevertheless, from a food security perspective, SFSCs significantly enhance autonomy and adaptive capacity, reducing reliance on fragile global supply chains and thereby bolstering the resilience, accessibility, and traceability of food systems. During systemic shocks such as pandemics or climate-related disruptions, localized networks tend to exhibit superior agility and responsiveness to community needs. Furthermore, SFSCs diversify distribution pathways and promote inclusive access to healthy, culturally rooted food, often through models like Community Supported Agriculture (CSAs) and farmers' markets.

In sum, SFSCs offer a holistic approach to reconciling sustainability and food security challenges, but their effectiveness depends on context-sensitive implementation, infrastructure innovation, and a balance between proximity and performance.

5.2. Supporting the Local Economy

A core economic benefit of SFSCs lies in their capacity to enhance the income of local farmers by eliminating intermediaries (Charatsari et al., 2020). This structural shift enables producers to capture a greater share of the final retail price, improving their financial viability (Zaninović & Skender, 2025). Proximity facilitates these direct links, retaining more currency within the community and stimulating a powerful local multiplier effect; studies indicate that each unit of currency spent locally can generate three to four times more value for the community (Kneafsey et al., 2008). Access to fair pricing mechanisms also empowers producers to reinvest in sustainable agricultural practices and improve their rural living conditions, contributing to the narrowing of urban–rural economic disparities.

Specialized studies affirm that Short Food Supply Chains (SFSCs) contribute substantially to the reduction of logistics and distribution costs, largely due to their decentralized architecture and geographic proximity between producers and final consumers. Direct sales modalities - such as farmers' markets (including mobile variants), on-farm sales, and cooperative retail outlets—not only bypass intermediary fees but also curtail expenditures associated with long-distance transportation, centralized storage infrastructure, and excessive packaging requirements.

This streamlined operational model enables producers to reallocate financial resources toward technological upgrades, sustainable production practices, and product quality enhancement, thereby improving the market competitiveness of local goods. Simultaneously, consumers benefit from lower transaction costs, which often translate into more affordable pricing, and gain improved access to fresh, healthy, and traceable food. Importantly, these direct interactions foster mutual trust, reinforce food literacy, and promote education around seasonality and environmental sustainability.

Consequently, SFSCs are not merely cost-saving instruments but represent a structural alternative to conventional agri-food supply chains. They operate as community-based reconnection mechanisms, reducing systemic vulnerability and enhancing food sovereignty - particularly in times of global disruption and supply chain fragility (Lucas et al., 2024).

5.3. Strengthening Community and Culture

LFSs foster direct, place-based interactions—such as those at farmers' markets—which help cultivate trust-based, transparent relationships and reinforce ethical values like fair wages and ecological agriculture (Goodman et al., 2012; Vittersø et al., 2019; Aouinait et al., 2022; Petropoulou et al., 2022). This transparent dialogue instills in customers a sense of assurance regarding the freshness, natural quality, and ethical sourcing of the products they acquire. This profound connection fosters a heightened awareness and responsibility in consumption practices, while simultaneously aiding in the preservation of local traditions. Geographic and relational proximity reconnects food with regional identity and culinary heritage, as exemplified by the Slow Food movement in Italy, which preserves culinary traditions and educates consumers on seasonality and sustainable practices (Sage, 2014; Jarosz, 2008).

This disintermediated structure fosters a symbiotic socio-economic link, rooted in transparent communication, food literacy, and adaptive market practices that align supply with local preferences and cultural expectations. Through direct engagement mechanisms - such as farmers' markets, community-supported models, and digital platforms - SFSCs enable producers to educate consumers about product seasonality, provenance, and sustainability, while simultaneously receiving feedback to adjust offerings in real time. This reciprocal relationship reinforces trust, co-responsibility, and a shared commitment to resilient, territorially grounded food systems.

The agency of Short Food Supply Chains (SFSCs) in modulating consumer behavior towards enhanced local product uptake is profoundly influenced by educational and strategic marketing endeavors. Such initiatives, aimed at elevating consumer consciousness regarding the merits of localized food systems, demonstrably impact purchasing patterns, as quantified by Onozaka et al. (2010) and Zepeda & Li (2006). Consumers' receptivity to marketing focused on salient attributes like freshness and sustainability translates into a notable increase (20-30%) in their inclination to select local products (Zepeda & Li, 2006), while broader campaigns have culminated in an approximate 35% surge in local market sales (Lucas et al., 2024). These data affirm the effectiveness of public acculturation concerning the holistic benefits—economic, social, and ecological—of prioritizing local consumption (Hyland et al., 2024). A direct corollary is the fostering of consumer fidelity to products of known local origin (Vittersø et al., 2019; Evola et al., 2022; Hyland et al., 2024), a factor pivotal for enhancing the resilience and sustainability of regional agri-food markets (Borsellino et al., 2020; Alessandrini, 2024) and, by extension, for underpinning local economic vitality and rural community development (Kneafsey et al., 2013; Jarzębowski et al., 2020; Doernberg et al., 2022).

5.4. Enhancing Resilience and Food Security

LFSs exhibit heightened adaptive capacity and systemic resilience in the face of global disruptions such as pandemics, geopolitical conflicts, and supply chain shocks. Their decentralized, proximity-based architecture reduces dependency on transnational logistics, enabling more responsive and autonomous food provisioning (Van der Ploeg, 2020). The COVID-19 pandemic underscored this resilience: regions with well-established LFS infrastructures, such as Québec, demonstrated superior continuity in food access (Blay-Palmer et al., 2021; Butu et al., 2020). Furthermore, SFSCs substantially improve the traceability and transparency of agri-food products, which is critical for food safety by reducing exposure to contamination risks associated with extended supply chains (Kiss et al., 2019; Vittersø et al., 2019; Zhang and Yu, 2021; Jia et al., 2024).

The contribution of Short Food Supply Chains (SFSCs) to enhanced food security is substantially predicated on their capacity to improve food system foundations through superior product traceability and heightened transparency. By furnishing consumers with explicit data on product origins and cultivation techniques, SFSCs address a critical deficit in conventional systems. This informational transparency is integral to food safety assurance, as SFSCs' attenuated logistical pathways inherently diminish vulnerability to contamination events prevalent in elongated and opaque supply chains (e.g., failures in cold chain integrity, extended handling). Robust food safety outcomes, further substantiated by improved traceability, are complemented by a reduced ecological impact attributable to minimized transportation and the adoption of sustainable practices. SFSCs thus emerge as a compelling model for synergistically achieving food safety, cultivating consumer trust, and reinforcing the ecological resilience of agri-food provisioning.

6. CHALLENGES AND LIMITATIONS OF LFS AND SFSCs

Despite the well-documented benefits, the expansion of LFSs and SFSCs is frequently constrained by a range of interconnected challenges. Numerous studies have underscored the structural vulnerabilities that impede the effective participation of small-scale actors, especially in regions lacking targeted investment or supportive policy frameworks (Ilbery & Maye, 2005; Martinez et al., 2010; Kneafsey et al., 2013). Small producers often struggle to secure the material assets, technological tools, and human capital necessary to professionalize operations and meet food safety standards. Collectively, these barriers threaten the long-term viability and inclusivity of SFSCs.

- **Limited Infrastructure and Seasonality Constraints:** The operational efficacy of LFSs and SFSCs is substantially constrained by agricultural seasonality and by pervasive infrastructural deficits. The lack of consistent, year-round product availability is compounded by deficiencies in cold chain logistics, storage, and distribution mechanisms, which precipitate inefficiencies and product losses (Renting et al., 2003; Kneafsey et al., 2013). For small-scale producers in rural peripheries, accessing urban consumer bases is often impeded by limited transportation and a scarcity of aggregation hubs, eroding their competitive standing against conventional supply chains (Aubry and Kebir, 2013; Alessandrini, 2024a).

- **Low Production and Processing Capacity:** A significant constraint is the limited production and processing capacity of small-scale agricultural enterprises. Many local producers operate on small landholdings with limited access to technology, which severely hampers their ability to scale operations or meet increasing consumer demand (Chiffoleau & Dourian, 2020; Bayir et al., 2022). This is compounded by the scarcity of certified, small-scale processing infrastructure, which is critical for developing value-added products and reinforcing the economic resilience of local food economies (Ilbery & Maye, 2005).
- **Regulatory Barriers and Standardization Issues:** The interface between regulatory regimes and the operational realities of small-scale producers presents notable challenges. Navigating the intricacies of food safety legislation, labelling conventions, and traceability demands—often designed for large-scale operators — entails significant bureaucratic effort, especially for those involved with artisanal products (Aouinait et al., 2022). These institutional impediments disproportionately disadvantage micro and smallholder enterprises, curtailing their growth and inhibiting their assimilation into formalized food supply networks (Kneafsey et al., 2013). Additionally, the absence of standardized quality frameworks in local markets may weaken consumer trust (Marsden et al., 2000; Chang et al., 2022; Hyland et al., 2024).
- **Affordability and Consumer Inclusion:** The higher cost of local and sustainable food often renders it inaccessible to lower-income consumers. This affordability gap can reinforce the notion that local food is a niche or luxury good, primarily reserved for wealthier consumer segments (Schanbacher, 2010; Smith et al., 2020). Without targeted policy interventions—such as income-based subsidies, public procurement programs, or adaptable CSA schemes—local food systems risk perpetuating social and economic inequalities (Feagan, 2007).
- **Fragmented Governance and Lack of Coordination:** The success and scalability of LFSs and SFSCs are closely tied to the presence of coordinated, multi-level governance that actively engages producers, consumers, civil society, and public institutions. However, the absence of integrated, place-based food governance strategies often results in fragmented initiatives, inconsistent policy support, and insufficient institutional continuity (Moragues-Faus & Morgan, 2015; Renkema & Hilletofth, 2022). These governance deficits manifest in siloed decision-making disconnected from broader regional planning, which compromises resilience and long-term viability (Renting et al., 2012).

- **Competition with Long Food Supply Chains (LFSCs):** SFSCs face persistent and often overwhelming competition from conventional distribution systems, particularly large supermarket chains. These commercial networks benefit from economies of scale, advanced logistical infrastructure, and aggressive pricing policies, enabling them to offer products at substantially lower costs (Ilbery and Maye, 2005; Sonnino and Marsden, 2006). In many regions, consumer behavior continues to reflect a strong preference for convenience and affordability over quality or sustainability, thus limiting the expansion potential of short supply chains (Tregear, 2011; Kneafsey et al., 2013).

7. CONCLUSIONS

The concepts of food sovereignty, local food systems (LFSs), and short food supply chains (SFSCs) are deeply interconnected and mutually reinforcing, forming the essential foundations for building sustainable, resilient, and equitable food systems. Food sovereignty is the guiding principle, actualized through the territorial framework of LFSs, which in turn are made operational by the relational proximity of SFSCs. This synergy generates significant economic, ecological, and social benefits, from boosting local economies and reducing environmental impact to strengthening community cohesion and resilience.

However, realizing this potential is not automatic. These systems face profound challenges, including infrastructural deficits, regulatory burdens unsuited for small-scale operators, limited production capacity, and critical issues of affordability and inclusion that can lead to social inequity. Furthermore, fragmented governance and intense competition from conventional food systems threaten the viability and scalability of these local initiatives.

To move from niche alternatives to foundational components of our food future, targeted interventions are essential. Success requires ongoing institutional support through enabling public policies; strategic investment in local infrastructure for processing and distribution; and robust consumer education to build awareness and loyalty. By intentionally aligning the principles of food sovereignty with the operational efficiency of LFSs and the responsiveness of SFSCs, communities can build food systems that are not only resilient to global shocks but also generate local prosperity while protecting environmental and cultural heritage.

A sustainable, resilient, and equitable agri-food system is achievable through the synergistic interplay of three core concepts: food sovereignty, Local Food Systems (LFSs), and Short Food Supply Chains (SFSCs). Food sovereignty provides the guiding political vision, giving communities the right to control their own food policies. This vision is put into practice within the territorial framework of LFSs, which are, in turn, made effective by the direct, transparent mechanisms of SFSCs. This powerful combination generates three principal categories of benefits:

1. **Fostering Local Prosperity:** By promoting local enterprises and reinvesting profits within the territory, LFSs and SFSCs build diversified local economies that are less dependent on volatile global markets.
2. **Promoting Environmental Stewardship:** Through minimized transportation ("food miles"), the efficient use of local resources, and the encouragement of sustainable farming methods, these systems reduce the overall ecological footprint of food production and consumption.
3. **Building Community and Empowering Citizens:** Direct producer-consumer relationships enhance traceability and build trust, while also empowering citizens to become active participants in the governance of their local food system, strengthening community bonds.

However, achieving this vision requires overcoming significant hurdles. The success of these systems is contingent upon:

- **Enabling Policy and Financial Support:** Consistent institutional backing through supportive public policies, accessible subsidies, and targeted training is needed to lower barriers for small-scale producers.
- **Strategic Investment in Infrastructure:** The development of local infrastructure for processing, storage, and logistics is crucial for LFSs and SFSCs to operate efficiently and serve broader markets.
- **Cultivating Informed Consumer Demand:** Ongoing consumer education and awareness campaigns are essential to build sustained loyalty for local products and encourage responsible consumption habits.

Ultimately, integrating the political vision of food sovereignty with the place-based structure of LFSs and the relational efficiency of SFSCs provides a robust pathway for communities to create food systems that are not only resilient but also prosperous, equitable, and culturally rooted.

7.1. Future Research Directions

While this paper provides a comprehensive conceptual framework, it also highlights several areas where further scholarly inquiry is needed to deepen our understanding and guide effective policy and practice. Based on the literature reviewed, future research should prioritize the following areas:

- **Nuanced Sustainability Assessments**: The manuscript notes that the economic and environmental advantages of SFSCs can exhibit considerable variability (Chiffoleau and Dourian, 2020). Future research should move beyond general assumptions and conduct more granular, comparative studies. Using methodologies like Life Cycle Assessment (LCA), research could identify the specific operational scales, logistical designs, and infrastructural conditions under which SFSCs achieve greater eco-efficiency than highly optimized conventional chains (Majewski et al., 2020).
- **Models for Effective Governance**: Fragmented governance was identified as a key challenge. Future research could conduct comparative case studies of existing food policy councils or other collaborative governance models to identify the specific institutional structures and participatory processes that are most effective at building resilient and scalable local food systems, thereby addressing the governance gaps identified by authors like Moragues-Faus & Morgan (2015) and Renting et al. (2012).
- **Health and Well-being Outcomes**: As noted by Chiffoleau and Dourian (2020), the health dimensions of LFS and SFSCs remain under-explored. Research is needed to move beyond general perceptions of freshness and quantitatively assess the impacts of participating in LFS on community health. This could include nutritional outcomes, mental health benefits derived from community engagement, and public health effects related to reduced exposure to contaminants in shorter chains.
- **Gender Equity and Social Inclusion**: This paper acknowledges the obligation for local food systems to promote gender equality, a point underscored in reports by organizations like UNIDO (2020). Future scholarship should move to empirically investigate this, focusing on women's roles, identifying systemic barriers to their economic empowerment and leadership, and evaluating which LFS models most effectively promote gender equity.
- **The Impact of Digitalization**: The rise of online platforms and food hubs is rapidly changing the LFS landscape (FAO, INRAE, 2020). Research is needed to understand how digitalization affects social proximity, trust, and inclusivity (Michel-Villarreal et al., 2021). Key questions include: How does technology change the producer-consumer relationship? Does it create new forms of exclusion or a "digital divide"? And what are the best practices for leveraging technology to enhance, rather than dilute, the social and cultural benefits of local food systems?

REFERENCES

Aiello, G., Giovino, I., Vallone, M., & Catania, P. (2017). A multi objective approach to short food supply chain management. *Chemical Engineering Transactions, 58*, 313–318. DOI: 10.3303/CET1758053

Alessandrini, M. (2024a). Final reflections—Short Food Supply Chains in the agri-food context: Charting the future agenda. In *Regulating Short Food Supply Chains in the EU* (Vol. 28). Springer., DOI: 10.1007/978-3-031-69390-8_8

Alessandrini, M. (2024b). Unpacking Short Food Supply Chains (SFSCs). A systematic classification of existing initiatives. In *Regulating Short Food Supply Chains in the EU* (Vol. 28). Springer., DOI: 10.1007/978-3-031-69390-8_3

Altieri, M. A., & Toledo, V. M. (2011). The agroecological revolution in Latin America: Rescuing nature, ensuring food sovereignty and empowering peasants. *The Journal of Peasant Studies, 38*(3), 587–612. DOI: 10.1080/03066150.2011.582947

Aouinait, C., Christen, D., Carlen, C., Mehauden, L., Mora, P., Massar, B., & Frederiks, M. (2022). Motivations and barriers for engagement in short food supply chains: Insights from European focus groups. *International Journal of Food Studies, 11*(SI), a8. DOI: 10.7455/ijfs/11.si.2022.a8

Aubry, C., & Kebir, L. (2013). Shortening food supply chains: A means for maintaining agriculture close to urban areas? The case of the French metropolitan area of Paris. *Food Policy, 41*, 85–93. DOI: 10.1016/j.foodpol.2013.04.006

Barry, C. (2012). *Commercialisation des produits agricoles. Un producteur sur cinq vend en circuit court.* Agreste Primeur, 275. http://agreste.agriculture.gouv.fr/IMG/pdf/primeur275.pdf

Bayir, B., Charles, A., Sekhari, A., & Ouzrout, Y. (2022). Issues and challenges in short food supply chains: A systematic literature review. *Sustainability (Basel), 14*(5), 3029. DOI: 10.3390/su14053029

Bazzani, C., & Canavari, M. (2017). Is local a matter of food miles or food traditions? *Italian Journal of Food Science, 29*(3), 505–517.

Berti, G., & Mulligan, C. (2016). Competitiveness of small farms and innovative food supply chains: The role of food hubs in creating sustainable regional and local food systems. *Sustainability (Basel), 8*(7), 616. DOI: 10.3390/su8070616

Bessière, J. (1998). Local development and heritage: Traditional food and cuisine as tourist attractions in rural areas. *Sociologia Ruralis, 38*(1), 21–34. DOI: 10.1111/1467-9523.00061

Bilska, B., Piecek, M., & Kołożyn-Krajewska, D. (2018). Food valorization in sustainable development. *Problems of World Agriculture, 18*(2), 22–28.

Blay-Palmer, A., Santini, G., Halliday, J., Malec, R., Carey, J., Keller, L., Ni, J., Taguchi, M., & van Veenhuizen, R. (2021). City region food systems: Building resilience to COVID-19 and other shocks. *Sustainability (Basel), 13*(3), 1325. DOI: 10.3390/su13031325

Borsellino, V., Schimmenti, E., & El Bilali, H. (2020). Agri-food markets towards sustainable patterns. *Sustainability (Basel), 12*(6), 2193. DOI: 10.3390/su12062193

Butu, A., Brumă, I. S., Tanasă, L., Rodino, S., Dinu Vasiliu, C., Dobo , S., & Butu, M. (2020). The impact of COVID-19 crisis upon the consumer buying behavior of fresh vegetables directly from local producers. Case study: The quarantined area of Suceava County, Romania. *International Journal of Environmental Research and Public Health, 17*(15), 5485. DOI: 10.3390/ijerph17155485

Canfora, I. (2016). Is the short food supply chain an efficient solution for sustainability in food market? *Agriculture and Agricultural Science Procedia, 8*, 402–407. DOI: 10.1016/j.aaspro.2016.02.036

Chang, B. P., Massri, C., Reipurth, M., Petropoulou, E., Hüttl-Maack, V., Gawlik, D., ... & Hieke, S. (2022). Barriers and facilitators of purchasing from short food supply chains: Evidence from consumer focus groups in Germany, Spain, Greece and Hungary. *International Journal of Food Studies, 11*(SI), 208-218. https://doi .org/DOI: 10.7455/ijfs/11.SI.2022.a7

Charatsari, C., Kitsios, F., & Lioutas, E. D. (2020). Short food supply chains: The link between participation and farmers' competencies. *Renewable Agriculture and Food Systems, 35*(6), 643–652. DOI: 10.1017/S1742170519000309

Chiffoleau, Y., & Dourian, T. (2020). Sustainable food supply chains: Is shortening the answer? A literature review for a research and innovation agenda. *Sustainability (Basel), 12*(23), 9831. DOI: 10.3390/su12239831

Csordás, A., Lengyel, P., & Füzesi, I. (2022). Who prefers regional products? A systematic literature review of consumer characteristics and attitudes in short food supply chains. *Sustainability (Basel), 14*(15), 8990. DOI: 10.3390/su14158990

Declaration of Nyéléni. (2007). *Declaration of Nyéléni*. https://nyeleni.org/IMG/pdf/DeclNyeleni-en.pdf

Doernberg, A., Piorr, A., Zasada, I., & Adewumi, M. O. (2022). Sustainability assessment of short food supply chains (SFSC): Developing and testing a rapid assessment tool in one African and three European city regions. *Agriculture and Human Values*, *39*(3), 885–904. DOI: 10.1007/s10460-021-10288-w

Evola, R. S., Peira, G., Varese, E., Bonadonna, A., & Vesce, E. (2022). Short food supply chains in Europe: Scientific research directions. *Sustainability (Basel)*, *14*(6), 3602. DOI: 10.3390/su14063602

FAO, & INRAE. (2020). *Enabling sustainable food systems: Innovators' handbook*. FAO.

Feagan, R. (2007). The place of food: Mapping out the 'local' in local food systems. *Progress in Human Geography*, *31*(1), 23–42. DOI: 10.1177/0309132507073527

Feenstra, G. W. (1997). Local food systems and sustainable communities. *American Journal of Alternative Agriculture*, *12*(1), 28–36. DOI: 10.1017/S0889189300007165

Felici, F. B., & Mazzocchi, G. (2022). Territory matters: A methodology for understanding the role of territorial factors in transforming local food systems. *Land (Basel)*, *11*(7), 1046. DOI: 10.3390/land11071046

Gillespie, A. H., & Smith, L. E. (2008). Food decision-making framework: Connecting sustainable food systems to health and well-being. *Journal of Hunger & Environmental Nutrition*, *3*(2-3), 328–346. DOI: 10.1080/19320240802244363

Goodman, D., DuPuis, E. M., & Goodman, M. K. (2012). *Alternative food networks: Knowledge, practice, and politics*. Routledge., DOI: 10.4324/9780203804520

Hinrichs, C. C. (2000). Embeddedness and local food systems: Notes on two types of direct agricultural market. *Journal of Rural Studies*, *16*(3), 295–303. DOI: 10.1016/S0743-0167(99)00063-7

Hinrichs, C. C. (2003). The practice and politics of food system localization. *Journal of Rural Studies*, *19*(1), 33–45. DOI: 10.1016/S0743-0167(02)00040-2

Hyland, J., Henchion, M. M., Olomo, O., Attard, J., & Gaffey, J. (2024). Sustainable and healthy food consumption in Europe: An analysis of consumer purchase patterns, motivations and barriers towards foods from SFSCs. *British Food Journal*, *126*(4), 1429–1455. DOI: 10.1108/BFJ-01-2023-0058

Ilbery, B., & Maye, D. (2005). Food supply chains and sustainability: Evidence from specialist food producers in the Scottish/English borders. *Land Use Policy*, *22*(4), 331–344. DOI: 10.1016/j.landusepol.2004.06.002

Jarosz, L. (2008). The city in the country: Growing alternative food networks in Metropolitan areas. *Journal of Rural Studies, 24*(3), 231–244. DOI: 10.1016/j.jrurstud.2007.10.002

Jarzębowski, S., Bourlakis, M., & Bezat-Jarzębowska, A. (2020). Short food supply chains (SFSC) as local and sustainable systems. *Sustainability (Basel), 12*(11), 4715. DOI: 10.3390/su12114715

Jia, F., Shahzadi, G., Bourlakis, M., & John, A. (2024). Promoting resilient and sustainable food systems: A systematic literature review on short food supply chains. *Journal of Cleaner Production, 435*, 140364. DOI: 10.1016/j.jclepro.2023.140364

Kiss, K., Koncz, G., Nagy-Demeter, D., Varró, B., Németh, M., & Ruszkai, C. (2019). Survey of consumers responsiveness to small-scale producers marketing in the Northern Hungary Region. [TMP]. *Theory Methodology Practice, 15*(1), 25–34. DOI: 10.18096/TMP.2019.01.03

Kneafsey, M., Cox, R., Holloway, L., Dowler, E., Venn, L., & Tuomainen, H. (2008). *Reconnecting consumers, producers and food: Exploring alternatives*. Bloomsbury Publishing. DOI: 10.5040/9781350047631

Kneafsey, M., Venn, L., Schmutz, U., Balázs, B., Trenchard, L., Eyden-Wood, T., ... & Blackett, M. (2013). *Short food supply chains and local food systems in the EU. A state of play of their socio-economic characteristics*. JRC Scientific and Policy Reports, European Commission. DOI: 10.2791/88784

Lee, K. S. (2023). Cooking up food memories: A taste of intangible cultural heritage. *Journal of Hospitality and Tourism Management, 54*, 1–9. DOI: 10.1016/j.jhtm.2022.11.005

Lucas, A., Moruzzo, R., & Granai, G. (2024). Farmers' markets contribution to the resilience of the food systems. *Agricultural and Food Economics, 12*(1), 50. DOI: 10.1186/s40100-024-00345-3

Lund, M. (2012). Multi-stakeholder co-operatives: Engines of innovation for building a healthier local food system and a healthier economy. *Journal of Co-operative Studies, 45*(1), 32–37.

Lutz, J., Smetschka, B., & Grima, N. (2017). Farmer cooperation as a means for creating local food systems—Potentials and challenges. *Sustainability (Basel), 9*(6), 925. DOI: 10.3390/su9060925

Lyson, T. A. (2004). *Civic agriculture: Reconnecting farm, food, and community*. University Press of New England.

Majewski, E., Komerska, A., Kwiatkowski, J., Malak-Rawlikowska, A., Wąs, A., Sulewski, P., Gołaś, M., Pogodzińska, K., Lecoeur, J.-L., Tocco, B., Török, Á., Donati, M., & Vittersø, G. (2020). Are short food supply chains more environmentally sustainable than long chains? A life cycle assessment (LCA) of the eco-efficiency of food chains in selected EU countries. *Energies*, *13*(18), 4853. DOI: 10.3390/en13184853

Malak-Rawlikowska, A., Majewski, E., Wąs, A., Borgen, S. O., Csillag, P., Donati, M., Freeman, R., Hoàng, V., Lecoeur, J.-L., Mancini, M. C., Nguyen, A., Saïdi, M., Tocco, B., Török, Á., Veneziani, M., Vittersø, G., & Wavresky, P. (2019). Measuring the economic, environmental, and social sustainability of short food supply chains. *Sustainability (Basel)*, *11*(15), 4004. DOI: 10.3390/su11154004

Marsden, T., Banks, J., & Bristow, G. (2000). Food supply chain approaches: Exploring their role in rural development. *Sociologia Ruralis*, *40*(4), 424–438. DOI: 10.1111/1467-9523.00158

Martinez, S., Hand, M., Da Pra, M., Pollack, S., Ralston, K., Smith, T., . . . Newman, C. (2010). *Local food systems: Concepts, impacts, and issues* (Report No. ERR-97). U.S. Department of Agriculture, Economic Research Service.

Mesić, Ž., Petljak, K., Borović, D., & Tomić, M. (2020). Segmentation of local food consumers based on altruistic motives and perceived purchasing barriers: A Croatian study. *Ekonomska Istrazivanja*, *34*(1), 221–242. DOI: 10.1080/1331677X.2020.1782243

Meyerding, S. G. H., Trajer, N., & Lehberger, M. (2019). What is local food? The case of consumer preferences for local food labeling of tomatoes in Germany. *Journal of Cleaner Production*, *207*, 30–43. DOI: 10.1016/j.jclepro.2018.09.224

Michel-Villarreal, R., Vilalta-Perdomo, E. L., Canavari, M., & Hingley, M. (2021). Resilience and digitalization in short food supply chains: A case study approach. *Sustainability (Basel)*, *13*(11), 5913. DOI: 10.3390/su13115913

Moragues-Faus, A., & Morgan, K. (2015). Reframing the foodscape: The emergent world of urban food policy. *Environment and Planning A. Environment & Planning A*, *47*(7), 1558–1573. DOI: 10.1177/0308518X15595754

Mundler, P. (2022). The role of proximity in food systems. In *Handbook on the Geographies of Proximity* (pp. 368–381). Edward Elgar Publishing. DOI: 10.4337/9781786434784.00027

Mundler, P., & Laughrea, S. (2016). The contributions of short food supply chains to territorial development: A study of three Quebec territories. *Journal of Rural Studies*, *45*, 218–229. DOI: 10.1016/j.jrurstud.2016.04.001

Onozaka, Y., Nurse, G., & McFadden, D. T. (2010). Local food consumers: How motivations and perceptions translate to buying behavior. *Choices*, *25*(1), 1–15. DOI: 10.22004/ag.econ.93822

Patel, R. (2009). Food sovereignty. *The Journal of Peasant Studies*, *36*(3), 663–706. DOI: 10.1080/03066150903143079

Paxton, A. (1994). *The food miles report: The dangers of long-distance food transport*. SAFE Alliance.

Petropoulou, E., Benos, T., Theodorakopoulou, I., Iliopoulos, C., Castellini, A., Xhakollari, V., ... & Petruzzella, D. (2022). Understanding social innovation in short food supply chains: An exploratory analysis. *International Journal of Food Studies, 11*(SI), a5. DOI: 10.7455/ijfs/11.si.2022.a5

Reich, B. J., Beck, J. T., & Price, J. (2018). Food as ideology: Measurement and validation of locavorism. *The Journal of Consumer Research*, *45*(4), 849–868. DOI: 10.1093/jcr/ucy027

Renkema, M., & Hilletofth, P. (2022). Intermediate short food supply chains: A systematic review. *British Food Journal*, *124*(13), 541–558. DOI: 10.1108/BFJ-06-2022-0463

Renting, H., Marsden, T. K., & Banks, J. (2003). Understanding alternative food networks: Exploring the role of short food supply chains in rural development. *Environment & Planning A*, *35*(3), 393–411. DOI: 10.1068/a3510

Renting, H., Schermer, M., & Rossi, A. (2012). Building food democracy: Exploring civic food networks and newly emerging forms of food citizenship. *International Journal of Sociology of Agriculture and Food*, *19*(3), 289–307.

Sage, C. (2014). The transition movement and food sovereignty: From local resilience to global engagement in food system transformation. *Journal of Consumer Culture*, *14*(2), 254–275. DOI: 10.1177/1469540514526281

Sanz-Cañada, J., Sánchez-Hernández, J. L., & López-García, D. (2023). Reflecting on the concept of local agroecological food systems. *Land (Basel)*, *12*(6), 1147. DOI: 10.3390/land12061147

Scaramuzzi, S., Gabellini, S., Belletti, G., & Marescotti, A. (2021). Agrobiodiversity-oriented food systems between public policies and private action: A socio-ecological model for sustainable territorial development. *Sustainability (Basel)*, *13*(21), 12192. DOI: 10.3390/su132112192

Schanbacher, W. D. (2010). *The politics of food: The global conflict between food security and food sovereignty*. Praeger. DOI: 10.5040/9798400698576

Sims, R. (2009). Food, place and authenticity: Local food and the sustainable tourism experience. *Journal of Sustainable Tourism, 17*(3), 321–336. DOI: 10.1080/09669580802359293

Smith, B., Lawrence, G., & Richards, C. (2020). Consumption, identity and local food: A symbolic interactionist perspective. *Sociologia Ruralis, 60*(3), 646–665. DOI: 10.1111/soru.12290

Sonnino, R., & Marsden, T. (2006). Beyond the divide: Rethinking relationships between alternative and conventional food networks in Europe. *Journal of Economic Geography, 6*(2), 181–199. DOI: 10.1093/jeg/lbi006

Tanasă, L. (2024). Implications of Short Food Supply Chains in the Local Agri-Food System of the North-East Development Region, *Annals of the Academy of Romanian Scientists - Series on Agri-culture, Silviculture and Veterinary Medicine Sciences*, Vol. 13, No. 2/2024, ISSN 2344-2085, pp. 5-19, 2024, https://aos.ro/wp-content/anale/AVol13Nr2Art.1.pdf

Tanasă, L. (2024). In Clujeană, P. U. (Ed.), *Sisteme agroalimentare locale i lan uri scurte de aprovizionare func ionale din jude ul Bacău, în Rezilien ă i sustenabilitate în sistemele rurale, coord.: Ioan Sebastian Brumă i Diana Elena Creangă* (pp. 227–262)., http://www.editura.ubbcluj.ro/bd/ebooks/pdf/4469.pdf

Tregear, A. (2011). Progressing knowledge in alternative and local food networks: Critical reflections and a research agenda. *Journal of Rural Studies, 27*(4), 419–430. DOI: 10.1016/j.jrurstud.2011.06.003

UNIDO. (2020). *Short food supply chains for promoting local food on local markets*. United Nations Industrial Development Organization.

Van der Ploeg, J. D. (2020). From biomedical to politico-economic crisis: The food system in times of Covid-19. *The Journal of Peasant Studies, 47*(5), 944–972. DOI: 10.1080/03066150.2020.1794843

Vittersø, G., Torjusen, H., Laitala, K., Tocco, B., Biasini, B., Csillag, P., & de Labarre, M. D. (2019). Short food supply chains and their contributions to sustainability: Participants' views and perceptions from 12 European cases. *Sustainability (Basel), 11*(17), 4800. DOI: 10.3390/su11174800

Wronka-Pośpiech, M., & Twaróg, S. (2024). Social enterprises and short food supply chains: Insights from exploratory case studies. *Scientific Papers of Silesian University of Technology. Organization & Management/Zeszyty Naukowe Politechniki Slaskiej. Seria Organizacji i Zarzadzanie, (212).* https://managementpapers.polsl.pl/wp-content/uploads/2025/02/212-Wronka-Po%C5%9Bpiech-Twar%C3%B3g.pdf

Zaninović, V., & Skender, P. (2025). *[Placeholder for forthcoming work].*

Zepeda, L., & Li, J. (2006). Who buys local food? *Journal of Food Distribution Research, 37*(3), 1–11.

Zhang, X., & Yu, X. (2021). Short supply chain participation, and agrochemicals' use intensity and efficiency: Evidence from vegetable farms in China. *China Agricultural Economic Review, 13*(4), 721–735. DOI: 10.1108/CAER-05-2020-0108

APPENDIX

Figure 6. Comparative matrix between Local Food Systems (LFSs), and Conventional/Long Food Supply Chains (LFSCs)

	SFSC	LAS	LFS
NUMBER OF INTERMEDIARIES	0-1	0-2	3+
TRANSPARENCY	High	High	Low
FLEXIBILITY	Very high	High	Low
TRANSPORTATION COSTS	Low	Minimal transport	High transpor costs
SOCIAL IMPACT	Strong local community support	Reinforces local identity and cohesion	Outsourced social challenges
PRODUCT QUALITY	High	Very high quality	Average to low quality
PRODUCT DIVERSITY	High diversity	Exceptional diversity	Standardized range
SEASONALITY	High seasonality	Very high seasonality	Moderate seasonality
PROCESSING & PACKAGING	Minimal processing & eco-friendly packsiing	Minimal processing & eco-friendly	Extensive processing & & packaging
ECONOMIES OF SCALE	Low economies of scale	Limited scale-economies	Significant impact
ECOLOGICAL IMPACT	Reduced impact	Very low impact	Significant impact
INNOVATION LEVEL	High innovation	Moderate innovation	High innovation
COMMUNITY INTEGRATION	High community integration	High community integration	Low community integration
SUPPORT POLICIES	pequire local policy support	Needs political and community backing	Supported by corporate/govemment trameworks
PRODUCT LIFECYCLE FOCUS	Durability and quality	Durability and quality	Efficiency and profitability

Source: Own computations based on ChatGPT software

Chapter 4
Bridging Green Innovation and Finance:
Circular Economy Transitions by Green Financial Instruments

Marijana Joksimović
https://orcid.org/0000-0002-5939-5137
Alfa BK University, Belgrade, Serbia

Biljana Grujić Vučkovski
https://orcid.org/0000-0003-2588-4888
Tamiš Research and Development Institute, Pančevo, Serbia

ABSTRACT

This paper explores relationship between green innovation and circular economy practices, emphasizing how green finance—a financial approach that supports environmentally sustainable investments—serves as a critical enabler in this transformation. While green innovation provides the technological and process solutions for circular models, it is green finance that mobilizes the capital needed to scale these solutions across industries. Key areas of focus include: The role of green bonds, sustainability-linked loans, and ESG (Environmental, Social, and Governance) investment frameworks in supporting circular initiatives. Case studies of enterprises and municipalities that have leveraged innovative financial instruments to fund circular economy projects such as sustainable packaging, renewable materials, waste-to-energy technologies, and product-as-a-service business models. The paper also identifies challenges such as inconsistent sustainability metrics, greenwashing risks, and the need for stronger collaboration between financial institutions, governments, and innovators.

DOI: 10.4018/979-8-3373-2898-0.ch004

THE SCENARIO

The increasing urgency of environmental challenges—ranging from climate change and biodiversity loss to rising levels of waste and resource scarcity—has accelerated the global push toward sustainable development. Traditional linear economic models, based on the extraction, consumption, and disposal of resources, have proven environmentally unsustainable and economically inefficient in the long term. In response, the circular economy has emerged as a transformative framework that seeks to redefine growth by decoupling economic activity from finite resource use and environmental degradation. It emphasizes principles of resource efficiency, product life extension, recycling, and regenerative design.

To support such systemic change, green innovation plays a critical role. It encompasses the development and deployment of environmentally friendly technologies, materials, business models, and production processes that contribute to ecological sustainability. However, the successful implementation and scaling of these innovations require more than technical feasibility—they demand substantial and sustained financial investment. This introduces the pivotal role of green finance, which refers to financial investments that generate environmental benefits and support sustainable development initiatives.

As a rapidly growing segment of the financial sector, green financial instruments—including green bonds, sustainability-linked loans, climate funds, and Environmental, Social, Governance (abbr. ESG) oriented investments—offer a pathway to mobilize capital toward circular economy objectives. These tools have the potential to not only fund green innovation but also shape market behavior and incentivize sustainable practices across industries and value chains.

Despite growing interest in aligning finance with environmental goals, the integration of green finance mechanisms into circular economy strategies remains underexplored and unevenly developed. Many innovative projects face barriers such as lack of access to capital, unclear sustainability metrics, and policy fragmentation. Therefore, understanding how green finance can more effectively support circular economy transitions is essential for building resilient and low-carbon economies.

This chapter aims to examine the nexus between green innovation, circular economy practices, and green finance, with a focus on how financial instruments can bridge the gap between technological potential and practical implementation. Through conceptual analysis and illustrative case studies, the study highlights enabling factors, challenges, and strategic pathways for aligning finance with circular economy objectives, ultimately contributing to a more sustainable and inclusive global economy.

Ultimately, the convergence of green finance and circular innovation represents a powerful pathway to not only mitigate environmental risks but also unlock new economic opportunities and resilience in the face of climate and resource challenges.

The global economy is facing unprecedented environmental challenges, from accelerating climate change and biodiversity loss to resource depletion and unsustainable waste generation. In response, a growing consensus among policymakers, businesses, and civil society is calling for a shift away from traditional linear economic models toward more sustainable, circular systems. The circular economy offers a transformative vision by promoting the continual use of resources, minimizing waste, and designing for durability, reuse, and regeneration.

However, realizing this vision at scale requires more than just technological solutions it demands a systemic approach where innovation and finance are aligned with sustainability objectives. Green innovation, encompassing environmentally friendly technologies, business models, and industrial processes, plays a pivotal role in enabling the transition to a circular economy. Yet, without adequate financial support, even the most promising innovations can struggle to achieve meaningful impact.

This is where green finance becomes essential. As an umbrella term for financial products and services that support environmental goals, green finance includes mechanisms such as green bonds, sustainability-linked loans, and ESG-aligned investment portfolios. These instruments are increasingly being mobilized to fund projects that drive decarbonization, improve resource efficiency, and support sustainable infrastructure. Importantly, they also have the potential to catalyze and scale circular economy initiatives.

This chapter explores how green financial instruments can bridge the gap between green innovation and the widespread implementation of circular economy practices. It examines the interplay between innovation and finance, identifies key enablers and barriers, and highlights case studies where financial tools have successfully supported circular solutions. By focusing on this nexus, the study aims to offer actionable insights into how stakeholders—from policymakers to private investors can collaborate to accelerate the global transition toward a more sustainable and resilient economy.

METHODOLOGY

This chapter employs a qualitative, multi-method research approach to explore the intersection between green innovation, circular economy practices, and green finance. The aim is to identify how green financial instruments can support and scale circular economy initiatives through innovation-driven solutions. The methodology integrates a thematic *literature review, data use in the chapter, case study analysis, expert input, analytical framework, conceptual framework,* and approach that enabling a comprehensive and contextual understanding of this emerging field (Joksimović et al., 2018).

Literature Review use in the chapter. A systematic review of academic literature, policy reports, and industry publications was conducted to establish the conceptual framework of the study. Key themes include: Definitions and scope of green innovation and circular economy The structure and functioning of green financial instruments (e.g., green bonds, ESG funds, sustainability-linked loans). Intersections between finance, innovation, and sustainability policy. Databases such as Scopus, Web of Science, and Google Scholar were used, alongside reports from institutions like the World Bank, UNEP, OECD, and the European Commission. This review provides the theoretical grounding and identifies knowledge gaps addressed by the empirical component (Balaban et al., 2023).

The intersection of green innovation, circular economy practices, and green finance has become an increasingly relevant area of research within the broader context of sustainable development. This literature review synthesizes key theoretical and empirical contributions that define each of these domains and explores how they interact to support sustainability transitions (Balaban et al., 2022).

Green innovation refers to the development and application of products, processes, services, and business models that reduce environmental harm and enhance resource efficiency (Kemp & Pearson, 2007). It plays a pivotal role in sustainability transitions by introducing alternatives to carbon-intensive and waste-generating systems (OECD, 2011). Scholars such as Rennings (2000) have emphasized that environmental innovations not only address ecological concerns but also have the potential to drive competitive advantage and economic growth.

The circular economy is conceptualized as an economic system that aims to eliminate waste and continuously reuse resources, in contrast to the traditional linear economy (Ellen MacArthur Foundation, 2013). It is grounded in principles such as designing out waste, keeping products and materials in use, and regenerating natural systems. Kirchherr et al. (2017) highlight that circular economy is not only an environmental necessity but also a driver of innovation and job creation. However, despite its promise, the transition to circular economy is often hindered by financial, regulatory, and market barriers (Lacy & Rutqvist, 2015).

Green finance encompasses financial instruments and investments that deliver environmental benefits in the context of sustainable development (UNEP, 2016). This includes green bonds, sustainability-linked loans, ESG investment portfolios, and climate-focused funds. The growth of green finance has been driven by both market demand and regulatory frameworks that encourage investment in low-carbon and resource-efficient technologies (Flammer, 2021; G20 Green Finance Study Group, 2016).

Several studies have pointed to green finance as a crucial enabler of green innovation and sustainable infrastructure (Zhang et al., 2011). However, issues such as inconsistent standards, greenwashing risks, and limited access to finance for small and medium-sized enterprises (SMEs) remain significant barriers (OECD, 2020).

While green finance and circular economy frameworks have largely evolved in parallel, a growing body of literature explores their integration. Studies suggest that financial mechanisms such as green bonds and sustainability-linked financing can be effectively tailored to support circular projects—ranging from renewable materials and product life extension to resource recovery and recycling (Pavlović et al., 2019, Popp et al., 2020; EIB, 2021).

Scholars have argued that aligning financial systems with circular goals requires a systems-thinking approach, cross-sectoral collaboration, and strong policy support (Merli et al., 2018). Moreover, investment in CE-related innovation must be underpinned by clear metrics, lifecycle assessments, and long-term value creation strategies (Bocken et al., 2014).

Data use in the chapter. This study relies on a combination of secondary data sources and qualitative case study evidence to analyze the role of green financial instruments in supporting circular economy innovation. The data collected serves to illustrate market trends, investment flows, policy frameworks, and practical applications of green finance in circular projects. (Živkov et al., 2021).

To assess the scale and growth of green financial instruments, the study uses publicly available datasets from leading global financial and sustainability organizations, including:

- Climate Bonds Initiative (abbr. CBI): Data on the issuance of green bonds globally, including sectoral allocation (e.g., energy, water, waste, circular economy) and issuer types (sovereign, municipal, corporate). Example: As of 2024, global cumulative green bond issuance surpassed USD 3.5 trillion, with a growing share directed toward circular economy projects such as waste management, sustainable agriculture, and closed-loop production systems (Climate Bonds Initiative, 2024).
- OECD and World Bank Reports: Indicators on green finance flows, policy instruments, and the role of public finance in leveraging private capital for green innovation. Example: The OECD (2023) notes that circular economy investments remain under 10% of total green finance flows, indicating a significant gap in capital mobilization.
- ESG Investment Trends (Morningstar, Bloomberg): data on asset management strategies that incorporate environmental, social, and governance criteria. Useful for understanding how investors are aligning portfolios

with sustainability objectives, including circular economy-related metrics (Joksimovic et al., 2017).

To understand how green finance supports circular economy projects, the study analyzes funding and innovation data in specific sectors such as *EU Circular Economy Finance Support Platform (European Commission).* This platform provides data on investment initiatives, innovation funding, and public-private partnerships (abbr. PPPs) targeting circular economy transitions across EU member states. Example: In 2022, the EU's Circular Economy Action Plan mobilized over EUR 10 billion in circular economy related investments, with significant support from the European Investment Bank (abbr. EIB, 2021). UNEP FI & Global Alliance for Circular Economy and Resource Efficiency (abbr. GACERE): Offers case data on financial innovation for circular economy, including sustainability-linked loans, blended finance, and risk-sharing mechanisms. Three case studies were selected to illustrate how green financial instruments have been applied to enable circular innovation. These cases include diverse sectors (urban development, packaging, industrial manufacturing), and data was sourced from: Company sustainability and financial reports (e.g., Philips, Veolia, Loop Industries); Project finance details from institutions like the European Bank for Reconstruction and Development (abbr. EBRD) and Asian Development Bank (abbr. ADB); third-party evaluations and lifecycle assessments (abbr. LCAs).

Each case study includes the following data points: Type of green financial instrument used (e.g., green bond, ESG loan) Investment size and duration Project objectives and alignment with circular economy principles reported environmental and economic outcomes (e.g., CO_2 reduction, material reuse, cost savings).

To support contextual analysis, the study includes policy and regulatory data relevant to green finance and circular economy integration: EU Taxonomy for Sustainable Activities, China's Green Bond Endorsed Projects Catalogue, Sustainable Finance Disclosure Regulation (abbr. SFDR). These frameworks provide the basis for assessing the alignment of financial flows with circular economy criteria.

Case Study Analysis. A series of purposefully selected case studies were analyzed to illustrate how green financial mechanisms have been used to support circular economy transitions in practice. Selection criteria included: Relevance to circular economy principles (e.g., waste reduction, resource efficiency, circular business models) Use of formal green financial instruments Availability of public data and documentation Case studies span multiple sectors, including manufacturing, energy, urban development, and agriculture. Each case was analyzed using a structured framework to assess: *a) The nature of the innovation; b) The financial mechanism employed; c) The measurable environmental and economic outcomes; d) Challenges and success factors.*

Expert Input. To complement the desk research, qualitative input was gathered from semi-structured interviews or existing expert commentaries (depending on scope and access). These included professionals in sustainable finance, policy advisors, and circular economy practitioners. The goal was to capture real-world insights on financial barriers, policy gaps, and innovation opportunities. Thematic coding was applied to extract key patterns and align findings with literature and case evidence (Grujić Vučkovski et al., 2022).

Analytical framework. Findings were synthesized using an integrative analytical framework that maps the relationships between green finance instruments, innovation drivers, and circular economy outcomes. This framework guided the comparison across case studies and facilitated the development of policy and strategic recommendations.

The primary aim of this research is to investigate how green financial instruments can effectively support the implementation and scaling of circular economy initiatives through green innovation. The study explores the dynamic interplay between finance, innovation, and sustainability, with a focus on identifying the enabling conditions for financial flows to drive system-wide circular transformation.

To guide this investigation, the study is structured around the following key research questions:

1. How do green financial instruments support green innovation within the context of the circular economy?
2. What types of circular economy projects are currently being funded through green finance mechanisms, and in which sectors?
3. What are the key barriers and enablers in aligning green finance with circular innovation at scale?
4. How can policy frameworks and market mechanisms be improved to enhance the impact of green finance on circular economy transitions?

To address the research questions, this study is guided by the following objectives:

- Objective 1: To examine the theoretical and practical connections between green innovation, circular economy models, and sustainable finance.
- Objective 2: To analyze real-world cases where green financial tools (e.g., green bonds, ESG funds, sustainability-linked loans) have supported circular economy projects.
- Objective 3: To identify challenges in mobilizing green finance for circular economy -related innovations and evaluate existing financial and regulatory frameworks.

- Objective 4: To propose actionable strategies and policy recommendations that foster stronger integration between green finance and circular innovation at both national and international levels.

This research adopts a global perspective, while drawing specific examples from both developed and emerging economies to reflect diverse policy contexts and financial ecosystems. The scope includes:

- Sectors analyzed: manufacturing, urban development, energy, waste management, and consumer goods.
- Types of financial instruments examined: green bonds, climate funds, blended finance, sustainability-linked loans, and ESG investment strategies.
- Stakeholders considered: public and private financial institutions, policy makers, innovators, corporations, and development banks.

By adopting a cross-sectoral and cross-disciplinary approach, this research contributes to the growing field of sustainable finance and circular economy studies, offering insights for both academic inquiry and practical application.

Conceptual Framework

The framework is built on the assumption that:

- Green innovation acts as a technical and process-driven foundation for circular economy solutions.
- Circular economy goals define the strategic direction and systemic transformation needed for sustainability.
- Green finance acts as a catalyst and scaling mechanism by channeling investment into green innovations that align with circular economy principles.

This study is grounded in a systems-thinking approach that links three interconnected domains: green innovation, the circular economy, and green finance. The conceptual framework illustrates how financial mechanisms serve as enablers that bridge innovation and implementation in circular models.

Core concepts defined of green innovation involves the development and application of technologies, products, services, and business models that reduce environmental harm and promote sustainability (Rennings, 2000). Circular Economy refers to an economic system that is restorative and regenerative by design, aiming to keep resources in use for as long as possible and minimize waste (Ellen MacArthur Foundation, 2013). Green Finance includes investments and financial instruments that provide environmental benefits and contribute to the sustainability transition (UNEP, 2016).

The framework posits the following mechanism:

1. **Findings and Analysis:** This section presents the key findings from the literature review, financial data analysis, and case study investigations. It highlights how green finance is being mobilized to support circular economy innovation, identifies gaps, and evaluates the effectiveness of financial instruments in achieving circular outcomes.
2. **Growing Integration of Green Finance and circular economy objectives:** Findings reveal a steady rise in the number of green financial instruments explicitly aligned with circular economy principles: according to the approximately 12% of global green bond issuances now include circular economy-related activities such as waste reduction, recycling infrastructure, sustainable material innovation, and product life extension (Climate Bonds Initiative, 2024); over EUR 2 billion in loans were allocated specifically to circular economy focused innovation projects, including renewable materials, reverse logistics, and circular product design.
3. Green Bonds and ESG Instruments as Key Enablers.

Several case studies illustrate how green financial tools are helping companies and cities scale circular solutions:

- **Case 1: Philips (Netherlands):** Issued €750 million in green innovation bonds, partly allocated to designing products for longevity and recyclability. *Impact*: Enabled over 90% of products sold to meet Eco Design standards, improving material efficiency and supporting a take-back program.
- **Case 2: City of Milan (Italy):** Used EU green funding to develop a city-wide food waste recovery and redistribution program. *Impact*: Over 100 tons of food recovered per year, with reductions in municipal waste costs and increased social equity outcomes.
- **Case 3: Loop Industries (USA):** Secured private equity backed by ESG-aligned investors to develop chemical recycling technology for plastics. *Impact*: Demonstrated a closed-loop PET plastic recycling model, attracting major brand partnerships.

These examples show that green financial mechanisms can significantly de-risk innovation, attract private capital, and support long-term circular economy goals. However, their impact is often dependent on clear sustainability metrics, project transparency, and investor confidence (Živkov et al., 2022).

RESEARCH AND DISCUSSION

The chapter provides a comprehensive analysis of the role green financial instruments play in bridging the gap between innovation and finance, specifically in the context of driving the transition to a circular economy. As industries and governments strive to meet sustainability targets, the chapter argues that innovative financial solutions are key to fostering the widespread adoption of circular economy principles. In continuing of the chapter we will analyze the following subheadings: *green financial instruments as catalysts for circular economy transitions; integration of innovation and finance; challenges and opportunities; role of policy and regulation; implications; future research directions.*

Green Financial Instruments as Catalysts for Circular Economy Transitions

The primary focus of the chapter is on how green financial instruments - *such as green bonds, green loans, and sustainability-linked financing* - serve as a vital tool in catalyzing the circular economy. Green financial instruments are designed to fund environmentally sustainable projects that promote resource efficiency, waste reduction, and long-term environmental benefits. These financial products are specifically designed to support environmentally sustainable projects and investments that contribute to addressing climate change, resource depletion, and environmental degradation. By channeling private and institutional capital into circular economy ventures, green financial instruments serve as catalysts for driving large-scale change in industries and markets.

The chapter emphasizes that these instruments not only help mobilize capital but also direct financial flows toward initiatives that contribute to a more sustainable economic system.

A key takeaway from the chapter is the concept of financing the circular economy, which requires a departure from traditional linear economic models of "take, make, dispose" toward models that promote reusability, recycling, and closed-loop production processes. Green financial instruments provide the necessary funding to support businesses that are adopting circular economy practices, such as recycling technologies, renewable energy solutions, and waste-to-value models.

The transition to a circular economy requires a profound shift in how businesses and governments approach resource management, waste reduction, and sustainability. Traditional economic models based on linear production and consumption are increasingly being challenged by the circular economy model, which emphasizes the reuse, recycling, and regeneration of materials and products. However, transitioning to this model demands significant investments in innovative technologies, sustainable business practices, and infrastructure that promotes resource efficiency.

Green Bonds: Financing Circular Economy Projects

Green bonds are one of the most well-known and widely used green financial instruments. They are debt securities issued by corporations, municipalities, or financial institutions with the specific intention of financing environmentally beneficial projects. These projects include investments in renewable energy, energy efficiency, sustainable waste management, and circular economy initiatives such as product lifecycle management and the recycling of materials.

Green bonds provide businesses with an opportunity to raise funds for circular economy projects while offering investors a way to support sustainable growth. By linking financing to specific environmental outcomes, green bonds help ensure that capital is directed toward projects that advance resource circularity and contribute to broader sustainability goals. The increasing popularity of green bonds reflects growing demand for green investments and demonstrates the significant potential for financial markets to support circular economy transitions.

Moreover, the green bond market has seen substantial growth in recent years, with both developed and emerging economies issuing bonds to fund circular economy projects. As the market matures, the issuance of green bonds is expected to expand further, enabling even more businesses to access affordable capital for sustainable innovation.

Green Loans and Sustainability-Linked Loans

In addition to green bonds, green loans and sustainability-linked loans (SLLs) are gaining prominence as financial instruments to support circular economy transitions. Green loans are similar to green bonds but involve direct lending arrangements between banks and borrowers for the purpose of financing green projects. These loans typically come with favorable terms, such as lower interest rates, in exchange for the borrower committing to specific environmental objectives or outcomes.

Sustainability-linked loans, on the other hand, are loans where the terms, such as interest rates, are linked to the borrower's performance on sustainability metrics. Unlike green loans, which finance specific green projects, SLLs are broader in scope and can be used for a variety of purposes as long as the borrower meets certain sustainability criteria. These instruments incentivize companies to improve their environmental performance by offering financial benefits tied to achieving specific circular economy targets, such as reducing waste, increasing resource efficiency, or adopting closed-loop production processes.

These financial products are particularly useful for companies that are transitioning to circular business models, as they provide the flexibility to invest in various stages of the circular economy, from design and manufacturing to recycling and waste management. The integration of sustainability metrics into loan agreements helps align the incentives of borrowers, lenders, and investors toward achieving circular economy goals.

Impact Investment Funds

Impact investment funds focus on investing in businesses and projects that generate positive environmental and social outcomes, in addition to financial returns. These funds often target high-impact sectors such as renewable energy, waste management, and sustainable agriculture, all of which play a critical role in advancing the circular economy.

Investors in impact funds seek both measurable financial returns and tangible, positive impacts on sustainability. By targeting sectors that are critical to circular economy transitions, impact funds provide capital to companies and projects that are directly working on innovations in material reuse, product design for circularity, and resource-efficient technologies. These funds enable businesses at all stages of the circular economy—from startups to large corporations—to access the capital they need to develop, scale, and commercialize their solutions.

Impact funds can also be structured to address specific circular economy challenges, such as financing the creation of recycling infrastructure, funding circular business model innovations, or supporting initiatives that reduce carbon footprints through sustainable manufacturing processes. By aligning investment strategies with long-term sustainability goals, impact investment funds are instrumental in fostering the circular economy's growth.

PPPs and Blended Finance

PPPs and blended finance structures are increasingly being recognized as critical tools in scaling circular economy transitions. These mechanisms combine public and private sector investments to support large-scale circular economy projects that would otherwise struggle to attract private capital due to perceived risks or long-term horizons.

Blended finance, in particular, leverages public funding or concessional capital to attract private investment into circular economy ventures. By reducing financial risks and providing guarantees or first-loss capital, blended finance can help mobilize private capital for projects that have strong environmental benefits but may not be immediately financially attractive to private investors. For instance, PPPs can be used to fund infrastructure projects like waste-to-energy facilities or recycling plants that are vital for enabling a circular economy but require substantial upfront investment.

Blended finance and PPPs have the potential to accelerate the deployment of circular economy technologies by overcoming financial barriers and attracting a broader pool of investors. Governments, development agencies, and financial institutions are increasingly exploring how these mechanisms can be tailored to meet the unique needs of circular economy projects.

The Role of Green Financial Instruments in Unlocking Investment for Circular Economy Innovations

Green financial instruments do more than just provide capital; they also signal market demand for circular economy solutions. The growing investor interest in sustainable and environmentally-friendly products and services is creating a shift in business practices, compelling companies to align their strategies with circular economy principles. As demand for green investments continues to rise, businesses and financial institutions are likely to increase their focus on circular economy initiatives to attract capital and meet the expectations of environmentally-conscious investors.

Moreover, the issuance and growth of green financial products help establish a sustainable investment ecosystem that supports circular economy ventures. The increasing transparency and standardization of green financial instruments through frameworks such as the Green Bond Principles and the Climate Bonds Standard provide both investors and companies with clear guidelines on what constitutes a credible and impactful green investment. This helps build trust in the market, encouraging more participants to engage in financing circular economy projects.

Green financial instruments play a pivotal role in driving the transition to a circular economy by channeling investment into sustainable and resource-efficient projects. By offering specialized funding options such as green bonds, green loans, sustainability-linked loans, and impact investment funds, these financial instruments help businesses access the capital needed to innovate and implement circular economy practices. The increasing popularity of green finance is a testament to the growing recognition that the future of business lies in sustainability. Moving forward, further collaboration between the public and private sectors, coupled with continued innovation in financial products, will be essential in accelerating the adoption of circular economy models and ensuring a sustainable, resource-efficient future.

Integration of Innovation and Finance

The transition to a circular economy requires an integrated approach that combines innovative technological advancements with financial mechanisms that support their development and deployment. However, while innovation is often the catalyst for change, securing the appropriate financing to scale and commercialize these innovations remains a critical barrier. The integration of innovation and finance is crucial for advancing the circular economy, as it ensures that emerging sustainable technologies, business models, and processes are adequately funded, tested, and brought to market.

The Role of Financial Instruments in Driving Green Innovation

Innovative technologies and business models are central to the circular economy, and many of these innovations emerge from the growing demand for sustainability across industries. These innovations include advances in materials recycling, waste-to-resource technologies, energy-efficient manufacturing, and product design for circularity. However, these innovations are often capital-intensive and require substantial investment, particularly in the early stages of development and commercialization.

Green financial instruments, such as green bonds, impact investment funds, and sustainability-linked loans, are designed to provide the capital needed for such innovations. These instruments help bridge the financing gap by aligning investor interest with the need for sustainable development. Specifically, financial products like green bonds enable large-scale investments in circular economy projects, while impact investing provides the flexible capital necessary to support early-stage innovation in areas like recycling technology or sustainable product design.

The integration of green finance and innovation is particularly evident in sectors like renewable energy, clean technology, and resource recovery. For example, the development of innovative recycling technologies, such as closed-loop recycling systems or chemical recycling of plastics, requires both strong research and development (R&D) efforts and substantial financial support to scale up. Green financial instruments provide the necessary funding for R&D and the scaling of these technologies, ensuring they move from prototype to market-ready solutions.

Stimulating Circular Business Models Through Green Finance

In addition to funding technological innovations, green financial instruments also support the development of circular business models that focus on resource efficiency, waste reduction, and the longevity of products. For example, businesses that adopt product-as-a-service models, repair and refurbishment services, or take-back schemes can access specialized green financing to support the transition from linear to circular models.

Circular business models often require significant upfront investment in infrastructure, logistics, and system redesign, which may deter companies from making the necessary investments without external financial support. Green loans or sustainability-linked loans provide a pathway for businesses to fund the development and implementation of circular models. These financial instruments offer favorable terms or incentives for companies that commit to specific sustainability targets or circular economy practices, creating a strong incentive for companies to innovate and integrate circularity into their operations.

Moreover, green finance encourages businesses to rethink their entire value chains and engage in closed-loop systems where materials are continuously reused, and waste is minimized. These business models not only reduce the environmental footprint of production and consumption but also offer long-term cost savings and new revenue streams. For instance, companies in the automotive or electronics sectors can shift from selling products to offering services such as leasing or subscription models, which help extend product life and facilitate efficient end-of-life recycling.

Innovation in Financial Instruments to Support Circular Economy Transitions

The relationship between innovation and finance is not one-sided. As businesses develop and scale circular economy solutions, the financial sector must also innovate to meet the unique needs of these new models. Traditional financial products often fail to address the specific challenges faced by circular economy initiatives, such as the long-term return on investment or the non-linear cash flow associated with resource recovery and product longevity.

To address these challenges, financial institutions and investors are developing new financial structures that are tailored to the needs of the circular economy. These innovations include blended finance, pay-for-performance models, and impact funds, all of which aim to lower the barriers to entry for circular economy projects and unlock greater amounts of capital.

For example, blended finance combines concessional funding (often from governments or philanthropic organizations) with private sector capital to finance circular economy projects that may otherwise be considered too risky or too long-term for traditional investors. This approach helps de-risk investments in innovative circular economy solutions and attracts private capital by offering financial guarantees or first-loss capital.

Pay-for-performance models are also emerging as a promising approach in the circular economy space. These models tie financial returns to the achievement of specific environmental or resource efficiency outcomes, incentivizing companies to meet targets related to waste reduction, energy efficiency, or resource recovery. For example, an investment fund might structure its financing terms so that the company only repays its loan if it successfully meets pre-agreed recycling or resource efficiency benchmarks. This performance-based structure ensures that financing is directly linked to the achievement of circular economy goals and promotes the successful implementation of sustainable innovations.

Encouraging Investment in Green Innovation Through Policy and Regulation

The integration of innovation and finance is further supported by favorable policy frameworks and regulatory environments that encourage both the development and financing of circular economy projects. Governments play a critical role in setting the stage for investment by introducing policies that incentivize the adoption of sustainable practices and technologies. These may include tax incentives for green investments, grants for R&D in sustainability, or regulations that mandate the recycling of certain materials.

For instance, the European Union has introduced several initiatives, such as the Circular Economy Action Plan, which provides policy support to businesses that implement circular models and innovations. These policies help create a clear signal to the market that circular economy transitions are not only desirable but also financially viable. This, in turn, attracts both public and private investment in innovative green technologies and business models.

Additionally, policy frameworks that standardize green financial products and provide clear definitions of what constitutes a "green" investment help foster investor confidence in the market. The alignment of innovation with finance is significantly bolstered when governments implement green finance standards, such as the EU Taxonomy for Sustainable Activities, which enables investors to identify and invest in circular economy projects with high environmental impact.

Scaling Innovation Through Collaborative Investment Models

As circular economy innovations are often complex and multifaceted, they require collaborative investment models to scale effectively. Partnerships between corporates, governments, financial institutions, and research organizations are essential to create the infrastructure and ecosystems necessary for circular economy transitions. These collaborations bring together diverse expertise and resources, from technical innovation to financing and policy support.

For example, large corporations can partner with financial institutions to create corporate venture funds that specifically target innovations in sustainability and circular economy solutions. These funds can help incubate and scale small startups working on innovative circular technologies, from advanced recycling systems to sustainable product designs. In return, corporate partners gain access to cutting-edge solutions that align with their sustainability goals, while financial institutions provide the capital to fund the innovation process.

The integration of innovation and finance is crucial for accelerating the transition to a circular economy. Financial instruments tailored to the unique needs of circular economy businesses provide the capital necessary for the research, development, and commercialization of sustainable technologies and business models. As the market for circular economy solutions continues to grow, innovation in both the technologies and financial products that support these solutions will be key to unlocking large-scale impact. By aligning financial mechanisms with the demands of circular economy innovation, the potential for achieving a sustainable, resource-efficient future becomes increasingly attainable.

One of the most significant insights from the chapter is the linkage between green innovation and finance. Innovation in the circular economy often involves cutting-edge technologies, new business models, and disruptive ideas that challenge traditional approaches to manufacturing and consumption. However, without appropriate financing mechanisms, even the most promising green innovations may struggle to reach commercial scale. The chapter argues that green financial instruments serve as a bridge between these two domains, providing the necessary capital to scale up innovative solutions and bring them to market.

The financing mechanisms discussed in the chapter are particularly important for SMEs and startups, which often lack the financial resources to fund large-scale circular economy initiatives. Green bonds and loans tailored to these companies can help address financing gaps and incentivize the adoption of sustainable practices across industries.

Challenges and Opportunities

The transition to a circular economy presents both significant challenges and valuable opportunities for innovation, finance, and policy. While the potential for sustainable growth through circular economy practices is immense, realizing this potential requires overcoming several barriers. These challenges, however, also give rise to new opportunities for collaboration, innovation, and growth, particularly within the context of green financial instruments. The role of green finance in addressing these challenges and capitalizing on opportunities is pivotal in accelerating the widespread adoption of circular economy practices across industries and regions.

Challenges in Catalyzing Circular Economy Transitions

We have identified four challenges that we consider the most important in terms of moving from a linear to a circular economy, namely:

1. **Lack of Standardization and Measurement Tools:** This is one of the primary challenges in scaling the circular economy through green financial instruments. There is no universally agreed-upon framework for assessing the environmental impact of circular economy projects, which makes it difficult for investors to assess risk, return, and actual sustainability outcomes. For example, the definition of what qualifies as "recyclable" or "sustainable" varies between regions and sectors, creating inconsistencies in reporting and verification. While frameworks such as the EU Taxonomy and the Green Bond Principles have made strides in defining sustainable activities, the lack of a comprehensive and globally recognized standard for measuring circularity continues to create confusion among stakeholders. This inconsistency limits the growth of green financial markets and makes it harder for investors to confidently direct capital into circular economy initiatives.
2. **Financial Risks and Uncertainty:** Investing in circular economy projects can involve higher perceived risks, particularly because many circular economy innovations require long-term investment horizons and substantial upfront capital. Traditional financial models, which often rely on short-term returns, may not align well with the longer payback periods characteristic of circular economy initiatives such as recycling infrastructure, waste-to-energy projects, or product-as-a-service models. Moreover, market risks related to the adoption of new business models or technologies, as well as the uncertainty of regulatory environments, further complicate financing decisions. Green finance products may struggle to attract investors if these risks are not mitigated or clearly communicated. The lack of clear and consistent regulations around green finance in different countries and industries contributes to this uncertainty.
3. **Insufficient Funding for SMEs:** SMEs often face significant challenges when seeking financing for circular economy projects. These businesses typically have limited access to traditional capital markets and may struggle to secure funding through green bonds or sustainability-linked loans, which tend to favor larger corporations with more established credit histories and higher asset bases. SMEs are also often perceived as riskier investments because they may lack the financial stability or capacity to implement large-scale circular economy projects. As a result, these businesses may miss out on the benefits of green financial instruments, even though they are often at the forefront of circular economy innovation.
4. **Regulatory and Policy Barriers:** A major challenge in scaling the circular economy is the lack of coherent and supportive regulatory frameworks. While some governments have implemented policies that incentivize circular practices (such as extended producer responsibility or deposit return schemes), many countries still lack the necessary infrastructure, incentives, or regulations to

support circular economy business models effectively. For example, without clear policies on waste management, material recovery, or eco-design requirements, businesses are less likely to invest in circular economy solutions, as they face uncertainty regarding future regulatory shifts. Additionally, inconsistent policy implementation across borders creates barriers to the cross-border flow of capital and expertise, further inhibiting the growth of global circular economy markets.

Opportunities in Bridging Green Innovation and Finance

Also, we have identified four challenges that we consider the most important in terms of moving from a linear to a circular economy, namely:

1. **Scaling Green Financial Products for Circular Economy:** This opportunity despite the challenges, the growing demand for sustainable investments presents a significant opportunity for the development and expansion of green financial products tailored to circular economy transitions. Green bonds, sustainability-linked loans, and impact investment funds are gaining popularity, and as demand for these instruments increases, financial institutions are likely to create more innovative solutions for financing circular economy projects. For instance, by refining and expanding financial instruments to support small-scale and early-stage circular economy ventures, investors can help unlock innovation in sectors such as waste management, material recovery, and closed-loop production systems. These innovative financial products can support SMEs and startups working on novel circular economy solutions, thus fostering a more inclusive transition to circularity. Additionally, the creation of green bond standards and circular economy certification schemes can help establish more clarity around what qualifies as a "green" investment, mitigating risks associated with misalignment and helping to attract more capital to circular economy projects.
2. **Policy and Regulatory Support as a Growth Driver:** This means that governments have a critical role to play in fostering an environment convenient to circular economy investments. There is a growing recognition that public policy and regulatory support can significantly catalyze green finance flows. Governments can incentivize businesses to adopt circular models by implementing clear, long-term policies that promote sustainable business practices, such as tax credits for circular economy projects, extended producer responsibility laws, and product design standards that encourage recyclability and reuse. Moreover, international cooperation and harmonized standards for green finance can provide clarity to investors and companies operating in multiple regions. By aligning policies across borders, governments can reduce market fragmentation

and create a more predictable investment landscape for circular economy projects. The European Union's initiatives, such as the Circular Economy Action Plan and the EU Green Deal, demonstrate how coordinated policy efforts can accelerate the adoption of circular economy practices and the development of green finance.

3. **Blended Finance Models to De-Risk Circular Economy Investments:** Blended finance, which combines concessional funding with private investment, represents a significant opportunity to unlock capital for circular economy projects that might otherwise be seen as too risky or long-term for traditional investors. Public-sector actors (such as development banks or government agencies) can provide initial funding or guarantees to de-risk investments in recycling technologies, circular supply chains, and sustainable product development. This helps attract private sector funding to scale up these projects. Blended finance is particularly relevant for projects in emerging markets, where there is significant untapped potential for circular economy solutions but where risks (such as regulatory uncertainty or infrastructure gaps) can be a deterrent to investment. By providing a financial cushion, blended finance can help ensure that investments in the circular economy reach their full potential, even in challenging environments.
   d. **Growing Consumer Demand for Sustainability:** A key opportunity in advancing the circular economy through green financial instruments lies in the growing consumer demand for sustainable products and services. As awareness of environmental issues rises, consumers are increasingly prioritizing sustainability in their purchasing decisions. This shift in consumer behavior creates a favorable market for businesses that adopt circular economy practices, such as offering repairable products, reusable packaging, or closed-loop services. Financial institutions can capitalize on this trend by directing more capital into businesses that cater to this growing demand. Additionally, aligning investments with consumer values can offer companies competitive advantages, such as improved brand reputation, customer loyalty, and access to new markets. Green financial products can further stimulate innovation by funding businesses that are ahead of the curve in developing products and services designed for circularity.

The challenges in financing the circular economy through green financial instruments are significant but not insurmountable. Issues such as lack of standardization, financial risks, and regulatory barriers present hurdles for investors and businesses alike. However, these challenges also offer opportunities for growth and innovation, including the creation of new financial products, the development of clearer policy frameworks, and the expansion of blended finance models. By harnessing these opportunities, green financial instruments can play a crucial role in accelerating the transition to a circular economy, helping to unlock the potential for a more sustainable and resource-efficient future.

While green financial instruments have made significant strides in facilitating the transition to a circular economy, several challenges remain. The chapter highlights the lack of standardization in green financial products, which can create confusion for investors and limit the effectiveness of these instruments. Inconsistent definitions of what constitutes a "green" investment, along with variations in reporting and certification practices, make it difficult for stakeholders to assess the environmental impact of their investments.

Moreover, the chapter discusses regulatory hurdles that continue to stymie the broader adoption of circular economy practices. Although some governments have introduced favorable policies and incentives to support green finance, there is still a lack of comprehensive regulatory frameworks that promote the integration of circular economy principles across industries. This regulatory uncertainty can discourage investment in circular economy projects and hinder the development of green financial instruments.

At the same time, the chapter also identifies significant opportunities for growth in green finance. As awareness of climate change and resource depletion grows, both investors and consumers are increasingly demanding sustainable products and services. This shift in consumer preferences presents a unique opportunity for companies to capitalize on the circular economy through innovation and the development of new financial products. Additionally, greater cooperation between governments, financial institutions, and businesses could lead to the establishment of more robust green financial markets and clearer frameworks for investment in circular economy initiatives.

Role of Policy and Regulation

The chapter emphasizes that the role of policy and regulation in promoting green financial instruments cannot be overstated. Governments play a critical role in setting the regulatory landscape that facilitates green finance. By implementing clear policies and creating incentives for sustainable investment, governments can reduce the risks associated with green investments and encourage more private sector participation. In particular, the chapter highlights the importance of tax incentives, carbon pricing, and green investment guidelines in attracting private capital to circular economy projects.

Moreover, global cooperation is crucial in addressing the challenges of climate change and sustainability. The chapter advocates for international harmonization of green finance standards to facilitate cross-border investment in circular economy initiatives. Such cooperation would not only increase the availability of capital for sustainable projects but also help develop common frameworks for measuring environmental impacts and defining what constitutes a "green" investment.

Implications

This section discusses the broader implications of the findings, focusing on how green finance can catalyze the transition to a circular economy. It also explores policy recommendations and strategic insights for stakeholders to overcome barriers, scale investments, and maximize the impact of circular economy innovations.

The Role of Green Finance in Scaling Circular Economy Innovations

The findings indicate that green finance plays a crucial role in bridging the funding gap for circular economy innovations, particularly in the scaling and commercialization of green technologies and sustainable business models. As demonstrated by case studies such as Philips and Loop Industries, green finance tools, including green bonds, sustainability-linked loans, and ESG investments, are enabling companies to scale circular business models by providing essential funding while de-risking long-term investments. (Joksimović & Stoimenov, 2024). To fully realize the potential of green finance in driving circular economy transitions, financial institutions must increase their commitment to financing circular innovations. Specifically, instruments like green bonds must be further tailored to support early-stage circular solutions, including those from small and SMEs. Moreover, aligning green finance mechanisms with impact measurement standards—such as life-cycle analysis and circularity metrics—can help ensure transparency and long-term sustainability.

Overcoming Barriers to Circular Economy Financing

The barriers to scaling circular finance identified in the findings such as the lack of standardized metrics, limited SME access, and incoherent policy frameworks—pose substantial challenges to achieving systemic circularity. Although green finance is growing, it remains fragmented, with varying levels of policy and market support across regions and sectors. Governments, financial regulators, and industry players must work collaboratively to standardize circular economy metrics and create policy coherence that aligns green finance with broader sustainability goals. The EU Taxonomy and Green Bond Principles can serve as models for developing universally accepted definitions and frameworks for circular investments. Moreover, tailored financing solutions such as blended finance models could help bridge the financing gap for SMEs engaged in circular innovation.

Policy and Regulatory Support for Circular Economy Transitions

The study also highlights the importance of policy support in driving the success of circular economy initiatives. Countries with clear circular economy action plans (e.g., the Netherlands, Finland) and integrated green finance policies have successfully attracted investment into circular projects. However, many other countries still lack comprehensive policies that provide a clear signal for businesses and investors to prioritize circular practices. For green finance to effectively support circular economy transitions, policy frameworks must incentivize circular innovation at every level. Governments should: *implement circular economy roadmaps and link them to existing green finance mechanisms; provide tax incentives and subsidies for businesses that adopt circular practices, such as product take-back programs, material reuse, and closed-loop manufacturing; foster cross-sector collaboration, where policymakers, businesses, and financial institutions come together to co-create funding opportunities for circular economy initiatives.*

The Need for Integrated Financial Models

The findings reveal that PPPs and blended finance mechanisms have been particularly effective in financing large-scale circular economy projects. For instance, cities and municipalities that engage in circular development (such as Milan's food waste recovery program) benefit from public funding that is leveraged by private investments. Financial instruments must evolve beyond traditional green bonds to incorporate blended finance approaches that combine philanthropic capital, government funds, and private sector investment. This model will be particularly effective for financing circular economy projects in emerging markets, where risks are higher, and capital is scarcer.

Encouraging Innovation Through Financial Incentives

The case studies illustrate that financial incentives, such as sustainability-linked loans, can drive innovation by rewarding companies that meet predefined sustainability targets. As seen in the Loop Industries example, financial institutions that incentivize innovation create an environment where companies are motivated to develop more sustainable, circular business models. Financial institutions should consider scaling performance-based incentives that reward firms for achieving specific circular economy outcomes, such as material recovery rates or CO_2 emissions reduction. By linking financial returns directly to sustainability targets, these instruments can foster innovation and speed up the adoption of circular economy practices across sectors.

Implications for Stakeholders

The following participants were identified as stakeholders:

1. **Financial Institutions:** There is a clear need for more tailored financial products that address the specific needs of the circular economy, particularly for SMEs and early-stage projects. Green bonds, blended finance, and sustainability-linked loans should be adapted to encourage investments in circular innovations and provide financing solutions for sectors traditionally underserved by sustainable finance.
2. **Policymakers:** Governments should prioritize circular economy policies that are complementary to green finance strategies. Creating a supportive regulatory environment will help lower investment risks and attract private capital. The creation of circular economy taxonomies, aligned with existing green finance taxonomies, will improve transparency and facilitate investment flows.
3. **Circular Economy Practitioners and Innovators:** Businesses should integrate circular principles into their core strategies and actively seek funding from green finance mechanisms. Collaboration with financial institutions to develop comprehensive sustainability performance metrics is essential for demonstrating the economic viability of circular economy innovations.

The findings underscore that green finance is a crucial enabler for advancing circular economy transitions. By aligning financial mechanisms with circular innovation, stakeholders can create a sustainable ecosystem that fosters long-term environmental, economic, and social benefits. However, overcoming the current barriers requires integrated action from governments, financial institutions, and businesses to create a cohesive and inclusive green finance landscape. Future research should focus on expanding the evidence base for the effectiveness of specific green financial instruments in different regions and sectors, particularly for SMEs and emerging markets.

Future Research Directions

The chapter concludes by identifying several areas for future research. First, it suggests further exploration into the impact of green financial instruments on the performance of circular economy businesses. While the relationship between finance and circular economy transitions is well-documented, more research is needed to quantify the effectiveness of specific green financial instruments in accelerating sustainability outcomes.

Additionally, the chapter calls for deeper investigation into innovative financial structures that could further enhance the flow of capital into circular economy initiatives. This includes exploring new financing mechanisms, such as impact investing, blended finance, and pay-for-performance models, that can better align the interests of investors, businesses, and society.

Lastly, the chapter suggests a focus on behavioral economics to understand how investors perceive and respond to green financial instruments. As the market for sustainable investments grows, understanding investor psychology and preferences will be essential to designing products that effectively meet the demand for green finance.

The chapter offers valuable insights into how green financial instruments can play a pivotal role in accelerating the transition to a circular economy. While challenges remain in terms of standardization, regulation, and market maturity, the opportunities for growth and innovation in green finance are significant. By fostering greater collaboration between governments, financial institutions, and businesses, and by continuing to refine and expand green financial products, it is possible to drive the necessary investments that will support the circular economy's success in the coming decades.

CONCLUSION

This chapter has examined the critical role that green financial instruments play in facilitating the transition to a circular economy with a focus on how these financial tools can support green innovation and help overcome systemic barriers to circularity. Through a comprehensive analysis of case studies, financial data, and literature on green finance, this research highlights both the potential and the current limitations of green finance mechanisms in driving the adoption of circular economy practices.

The key findings from the study show that while the integration of green finance with circular economy goals is still in the early stages, there is significant momentum in certain sectors such as manufacturing, waste management, and urban infrastructure. Green financial instruments, such as green bonds, sustainability-linked loans, and blended finance, are already being used to fund projects that drive circular solutions, enabling companies and municipalities to implement innovations that reduce waste, conserve resources, and minimize environmental impacts.

Through cross-analysis of case data and financial trends, the following leverage points emerge:

- Clear Impact Measurement - Projects with defined life-cycle metrics and ESG impact reporting attract more stable financing.
- Policy- Driven Innovation Clusters - Countries with national circular economy strategies and innovation grants (e.g., the Netherlands, Finland) see higher levels of green circular economy investment.
- PPPs - Joint financing models (e.g., EIB-backed city projects) are critical for de-risking early-stage circular economy ventures.

However, the research also identifies several key barriers to scaling up these financial instruments for broader circular economy applications. These include:

- Lack of standardized metrics to assess the circularity of projects, which leads to inconsistent project evaluation and increases the risk of greenwashing.
- Access to finance for small and SMEs, which are often at the forefront of circular innovations but face challenges in securing funding due to high risk and a lack of financial infrastructure tailored to their needs.
- Policy incoherence, where existing green finance frameworks are not fully aligned with circular economy goals, hindering the widespread adoption of circular practices. Many countries lack integrated policies that link green finance regulations with circular economy roadmaps or innovation strategies.

Despite these challenges, the chapter underscores the growing alignment between green finance and circular economy objectives, particularly as more companies and governments recognize the economic and environmental benefits of circularity. PPPs have proven effective in leveraging green finance for large-scale circular economy projects, such as those seen in Milan's food waste recovery programs and Philips' circular product design initiatives. These examples illustrate that, when properly structured, green finance tools can unlock the potential for circular innovations to scale and drive systemic change.

From a policy perspective, the research highlights the importance of creating clear regulatory frameworks that provide a coherent and unified approach to integrating green finance with circular economy practices. Governments must introduce policies that incentivize circular business models, such as tax incentives for material recovery, product take-back schemes, and support for innovation in sustainable materials. Additionally, standardizing metrics to measure the environmental and economic impacts of circular projects will help improve transparency, attract more investment, and enhance the credibility of green financial products.

In summary, green finance has immense potential to act as a catalyst for the circular economy transition, but this potential is far from fully realized. The scaling of circular innovations will depend on a collaborative effort from financial institutions, policymakers, businesses, and investors to address existing barriers and create a supportive ecosystem that enables circular solutions to thrive. Key actions, such as the development of new financial instruments tailored for circular projects, improved access to funding for SMEs, and the alignment of policy frameworks, are crucial to ensuring that green finance drives meaningful and sustained progress toward a circular and sustainable economy.

The findings of this research contribute valuable insights into the ways that green finance can accelerate circular transitions. Further studies should explore sector-specific challenges, refine the metrics for circular economy investments, and evaluate the effectiveness of emerging green financial products in different regions and industries. Only by bridging these gaps can we unlock the full potential of green finance to foster a truly circular economy that is both economically viable and environmentally regenerative.

This chapter has explored the critical role of green financial instruments in catalyzing the transition to a circular economy, focusing on how these financial tools can support green innovation and promote systemic change. Through the analysis of case studies, financial market data, and the current state of circular economy investments, it is clear that green finance is pivotal in bridging the gap between innovation and implementation of circular solutions.

The findings suggest that while the integration of green finance and circular economy practices is growing, it remains underutilized and faces several challenges, including a lack of standardized metrics, limited access to funding for SMEs, and policy incoherence. However, significant progress is being made in sectors like manufacturing, waste management, and urban development, where green finance has already demonstrated its potential to drive positive environmental and economic outcomes.

Key takeaways from the research include:

1. The growing alignment between green finance and circular economy objectives, especially in areas like waste reduction, sustainable materials, and energy efficiency.
2. The effectiveness of green financial tools—such as green bonds, ESG investments, and blended finance - in scaling circular innovations, particularly for large enterprises and city-level projects.
3. Barriers to further scale that need addressing, particularly the need for standardized metrics, policy coherence, and expanded access to capital for smaller players in the circular economy space.
4. The importance of policy support and cross-sector collaboration in overcoming barriers and incentivizing greater investment in circular economy innovations.

The analysis points to the need for further policy harmonization and financial innovation to unlock the full potential of green finance in supporting circular economy transitions. Governments and financial institutions must work together to create regulatory frameworks that ensure that green finance is effectively mobilized towards circular economy objectives. Furthermore, performance-based financial incentives, better access to finance for SMEs, and stronger investment in sustainability metrics are essential to drive long-term success.

In conclusion, green finance can be a powerful enabler of circular economy transformations if its potential is fully leveraged. The continued development of tailored financial instruments, the standardization of sustainability criteria, and the creation of supportive policy ecosystems will be key to ensuring that circular economy innovations are funded, scaled, and adopted at a global level. The research has provided a foundation for further exploration into this area and offers practical insights for stakeholders committed to fostering a sustainable future.

ACKNOWLEDGEMENT

Chapter is a part of research financed by the Ministry of Science, Technological Development and Innovation of the Republic of Serbia and agreed in decision no. 451-03-136/2025-03/200054 and research result on project U 01/2023 Green Economy in The Era of Digitization, Faculty of Finance, Banking, and Auditing, Alpha BK University in Belgrade, Republic of Serbia.

REFERENCES

Balaban, S., Joksimović, M., & Stoiljković, B. (2022). The determinants of growing agri-food export: The case of CEE countries. *Ekonomika Poljoprivrede*, *69*(3), 877–886. DOI: 10.5937/ekoPolj2203877B

Balaban, S., Milenkovic, I., & Joksimović, M. (2023). *The euro exchange rate's resistance to the exogenous shock caused by COVID-19*. Strategic Management-International Journal of Strategic Management and Decision Support Systems in Strategic Management.

Bocken, N. M. P., Short, S. W., Rana, P., & Evans, S. (2014). *A literature and practice review to develop sustainable* business *model archetypes. Journal of Cleaner Production*, *65*, 42–56. DOI: 10.1016/j.jclepro.2013.11.039

Climate Bonds Initiative. (2024). *Sustainable Debt Market Summary 2024*

Ellen MacArthur Foundation. (2013). *Towards the Circular Economy: Economic and business rationale for an accelerated transition.*

European Investment Bank (EIB). (2021). *The EIB Circular Economy Guide: Supporting the circular transition.*

Flammer, C. (2021). Corporate green bonds. *Journal of Financial Economics*, *142*(2), 499–516. DOI: 10.1016/j.jfineco.2021.01.010

G20 Green Finance Study Group. (2016). *G20 Green Finance Synthesis Report.*

Grujić Vučkovski, B., Paraušić, V., Jovanović Todorović, M., Joksimović, M., & Marina, I. (2022). Analysis of influence of value indicators agricultural production on gross value added in Serbian agriculture. *Custos e Agronegocio*, *18*(4), 349–372.

Joksimovic, M., Grujic, B., & Joksimovic, D. (2017). Foreign direct investment and their impact on economic development countries in transition. Progress in Economic Sciences, (4), 239-246.ceedings, 217-221.

Joksimović, M., Grujić, B., & Joksimović, D. (2018). Correlation and regression analysis of the impact of leasing on agricultural production in Republic of Serbia. Economic of agriculture, 65(2), 583-600.

Joksimovic, M., & Stoimenov, S. (2024). The importance of green bonds for the development of the green economy. *Bizinfo (Blace)*, *15*(1), 107–111. DOI: 10.5937/bizinfo2401107J

Kemp, R., & Pearson, P. (2007). *Final report MEI project about measuring eco-innovation*. European Commission.

Kirchherr, J., Reike, D., & Hekkert, M. (2017). Conceptualizing the circular economy: An analysis of 114 definitions. *Resources, Conservation and Recycling*, *127*, 221–232. DOI: 10.1016/j.resconrec.2017.09.005

Lacy, P., & Rutqvist, J. (2015). *Waste to Wealth: The Circular Economy Advantage*. Palgrave Macmillan.

Merli, R., Preziosi, M., & Acampora, A. (2018). How do scholars approach the circular economy? A systematic literature review. *Journal of Cleaner Production*, *178*, 703–722. DOI: 10.1016/j.jclepro.2017.12.112

OECD. (2011). *Fostering Innovation for Green Growth.*

OECD. (2020). *Developing Sustainable Finance Definitions and Taxonomies.*

OECD. (2023). *Towards Orderly Green Transition: Investment Requirements and Managing Risks to Capital Flows*

Pavlović, V., Knežević, G., Joksimović, M., & Joksimović, D. (2019). Fraud detection in financial statements applying Benford's law with Monte Carlo simulation. *Acta Oeconomica*, *69*(2), 217–239. DOI: 10.1556/032.2019.69.2.4

Popp, D., Hafner, T., & Johnstone, N. (2020). Environmental policy and innovation: A decade of research. *International Review of Environmental and Resource Economics*, *14*(3-4), 265–337. DOI: 10.1561/101.00000111

Rennings, K. (2000). Redefining innovation—Eco-innovation research and the contribution from ecological economics. *Ecological Economics*, *32*(2), 319–332. DOI: 10.1016/S0921-8009(99)00112-3

UNEP. (2016). *Definitions and Concepts: Background Note for G20 Green Finance Study Group.*

Zhang, , BYang, , YBi, , J. (2011). Tracking the implementation of green credit policy in China: Top-down perspective and bottom-up reform. *Journal of environmental management, 92*(4), 1321-1327.

Živkov, D., Balaban, S., & Joksimović, M. (2022). Making a Markowitz portfolio with agricultural commodity futures. *Zemedelská Ekonomika, 68*(6), 219–229. DOI: 10.17221/78/2022-AGRICECON

Živkov, D., Joksimović, M., & Balaban, S. (2021). Measuring parametric and semi-parametric downside risks of selected agricultural commodities.

Chapter 5
Digital Transformation in the Dairy Sector:
A Multidisciplinary Approach to Rural Economic Growth

Andra-Sabina Neculai-Văleanu
Romanian Academy, Iasi, Romania & Academy of Romanian Scientists, Romania

Catalina Sanduleanu
https://orcid.org/0009-0009-3653-1085
Romanian Academy, Iasi, Romania & Academy of Romanian Scientists, Romania

Diana Elena Creangă
Romanian Academy, Iasi, Romania

Ioan Sebastian Brumă
https://orcid.org/0000-0002-0549-5474
Romanian Academy, Iasi, Romania

Gabriel Vasile Hoha
"Ion Ionescu de la Brad" Iasi University of Life Sciences, Romania

ABSTRACT

The chapter investigates how digital technologies transform the worldwide dairy industry by analyzing their effects on productivity levels, environmental sustainability and rural economic growth. The chapter examines IoT sensors and artificial intelligence used for herd health monitoring, blockchain technology for supply chain traceability and advanced data analytics to explain how these technologies will enable precision farming, optimize resource allocation, and improve animal welfare. The analysis recognizes the wider social and structural effects, which include changes in

DOI: 10.4018/979-8-3373-2898-0.ch005

labor needs and requirements for new skills and ongoing digital inclusion problems in rural areas. The chapter examines policy frameworks that appear necessary for achieving sustainable digital adoption that benefits all stakeholders. The analysis positions digital transformation as a complex socio-economic phenomenon rather than viewing technology as a universal solution, thereby providing strategic guidance for dairy industry stakeholders who aim to sustain innovation while ensuring inclusivity and resilience.

1. INTRODUCTION: THE GLOBAL DAIRY SECTOR AND THE DIGITAL IMPERATIVE

Farm animal production is an essential and unique contributor to global economic growth and stability, with an estimated 608 million farmers and herders worldwide being heavily dependent on livestock as a major source of nutrition, income, and ultimately, as an insurance policy in their lives (FAO, 2021). According to the OECD/FAO 2025 Report, global livestock are projected to expand by 7% by 2034, with the output of livestock products expected to grow by 17%. The global production of bovine milk, comprising cattle and buffalo milk, accounted for a staggering 96 percent of the world's milk production in 2022, reaching a volume of 897 million tonnes (The World Dairy Situation Report, 2023). This figure represents a significant increase of 340 million tonnes, or approximately 61 percent, compared to the year 2000. In 2022, Asia emerged as the largest milk-producing region, contributing 45 percent of the total milk production, followed by Europe at 25 percent, the Americas at 22 percent, Africa at 5 percent, and Oceania at 3 percent (FAO, 2021).

This important industry also supports approximately 300 million jobs worldwide, as successful, creative practices work to spur rural economic development and create opportunities to make poverty reduction a reality in many communities and households (Banu & Fazal, 2025). However, they face overwhelming challenges, such as a complex and challenging business landscape that is difficult to navigate and succeed in and significant constraints that limit their progress and development, suggesting that they require holistic support and sustainable solutions to build industry resilience. New technologies such as the industrial Internet of Things (IoT), artificial intelligence (AI), blockchain, robotics, and big data analytics have transformed industries globally and have enormous potential to enhance productivity along the agricultural value chain.

Emerging technologies of the fourth revolution, especially automation, artificial intelligence, and extreme processing, are the game-changing tools that are now being used to address various challenges in this sector (McFadden et al., 2022). Within Agriculture 4.0, applications are divided into four overarching groups: monitoring, which includes smart systems and automated data collection in real-time for quick responsive action and control; prediction, supporting proactive optimisation through advanced forecasting with real-time coupled with historical context; logistics, focusing on supply chains and frameworks while optimising transparency and efficiency; and control, sustaining process management through feedback mechanisms such as automated and smart irrigation, fertilisation, and more sophisticated process management (Tangorra et al., 2024).

Digital transformation is an evolutionary process in which farms seek to achieve a dynamic equilibrium. The utilisation of digital technologies is not a singular event; rather, it represents a long and ongoing adaptation journey. Farms need to consistently refine their strategies, align all systems, and effectively manage uncertainties and potential downsides (Vahdanjoo et al., 2025). Policy designs and supporting mechanisms for rural economic development must be flexible and iterative because farmers and other rural businesses need to be able to change their digital strategies over time, respond to emerging risks (e.g., data privacy, cybersecurity), and keep identifying value chain alignments to maximise positive outcomes and sustainability. Transformation requires a holistic approach that includes technology, business strategy, and risk management.

Recognising Precision Agriculture (PA) as the foundation of the digital revolution in agriculture is important, as it has introduced data-driven decision-making and individualised management (Neculai-Valeanu et al., 2025a). Digital technologies are powerful innovations that not only foster operational efficiency but are also key drivers toward social and environmental sustainability. The digital economy is an important driver for agricultural and rural economic expansion (Vahdanjoo et al., 2025).

The phenomenon described is both complex and wide-ranging, and this chapter adopts a holistic multidisciplinary approach to explain these manifold effects. The involvement of digital tools leads to a fundamental change in the relationship between different actors, such as technology suppliers, input suppliers, farms, traders, processing units, retailers, and, in the end, consumers. This evolution is opening a new world of connectivity and productivity to develop more sustainable farming throughout the whole value chain.

2. DIGITAL TECHNOLOGIES REVOLUTIONIZING DAIRY FARMING AND PROCESSING

The dairy industry is changing rapidly due to the adoption of intelligent agricultural technologies. Technology allows real-time monitoring, early illness or stress detection, predictive analytics, and proactive decision-making. Farmers can now anticipate problems, optimise processes, and act promptly (Neculai-Valeanu et al., 2025a). Proactive management optimises biological processes like breeding cycles and milk yields to maximise productivity, reduce waste (feed, water, and medication), and improve animal health (fewer severe illnesses and lower mortality). Farming today requires more analytical and decision-making skills than physical labour, which can attract new type workers.

2.1. Internet of Things (IOT), Sensor and Automation in Dairy Operations

The Internet of Things (IoT) plays a pivotal role in facilitating advancements across the dairy value chain by enabling the digitisation of various components. In addition to tracking animals, IoT technologies improve crop resource efficiency in animal production. IoT applications for the automatic irrigation and fertilisation of agricultural fields reduce water and fertiliser losses significantly. To optimise dairy processing, sensors and IoT devices are connected to Manufacturing Execution Systems (MES) to read and provide real-time temperature, pressure, and humidity data (Mantravadi et al., 2023). The economic value of IoT applications is considerably, Precision tracking and optimisation with IoT monitoring systems could reduce feed costs by 15%, saving $470 per cow annually. These technologies could save nearly 15% of summer energy costs by triggering the cooling system when ambient conditions require it (Tangorra et al., 2024).

Wearable sensors and real-time monitoring are changing animal management worldwide (Lee and Seo, 2021). These devices monitor all animal health conditions to determine instant health status and improve animal welfare. Wearables like pedometers and collars record their behaviour and health, as well as their fertility. The monitoring system uses machine learning algorithms to predict and diagnose health issues so farmers can make informed herd health and reproduction decisions.

Automation in dairy production focuses on labour-saving and relieving farmers of physically demanding work. A major technological advancement of the past few decades is the robotic milking system from DeLaval and Lely, saving farmers time and increasing milk yields and animal health (Lavrijsen-Kromwijk et al., 2024). Beyond milking, other automated systems are enhancing various aspects of dairy operations. Precision feeding systems, for example, use digital technology to create tailored-fit feed rations for each cow based on their nutritional needs, optimising milk production and reducing feed waste.

Automatic manure removal, achieved through scrapers or robots, has been shown to ensure better cleanliness and to decrease infectious claw diseases and lameness (Gaworski et al., 2024). The influence of automation on animal welfare is notable, with research suggesting that increased automation can have beneficial effects on animal behaviour and human-animal interactions. Cows in highly automated farms have less disturbance and more autonomy, allowing them to establish routines (Lage et al., 2024). Automated milking systems may even enable early detection of udder infections by continuously monitoring somatic cell scores at each milking.

Automated dairy sanitation systems guarantee consistent and precise cleaning while adhering to stringent hygiene standards and optimising resource conservation. This fosters more sustainable farms and liberates staff time to concentrate on other critical tasks, thereby enhancing productivity.

2.2. Artificial Intelligence (AI) and Data Analytics for Enhanced Management

Similar to IoT, Artificial Intelligence (AI) and Machine Learning (ML) technologies have emerged as powerful tools in agriculture. They support advanced activities like crop and soil monitoring, precision farming, agri-robotics, predictive analytics, and livestock monitoring (Ahmed & Shakoor, 2025). AI supports dairy scientists and farmers to interpret large data sets more precisely and quickly for improved decision-making in key areas such as feeding strategies, disease control, or genetic selection (Gontijo et al., 2025; Palma et al., 2025). AI-driven predictive analytics maximises the accuracy of milk yield estimates and improves reproductive management by identifying optimal breeding protocols; hence, it increases total herd productivity and profitability. A study indicated that enhancing dietary precision with AI lowered feed expenses by $31 per cow per year and markedly diminished nitrogen excretion. (Bull Vine, 2025).

Machine learning systems have exhibited the capacity to predict mastitis cases with an accuracy ranging from 94% to 98%, highlighting AI's promise for preventive health management (Luo et al., 2023). Dairy farming is increasingly using computer vision systems (CVS) for animal identification, behaviour observation, feed intake assessment, body weight estimation, and disease identification. Facial recognition technology enhances cow welfare by enabling farmers to accurately identify individual cows and track their health status, resulting in targeted care and expedited medical intervention. A notable instance of AI integration is the "Dairy Brain project" at the University of Wisconsin–Madison (Cabrera, 2025). This system employs real-time data from many sources, such as sensors on milking apparatus, feed intake monitors, and animal health trackers. Through the analysis of this data using sophisticated AI algorithms, Dairy Brain delivers actionable insights for real-time decision-making, enhances milk production results, and promotes environmental sustainability via improved resource utilisation.

Big data analytics, with its Vs, including Volume, Velocity, Variety, and Veracity, covers a range of technologies for the collection, storage, management, and analysis of an organisation's large datasets. These analytic tools and sensor developments are key for better supporting decision-making for accurate milk predictions and the early intervention in, for example, the case of lameness and mastitis on dairy farms (Lokhorst et al., 2019; Palma et al., 2025). Data integration and analysis are essential for the progress of the dairy industry. Predictive analytics and data-based decision-making are rapidly becoming an integral part of dairy farming in today's world. Farm management software like this, for example, is capable of gathering all-encompassing information about the performance of individual cows, enabling farmers to make very specific decisions in matters such as breeding, nutrition, and health management.

The combination of AI and big data takes on an additional significance because it is possible to refine the management of various raw resources used in farm operations. Integration of these units guarantees that the water, energy, and feed going in are utilised to the maximum, which has led to a significant decrease in the dairy industry's environmental footprint. This comprehensive approach to data utilisation takes raw information and turns it into actionable knowledge that dairy producers can use to work more efficiently, sustainably, and profitably.

2.3. Building Trust with Blockchain in Dairy

Blockchain has been recognised as an important tool for improving food safety and product traceability throughout the dairy supply chain—including the management and sharing of milk testing data. Its fundamental worth is in developing a trustworthy system for tracking decision-making and real-time data across the agricultural value chain in a way that is independent, immutable, and accessible. One of the key strengths of blockchain is its data immutability, which ensures that test results from milk analysis cannot be manipulated or altered without the consent of various stakeholders, including regulatory bodies (Sharma et al., 2023).

Such an attribute increases protection for not only the consumer but also the producer, ensuring their reputation is still intact if any food-related issues arise further down the pipeline. A cryptographic process achieves immutability, requiring an entity to use computational power to solve a "hash puzzle" in order to add a new block of data. Any modification of the data afterwards would cause all hashes that referred to the data to be immediately invalid since everyone who relies on that data may tell that it has been modified, thus making it impossible to tamper with without everyone knowing about it (Montenegro Hernandez, 2024; Miranda & Shukla, 2025). In addition to test data security, the supply chain can benefit from blockchain in a multi-faceted way by making the whole supply scenario more resilient in the face of increased risk and uncertainty, adding transparency to the process, and tracing an item from the farm to the consumer (Sharma et al., 2023).

For practical dairy applications, a private, permissioned blockchain is often recommended. In such a system, only authorised entities or individuals involved in milk processing have been granted access, with dairy producers having privileges to create blocks and state inspection services having assessment access. Furthermore, raw data can be stored off-chain, with only the cryptographic hash value of the data stored on the blockchain for verification, balancing data integrity with storage efficiency and privacy.

3. ECONOMIC GROWTH AND PROFITABILITY THROUGH DIGITALISATION

Digital transformation is a pivotal factor influencing rural and agricultural development, with the digital economy serving as a powerful engine for agricultural and rural economic growth. It offers significant opportunities for enhancing farm profitability, optimising operations, and fostering new market avenues.

3.1. Efficiency Gains and Cost Reductions

Digital tools and technologies are instrumental in improving productivity across the agriculture sector by fundamentally enhancing the innovation capability and quality of agribusinesses. The integration of artificial intelligence may improve dairy management, including operational efficiency, and economic performance, as shown in Table 1. Automated milking systems (AMS) can increase milking frequency by 0.5 per day while simultaneously reducing labour requirements (Lage et al., 2024). By milking cows at physiologically optimal intervals rather than human schedules, this cow-driven approach has increased productivity by 10% on many operations. Manufacturing Execution Systems (MES) enable real-time resource tracking, processing condition monitoring, and product quality assurance in dairy processing.

Table 1. Quantifiable Economic Benefits of Digital Adoption in Dairy

Benefit Category	Specific Digital Technology/ Interventions	Quantifiable Impact	References
Feed Cost Reduction	IoT monitoring systems, AI-driven diet optimisation; Precision feeding systems	15% reduction; $470/cow annually;	Chase and Fortina, 2023
Labour Efficiency Gains	Digital recordkeeping; Automated milking systems	40% administrative time slash; 20-30% reduction in labour requirements (AMS)	Lage et al., 2024; Lavrijsen-Kromwijk t.al.,2024
Robotic Milking Systems Payback Period	Robotic milking systems	Payback in 6 years (down from 9-10 years); Cost $185,000-$275,000/unit	Lage et al., 2024
Milk Quality	Digital monitoring (e.g., somatic cell count reduction)	$0.85 per hundredweight increase; $150,000 annually (2,800-head operation)	Bullvine, 2025
Reproductive Management	Digital systems (e.g., improved conception rates)	over 30% improvement in conception rates;	Kaewbang et al., 2024
Energy Cost Reduction	IoT sensors for cooling	15% reduction during the summer months	Buckley et al., 2025
Production Efficiency (Processing)	Manufacturing Execution Systems (MES)	Up to 1% increase in production yields; Up to 2% reduction in product giveaway	Mantravadi et al., 2023
Overall Profit/ Efficiency	Comprehensive digital transformation	13.8% year-on-year increase in total profit; Inventory turnover reduced; Over 9% reduction in scheduling costs	Cui, 2025

MES implementation has been shown to increase production efficiency by up to 1% (Mantravadi et al., 2023). Furthermore, digital technology may effectively substitute manual labour and substantially improve farmers' monitoring and management capacities, potentially addressing the historical inverse relationship between farm size and productivity.

Ongoing studies indicate that IoT monitoring systems can deliver a 15% reduction in feed costs through precision tracking and optimisation, translating to potential savings of $470 per cow annually (BullVine, 2025). Digital recordkeeping significantly enhances labour efficiency by slashing administrative time by 40%, thereby freeing up labour. Predictive maintenance solutions avert expensive equipment malfunctions and prolong machinery lifespan by 20-30% (Vlaicu et al., 2024).

Although earlier forecasts for robotic milking systems suggested a nine-year return on investment, numerous enterprises are already seeing profits in slightly over six years. Although the initial cost of these systems ranges from $185,000 to $275,000 per unit, the compelling return on investment is becoming increasingly apparent. Improved milk quality, often achieved through digital monitoring (e.g., somatic cell count reduction), can lead to significant premiums, such as an increase of $0.85 per hundredweight, resulting in approximately $150,000 annually for a 2,800-head operation.

In dairy processing, the implementation of Manufacturing Execution Systems (MES) can lead to up to a 2% reduction in product giveaway, optimising ingredient use and minimising waste. MES also significantly reduces the time required for traceability audits to as little as 30 minutes, implying a more efficient and less costly process for handling potential issues. Mengniu Dairy, a leading Chinese dairy company, serves as a compelling case study: its digital transformation resulted in a 13.8% year-on-year increase in total profit in 2023, improved inventory turnover from 38.6 to 32.5 days, and a 9% reduction in scheduling costs within its supply chain (Cui, 2025).

3.2. Unlocking Revenue and Competitiveness

Digital economies possess the capacity to significantly promote the marketing of agricultural products and stimulate rural industrial development. Mobile solutions, in particular SMS-based technologies and apps like iCow, have taken off in Kenya, providing farmers with instant market prices, wider buyer networks, and valuable extension services. Mobile transactions enhance financial inclusion for dairy farmers by offering direct payment and secure virtual transactions, such as M-Pesa. E-commerce platforms are changing the landscape of dairy marketing by connecting directly with farmers, processors, and the ultimate consumers. The Direct-to-Consumer (D2C) model, for example, enables companies to circumvent wholesalers and retailers, providing them with more control over their brand, marketing, and sales methods (CGIAR Platform for Big Data in Agriculture, 2022).

These farm-to-fork models, supported by technology, enable farmers to reach out to urban areas independently, thereby simplifying their market access. Rural areas can incorporate a blend of physical and digital technologies alongside conventional agriculture to diversify into new ventures such as rural tourism, agri-processing, hyperlocal logistics, and local entrepreneurship.

Digitalisation is not only a critical factor for dairy farmers to remain competitive in a fast-paced market. While the larger farms have traditionally been first in line to embrace agritech, there's an emerging interest and hunger for these tech-driven tools among mid-size and smaller farms as well, partly prompted by growing economic pressures. According to a study carried out by Cui (2025), larger farmers generally possess a greater capacity to adopt digital technologies due to their need for more sophisticated tools to manage complex production systems and their ability to benefit economically.

Although there are many advantages, high costs of initial investment and lack of capable labour are major inhibitors for technology becoming widely accepted, particularly for small farms. This risks a "digital divide" between farms actively using and embedding AI and other digital technologies into their farms and those that do not—that may lead to the latter seeking just to "survive" the market rather than compete. The contrary case presented by successful companies like Mengniu Dairy is full digital transformation that creates an excellent effect on overall operational performance and market competitiveness. Tech-enabled businesses are better equipped to adjust and thrive during labour shortages, rising feed costs, or fluctuating energy prices, while their competitors may struggle to survive. For instance, IoT-based monitoring systems can cut feed costs by 15% and energy costs by 10% (Tangorra et al., 2024). This ability to quickly adapt operations with the help of real-time data and automation will help limit the impact of higher-cost inputs and labour shortages, turning potential crises into a business advantage. The rationale for digital transformation as a strategy for risk management and business continuity is more compelling now than ever in a more volatile world. Policymakers should explore incentives that promote digital adoption as a type of agricultural insurance or resilience, especially among smaller farms that may be at greater financial risk from market volatility (Eastwood et al., 2023).

This points to an important policy challenge: how to ensure digital technology adoption can take place on all farm sizes so that small and medium-sized farms do not fall further behind. Strategies must include flexible pricing models, tailored solutions for diverse farmer needs, accessible financing, and robust extension services that focus on capacity building for smaller operations. Without such targeted interventions, digital transformation runs the risk of strengthening the power and wealth of already bigger agribusinesses at the expense of rural economic inclusion.

4. SOCIAL IMPLICATIONS: TRANSFORMING RURAL LIVELIHOODS AND COMMUNITIES

Digital transformation in the dairy sector goes beyond purely economic metrics, profoundly impacting rural livelihoods, labour dynamics, and community well-being. It presents both significant opportunities for empowerment and notable challenges related to equity and access.

4.1. Shifting Labour Demands and Workforce Evolution

Automation in dairy farming offers increased labour flexibility and necessitates a shift in the required farmer skill sets towards technological and data management.

Tasks with a physical nature, such as feeding or milking, are more replaced by tasks that revolve around management, such as consulting data, monitoring alerts, and maintaining digital tools. This knowledge necessitates the development of new skills in farmers, such as technology literacy and data handling expertise. Although this type of work will increase the efficiency pressure on farmers, it will also help ease the emotional pressure of detecting animal health problems. The impact of digital agriculture on knowledge and skills is a topic of significant discussion (Glover & Sumberg, 2025). 'Deskilling?' In highly digitalised agricultural processes, there may be experiences of 'skill' decimation—often referred to as the 'deskilling' of agriculture—and over time, the ability to make decisions may suffer due to increasingly sophisticated digital agriculture, especially in its most automated forms.

This perspective argues that rapid data generation and prescriptive actions could make farmers "mechanical" implementers, and in doing so erode their experiential wisdom and tacit knowledge. Farmers, managers, and workers may find themselves restricted to idle interaction with tablets or computers, raising doubts about their future knowledge and capabilities.

On the other hand, researchers stress the "reskilling" and "upskilling" and point out that, although part of traditional knowledge may be lost, digital agriculture requires new skills linked with the use of digital technologies (Glover & Sumberg, 2025). The effects on skills are not uniform but instead conditioned upon various factors: the capacities and logic of digital tools themselves (e.g., whether they propose prescriptive solutions or favour active interpretation), the logic of the business model and of the developer team, the digital proficiency and literacy of the users, and a broader social and environmental context and institutional framework.

Automation's impact on labour is dual, involving both displacement and transformation. Although automation undoubtedly conserves labour and diminishes manual tasks, successful implementations frequently redefine roles rather than eliminate them. Automated systems perform repetitive duties, such as milking, freeing humans to concentrate on more complicated responsibilities, like cow health monitoring, breeding decisions, and nutrition management. The "deskilling" risk, where farmers become mere button-pressers, is a valid concern, but the potential for "reskilling" allows for more meaningful, analytical work. This recognition underscores a growing need in rural areas for proactive workforce information strategies. Schools and extension services should modify their curricula to incorporate digital literacy, data analysis, and technology management. Policies must also promote training and reskilling programmes for the existing rural workforce so that they can be shifted into these new roles rather than risk being left unemployed because of skills mismatches.

Dairy farms across many regions face a simmering crisis characterised by labour shortages and an ageing workforce, with the average age of farmworkers steadily rising to the late 50s (Calvo-Sotomayor et al., 2019). This demographic shift prompts critical enquiries about who will assume leadership roles in the future. Digital tools, including IoT sensors and robotics, offer a compelling solution by promising increased productivity and appealing to younger generations through an innovative and tech-savvy environment.

By showcasing the innovation and immense potential of a modern dairy farm, the industry can effectively shift the narrative away from common misconceptions about farm life, such as early mornings, monotonous work, and modest pay. This reframing presents farming as a forward-thinking sector that aligns with the tech-savvy skills and interests of younger, digitally advanced generations who might otherwise prefer office environments. Furthermore, enhanced animal welfare practices made possible by digital tools, such as real-time health monitoring and predictive diagnostics, can appeal to younger individuals who are increasingly prioritising ethical and sustainable practices.

4.2. Addressing the Digital Divide and Promoting Inclusivity

Digital technologies can significantly enhance access to basic services such as healthcare, education, and finance in rural areas, thereby making substantial contributions to community well-being. Digital classrooms can link students in rural regions with instructors, transcending constraints of physical facilities and teacher accessibility. This facilitates remote learning opportunities, provides access to a wider range of educational resources, and potentially leads to higher quality instruction, which can improve educational attainment and future prospects for rural youth. In the financial sector, fintech tools can empower the unbanked population in rural regions to securely save, borrow, and insure. This provides access to essential financial services that can improve the economic resilience of people living in rural areas. These services enable people to better manage their finances, invest in livelihoods, and protect themselves against unforeseen events. (Garlinska et al., 2023).

Beyond these services, access to information and digital communities can promote a sense of solidarity and inclusion among dairy farmers, lessening social isolation and potentially impacting emotional well-being and mental health positively. Automation helps improve the well-being of farmers by reducing the amount of labour required to employ physically demanding techniques.

A significant barrier to widespread digital adoption in the dairy sector is the pervasive digital divide. Most smallholder farmers, particularly those in developing regions, often lack access to essential digital infrastructure, including smartphones and reliable internet connectivity, as well as the necessary digital literacy to effectively utilise these technologies (Magesa et al., 2023). The high costs associated with implementing digital technologies—particularly mature AI, IoT, and blockchain solutions—create significant barriers for agri-farmers and cooperatives because of their limited resources.

Additionally, the limited level of digital skills among women, who constitute a strong majority of the casual workforce in some areas, remains a significant challenge. However, studies have shown that enhancing digital literacy can not only increase dairy productivity but also foster social capital and confidence, especially among under-represented groups (Antonio & Tuffley, 2014). The digital divide is not merely a technical inconvenience; it is a fundamental impediment to equitable rural economic growth and social well-being. It prevents smallholder farmers from accessing essential market information and financial services, as well as productivity-enhancing technologies, thereby exacerbating existing inequalities and limiting their ability to participate fully in the digital economy. This results in a two-tiered agricultural system in which digitally connected farms are able to thrive, while those that remain disconnected face the risk of falling further behind.

To bridge this divide, a multi pronged, coordinated effort is required. Solutions include developing contextually appropriate and user-centric digital solutions, such as mobile applications with intuitive interfaces that function effectively with limited connectivity and provide information in local languages. The proliferation of affordable and accessible hardware, potentially built on open-source designs, is important for democratising technology access, allowing even smallholder farmers to engage in precision agriculture (Yuan & Sun, 2024). Robust frameworks for data governance and ownership are also essential to build trust, ensuring farmers retain control over their information and its usage. Digital literacy programmes, delivered through community centres and agricultural extension services, are vital for equipping farmers with the skills and critical thinking necessary to navigate the digital landscape effectively. Finally, open-source agricultural technologies can democratise access to innovation by enabling collaborative development and the sharing of tools and knowledge, which fosters a collective community for agricultural advancement. Without addressing the digital divide comprehensively, the promise of digital transformation for inclusive rural economic growth will remain largely unfulfilled.

5. ENVIRONMENTAL SUSTAINABILITY: REDUCING IMPACT AND OPTIMIZING RESOURCES

Digital transformation is essential for tackling the environmental issues confronting the dairy industry and plays an important role in promoting sustainable agricultural practices, resource optimisation, and climate change mitigation.

5.1. Resource Efficiency in the Circular Dairy Economy

Digital tools are indispensable for farmers aiming to operate their farms in a sustainable and profitable manner. These technologies provide instant information and analysis, enabling better management of critical resources such as water, energy, and land. For instance, robotic milking helps farmers make more milk with fewer cows, which in turn has a smaller environmental footprint through reduced carbon dioxide emissions, water, and feed use. AI-driven systems are essential for optimising feed timing and amounts, thereby maximising milk output per feed unit and significantly minimising waste.

Research has reported that diet precision with the assistance of AI can reduce feed costs and have a substantial influence on nitrogen excretion, being both economically and environmentally friendly (Chase and Fortina, 2023). Moreover, precision feeding digital technology has a significant impact on the carbon emission efficiency of dairy farms through reducing the waste generated from excessive feed input. AI optimises feed composition, as well as energy management that enables the integration of renewable energy—such as solar and biogas on the farm—replacing fossil fuels.

The dairy industry relies on the efficient use of water as a key factor in achieving both environmental sustainability and cost-effective operation. Automated cleaning systems precisely track the use of chemicals and water, ensuring consistency while minimising waste. While energy use is a small proportion of dairy sector greenhouse gas (GHG) emissions, fostering energy management on farms can result in cost savings and reducing the carbon footprint. An integration of different energy-saving technologies, e.g., speed control devices and waste heat recovery systems, may save one-third of the electricity (Shine et al., 2020).

The implementation of digital transformation can also have a genuine and positive impact on the environment by contributing to the preservation of natural resources, the reduction of pollution and waste, and the reduction of carbon emissions produced by farms. Digital solutions can help implement a circular economy by integrating the digital and physical landscapes for advanced digital waste governance. Using landfills or incinerators is discouraged in zero-waste cities. In circular economics, waste is turned into a resource that can be recovered, recycled, and reused regularly (Almansour & Akrami, 2024). The Water-Energy-Food (WEF) nexus holistic approach is increasingly being used as a tool for supporting the transition towards sustainable development in initiatives involving the concept of circular economy, as Rhouma et al. (2024) pointed out. This is done in order to support the transition towards sustainable development.

The dairy industry presents a significant opportunity to implement the principles of the circular economy, particularly through the integration of the Water-Energy-Food (WEF) nexus. By viewing these interconnected resources holistically, dairy operations can optimise resource utilisation and minimise waste. For example, wastewater generated from dairy processing can be treated and reused for irrigation, thereby reducing water consumption while simultaneously enhancing the sustainability of agricultural practices. Additionally, the energy derived from biogas produced during the anaerobic digestion of dairy waste can be harnessed to power operations, further contributing to energy efficiency and reducing reliance on fossil fuels.

Moreover, the adoption of circular economy practices in the dairy sector can lead to innovative solutions that enhance overall productivity and sustainability. By focusing on the recovery and recycling of by-products, such as whey and other dairy residues, companies can create value-added products, thereby diversifying their revenue streams. This not only minimises waste but also aligns with growing consumer demand for sustainably produced food. Overall, the dairy industry's commitment to these sustainable practices can greatly aid sustainable development and circular economy implementation.

5.2. Managing Environmental Impacts and Emerging Risks

Artificial intelligence (AI) is becoming increasingly recognised as a pioneer in the development of countermeasures to methane emissions, which are a significant contributor to climate change and produced by the dairy industry. To reduce the amount of enteric fermentation and improve manure management practices, artificial intelligence is leading initiatives such as dietary optimisation (Cabrera, 2025). These initiatives not only aim to lower methane output but also enhance overall farm efficiency and sustainability. By integrating AI-driven solutions, farmers can make more informed decisions that promote environmental stewardship while maintaining productivity. An estimated fifteen percent reduction in global carbon emissions could be achieved through the implementation of digital technologies in agricultural and land-based settings, according to projections made by Ferguson et al. (2024).

Through increased feed efficiency and decreased waste, automated systems in the dairy industry contribute to a reduction of as much as 12–18% in the amount of greenhouse gas emissions that are produced per unit of milk. The United States Dairy Net Zero Initiative (NZI) is an example of a concerted effort to achieve greenhouse gas neutrality by the year 2050. The NZI focuses on optimising water and manure nutrients use. These initiatives not only aim to enhance sustainability within the industry but also promote better practices among farmers, encouraging the adoption of innovative technologies. As a result, the dairy sector is moving towards a more environmentally responsible future, benefiting both producers and consumers alike.

Digital innovations are also making major contributions to improving animal welfare. AI-powered wearables, for instance, revolutionise animal welfare by offering real-time health insights. Continuous monitoring of health data, facilitated by AI, enables the early detection of subtle changes in an animal's behaviour or physiology that may indicate illness or stress (Vlaicu et al., 2024). Such information enables interventions to be carried out in a timely and precise manner, which not only enhances the welfare of animals as a whole but also lessens the likelihood of losses resulting from disease outbreaks (Neculai-Valeanu et al., 2025b).

Automation may improve animal behaviour and human-animal interactions (Lage et al., 2024). Higher automation has been linked to a decrease in the prevalence of severe lameness and has improved leg cleanliness. This improvement is primarily due to effective bedding systems and automatic manure removal. Robotic milking machines can also record somatic cell scores during milking to detect udder infections early. Ruchay et al. (2024) report that facial recognition technology is improving cow welfare. For animal health, this technology accurately identifies and tracks cows and allows farmers to provide more targeted care and faster medical attention based on subtle signs like facial features. If the livestock industry can enhance animal welfare with the help of digital technology, cows will be healthier, have extended lactations, and increase their production.

While digital systems offer immense efficiency gains in environmental control and animal welfare, they may also introduce new vulnerabilities. The increasing reliance on interconnected digital systems for critical functions in dairy farms presents a dual reality: immense efficiency gains alongside significant vulnerability. Cybersecurity threats, for instance, can lead to devastating losses and serious animal welfare concerns. Adewusi et al. (2022) conducted a comprehensive literature review on cybersecurity in agricultural supply chains, noting that compromised IoT and environmental controls can lead to cascading animal health impacts and reputational damage. It is possible for disruptions to rapidly escalate from problems with productivity to significant concerns regarding animal welfare, thereby increasing the risks associated with both ethics and operations (Neethirajan, 2025). This means that the very efficiency and integration that drive sustainability benefits also introduce new, potentially catastrophic, environmental and animal welfare risks if systems are compromised.

Ransomware attacks involve malicious actors encrypting vital farm data or locking essential digital systems. It is possible that such incidents will result in significant disruptions to operations until a ransom is paid. Attacks, often motivated by ideological objectives such as animal welfare concerns or environmental impacts of intensive agriculture, can damage a farm's reputation and erode consumer trust through tactics like data disclosures or website defacements. Furthermore, hacks may concentrate on critical control systems, precision agricultural algorithms, or private genetic data, which has the potential to cause significant disruptions in supply chains and economic instability (Adewusi et al., 2025).

This demonstrates the critical importance of implementing robust cybersecurity and biosecurity protocols as fundamental components of digital transformation strategies. Policy should mandate robust cybersecurity measures, data backup, and redundancy planning. Research and development must focus on developing resilient, secure digital systems tailored for agricultural environments. Farmers and industry stakeholders need training not only in using these technologies but also in identifying and mitigating cyber risks, recognising that a digital attack can have direct, severe physical and environmental consequences for livestock and farm operations (Neethirajan, 2025).

6. POLICY AND REGULATORY FRAMEWORKS FOR AN EQUITABLE DIGITAL TRANSITION

It is contingent upon the development and implementation of supportive policy and regulatory frameworks that address technological, economic, social, and environmental considerations in a comprehensive manner for the dairy industry to undergo a digital transformation that is both successful and equitable.

6.1. Ensuring Data Privacy, Security and Governance

In the dairy industry, data governance has emerged as a critical issue as a result of the significant lack of legal restrictions regarding data usage. Critical challenges include concerns about data ownership, privacy, and the monetisation of data. Companies are often reluctant to share data due to perceived limited value or competitive disadvantages. Farmers, on the other hand, frequently lack control over data exchange costs and need to retain control over who accesses their valuable information. In Europe, the Data Act, set to enter into force in 2025, aims to facilitate fair data sharing across sectors by defining rights to access and use data. The European Union Code of Conduct on the Sharing of Agricultural Data provides direction with regard to the utilisation of data and the rights to access it. The Common European Agricultural Data Space (CEADS) is currently in the process of being developed with the intention of facilitating the reliable sharing of agricultural data between private stakeholders and public authorities. This is being done with the intended purpose of improving the economic and environmental performance of the agricultural sector.

The criticality of trust in data governance for widespread adoption cannot be overstated. Farmers have expressed significant concerns regarding the absence of clear information about data ownership, usage, and control. A prevailing sentiment is that farmers do not trust agribusiness companies when it comes to collecting, managing, and processing their data. To establish the trust necessary for participation, it is essential to ensure that the agreements are transparent, as this transparency is important for building trust (Cue et al., 2021). This means that the lack of clear, legally binding data governance frameworks and the resulting farmer distrust are not just minor impediments but fundamental barriers to widespread digital adoption. Farmers will be hesitant to invest in and use technologies that generate data if they don't trust how it will be used, even if it could be profitable. This trust deficit directly affects the scalability and efficacy of digital transformation initiatives.

Policy efforts, such as a "Farmers Bill of Rights", are not merely about legal compliance but about building a foundation of trust that is essential for a thriving data economy in agriculture. This requires moving beyond voluntary codes to legally enforceable standards, ensuring data transparency, clear ownership, and fair monetisation models. Without addressing this trust deficit, the full potential of data-driven agriculture for rural economic growth will remain untapped, as farmers will continue to operate in silos, limiting collective intelligence and innovation.

6.2. Closing the Digital Divide: Infrastructure and Adoption Barriers

A significant challenge to digital transformation in the dairy sector is the stark infrastructure gap in high-speed internet access between rural and urban areas. Data indicates that 80% of Americans living in households without access to a fixed terrestrial broadband provider reside in rural areas. In the absence of dependable and cost-effective high-speed internet connectivity, both at the farmhouse and in the field, numerous advanced digital technologies are unable to achieve their full potential. Both the low population densities in rural areas and the high cost of installing and operating internet infrastructure present a non-viable proposition for private service providers, which means that large-scale private investment is discouraged as a result. Consequently, unreliable broadband access continues to be a significant barrier to the widespread adoption of technologies that are based on Internet of Things sensors and precision agriculture, respectively.

Table 2. Key Challenges and Policy Solutions for Digital Transformation in Dairy

Challenge Category	Specific Challenge Description	Proposed Policy/Strategic Solution	References
Infrastructure Limitations	Lack of reliable rural broadband connectivity; Inadequate IT infrastructure on farms	Government funding for rural broadband; Development of Digital Public Infrastructure and National Agricultural Data Infrastructure	Trendov et al., 2019
Financial Constraints	High upfront costs of digital technologies; Limited access to affordable financing for small/ medium farms	Targeted financial incentives, grants, and tailored loan programmes; Modifying eligibility criteria for existing assistance programmes	Yuan & Sun, 2024
Digital Literacy/ Skills Gap	Insufficient technical knowledge and digital literacy among farmers; Ageing workforce and labour misconceptions	Expanded agricultural extension services and vocational training programmes; Digital literacy programmes through community centres; Promoting new skill sets for data management and tech operation	Cabrera, 2025; Hassoun et al., 2023; Magesa et al., 2023
Data Governance Concerns	Lack of legal regulation on data usage; Concerns about data ownership, privacy, and monetisation; Farmer distrust of agribusiness data practices	Enact clear, legally binding policies (e.g., "Farmers Bill of Rights"); Promote transparency in data sharing agreements; Establish Common European Agricultural Data Space	Ronzhin et al., 2025; Eastwood et al., 2023
Farmer Resistance to Change	Preference for traditional management methods; Complexity of implementing new technologies	User-centric design of digital tools; Clear demonstration of tangible benefits and return of investment; Collaborative co-creation of solutions with farmers; Peer learning and social innovation	Wu. 2024
Environmental Risks	Cybersecurity threats to automated farm systems (e.g., climate control, milking routines); Potential for data manipulation	Mandated or incentivised robust cybersecurity protocols; Development of resilient, cyber-secure farm systems; Training on identifying and mitigating cyber risks	Neethirajan, 2025
Lack of Interoperability Standards	Proprietary data formats; Inconsistent data standards across different systems/manufacturers	Support industry discussions to establish equipment interoperability and data communication standards; Promote open standards and open-source solutions	Ronzhin et al., 2025; Ahmadzai et al., 2021

Efforts to bridge this gap are underway. The USDA's ReConnect Broadband Funding Pilot Program, launched in 2019, aims to expand eligibility for federal funding for rural broadband and encourage public-private partnerships. Digital Public Infrastructure (DPI) and National Agricultural Data Infrastructure (NAgDI) are also crucial initiatives. DPI provides essential building blocks for seamless digital integration, promoting connectivity, communication, and innovation in agrifood systems. NAgDI, a specific DPI model, focuses on creating decentralised, secure, and interoperable shared spaces for data exchange in agriculture, providing a robust foundation for digital agricultural innovation.

As presented in Table 2, several key barriers impede the broader adoption of digital technologies in dairy farming. There are high upfront acquisition costs, concerns about farm data sharing and ownership, no uniform standards for technology interoperability, and limited technical support. Farmer resistance to change, often due to a preference for traditional management, can also hinder adoption. Various solutions are proposed like changing the eligibility requirements for government financial assistance programs and increasing funding. Also important is expanding agricultural extension services to help farmers with technical issues. Data standards improve equipment interoperability, allowing systems to communicate seamlessly. Data integration can be made more accessible to farmers by creating user-friendly tools that don't require IT expertise. The cooperation of all relevant parties is essential to the development of dairy farming communities that are economically robust, digitally literate, and welcoming to all members of the community. This includes farmers, participants in the industry, suppliers of technology, researchers, organisations affiliated with the government, and organisations that are not affiliated with the government.

The successful adoption of digital technologies in agriculture is deeply interdependent on robust infrastructure, supportive policy environments, and developed human capital (Hassoun et al., 2023). Poor broadband connectivity, financial incentives, or digital skills can significantly reduce the effectiveness of investments in other areas. Farmers need technology, but they also need to afford, connect to, and use it, and this requires holistic, integrated policies. First, governments should invest in rural broadband infrastructure and provide financial aid to lower adoption costs. These efforts should be accompanied by comprehensive education and training programmes to improve farmers' technical skills and digital literacy. When it comes to addressing these challenges, a fragmented approach will result in uneven adoption and unequal distribution of resources.

7. CHARTING THE FUTURE OF DIGITAL DAIRY FOR RURAL PROSPERITY

The digital transformation of the dairy sector represents a dynamic and evolving process with profound implications for rural economic growth. This chapter has examined various multidisciplinary aspects of the transformation, emphasising technological advancements, economic benefits, social implications, environmental contributions, and key policy considerations.

7.1. Synthesis of Key Findings

The production and processing of dairy products are undergoing a tremendous transformation as a result of the implementation of digital technologies such as the Internet of Things (IoT), artificial intelligence (AI), blockchain, big data analytics, automation, and precision agriculture. This shift is moving the industry toward a proactive, data-driven management paradigm that enables real-time monitoring, predictive analytics, and automated operations. The economic benefits derived from this transformation are substantial. These benefits include higher productivity, measurable savings in costs like feed, labour, and maintenance, better overall profits, and new ways to reach customers directly and support different rural jobs. Socially, digitisation is fundamentally transforming labour roles within dairy farming, necessitating the development of new skill sets focused on data management and technological literacy. It also offers opportunities to attract a younger, tech-savvy workforce. Furthermore, digital advancements enhance farmer well-being by reducing physical burdens and improving access to essential basic services like healthcare, education, and finance in rural areas.

From an environmental perspective, digital tools are critical for optimising resource use (water, energy, feed), reducing waste, and mitigating greenhouse gas emissions, thereby aligning with broader sustainability goals. Additionally, there are increased risks associated with reliance on digital systems. These risks include vulnerabilities in cybersecurity, which can disrupt essential farm operations and affect regulations governing environmental and animal welfare. Policy and regulatory frameworks are needed to guarantee an equitable digital transition. Key areas of focus include data governance (addressing ownership, privacy, and security concerns), bridging the persistent rural broadband gap, and providing essential government support and incentives for technology adoption. The digital divide constitutes a substantial obstacle, particularly for smallholder farmers, impeding the extensive and inclusive adoption of digital technologies.

Ultimately, successful digital transformation in the dairy sector is highly context-specific, requiring tailored solutions and a synergistic approach that integrates technological innovation with social innovation and trust-building initiatives.

7.2. Future Research Directions

To clarify our knowledge about digital transformation in the dairy industry and facilitate its practical application, several key areas require further empirical investigation:

- ***Socio-Economic Impact Assessment***: More empirical research is needed to quantify the long-term social and economic impacts of digital transformation, particularly on small and medium-sized dairy farms and marginalised rural communities, to ensure that the benefits are equitable and widely distributed.
- ***Technology Adaptation and Accessibility***: Research should focus on the development of open-source and affordable digital technologies specifically adapted for diverse agro-ecological conditions and resource-constrained environments, to address existing barriers to adoption.
- ***Advanced Data Governance Models***: Investigation into robust, decentralised data governance models that empower farmers with data ownership and control. This could explore leveraging blockchain technology beyond mere traceability to facilitate broader data monetisation and collective benefits for farming communities.
- ***Skill Development Effectiveness***: Studies on the effectiveness of different training and capacity-building programmes in enhancing digital literacy and new skill sets among the dairy workforce are needed. This research should aim to provide empirical evidence to inform the ongoing deskilling/reskilling debate and ensure effective workforce transitions.
- ***Environmental Impact and Cybersecurity Resilience***: Continued research on the environmental impacts of digital technologies is necessary, including more precise measurement of greenhouse gas emission reductions from specific digital interventions. Concurrently, there is a critical need for research into the development of resilient, cyber-secure farm systems to mitigate emerging risks posed by digital dependence.
- ***Innovative Business Models and Partnerships***: Exploration of innovative business models and public-private partnerships that effectively facilitate technology adoption, financing, and technical support in rural areas, especially for small-scale producers, is vital for scaling digital solutions equitably.

7.3. Strategic Recommendations for Stakeholders

A collaborative effort among all industry stakeholders is essential to achieve a prosperous and equitable digital future for the dairy industry. Taking this into consideration, the following suggestions have been developed:

For Policymakers and Governments

Investing in basic infrastructure is essential to ensure that rural broadband is treated as a critical public utility: affordable, reliable, and accessible for everyone, not just the largest operators. This creates the foundation upon which digital agriculture can flourish. Alongside this, it is important to establish equitable data governance by adopting clear rules on data ownership, privacy, and security that protect the rights of all actors across the agricultural supply chain, from smallholders to larger enterprises. To further enable adoption, targeted incentives and financing mechanisms, including financial aid and customised loan programmes, can offset the high upfront costs of digital technologies, making them more accessible for small and medium-sized farms. Complementing these measures, strengthening skill development and extension services is vital, with a focus on agricultural training, digital literacy, and adaptive management skills that prepare farmers and rural workers for evolving roles. Finally, promoting public-private partnerships between governments, academia, and technology providers can ensure the co-development of context-specific, user-centred solutions while supporting their sustainable deployment and use in practice. Together, these efforts create a more inclusive, resilient, and digitally empowered agricultural sector.

For Industry and Technology Providers

Interoperability and ease of use should be established as primary design goals for agricultural innovations. Solutions must be developed using open standards and intuitive, user-friendly interfaces that integrate seamlessly with existing farm systems, reducing complexity and lowering adoption barriers for farmers. In parallel, flexible business models should be adopted to ensure accessibility and financial viability across farms of different scales. Options such as subscription services, pay-per-use schemes, or tiered pricing structures can make digital tools more attainable, particularly for smaller farms with limited resources. Building trust and transparency is equally critical, requiring open communication about how data is collected, managed, and shared, while actively engaging farmers to address concerns around ownership and privacy. Finally, comprehensive support must be provided through robust technical assistance, ongoing training, and readily available educational resources. Such measures will help farmers maximise the value of their digital investments, overcome challenges, and fully harness the benefits of digital agriculture.

For Farmers and Rural Communities

Farmers are encouraged to embrace lifelong learning by actively pursuing opportunities for digital literacy and skill development, recognising that continuous adaptation is essential to keeping pace with the evolving technological demands of modern dairy farming. Equally important is the need to engage proactively with policymakers and government representatives to highlight critical issues such as broadband access, data rights, and financial support for digital adoption, ensuring that farmers' perspectives shape future policy frameworks. Collaboration and knowledge sharing also play a pivotal role, with networks, cooperatives, and digital communities providing helpful forums for exchanging best practices, learning from shared experiences, and collectively strengthening the ecosystem for innovation. Finally, the adoption of digital technologies should be strategy-based and incremental, prioritising the resolution of pressing challenges while gradually building redundancy and resilience in farm systems. This deliberate phased approach fosters smoother transitions, minimises risks, and maximises long-term benefits.

In conclusion, the transition from analogue to digital in the dairy industry is not a process of leapfrogging but rather a journey. It has been demonstrated by early adopters that it is possible to achieve more profitable, efficient, and sustainable dairying that also provides a better life for farmers. How can we scale up these numerous examples of success to make them the norm, not the exception? Utilising concepts from a wide range of fields and experiences, as we have done in this chapter, stakeholders can develop strategies that maximise the potential for gains and avoid the occurrence of shortcomings. If managed effectively, the digital revolution in dairy farming has the potential to serve as a model for other farming types. The outcome would demonstrate how combining tradition and innovation can lead to a resilient and prosperous future for rural communities all over the world.

ACKNOWLEDGMENT

This material is the result of research actions carried out within the project *TWIN-IN – Promoting responsible TWIN transition in European agrifood systems through INnovation and learning alliances*, funded by the European Commission under the Grant Agreement ID 101187101-ERASMUS-EDU-2024-PI-ALL-INNO-EDU-ENTERP, coordinated at the Romanian Academy Iasi Branch, whose institutional resources and academic environment were essential for the successful completion of this work.

The information presented in this material does not necessarily represent the official positions of the European Commission or the programmes that finance these projects. Responsibility for the data and opinions presented lies exclusively with the authors who contributed to the production of this material.

REFERENCES

Adewusi, A. O., Chiekezi, N. R., & Eyo-Udo, N. L.Adebunmi Okechukwu AdewusiNjideka Rita ChiekezieNsisong Louis Eyo-Udo. (2022). Cybersecurity threats in agriculture supply chains: A comprehensive review. *World Journal of Advanced Research and Reviews*, *15*(3), 490–500. DOI: 10.30574/wjarr.2022.15.3.0888

Ahmadzai, H., Tutundjian, S., & Elouafi, I. (2021). Policies for Sustainable Agriculture and Livelihood in Marginal Lands: A Review. *Sustainability (Basel)*, *13*(16), 8692. DOI: 10.3390/su13168692

Ahmed, N., & Shakoor, N. (2025). Advancing agriculture through IoT, Big Data, and AI: A review of smart technologies enabling sustainability. *Smart Agricultural Technology*, *10*, 100848. DOI: 10.1016/j.atech.2025.100848

Almansour, M., & Akrami, M. (2024). Towards Zero Waste: An In-Depth Analysis of National Policies, Strategies, and Case Studies in Waste Minimisation. *Sustainability (Basel)*, *16*(22), 10105. DOI: 10.3390/su162210105

Antonio, A., & Tuffley, D. (2014). The Gender Digital Divide in Developing Countries. *Future Internet*, *6*(4), 673–687. DOI: 10.3390/fi6040673

Banu, N., & Fazal, S. (2025). Climate Change, Livelihood Crisis and Resilience: An Introduction. In *Livelihoods and Well-Being in the Era of Climate Change*. Springer., DOI: 10.1007/978-3-031-81132-6_1

Buckley, F., Upton, J., Shalloo, L., & Murphy, M. D. Optimizing the Cooling Schedule of Stored Milk on Dairy Farms to Reduced Costs and Carbon Emissions. Available at *SSRN* 5222087.

Bullvine (2025). AI Slashes Feed Costs $31 Per Cow While Your Competitors Pull Further Ahead: The Data-Driven Revolution Reshaping Dairy's Future. https://www.thebullvine.com/news/ai-slashes-feed-costs-31-per-cow-while-your-competitors-pull-further-ahead-the-data-driven-revolution-reshaping-dairys-future/

Cabrera VE. (2025). Artificial intelligence applied to dairy science: insights from the Dairy Brain Initiative. Anim Front. Jan 4;14(6):60-63. DOI: 10.1093/af/vfae040

Calvo-Sotomayor, I., Laka, J. P., & Aguado, R. (2019). Workforce Ageing and Labour Productivity in Europe. *Sustainability (Basel), 11*(20), 5851. DOI: 10.3390/su11205851

Chase, L. E., & Fortina, R. (2023). Environmental and Economic Responses to Precision Feed Management in Dairy Cattle Diets. *Agriculture, 13*(5), 1032. DOI: 10.3390/agriculture13051032

Cue, R., Doornink, M., George, R., Griffiths, B., Jorgensen, M. W., Rogers, R., Saha, A., Taysom, K., Cabrera, V. E., Wangen, S. R., & Fadul-Pacheco, L. (2021, October 15). Data Governance in the Dairy Industry. *Animals (Basel), 11*(10), 2981. DOI: 10.3390/ani11102981

Cui, X. (2025). The Impact of Digital Transformation on Enterprises—Taking Mengniu Dairy as an Example. Advances in Economics. *Management and Political Sciences, 177*, 181–186. DOI: 10.54254/2754-1169/177/2025.22480

Da Costa Miranda, C. N., & Shukla, M. (2025). Blockchain-based smart dairy supply chain: Catching the momentum for digital transformation. *Asian Journal of Management and Commerce, 6*(1), 502–514. DOI: 10.22271/27084515.2025.v6.i1f.493

Eastwood, C. R., Knook, J., Turner, J. A., & Renwick, A. (2023). Policy approaches for enhanced dairy sector innovation – a review of future pathways and policies for effective implementation of digital agriculture. *New Zealand Economic Papers, 57*(2), 164–171. DOI: 10.1080/00779954.2022.2161935

FAO (Food and Agriculture Organization). (2021). The State of Food and Agriculture 2021: Transforming Food Systems for Affordable Healthy Diets. FAO (https://www.fao.org/publications/sofa/2021/en/)

Ferguson, H. J., Bowen, J. M., McNicol, L. C., Bell, J., Duthie, C.-A., & Dewhurst, R. J. (2024). The impacts of precision livestock farming tools on the greenhouse gas emissions of an average Scottish dairy farm. *Frontiers in Sustainable Food Systems, 8*, 1385672. DOI: 10.3389/fsufs.2024.1385672

Food and Agriculture Organization of the United Nations. (2024). Statistical Yearbook 2024: Chapter 2 Production of livestock and livestock commodities. https://openknowledge.fao.org/server/api/core/bitstreams/d784864f-7f28-49d2-903e-6680d09a9d97/content/cd2971en.html#chapter-2_2

Garlinska, M., Osial, M., Proniewska, K., & Pregowska, A. (2023). The Influence of Emerging Technologies on Distance Education. *Electronics (Basel), 12*(7), 1550. DOI: 10.3390/electronics12071550

Gaworski, M., & Kic, P. (2024). Assessment of Production Technologies on Dairy Farms in Terms of Animal Welfare. *Applied Sciences (Basel, Switzerland), 14*(14), 6086. DOI: 10.3390/app14146086

Glover, D., & Sumberg, J. (2025). Skill and deskilling in an uncertain agricultural world: Introduction to the special issue. *Outlook on Agriculture, 54*(2), 123-132. (Original work published 2025)DOI: 10.1177/00307270251337112

Gontijo, D., Santana, D. R., de Assis Costa, G., Cabrera, V. E., & de Andrade Freitas, E. N. (2025). Dairy GPT: Empowering dairy farmers to interact with numerical databases through natural language conversations. *Smart Agricultural Technology, 12*, 101097. DOI: 10.1016/j.atech.2025.101097

Hassoun, A., Garcia-Garcia, G., Trollman, H., Jagtap, S., Parra-Lopez, C., Cropotova, J., Bhat, Z. F., Centobelli, P., & Aït-Kaddour, A. (2023). Birth of dairy 4.0: Opportunities and challenges in adoption of fourth industrial revolution technologies in the production of milk and its derivatives. *Current Research in Food Science, 7*, 100535. DOI: 10.1016/j.crfs.2023.100535

Kaewbang, J., Lohanawakul, J., Ketnuam, N., Prapakornmano, K., Khamta, P., Raza, A., Swangchan-Uthai, T., Makararpong, D., & Inchaisri, C. (2024). Smart sensors in Thai dairy reproduction: A case study. *Veterinary World, 17*(6), 1251–1258. DOI: 10.14202/vetworld.2024.1251-1258

Lage, C. F. A., Marques, T. C., Bruno, D. R., Endres, M. I., Ferreira, F., Pires, A. P. A., Leão, K., & de Lima, F. S. (2024). Farmers' Perceptions on Implementing Automatic Milking Systems in Large USA Dairies: Decision-Making Process, Management Practices, Labor, and Herd Performance. *Animals (Basel), 14*(2), 218. DOI: 10.3390/ani14020218

Lavrijsen-Kromwijk, L., Demba, S., Müller, U., & Rose, S. (2024). Impact of Automation Level of Dairy Farms in Northern and Central Germany on Dairy Cattle Welfare. *Animals (Basel), 14*(24), 3699. DOI: 10.3390/ani14243699

Lee, M., & Seo, S. (2021). Wearable Wireless Biosensor Technology for Monitoring Cattle: A Review. *Animals (Basel), 11*(10), 2779. DOI: 10.3390/ani11102779

Lokhorst, C., de Mol, R. M., & Kamphuis, C. (2019). Invited review: Big Data in precision dairy farming. *Animal, 13*(7), 1519–1528. DOI: 10.1017/S1751731118003439

Luo, W., Dong, Q., & Feng, Y. (2023). Risk prediction model of clinical mastitis in lactating dairy cows based on machine learning algorithms. *Preventive Veterinary Medicine, 221*, 106059. DOI: 10.1016/j.prevetmed.2023.106059

Magesa, M., Jonathan, J., & Urassa, J. (2023). Digital Literacy of Smallholder Farmers in Tanzania. *Sustainability (Basel), 15*(17), 13149. DOI: 10.3390/su151713149

Mantravadi, S., Srai, J. S., & Møller, C. (2023). Application of MES/MOM for Industry 4.0 supply chains: A cross-case analysis. *Computers in Industry, 148*, 103907. DOI: 10.1016/j.compind.2023.103907

McFadden, J.. (2022). The digitalisation of agriculture: A literature review and emerging policy issues. In *OECD Food, Agriculture and Fisheries Papers, No. 176*. OECD Publishing., DOI: 10.1787/285cc27d-

Montenegro Hernandez, J. (2024). Blockchain Applications in the Food Industry: A Systematic Literature Review. *International Journal of Applied Research in Business and Management, 5*(2). Advance online publication. DOI: 10.51137/ijarbm.2024.5.2.23

Neculai-Valeanu, A.-S., Sanduleanu, C., Amaritii, G., & Bruma, I. S. (2025b). Precision livestock farming and its role for assuring a sustainable cattle management – A study case on connected cow. *Scientific Papers. Series Management, Economic Engineering in Agriculture and Rural Development, 25*(1), 689–696. ISSN 2284-7995.

Neculai-Valeanu, A.-S., Sanduleanu, C., & Porosnicu, I. (2025a). From tradition to precision: Leveraging digital tools to improve cattle health and welfare. *Frontiers in Veterinary Science, 12*, 1549512. Advance online publication. DOI: 10.3389/fvets.2025.1549512

Neethirajan, S. (2025). Safeguarding digital livestock farming: A comprehensive cybersecurity roadmap for dairy and poultry industries. *Frontiers in Big Data, 8*, 1556157. Advance online publication. DOI: 10.3389/fdata.2025.1556157

Palma, O., Plà-Aragonés, L. M., Mac Cawley, A., & Albornoz, V. M. (2025). AI and Data Analytics in the Dairy Farms: A Scoping Review. *Animals (Basel)*, *15*(9), 1291. DOI: 10.3390/ani15091291

Rhouma, A., El Jeitany, J., Mohtar, R., & Gil, J. M. (2024). Trends in the Water–Energy–Food Nexus Research. *Sustainability (Basel)*, *16*(3), 1162. DOI: 10.3390/su16031162

Ronzhin, A., Figurek, A., Surovtsev, V., & Dibirova, K. (2025). Digital Transformation and Precision Farming as Catalysts of Rural Development. *Land (Basel)*, *14*(7), 1464. DOI: 10.3390/land14071464

Ruchay, V. K., Guo, H., & Pezzuolo, A. (2024). On-barn cattle facial recognition using deep transfer learning and data augmentation. *Computers and Electronics in Agriculture*, *225*, 109306. DOI: 10.1016/j.compag.2024.109306

Sharma, A., Goar, V., Kuri, M., & Chowdhary, C. L. (2023). Supply chain management using blockchain security enhancement. In V. Goar, M. Kuri, R. Kumar, & T. Senjyu (Eds.), *Advances in Information Communication Technology and Computing* (Lecture Notes in Networks and Systems, Vol. 628, pp. 221–233). Springer, Singapore. DOI: 10.1007/978-981-19-9888-1_15

Shine, P., Upton, J., Sefeedpari, P., & Murphy, M. D. (2020). Energy Consumption on Dairy Farms: A Review of Monitoring, Prediction Modelling, and Analyses. *Energies*, *13*(5), 1288. DOI: 10.3390/en13051288

Tangorra, F. M., Buoio, E., Calcante, A., Bassi, A., & Costa, A. (2024). Internet of Things (IoT): Sensors Application in Dairy Cattle Farming. *Animals (Basel)*, *14*(21), 3071. DOI: 10.3390/ani14213071

Trendov, N. M., Varas, S., & Zeng, M. (2019). *Digital technologies in agriculture and rural areas: Status report*. Food and Agriculture Organization of the United Nations., https://www.fao.org/3/ca4985en/ca4985en.pdf

Vahdanjoo, M., Grøn Sørensen, C., & Nørremark, M. (2025). Digital transformation of the agri-food system. *Current Opinion in Food Science*, *63*, 101287. Advance online publication. DOI: 10.1016/j.cofs.2025.101287

Vlaicu, P. A., Gras, M. A., Untea, A. E., Lefter, N. A., & Rotar, M. C. (2024). Advancing livestock technology: Intelligent systemization for enhanced productivity, welfare, and sustainability. *AgriEngineering*, *6*(2), 1479–1496. DOI: 10.3390/agriengineering6020084

Wu, J. (2024). Digitizing Agriculture: Strategic Insights into Traditional Challenges and Modern Management Solutions. Advances in Economics. *Management and Political Sciences*, *121*(1), 215–219. DOI: 10.54254/2754-1169/121/20242631

Yuan, Y., & Sun, Y. (2024). Practices, Challenges, and Future of Digital Transformation in Smallholder Agriculture: Insights from a Literature Review. *Agriculture*, *14*(12), 2193. DOI: 10.3390/agriculture14122193

Chapter 6
EU Policies for Sustainable Rural Development Emphasising Multifunctional Farming and Farm Entrepreneurship Engaged in Diversification

Sotiris Apostolopoulos
https://orcid.org/0000-0002-1065-891X
Neapolis University, Pafos, Cyprus

ABSTRACT

The current chapter examines the European sustainable rural development policies based on multifunctional farming and farm entrepreneurship linked to diversification. When it comes to sustainable development policies,multifunctional farming and farm entrepreneurship engaged in diversification are part of the agenda as well. Furthermore, the views, experiences and expectations of rural residents involved in the aforementioned field are of particular importance for evaluating the effectiveness of the European rural development policies drawn in this study. Empirically,

DOI: 10.4018/979-8-3373-2898-0.ch006

a qualitative approach has been employed utilising semi-structured interviews with sixteen farmers and rural residents to detect their opinions on the European funded programmes wherein they are involved and to assess the effectiveness of European rural development policies. The study revealed, among others, that European support policies are vital despite any existing obstacles indicated that European programmes contribute to changing the way agriculture is produced and lead to sustainability.

1. INTRODUCTION

The EU has been constantly supporting sustainable rural development through its policy interventions, actions and initiatives (Carayannis et al., 2020). In this light, it pursues policies for agricultural production, agribusiness, addressing aging population, job creation, connectivity, solid waste management, green and digital transition and generally meeting the social, economic and environmental challenges of rural areas (Kusio et al., 2022; Dan & Popescu, 2017). However, many European funding programmes have not delivered the desired results as they have relied on subsidised production only, favouring oftentimes the larger agricultural holdings. It is evident that a concrete vision and holistic planning for the countryside, its inhabitants and production was ultimately missing. The EU had to address this issue in 2021 with the implementation of the long-term vision "The EU rural vision" with a timeframe up to 2040 (European Commission, 2021). It represents a long-term vision for a stronger, more resilient, sustainable and prosperous countryside by 2040 covering 83% of the EU's territory and 137 million people lyring in those areas (European Commission, 2021). Additionally, a key factor in making the vision become a reality involves changing the model of agricultural production by building a new sustainable model that is pro-environmental and does not use natural resources unwisely (Carayannis et al., 2020; Apostolopoulos et al, 2020a). This implies changing the current model of agricultural production and replacing it with sustainable systems one of them includes multifunctional farming and farm entrepreneurship linked to diversification (Martinho, 2020; Apostolopoulos et al., 2018; Vesala & Vesala, 2010). Thus, "The EU rural vision" foresees rebooting rural development towards robust, well-connected, prosperous and resilient rural areas via a set of diversified activities leading to the diversification of the rural economy (Cardillo et al, 2023). These goals have direct reference to the competitiveness of multifunctional agriculture (Bartolini et al, 2014).

Moreover, the European framework through targeted initiatives and actions contributes significantly to support multifunctional agriculture and sustainability in order to overcome barriers and achieve sustainable rural development (Dan & Popescu, 2017; Seuneke et al., 2013; Morgan et al, 2010). That kind of support leads to increasing activities that complement agricultural production by using its resources for both agricultural and non-agricultural production, such as agro-tourism and photovoltaic energy (Apostolopoulos et al, 2020b; Karagianni et al., 2019; Iakovidou et al., 2002). Many scholars argue that supportive policies for multifunctional agriculture contribute to its transformation (Losch, 2004) and to environmental protection (Léon, 2005). Multifunctional agriculture stands at the core of EU policies and constitutes the one that integrates the interdependent objectives of agriculture and rural society (Gargano et al., 2021; Knickel et al., 2004). In this regard, the European model of agricultural production asserts that agriculture encompasses more functions such as environmental and natural resource protection and landscape conservation which contributes to the socio-economic sustainability of rural areas (Song et al., 2020; Brummel & Nelson, 2014; Belletti, et al., 2003). For the EU, the multifunctional model of agriculture within the Common Agricultural Policy is a cornerstone (Volanen, 2000).

Simultaneously, farm entrepreneurship linked to diversification contributes to sustainable development and increased incomes of rural residents engaged in agriculture (Ragkos et al., 2018; Milestad et al., 2012; Meert et al., 2005). Furthermore, according to Ilbery (1991), diversification provides unconventional activities like organic production, snail farming, processing, agro-tourism with farm resources such as land and buildings.

The current chapter examines how do European policies that shape the vision for a sustainable and prosperous countryside by 2040 relate to sustainable multi-functional farming and sustainable farm entrepreneurship linked to diversification. This relationship is not being explored from the perspective of those who designed and currently implement it, but through the views and perceptions of rural residents who are utilising European funding programmes in the pursuit of sustainable multifunctional farming and farm entrepreneurship. Such an approach is missing from the global literature and it is vital to be informed and enriched by the experiences and expectations of the key actors of the relevant European programmes which are definitely the rural populations. After all, the success of "The EU rural vision" with a time horizon of 2040 will depend on the participation and active support of rural residents.

2. LITERATURE REVIEW

Multifunctional farming and farm entrepreneurship linked to diversification as an alternative in different types of agricultural contexts have attracted increasing research interest in recent decades (Agoraki et al., 2024; Cardillo et al., 2023; Apostolopoulos et al, 2020b). Certain research findings show the contribution of the aforementioned field to agricultural revitalization even in mountainous and remote rural areas (Sivini & Vitale, 2023; Arru et al, 2021). Multifunctional agriculture has also sparked significant research interest after the Rio Earth Summit where the concept of "multifunctionality" gained importance in Agenda 21 documents with regard to sustainable development (Poojari et al., 2024; Barot et al., 2017; Huang et al, 2015). According to Tohidyan & Rezaei-Moghaddam (2019), entrepreneurship is at the heart of multifunctional agriculture. This is a form of entrepreneurship based on technological and economic synergies whilst oriented towards sustainable rural development (Gittins et al, 2025; Agoraki et al, 2024). Notably, multifunctional agribusinesses vastly contribute to the sustainable development goals as the latter were identified by the United Nations (Apostolopoulos et al., 2018). However, agricultural crops in combination with other economic activities such as tourism should guarantee the improvement of livelihoods that contribute to the quality of life of rural residents (Renting et al., 2009).

Rural entrepreneurship is a distinct case of the general entrepreneurship sector since countrysides have their own characteristics and peculiarities that distinguish them from urban centres (Lans et al., 2014; Vik & McElwee, 2011). However, contrary views have been reflected in the international literature. These do not differentiate entrepreneurship in urban centres from that in rural areas, merely accepting that entrepreneurship outside urban settings has disadvantages, identified in the difficulty of accessing the market and consumers (Stathopoulou et al, 2004). In fact, many of these barriers are considered to have been removed by the evolution of digitalisation (Nedilska & Oleniuk, 2020; Carmela Annosi et al., 2020). Moreover, research by Phillipson et al (2019) revealed that there are no findings to suggest that rural businesses are underperforming relative to their urban counterparts. Meanwhile, rural entrepreneurship has stimulated considerable research efforts (Asmit, 2024; Mulibana & Tshikovhi, 2024; Dias et al, 2019). Studies indicate that the rural environment is linked to rural entrepreneurship and they are mutually dependent on each other (Filatotchev et al., 2022; Bosworth, 2012). Rural enterprises add value to the economy and citizens' well-being (Bannor et al, 2021; Phillipson et al, 2019; Smit, 2004) while playing a pivotal role in enhancing regional development (Kusio & Fiore, 2022; Patel & Chavda, 2013; Saxena, 2012). Simultaneously, the regional entrepreneurial ecosystem creates business opportunities (Wu et al, 2021). Additionally, various studies have shown that entrepreneurship creates value for rural communities (Korsgaard et al., 2015; Morgan et al., 2010). Furthermore, digital transformation is seen as creating fourth revolution conditions for agriculture and rural businesses (Hrustek, 2020; Sott et al, 2020; Knierim et al, 2019). In this regard, the penetration of new technologies in agribusinesses is crucial for their operation, growth, and entering new markets and in keeping them up-to-date (Botsiou & Dagdilelis, 2013).

There exists research interest in farm diversification within various international contexts (Refai et al, 2024; Gittins & McElwee, 2023; Refai & McElwee, 2023). Through farm diversification, enterprises are established with the potential to increase total income by retaining the rural population in the countryside (Anderson et al, 2006; Pyysiäinen, et al., 2006). According to the global literature, the motivations that drive farmers to diversify their crops fall along a wide spectrum between economic returns and creating opportunities for increasing overall income (Lokier et al, 2021; De Rosa et al, 2019; McElwee, 2008). Specifically, such alternative forms of income revitalize farms and contribute to rural development (Daskalopoulou & Petrou, 2002). The concrete status lead to new products and generate incomes ultimately contributing to the improvement of farmers' quality of life (Greenberg et al., 2018).

A growing body of research has increasingly focused on how European policies and European funding support multifunctional agriculture, farm diversification and agribusinesses to make rural areas vibrant, interlinked, resilient and prosperous (Oltean & Arion, 2023, Aronica et al., 2023, Chartier et al., 2021, Vásáry et al., 2021). The European vision "The EU rural vision" (with a time horizon of 2040) was also identified in the research focus (Makris et al, 2025; Alonso & Pozas, 2024; Aronica et al, 2023). The European vision should be based on digitalisation to improve the socio-economic conditions of rural areas (Vásáry et al, 2021) and support sustainable entrepreneurship by strengthening the local identity of rural communities (Aronica et al., 2023; Chartier et al., 2021; Vásáry & Szabolcs, 2020).

3. METHODOLOGY

Qualitative research approach was adopted since, based on the international literature, it is considered adequate and effective in detecting and capturing personal perceptions, beliefs and experiences (Tuli, 2010; Fossey et al., 2002; Al-Busaidi, 2008). The particular research method positively contributes to the diversity of entrepreneurship issues (Javadian et al., 2020), clarifies and explains accurately the complexity of the phenomenon under investigation (Neergaard & Ulhøi, 2007) whilst analyses entrepreneurship in depth (Drakopoulou-Dodd et al., 2014) and emphasises the notions, perspectives and opinions of the participants (Al-Busaidi, 2008).

Moreover, it reliably clarifies and interprets social, economic, and business environments (Neergaard, & Ulhøi, 2007; Denzin & Lincoln, 2005). Qualitative research is particularly effective in studying aspects that are difficult to measure such as daily behaviours, entrepreneurial identity, family integration in business operations, persistence, and emotions (Van Burg et al, 2020; Welter et al, 2017). The sample was collected using semi-structured interviews since based on the literature these are suitable and effective in qualitative methods and significantly enhance the objectivity and reliability of the examined subject (DeJonckheere & Vaughn, 2019; Kallio et al., 2016).

Semi-structured interviews create a flexible discussion framework (Patton, 1990). Twelve semi-structured interviews were conducted with producers coming from various regional units of Greece. Previously, convenience sampling strategy (Moser & Korstjens, 2018) was employed to identify the sample. Table 1 captures key facets of the sample such as the respondent's status, age and area of residence.

Table 1. Description of study sample

Respondent	Status	Age	Area
R1	Apple producer with refrigeration business for fruit preservation	55	Arcadia Regional Unit
R2	Cherry producer with juice pressing plant	51	Arcadia Regional Unit
R3	Olive oil producer with olive oil mill and agritourism establishment	64	Hlia Regional Unit
R4	Nut producer with a nut processing plant and a treatment plant	42	Arcadia Regional Unit
R5	Pomegranate producer with a juice pressing unit and an agritourism establishment	55	Arcadia Regional Unit
R6	Producer of fruit and vegetables in greenhouses with a processing unit	47	Hlia Regional Unit
R7	Olive oil producer with a processing plant and a traditional café	40	Messinia Regional Unit
R8	Wine producer owning a winery	53	Arcadia Regional Unit
R9	Fruit and vegetable producer in greenhouses owning a processing plant and short-term rental accommodation	38	Messinia Regional Unit
R10	Olive oil producer owining an olive oil mill	50	Lakonia Regional Unit
R11	Olive oil producer owning an oil processing plant and a feed mill	42	Lakonia Regional Unit
R12	Wine producer owning a winery	67	Drama Regional Unit

On average each interview lasted one hour. The interviews were conducted in January and February 2025 and were carried out using phone calls and on-line meetings since according to the international literature, data collection via telephone and internet is as reliable as face-to-face interviews (Deakin & Wakefield, 2014; Cachia & Millward, 2011). Relying on an inductive approach, the twelve interviews were examined and cross-checks were performed based on the themes (Yin, 1994). Moreover, by using inductive reasoning, emerging themes were generated in relation to the research questions (Gioia et al., 2013). Table 2 illustrates the relevant emerging themes and sub-themes.

Table 2. Thematic Analysis

Theme	Sub-theme
Multifunctional farming	• Environmental dimension • Economic dimension • Social dimension • Application of contemporary technologies
Farm enterprises	• Selection incentives • Digitalisation • Impact on local communities
Crop diversification policies	• Selected incentives • Diversification as a business strategy • Barriers and constraints • Benefits
European policies to support multifunctional agriculture, farm enterprises and crop diversification	• Diffusion of European policies in relation to the European vision • Financial instruments • Inclusion in European programmes (experiences and obstacles) • Green and digital transition

4. FINDINGS ANALYSIS

The findings for European sustainable rural development policies towards multifunctional farming and farm entrepreneurship linked to diversification were structured on the basis of the following four thematic sections: Towards the area related to multifunctional farming, the area related to rural enterprises, the area related to crop diversification policies and lastly the area related to European policies for supporting multifunctional farming, agribusiness and crop diversification

Multifunctional Farming

Research revealed that multifunctional farming is redefining the role of agriculture by helping to balance agricultural production with the preservation of the natural environment and the sustainability of rural areas. It is directly linked to climate change and biodiversity loss. The technological evolution is contributing to risk reduction and food security.

'Multifunctional farming brings agriculture closer to sustainability while taking into account environmental protection. Technological developments in agriculture today play a significant role in preserving the natural environment' (R1)

Additionally, interviewees have stated that multifunctional farming is of particular importance for the economic development of rural communities. According to their views, it beneficially contributes to employment and the creation of new economic activities within rural communities.

'Multifunctional agriculture contributes to the economic development and prosperity of rural citizens. It creates opportunities and generates relevant income while improving economic cohesion' (R9)

The multifunctional agriculture enhances rural population retention in countrysides. At the same time, it enhances the preservation of cultural heritage while bringing agriculture closer to the demands of society.

'Retaining the population in rural areas requires output, jobs and decent incomes. Then rural areas can be developed while preserving their cultural heritage' (R5)

Respondents have claimed that multifunctional farming needs contemporary technologies engagement in order for farming systems to be managed properly.

'Today, technology is needed everywhere, especially in agriculture. Let's be honest, only through the use of new technologies, we would produce and promote healthy products and simultaneously protect the environment.' (R11)

Farm Enterprises

The present research has shown that a key motivation for farmers in establishing agribusinesses is the creation of value in their products. Processing, standardization and branding enter markets easily and create cash flows for farmers.

'In order not to have our products taken away from us at low prices and exploited by others, there was no other way than to brand our products, standardize them and market them on our own.' (R6)

The research revealed that communication networks and digitalisation have enabled countryside to overcome rural isolation and facilitated the creation of agribusinesses by farmers themselves.

'Rural areas have been isolated for years. Travel was difficult and there were barriers to accessing public services and banks. Today, technology has addressed this' (R8)

The research revealed that sustainable entrepreneurship in the agricultural sector is transforming traditional systems, creating jobs and reducing poverty. It also generates income and contributes to the sustainable development of rural communities.

'There exist many benefits that are created by an agribusiness linked to crops. It creates income, jobs and contributes to the development of the region.' (R4)

Crop Diversification Policies

The research indicates that the motivation for farmers' decision to diversify their crops lies in seeking to exploit opportunities for increasing incomes through the new product development. Also, to build resilience towards their economic activities by reducing risks.

'It was a difficult decision. But we had to utilise the opportunity to reduce risks and strengthen our financial position. The result confirmed our family's decision' (R7)

The research has shown that the diversification strategy creates resilience in the business. However, it requires skills from farmers, existence of infrastructure, human and financial resources as well as digital technologies.

'Diversification is not a simple process. We struggled because it required skills and knowledge that we did not have. We had to secure capital and acquire the capacity to use digital technologies' (R3).

Survey participants consider that the most serious barriers to someone deciding to diversify their farming are bureaucracy, difficulty in joining support programmes, inefficient institutional framework and difficulties in securing bank loans.

'The barriers and difficulties are so many that they act as a deterrent. To join a support programme or to secure bank lending is not an easy task. Everywhere you are confronted with the 'beast' of bureaucracy'. (R9)

Research has shown that diversification creates benefits. It increases income. It helps to keep the population in the countryside. Farmers respond better to the challenges of sustainable development.

'I don't regret the decision. We were able and strengthened our position by increasing our incomes. I once thought about leaving the agricultural sector. Today both my family and I feel justified in our choice'. (R5)

European Policies to Support Multifunctional Farm, Rural Entrepreneurship and Crop Diversification

Interviewees didn't know so much towards the European vision "The EU rural vision". It was detected that there is a lack of information and awareness of European policies concerning multifunctional agriculture, agribusiness and diversification. However, they expressed the desire to create information and information mechanisms.

'I know very little about European policies and the European vision you are asking me about. The only source of information for us is television' (R12).

Study revealed that European funding programmes are crucial despite existing obstacles. They help to change the way in which agriculture is produced and lead to sustainability, provided that they are flexible and linked to the real needs of crops and farms.

'Agricultural production and rural businesses need European and domestic support programmes, as they contribute to the modernisation of crops, the development of businesses and the prosperity of our villages' (R1).

It was highlighted that there exist barriers to farmers' participation in European programmes and these are mainly related to lack of information, bureaucracy and ensuring their own participation. Strong administrative barriers were also identified.

'I cannot claim that my experience has been positive in trying to join a European programme. The system is complex, demanding and bureaucratic. It is also difficult for us to ensure the same level of participation under the conditions required by the programme' (R5)

Interviewees consider the green and digital transition important. However, they claim that it has financial costs that they alone are unable to overcome.

'The importance of the green and digital transition is certainly undeniable. We consider it both useful and necessary. The problem is that this transition has an economic cost, so the state and the EU have to bear this cost' (R9).

5. DISCUSSION

Research indicated that multifunctional farming integrates socio-economic and environmental dimensions. It redefines the role of agriculture. Additionally, it contributes to balancing agricultural production through the preservation of the natural environment as well as the sustainability of agricultural production and rural communities. On top of that, it fosters economic development by creating jobs and establishing new economic activities within rural communities. In this light, it positively contributes to the retention of the population lying in rural areas, the preservation of cultural heritage and brings farming closer to the demands of society, respectively. Multifunctional farming needs to be aligned with the contemporary technologies in order to grow generally. Comparing these findings with the results of other studies via the international literature, we observe that multifunctional agriculture integrates economic, social and environmental dimensions (Peng et al., 2015; Hediger & Knickel, 2009; Meeus, 1993) bringing agriculture in line with rural citizens'current needs.

It reframes the role of modern agriculture (Losch, 2004) on the basis of the changes required by the new production model (Van der Ploeg & Roep, 2003). It adequately utilises endogenous resources (Potter & Tilzey, 2005). According to Romstad (2002), the key elements of multifunctional farming include the environment, food quality and safety, and the sustainability of rural areas by retaining the local population, sustaining cultural heritage and stimulating the deployment of new economic activities. In order for the multifunctional farming to be developed, it requires the support of modern technological advances (Tohidyan Far & Rezaei-Moghaddam, 2019; (Tohidyan Far & Rezaei-Moghaddam, 2019; Kanniainen & Vesala, 2005; Kreft & Sobel, 2005; Wilson, 2001).

The current research has revealed that the main motivation for setting up an agribusiness is to secure economic flows through the standardisation, processing and production of branded products by the farmers themselves. Communication and digitalisation networks have brought rural areas out of isolation and created a favourable environment for the creation of agri-enterprises. Additionally, the study indicated that sustainable entrepreneurship enhances job creation, incomes and promotes the sustainable development of rural communities. The latter resides In consistency with the findings of existing studies derived from the international literature, where it is evident that sustainable entrepreneurship creates jobs and incomes (Makris et al., 2024; Polas et al., 2022; Dzingirai, 2021; Mbam, & Nwibo, 2013). On top of that, research revealed that communication and digitalisation networks have created an conducive environment for rural enterprises (Makris et al., 2025; Makris et al., 2025; Apostolopoulos et a.l, 2024; Paunović et al., 2024; Masouras, et al., 2024).

Moreover, this study has demonstrated that farmers are motivated to diversify their crops in search of ways to make their economic activities more resilient while increasing their income. However, diversification requires skills and knowledge in digital technologies, financial resources and infrastructure. Certain barriers to diversification include an inefficient institutional framework that creates bureaucracy and ambiguity, difficulties in securing bank loans and the difficulty of accessing support programmes. Diversification drives income generation, retains the population in rural areas and better responds to the challenges of sustainable development. Diversification enables farmers to better respond to the challenges of their sector which is consistent with the findings of other studies in the field (Gittins et al., 2025). Among the motivations for diversification are the pursuit of income growth, farm revitalisation and the development of resilience towards agribusinesses (Lokier et al., 2021; McElwee, 2008; Daskalopoulou & Petrou, 2002). Diversification fosters entrepreneurial activities by developing new products whilst improving rural residents' living conditions (Greenberg et al., 2018). Various studies show that diversification as a strategy is a complex process that reduces risks, creates resilience and economic flows (Benedek et al., 2021; Dai et al., 2019; Meuwissen et al., 2019; Chirico et al., 2011). However, diversification requires expertise by farmers (Sisto et. al., 2018; McElwee & Smith, 2012). It also requires financial, physical and human resources, infrastructure and technologies (Adhikari et al., 2023). Obstacles feature bureaucratic challenges, limited access to grants and difficulties in bank lending (Bonell et al.,

2022; Zhuravlova, 2019). Research has shown that diversification produces family and social benefits (Gittins et al., 2025; Lokier et al., 2021). In this regard, it has the capacity to strengthen family ties, offer incetives to the rural population in order for the latter to be attracted to the countryside utilmately generating incomes and jobs (Lokier et al., 2021; López-i-Gelats et al., 2011; Jervell, 2011).

The present study revealed that there is a lack of information and awareness of European policies and European funding programmes. However, farmers are willing to be informed and consider it necessary to set up information structures on European policies affecting their crops and farm enterprises. The survey also showed that the European funded programmes contribute to the change of production patterns while supporting processing and standardisation. However, joining European funded programmes is a complex process with many bureaucratic obstacles and strong administrative barriers. Correlating these findings with the findings of other studies derived from the international literature, we found that European funding programmes need to be flexible, support sustainable entrepreneurship and create growth opportunities (Ahlmeyer & Volgmann, 2023; Chartier et al., 2021; Michalcewicz-Kaniowska & Zajdel, 2019; Adamowicz & Zwolińska-Ligaj, 2018).

There exist also research revealing that many European programmes fail because they do not take into account the specificities of rural communities and do not address bureaucracy and administrative barriers (Dan & Popescu, 2017; Panyik, 2015; Furmankiewicz, 2015; Ribeiro & Marques, 2002). Research has also indicated that European programmes should take into account the specificities of rural communities, be flexible and meet the needs of production and rural residents (Ahlmeyer & Volgmann, 2023; Chartier et al., 2021).

6. CONCLUSION

The expansion of communication networks and digitalisation in rural areas combined with the effort to change the production model due to climate change have changed the traditional forms of cultivation and marketing of agricultural products. The adoption of multifunctional farming, the development of agribusinesses by farmers themselves and the willingness to diversify crops have created a new driving force for the agricultural sector. In this light, European support policies are crucial despite the existing obstacles. European programmes are helping to change the way in which agriculture is produced and to make it sustainable. On top of that, activities complementary to agricultural production, such as agricultural entrepreneurship, are increasingly linked to diversification, which strengthens agricultural production. EU policies for the agricultural sector are accompanied by funded programmes in the direction of sustainable rural development. Notably, many of the European policies have not been effective because a comprehensive and long-term vision for the countryside has been lacking. This integrated long-term vision "The EU rural vision" with a time horizon of 2040 was implemented in 2021. However, the survey showed that the rural world is not informed properly about this long-term vision.

The current chapter adds to the international literature on multifunctional agriculture, agribusiness and crop diversification in relation to European policies and European funded programmes. The findings of the present research are useful for those involved in agricultural sector policies at European, national and local level. Simultaneously, the findings are useful for farmers themselves and for students who will in the future be involved in the agricultural sector. Like any research, this research is not exempt from limitations. This research examines multifunctional farming, agribusiness, crop diversification and current European policies through the perspective and experiences of farmers. However, future research should also approach these issues from the perspective of policy makers in the agricultural sector.

REFERENCES

Adamowicz, M., & Zwolińska-Ligaj, M. (2018). New concepts for rural development in the strategies and policies of the European Union. *Economic and Regional Studies/Studia Ekonomiczne i Regionalne, 11*(3), 7-31.

Adhikari, L., Komarek, A. M., de Voil, P., & Rodriguez, D. (2023). A framework for the assessment of farm diversification options in broadacre agriculture. *Agricultural Systems, 210*, 103724. DOI: 10.1016/j.agsy.2023.103724

Agoraki, K. K., Deirmentzoglou, G. A., Psychalis, M., & Apostolopoulos, S. (2024). Types of Innovation and Sustainable Development: Evidence from Medium-and Large-Sized Firms. [IJITM]. *International Journal on Management of Innovation & Technology, 21*(02), 1–18. DOI: 10.1142/S0219877024500135

Ahlmeyer, F., & Volgmann, K. (2023). What Can We Expect for the Development of Rural Areas in Europe?—Trends of the Last Decade and Their Opportunities for Rural Regeneration. *Sustainability (Basel), 15*(6), 5485. DOI: 10.3390/su15065485

Al-Busaidi, Z. Q. (2008). Qualitative research and its uses in health care. *Sultan Qaboos University Medical Journal, 8*(1), 11–19. DOI: 10.18295/2075-0528.2688

Alonso, I. B., & Pozas, B. M. (2024). Following the circular economy in European rural municipalities through the Spanish Urban Agenda. *Ecological Economics, 224*, 108263. DOI: 10.1016/j.ecolecon.2024.108263

Anderson, A., McElwee, G., & Vesala, K. (2006). Developing the entrepreneurial skills of farmers: Some myths explored. *International Journal of Entrepreneurial Behaviour & Research, 12*(1).

Apostolopoulos, N., Al-Dajani, H., Holt, D., Jones, P., & Newbery, R. (2018). Entrepreneurship and the sustainable development goals. In *Entrepreneurship and the sustainable development goals* (pp. 1–7). Emerald Publishing Limited. DOI: 10.1108/S2040-724620180000008005

Apostolopoulos, N., Liargovas, P., Stavroyiannis, S., Makris, I., Apostolopoulos, S., Petropoulos, D., & Anastasopoulou, E. (2020b). Sustaining rural areas, rural tourism enterprises and EU development policies: A multi-layer conceptualisation of the obstacles in Greece. *Sustainability (Basel), 12*(18), 7687. DOI: 10.3390/su12187687

Apostolopoulos, N., Ratten, V., Stavroyiannis, S., Makris, I., Apostolopoulos, S., & Liargovas, P. (2020a). Rural health enterprises in the EU context: A systematic literature review and research agenda. *Journal of Enterprising Communities: People and Places in the Global Economy, 14*(4), 563–582. DOI: 10.1108/JEC-04-2020-0070

Apostolopoulos, S., Makris, I., Macaulay, B., & Dimitrakopoulos, P. (2024). Private Enterprises and Innovative Interventions in Long-Term Care for Older People: Insights Into Residual Stereotypes of Greek Rural Areas. In *European Conference on Innovation and Entrepreneurship* (pp. 54-61). Academic Conferences International Limited. DOI: 10.34190/ecie.19.1.2402

Aronica, M., Cracolici, M. F., Insolda, D., Piacentino, D., & Tosi, S. (2023). A long-term vision for rural areas: A case study of Sicilian farms. *Regional Studies, Regional Science*, *10*(1), 640–658. DOI: 10.1080/21681376.2023.2225569

Arru, B., Furesi, R., Madau, F. A., & Pulina, P. (2021). Economic performance of agritourism: An analysis of farms located in a less favoured area in Italy. *Agricultural and Food Economics*, *9*(1), 1–21. DOI: 10.1186/s40100-021-00199-z

Asmit, B., Simatupang, T. M., Rudito, B., & Novani, S. (2024). Uncovering the building blocks of rural entrepreneurship: A comprehensive framework for mapping the components of rural entrepreneurial ecosystems. *Heliyon*, *10*(1), e24139. DOI: 10.1016/j.heliyon.2024.e24139

Bannor, R. K., Ros-Tonen, M. A., Mensah, P. O., Derkyi, M., & Nassah, V. F. (2021). Entrepreneurial behaviour among non-timber forest product-growing farmers in Ghana: An analysis in support of a reforestation policy. *Forest Policy and Economics*, *122*, 102331. DOI: 10.1016/j.forpol.2020.102331

Barot, S., Allard, V., Cantarel, A., Enjalbert, J., Gauffreteau, A., Goldringer, I., Lata, J.-C., Le Roux, X., Niboyet, A., & Porcher, E. (2017). Designing mixtures of varieties for multifunctional agriculture with the help of ecology. A review. *Agronomy for Sustainable Development*, *37*(2), 1–20. DOI: 10.1007/s13593-017-0418-x

Bartolini, F., Andreoli, M., & Brunori, G. (2014). Explaining determinants of the on-farm diversification: Empirical evidence from Tuscany region. *Bio-Based and Applied Economics*, *3*(2), 137–157.

Belletti, G., Brunori, G., Marescotti, A., & Rossi, A. (2003). Multifunctionality and rural development: a multilevel approach.

Benedek, Z., Fertő, I., Galamba Marreiros, C., Aguiar, P. M. D., Pocol, C. B., Čechura, L., Põder, A., Pääso, P., & Bakucs, Z. (2021). Farm diversification as a potential success factor for small-scale farmers constrained by COVID-related lockdown. Contributions from a survey conducted in four European countries during the first wave of COVID-19. *PLoS One*, *16*(5), e0251715. DOI: 10.1371/journal.pone.0251715

Bonell, F. E., & Vaccaro, I. (2022). Techno-herds and cyborg-shepherds in the age of spectacularized bucolism: What lies behind the postcard. *Journal of Rural Studies*, *95*, 40–49. DOI: 10.1016/j.jrurstud.2022.07.025

Bosworth, G. (2012). Characterising rural businesses–Tales from the paperman. *Journal of Rural Studies*, *28*(4), 499–506. DOI: 10.1016/j.jrurstud.2012.07.002

Botsiou, M., & Dagdilelis, V. (2013). Aspects of incorporation of ICT in the Greek agricultural enterprises: The case of a prefecture. *Procedia Technology*, *8*, 387–396. DOI: 10.1016/j.protcy.2013.11.051

Brummel, R. F., & Nelson, K. C. (2014). Does multifunctionality matter to US farmers? Farmer motivations and conceptions of multifunctionality in dairy systems. *Journal of Environmental Management*, *146*, 451–462. DOI: 10.1016/j.jenvman.2014.07.034

Cachia, M., & Millward, L. (2011). The telephone medium and semi-structured interviews: A complementary fit. *Qualitative Research in Organizations and Management*, *6*(3), 265–277. DOI: 10.1108/17465641111188420

Carayannis, E., Jones, P., Liargovas, P., & Apostolopoulos, N. (2020). Entrepreneurship and the European Union policies after 60 years of common European vision: Regional and spatial perspectives. *Journal of Small Business and Entrepreneurship*, *32*(6), 517–522. DOI: 10.1080/08276331.2020.1769883

Cardillo, C., Cimino, O., De Rosa, M., & Francescone, M. (2023). The evolution of multifunctional agriculture in Italy. *Sustainability (Basel)*, *15*(14), 11403. DOI: 10.3390/su151411403

Carmela Annosi, M., Brunetta, F., Capo, F., & Heideveld, L. (2020). Digitalization in the agri-food industry: The relationship between technology and sustainable development. *Management Decision*, *58*(8), 1737–1757. DOI: 10.1108/MD-09-2019-1328

Chartier, O., Salle, E., Kull, M., Miller, D., Nieto, E., Vestergård, L., & Iadecola, F. (2021). *Long-yerm vision of rural areas: contribution from the SHERPA science-society-policy platforms: SHERPA position paper*. SHERPA.

Chirico, F., Sirmon, D. G., Sciascia, S., & Mazzola, P. (2011). Resource orchestration in family firms: Investigating how entrepreneurial orientation, generational involvement, and participative strategy affect performance. *Strategic Entrepreneurship Journal*, *5*(4), 307–326. DOI: 10.1002/sej.121

Dai, X., Wu, Z., Fan, Y., Li, B., Yang, Z., Nan, B., & Bi, X. (2019). Characteristics and determinants of livelihood diversification of different household types in far Northwestern China. *Sustainability (Basel)*, *12*(1), 64. DOI: 10.3390/su12010064

Dan, M. C., & Popescu, C. (2017). Entrepreneurship in the rural areas of Romania. The impact of the 2007-2013 EU funding programmes. In *Proceedings of the International Conference on Business Excellence* (Vol. 11, No. 1, pp. 1129-1136). DOI: 10.1515/picbe-2017-0116

Daskalopoulou, I., & Petrou, A. (2002). Utilising a farm typology to identify potential adopters of alternative farming activities in Greek agriculture. *Journal of Rural Studies, 18*(1), 95–103. DOI: 10.1016/S0743-0167(01)00027-4

De Rosa, M., McElwee, G., & Smith, R. (2019). Farm diversification strategies in response to rural policy: A case from rural Italy. *Land Use Policy, 81*, 291–301. DOI: 10.1016/j.landusepol.2018.11.006

Deakin, H., & Wakefield, K. (2014). Skype interviewing: Reflections of two PhD researchers. *Qualitative Research, 14*(5), 603–616. DOI: 10.1177/1468794113488126

DeJonckheere, M., & Vaughn, L. M. (2019). Semistructured interviewing in primary care research: A balance of relationship and rigour. *Family Medicine and Community Health, 7*(2), e000057. DOI: 10.1136/fmch-2018-000057

Denzin, N. K., Lincoln, Y.S., (2005). Introduction: The discipline and practice of qualitative research.

Dias, C. S., Rodrigues, R. G., & Ferreira, J. J. (2019). What's new in the research on agricultural entrepreneurship? *Journal of Rural Studies, 65*, 99–115. DOI: 10.1016/j.jrurstud.2018.11.003

Drakopoulou-Dodd, S., McDonald, S., McElwee, G., & Smith, R. (2014). A Bourdieuan analysis of qualitative authorship in entrepreneurship scholarship. *Journal of Small Business Management, 52*(4), 633–654. DOI: 10.1111/jsbm.12125

Dzingirai, M. (2021). The role of entrepreneurship in reducing poverty in agricultural communities. *Journal of enterprising communities. People and Places in the Global Economy, 15*(5), 665–683.

European Commission, (2021). A long-term Vision for the EU's Rural Areas-Towards stronger, connected, resilient and prosperous rural by 2040, SWD (2021) 166 final.

Filatotchev, I., Ireland, R. D., & Stahl, G. K. (2022). Contextualizing management research: An open systems perspective. *Journal of Management Studies, 59*(4), 1036–1056. DOI: 10.1111/joms.12754

Fossey, E., Harvey, C., McDermott, F., & Davidson, L. (2002). Understanding and evaluating qualitative research. *The Australian and New Zealand Journal of Psychiatry, 36*(6), 717–732. DOI: 10.1046/j.1440-1614.2002.01100.x

Furmankiewicz, M.,Knieć, W., & Atterton, J. (2015). Rural governance in the new EU member states: The experience of the Polish LEADER+ Pilot Programme (2004–2008). *Governance in transition*, 133-153.

Gargano, G., Licciardo, F., Verrascina, M., & Zanetti, B. (2021). The agroecological approach as a model for multifunctional agriculture and farming towards the European Green Deal 2030—Some evidence from the Italian experience. *Sustainability (Basel)*, *13*(4), 2215. DOI: 10.3390/su13042215

Gioia, D. A., Corley, K. G., & Hamilton, A. L. (2013). Seeking qualitative rigor in inductive research: Notes on the Gioia methodology. *Organizational Research Methods*, *16*(1), 15–31. DOI: 10.1177/1094428112452151

Gittins, P., Apostolopoulos, S., Anastasopoulou, E. E., & Apostolopoulos, N. (2025). Responding to Greece's constrained agricultural context: Farm diversification strategies used by family farmers. *Journal of Rural Studies*, *113*, 103522. DOI: 10.1016/j.jrurstud.2024.103522

Gittins, P., & McElwee, G. (2023). Constrained rural entrepreneurship: Upland farmer responses to the socio-political challenges in England's beef and sheep sector. *Journal of Rural Studies*, *104*, 103141. DOI: 10.1016/j.jrurstud.2023.103141

Greenberg, Z., Farja, Y., & Gimmon, E. (2018). Embeddedness and growth of small businesses in rural regions. *Journal of Rural Studies*, *62*, 174–182. DOI: 10.1016/j.jrurstud.2018.07.016

Hediger, W., & Knickel, K. (2009). Multifunctionality and sustainability of agriculture and rural areas: A welfare economics perspective. *Journal of Environmental Policy and Planning*, *11*(4), 291–313. DOI: 10.1080/15239080903412453

Hrustek, L. (2020). Sustainability driven by agriculture through digital transformation. *Sustainability (Basel)*, *12*(20), 8596. DOI: 10.3390/su12208596

Huang, J., Tichit, M., Poulot, M., Darly, S., Li, S., Petit, C., & Aubry, C. (2015). Comparative review of multifunctionality and ecosystem services in sustainable agriculture. *Journal of Environmental Management*, *149*, 138–147. DOI: 10.1016/j.jenvman.2014.10.020

Iakovidou, O., Koutsouris, A., & Partalidou, M. (2002). The development of rural tourism in Greece, through the initiative Leader II: The case of northern and central Chalkidiki. *A Mediterranean Journal of Economics, Agriculture and Environment. New Medit. Journal*, *1*(4), 35–38.

Ilbery, B. W. (1991). Farm diversification as an adjustment strategy on the urban fringe of the West Midlands. *Journal of Rural Studies, 7*(3), 207–218. DOI: 10.1016/0743-0167(91)90085-7

Javadian, G., Dobratz, C., Gupta, A., Gupta, V. K., & Martin, J. A. (2020). Qualitative Research in Entrepreneurship Studies: A State-of-Science. *The Journal of Entrepreneurship, 29*(2), 223–258. DOI: 10.1177/0971355720930564

Jervell, A. M. (2011). The family farm as a premise for entrepreneurship. In *The handbook of research on entrepreneurship in agriculture and rural development.* Edward Elgar Publishing. DOI: 10.4337/9780857933249.00009

Kallio, H., Pietilä, A. M., Johnson, M., & Kangasniemi, M. (2016). Systematic methodological review: Developing a framework for a qualitative semi-structured interview guide. *Journal of Advanced Nursing, 72*(12), 2954–2965. DOI: 10.1111/jan.13031

Kanniainen, V., & Vesala, T. (2005). Entrepreneurship and labor market institutions. *Economic Modelling, 22*(5), 828–847. DOI: 10.1016/j.econmod.2005.05.002

Karagianni, M., Georgakopoulou, S., & Delitheou, V. (2019). Agrotourism: A lever for rural development based on the cultural reserve of Greece. In *Smart Tourism as a Driver for Culture and Sustainability: Fifth International Conference IACuDiT, Athens 2018* (pp. 193-206). Springer International Publishing. DOI: 10.1007/978-3-030-03910-3_14

Knickel, K., Renting, H., & Van der Ploeg, J. D. (2004). Multifunctionality in European agriculture. *Sustaining agriculture and the rural economy: Governance, policy and Multifunctionality. Edward Elgar Publishing Inc*, 81-103.

Knierim, A., Kernecker, M., Erdle, K., Kraus, T., Borges, F., & Wurbs, A. (2019). Smart farming technology innovations–Insights and reflections from the German Smart-AKIS hub. *NJAS Wageningen Journal of Life Sciences, 90*(1), 100314. DOI: 10.1016/j.njas.2019.100314

Korsgaard, S., Müller, S., & Tanvig, H. W. (2015). Rural entrepreneurship or entrepreneurship in the rural–between place and space. *International Journal of Entrepreneurial Behaviour & Research, 21*(1), 5–26. DOI: 10.1108/IJEBR-11-2013-0205

Kreft, S. F., & Sobel, R. S. (2005). Public policy, entrepreneurship, and economic freedom. *The Cato Journal, 25*, 595.

Kusio, T., & Fiore, M. (2022). Which Stakeholders' Sector Matters in Rural Development? That Is the Problem. *Energies, 15*(2), 454. DOI: 10.3390/en15020454

Kusio, T., Kudełko, J., Borges, A., Delic, A., & Stroila, I. (2022). Are there any differences in rural development challenges within European countries? Social and economic contexts from EU rural leaders. *The International Food and Agribusiness Management Review*, *25*(5), 737–756. DOI: 10.22434/IFAMR2021.0147

Lans, T., Van Galen, M. A., Verstegen, J. A. A. M., Biemans, H. J. A., & Mulder, M. (2014). Searching for entrepreneurs among small business ownermanagers in agriculture. *NJAS Wageningen Journal of Life Sciences*, *68*(1), 41–51. DOI: 10.1016/j.njas.2013.12.001

Léon, Y. (2005). Rural development in Europe: A research frontier for agricultural economists. *European Review of Agriculture Economics*, *32*(3), 301–317. DOI: 10.1093/eurrag/jbi012

Lokier, J., Morris, W., & Thomas, D. (2021). Farm shop diversification: Producer motivations and consumer attitudes. *International Journal of Entrepreneurship and Innovation*, *22*(4), 215–228. DOI: 10.1177/1465750320985364

López-i-Gelats, F., Milán, M. J., & Bartolomé, J. (2011). Is farming enough in mountain areas? Farm diversification in the Pyrenees. *Land Use Policy*, *28*(4), 783–791. DOI: 10.1016/j.landusepol.2011.01.005

Losch, B. (2004). Debating the multifunctionality of agriculture: From trade negotiations to development policies by the South. *Journal of Agrarian Change*, *4*(3), 336–360. DOI: 10.1111/j.1471-0366.2004.00082.x

Makris, I., Apostolopoulos, S., & Dimitrakopoulos, P. (2024). Analysing supporting mechanisms, cultural shaping and incentives for circular economy: The case of local governments. *Interdisciplinary Environmental Review*, *23*(3), 218–235. DOI: 10.1504/IER.2024.139254

Makris, I. A., Apostolopoulos, S., & Masouras, A. (2025). EU policies and female entrepreneurship in Greek rural areas in relation to digital challenges. In *Real-World Tools and Scenarios for Entrepreneurship Exploration* (pp. 203–222). IGI Global.

Martinho, V. J. P. D. (2020). Agricultural entrepreneurship in the European Union: Contributions for a sustainable development. *Applied Sciences (Basel, Switzerland)*, *10*(6), 2080. DOI: 10.3390/app10062080

Masouras, A., Anastasiadou, S., Constantelou, A., & Apostolopoulos, S. (Eds.). (2024). *Real-world Tools and Scenarios for Entrepreneurship Exploration*. IGI Global. DOI: 10.4018/979-8-3693-3100-2

Mbam, B. N., & Nwibo, S. U. (2013). Entrepreneurship development as a strategy for poverty alleviation among farming households in Igbo-Eze North Local Government Area of Enugu State, Nigeria. *Greener Journal of Agricultural Sciences*, *3*(10), 736–742. DOI: 10.15580/GJAS.2013.3.100613883

McElwee, G. (2008). A taxonomy of entrepreneurial farmers. *International Journal of Entrepreneurship and Small Business*, *6*(3), 465–478. DOI: 10.1504/IJESB.2008.019139

McElwee, G., & Smith, R. (2012). Classifying the strategic capability of farmers: A segmentation framework. *International Journal of Entrepreneurial Venturing*, *4*(2), 111–131. DOI: 10.1504/IJEV.2012.046517

Meert, H., Van Huylenbroeck, G., Vernimmen, T., Bourgeois, M., & van Hecke, E. (2005). Farm household survival strategies and diversification on marginal farms. *Journal of Rural Studies*, *21*(1), 81–97. DOI: 10.1016/j.jrurstud.2004.08.007

Meeus, J. H. (1993). The transformation of agricultural landscapes in Western Europe. *The Science of the Total Environment*, *129*(1-2), 171–190. DOI: 10.1016/0048-9697(93)90169-7

Meuwissen, M. P., Feindt, P. H., Spiegel, A., Termeer, C. J., Mathijs, E., De Mey, Y., & Reidsma, P. (2019). A framework to assess the resilience of farming systems. *Agricultural Systems*, *176*, 102656. DOI: 10.1016/j.agsy.2019.102656

Michalcewicz-Kaniowska, M., & Zajdel, M. (2019). Rural development in European Union policy. *Economic science for rural development, 50*, 140-146.

Milestad, R., Dedieu, B., Darnhofer, I., & Bellon, S. (2012). Farms and farmers facing change: The adaptive approach. In Darnhofer, I., Gibbon, D., & Dedieu, B. (Eds.), *Farming Systems Research into the 21st Century: The new Dynamic* (pp. 365–385). Springer. DOI: 10.1007/978-94-007-4503-2_16

Morgan, S. L., Marsden, T., Miele, M., & Morley, A. (2010). Agricultural multifunctionality and farmers' entrepreneurial skills: A study of Tuscan and Welsh farmers. *Journal of Rural Studies*, *26*(2), 116–129. DOI: 10.1016/j.jrurstud.2009.09.002

Moser, A., & Korstjens, I. (2018). Series: Practical guidance to qualitative research. Part 3: Sampling, data collection and analysis. *The European Journal of General Practice*, *24*(1), 9–18. DOI: 10.1080/13814788.2017.1375091

Mulibana, L., & Tshikovhi, N. (2024). Rural Entrepreneurship and Innovation in BRICS Economies: Secondary Evidence from Rural Areas in South Africa. *Sustainability (Basel)*, *16*(6), 2408. DOI: 10.3390/su16062408

Nedilska, L., & Oleniuk, D. (2020). Agribusiness digitalization: Trends and funding sources. *Scientific Horizons*, *6*(91), 26–32. DOI: 10.33249/2663-2144-2020-91-6-26-32

Neergaard, H., & Ulhøi, J. P. (Eds.). (2007). *Handbook of qualitative research methods in entrepreneurship*. Edward Elgar Publishing. DOI: 10.4337/9781847204387

Oltean, R. C., & Arion, F. H. (2023). The European rural development vision in Romanian context, 72-75

Panyik, E. (2015). Rural tourism governance: Determinants of policy-makers' support for tourism development. *Tourism Planning & Development*, *12*(1), 48–72. DOI: 10.1080/21568316.2014.960603

Patel, B., & Chavda, K. (2013). Rural entrepreneurship in India: Challenge and problems. *International Journal of Advance Research in Computer Science and Management Studies*, *1*(2).

Patton, M. Q. (1990). *Qualitative evaluation and research methods*. SAGE Publications, inc.

Paunović, I., Apostolopoulos, S., Miljković, I. B., & Stojanović, M. (2024). Sustainable rural healthcare entrepreneurship: A case study of Serbia. *Sustainability (Basel)*, *16*(3), 1143. DOI: 10.3390/su16031143

Peng, J., Liu, Z., Liu, Y., Hu, X., & Wang, A. (2015). Multifunctionality assessment of urban agriculture in Beijing City, China. *The Science of the Total Environment*, *537*, 343–351. DOI: 10.1016/j.scitotenv.2015.07.136

Phillipson, J., Tiwasing, P., Gorton, M., Maioli, S., Newbery, R., & Turner, R. (2019). Shining a spotlight on small rural businesses: How does their performance compare with urban? *Journal of Rural Studies*, *68*, 230–239. DOI: 10.1016/j.jrurstud.2018.09.017

Polas, M. R. H., Raju, V., Muhibbullah, M., & Tabash, M. I. (2022). Rural women characteristics and sustainable entrepreneurial intention: A road to economic growth in Bangladesh. *Journal of Enterprising Communities: People and Places in the Global Economy*, *16*(3), 421–449. DOI: 10.1108/JEC-10-2020-0183

Poojari, M., Hanumanthappa, H., Prasad, C. D., Jathanna, H. M., Ksheerasagar, A. R., Shetty, P., Shanmugam, B. K., & Vasudev, H. (2024). Computational modelling for the manufacturing of solar-powered multifunctional agricultural robot. [IJIDeM]. *International Journal on Interactive Design and Manufacturing*, *18*(8), 5725–5736. DOI: 10.1007/s12008-023-01291-y

Potter, C., & Tilzey, M. (2005). Agricultural policy discourses in the European post-Fordist transition: Neoliberalism, neomercantilism and multifunctionality. *Progress in Human Geography*, *29*(5), 581–600. DOI: 10.1191/0309132505ph569oa

Pyysiäinen, J., Anderson, A., McElwee, G., & Vesala, K. (2006). Developing the entrepreneurial skills of farmers: Some myths explored. *International Journal of Entrepreneurial Behaviour & Research*, *12*(1), 21–39. DOI: 10.1108/13552550610644463

Ragkos, A., Koutsou, S., Theodoridis, A., Manousidis, T., & Lagka, V. (2018). Labor management strategies in facing the economic crisis. Evidence from Greek livestock farms. *New Medit*, *17*(1), 59–72. DOI: 10.30682/nm1801f

Refai, D., Elkafrawi, N., & Gittins, P. (2024). Creating a sustainable ripple in rural entrepreneurship–the case of Deserttulip in resource-constrained rural Jordan. *International Journal of Entrepreneurial Behaviour & Research*, *30*(1), 180–199. DOI: 10.1108/IJEBR-02-2023-0168

Refai, D., & McElwee, G. (2023). Refugee subentrepreneurship: The emergence of a liquid cage. *Work, Employment and Society*, *37*(4), 1032–1051. DOI: 10.1177/09500170211062817

Renting, H., Rossing, W. A., Groot, J. C., Van der Ploeg, J. D., Laurent, C., Perraud, D., Stobbelaar, D. J., & Van Ittersum, M. K. (2009). Exploring multifunctional agriculture. A review of conceptual approaches and prospects for an integrative transitional framework. *Journal of Environmental Management*, *90*, S112–S123. DOI: 10.1016/j.jenvman.2008.11.014

Ribeiro, M., & Marques, C. (2002). Rural tourism and the development of less favoured areas—Between rhetoric and practice. *International Journal of Tourism Research*, *4*(3), 211–220. DOI: 10.1002/jtr.377

Romstad, E. (2002). Policies for promoting public goods in agriculture. Paper presented at the 10th EAAE Congress in Zaragoza, Spain, 28-31

Saxena, S. (2012). Problems Faced By Rural Entrepreneurs and Remedies to Solve. *Journal of Business and Management*, *3*(1), 23–29.

Seuneke, P., Lans, T., & Wiskerke, J. S. (2013). Moving beyond entrepreneurial skills: Key factors driving entrepreneurial learning in multifunctional agriculture. *Journal of Rural Studies*, *32*, 208–219. DOI: 10.1016/j.jrurstud.2013.06.001

Sisto. R., Lopolito, A, van Vliet, M. 2018. Stakeholder participation in planning rural development strategies: Land Use Policy 7- 442-450.

Sivini, S., & Vitale, A. (2023). Multifunctional and Agroecological Agriculture as Pathways of Generational Renewal in Italian Rural Areas. *Sustainability (Basel), 15*(7), 5990. DOI: 10.3390/su15075990

Smit, A. B. (2004). Changing external conditions require high levels of entrepreneurship in agriculture. In *XV International Symposium on Horticultural Economics and Management 655* (pp. 167-173). DOI: 10.17660/ActaHortic.2004.655.21

Song, B., Robinson, G. M., & Bardsley, D. K. (2020). Measuring multifunctional agricultural landscapes. *Land (Basel), 9*(8), 260. DOI: 10.3390/land9080260

Sott, M. K., Furstenau, L. B., Kipper, L. M., Giraldo, F. D., Lopez-Robles, J. R., Cobo, M. J., Zahid, A., Abbasi, Q. H., & Imran, M. A. (2020). Precision techniques and agriculture 4.0 technologies to promote sustainability in the coffee sector: State of the art, challenges and future trends. *IEEE Access : Practical Innovations, Open Solutions, 8*, 149854–149867. DOI: 10.1109/ACCESS.2020.3016325

Stathopoulou, S., Psaltopoulos, D., & Skuras, D. (2004). Rural entrepreneurship in Europe: A research framework and agenda. *International Journal of Entrepreneurial Behaviour & Research, 10*(6), 404–425. DOI: 10.1108/13552550410564725

Tohidyan Far, S., & Rezaei-Moghaddam, K. (2019). Multifunctional agriculture: An approach for entrepreneurship development of agricultural sector. *Journal of Global Entrepreneurship Research, 9*(1), 1–23. DOI: 10.1186/s40497-019-0148-4

Tuli, F. (2010). The basis of distinction between quantitative and qualitative in social science: Reflection on ontological, epistemological and methodological perspectives. *Ethiopian Journal of Education and Sciences, 6*(1), 97–108.

Van Burg, E., Cornelissen, J., Stam, W., Jack, S., (2020). Advancing Qualitative Entrepreneurship Research: Leveraging Methodological Plurality for Achieving Scholarly Impact.

Van der Ploeg, J. D., & Roep, D. (2003). Multifunctionality and rural development: the actual situation in Europe. *Multifunctional agriculture: a new paradigm for European agriculture and rural development, 3*, 37-54.

Vásáry, V., Biró, S., Kis, M., & Varga, E. (2021). Long-Term Vision For Rural Areas. *Multidiszciplináris kihívások, sokszínű válaszok-Gazdálkodás-és Szervezéstudományi folyóirat*, (1), 51-77.

Vásáry, V., & Szabolcs, B. (2020). Long-term vision of rural areas in Hungary, focusing on foresights. *Rural Areas and Development, 17*, 90–104.

Vesala, H. T., & Vesala, K. M. (2010). Entrepreneurs and producers: Identities of Finnish farmers in 2001 and 2006. *Journal of Rural Studies*, *26*(1), 21–30. DOI: 10.1016/j.jrurstud.2009.06.001

Vik, J., & McElwee, G. (2011). Diversification and the entrepreneurial motivations of farmers in Norway. *Journal of Small Business Management*, *49*(3), 390–410. DOI: 10.1111/j.1540-627X.2011.00327.x

Volanen, R. (2000). For Harmony of functions: On governance of multifunctionality and its scientific support–the point of view of the ecological function. In *Seminar "Science and Governance: CAP and Multifunctionality of Agriculture within the European Research Area* (pp. 23-24).

Welter, F., Baker, T., Audretsch, D. B., & Gartner, W. B. (2017). Everyday entrepreneurship-a call for entrepreneurship research to embrace entrepreneurial diversity. *Entrepreneurship Theory and Practice*, *41*(3), 311–321. DOI: 10.1111/etap.12258

Wilson, G. A. (2001). From productivism to post-productivism… and back again? Exploring the (un) changed natural and mental landscapes of European agriculture. *Transactions of the Institute of British Geographers*, *26*(1), 77–102. DOI: 10.1111/1475-5661.00007

Wu, A., Liu, Y., & Song, D. (2021). The Impact of Regional Entrepreneurial Ecosystem on Farmers' Performance and Efficiency-Empirical Evidence from Zhejiang Province. *Agricultural Technology Economy*, (1), 12.

Yin, R. K. (1994). Discovering the future of the case study. Method in evaluation research. *Evaluation Practice*, *15*(3), 283–290.

Zhuravlova, T. (2019). BANK LENDING OF AGRICULTURAL ENTERPRISES. *Інвестиції: практика та досвід*, (23), 35-41.

Chapter 7
Importance of Promotion for Development of Rural Tourism and Agricultural Entrepreneurship in the Republic of Serbia

Gordana Radović
https://orcid.org/0000-0001-9770-6306
Institute of Agricultural Economics, Belgrade, Serbia

Predrag Miroslav Vuković
https://orcid.org/0000-0002-4723-9815
Instite of Agricultural Economics, Belgrade, Serbia

ABSTRACT

Serbia has high-quality natural, social and human resources for the development of rural tourism. The problem of rural tourism is that supply is located in rural areas and demand is located in city centers. Role of marketing is to connect supply and demand. Until now demand for rural tourism is mostly come from domestic market, but the interest of tourists come from a broad. The promotion of rural tourism, as an additional activity on agricultural farms, is important in many ways. Primarily for the purpose of increasing tourist traffic, but also the development of agrarian entrepreneurship, increasing the income of agricultural farms, as well as stopping process of depopulation rural areas in the Serbia. Nowadays exsist many maketing tools how to communcate opposite sides of market – supply and demand. In order to

DOI: 10.4018/979-8-3373-2898-0.ch007

develop promotion in rural tourism, adequate investments are also needed. The aim of the paper is to analyze the current forms of promotion of rural tourism, as well as to present development opportunities in this important segment of the marketing mix.

INTRODUCTION

Modern trends in tourism are increasingly moving away from concept of mass tourism, which involves vacations at sea or mountain tourist destinations. Instead, efforts are being made to include all forms of tourist demand in order to develop tourism as successfully as possible. Therefore, countries and destinations that do not have the natural conditions for the development of mass tourism are seeking their place in the market by offering alternative forms of tourism types. One of such forms of tourism is rural tourism (Vuković, P. et al 2015). Rural tourism is a common name for all forms of tourism that can take place in rural areas. According to the definition of rural tourism stated in the Encyclopedia of Tourism (Jafari & Xiao, 2024), it was pointed out that the rural area is the basic resource for the development of rural tourism. In everyday use, the name "village tourism" is also used as a synonym for "rural tourism". We believe that this is not entirely correct. The difference is not terminological, but essential. Rural tourism means only tourism in villages. Rural tourism includes tourism in smaller places, in which the population density does not exceed 150 inhabitants per km^2, that is, which are considered rural areas in accordance with the Organization for Economic Cooperation and Development (OECD) categorization. Different forms of rural tourism are defined according to the reasons for which tourists come to rural areas, and there are more than 50 of them today. The most represented is agrotourism, which includes the stay of tourists on agricultural farms, as well as the possibility for tourists to get involved in agricultural work performed by their hosts. A common characteristic for all forms of rural tourism is seasonal demand, which conditions the low occupancy of capacities on an annual basis. Therefore, the role of marketing in the development of rural tourism is very important, especially continuous and adequate promotion.

Rural tourism in Europe began to develop more intensively in the 70s of the 20th century for two reasons. The first reason was related to the increasingly pronounced depopulation of rural areas and the need to ensure the economic development of these areas - rural development. The second reason was related to the increasingly pronounced tourist demand at the global level for a differentiated tourist offer, that is, to the decreasing demand for mass tourism. Tourist demand is directed towards rural areas, because they are the guardians of traditions and treasures of culture, customs, habits, way of life and diet of certain peoples. The development of rural tourism is a long-term process. Today, France has the largest rural tourism offer in Europe, i.e. the largest number of beds, but it took more than 50 years for this country to reach its current level of development.

The successful development of rural tourism in recent decades has been recorded in Austria, Slovenia, Croatia, Hungary and Romania. In these countries, the development of rural tourism was implemented with strategic and financial support from the state, which included support in education and promotion, as well as in the organization of rural tourism, but also continuous administrative support (Radović, 2017). For the purpose of financing the development of rural tourism, the full and adequate use of funds from the pre-accession funds of the European Union is of utmost importance, as was the case in Romania (Radović, et al., 2024). In this country, special attention is paid to the development of rural tourism in certain areas. A group of authors (Popescu et al., 2022) cite the example of the Moieciu area, where the number of accommodation capacities in tourism, especially in rural tourism, has doubled in the last decade. In the current period, the development of rural tourism is also the result of an interactive approach, i.e., respecting the opinions of tourists on which direction the development of rural tourism should be directed, i.e., on which segments the emphasis should be placed. As the cited authors state, tourists believe that in the coming period, the development of rural tourism in this area should, among other things, be based on the development of tourist content and an increase in promotional activities. Non-boarding (non - pansion) activities that are offered in tourist destinations enable new experiences and have a positive effect on the appropriate degree of satisfaction during the stay, thus influencing the decision of tourists to visit a certain place, i.e. to repeat their experience, which in the long term has a positive effect on the competitiveness of the destination itself. (Vuković et al., 2024)

A significant incentive for the development of rural tourism in the European Union was the measures of the Common Agricultural Policy (CAP) defined within the planning document AGENDA 2000. This planning document highlighted the importance of the development of non-agricultural activities in rural areas, and within which the importance of rural tourism was particularly emphasized. AGENDA 2000 also defined the amendments to the Common Agricultural Policy (CAP), which established the so-called second pillar (second pillar) within which a set of measures for financing rural development was defined. The latest amendments to the Common Agricultural Policy of the European Union have placed the emphasis on sustainable rural development and environmental protection (EP, 2023). Rural tourism should also play a significant role in contributing to the implementation of the Green Deal, as a key EU strategy in the current period (EC, 2021). This strategy has as its main goal to achieve climate neutrality by 2050. The contribution of rural tourism should be in terms of its sustainable development in all segments: environmental, economic and social. The above documents significantly guide the development of rural tourism, as well as tourism in general. It is known, and as the group of authors (Buchalis et al., 2023) points out, that tourism plays a decisive role in the implementation of sustainable development goals and providing income for the sustainable economic development of rural areas. The results of research by Radović et al. (2020a), which was carried out in Serbia, indicate that parallel development of tourism and agriculture is necessary in order to ensure the economic sustainability of rural tourist households.

Rural areas cover 79.5% of the total territory of the Republic of Serbia (IPARD III 2021-2027) and there lives 38% of the total population, according to the results of the last population census (RIS-TPS-2022). According to the results of the last Agricultural Census, which was carried out in 2023, there are a total of 508,365 agricultural holdings in Serbia, of which 99.6% are family agricultural holdings, and the average size of an agricultural holding is 6.4 ha (RIS-RCA-2023). This is a small size of an agricultural holding for the development of profitable agricultural production, and it is necessary to increase the income of holdings through non-agricultural activities. One of the possibilities is rural tourism. Does Serbia have the necessary resources to develop this industry? In order to define the answer to this question, it is necessary to analyze the natural, social, physical, human and financial resources, which together represent a platform for the development of rural tourism.

The Republic of Serbia has high-quality natural resources for the development of rural tourism. These include: natural beauty, pleasant climate, relatively unpolluted air, water and soil in rural areas, the richness and diversity of plants and animals,... The territory of the Republic of Serbia is, according to the criteria of the World Conservation Union (IUCN), one of six European and 153 global centers of biological diversity (RARIS, 2012). In the past, the natural resources of rural areas were primarily used for the development of agriculture, and in the future, the development of rural tourism should valorize natural resources on the tourist market, "where higher prices for agricultural products can be achieved" (Cvijanović et al., 2016, 43). Human resources are increasingly a limiting factor for the development of rural tourism due to the current depopulation of rural areas. For example, according to the 2002 Census, 55% of the total population in the Republic of Serbia lived in rural areas, while according to the 2022 Census, only 38% of the total population lived in rural areas. According to data from the 2024 Labor Force Survey, only 12% of the population of rural areas was in the 15-24 age group. According to the aforementioned source, 15% of the total population was unemployed. The structure of the unemployed is dominated by rural residents with secondary education, who in 2024 accounted for 62% of the total number of unemployed, with 26% having a lower education, and only 11% of the total number of unemployed rural residents with a higher education (ARS-RS, 2025). Therefore, in addition to the increasingly pronounced depopulation of rural areas, a limiting factor for the development of rural tourism is the unfavorable age and educational structure of the population in these areas.

Physical resources are: cultural and historical monuments, museums, galleries, libraries, located in rural areas, religious buildings, public infrastructure and tourist signage. As he concludes (Radović, 2015), Serbia has quality physical resources for the development of rural tourism, but the lack is represented by the insufficient representation of tourist signage, as well as the poor quality of public infrastructure (traffic, utility, energy and telecommunication infrastructure). Social resources of importance for the development of rural tourism in the Republic of Serbia include: rich cultural and historical heritage, preserved characteristic ethnic features and gastronomy, folklore, traditional handicrafts, folk customs, old crafts and numerous ethnographic and gastronomic manifestations. Financial resources represent one of the biggest limitations for the development of rural tourism in the Republic of Serbia (Radović, 2015). Bearing in mind that agriculture has an unfavorable economic position, due to numerous problems that have been current for several decades, most agricultural farms do not have their own accumulation, which they would direct to the development of rural tourism, but for this purpose they need external sources of financing Radović (2016a).

Bearing in mind the mentioned resources and the need to stop depopulation and speed up the economic development of rural areas through the development of rural tourism, the aim of the work is to analyze the current forms of promotion of rural tourism in the Republic of Serbia and consider the possibilities for their innovation. Active and adequate promotion would enable higher occupancy of accommodation facilities in rural areas, which should have an impact on increased employment in this industry, and through the multiplier effect of tourism, it would also affect the development of other economic activities, i.e. the entire rural economy.

LITERATURE REVIEW

Rural tourism is a complex tourist product, composed of numerous partial tourist products that are interconnected into a functional, economic, sociological and spatial, as well as touristic whole (Kušen, 2007). In addition to the evident diversity, i.e. the quality of the rural tourist product, an active role is also needed for other elements of the marketing mix, i.e. an adequate price, promotion and sales policy. Rural tourism includes all tourist activities that can take place in rural areas and that can be included in the tourist offer of those areas. The key characteristics of rural tourism are, as stated by Roberts & Hall (2003), that it is related to the rural area, that it is characterized by direct guest-host contact, that it offers the opportunity for the tourist to participate in the traditional activities and lifestyle of the local population, as well as that it has a feature of the tradition of a rural area. Ivona (2021) indicates that tourism can play a key role in the development of rural areas, that is, it can realize the diversification of rural economies and improve the quality of life of the local population. This position is also agreed by (Wang & Lu, 2025), as well as by a group of authors (Liu et al., 2023), who state that rural tourism is a "revitalization strategy" of rural areas, i.e., it provides an incentive for the economic, socio-cultural and ecological development of rural areas. A rural area can be defined as an area with a small concentration of inhabitants, whose main occupation is agriculture, and which is characterized by special customs and village identity (Štetić & Cvijanović & Šimičević, 2014).

The basic characteristics of rural tourism, from the aspect of its economic, i.e. financial importance, are the impact on the economic development of local economic communities and regions and the impact on the growth of the population's standard of living (Boyne, 2005). According to Mitchell & Hall (2005), rural tourism is one of the most labor-intensive industries, which represents a potential contribution to the creation of new jobs and the economic development of rural areas, and which is often the most important element in rural development strategies. Jing (2006) agrees with this position, who points out that precisely because rural tourism enables direct and indirect employment of the rural population, the World Tourism Organization is of the opinion that the greatest economic importance of rural tourism lies in the fact that this activity helps eliminate poverty - "tourism helps poverty elimination".

According to (Đekić & Vučić, 2003, 171), the economic importance of rural tourism at the micro level, i.e. the importance for the development of the local economic community, can be abbreviated with the term "CARE". This term implies: creation of new jobs (Create New Jobs), attraction of new jobs (Attract New Business), preservation of existing firms (Retain Existing Firms), expansion of existing firms (Expand Existing Firms). A group of authors (Roberts & Mitchell & Hall, 2005) introduces the term "rural capital", which according to these authors can be defined as the capacity that provides resources for development, which can be identified as: economic, natural, human, social and cultural resources. According to (Todorović & Štetić, 2009), tourism is a factor in the development tendencies of rural areas, a supplementary activity for the rural population, a market for agricultural products, a factor in the development of agriculture and a "softener" of depopulation flows. According to (Pejanović, 2013, 201), the development of rural tourism enables: stabilization of overall regional development, full valorization of natural and anthropogenic values of rural space, preservation of tradition, culture and recognizable identity of rural communities, optimization of the relationship between rural and urban units of the region, raising the competitiveness of the region as a tourist destination, creating a balance between all economic activities in the region, as well as the development of entrepreneurship in rural areas.

Rural tourism enables economic, i.e. rural development, but also an increase in the income of agricultural farms, because it enables the placement of agricultural products at higher prices within the "market in one's own backyard". Rural tourism also enables the marketing of products of old crafts and domestic handicrafts, provides additional employment for residents of rural areas, and enables the valorization of the work of women in agricultural households. All of the above affects the growth of the income of the rural population, the growth of living standards, and thus the development of rural areas (Radović & Pejanović & Njegovan 2012). Rural tourism should be developed on a sustainable basis as part of integral rural development, which is defined in the literature as "a modern concept that represents the complex development of a certain rural area based on available natural, material, infrastructural and human resources that are managed with due care to preserve the balance of man and nature" (Njegovan & Pejanović, 2009, p. 180). According to Roberts & Hall (2003, p. 3), rural tourism can be a relatively "sensitive" element of rural development considering that it includes many micro-enterprises, this type of tourism is engaged in by rural entrepreneurs, such as farmers from small towns and villages, but also by local officials who often do not have the specific qualifications required for tourism.

In order to develop rural tourism, as a form of entrepreneurship in rural areas, the application of modern information and digital technologies is of great importance (Cheng et al., 2024; Pan & Zhang & Zhang, 2024). Modern digital technologies, as pointed out by the group of authors (Samsudin et al., 2024), play a key role in the development of sustainable rural entrepreneurship, because they enable access to innovative solutions, improve business sustainability, encourage economic development, and thus fight against the depopulation of rural areas and contribute to environmental and social sustainability. The author Buhalis (2022) indicates that in order to sustainably develop tourism, it is necessary to apply the achievements of modern (smart) technologies, and the quoted author also emphasizes the importance of adequate management in tourism, as well as the importance of marketing.

Marketing in rural tourism, as well as in tourism in general and in all service activities, is specific. The specificity of marketing in service activities was emphasized by many authors in the available literature (Ferrell, 2021; Zeithaml & Bitner & Gremler, 2018; etc.). Author group Kotler & Bowen & Makens (2017); Kotler et al. (2021) highlight four basic characteristics of services, namely: intangibility, inseparability (production and consumption cannot be spatially and functionally separated), transience (the service does not exist before purchase, nor can it be stored), as well as variability (the service cannot be standardized, because it depends on direct contact between the seller and the buyer - tourists).

Promotion, like a quality tourist product, an adequate price and distribution channels, is a very important element of the marketing mix in rural tourism. As the authors point out (Dobre et al., 2024), promotion plays a key role in the development of rural tourism, as it contributes to raising awareness of the authenticity of rural areas, strengthening the brand image, attracting tourists and encouraging economic growth in rural local economic communities. According to (Milisavljević, 1996, p. 354) "promotion is the process of communicating with customers (tourists) with the aim of creating a positive attitude about products and services that leads to their favoring in the purchase process on the market". The cited author points out that the target audience significantly influences decisions: "what to say, when, how, where and to whom to say it" (Ibid, p. 394). The authors (Senić & Senić, 2016, p. 551) state that "promotion is used to spread the word to potential guests." The best promotion of tourist services is realized at the point of consumption, and a satisfied tourist is the best seller. The promotional mix could be defined as a combination of propaganda, sales promotion, public relations, personal selling and publicity, and the optimal combination of these elements should ensure optimal results (Cvijanović, 2016, p. 139).

The problem with rural tourism lies in the fact that supply and demand are dislocated. Namely, supply is located in rural areas, while demand comes from urban city centers. Therefore, communication between supply and demand plays a crucial role in the success of a rural tourist destination. In this sense, the management of rural tourist destinations has various techniques of mass and direct communication with the market. (Vuković, P. 2019). Jobber D., & Fahy J., (2022) made distinguish between mass and direct communication techniques. Mass communication techniques include: integrated marketing communications (offline communications techniques such as traditional channels: TV, radio, newspapers, direct post and on-line communications techniques such as digital channels, social medias, e-mails, web, etc.), propaganda, sales promotion, public relations and publicity, sponsorships, fairs and exhibitions. On the other hand, direct communication techniques include: database-based marketing, customer relationship management (tourist), direct marketing, Internet marketing, computer reservation systems, personal selling, ales management. Considering the nature of rural tourism and the low level of education of people in rural areas, one of the important tasks will be education and appropriate training and seminars to familiarize all stakeholders with communication techniques, both mass and direct. Today, an important role in this in the Republic of Serbia is played by the Tourist Organization of Serbia, whose function is primarily focused on promotion, but also by other stakeholders from the public and private sector. Public sector includes governmental and local administrations, regional chambers of commerce, regional development agencies, institutions supporting the development of rural tourism, etc., and private sectors include family farms, private associations and cooperatives, small and medium-sized enterprises, private investors and entrepreneurs, etc. (Vuković, P. et al. 2024).

According to (Gonroos, 1987), the tourist product can be divided into four levels: (1) the basic product - represents what the tourist buys; (2) expected product - represents what the tourist expects; (3) additional product – provides additional value to the basic product, that is, it provides a difference in relation to the competition; (4) extended product - it implies a variety of services and tourist contents that are offered to tourists in order to increase the quality level of the basic product, and communication with tourists is very important here. Planning and developing a tourism product involves a combination of five "right" elements: planning the "right" product, selling it at the "right" price, placing it through the "right" distribution channels, selling it at the "right" time, and selling it in the "right" quantity (Mcintosh & Goeldner, 1984). According to (Bakić, 2010), in a promotional performance it is always necessary to: identify potential market segments, carefully create a message, choose an adequate medium, determine the time, frequency and impact of the media, determine the budget and measure the results. The authors (Kotler & Levy 1969) point out that the tasks of public relations are: (a) to help launch new products; (b) to help reposition the mature product; (c) to generate interest in a product whose population is declining; (d) to "defend" a product that has failed in public; (e) to influence a specific target group of consumers; (f) to create an image of the company in such a way as to project favorable things about the product or service.

For the development of rural, as well as other types of tourism is necessary to study, knowledge of marketing, and the application of the best marketing solutions Vuković (2019). The promotion of rural tourism, as an additional activity on agricultural farms, is important in many ways. First of all, in order to increase the occupancy of tourist capacities, i.e. the growth of tourist traffic and income from tourism for these entities (Radović, 2015). Authors Radović & Pejanović (2019) indicate that in order to develop rural tourism in Serbia, active promotion of this activity in specialized media is needed, in order to set an example for other agricultural farms to dare and start this entrepreneurial venture.

Significant of promotions for development of rural tourism have also been the subject of research by other authors, primarily in neighboring countries. A significant example is the Republic of Croatia, where this activity has been developing in approximately the same time period as in the Republic of Serbia. The authors (Rakić & Hanžek, 2022; Nejašmić & Barišić, 2021) have highlighted and analyzed the role and importance of promotion for the development of rural tourism. Significant promotions for the development of rural tourism have also been recognized in other neighboring countries. For example, in the Republic of Slovenia, the Chamber of Agriculture and Forestry played a very significant role in the initial phase of rural tourism development, and also organized education in the field of rural tourism promotion Radović (2016b). In order to develop rural tourism in the Republic of Serbia, it is necessary to form an agile association of service providers at the national level, which should have its own branches (branches) in all circles. The task of this association should be the active promotion and sale of rural tourism products, as well as the education of rural tourism entities Radović, (2020b).

he development of rural tourism in the Republic of Serbia is an extremely complex process, given that rural areas are among the most heterogeneous in Europe in terms of natural, economic, demographic and social conditions. Therefore, it is necessary that in the coming period, the development of rural tourism should be viewed from a multi-sector perspective, to be based on an adequate legal and strategic framework, with precise action plans developed, which will define financing modalities, but also control the realization of goals (Radović & Pejanović, 2019).

CHARACTERISTICS OF SUPPLY AND DEMAND IN RURAL TOURISM

Factors that affect the quality of the tourist supply are: the attractiveness of the location - natural and social characteristics, the quality and capacities of accommodation and catering services, the quality of the traffic infrastructure, as well as tourist mediation and promotion (Cvijanović, 2016). Bearing in mind that in rural tourism exsist direct communication between guest and host, the quality of the tourist supply is also influenced by hospitality, communicativeness of the host, knowledge of foreign languages, as well as the general level of education. The quality of the tourist supply also depends on the availability and variety of tourist content, the quality of communal infrastructure, internet communication, etc. Tourist demand is influenced by objective and subjective factors. Objective factors are: available financial means for purchasing a tourist product, available free time, health condition of tourists, etc. Subjective factors of tourist demand are tourist affinities, level of education, age, gender, etc.

Table 1. Characteristics of rural tourism supply and demand

Rural tourist supply:	**Rural tourist demand::**
– dislocated	– conditioned by: motivation, awareness, emotions, knowledge (which shape tourist behavior).
– seasonal	– seasonal
– static	– susceptible to trend
– inelastic	– spiritually and price elastic
Imperative: it is effective to connect with rural tourism demand	*Imperative: recognize the demands of tourists and incorporate them into the rural tourism supply*

Source: (Radović, 2015 na osnovu Muhi, 2009; Roberts, L. & Simpson, F. 2005).

All the mentioned characteristics of rural tourist offer and rural tourist demand shown in table no. 1 should give dimension to the promotional mix of the rural tourism product.

RURAL TOURISM AS A FACTOR OF DEVELOPMENT AGRICULTURAL ENTREPRENEURSHIP

The development of rural tourism should be based on the development of small and medium-sized enterprises, ie. on agricultural entrepreneurship. Agrarian entrepreneurship is defined as "a new organizational form of entrepreneurship", which can be developed in all activities that include multifunctional agriculture (Pejanović, 2013, p. 295). Multifunctional agriculture is an integral, territorially rounded rural economy, which, in addition to agriculture, i.e. primary agricultural production, also includes activities related to it. Therefore, multifunctional agriculture is often called "agrarian entrepreneurship" in the literature. (Ibid, p. 300).

The most important segment of multifunctional agriculture is rural tourism, given that it can create the fastest diversification and development of the rural economy. The importance of rural tourism is derived from the multiplicative impact of tourism on economic development. Rural tourism is directly linked to agriculture, trade, transport, and indirectly to other economic activities. Unković & Zečević (2011, p.35) define the multiplication factor as "the number of turnovers of money received from foreign tourists during one calendar year." The cited authors point out that "the greater the number of hands through which foreign money passes, the greater the effect of tourism on the host economy" (Ibid., p. 36).

The main goal of the concept of the development of multifunctional agriculture is the development of rural economies, the reduction of differences in economic development between urban and rural areas and the stopping of the process of demographic emptying of rural areas. Limitations in the development of the concept of multifunctional agriculture, which the member countries of the European Union encountered, as stated (Vasilevska, 2009, p. 42-43), are: inadequate human resources (unfavorable age and educational structure), inadequate physical resources and lack of financial resources, inadequate market institutions and lack of political will to realize the concept of multifunctional agriculture.

In the Republic of Serbia, entrepreneurship is underdeveloped, and according to developed countries, entrepreneurship should become a new development philosophy. The limitations are the lack of state support, as well as the "lack of entrepreneurial spirit and mentality in our region". Also, the problem in the development of entrepreneurship in domicile conditions is the complicated bureaucratic procedure and the lack of quality credit funds (Pejanović, 2013, 299-303). As part of the agrarian policy measures, there is credit support, which has been paid to agricultural subjects continuously since 2004 in the form of subsidizing interest on loans from commercial banks. The average utilization of these subsidies is high, amounting to 73% in the period 2014-2022. year (Radović & Popović & Grujić-Vučkovski, 2024, p. 72). There are also interest subsidies for loans for the development of tourism and entrepreneurship, but the available funds are generally insufficient to meet the needs of the economy. Therefore, a greater quantity of quality sources of financing should be provided. which would be marketed in order to develop small and medium-sized enterprises within the activities that include multifunctional agriculture, and where the priority should be the development of rural tourism.

The Republic of Serbia is one of the most agrarian European countries considering that the majority of the working-age population in rural areas is engaged only in primary agricultural production, and in rural areas "diversification of household income, not activity, dominates" (Bogdanov, 2007, p. 117). There are also big differences in the economic development of individual regions, and that is why rural tourism, as a factor in the development of agrarian entrepreneurship, is of great importance for mitigating this imbalance. Observed regionally, the economically least developed regions are Southern Serbia and Eastern Serbia.

According to the results of the Agricultural Census in 2012, in the Republic of Serbia, there were a total of 628,552 agricultural farms, and only 78,301 or 12.4% of the total number of agricultural farms were engaged in activities other than agriculture and other profitable activities (Cvijanović & Paraušić & Subić, 2014). According to research (Bogdanov & Babović, 2014), in 2012, less than 1% of the total number of agricultural holdings in the Republic of Serbia engaged in rural tourism. According to the results of the Census of Agriculture in 2023, there were a total of 508,325 agricultural farms in the territory of the Republic of Serbia (Census of Agriculture, 2023), and 101,172 or 19.9% of the total number of agricultural farms were engaged in activities other than agriculture and other profitable activities. According to research (Zarić, 2025), in 2023 only 880 or 0.87% of the total number of agricultural holdings (PGs) engaged in other profitable activities in the Republic of Serbia engaged in rural tourism (table 2). It can be concluded that only 0.2% of the total number of agricultural holdings (PG) in the Republic of Serbia were involved in rural tourism in 2023. This is an extremely small number of agricultural farms when the available natural, social, physical, as well as human and financial resources are considered in the analysis.

Table 2. Types of other profitable activities at PG in 2023.

Type of activity	**Number of family farms**	**Participation in the total number of family farms engaged in other profitable activities (in %)**
„Roasting“ brandy	28.042	27,72
Fruit and vegetable processing	16.676	16,48
Milk processing	16.558	16,37
Other activities	8.887	8,78
Processing other agricultural products	8.318	8,22
Forestry activities	6.375	6,30
Meat processing	6.039	5,97
Woodworking	3.142	3,11
Contract work in another field	2.467	2,44
Contract work in the field of agriculture	1.721	1,70
Folk craft	1.637	1,62
Tourism	*880*	*0,87*
Providing health, social or educational services	214	0,21
Fish farming	186	0,18
Energy production from renewable sources	30	0,03
TOTAL	101.172	100,00

Source: Zarić, 2025, str. 62. Dostupno na: https://publikacije.stat.gov.rs/G2025/Pdf/G202512005.pdf.

The development of multifunctional agriculture, and above all rural tourism, in the Republic of Serbia is a development perspective of rural areas. The average size of agricultural holdings, according to the results of the last Census of Agriculture, is only 6.4 ha (Census of Agriculture, 2023). On such small holdings, there are no conditions for the development of competitive agricultural production, so the development of activities that rely on agriculture is a necessity for the purpose of sustainable economic development of these agricultural entities.

DEVELOPMENT OF RURAL TOURISM IN THE REPUBLIC OF SERBIA

In order to analyze the development of rural tourism in the Republic of Serbia, we will analyze the current supply - the number of rural tourist households (RTH) and the demand in rural tourism - the number of tourist arrivals and overnight stays in rural tourist households (RTH). It is important to note that according to the current Act on Tourism (Act on Tourism, 2019), the offer in rural tourism in the Republic of Serbia includes, in addition to rural tourist households (RTH), and subjects that are defined as domestic handicrafts (DHC). Considering that there are no available statistical data for the subjects that are categorized as domestic crafts, the analysis of their offer, as well as the demand of tourists, will not be the subject of analysis in this paper.

Analysis of the development of the supply in rural tourism in the Republic of Serbia

As already stated in the previous considerations, in 2023 only 880 agricultural farms (Zarić, 2025) or only 0.2% of the total number of agricultural farms (AF) in the Republic of Serbia were engaged in rural tourism in the Republic of Serbia (Census of Agriculture, 2023). The regional distribution of these farms is presented in table 3.

Table 3. Regional distribution of PGs that dealt with tourism in 2023

Region	Number of family households engaged in tourism
Region of Šumadija and Western Serbia	572
Region of Southern and Eastern Serbia	185
Region of AP Vojvodina	88
Belgrade region	35
Total:	880

Source: Zarić, 2025, str. 63. Dostupno na: https://publikacije.stat.gov.rs/G2025/Pdf/G202512005.pdf. Obrada autora.

Based on the tabular representation (table __), it can be noted that there is a significant regional unevenness in the development of this activity. In terms of the development of the offer, the region of Šumadija and Western Serbia is in first place, where rural tourism first began to develop. It is a well-known historical fact that the first tourists were received by households in the village of Devići, which is located in the territory of the municipality of Ivanjica in Western Serbia. It was in the 70s of the 20th century and represents the beginning of rural tourism in the Republic of Serbia, as well as in the entire then Socialist Federal Republic of Yugoslavia (Marković & Ostojić, 2012).

According to current data from the Ministry of Tourism, from the eTourist electronic register, in the Republic of Serbia at the beginning of April 2025, there were 1,486 rural tourist households with a total of 7,012 beds. This represents about four beds per household. Bearing in mind that according to the current legislation, it is possible for households in rural tourism to have up to 30 beds, the above data indicates the insufficient current development of the offer in rural tourism in the Republic of Serbia.

Analysis of the development of demand for rural tourism in the Republic of Serbia

Statistical data on tourist traffic (tourist arrivals and overnight stays) in rural tourist households have been available since 2014. In order to analyze the participation of the demand for rural tourism in the total demand for all types of tourism in the Republic of Serbia, the data are shown in table 4.

Table 4. Share of tourist arrivals and overnight stays in rural tourist households (RTH) in the total number of tourist arrivals and overnight stays in the Republic of Serbia 2014-2023.

Year	The share of tourist arrivals in RTH...		Participation of tourist overnight stays in RTH...	
	...in the total number of tourist arrivals (in %)	...in the total number of foreign tourist arrivals (in %)	... in the total number of overnight stays by tourists (in %)	...in the total number of overnight stays by foreign tourists (in %)
2014.	0,01	-	0,01	-
2015.	0,06	0,02	0,07	0,03
2016.	0,16	0,02	0,19	0,03
2017.	0,16	0,02	0,19	0,02
2018.	0,16	0,03	0,16	0,03
2019.	0,23	0,05	0,24	0,07
2020.	0,64	0,07	0,63	0,21
2021.	0,47	0,13	0,60	0,41
2022.	0,75	0,38	0,96	0,44
2023.	0,70	0,41	0,83	0,39

Source: *Statistički godišnjak 2014-2023.* Processing by the author.

The demand for the tourist product of rural tourism recorded a very mild and gradual growth in the analyzed period 2014-2023. year. However, in the entire analyzed period, neither the participation of the number of tourist arrivals in rural tourism in the total number of tourist arrivals, nor the participation of the number of tourists overnight stays in rural tourism in the total number of tourist overnight stays, was not even 1% (table 5).

Table 5. Number of tourist arrivals and overnight stays in rural tourist households (RTH) 2014-2023.

Year	Number of tourist arrivals	Number of tourists overnight stays
2014	164	502
2015	1.523	4.910
2016	4.335	14.497
2017	5.061	16.040
2018	5.584	15.039
2019	8.529	24.677
2020	11.673	38.981
2021	12.214	48.838
2022	29.119	117.320
2023	29.148	103.342

Source: *Statustički godišnjak 2014-2023.*

Tourist demand in rural tourism recorded growth when analyzing the number of arrivals and the number of overnight stays. The growth is particularly pronounced since 2020, i.e. since the "corona period", when many domestic tourists stayed in Serbia due to the "closing of the borders". It is significant that the growth trend continued in the following years. A slight decrease in the number of overnight stays by tourists in rural tourism was recorded in 2023 compared to 2022, by 12% (table _).

Based on the conducted research, we can conclude that rural tourism is not sufficiently developed in the Republic of Serbia, despite the recorded growth trend, both in the supply segment and in the demand segment. What are the problems in the development of this activity?

PROBLEMS IN THE DEVELOPMENT OF RURAL TOURISM IN THE REPUBLIC OF SERBIA

According to the results of earlier research (Radović, 2013; Radović 2015), the problems in the development of rural tourism in the Republic of Serbia are:

- lack of adequate funding sources;

- non-existence of the Register of entities providing services in rural tourism;
- the absence of defined standards for the development of rural tourism;
- inconsistency of rural tourism entities defined by the Law on Tourism with the current situation in practice;
- insufficient offer of tourist content;
- underdevelopment of infrastructure (traffic and communal);
- underdevelopment of tourist signage;
- insufficient involvement of travel agencies in the sale of rural tourism products;
- insufficient association of service providers in rural tourism;
- insufficient education of service providers in rural tourism;
- insufficient specialization of services in rural tourism;
- insufficient and inadequate promotion of the tourist product of rural tourism.

In the previous decade, efforts were made by competent state institutions with the aim of developing rural tourism in the Republic of Serbia, but it can be stated that most of the mentioned problems are still current today. For example, the current Law on Tourism (2019) recognizes as service providers in rural tourism in the Republic of Serbia only rural tourist households and home-made facilities. However, in current practice the subjects of rural tourism are also: ethnic villages, hotels and motels in rural areas, inns, log cabins, sculptures, etc. (www.selo.co.rs).

Regarding the register of rural tourism, it has been introduced in the meantime in the form of eTurista, but the data within it are not publicly available. Also, a national association of service providers in rural tourism has not been formed, providers are not specialized in certain services, and their education is insufficient. The underdevelopment of infrastructure (utility and traffic) is still a big problem, as is the lack of tourist signage. The offer lacks diverse and high-quality tourist content, and travel agencies are insufficiently interested in selling this tourist product. Also, there are no defined standards within which this activity would be developed.

We are of the opinion that the problem of financing is still the biggest problem in the development of this activity, despite the fact that in recent years funds from the IPARD II and IPARD III programs (within Measure 7) have been available to rural tourism entities, as if there were subsidies from competent state institutions. The aforementioned financial resources were mainly intended for the construction and renovation of accommodation facilities. However, as we pointed out in one of the earlier studies (Radović et al., 2018), for the development of rural tourism, it is necessary to "define the modalities of financing all segments of the rural tourism offer: accommodation capacity, hospitality sector, tourist content, promotion, sales channels, as well as the development and training of personnel and the development of rural infrastructure (Radović et al., 2018, 423-424). For the purpose of developing rural tourism in the Republic of Serbia, we believe that it would be useful to adopt a Strategy development of rural tourism, as well as defining action plans for each year of the defined period within this strategic document.

The problem of insufficient and inadequate promotion of rural tourism is also a significant development problem. What are the current forms of promotion of rural tourism in the Republic of Serbia, will be stated in further research.

METHODS OF PROMOTING RURAL TOURISM IN THE REPUBLIC OF SERBIA

In order to analyze the current ways of promoting rural tourism entities, a survey was carried out in which 238 rural tourism entities were involved in the Republic of Serbia. The research included subjects of rural tourism that are in the database of the Tourist Organization of Serbia (TOS, 2017). The research was carried out by telephone and internet search in April and May 2025.

Table 6. Current ways of promoting rural tourism entities in the Republic of Serbia.

Republic of Serbia	Number of subjects of rural tourism	Promotion methods		
		Web site/catalogues of tourist organizations	Own website	Website of association
AP Vojvodina	53	24	23	6
Participation in (%)	100,00	45,28	43,40	11,32
Central Serbia	88	65	23	-
Participation in (%)	100,00	73,86	26,14	-
Western Srbia	62	43	19	-
Participation in (%)	100,00	69,35	30,65	-
Eastern Serbia	35	26	7	2
Participation in (%)	100,00	74,29	20,00	5,71
TOTAL:	**238**	**158**	**72**	**8**
Participation in (%)	**100,00**	**66,39**	**30,25**	**3,36**

Source: Author's research.

The results of the conducted research show that the largest number of rural tourism entities in the Republic of Serbia use catalogs and websites of tourist organizations for promotion. This is in accordance with the defined role of tourist organizations, which is stated in the Law on Tourism, where it is defined that the promotion of tourism in the Republic of Serbia is carried out by the "Tourist Organization of Serbia, the tourist organization of the autonomous region and tourist organizations of local self-governments" (Law on Tourism, 2019, Article 30). This method of promotion is used by 158 rural tourism entities or 66.39% of the total number of rural tourism entities that were included in the research. Promotion through their own website is used by 72 subjects (30.25% of the total number of subjects included in the research), and promotion through association websites is used by 8 subjects (3.36% of the total number of subjects included in the research). It is important to note that all entities that have their own website or use the association's website, in parallel use the available promotion opportunities through tourist organizations as a means of promotion (table 6).

When the research results are analyzed by individual regions, the following can be concluded.

- in AP Vojvodina: 45.28% of the total number of subjects included in the research use promotion through catalogs and websites of tourist organizations; 43.40% of the total number of subjects included in the research also have their own website (in parallel, they also use promotion through tourist organizations); 11.32% of the total number of subjects included in the research uses for promotion the website of the association in which it is a member (in parallel, it also uses promotion through tourist organizations);
- in Central Serbia: 73.86% of the total number of subjects included in the research use promotion through catalogs and websites of tourist organizations; 26.14% of the total number of subjects included in the research also have their own website (in parallel, they also use promotion through tourist organizations);
- in Western Serbia: 69.35% of the total number of subjects included in the research use promotion through catalogs and web sites of tourist organizations; 30.65% of the total number of subjects included in the research have their own website (in parallel, they also use promotion through tourist organizations);
- in Eastern Serbia: 74.29% of the total number of subjects included in the research use promotion through catalogs and websites of tourist organizations; 20.00% of the total number of subjects included in the research have their own website (in parallel, they also use promotion through tourist organizations); 5.71% of the total number of subjects included in the research uses for promotion the website of the association in which it is a member (in parallel, it also uses promotion through tourist organizations).

In addition to the mentioned methods of promotion, almost all subjects who were involved in the research used social networks (Facebook or Instagram) as a form of promotion, and all of them used the method of promotion, which can be called "word-of-mouth promotion", that is, the recommendation of friends or satisfied guests.

CONCLUSION

Rural tourism in the Republic of Serbia is currently not sufficiently developed, despite the existence of respectable resources for development. More precisely, based on data from Statistical Office of the Republic of Serbia, it is a matter of stagnation in development, given that in the period from 2012 to 2023, less than 1% of the total number of agricultural holdings were engaged in rural tourism. Also, in the period from 2014 to 2023, the average share of the number of tourist arrivals in rural tourism in the total number of tourist arrivals, as well as the average share of the number of tourist overnight stays in rural tourism in the total number of tourist overnight stays, was less than 1%.

The development of rural tourism represents a significant potential for initiating rural development, which would also influence balanced economic development across various regions, especially considering that, according to the OECD classification, nearly 80% of the total territory of the Republic of Serbia is considered rural. The development of rural tourism is also an important factor in the advancement of agrarian entrepreneurship, which could contribute to mitigating regional development disparities. Specifically, the economically least developed regions are Southern and Eastern Serbia, and these very regions possess high-quality, primarily natural, resources for the development of rural tourism. Furthermore, the development of rural tourism plays a crucial role in halting the depopulation of rural areas. The percentage of people living in rural areas decreased by 31% in the period from 2002 to 2022.

The development of rural tourism is also a necessity, considering that the average size of an agricultural holding is only 6.4 ha, according to the results of the Agricultural Census carried out in 2023. On such small holdings, it is impossible to ensure the necessary productivity, economy and profitability, i.e. the competitiveness of agricultural production. In such conditions, it is also impossible to implement the system of precision agriculture, which is imperative in the modern development of agriculture. However, in such conditions, the development of non-agricultural activities on agricultural farms is of great importance, in order to ensure their survival, but also to enable development. Within non-agricultural activities, rural tourism should have primacy, which, due to the multiplier effect of tourism, can initiate the fastest diversification and development of rural economies.

Considering the above reasons, i.e. the necessities for the development of rural tourism in the Republic of Serbia, as well as the relatively satisfactory resource base, what are the problems in the development of this activity? They are numerous, and one of the most significant is the insufficient and inadequate promotion of this type of tourism. Adequate promotion of rural tourism could affect the growth of demand from tourists from abroad, i.e. the growth of "invisible exports", as this type of tourist traffic is often called in the literature. In order to develop promotion, as a very important segment of the marketing mix, adequate financing modalities are also needed. In the current period, rural tourism entities are available subsidies and loans with subsidized interest for the construction, expansion or reconstruction of accommodation and/or catering capacities, but not for promotion. Therefore, the current forms of promotion of rural tourism are modest, i.e. insufficiently developed.

The subject of research in this paper was the most significant current forms of rural tourism promotion in the Republic of Serbia. These are: promotion through tourist organizations at the republican, provincial and local levels, which, according to the current Law on Tourism, are responsible for this activity. In addition to the above form of promotion, more and more rural tourism entities in the Republic of Serbia have their own websites, and some also use the websites of associations of rural tourism service providers.

According to the results of the research conducted in this paper, 66.39% of rural tourism entities use promotion through tourist organizations as the primary form of promotion, 30.25% of the total number of entities included in the research have their own website, and promotion through association websites is used by only 3.36% of the total number of entities included in the research. Regionally, in the AP Vojvodina the largest number of entities have their own website (43.40% of the total number of entities included in the research). All entities that have their own website or use an association website, in parallel, as a method of promotion, also use available promotion opportunities through tourist organizations, as well as recommendations from friends and satisfied guests, but increasingly also social networks.

The number of rural tourism entities in the Republic of Serbia that use promotion through the media is negligible, and if they do, they are most often specialized media. Promotion at fairs in the country and abroad is also insufficiently represented when we look at the individual level, i.e. independent appearances of service providers in rural tourism. The reasons are mainly the lack of available financial resources for this form of promotion. Truth be told, this form of promotion is also present, but through tourist organizations. However, they often do not have the necessary human resources to qualitatively convey certain "experiences" of rural tourism in certain regions in Serbia, which are the most interesting for the modern tourist.

Bearing in mind the increasing influence of social networks and digital technologies, it would be useful in future research to analyze their presence as a form of rural tourism promotion in the Republic of Serbia. In order to comprehensively develop this tourism product, we believe that it is necessary to adopt a Rural Tourism Development Strategy in the Republic of Serbia. This document should also include a promotion development strategy, as well as opportunities for providing adequate financing modalities and this important element of the marketing mix.

ACKNOWLEDGEMENT

Paper is a part of research financed by the MSTDI RS, agreed in decision no. 451-03-136/2025-03/200009 from 04.02.2025.

REFERENCES

Bakić, O. (2010). *Marketing u turizmu.* Univerzitet Singidunum.

Bogdanov, N. (2007). Mala ruralna domaćinstva u Srbiji i ruralna nepoljoprivredna ekonomija, MPŠV RS, UNDP, Beograd.

Bogdanov, N., & Babović, M. (2014). Radna snaga i aktivnosti poljoprivrednih gazdinstava, Republički zavod za statistiku, Beograd.

Boyne, S. (2005). New Directions in Rural Tourism Impact Research. In Hall, D., Roberts, L., & Mitchell, M. (Eds.), *New Directions in Rural Tourism* (pp. 19–37). Ashgate Publishing Limited.

Buhalis, D. (2022). Tourism Management and Marketing in Transformation: Introduction and Editor's Statement. In Buhalis, D. (Ed.), *Encyclopedia of Tourism Management and Marketing*. Edward Elgar Publishing., https://www.elgaronline.com/view/nlm-book/9781800377479/b9781800377486.tourism.management.marketing.xml

Cheng, C., Gao, Q., Ju, K., & Ma, Y. (2024). How digital skills affect farmers' agricultural entrepreneurship? An explanation from factor availability. *Journal of Innovation & Knowledge*, *9*(2), 100477. DOI: 10.1016/j.jik.2024.100477

Cvijanović, D. (2016). *Marketing u turizmu*, Univerzitet u Kragujevcu Fakultet za hotelijerstvo i turizam, Vrnjačka Banja.

Cvijanović, D., Paraušić, V., & Subić, J. (2014). *Popis poljoprivrede u 2012 – Poljoprivredna gazdinstva prema ekonomskoj veličini i tipu proizvodnje u Republici Srbiji*, Republički zavod za statistiku, Beograd.

Cvijanović, D., Radović, G., & Cvijanović, G. (2016). Resources and the rural tourism development in the Republic of Serbia, *Horizons International Scientific Journal*, Series A, Social Sciences and Humanities, Year X, Volume 20, 41-51. Dostupno na: https://www.uklo.edu.mk/tabs/view/d95527c021a7b5c063ab1e094136937c

Đekić, S., & Vučić, S. (2003). Savremeni ruralni turizam i rekreacija, Zbornik radova, Drugi Forum: *Ruralni turizam i održivi razvoj Balkana*, Kragujevac, 7-9. maj 2003,169-174.

Dobre, C. A., Stoian, M., Hontus, A. C., Chiurciu, I. A., & Soare, E. (2024). Component of marketing in authentic Romanian rural tourism. *Scientific Papers. Series Management, Economic, Engineering in Agriculture and Rural Development, 24*(1), 335–340.

EC. (2021). Rural Tourism and the Green Deal: A Path Towards Sustainability. European Commission (EC), Brussels, Belgium.

EP. (2023). Rural tourism. European Parliament (EP), Brussels, Belgium.

Ferrell, O. C. (2021). *Marketing Strategy* (5th ed.). South Western Cengage Learning.

Ivona, A. (2021). Sustainability of rural tourism and promotion of local development. *Sustainability (Basel), 13*(16), 8854. DOI: 10.3390/su13168854

Jafari, J., & Xiao, H. (2024), (eds.). Encyclopedia of Tourism. 2nd edition, Springer, Cham, Switzerland, Dostupno na: https://doi.org/ (pristup: 11.05.2025.).DOI: 10.1007/978-3-030-74923-1

Jing, X. (2006). *Rural Tourism and Sustainable Community Development*, International Forum on Rural Tourism, China, September, 4-6, 2006, Final Report World Tourism Organization.

Jobber, D., & Fahy, J. (2022). *Foundations of Marketing*. McGraw-Hill Education (UK) Ltd. (Paperback) ISBN 978-1-5268-4900-7 (eBook): ISBN 978-1-5268-4901-4.

Kotler, P., Bowen, J. T., Makens, J. C., & Baloglu, S. (2021). *Marketing for hospitality and tourism* (8th ed.). Pearson Education.

Kotler, P., Bowen, J. T., & Makens, J. T. (2017). *Marketing for Hospitality and Tourism*. Pearson Education.

Kotler, P., & Levy, S. J. (1969). Broadening the concept of marketing. *Journal of Marketing, 33*(1), 10–15. DOI: 10.1177/002224296903300103 PMID: 12309673

Kušen, E. (2007). Kako ugostiti turiste na vlastitom imanju, Institut za turizam, Zagreb.

Liu, Y. L., Chiang, J. T., & Ko, P. F. (2023). The benefits of tourism for rural community development. *Humanities & Social Sciences Communications, 10*(1), 1–12. DOI: 10.1057/s41599-023-01610-4 PMID: 37016690

Marković, S., & Ostojić, M. (2012). Četiri decenije seoskog turizma u Moravičkom kraju, Zbornik radova, Prvi stručni skup o ruralnom turizmu i održivom razvoju, Kragujevac, 28-40.

Mcintosh, R. W., & Goeldner, S. R. (1984). *Tourism – Phnciples, Practices*, Philosophies, John Wiley and Sons, New York.

Milisavljević, M. (1996). *Marketing*, Savremena administracija, Beograd.

Mitchell, M., & Hall, D. (2005). Rural Tourism as Sustainable Business: Key Themes and Issues. In Hall, D., Kirkpatrick, I., & Mitchell, M. (Eds.), *Rural Tourism and Sustainable Business* (pp. 1–15). Channel View Publications. DOI: 10.2307/jj.27195513.6

Muhi, B. (2009). *Primena marketinga u seoskom turizmu Vojvodine*, Univerzitet Educons, Fakultet poslovne ekonomije, Sremska Kamenica.

Nejašmić, P., & Barišić, P. (2021). Analiza situacije digitalnog marketinga ruralnog turizma u Republici Hrvatskoj. In: *Prema sigurnijoj socijalnoj budućnosti. Istraživanje o socijalnim uslugama u Belom Manastiru,* 1-27.

Njegovan, Z., & Pejanović, R. (2009). Ruralna regionalizacija AP Vojvodine, Monografija, Univerzitet u Novom Sadu, Poljoprivredni fakultet, Departman za ekonomiku poljoprivrede i sociologiju sela, Novi Sad.

Pan, Y., Zhang, S., & Zhang, M. (2024). The impact of entrepreneurship of farmers on agriculture and rural economic growth: Innovation-driven perspective. *Innovation and Green Development, 3*(1), 100093. DOI: 10.1016/j.igd.2023.100093

Pejanović, R. (2013). Ogledi iz agrarne i ruralne ekonomije, Monografija, Univerzitet u Novom Sadu, Poljoprivredni fakultet, Departman za ekonomiku poljoprivrede i sociologiju sela, Novi Sad.

Popescu, G., Popescu, C. A., Iancu, T., Brad, I., Pe , E., Adamov, T., & Ciolac, R. (2022). Sustainability through rural tourism in Moieciu area-development analysis and future proposals. *Sustainability (Basel), 14*(7), 4221. DOI: 10.3390/su14074221

Radović, G. (2013). Problemi razvoja ruralnog turizma u Republici Srbiji. *Agroekonomika, Br., 59-60*, 114–123.

Radović, G. (2015). Modaliteti finansiranja ruralnog turizma u Republici Srbiji, Doktorska disertacija, Univerzitet u Novom Sadu, Poljoprivredni fakultet, Departman za ekonomiku poljoprivrede i sociologiju sela, Novi Sad.

Radović, G. (2016a). Sources of finance for rural tourism in the Republic of Serbia, *Economics of Agriculture, 63*(3), 1053-1065. ISSN 0352-3462. COBISS.SR-ID 27671. UDC: 338.48-44(1-22)(497.11). https://bsaae.bg.ac.rs/images/Ekonomika%20kompletna/2016/EP%203%202016lq.pdf

Radović, G. (2016b). Razvoj ruralnog turizma u Sloveniji - moguće smernice Srbiji, *HiT Menadžment – Menadžment u hotelijerstvu i turizmu, 4* (2/2016), 103-111.

Radović, G. (2017). *Experience of foreign countries in rural tourism development - lessons for Serbia,* In: Cvijanović, D. et al. (Eds), 2nd International Scientific Conference "Tourism in Function of Development of the Republic of Serbia – Tourism Product as a Factor of Competitiveness of the Serbian Economy and Experiences of other Countries", University of Kragujevac, Faculty of Hotel Management and Tourism, Vrnjačka Banja, Serbia, June 1-3, 2017, Thematic Proceedings II, 429-443. http://www.tisc.rs/proceedings/index.php/hitmc/article/view/112/109

Radović, G. (2020b). Underdevelopment of rural tourism in Serbia: Causes, consequences and possible directions of development, *Economics of Agriculture, 67*(4), 1337-1352. ISSN 0352-3462. COBISS.SR-ID 27671. https://doi:DOI: 10.5937/ekoPolj2004337R

Radović, G., Drãcea, R. M., Vuković, P., & Zejak, D. (2024). *Financing of Rural Tourism in Romania, Serbia and Montenegro in the Period of Integration into the European Union,* In: Proceedings of the 18th International Conference on Business Excellence Smart Solutions for a Sustainable Future (ICBE 2024), 21-23 March 2024, Bucharest, Romania, 2664-2684. https://sciendo.com/article/10.2478/picbe-2024-0223

Radović, G., Košić, K., & Demirović, D. (2018). Financing as a key factor of the Strategy of sustainable rural tourism development in the Republic of Serbia, *Economics of Agriculture, 65*(1), 413-426. ISSN 0352-3462. COBISS.SR-ID 27671. . www.ea.bg.ac.rs/index.php/EA/issue/view/1/Volume%2065%20Issue%20%601%20 2018DOI: 10.5937/ekoPolj1801413R

Radović, G. & Pejanović, R. (2019). Importance of Promotion in Specialized Media for the Development of Rural Tourism in Serbia, *Media dialogues,* Vol. 12, No. 3, 97-108.

Radović, G., Pejanović, R., & Njegovan, Z. (2012). Značaj i uloga integrisanog ruralnog turističkog proizvoda u Republici Srbiji, *Ekonomski vidici - tematski broj: Privredni preobražaj Srbije – mogućnosti i ograničenja*, God. XVII. *Broj, 4*, 577–591.

Radović, G., Petrović, D. M., Demirović-Bajrami, D., Radovanović, M., & Vuković, N. (2020a). Can Proper Funding Enhance Sustainable Tourism in Rural Settings? Evidence from a Developing Country, *Sustainability, 12*(18), 7797, 1-16. COBISS. *SR-ID, 64033033.* Advance online publication. DOI: 10.3390/su12187797

Radović, G., Popović, V., & Grujić-Vučkovski, B. (2024). Incentives for Credit Support of Agriculture in the Republic of Serbia [WBJAERD]. *Western Balkan Journal of Agricultural Economics and Rural Development, 6*(1), 65–75. DOI: 10.5937/WBJAE2401065R

Rakić, T., & Hanžek, M. (2022). Promocija ruralnih turističkih destinacija: analiza službene web stranice za Hrvatsku kao turističku destinaciju. In: *2nd International Scientific and Professional Conference for the Development of Rural Tourism: Sustainable and responsible development of the rural area,* 116-133.

RARIS. (2012). Vodič za ruralni turizam, Regionalna agencija za razvoj Istočne Srbije, Dostupno na: http://www.raris.rs (pristup: 14.05.2025.)

Roberts, L., & Hall, D. (2003). *Rural tourism and Recreation: Principles to Practise.* CABI Publishing.

Roberts, L., Mitchell, M., & Hall, D. (2005). New Directions in Rural Tourism: Local Impacts and Global Trends. In Hall, D., Roberts, L., & Mitchell, M. (Eds.), *New Directions in Rural Tourism* (pp. 225–233). Ashgate Publishing Limited.

Roberts, L., & Simpson, F. (2005). Encouraging Responsible Access to the Countryside. In Hall, D., Roberts, L., & Mitchell, M. (Eds.), *New Directions in Rural Tourism* (pp. 67–79). Ashgate Publishing Limited.

Samsudin, N., Zakaria, T., Osman, J., Ramdan, M. R., Khalid, I. K. M., Mohamad, N., & Sastraredja, S. (2024). The Digitalization Technology for Sustainable Rural Entrepreneurship: A Structured Review. *Journal of Advanced Research in Applied Sciences and Engineering Technology, 42*(1), 14–30. DOI: 10.37934/araset.42.1.1430

Senić, R. & Senić, V. (2016): *Marketing menadžment u turizmu,* Univerzitet u Kragujevcu, Fakultet za hotelijerstvo i turizam, Vrnjačka Banja.

Štetić, S., Cvijanović, D., & Šimičević, D. (2014). Posebni oblici turizma Dunavskog regiona, Monografija, Institut za ekonomiku poljoprivrede, Beograd.

Todorović, M., & Štetić, S. (2009). Ruralni turizam, Univerzitet u Beogradu, Geografski fakultet, Beograd.

Unković, S., & Zečević, B. (2011). Ekonomika turizma, Univerzitet u Beogradu, Ekonomski fakultet, Centar za izdavačku delatnost, Beograd.

Vasilevska, Lj. (2009). Ruralni turizam u okviru multifunkcionalne poljoprivrede – mogućnosti i ograničenja, Zbornik radova, *Prva regionalna turistička konferencija: Regionalna saradnja u razvoju turizma*, Privredna komora Beograd, Beograd, 35-46.

Vuković, P. (2019). Informaciono-komunikacione tehnologije kao pretpostavka uspešnog razvoja ruralnog turizma u Republici Srbiji. Journal: *Zbornik Matice srpske za društvene nauke*, 169 (1). pp. 109-123. ISSN 0352-5732.

Vuković, P. (2019). Konkurentnost ruralnih turističkih destinacija u području Donjeg Podunavlja u Republici Srbiji, Monografija, Institut za ekonomiku poljoprivrede, Beograd.

Vuković, P., Andrei, J. V., Kljajic, N., & Arsic, S. (2024). Vasile, Jean A., Kljajić, N. and Arsić, S. (2024). Possibilities for active tourist holidays in rural areas in the region of AP Vojvodina, Serbia. *Journal of Tourism Management Research, 11*(1), 98–110. DOI: 10.18488/31.v11i1.3780

Vuković, P., Čavlin, G., & Čavlin, M. (2015). Complementarity in the development of rural tourism with the development of thermal baths, spa and welness tourism. Journal: *Ekonomika poljoprivrede/Economic of Agriculture*, No.1, Vol. 62. pp.259-270.

Wang, H., & Lu, X. (2025). A Comparative Study on the Promoting Effects of Different Tourism Development Models on Rural Revitalization: Case Studies from Two Typical Villages in China. *Sustainability (Basel), 17*(2), 714. DOI: 10.3390/su17020714

Zarić, V. (2025). *Struktura, ekonomska snaga i marketing proizvoda poljoprivrednih gazdinstva u Srbiji*, Republički zavod za statistiku, Beograd. Dostupno na: https://publikacije.stat.gov.rs/G2025/Pdf/G202512005.pdf

Zeithaml, V. A., Bitner, M. J., & Gremler, D. D. (2018). *Services marketing: Integrating customer focus across the firm*. McGraw-Hill.

Chapter 8
Rural Development of Serbia in the Era of the Digital Economy

Branko Mihailović
https://orcid.org/0000-0002-2398-6568
Institute of Agricultural Economics, Belgrade, Serbia

Vesna Popović
https://orcid.org/0000-0003-1018-2461
Institute of Agricultural Economics, Belgrade, Serbia

ABSTRACT

This chapter looks at Serbian rural development in the context of the digital economy, covering a variety of socioeconomic initiatives aimed at rural communities and defined by rural policy. Therefore, this chapter's goal is to examine Serbian rural growth in the digital economy from two perspectives: (1) the application of digital marketing and (2) the deployment of precision agriculture technologies. For businesses looking to achieve sustainable success in Serbia's dynamic agro-product trade, digital marketing is an essential component. The authors also examine examples of rural areas in Serbia that have successfully implemented modern digital technologies, with the aim of establishing a framework for effective transformation and modernization in this domain. The research findings may contribute to the advancement of rural areas in Serbia, specifically through the application of digital marketing strategies and the adoption of precision agriculture systems.

DOI: 10.4018/979-8-3373-2898-0.ch008

INTRODUCTION

This chapter analyzes Serbian rural development within the context of the digital economy, including a range of socioeconomic activities that are characterized by rural policies targeted at rural communities. Through a range of strategies, such as investing in agricultural production resources, building and modernizing rural infrastructure, educating and training the rural populace, promoting traditional and cultural values, protecting the environment, fostering rural tourism, and more, these initiatives aim to improve the standard of living and spur economic growth in rural areas. New prospects for a thorough post-pandemic resurgence based on the green and digital transition are presented to rural communities, which are valued for their food production, tourism, and management of natural resources and climatic hazards but also face the exodus of women and young (Popović & Mihailović, 2023).

Developmental disparities and polarization in many rural traits were caused by the disparate rates of development, diversity of potentials, and spatial dispersion of socioeconomic processes in rural areas (Drobnjaković et al., 2022). Different countries use different criteria to identify different kinds of communities because there isn't a single, universal norm in this area.

Depending on particular demands and conditions, settlements are separated into rural and urban zones. The OECD defines rurality at two distinct territorial unit groups (Dax, 1996): 1) Local level: Settlements having a population density of less than 150 people per km^2 are classified as rural regions by the OECD; 2) Regional level: The OECD uses the proportion of a region's population that lives in rural areas to establish more expansive administrative and functional organizations at the regional level. Specifically, mostly rural or transitional areas, where 15% to 50% of the population resides in rural settlements; primary rural areas, where more than 50% of the population resides in rural settlements; and predominantly urban areas, where fewer than 15% of the population resides in rural settlements. (Dax, 1996). Supporting the creation of regional and local organizations devoted to rural development and strengthening the Ministry of Agriculture's collaboration with local governments are essential, depending on the unique requirements of each rural area. Furthermore, focusing aid on the digitization and diversification of Serbian rural communities is crucial, as is expanding funding for rural development.

The development of technologies itself, the facilitation of the availability of information and communication technologies (ICT), and the expansion of knowledge and skills that enable people access, communication, and economic exchange are all implied by the digital economy and society (Arsić et al., 2022). The information economy and the virtual Internet, the progeny of the industrial revolution, are successfully impacting many facets of business, the economy, and daily life while also altering norms and standards. The digital revolution and computer technology are fundamentally changing our conceptions of space, time, and substance. Nowadays, a firm doesn't need a large physical site because it may work electronically and remotely. By linking operations with customers and with one another, a seamless virtual network can be established. E-commerce, sometimes referred to as online or Internet-based commerce, is rapidly growing in significance and replacing conventional retail methods. The degree of ICT adoption in business is used to evaluate a country's competitiveness. Stated differently, all parties involved in the business process must possess a new degree of information literacy due to the global nature of company (Arsić et al., 2022).

The European Union's "Europe 2020" agenda includes the concepts of the economy and the digital society (Borowiecki et al., 2021). In established market economies, the agriculture sector has already been impacted by the Internet. Among its marketing applications are online advertising, online purchasing (or selling), and online services. Market and environmental research, information sharing through website development, communication, direct online sales and purchases, swaps, auctions, and more are just a few of the many uses for the Internet by businesses.

For instance, the most recent local weather forecasts are constantly available online. Furthermore, seeds and fertilizer can be purchased and completed goods sold via the global computer network. Interestingly, the internet is being used by younger, more educated, and more motivated farmers worldwide to increase productivity and profitability. Existing methodologies and tools for managing companies are constantly changing and being revised in compliance with the global business transformation and the rapid development of digitalization processes in the global economy (Al-Ababneh, 2020). Under these circumstances, a more thorough integration of rural agricultural producers is necessary for the growth of Serbia's agro-complex system.

The agro-complex, a major sector of the national economy, is crucial to modern agricultural productivity. This agro-complex includes primary agricultural production, the industry that transforms agricultural products into finished industrial food and non-food items, the marketing of agricultural and food products, the industry that provides inputs for agricultural production, and the final meal intake. For many years, the largest creditor of retail chains in Serbia has been the agricultural sector. The high listing fees have an especially negative impact on small and medium-sized businesses (Popović et al., 2018).

The intricacy of functional connections, as well as the interdependence and mutual conditioning among distinct components, are the primary features of this sizable subsystem. Therefore, farmers see the ease and speed of accessing a wealth of information, as well as the potential to conduct business, buy, and sell directly from their "own backyard," removing the need for middlemen, as the justification for the adoption of digital marketing in Serbian rural areas, or the Internet in agriculture. However, rural areas also had a much lower spread of broadband internet connections. Despite recent improvements in internet infrastructure, knowledge, and technology, there is still a discernible digital divide between rural and urban communities (Dašić et al., 2023).

Today's young farmers want to use all the tools and opportunities offered by the digital economy, including applications, the Internet, satellites, machine learning, and biotechnology, so they can accomplish a lot more work in less time. In order to create a framework for successful transformation and modernization in this area, the authors of this chapter analyze Serbian rural growth in the digital economy from three perspectives: the use of digital marketing; the application of precision agriculture technologies; and examples of Serbian rural areas that have successfully implemented modern digital technologies.

BACKGROUND

The global nature of the digital economy "leaked" to us, and the government's digitization process was established as one of the three fundamental elements of Serbia's development, in addition to economic growth and education (Djorić, 2020). In the majority of industrial areas and for the majority of communities, information technologies are the primary force behind the major changes in the global economy as well as the innovation and development processes themselves (Miletić et al., 2017).

Serbia must articulate its priorities in the context of the new industrialization. ICT and infrastructure are top priorities (Djuričin & Vuksanović, 2016). For producers hoping to achieve long-term success in Serbia's vibrant agro-product industry, digital marketing is essential. Modern marketing strategies must be updated in light of global shifts, the quick development of technology, and changing consumer behavior. The agro-sector, a crucial component of Serbia's economic structure, faces both opportunities and difficulties as a result of digitization. Customers are increasingly depending on digital channels to investigate products and form opinions about purchases as a result of the extensive availability of mobile devices and the ubiquitous use of the internet. The development of digital technologies makes participation and presentation easier to grasp, which helps to meaningfully include stakeholders in places with higher rates of disability, lower educational attainment, and older demographics (Pantić & Čolić, 2023).

The majority of Serbia is made up of rural areas, which vary greatly in terms of infrastructure, income, employment, production capacities, level of living, and natural conditions for development (Popović et al., 2011). One crucial tactic for rural revival is digital rural construction (Cao et al., 2023). The connections between different players in the agricultural value chain could be drastically changed by the digitalization process. This entails changing the relationships between farmers, traders, processing facilities, input and technology suppliers, merchants, and consumers. A new approach to education has been brought about by globalization and the rapid advancement of new technology (Mihailović et al. 2014).

The entire agricultural ecosystem is changing as a result of the new opportunities and efficiency that digitalization offers, as well as the way that decisions are made, transactions are carried out, and information is shared. Every link in the value chain will be impacted by this digital transformation, which will also encourage cooperation, openness, and creativity for sustainable agricultural methods. The correlation analysis's findings demonstrate a strong positive linear relationship between digital skills and GDP per capita, underscoring the significance of national development in fostering the development of sufficient levels of digital skills, which are essential for the twenty-first century, and vice versa (Antonijević et al., 2023). Farmers' digital abilities must be improved in order to establish a digitally competitive and sustainable environment. This will increase farmers' output and cut down on wasteful spending (Rađenović et al., 2025)

Production-oriented agriculture that did not adhere to market demands predominated in Serbia in the past (Cvijanović et al., 2015). It is possible to overcome this disadvantage with the use of digital marketing. Additionally, internet marketing successfully connects Serbian farmers in rural areas with customers directly. Therefore, direct response ad campaigns, an effective and well-designed database, and the establishment of direct consumer connections are the three key elements of direct marketing that are necessary to boost sales volume, market share, and profitability. Direct marketing identifies customers by name, address, and purchase behavior, in contrast to mass marketing, which views customers as a group with shared demographic traits.

Precision agriculture (PA), on the other hand, is a method of food production in which agrotechnical measurements and inputs are used locally rather than uniformly over the plot. The goal of precision agriculture is to introduce the essential technology components for its production, including sensing, data processing and interpretation technologies, intelligent machinery, field robots, and crop modeling (Zhang, 2016).

Specifically, since it is carried out in accordance with the locally specialized resources of a particular rural place, the term "site-specific agriculture" would be more appropriate. Through appropriate resource use and management, precision agriculture has opened the possibility of converting traditional agriculture into a sustainable, ecologically friendly industry (Mondal & Basu, 2009). Although the concept is not new, the realization of such agricultural production was made possible by the development of modern positioning technology, specifically the use of GPS (Geographic Information System). Numerous pillars can support the implementation of site-specific agriculture. By identifying resources, potentials, and requirements and using mapping to visually express them by location, the foundation for certain activities is created. Conversely, farmers embrace new technology because they anticipate its benefits. Profitability is the driving force behind innovation in a market economy. Increasing productivity or lowering manufacturing costs are the two main ways that PA does this, which also results in lower production costs per unit (Erickson & Fausti, 2021).

The poor development of Serbia's rural regions can be attributed to a number of factors, including the movement of rural populations to urban areas, an unfavorable age distribution, a lack of investment in rural areas, and the linkage of rural development with agriculture while disregarding non-agricultural activity. It is essential to adopt a situational or regional approach when creating aid measures because Serbian rural areas have distinct regional characteristics and differing degrees of rural development. Opportunities to use digital marketing and precision agriculture technologies to improve rural areas in Serbia will be carefully studied in light of the existing state of affairs in this region.

DISCUSSION

Implementing of Digital Marketing in the Rural Areas

Researchers from a wide range of fields have been interested in the causes and effects of this urban-rural gap since the Internet was introduced to the consumer market, leading to a sizable and expanding body of literature. However, the debate is rather divided because the topical challenges for rural development are frequently discussed inside (sub)disciplines (Salemink et al., 2017). The fundamental theoretical elements of digital marketing that have been described enable us to assert that there is no one conceptual method in marketing theory that can be used to identify the key characteristics and patterns of the global development of digital marketing. One should examine its essential elements while keeping in mind current developments in the global digital economy in order to support the primary distinctive characteristics of digital marketing. Without defining conceptual milestones in the development of marketing within the digitalization of the modern space, it is impossible to justify the main trends in the development of digital marketing. This will also highlight the distinctions between digital marketing and Internet marketing.

The process of validating the conceptual characteristics and current trends in the global development of digital marketing will be made possible by the consolidation of all the essential elements of the field. The marketing system as a whole, including its constituent aspects and components that each firm chooses for itself based on strategic goals and ambitions, is greatly impacted by the global economy's transformational processes.

It is important to note that the swift use of digital technologies for business purposes defines the topic's importance and the necessity of a more thorough examination and analysis of contemporary development patterns. A key component of contemporary marketing strategy is the utilization of digital technologies, which enable firms to reduce expenses and start reengineering their current business processes by optimizing digitalization (Al-Ababneh, 2020). The unequal ways that people have access to digital technologies are referred to as “digital divides.” Numerous variables contribute to this, such as the availability of various technologies (e.g., costly equipment), the provision of technologies (e.g., the telecommunications infrastructure), and education (e.g., lack of knowledge about various technologies) (Roberts et al., 2017).

Businesses primarily utilize digital marketing solutions that are based on these technologies or that are sold online. Because Internet marketing solely uses the Internet for communication, but digital marketing makes use of additional communication networks including Bluetooth, Wi-Fi, GPS, gsm, and gprs, it is important to note that Internet marketing is a subset of digital marketing. The primary goal of digital marketing is to draw in more and more target audiences for its continued push into the digital realm, and it is also starting to infiltrate traditional forms of communication. The fundamental instruments of digital marketing, which are shown in Table 1, are worth taking into consideration for a more thorough analysis and identification of the major trends in the global development of digital marketing (Al-Ababneh, 2020).

Table 1. Classification Basic Digital Marketing Tools

Digital marketing tools	Characteristic	Key Features
Content	The process of filling the media space with information about a product and service in order to attract and expand the target audience.	Content creation is the foundation of in bound marketing, and its quality plays a key role.
SMM	Social marketing is aimed at getting traffic and increasing audience attention through social networks.	The activity of the audience on social networks is used as part of maintaining the brand, and to expand the audience and even for active sales.
Landing pages	A page / website that describes the features of a product and its benefits.	Landing is the main tool for obtaining users (leads), its conversion is the main indicator of the effectiveness . of your site.

continued on following page

Table 1. Continued

Digital marketing tools	Characteristic	Key Features
Appstore	Application store where the application / game is presented, but this tool does not allow you to manage this resource.	Application store shave the iron promotion mechanisms: ratings, reviews, popularity, phishing.
SEO	The process of obtaining traffic from "free", "organic", or "editorial" search results in search engines.	SEO is a slow and long-term tool aimed at optimizing the site architecture, working with HTML and links, as well as with content.
Work with the press	Managing the dissemination of information through electronic and traditional media.	Working with the press has a lot to do with creating content, but here you need to fully control product information.
User support	The provision of services to customers before, during and after the purchase of a product.	The user should feel the care and desire to improve their product and for this they will be ready to endure inconvenience.
UX	User experience – human product interactions, including interface, graphics, design, content, physical interaction.	If the product is not unique in the market, then UX will be one of the main indicators affecting the choice of the user.
Strategic partnership	Mutually beneficial relationships.	Increasing brand awareness, expanding the audience through cooperation with other organizations.
Marketing channel	Product promotion by other marketing companies.	The organization carries minimal risks and pays for a specific result.
E-mail	Email production for motion to a group of recipients.	With proper customer segmentation, an email sales channel can be quite effective.

Source: Al-Ababneh, 2020.

The study, which had 218 individuals who produced organic agricultural goods inside the Republic of Serbia, is intriguing. The owners of registered farms who participated in the survey offered their responses. This method enables us to determine if a representative sample was used for the survey process, which is consistent with the research's intended participant model. From May to December 2023, in-person interviews and email correspondence were used to obtain the data (Stojanović et al., 2024).

The existence of varying sentiments among respondents about regions in three statements is displayed in Table 2. The sentiments of respondents from Vojvodina differed significantly from those of farm owners and organic producers in Central and Eastern Serbia, as well as Southern and Western Serbia, according to ad hoc tests (Stojanović et al., 2024).

Social networks are a crucial tool in the area of e-business that deals with this subject, Internet marketing and promotion. When it comes to using contemporary digital technology to develop marketing strategies for the promotion and sale of their products, farmers and the agriculture industry are still getting used to the idea of Internet marketing and its subset, Internet promotion. Making the process of promoting, selling, distributing, and purchasing agricultural products simpler and more effective is the aim of Internet use in this sector. Agricultural producers can swiftly increase their clientele, reach a larger audience, and fortify their competitive edge by utilizing contemporary technologies (Dašić et al., 2023).

Table 2. One-way analysis of variance based on the region to which the owners of the plots where organic agricultural production takes place belong

Statement	Vojvodina	Belgrade Region	Central and Western Serbia	Southern and Eastern Serbia	F	p
Online sales channels can enhance the overall sales of organic agricultural products	4.29	04.05	3.82	3.30	3.86	14
Digital communication channels create new markets for organic agricultural products	4.35	04.02	3.94	3.30	3.90	25
Social media is a particularly significant communication channel with consumers of organic agricultural products	4.41	4.33	3.88	3.46	04.02	17

Source: Stojanović et al., 2024.

The following research is noteworthy in this regard: "Digital mapping of business performance indicators of agricultural holdings in Serbia" (Rađenović et al., 2025). An earlier analysis of the body of research and identified deficiencies in the management of agricultural holdings served as the foundation for the inquiries. There are multiple sets of questions in the questionnaire. The demographics of agricultural holdings' representatives and the regions in which they operate are covered by the first set of questions (Rađenović et al., 2025). The second series of questions was designed to evaluate their expertise in the area of agricultural digitalization, while the third set of questions focuses on using digital tools and technology for agricultural management, as indicated in Table 3. The target group included agricultural holdings from Southern and Eastern Serbia, while the research sample included 45 representatives of agricultural holdings. The majority of research participants came from the areas of Nišava, Toplica, Jablanica, Pčinj, Pirot, Rasina, and Zaječar (Rađenović et al., 2025). The majority of responders (47%) were between the ages of 40 and 55, whereas the same percentage (27%), however, were between the ages of 25 and 40 and 55 and 70. Given that the questionnaire was sent by email in an online format, the sample's age distribution may reflect younger farmers' increased usage of computers and the Internet (Rađenović et al., 2025).

Table 3. Digital agricultural tools examination for analysed issues

Analysed agricultural digital issues	Utilized digital agricultural assets - "Smart" phone	Utilized digital agricultural assets - PC	Utilized digital agricultural assets - Drone, GPS
Type of technology for managing agricultural holdings	"Smart" phone	PC	Drone, GPS
Agricultural applications for managing agricultural holdings	E-mail Social media Cloud systems	Internet Browse options	Local government agricultural apps
Type of agricultural digital service for managing agricultural holdings	Digital agricultural platforms	Information-oriented apps for rural areas	Municipality agro-platforms
Type of agricultural activities which utilized agricultural digital toolbox	Weather forecast Market condition Efficient resource allocation	Process automatization Subsidies Supply chain management	Revenues/Expenses Import/ Export Education of farmers through digital platforms

Source: Rađenović et al., 2025.

The Application of Technology in Precision Agriculture

According to site conditions, precision agriculture is a production strategy that encourages varied management techniques in a field. The new tools and information sources made possible by contemporary technologies form the foundation of this system. These consist of remote sensing, soil, plant, and pest sensors, yield monitoring devices, geographic information systems (GIS), the global positioning system (GPS), and variable-rate technology for input applicators (Seelan et al., 2003).

The application of precision agriculture components creates a sizable commercial opportunity for the global expansion of the agro-industrial sector. Depending on the soil quality, labor intensity, fixed capital, and material resources, we have suggested that the coefficient of regulatory resource intensity development indicates an average level of resource consumption in the examined agricultural enterprises of grain specialty (Gusev et al., 2019). Implementing digital marketing tactics in both online and offline settings is made possible by the rapid development of electronic devices and specialized software. In the present business world, each organization may have a varied set of tools. While some organizations can use these tools and grow successfully, others will just cause losses or, at most, be ineffectual. It is important to remember that the global market's revolution and the economy's digitization force top management to figure out all of the digital marketing channels and select the best collection of instruments. The primary digital marketing channels should be taken into consideration for a more thorough examination of current developments in the field worldwide (Al-Ababneh, 2020).

In addition to administrative records from the food chain (such as invoices and lab results) and external sources (such as weather data and environmental conditions), smart agriculture collects data from the field regularly and precisely. After analyzing and interpreting the combined data, insights are produced to help farmers make better decisions (Radić et al., 2022). The Internet of Things (IoT) adds an additional aspect to the field of agriculture and smart farming. Agricultural and farming bases located in rural areas can be effectively connected through the use of fog computing and WiFi-based long distance networks in the Internet of Things (Ahmed et al., 2018). The necessity for agricultural technology advancement and the uptake of new technologies by farmers are important factors in preserving agriculture's competitiveness in the global economy. The Internet of Things (IoT) is one area of information technology that has seen tremendous development in recent years. More consumers, equipment, services, and applications can be connected to the Internet thanks to IoT technologies. Both direct and indirect data sharing is possible between devices that are connected to other devices and apps. End users administer and maintain IoT systems, configure device configurations, and access this data through mobile applications and the internet (Radić et al., 2022). Automation and sophisticated gear can then be used to implement these decisions, and farmers can receive real-time process monitoring and feedback. Sensors, communication networks, edge computing, platforms, unmanned aerial systems, artificial intelligence, and the Internet of Things (IoT) are among the technologies utilized. Some advantages of IoT use in the agri-food industry are displayed in Table 4.

Table 4. Benefits of IoT in the agri-food sector

1. Collect data using sensors and IoT devices to track agri-food processes, equipment efficiency, fertilisers needed, and ensure uniform quality of the food.
2. Sustainable cost management and waste optimisation using efficient control over production by identifying anomalies in crop growth or livestock health, to mitigate risks.
3. Improving the functioning of the food chain by making farm data available to other actors and trigger consumers to buy more sustainable food.
4. Process automation during the production cycle using IoT, digital technologies and platforms (e.g., fertilization, irrigation, pest control).
5. Effective control of production processes to maintain high quality and volume of products.
6. Accelerate the transition to sustainable fair food systems with a neutral or positive environmental impact, and ensure food security, nutrition, public health, preserve affordability of food while generating fairer economic returns, and promoting fair trade.

Source: Project "Internet of Food and Farm 2020", EU, 2021.

It is clear that there are advantages to making sure IoT solutions are developed, implemented, and used successfully in the agriculture industry. From an economic perspective, it makes sense (higher productivity, lower long-term costs, and less expensive waste, as well as greater industrial growth) (Radić et al., 2022). A wide range of methods, crops, and nations have adopted the idea. It is gradually adopted or assessed globally, while acceptance varies greatly by cropping system, area, and nation. A wider adoption is constrained by a number of issues, including technological, agronomic, and socioeconomic. Costs and a lack of expertise are the main socioeconomic hurdles. Lack of fundamental knowledge, poor scouting and sample practices, no site-specific fertilizer recommendations, information misuse, and a shortage of skilled agronomic services are agronomical difficulties. Numerous technological obstacles pertain to remote sensing, software, GPS, sensors, and machines (Robert, 2002). One of the main obstacles to the adoption and use of IoT solutions was technological constraints (Table 5). These restrictions were extensive, and overcoming them will need a coordinated effort from technology companies and legislators. Case studies of IoT application in EU nations have shown numerous technological and legal variations among nations, including those related to bandwidth, internet access, and IoT solutions (Radić et al., 2022).

Table 5. Technological limitations IoT

1. Transnational and national policymakers need to find greater convergence on regulation to ensure easy, effective, and mutually beneficial transitions between borders, allowing easier adoption of new agricultural IoT technologies.
2. There needs to be clear policy to support technological innovation and adoption through economic incentives, advice, integration, and education.
3. Implement sufficient internet connections in rural areas, ensuring fast, widespread, and reasonably priced availability. Ensure that rural areas have sufficient mains/electricity for IoT connectivity, promote an awareness of this availability, and education of how the sector can benefit from cloud-based services and online business channels.
4. Make specific policy efforts for fair access to, and education of, technology to avoid the "digital divide" and information asymmetries. The digital divide is caused when there are those who benefit from, have access to, and can use digital technologies, while others cannot.
5. Technology standards and the use of performance standards need to be set, along with policy decisions including holistic consideration of benefits, costs, effects of digital technologies, climate, re-use, and recycling. The technology itself must be robust and reliable, achieved through independent testing facilities to ensure they are effective.

Source: Project "Internet of Food and Farm 2020", EU, 2021.

The application of cutting-edge technology, such as WSN, IoT, cloud computing, artificial intelligence (AI), and machine learning (ML), to increase crop productivity is known as precision agriculture. The majority of current research suggests that PA-based practices significantly impact productivity and sustainability. Providing decision support systems based on various crop characteristics, such as soil nutrients, soil water level, wind speed, sunshine intensity, temperature, humidity, chlorophyll content, etc., is the aim of PA (Shafi et al., 2019). Managers of agricultural enterprises can now get accurate, up-to-date information on production circumstances thanks to the use of digital technologies. As a result, this optimizes resource use, lowers manufacturing costs, and supports well-informed decision-making processes. It has been shown that digitalization increases an organization's ability to withstand market shocks, which in turn promotes increases in output and income (Tomashuk et al., 2025).

Successful Digitalization Case Studies in Rural Areas

Territorial competitiveness and the explanation of different development outcomes under similar development conditions can be significantly influenced by regional differences in the capacity of local actors (knowledge, abilities, shared principles, mindsets, customs, culture, in building engagement, pronounced local identity, and quality of life) and the quality of their formal and informal, internal and external networks (Popović et al., 2010). One aspect of human capital is digital literacy, which encompasses abilities in communication, information flow, safety, content production, and problem-solving in a digital setting (Pāvulēns & Vilka, 2024). Accordingly, the following are examples of successful digitalization in rural areas.

- The municipality of Sokobanja and the village of Vrmdža adopted contemporary digital technology and established a so-called rural hub that serves as a location for contemporary freelance work. They dubbed this strategy "rural," which combines urban and rural development as the name suggests. This choice turned out to be very wise because many young married couples, primarily millennials, chose to live in this town and work there. (Manasijević et al., 2019). But now that new digital technologies are available, there is room for several communities in the Republic of Serbia to be revitalized. In other words, our nation is completely at odds with the current trend in Western nations. Many professions are no longer site-specific due to the growing number of tasks that may be completed using digital technologies. This enables people to relocate their business operations from largely polluted cities to rural areas where they naturally require favorable working circumstances (digital technology) (Manasijević et al., 2019).
- "Smart" villages gain from a variety of partnerships and partnerships with other communities, which may be founded on pre-existing projects and fi-

nanced by a range of public and private sources. According to the report, the municipality of Petrovac na Mlavi is one of the Republic of Serbia's less developed areas. Specifically, while they may not be as directly related to smart cities, agriculture and food production are essential to the idea of smart villages. The continuous technology revolution in agriculture will undoubtedly facilitate and impact the development and use of any smart village concept (Azevedo, 2019). The way the local community has developed new practices and discovered answers in line with its own context, in its own distinctive and creative style, in response to the demands and the endeavor to alter things and solve particular issues, is demonstrated (Stamenović, 2024). Thanks to creative thinking and the so-called smart approach, the municipality of Petrovac na Mlavi has been able to find its place in the market and establish a relatively good position on the tourist map. This is because it falls into the fourth group of local self-government unit development in the Republic of Serbia, which is devastated areas, the most underdeveloped local self-government units. Rich local, traditional, and cultural history, a healthy atmosphere, a distinctive and alluring atmosphere, genuine cuisine, and a wealth of appealing material are the cornerstones upon which the goal is to grow ("Smart village: the new EU rural development frontier", 2023). As the first phase, the municipality of Petrovac na Mlavi has started by creating and adopting the required planning and program documents, wherein rural smart development is crucial to the municipality's future growth. A digital display in the municipality of Petrovac na Mlavi provided a new and efficient means of collaboration and information sharing with tourists, focusing on three primary development concepts: economic sustainability, society, and environmental protection (Stamenović, 2024). Using the municipality of Petrovac na Mlavi as an example, the idea of smart rural development gives local communities fresh chances to implement creative solutions in the domains of industry, tourism, and agriculture by leveraging their own potential (Stamenović, 2024).

- In order to determine the reasons behind Serbian agriculture's sluggish adoption of advanced technology, BioSense carried out an extensive survey. The results were compared with those of other European countries as part of the SmartAkis project, which was supported by the European Union (Horizon H2020, Project ID: 696294). Of the 36 farmers interviewed, 44% farmed arable crops, 28% planted orchards, and 28% planted vineyards, using the most popular cropping practices in Serbia (Tagarakis, 2018). Only 14% of the farmers polled have implemented smart farming technologies, according to the results. The second country from the end had an adoption rate that was roughly double that of the other countries (France, Germany, Greece, Spain, Netherlands, and the United Kingdom), making it the lowest adoption rate among the countries that participated in the analysis. Additionally, 92% of the farmers surveyed felt that incorporating technology into agriculture may enhance farming, and 36% said that smart farming technologies might increase revenue. This appears more likely to happen in Serbia than in wealthy countries because of the comparatively low yields caused by bad management using subpar quality and quantity of inputs, allowing a larger margin for improvement. (Tagarakis, 2018).

- Agri-food product digital marketing: Braničevo Podunavlje (BP) region's development potential. Digital marketing of food and agricultural products is mandated as one of the answers in light of the shock that the tourism industry and rural tourism have endured. Agriculture in the BP region would provide enough revenue for agricultural holdings by generating competitive agri-food products, concentrating its operations on satisfying consumer demands and preferences, and collaborating closely with the food processing sector. (Mihailović, Radić-Jean, 2019). In order to connect farmers and rural business owners with buyers and to keep them updated on agricultural innovations, weather, input availability, financial services, and market prices, information and communications technology are becoming more and more crucial (FAO, 2017). Responses to the question: Do you use contemporary IT technology to market and promote your product have been as follows (Mihailović, Radić-Jean, 2019): I own a website for a product or agricultural holding: 27.78%; I have a product or agricultural holding Facebook page: 41.11%; I have a product or agricultural holding Instagram page: 13.33%; 17.78% that they don't employ contemporary IT technology for marketing and promotion. Given that Facebook is a free advertising platform, it makes sense that the majority of producers (47.11%) have a page for their agricultural holding or product (Mihailović, Radić-Jean, 2019). The necessity for manufacturers to receive training and education in this area is further increased by the fact that nearly 18% of producers questioned do not use contemporary IT technologies for marketing and promotion (Mihailović, Radić-Jean, 2019).
- Local Market (Local Market, 2019) is a multisectoral, regional project that supports Braničevo-Podunavlje producers of food and drinks as well as other agricultural products. Through free producer advertising on the Internet portal or extensive online, social media, and local media promotional campaigns, the initiative seeks to promote the purchase of local goods by educating and motivating locals to get in touch with producers and obtain the desired goods (Local Market, 2019). In times of heightened global competition, digitization helps small farmers to thrive and solidify their place in the market. The effects of economies of scale, size, and breadth are attained

through digital cooperation, which can function as a single huge agricultural producer (Mihailović & Popović, 2021).

Since they serve as the foundation for the growth of rural tourism, Table 6 lists all of the incentives for regional development in the Republic of Serbia for the years 2018–2021. Incentives obtained from the state budget, which accounted for 62% of the entire structure, dominate their structure (Radović et al., 2024). The State Audit Institution's examination, however, found that because "they are not directed towards regional development priorities," these incentives did not substantially lessen regional development disparities in the Republic of Serbia (SAI, 2023).

Table 6. Incentives for regional development in the Republic of Serbia 2018-2021. year

Sources of funding incentives	**Total incentive amounts 2018-2021. (in billions of dinars)**
Ministry of Education, Science and Technological Development	196
Ministry for European Integration	169
Ministry of Construction, Transport and Infrastructure	153
Other sources of funding	311
Total:	829

Source: State Audit Institution - SAI, 2023.

SOLUTIONS AND RECOMMENDATIONS

In order to provide sustainable intensification of global agriculture, scientists are searching for technical solutions based on the producing more with less model, which increases returns on current agricultural land with environmentally appropriate input utilization (Popović et al., 2012). Despite being a worldwide phenomenon, climate change has a variety of local effects. The effects of climate change on the agricultural and forestry sectors, as well as their capacity for adaptation and mitigation, will depend on a number of factors, including current agro-ecological conditions, production structure, different production systems, technological advancements, socio-economic considerations, international competition, and policy decisions (Popović & Mijajlović, 2014). A set of guidelines and recommendations for the future development and application of digitalization processes in forestry, agriculture, and rural areas are presented in this section. A successful digitalization strategy in rural areas requires three fundamental elements: economic gains, human capital, and technological infrastructure. The first requirement is that all European rural communities have access to first-rate internet and digital infrastructure. Since internet access has become essential, it should be promoted using a rights-based strategy. Market failures should be identified promptly, and where required, public action should take the place of private initiative. The second fundamental requirement is human capital. One of the biggest problems facing businesses in the twenty-first century is the utilization of digital technologies. The extensive usage of information technologies at various points throughout a sector's value chain is what defines this digitalization (Ciruela-Lorenzo et al., 2020). Only when local stakeholders acknowledge their value and possess the necessary abilities and competencies can digitalization occur. In order to facilitate digitalization, rural communities need to have access to middlemen, digitalization brokers, and "spaces." Co-working spaces, living labs, fab labs, digital hubs, and other intermediary organizations can support the growth of local capacity for innovation, creation, and contribution to new smart goods and services (Brunori et al., 2021).

- Connecting sustainable development to digitalization. As long as digitalization tactics and procedures are in line with the Sustainable Development Goals (SDGs), it can promote sustainable development. The territorial capital of rural regions and their industries can be enhanced by digitalization, and digital solutions can meet the demands and expectations of rural businesses and communities while tackling societal issues in Europe.
- Adapting digitalization to various settings. A number of the topics discussed in the digitalization debate are complex and require consideration from multiple levels and actors. For instance, in regions where the average age of farmers is rising and labor is in limited supply, robotization may prevent farming from diminishing; in other regions, however, it may result in farm concentration and job loss.
- Favoring inclusion through digital means. Digitalization can lead to unequal development even in a level playing field because early adoption can give certain people a competitive edge over late adopters. Active measures should be implemented to prevent digital exclusion and to guarantee that no one is left behind in order to prevent this from resulting in marginalization and polarization and to provide equal access to the opportunities brought about by digitalization.
- The creation of digital ecosystems. "Connectors," or people and organizations who facilitate digital coordination of local actors, choose the best technology, and encourage data sharing and interoperability, are linked to the establishment of favorable digitalization ecosystems.
- Constructing models of adaptive governance. A key tenet for realizing the intended digital future is the obvious necessity of altering existing gover-

nance structures and creating new ones that coherently and consistently address regional concerns including infrastructure, skills, data, innovation, and digital inclusion. Governance models must change from reactive to proactive in order to accomplish this.

- Creating policy instruments for digitalization that is sustainable. Since it examines how digital technologies can lead to a reconfiguration of social and economic connections, sustainable digitalization is an ambitious agenda of social transformation. Because of this, all laws that have an impact on agriculture, forestry, and rural areas should be updated and redesigned to take into account both the benefits and risks that come with digitalization. It takes committed organizations with the necessary skills to support successful digitalization.

Requirements engineers should carefully take into account the unique socio-economic features of rural areas when creating new systems in order to maximize possible benefits and minimize drawbacks. Economic factors, such as the potential for cost savings, and regulatory factors, such as the push by institutions for more accurate production tracking and monitoring, are the main drivers, according to the experts. Barriers include a lack of connectivity as well as mistrust of technology and other sociocultural factors. Positive effects include increased productivity and a decrease in manual labor, while negative effects include the potential for dependency on technology, which could result in a loss of practical expertise, and the marginalization of specific actors, such as small farms and subjects with limited education (Ferrari et al., 2022). We live in an era of communication, and almost every facet of human endeavor is impacted by or touched by communication. For instance, ICT (information and communication technology) has connected once-adverse individuals on platforms that benefit both parties. By replacing real-world distances with virtual ones, ICT has lowered the cost of conducting business. With a mobile phone, a farmer may now check his bank account balance, conduct bank transactions, and communicate with his agro-dealers or buyers of produce in both urban and rural areas without leaving his rural surroundings. There are currently several platforms along a particular value chain, which together should have a good impact on participants' revenue, productivity, and adoption of agricultural technologies. Agricultural production and technology adoption are now mediated by ICT use for extension message delivery (Phillip & Ndirpaya, 2020). In actuality, digitalization greatly affects society by encouraging convergence in a number of fields. (Stojanova et al., 2022). Since digitization is pervasive across all social spheres and has affected practically every aspect of life, it highlights the connection between technological advancements and rapid social change, demonstrating that technology and society are intertwined (Musik & Bogner, 2019).

FUTURE RESEARCH DIRECTIONS

In addition to digitalization, other megatrends include population transition and urbanization. According to UN predictions, rural populations are expected to decline as urbanization continues to rise. In contrast to 1950, when just 30% of the world's population resided in urban regions, the results show that 68% of people would live in urban areas by 2050 (Richter et al., 2019). This is in contrast to the difficulties that rural areas face due to their declining populations. The average life expectancy is rising due to population shift, which is another factor driving this growth. In conclusion, the megatrends will have an unforeseeable impact on modern living. Because of this, it is critical to recognize these megatrends' problems early on and take the appropriate action (Richter et al., 2019). In the future, the creation of agri-food products with added value that are aimed at satisfying customer demands and desires must be prioritized, with a focus on quality, innovation, and strict adherence to food safety and hygiene regulations (Mihailović & Radić Jean, 2019). Digital marketing and precision farming are key components to achieving this in the future.

Future studies should suggest a framework for tackling the ecological and digital "twin transition" using transformative policies founded on directionality, market integration, and reflexivity in accordance with the Green Deal. The foundation of the framework is the idea that digitalization is a socio-technical process, which means considering the social effects of each technology's advancement and focusing innovation strategies on precisely identifying the issues that need to be resolved (Brunori, 2022). Future studies should therefore develop the idea of a socio-cyber-physical system as a paradigm for innovation and strategic policies, and take into account its implications for sustainable digitalization initiatives in Serbia's rural areas and agricultural sector. Agriculture may significantly contribute to the nation's economic development with proper strategic planning (Mihailović et al., 2018).

CONCLUSION

In the framework of the digital economy, this chapter examines Serbian rural development, encompassing a range of socioeconomic programs targeted at rural populations and characterized by rural policy. Thus, the objective of this chapter is to analyze Serbian rural growth in the digital economy from two angles: the use of precision agriculture technologies and digital marketing. Digital marketing is crucial for companies trying to succeed over the long term in Serbia's vibrant agro-product sector. The swift development of technology and changing customer habits both call for a reworking of conventional marketing strategies. The agricultural industry has already been influenced by the Internet in developed market economies, and its usage for marketing goals is wide-ranging, ranging from online advertising to online buying (or purchasing) and services. Market and environmental research, communication, information sharing by setting up a website, direct online purchasing and selling, exchanges, auctions, and more can all be done by businesses via the Internet. If there are insufficient digital abilities in rural areas, making investments in digital infrastructure would be a waste. Rural communities must plan their skill development pathways in order to ensure that they have the skills they require to access planned or current digital infrastructure, understand and utilize the services that result, and take part in the co-design of new initiatives and services.

Now that new digital technologies are available, there is room for several communities in the Republic of Serbia to be revitalized. In other words, our nation is completely at odds with the current trend in Western nations. Many professions are no longer site-specific due to the growing number of tasks that may be completed using digital technologies. This enables people to relocate their commercial operations from largely polluted cities to countryside, where they naturally require better working environments. The territorial capital of rural regions and their industries can be enhanced by digitalization, and digital solutions can meet the demands and expectations of rural businesses and communities while tackling the social problems in Europe. Connecting rural and urban areas, lowering the vulnerability of delicate environments, enhancing local communities' ability to prepare for ecological shocks and strains, fostering the development of new services to make rural economies more productive, and improving access to markets for rural products and services are all the objectives of digitalization. Precision agriculture, on the contrary, is a method of agricultural production in which agrotechnical inputs and measurements are used locally, rather than uniformly over the entire plot. Since it is carried out in accordance with the locally specialized resources of a particular rural area, site-specific agriculture would be a more suitable title. Geographically specific agriculture can be implemented on a number of different platforms. Pillars for specific activities are formed by identifying possibilities, strengths, and requirements and using mapping to graphically represent them by location. According to site conditions, precision agriculture is a production strategy that encourages varied management techniques in a field. The new tools and information sources made possible by contemporary technologies form the foundation of this system.

In order to provide a foundation for successful modernization and transformation in this field, the authors also look at Serbian rural areas that have effectively adopted contemporary digital technologies. Through the use of digital marketing techniques and the implementation of precision agriculture technologies, the research findings may help Serbia's rural communities progress.

ACKNOWLEDGMENT

Paper is a part of research financed by the MSTDI RS, agreed in decision no. 451-03-136/2025-03/200009 from 4.2.2025.

REFERENCES

Ahmed, N., De, D., & Hussain, I. (2018). Internet of Things (IoT) for smart precision agriculture and farming in rural areas. *IEEE Internet of Things Journal, 5*(6), 4890–4899. DOI: 10.1109/JIOT.2018.2879579

Al-Ababneh, H. A. (2020). Modern trends of digital marketing development in the world. *PalArch's Journal of Archaeology of Egypt/Egyptology, 17*(8): 121-139.

Antonijević, M., Bradić-Martinović, A., Banović, J., & Ivanović, Đ. (2023). Is There a Relationship Between Country Development and Citizens' Level of Digital Skills?. *Economic Analysis: journal of emerging economies 56*, 57-68, https://doi .org/.DOI: 10.28934/ea.23.56.1

Arsić, S., Stojanović, A., Milošević, I., & Gajić, M. (2022). Positioning of the Republic of Serbia according to the index of digital economy and society in South-East Europe. *An international serial publication for theory and practice of Management Science*, International May Conference on Strategic Management – IMCSM22, May 28, 2022, Bor, Serbia, 300-309.

Azevedo, D. (2019). Precision agriculture and the smart village concept. In *Smart Villages in the EU and Beyond* (pp. 83–97). Emerald Publishing Limited. DOI: 10.1108/978-1-78769-845-120191007

Borowiecki, R., Siuta-Tokarska, B., Maroń, J., Suder, M., Thier, A., & Żmija, K. (2021). Developing digital economy and society in the light of the issue of digital convergence of the markets in the European Union countries. *Energies, 14*(9), 2717. 7. DOI: 10.3390/en14092717

Brunori, G. (2022). Agriculture and rural areas facing the "twin transition": Principles for a sustainable rural digitalisation. [REA]. *Rivista di Economia Agraria, 77*(3), 3–14. DOI: 10.36253/rea-13983

Brunori, G., Nieto, E., Casares, B., Debruyne, L., Tisenkopfs, T., & Brunori, A. (2021). Experts' recommendations to boost sustainable digitalisation of agriculture, forestry and rural areas by 2040. *Pisa, Italy*.

Cao, X., Yan, M., & Wen, J. (2023). Exploring the level and influencing factors of digital village development in China: Insights and recommendations. *Sustainability (Basel), 15*(13), 10423. DOI: 10.3390/su151310423

Ciruela-Lorenzo, A. M., Del-Aguila-Obra, A. R., Padilla-Meléndez, A., & Plaza-Angulo, J. J. (2020). Digitalization of agri-cooperatives in the smart agriculture context. proposal of a digital diagnosis tool. *Sustainability (Basel), 12*(4), 1325. DOI: 10.3390/su12041325

Cvijanović, D., Mihailović, B., Čavlin, M., & Čavlin, G. (2015). Impact of marketing consulting on performances of agrarian clusters in Serbia. *Sustainability (Basel), 7*(2), 1099–1115. https://doi.org/doi:10.3390/su7021099. DOI: 10.3390/su7021099

Dašić, D., Ratković, M., Marčetić, A., & Tošić, M. (2023). Promotion on the internet as a function of agribusiness development in Central Serbia. *Ekonomika Poljoprivrede, 70*(2), 479–491. DOI: 10.59267/ekoPolj2302479D

Dax, T. (1996). Defining rural areas–International comparisons and the OECD indicators1. *Rural Society, 6*(3), 3–18. DOI: 10.5172/rsj.6.3.3

Djorić, Ž. (2020). Digital economy-basic aspects and the case of Serbia. *Economic Outlook/Ekonomski Pogledi, 22*(2), 73-96.

Djuričin, D., & Vuksanović, I. (2016). The future of Serbia and how to survive IT: Catching up and convergence with the EU. *Economics of Enterprise, 64*(1-2), 15–36. DOI: 10.5937/ekopre1602015D

Drobnjaković, M., Stojanović, Ž., & Josipović, S. (2022). Rural areas and rural economy in Serbia. *The Geography of Serbia: Nature, People, Economy*, 289-303. https://DOI: 10.1007/978-3-030-74701-5_22

Erickson, B., & Fausti, S. W. (2021). The role of precision agriculture in food security. *Agronomy Journal, 113*(6), 4455–4462. DOI: 10.1002/agj2.20919

Ferrari, A., Bacco, M., Gaber, K., Jedlitschka, A., Hess, S., Kaipainen, J., Koltsida, P., Toli, E., & Brunori, G. (2022). Drivers, barriers and impacts of digitalisation in rural areas from the viewpoint of experts. *Information and Software Technology, 145*, 106816. DOI: 10.1016/j.infsof.2021.106816

Food and Agriculture Organization of the United Nations - FAO. (2017). *The future of food and agriculture – Trends and challenges,* Retrieved February 02, 2019 from https://www.fao.org/3/i6583e/i6583e.pdf

Gusev, A. S., Beznosov, G. A., Ziablitckaia, N. V., Kholmanskikh, M. V., Novopashin, L. A., Denyozhko, L. V., & Sadov, A. A. (2019). An analysis of research areas in precision agriculture. *International Transaction Journal of Engineering Management & Applied Sciences & Technologies, 10*(10), 1–10.

Local Market. (2019). Retrieved December 12, 2021 from https://www.lokalnipazar.rs/o-inicijativi

Manasijević, A., Milojković, M., & Mastilo, D. (2019). Digital Village Transformation: A Model for Relativizing Regional Disparities in the Republic of Serbia. *Economics-časopis za inovacijska i ekonomska istraživanja, 7*(2), 125-138. DOI: 10.2478/eoik-2019-0013

Mihailović, B., Birmančević, B., & Obradović, M. (2014). The selection factors of consultants in Serbian agro-sector. *Ekonomika Poljoprivrede, 61*(1), 149–162. DOI: 10.5937/ekoPolj1401149M

Mihailović, B., & Popović, V. (2021). Digital marketing of agri-food products in support of rural tourism during the Covid pandemic. In *Tourism International Scientific Conference Vrnjačka Banja-TISC,* Vol. 6, No. 1, 111-126. DOI: 10.52370/TISC21111BM

Mihailović, B., & Radić Jean, I. (2019). Resources and potential of agri-food products with added value in Braničevo-Podunavlje region. *Ekonomika Poljoprivrede, 66*(3), 669–680. DOI: 10.5937/ekoPolj1903669M

Mihailović, B., Simonović, Z., & Brzaković, T. (2018). Strategic planning of sustainable development of agriculture of Lajkovac Municipality. *Ekonomika Poljoprivrede, 65*(2), 465–884. DOI: 10.5937/ekoPolj1802475M

Miletić, D., Vojvodić, A., & Vojvodić, M. (2017). The basic characteristics of the information technology sector in Serbia. *SEER: Journal for Labour and Social Affairs in Eastern Europe*, 5-20.

Mondal, P., & Basu, M. (2009). Adoption of precision agriculture technologies in India and in some developing countries: Scope, present status and strategies. *Progress in Natural Science, 19*(6), 659–666. DOI: 10.1016/j.pnsc.2008.07.020

Musik, C., & Bogner, A. (2019). Book title: Digitalization & society: A sociology of technology perspective on current trends in data, digital security and the internet. *Osterreichische Zeitschrift fur Soziologie, 44*(S1), 1–14. DOI: 10.1007/s11614-019-00344-5

Pantić, M., & Čolić, N. (2023). Digital participation framework for mountain areas in Serbia. *Transylvanian Review of Administrative Sciences, 19*(68), 78–95. DOI: 10.24193/tras.68E.5

Pāvulēns, E., & Vilka, L. (2024). Digitalisation in the provision of social services: Rural counties perspective. In *SHS Web of Conferences* (Vol. 184, p. 05002). EDP Sciences.

Phillip, D., & Ndirpaya, Y. D. (2020). Digitalization in Agriculture. *Food and Nutrition-A Case Study of Nigeria. FARA Research Report*, *5*(10), 66.

Popović, V., Katić, B., & Savić, M. (2011). Rural development in Serbia and the local communities. *Economics of Agriculture, 58*(1), 33–44.

Popović, V., Katić, B., & Živanović-Miljković, J. (2010). Rural development network and territorial competitiveness. *Economics of Agriculture, 57*(Special nu), 111-120.

Popović, V., & Mihailović, B. (2023). Women Entrepreneurship in multifunctional agriculture for rural revival in Serbia. In *Sustainable growth and global social development in competitive economies* (pp. 225–247). IGI Global. DOI: 10.4018/978-1-6684-8810-2.ch012

Popović, V., Mihailović, B., & Simonović, Z. (2018). Modern Food Retail and Unfair Trading Practices. *Ekonomika Poljoprivrede*, *65*(4), 1499–1512. DOI: 10.5937/ekoPolj1804499P

Popović, V., & Mijajlović, N. (2014). Climate change and sustainable development in agriculture and forestry. In *Sustainable practices: Concepts, methodologies, tools, and applications* (pp. 18–48). IGI Global. DOI: 10.4018/978-1-4666-4852-4.ch002

Popović, V., Sarić, R., & Jovanović, M. (2012). Sustainability of agriculture in Danube basin area. *Economics of Agriculture*, *59*(1), 73–87.

Project "Internet of Food and Farm 2020", EU, 2021. Retrieved May 03, 2025 from https://cordis.europa.eu/project/id/731884

Rađenović, Ž., Janjić, I., Talić, M., Đokić, M., Rađenović, T., Boskov, T., & Krstić, B. (2025). Digital mapping of business performance indicators of agricultural holdings in Serbia. *Ekonomika Poljoprivrede*, *72*(1), 225–240. DOI: 10.59267/ekoPolj2501225R

Radić, V., Radić, N., & Cogoljević, V. (2022). New technologies as a driver of change in the agricultural sector. *Ekonomika Poljoprivrede*, *69*(1), 147–162. DOI: 10.5937/ekoPolj2201147R

Radović, G., Subić, J., & Pejanović, V. (2024). Analysis of implementation of the IPARD II program in Serbia. *Economics of agriculture, 71*(3), 1017-1031. DOI: 10.59267/ekoPolj24031017R

Richter, A., Waidelich, L., Kölmel, B., Bulander, R., Glaser, P., Proske, M., & Brügmann, S. (2019). Digitalisation and Future Challenges in Rural Areas: An Open Innovation based Research. In *ICETE (1)*, 153-159.

Robert, P. C. (2002). Precision agriculture: a challenge for crop nutrition management. In *Progress in Plant Nutrition: Plenary Lectures of the XIV International Plant Nutrition Colloquium: Food security and sustainability of agro-ecosystems through basic and applied research* (pp. 143-149). Springer Netherlands. DOI: 10.1007/978-94-017-2789-1_11

Roberts, E., Beel, D., Philip, L., & Townsend, L. (2017). Rural resilience in a digital society. *Journal of Rural Studies, 54*, 355–359. DOI: 10.1016/j.jrurstud.2017.06.010

Salemink, K., Strijker, D., & Bosworth, G. (2017). Rural development in the digital age: A systematic literature review on unequal ICT availability, adoption, and use in rural areas. *Journal of Rural Studies, 54*, 360–371. DOI: 10.1016/j.jrurstud.2015.09.001

Seelan, S. K., Laguette, S., Casady, G. M., & Seielstad, G. A. (2003). Remote sensing applications for precision agriculture: A learning community approach. *Remote Sensing of Environment, 88*(1-2), 157–169. DOI: 10.1016/j.rse.2003.04.007

Shafi, U., Mumtaz, R., García-Nieto, J., Hassan, S. A., Zaidi, S. A. R., & Iqbal, N. (2019). Precision agriculture techniques and practices: From considerations to applications. *Sensors (Basel), 19*(17), 3796. DOI: 10.3390/s19173796

Stamenović, A. P. (2024). The concept of smart rural development on the example of the municipality of Petrovac na Mlavi. In *Proceedings The First International Conference FUTURE-BME 2024 (Forging the Future: Pioneering Approaches in Business, Management and* Economics Engineering to Overcome Emerging Global Challenges), 279-285.

State Audit Institution – SAI. (2023). *Audit and Performance Audit Report: The Impact of Regional Development on Demographic Trends in the Republic of Serbia – Parallel Performance Audit*. Presentation.

Stojanova, S., Cvar, N., Verhovnik, J., Božić, N., Trilar, J., Kos, A., & Stojmenova Duh, E. (2022). Rural digital innovation hubs as a paradigm for sustainable business models in europe's rural areas. *Sustainability (Basel), 14*(21), 14620. DOI: 10.3390/su142114620

Stojanović, M., Gligorijević, J., Grubor, M., Popović, M., Ćorić, B., Zarev, D., & Šmelcerović, M. (2024). the potential of digital marketing in the promotion of organic agricultural products. *Ekonomika Poljoprivrede, 71*(4), 1237–1251. DOI: 10.59267/ekoPolj24041237S

Tagarakis, A. C., van Evert, F., Kempenaar, C., Ljubicic, N., Milic, D., Crnojevic-Bengin, V., & Crnojevic, V. (2018). Opportunities for precision agriculture in Serbia. In *Proceedings of the 14th International Conference on Precision Agriculture,* Montreal, QC, Canada (Vol. 24), 1-12.

Tomashuk, I., Koliadenko, S., & Burdiak, M. (2025). The impact of digital innovations on the development of agricultural business. *Baltic Journal of Economic Studies, 11*(1), 361–375. DOI: 10.30525/2256-0742/2025-11-1-361-375

Zhang, Q. (2016). *Precision agriculture technology for crop farming*. Taylor & Francis.

ADDITIONAL READING

Bajraktari, N., & Ahmeti, A. (2018). Application of Marketing in Interest as a Factor of Development of Enterprises in Digital Economy. *Prizren Social Science Journal, 2*(1), 36–51.

Cochrane, N., Reed, M., & Jovanović, Z. (2007). Designing a Rural Development Strategy for Serbia: Training Local Actors to Mobilize Local Assets.

Djukic, G. P. (2022). Digital inclusion for vulnerable groups and transformation: A comparative case study. In *Handbook of Research on Global Institutional Roles for Inclusive Development* (pp. 19–38). IGI global. DOI: 10.4018/978-1-6684-2448-3.ch002

Kljajić, N., Paraušić, V., & Subić, J. (2024). Socio-environmental aspects of digitalisation in Serbian agriculture: Farmers' perceptions. *Scientific Papers. Series Management, Economic, Engineering in Agriculture and Rural Development, 24*(3), 487–496.

Kovljenić, M., Škorić, J., Galetin, M., & Škorić, S. (2023). Digital technology in agriculture: evidence from farms on the territory of AP Vojvodina. *Economics of agriculture, 70*(2), 583-596.

Krstić, A. (2014). Digital switchover in Serbia in a comparative perspective. *International Journal of Digital Television, 5*(3), 237–253. DOI: 10.1386/jdtv.5.3.237_1

Mićić, L. (2017). Digital transformation and its influence on GDP. *Economics-Innovative and Economics Research Journal*, *5*(2), 135–147.

Stojanović, A., Radić, A., Arsić, S., & Milošević, I. (2022). Investigating digital divide in European rural areas as a barrier to knowledge sharing. *PaKSoM, 2022*, 343.

Tankosić, J. V., Mirjanić, B., Prodanović, R., Lekić, S., & Carić, B. (2024). Digitalization in Agricultural Sector: Agriculture 4.0 for Sustainable Agriculture. *Journal of Agronomy, Technology and Engineering Management*, *7*(1), 1036–1042. DOI: 10.55817/GEQW8736

Wang, F., & Shen, S. (2024). Does the digital economy development improve or exacerbate income inequality? International evidence. *MDE. Managerial and Decision Economics*, *45*(6), 4012–4038. DOI: 10.1002/mde.4231

KEY TERMS AND DEFINITIONS

Digital Economy: The term "digital economy" describes the economic activity that results from the use of digital technology to link people, companies, devices, data, and operations.

Digital Infrastructure: The actual hardware and software-based technologies that make digital services possible are known as digital infrastructure. It comprises the networks and IT systems that let businesses function and interact.

Digital Literacy: The capacity to locate, assess, and share information via typing or digital media platforms is known as digital literacy.

Digital Marketing: Using websites, apps, mobile devices, social media, search engines, and other digital tools to advertise and sell goods and services is known as digital marketing.

Precision Agriculture: Determining the causes of yield variations in the field, coming up with potential remedies based on economic rationality, putting new technology into place, and repeating the process are all part of precision agriculture.

Rural Development: The goal of rural development is to enhance the social and economic well-being of a particular population: the rural poor. It entails providing the poorest people who are looking for work in rural areas with the advantages of development.

Smart Villages: Smart Villages are rural communities that build on local opportunities and strengths by enhancing their resilience through creative solutions.

Chapter 9

Prospects for Carbon Farming in Serbian Agriculture

Vesna Popović
https://orcid.org/0000-0003-1018-2461
Institute of Agricultural Economics, Belgrade, Serbia

Jelena Živanovic Miljković
http://orcid.org/0000-0003-2559-7870
Institute of Architecture and Urban and Spatial Planning of Serbia, Serbia

Branko Mihailović
https://orcid.org/0000-0002-2398-6568
Institute of Agricultural Economics, Belgrade, Serbia

ABSTRACT

The research objective is carbon farming, here encompassing sustainable soil management practices for soil organic carbon sequestration and/or soil GHG emissions reduction in croplands and grasslands, and business model that generates farmers reward for climate change mitigation outcomes and co-benefits for environment and society. After reviewing the main issues of carbon farming and its role in climate change mitigation policy, the authors analyzed pedoclimatic conditions, land use dynamics and management, carbon content in agricultural soils, and farm structure in main agricultural regions of Serbia-Vojvodina and Central Serbia. The research results, together with findings on carbon farming mechanisms, allow the authors to consider the region-specific combination of carbon farming practices and business

DOI: 10.4018/979-8-3373-2898-0.ch009

models relevant to Serbian agriculture on the path to EU membership, as well as the main barriers to their adoption. Further research should include engaging stakeholders in testing identified carbon farming solutions to ensure fine-tuned policy design.

INTRODUCTION

The global warming reached 1.1°C above pre-industrial levels in 2011-2020 in response to ongoing greenhouse gas (GHG) emissions arising from unsustainable energy use, land use and land-use change, and production and consumption patterns (Lee & Romero, 2023). Climate changes already have adverse impacts on global ecosystems, economy and human health and the projections of end-of-century global warming of 1.5°C to $\geq$4°C indicated that these impacts will intensify depending on future GHG emissions (Lee & Romero, 2023; Anderson et al., 2016).

The UNFCCC Paris Agreement (2015) binds signatory countries to keep global average temperature well below 2°C above pre-industrial levels and preferably at 1.5°C with no or limited overshoot, achieving a balance between anthropogenic GHG emissions and removals in the second half of this century. National targets of net-zero emissions by 2050 and net-zero pledges of non-state entities encouraged by the UNFCCC Race to Zero campaign (2019), have proliferated in recent few years (Hans et al., 2022). However, according to UNEP's 2024 Emissions Gap Report, nationally determined contributions (NDCs) are insufficient to meet the Paris Agreement's temperature limits and net zero targets, putting the world on track for best-case global warming of 2.6°C by 2100. Moreover, existing mitigation policies do not have the capacity to meet even these insufficient NDCs, indicating an implementation gap that leads to a median global warming of 3.1°C (UNEP, 2024). The 2025 NDCs (NDCs 3.0) and their implementation policies need to be more progressive and ambitious to align the global emissions trajectory with the goals of the Paris Agreement.

A high overshoot of 1.5°C target increases reliance on large-scale carbon removals to offset higher emissions before 2030 (Pathak et al., 2022). Intensively-managed under climate change, agricultural mineral soils are among the most depleted terrestrial carbon stocks and have a good prospect for soil organic carbon (SOC) sequestration and soil quality improvement (Sanderman et al, 2017; Lal, 2018; Poeplau, 2023). According to Pathak et al. (2022), the SOC sequestration in croplands and grasslands has a high technology readiness level, is cost-effective (-45–\$100/ tCO_2eq) and has a mitigation potential at global level of 0.6–9.3 $GtCO_2yr^{-1}$. However, it also carries risks of reversal and faces biophysical constraints related to SOC saturation capacity and deficit dynamics influenced by pedoclimatic conditions, land use and land management practices (Chenu et al., 2019; Rumpel et al., 2020; Moinet, 2023).

Agricultural soil carbon projects have rarely been included in carbon markets and NDCs in the past, mostly due to the complex MRV mechanisms but also other, economic, social, institutional and other barriers (Bossio et al., 2020; Wiese et al., 2021). However, the number of countries that referred to SOC in mitigation measures increased in new and updated 2022 NDCs (Rose et al., 2022). An increase in SOC sequestration for climate action, soil health and soil fertility has been advocated by several UNFCCC initiatives such as the 4p1000 Initiative (Rumpel et al., 2020) and Koronivia joint work on agriculture (UN, 2019). The FAO-hosted Global Soil Partnership calls for recarbonization of global agricultural soils within RECSOIL initiative (FAO, 2019). At COP 29, Parties agreed on rules for international co-operation through carbon markets under the Paris Agreement (Article 6) to help countries leverage carbon-related climate finance and deliver their NDC targets, and thus support faster global decarbonization (UN, 2025).

In its 2022 updated NDC, the Republic of Serbia committed to an unconditional emissions reduction target of 13.2% compared to 2010 levels, or 33.3% compared to 1990 levels, without the land use, land use change and forestry (LULUCF) by 2030 (MEP, 2022). The net GHG emissions target for Serbia, set within the net GHG emissions targets of the EU Energy Community Ministerial Council for 2030 compared to 1990 levels (Decision 2022/02/MC-EnC10), is -40.3%, including LULUCF. As a signatory to the Sofia Declaration on the Green Agenda for the Western Balkans, Serbia has pledged to working with the EU towards its 2050 target of a carbon-neutral continent (RCC, 2021).

The EU Climate Law (EU/2021/1119) set the objective of balanced GHG emissions and removals within the European Union at the latest by 2050 and confirmed the 2030 objective of at least 55% reduction in net GHG emissions compared to 1990 without the use of international credits. To leverage opportunities for climate action, the revised LULUCF Regulation (EU/2023/839) set ambitious net carbon removal national targets for the land use sector. These targets form the backbone of the EU NDC for the 2021-2030 period (EC, 2023). The EU Farm to Fork Strategy (COM (2020) 381 final) considers carbon farming as a new green business model and highlights a potential role of the CAP and other public and private initiatives in its financing. The Carbon Removals and Carbon Farming (CRCF) Regulation (EU/2024/3012) has created the first EU-wide voluntary framework for certifying carbon farming outcomes across Europe. All carbon removals and soil emission reductions certified under this certification framework should contribute to the achievement of its NDC and climate objectives as well as to the nature restoration targets, by implementing activities that generate biodiversity co-benefits (EU/2024/1991). Furthermore, recent DG CLIMA's studies consider a range of policy options for climate mitigation incentives across the agri-food value chain, including agri-food emission trading system (AgETS) combined with LULUCF removals reward models (EC DG CLIMA, 2023, 2024).

After introductory review of the role of carbon farming in climate mitigation policy and theoretical background dedicated to main carbon farming issues, the authors will analyse soil types, climate and topography, land use and land use dynamics, land management and soil carbon levels in the two main agro-ecological regions of Serbia – Vojvodina and Central Serbia (without data for Kosovo i Metohija under UNMIK). These research results, in conjunction with the findings contained in scientific papers, project reports, and solutions adopted in climate legislation, will allow the authors to consider the region-specific combination of carbon farming practices and business models relevant to Serbian agriculture on the path to EU membership, as well as the main barriers to their adoption. This will be elaborated and summarized in solutions and recommendations. Further research should include stakeholder engagement and active participation in testing identified carbon farming solutions, thereby enabling fine-tuning of carbon farming policy design.

BACKGROUND

According to EU legislation (EU/2024/3012), carbon farming refers to any practice or process carried out over a period of activity of at least five years, which relates to the management of terrestrial or coastal environments and results in the capture and temporary storage of atmospheric or biogenic carbon in biogenic carbon pools or the reduction of greenhouse gas emissions from soil carbon pools. The EU carbon farming initiative (COM (2021) 800 final) defined carbon farming as a green business model that allows farmers to generate income for climate change mitigation results, while respecting ecological principles favourable to biodiversity and natural capital as a whole.

The SOC sequestration potential and soil emissions reduction in croplands and grasslands can be realized by carbon farmers through the adoption of site-specific, sustainable soil management (SSM) practices that enhance carbon removal and/or reduce GHG emissions from agricultural soils, supported by effective measuring/ monitoring, reporting and verification (MRV) methodologies and sound and just policy- and/or market-based incentive mechanisms (Lal et al., 2018; FAO, 2019).

The FAO's RECSOIL technical manual of recommended management practices gives a comprehensive overview of cropland and grassland practices that ensure sufficient soil organic cover (cover cropping, organic mulch), decrease decomposition rates of soil organic matter (reduced- or no-tillage) and maintain/increase SOC content (soil and water conservation techniques, crop diversification, nutrient management, grassland conservation and restoration and grazing management), including various forms of integrated farming systems. Moreover, agroecology, climate-smart agriculture, regenerative agriculture, organic agriculture and precision farming, being all complex and not mutually exclusive agricultural systems, encompass a range of production practices that have a significant positive impact on soil organic carbon depending on local climate, soil type and land use (FAO & ITPS, 2021).

The majority of these practices provides multiple co-benefits for the environment, people and economy by enhancing climate resilience and biodiversity, combating desertification and land degradation and improving soil properties, food security and livelihoods of farming communities (Shukla et al., 2019, Vermeulen et al., 2019; Bossio et al., 2020). However, some of them are also linked to significant trade-offs, costs and conflicts with other practices and need reassessment, particularly in terms of their potential to contribute to both carbon storage and yield improvement (Lugato et al., 2018; Chenu et al., 2019; Paul et al., 2023; Moinet, 2023). As with other approaches to sustainable agriculture, there is a need to assess certain land uses or mitigation actions at regional and landscape level to provide integrated solutions suitable for local ecosystems, prevent leakage effects and promote regional value chains and marketing strategies (Weltin et al., 2018; Paul et al., 2023; Amelung et al., 2020).

Farmers are willing to implement SOC-focused SSM practices primarily if there are clear co-benefits in terms of increased yields and profitability. Small per hectare sequestration rates and still challenging MRV process further demotivate carbon farmers (Pathak et al., 2022). Measuring, monitoring, reporting and verifying the addition and permanence of SOC constitutes a crucial step for carbon farming projects, especially those dealing with result-based financial incentives (FAO, 2019, 2020). To be used effectively, these methods need to be robust, scalable and affordable to farmers (van der Voort, 2023). Relying on standardized baselines and remote sensing technologies, the EU CRCF Regulation aims to streamline certification processes, making them cost-effective, yet robust.

The financial incentives for carbon farmers can come from public or private sources, rewarding them either for their SOC-centred SSM actions or the amount of additional carbon removals or soil emission reductions generated in comparison to a baseline, including hybrid models, which mix action- and result-based payments. Public financing usually involves action-based SSM practices, although it can also refer to credit purchases as a public policy tool to encourage mitigation (McDonald et al., 2021; Verschuuren, 2017). Agri-food companies can pay carbon farmers within supply chain by counting on price premiums from customers or for meeting their own climate objectives. Nevertheless, private financing dominates the business models linked to voluntary carbon markets, with higher MRV requirements that ensure quality carbon offsets. Most transactions there occur through a third-party entity, which links farmers to buyers (McDonald et al., 2021; Shockley & Snell, 2021).

Pilot project developers are often among them, usually coming with agribusiness partners to initially document carbon accumulation on contracted farmlands, then continuing to act in the longer term as intermediaries between farmers and carbon offsets buyers (McDonald et al., 2021; Aiken, 2021). Carbon funds and innovative funding mechanisms like advance market commitments (AMCs) can boost investment in now removal technologies and nature-based solutions. Blended public-private finance would leverage public money to reduce commercial risk and attract additional capital (EC DG CLIMA, 2025).

Around 40% of carbon pricing instruments in operation worldwide allow for the use of carbon credits to offset liabilities, while the international compliance markets aim to enable countries voluntarily purchasing correspondingly adjusted credits recognized under international treaties to meet their NDCs (World Bank, 2024). Many of them, such as Australia, Alberta and California ETSs have included agricultural emissions and removals as offsets (Verschuuren, 2022). When it comes to the EU, there is no legal possibility to date to use carbon credits for compliance with the EU ETS liabilities (Directive 2003/87/EC). The EU CRCF Regulation excludes carbon removals and soil emission reductions generated under the Regulation from use towards third-party-NDCs or international compliance schemes. However, the EU is considering integrating carbon removal credits issued for permanent carbon removal technologies into the EU ETS, as well as Article 6 carbon credits into its 2040 climate target (Schuett, 2024; Abnett, 2025). Moreover, the EU is considering different options of applying the polluter-pays principle to GHG emissions along the agri-food value chain via emissions trading (AgETS), and beyond, to linking AgETS to LULUCF removals - indirectly by using revenues collected from AgETS or directly using carbon credits to offset AgETS obligations in a way that incentivise removals without risking of emission deterrence (EC DG CLIMA, 2023).

Many questions remain regarding high costs for carbon farmers and impacts on competitiveness, income and consumer prices. It is crucial to understand the costs and risks of implementing new practices before engaging in carbon market programs and the responsibilities of farmers during the term of the agreement (Paustian et al., 2019; Shockley & Snell, 2021). Hybrid models that combine up-front grants with result-based rewards and public risk management instruments such as price floors or loan guarantees can help farmers cover initial transition costs and manage liquidity risks (EC DG CLIMA, 2025). Other challenges to carbon farming relate to socio-cultural and institutional barriers and include farmers' conservative value systems and a high preference for autonomy, low human and social capital for adopting innovative practices, knowledge gaps, weak governance and low public awareness (Henry et al., 2023; Naftel, 2022).

Maximising synergies and managing trade-offs require effective legislation and governance, research and innovation, knowledge transfer, investments and markets, raised public awareness and strong farmer organisations, integrated within a framework of fair and just joint action to meet the multiple sustainable development objectives. As Stabinsky (2021) stated, "schemes where nature is reduced to its constituent carbon to be sold to the highest bidder, will never be solutions" (p. 44).

CARBON FARMING IN SERBIAN AGRICULTURE

Study Area

Serbia is a landlocked country in south-eastern Europe. The northern part of Serbia consists of lowlands, while the southern part of the country is dominated by hills and mountains. Climate is continental in the north, moderate continental in the south and alpine in the high mountains. Winters are short, cold and snowy, while summers are warm. Thirteen of the fifteen warmest years in Serbia were registered after the year 2000. Serbia is highly water-stressed country, with high risk of erosion and flooding in most parts of the territory (MEP, 2024a).

Many factors affect SOC stock level and dynamic, such as soil type, climate and topography, current and previous land use, and land management. Therefore, the SOC sequestration potential is region-specific as well as the mix of SSM practices for its maintenance and enhancement.

Soil Type, Climate and Topography

Based on findings of Čirič and Filipovski (1972) and Filipovski (1974), Dinić (1997) elaborated four pedogeographic regions of Serbia, with following soil types:

- *Vojvodina lowlands of Pannonian Basin*, with chernozem on loess plateaus and chernozem, humifluvisols and halomorphic soils on loess terraces; fluvisols, humifluvisols, humogleys and halomorphic soils on alluvial plains and river terraces; arenosols, chernozems and redzinas in Deliblato and Subotica sands; and rankers, rendzinas, eutric and dystric cambisols, luvisols and colluvial soils on Pannonian basin' island mountains.
- *The southern hilly edge of the Pannonian Basin in Central Serbia*, with vertisols and eutric cambisols on lake sediments; oases of chernozems and pseudogleys; fluvisols, humofluvisols, humogleys and eugleys on alluvial plains and low river terraces; and colluvial soils in the erosion-prone southern parts of the region.
- *Northwestern part of Central Serbia*, with a more humid climate and high altitudinal variety of soil cover - from fluvisols and eugleys at the bottom of

river valleys, through chernozems and luvisolic eutric cambisols, to luvisols, rendzinas and regosols on mountain slopes;

- *Vast mountainous areas of eastern and western parts of Central Serbia*, with chalcocambisols, luvisols and chalcomelanosols on a limestone substrate; distric cambisols and rankers on acidic silicate rocks; and vertisols, eutric cambisols, luvisols and rankers on strongly alkaline rocks.

Climate and topography further influence soil carbon stocks and land suitability for crop production within different agro-climatic zones, as defined in Rulebook on cadastral classification and land evaluation (Official Gazette of the Republic of Serbia – OG RS, 63/2014):

- *The lowlands* extend up to an altitude of 250 meters. The average annual temperature is higher than 10.5°C, the average annual precipitation is up to 700 mm, while the amount of precipitation during the growing season is on average 350 mm. Most of the lands are of the first to fourth quality class and there are no restrictions on crop cultivation. This is a zone of intensive crop production, primarily of grains and oilseeds.
- *The hilly zone* extends at an altitude of 250 to 650 meters above sea level. The average annual temperature is higher than 9.5°C, the average annual precipitation is up to 750 mm, and during the growing season up to 400 mm. All agricultural crops are grown, with very few restrictions, and the lands are mainly of the second to the fifth capability classes. An intensive grain and forage production is mixed with indoor livestock rearing, mainly on the family farms.
- *The hilly-mountainous zone* extends at an altitude of 650 to 1000 meters above sea level. The average annual temperature is up to 8°C, the average annual precipitation is up to 800 mm, and the amount of precipitation during the growing season is over 400 mm. The number of crops is limited; there cannot be grown maize or vineyards and the lands are mainly of the fourth to the sixth capability classes. Its western part is known by production of raspberries and potatoes.
- *The mountain zone* includes areas at an altitude of over 1,000 meters, with an average annual temperature below 6 °C and an average annual rainfall of 900 mm or more, while during the growing season it exceeds 450 mm. The number of crops is limited to spring cereals, while vineyards or orchards cannot be grown. There are mostly lands from the fifth to the eighth capability classes. This is the area for livestock grazing and low-intensive crop production.

Land Use and Land Use Change

According to 2023 Census of Agriculture (SORS, 2024c), utilised agricultural area (UAA) in the Republic of Serbia covers 3,239,374 ha, which represents 41.8% of the country's territory. This land is managed by 503,044 agricultural holdings, almost all family farms, of which more than two-thirds are smaller than 5 hectares. The largest share of the UAA is occupied by arable land and gardens (78.8%), followed by permanent grasslands (14.5%), fruit and berry plantations (6.1%) and vineyards (0.6%).

The regional distribution of these land use categories is largely determined by pedo-climatic advantages. Close to half of the total UAA in the country and 56.1% of arable land and gardens is located in the Vojvodina lowlands, while the majority of permanent grasslands, fruit and berry plantations and vineyards are in the predominantly hilly and mountainous Central Serbia. Vojvodina has one fifth of all farms in the country, with the rest in Central Serbia. The share of small farms (smaller than 5 ha) here is 47.9%, while medium-scale farms (5 to 20 ha) are 35.5%, and those over 20 ha 16.5%. In Central Serbia, these shares are 73.5%, 24.6% and 2.0%, respectively. Being part of the crop rotation, one-year fallow covered 8,247 ha (27.1% was in Vojvodina and 72.9% in Central Serbia), while unutilised agricultural land occupied 98,484 ha (5,939 ha in Vojvodina and 92,545 ha in Central Serbia).

Agricultural areas identified in Serbia in 2018 under CORINE Land Cover nomenclature comprise six third-class level categories of land cover: non-irrigated arable land (211), vineyards (211), fruit trees and berry plantations (222), pastures (231), complex cultivation patterns (242) and land principally occupied by agriculture, with significant areas of natural vegetation (243). Land cover statistics derived from the CORINE land cover data series confirm that non-irrigated land dominates and is mostly located in Vojvodina, while mosaic farmland prevails in the agricultural land structure in Central Serbia (EEA, 2023). During the period 2000-2018, total agricultural land in Serbia decreased by 120 km^2, dominantly in Central Serbia (decreased by 110 km^2), with the largest decrease recorded in pastures and mosaic farmland (Figure 1).

Figure 1. Diagram of CLC agricultural land cover flows in Serbia, 2000-2018 (km²)

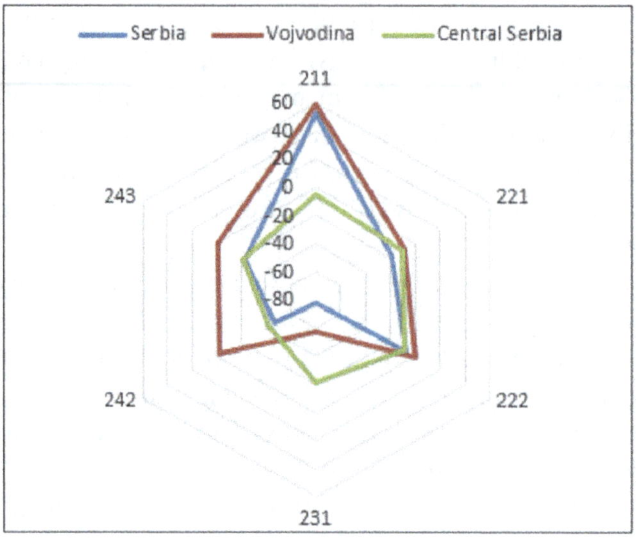

Source: Authors' composition based on EEA, 2023.

These values are net results of land formation data that refer to the amount of land of certain land cover category created elsewhere, and land consumption data, which register the amount of decreasing land cover areas, as defined in the EEA Land and Ecosystem Accounting (LEAC) statistics (Table 1).

Table 1. Land formation and land consumption in land cover flows, 2000-2018 (km²)

	Arable land & permanent crops	Pastures	Mosaic farmland	Total agricultural areas
Land formation	187	26	23	236
Land consumption	160	104	92	356
Land cover change	27	-78	-69	-120

Source: Authors' composition based on EEA, 2023.

According to LEAC statistics (EEA, 2023), internal conversions in agriculture prevailed among the causes of the formation of arable land and permanent crops, as well as pastures and mosaic farmland during the observed period 2000-2018. Close to half of the newly created arable land and permanent crops came from the conversion of grassland. Conversion of permanent crops to arable land was also present as well as the reverse, conversion from arable land to permanent crops. Pastures were mainly created by expansion of grassland and long-term fallow land

and semi-natural creation and rotation, whereas new mosaic farmland was formed by internal conversion of complex agricultural classes and expansion of semi-natural areas on agricultural land (Figure 2).

Figure 2. Agricultural land cover change, 2000-2018 (km²)

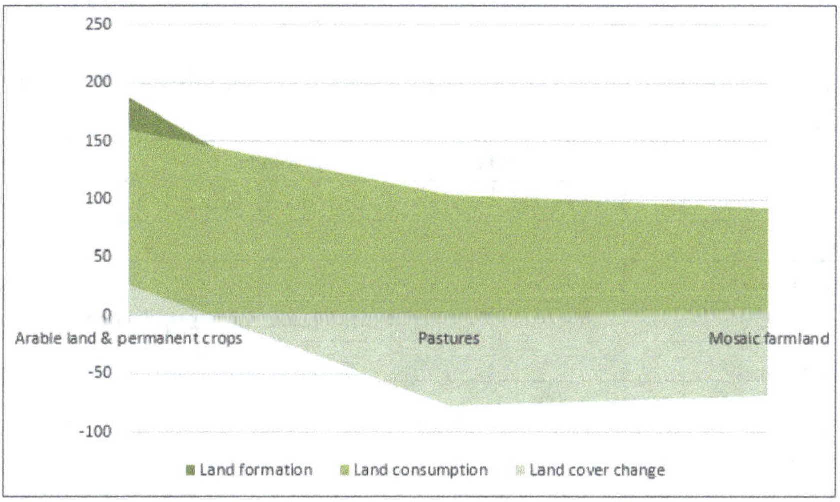

Source: Authors' composition based on EEA, 2023.

In terms of consumption, agricultural internal conversions have the largest share in arable land and permanent crops reduction (64.8%), followed by the expansion of economic sites and infrastructure (22.7%). Pastures were mostly converted to arable land and permanent crops (63.2%), and to a lesser extent to forests and shrub on agricultural land (14.3%), while mosaic agricultural land was lost in favour of forests and shrub on agricultural land (30.8%), expansion of mines and quarrying areas (14.7%), and urban diffuse residential expansion (13.7%).

The expansion of urban housing settlements has been carried out almost entirely at the expense of agricultural land, as well as most of the expansion of economic locations and infrastructure, often causing serious land use concerns, conflicts and trade-offs (Popović et al., 2015; Živanović Miljković et al., 2022; Živanović Miljković et al., 2025).

Land Management

The Agricultural Land Law established an obligation for owners and users of agricultural land to use it by "acting as good stewards and in accordance with the rules of the Code of Good Agricultural Practice" (OG RS, 41/2009, Art. 59). Since the Regulation on the Code of Good Agricultural Practices (OG RS, 23/2023) was adopted only recently, the 2023 Census of Agriculture registered the number of farms and land areas on which farmers voluntarily applied sustainable soil management and conservation practices in order to increase resource use efficiency and thereby increase profitability (Table 2).

Table 2. Soil management and conservation practices: number of farms and area (ha), 2023.

	Serbia		Vojvodina		Central Serbia	
	Areas (ha)	**Farms**	**Areas (ha)**	**Farms**	**Areas (ha)**	**Farms**
Tillage						
Conventional tillage	2,011,544	379,905	1,189,199	91,852	822,345	288,053
Conservation tillage	153,173	17,741	106,454	2,542	46,719	15,199
Zero tillage	32,989	15,986	6,485	522	26,504	15,465
Soil cover						
Bare soils after main crops	1,273,098	238,620	784,575	58,424	488,523	180,196
Winter crops	696,071	152,858	412,785	35,366	283,287	117,492
Catch and cover crops	40,082	16,032	19,374	1,031	20,708	15,001
Plant residues, mulching	203,295	69,477	86,579	9,936	116,716	59,541
Nutrient management						
Mineral fertilisers	2,049,333	436,415	1,190,542	88,240	858,792	348,174
Manure	687,776	350,865	235,787	67,468	451,990	283,396
Irrigation						
Irrigation areas	268,305	138,139	143,999	20,809	124,307	117,330

Source: SORS, 2024b, 2024d, 2024e, 2025a.

Among farms that apply conservation and zero tillage in Vojvodina, the majority are those larger than 20 ha and medium-sized farms, from 5 to 20 ha. In Central Serbia, nearly half of the farmers who have opted for reduced and zero tillage apply it on farms smaller than 5 ha (SORS, 2025a). The structure of agricultural holdings is different when it comes to the use of cover crops and harvest residues and/or mulching, which is most prevalent on small farms, both in Central Serbia and in the Vojvodina region, with a share of 69.4% and 58.0%, respectively. However, the share of farms larger than 20 ha in the use of these SSM measures in Vojvodina is 19%, while in Central Serbia it is only 2.8% (SORS, 2024e).

Mineral fertilizers are applied to 53.3% of the UAA. This percentage is higher in Vojvodina, reaching 79.4%, while in Central Serbia it is 49.4%. Manure is applied to a fifth of the UAA, in Vojvodina to less than 16%, while in Central Serbia, with the predominant part of the country's livestock, this percentage is higher and amounts to 26% (SORS, 2024a, 2024b).

According to the 2012 AgCensus, 10.8% of arable land and gardens was not covered by the planned crop rotation (in Vojvodina 5.5% and in Central Serbia 18.3%) (SORS, 2012).

Serbia irrigates 8.3% of the UAA, predominantly arable land and gardens, and in a lesser extent fruit and berry plantations. Vojvodina has 57.3% of the total irrigated area, mainly arable land, while in Central Serbia most of it is under fruit and berries (SORS, 2024a, 2024d).

Integrated farming and livestock systems refer to Central Serbia, but due to long-term decline in livestock production, their potentials for development remain untapped. Free range pigs, sheep and poultry rearing in forests patches and extensively managed orchards used as farmyards is traditionally practised on small-scale farms in Central Serbia as well as the sheep and cattle grazing in flooded forests with high proportion of grassland cover on the riverbanks in Vojvodina. These low-intensity farming systems with high biodiversity and landscape benefits were considered for HNV farming (Cooper et al., 2010), and represent a good basis for agroforestry development.

Areas under organic crop production including areas under conversion, in 2023 accounted for 28,935 ha (0.85% of UAA). Areas under fruits and berries dominate (33.4%), followed by cereals (31.4%) and fodder crops (17.5%) (SEPA, 2024). More than two-thirds of the total organic area is located in Central Serbia, and the rest is in Vojvodina. Although the total organic area remains small, it increased steadily, with significant potential for further development, especially in Central Serbia (Simić, 2025).

The promotion of regenerative agriculture has been intensified in recent years. The Regenerative Agriculture Alliance of Serbia, founded in 2024, aims to address systemic issues within the local regenerative agriculture ecosystem by operating through working groups dedicated to: education and knowledge transfer; demo farms; research, innovation and projects; digital technologies and mechanization; and financial and social support (ABE, 2024).

By optimizing the use of agricultural inputs, precision agriculture can result in lower GHG emissions. Smart machinery and equipment are mainly implemented on larger farms, while small farmers are still oriented towards web and android digital platforms for public use. In its Third National Communication to the UNFCCC, the country included the development of precision farming among additional measures to reduce GHG in the period 2030-2050, which will rely entirely on international support (MEP, 2024a).

Soil Organic Carbon and Soil GHG Emissions

Based on humus content data from soil fertility monitoring in 2023, the average organic carbon content in agricultural soil at a depth of 0-30 cm in the Vojvodina region is 1.90% and falls into the low organic carbon content category (1.01-2.0%). The average organic carbon content in arable land and gardens is 1.91%, in vineyards 1.33%, in orchards 1.99% and in meadows and pastures 1.98%. In Central Serbia, the average organic carbon content measured in agricultural soil at a depth of 0-30 cm is 2.20% and falls into the medium content category. The average organic carbon content in arable land and gardens is 2.21%, in vineyards 1.93%, in orchards 2.09% and in meadows and pastures 2.40% (SEPA, 2024).

Using the CENTURY agroecosystem model and six alternative management practices scenarios applied versus business as usual (BAU) practices, Lugato et al. (2014) assessed the pan-European carbon sequestration potential in agricultural soils by 2050, including Serbia. Carbon sequestration potential was registered in the Vojvodina lowlands and on the southern hilly edge of the Pannonian Basin in central Serbia, with higher values of organic carbon stock change in Vojvodina. The RECSOIL global map of soil organic carbon sequestration potential allows users to identify regions, soil types and farming systems with greater potential for increasing soil organic carbon stocks. Serbia is included in the map using a gap-filling layer, without providing national GSOCseq layers (FAO, 2022a).

In 2021, total agricultural emissions in Serbia were 4,733 Gg CO2 eq, while LULUCF net sinks amounted to 4,181 Gg CO2 eq. Soil emissions associated to carbon farming were 1287 Gg CO2 eq, of which 95.5% are agricultural land emissions that decreased in 2010-2021 period for 30.5%, while LULUCF emissions from cropland and grassland were 58 Gg CO2 eq and had a stable emission trend (MEP, 2024a).

Carbon Farming Business Models

Serbian farmers who opt for SSM practices can count on action-based payments from national budget and the EU IPARD fund sources, while some of them have participated in several pilot projects dedicated to carbon farming and regenerative agriculture.

According to Regulation on the distribution of incentives in agriculture and rural development in 2025 (OG RS, 8/2025), agricultural policy measures in the area of preservation and improvement of the environment and natural resources are focused on support to organic production and certification of organic products. The implementation of agri-environment measures, and measure of HNV farmland preservation has been postponed until the start of Land Parcel Identification System (LPIS) and formal mapping of HNV areas. Small- and medium-scale farms can benefit from incentives for investment in fertilization, irrigation and fertigation equipment. Public support is also directed to technical and technological development and innovative projects in agriculture and rural development as well as to agricultural advisory services.

The IPARD III program for the Republic of Serbia 2021-2027 (OG RS, 118/2023) currently supports large farms, with more than 100 ha of cereals and industrial crops for investment in mechanization and machinery for conservation tillage. The preparation of a procedural framework for the accreditation of agri-environment-climate and organic farming measure is underway, with the aim of preparing the sector for the introduction of EU methodologies and practices. The measure will cover: 1) crop rotation on arable land that include intercrops and green fallow, 2) inter-row grass cover-cropping in orchard, vineyard and berry plantations 3) establishment and maintenance of pollinator strips, and 4) sustainable management of meadows and pastures, including late mowing and stocking density limits. The support, based on income foregone and additional costs incurred, is intended for farmers who voluntarily agree to adhere to agri-environment-climate commitments that go beyond a baseline defined by national legislation and good agricultural practice for a period of at least 5 years.

The project dedicated to development of innovative methods in organic plant production to increase the climate neutrality of agriculture has been implemented by the Institute for Soil Science, and supported by the MAFWM in 2021-2022, on two organic farms, in Vojvodina and Central Serbia, which have continued to serve as demo farms for long-term site-specific field research and education of carbon farmers as well as advisers from the extension service (Ugrenović et al, 2022).

The implementation of the C-FARMS project, leading by Institute of Field and Vegetable Crops, Novi Sad, began in 2024 within the framework of the Interreg IPA VI-A Hungary-Serbia program (2021-2027), with the aims of establishing soil health living labs and engaging farmers, cooperatives, policymakers and academia to test and demonstrate various carbon sequestration and soil recarbonization solutions and accompanying digital technologies (Interreg IPA Hungary-Serbia, 2024).

The Horizon 2020 AgriCaptureCO2 project (2021-2023), with Serbia as one of five case studies, went a step further and, in addition to engaging in the promotion of regenerative agricultural practices and digital solutions for assessing the effects of their implementation, had the objective of developing a methodology for certification of carbon credits under recognised global frameworks. A number of medium-sized family farms were involved in the project within Serbian case study, most of them already familiar with regenerative practices, but also newcomers. A transparent and cost-effective MRV platform based on satellite data and soil sampling, as well as financial benefits from voluntary carbon credit markets could give a new impetus for the uptake and scale up regenerative agriculture and carbon farming among farmers (AgriCaptureCO2,2023).

Discussion

Due to different soil properties such as parent material, initial SOC content, soil profile characteristics, soil biodiversity, topography, climate, land use and land management, soils have different SOC storage potentials (Lal et al., 2018; Chenu et al., 2019; Wiesmeier et al., 2019). Clay is considered as one of the key materials for carbon sequestration as it tends to bind organic matter in the soil. However, enhanced degradation of clay-associated organic carbon has been observed under certain conditions and the mechanisms of clay and SOC interactions in these conditions are not fully understood (Yang et al., 2021). Rising temperature leads to increased microbial decomposition and carbon loss (Walker et al., 2018). Nevertheless, some recent research indicates that microbial decomposition contributes to long-term carbon sequestration by maintaining its downward movement through the soil profile (Dynarski et al., 2020). In general, there are still many unknowns related to carbon storage that make it difficult to assess the overall benefits of a particular SSM practice for carbon sequestration and crop yields under specific pedoclimatic conditions and land use (Jat et al., 2022; Moinet, 2023).

The decrease in carbon level, especially on fertile arable lands in Vojvodina, is mainly caused by decades-old practice of deep ploughing, leaving bare soils after main crops, crop rotations with reduced lay crops presence, insufficient application of manure, and removal of harvest residues. Climate change and underdeveloped irrigation systems further exacerbated this process. Regardless, it is well established that SOC-depleted soils can store more additional carbon than carbon-rich soils (Sanderman et al., 2017; Amelung et al., 2020). Sequestration of SOC and soil emissions reduction happen there using region-specific sustainable land management practices that respect local biophysical, technological, economic and socio-cultural features (Popović and Mijajlović, 2013; Lal et al., 2018; Henry et al., 2023). Carbon sequestration potential assessed by Lugato et al. (2014) in Vojvodina and the southern hilly edge of the Pannonian Basin in Central Serbia pointed to good opportunities for carbon farming development.

Many of these practices are already incorporated in existing environmental legislation and good agricultural practice, as well as in national documents as obligations under international agreements. Thus, Low Carbon Development Strategy 2023-2030/2050 (OG RS, 46/2023) calls for incentives for increasing legume share in fodder area and promotion of winter cover crops planting for GHG emission reduction in agriculture sector. The latter is the main measure in agriculture in Third National Communication to the UNFCCC, while Integrated National Energy and

Climate Plan up to 2030/2050 (OG RS, 70/2024) focuses on conversion of heaths on inclined terrains into grassland and integrated nutrient management. Serbian NDC for the 2021-2030 highlights the mitigation potential of nutrient management, incorporation of legumes into pastures, and grazing management.

Agroforestry, conservation agriculture, nutrient management, pasture management, and restoration of abandoned agricultural areas, including by agroforestry, were considered as practices with climate mitigation potential that can be incorporated into nature-based solutions (NbS) context (Vuković Vimić, et al., 2021). The Draft Environmental Protection Strategy Action Plan 2024-2028 aims to provide guidelines for the implementation of large-scale NbS and their integration into strategic and planning documents by the end of 2025, and to incentivize scientific research projects, pilot projects and case studies for deployment of NbS, inter alia in agriculture, by the end of 2027 (MEP, 2024b).

State incentives currently are mainly directed to organic farming. FAO (2022b) advocates for wider uptake of agroforestry. Payments for carbon sequestration could further incentivize agroforestry adoption, but a 5-year support commitment is a significant barrier for the permanence and additionality in general, as well as in agroforestry. More tangible results related to the implementation of SSM practices and the sector's alignment with the EU methodologies in this area are expected from implementation of IPARD III agro-environment-climate measure, which accreditation is in progress. However, the European Court of Auditors found that most of the mitigation measures supported by the CAP in 2014-2020 had low potential for mitigating climate change and did not consider that the CAP after 2020 will improve the situation (ECA, 2021). Verschuuren (2022) emphasized several gaps in the post-2030 CAP toolbox that need to be filled in order to use set of instruments that together facilitate a transition towards a climate- and biodiversity-friendly, nutritious and healthy food system. It is obvious that Serbia's agricultural policy will undergo continuous adjustments on the path to membership, parallel with dynamic EU reforms, and the current delays in the accession process are not encouraging.

Despite these institutional weaknesses and delays, carbon farming adoption face a number of other challenges. High establishment costs and longer-term returns, poor access to knowledge, capital and markets and weak institutional support all represent significant barriers to the carbon farming uptake by farmers. There are also significant regional socio-economic and cultural barriers, including farm size, ageing farmer population, depopulation and land abandonment, as well as traditional norms regarding the business orientation of a prosperous farmer (ABE, 2023; SORS, 2025b).

SOLUTIONS AND RECOMMENDATIONS

Intensively-managed under climate change, arable lands, orchards and vineyards in Vojvodina and Central Serbia have a priority for soil quality improvement and carbon sequestration using cropland SSM practices while the hilly-mountainous parts of Central Serbia with large unutilised agricultural area are predisposed to agroforestry, mixed farming, and pasture management on the predominant smallholder farms. Farmers, especially smallholders, need support for knowledge and skills upgrading to operate with digital soil data, and enhancing collaborative capacity (e.g. within machinery rings) to secure access to specialized farm equipment. State engagement is also needed for the adoption of EU rules on Good Agricultural and Environmental Condition (GAEC) and the Land Parcel Identification System (LPIS), both of which are planned for the end of 2026 (The Government of the RS, 2024).

When it comes to carbon farming mechanisms, action-based budgetary payments from national and IPARD sources will dominate in the near future. Later, a hybrid model that combines up-front investment support and result-based rewards for carbon and other environmental outcomes generated by nature-based solutions could be an effective policy option towards market-based approaches aligned with EU legislation. A policy framework is necessary for all of the above activities. As seen earlier, the EU Farm to Fork Strategy considers carbon farming as a new green business model and highlights a potential role of the CAP and other public and private initiatives in its financing. The Strategy for Agriculture and Rural Development of the Republic of Serbia for the period 2025-2032 is currently being drafted and is expected to follow this pathway.

FUTURE RESEARCH DIRECTIONS

The assessment and demonstration of cost-effective carbon farming practices and their co-benefits in different pedo-climatic conditions is linked to accurate spatial data for model inputs as well as validation data for land use and land management from long-term field trials. A participatory approach that involves farmers and local experts and institutions in research activities is of vital importance there.

The bottom-up approach is also a key factor in preparation and upgrading of SOC sequestration map layers. Developed and validated by local experts using standardized procedures and best available local data, these inputs are reliable and useful tool in designing a site-specific set of SSM practices, and creating policy, investment or research priorities.

The SSM practice policy design involves an integrated assessment of their climate and other co-benefits and tradeoffs, as well as their interactions at landscape level, in particular those related to environmental integrity, land competition and food production.

The highly fragmented and regionally differentiated economic and social structure of the farming sector requires careful policy tailoring. Many farmers are faced with economic insecurity and land abandonment caused by climate vulnerability, market uncertainties and policy inertia. Further research should be necessary to testing identified carbon farming mechanisms, including evaluation of their effects on yield, input costs and farm income. Strengthening farm networks, including demo farms, living labs and regional carbon farming hubs, enables knowledge transfer and reduces adoption barriers.

CONCLUSION

A high overshoot of the Paris Agreement's temperature limit of 1.5°C increases reliance on large-scale carbon removals to offset higher emissions before 2030. Intensively-managed under climate change, agricultural mineral soils are among the most depleted terrestrial carbon stocks and have a good prospect for soil organic carbon sequestration and soil quality improvement. The decrease in carbon level in agricultural land in Serbia, especially on fertile arable lands in Vojvodina region, is mainly caused by decades-old practice of deep ploughing, leaving bare soils after main crops, crop rotations with reduced lay crops presence, insufficient application of manure, and removal of harvest residues. Carbon sequestration potential assessed in a previous study in Vojvodina and the southern hilly edge of the Pannonian Basin in Central Serbia pointed to good opportunities for carbon farming development. Intensively-managed arable lands, orchards and vineyards in these areas have a priority for soil quality improvement and carbon sequestration using cropland SSM practices, while the hilly-mountainous parts of Central Serbia with large unutilised agricultural area are predisposed to agroforestry, mixed farming, and pasture management on the predominant smallholder farms. When it comes to carbon farming mechanisms, action-based budgetary payments from national and IPARD sources will dominate in the near future. Later, a hybrid model that combines up-front investment support and result-based rewards for carbon and other environmental outcomes generated by nature-based solutions could be an effective policy option towards market-based approaches aligned with EU legislation. Strengthening farm networks, including demo farms, living labs and regional hubs is necessary to enable knowledge transfer and reduce adoption barriers.

ACKNOWLEDGMENT

Paper is a part of research financed by the MSTDI RS, agreed in Decision no. 451-03-136/2025-03/200009 from 04.02.2025 and Decision no. 451-03-136/2025-03/200006 from 04.02.2025.

REFERENCES

Abnett, K. (2025, April 7). EU considering international CO2 credits to meet new climate goal, sources say. *Reuters*. https://www.reuters.com/sustainability/cop/eu-considering-international-co2-credits-meet-new-climate-goal-sources-say-2025-04-07/

AgriCaptureCO2. (2023). Project plan and deliverables. https://agricaptureco2.eu/project-plan-and-deliverables/

Aiken, J. D. (2021, April 21). Ag carbon credits. *Cornhusker Economics*. https://agecon.unl.edu/ag-carbon-credits

Amelung, W., Bossio, D., de Vries, W., Kögel-Knabner, I., Lehmann, J., Amundson, R., Bol, R., Collins, C., Lal, R., Leifeld, J., Minasny, B., Pan, G., Paustian, K., Rumpel, C., Sanderman, J., van Groenigen, J. W., Mooney, S., van Wesemael, B., Wander, M., & Chabbi, A. (2020). Towards a global- scale soil climate mitigation strategy. *Nature Communications*, *11*(1), 5427. DOI: 10.1038/s41467-020-18887-7

Anderson, T. R., Hawkins, E., & Jones, P. D. (2016). CO2, the greenhouse effect and global warming: From the pioneering work of Arrhenius and Callendar to today's Earth System Models. *Endeavour*, *40*(3), 178–187. DOI: 10.1016/j.endeavour.2016.07.002

Bossio, D. A., Cook-Patton, S. C., Ellis, P. W., Fargione, J., Sanderman, J., Smith, P., Wood, S., Zomer, R. J., von Unger, M., Emmer, I. M., & Griscom, B. W. (2020). The role of soil carbon in natural climate solutions. *Nature Sustainability*, *3*(5), 391–398. DOI: 10.1038/s41893-020-0491-z

Chenu, C., Angers, D. A., Barré, P., Derrien, D., Arrouays, D., & Balesdent, J. (2019). Increasing organic stocks in agricultural soils: Knowledge gaps and potential innovations. *Soil & Tillage Research*, *188*, 41–52. DOI: 10.1016/j.still.2018.04.011

Cooper, T., Pezold, T., Keenleyside, C., Đorđević-Milošević, S., Hart, K., Ivanov, S., Redman, M., & Vidojević, D. (2010). *Developing a National Agri-Environment Programme for Serbia*. IUCN.

Čirič, M., Filipovski, Gj. (1972). Regional'nye počvenno-geografičeskie zakonomernosti v Jugoslavii [Regional pedo-geographical features in Yugoslavia], Počvovedenie, AN SSSR, Moskva, 2, 34–38.

Dinić, J. B. (1997). *Prirodni potencijal Srbije. Ekonomsko-geografska analiza i ocena* [The natural potential of Serbia. Economic-geographical analysis and evaluation]. Univerzitet u Beogradu. Ekonomski fakultet.

European Commission. (2023). The update of the nationally determined contribution of the European Union and its member states. https://unfccc.int/sites/default/files/NDC/2023-10/ES-2023-10-17%20EU%20 submission%20NDC%20update.pdf

European Commission, DG CLIMA. (2023). *Pricing agricultural emissions and rewarding climate action in the agri-food value chain*. Study. Trinomics. https://doi:.DOI: 10.2834/200

European Commission. DG CLIMA. (2024). *Incentivizing climate action for a sustainable and competitive agri-food value chain*. Follow-up study presentation. Trinomics, IEEP, Ricardo, and WUR. https://climate.ec.europa.eu/document/ download/f76a263a-69b4-4032-a604-e9cf6caa3944_en?filename= policy_crcf_agrifood_ws_ ieep_en.pdf

European Commission, DG CLIMA. (2025). *Support to the design of policy options for financial incentives for carbon farming*. Deloitte. .DOI: 10.2834/3087542

European Court of Auditors. (2021). *Common Agricultural Policy and climate. Half of EU climate spending but farm emissions are not decreasing*. Special Report. .DOI: 10.2865/285879

European Environment Agency – EEA. (2023). *Land cover and change accounts 2000-2018*. https://www.eea.europa.eu/en/analysis/maps-and-charts/land-cover-and-change-statistics-dashboards. Published 25 Sept 2019, Modified 22 Aug 2023.

FAO. (2019). *Recarbonization of global soils. A tool to support the implementation of the Koronivia joint work on agriculture*. FAO.

FAO. (2020). *A protocol for measurement, monitoring, reporting and verification of soil organic carbon in agricultural landscapes – GSOC-MRV Protocol*. FAO., DOI: 10.4060/cb0509en

FAO. (2022a). *Global Soil Organic Carbon Sequestration Potential Map – GSOCseq v.1.1*. Technical report. .DOI: 10.4060/cb9002en

FAO. (2022b). *The State of the World's Forests 2022. Forest pathways for green recovery and building inclusive, resilient and sustainable economies*. FAO., DOI: 10.4060/cb9360en

FAO & ITPS. (2021). *Recarbonizing global soils: A technical manual of recommended management practices. Volume 3: Cropland, Grassland, Integrated systems and farming approaches – Practices overview*. FAO. .DOI: 10.4060/cb6595en

Filipovski, Gj. (1974). *Pedologija* [Pedology], (2nd revised edition). Univerzitet "Kiril i Metodij" Skopje.

Hans, F., Kuramochi, T., Black, R., Hale, T., & Lang, J. (2022). *Net Zero Stocktake 2022*. NewClimate Institute, Oxford Net Zero, Energy & Climate Intelligence Unit, Data-Driven EnviroLab.

Henry, B., Dalal, R., Harrison, M. T., & Keating, B. (2023). Creating frameworks to foster soil carbon sequestration. In Rumpel, C. (Ed.), *Understanding and fostering soil carbon sequestration* (pp. 767–808). Burleigh Dodds Science Publishing., DOI: 10.19103/AS.2022.0106.25

Interreg, I. P. A. Hungary-Serbia. (2024). Climate Smart Soil for ZERO-CARBON farms. https://hungary-serbia.eu/projects/c-farms

IPCC. (2019). Summary for Policymakers. In Shukla, P.R., Skea, J., Calvo Buendia, E., Masson-Delmotte, V., Pörtner, H.- O., Roberts, D. C., Zhai, P., Slade, R., Connors, S., van Diemen, R., Ferrat, M., Haughey, E., Luz, S., Neogi, S., Pathak, M., Petzold, J., Portugal Pereira, J., Vyas, P., Huntley, E., …Malley, J. (Eds.), *Climate Change and Land: an IPCC special report on climate change, desertification, land degradation, sustainable land management, food security, and greenhouse gas fluxes in terrestrial ecosystems*. IPCC.

IPCC. (2023). Summary for Policymakers. In Lee, H., & Romero, J. (Eds.), *Climate Change 2023: Synthesis Report of the IPCC Sixth Assessment Report (AR6)* (pp. 1–34). IPCC., DOI: 10.59327/IPCC/AR6-9789291691647

Jat, M. L., Chakraborty, D., Ladha, J. K., Parihar, C. M., Datta, A., Mandal, B., Nayak, H. S., Maity, P., Rana, D. S., Chaudhari, S. K., & Gerard, B. (2022). Carbon sequestration potential, challenges, and strategies towards climate action in smallholder agricultural systems of South Asia. *Crop and Environment*, *1*(1), 86–101. DOI: 10.1016/j.crope.2022.03.005

Lal, R., Smith, P., Jungkunst, H. F., Mitsch, W. J., Lehmann, J., Nair, P. K. R., McBratney, A. B., Sá, J. C. M., Schneider, J., Zinn, Y. L., Skoru-pa, A. L. A., Zhang, H., Minasny, B., Srinivasrao, C., & Ravindranath, N. H. (2018). The carbon sequestration potential of terrestrial ecosystems. *Journal of Soil and Water Conservation*, *73*(6), 145A–152A. DOI: 10.2489/jswc.73.6.145A

Lugato, E., Bampa, F., Panagos, P., Montanarella, L., & Jones, A. (2014). Potential carbon sequestration of European arable soils estimated by modelling a comprehensive set of management practices. *Global Change Biology*, *20*(11), 3557–3567. DOI: 10.1111/gcb.12551

Lugato, E., Leip, A., & Jones, A. (2018). Mitigation potential of soil carbon management overestimated by neglecting N2O emissions. *Nature Climate Change*, *8*(3), 219–223. DOI: 10.1038/s41558-018-0087-z

McDonald, H., Frelih-Larsen, A., Lóránt, A., Duin, L., Pyndt Andersen, S., Costa, G., & Bradley, H. (2021). *Carbon farming. Making agriculture fit for 2030*. European Parliament. Policy Department for Economic, Scientific and Quality of Life Policies. https://www.europarl.europa.eu/supporting-analyses

Ministry of Environmental Protection – MEP. (2022). *Nationally determined contribution (NDC) of the Republic of Serbia for the 2021–2030*. https://unfccc.int/sites/default/files/NDC/2022-08/NDC%20Final_ Serbia%20english. pdf

Ministry of Environmental Protection – MEP. (2024a). The third national communication of the Republic of Serbia to the UNFCC. https://unfccc.int/sites/default/files/resource/3NC_Serbia.pdf

Ministry of Environmental Protection – MEP. (2024b). *Nacrt Akcionog plana Strategije zaštite životne sredine za 2024-2028* [Draft Environmental Protection Strategy Action Plan for 2024-2028]. https://www.ekologija.gov.rs/informacije-od-javnog-znacaja/javne-rasprave

Moinet, G. Y. K., Hijbeek, R., van Vuuren, D. P., & Giller, K. E. (2023). Carbon for soils, not soils for carbon. *Global Change Biology*, *29*(9), 2384–2398. DOI: 10.1111/gcb.16570

Naftel, H. (2022). *Understanding the Barriers to Carbon Farming on Private Lands*. All Graduate Plan B and other Reports. 1677. https://digitalcommons.usu.edu/gradreports/1677

Pathak, M., Slade, R., Shukla, P. R., Skea, J., Pichs-Madruga, R., & Ürge-Vorsatz, D. (2022). Technical Summary. In *Climate Change 2022: Mitigation of Climate Change. Contribution of WG III to the IPCC Sixth Assessment Report (AR6)*. Cambridge University Press., DOI: 10.1017/9781009157926.002

Paul, C., Bartkowski, B., D nmez, C., Donc, A., Mayerd, S., Steffens, M., Weigl, S., Wiesmeierd, M., Wolfg, A., & Helming, K. (2023). Carbon farming: Are soil carbon certificates a suitable tool for climate change mitigation? *Journal of Environmental Management, 330*, 117142. https://doi.org/. 2022.117142.DOI: 10.1016/j.jenvman

Paustian, K., Larson, E., Kent, J., Marx, E., & Swan, A. (2019). Soil C Sequestration as a Biological Negative Emission Strategy. *Frontiers in Climate*, *1*, 8. DOI: 10.3389/fclim.2019.00008

Poeplau, C., & Dechow, R. (2023). The legacy of one hundred years of climate change for organic carbon stocks in global agricultural topsoils. *Scientific Reports*, *13*(1), 7483. DOI: 10.1038/s41598-023-34753-0

Popović, V., & Mijajlović, N. (2013). Climate Change and Sustainable Development in Agriculture and Forestry. In Jean-Vasile, A., Adrian, T., Subic, J., & Dusmanescu, D. (Eds.), *Sustainable Technologies, Policies, and Constraints in the Green Economy* (pp. 140–171). IGI Global Scientific Publishing., DOI: 10.4018/978-1-4666-4098-6.ch008

Popović, V., Miljković, J. Ž., Subić, J., Jean-Vasile, A., Adrian, N., & Nicolăescu, E. (2015). Sustainable Land Management in Mining Areas in Serbia and Romania. *Sustainability (Basel)*, *7*(9), 11857–11877. DOI: 10.3390/su70911857

Regional Cooperation Council – RCC. (2021). Action Plan for the Implementation of the Sofia Declaration on the Green Agenda for the Western Balkans 2021-2030. https://www.rcc.int/pubs/183/action-plan-for-the-implementation-of-the-sofia -declaration-on-the-green-agenda-for-the-western-balkans-2021-2030

Rose, S., Khatri-Chhetri, A., Stier, M., Wiese-Rozanova, L., Dittmer, K. M., Shelton, S., & Wollenberg, E. (2022). *Ambition for SOC sequestration in the new and updated NDCs: 2020-2022. Analysis of agricultural sub-sectors in national climate change strategies*. CCAFS Info Note. https://cgspace.cgiar.org/server/api/core/bitstreams/056fa862-9e65-4a0f-b72f-bc13eb83212c/content

Rumpel, C., Amiraslani, F., Chenu, C., Garcia Cardenas, M., Kaonga, M., Koutika, L.-S., Ladha, J., Madari, B., Shirato, Y., Smith, P., Soudi, B., Soussana, J.-F., Whitehead, D., & Wollenberg, E. (2020). The 4p1000 initiative: Opportunities, limitations and challenges for implementing soil organic carbon sequestration as a sustainable development strategy. *Ambio*, *49*(1), 350–360. DOI: 10.1007/s13280-019-01165-2

Sanderman, J., Hengl, T., & Fiske, G. J. (2017). Soil carbon debt of 12,000 years of human land use. *Proceedings of the National Academy of Sciences of the United States of America, 114*(36), 9575–9580. DOI: 10.1073/pnas.1706103114

Schuett, L. (2024). Permanence and liability: Legal considerations on the integration of carbon dioxide removal into the EU emissions trading system. *Transnational Environmental Law, 13*(1), 87–110. DOI: 10.1017/S2047102524000013

Serbian Environmental Protection Agency – SEPA. (2024). *Report on the state of the environment in the Republic of Serbia 2023.* https://sepa.gov.rs/wp-content/uploads/2025/02/ZivotnaSredina2023.pdf

Shockley, J., & Snell, W. (2021, April 29). Carbon markets 101. *Economic and Policy Update, 21*(4), 1-3. https://agecon.ca.uky.edu/files/carbon_markets_101.pdf

Simić, I. (2025, May 18). *Organska proizvodnja u Srbiji na tek 0,85 odsto površina, uglavnom se izvozi* [Organic production in Serbia is only 0.85 percent of the area, mostly exported]. N1 News. https://n1info.rs/biznis/organski-proizvodi-izvoz-srbija/

Stabinsky, D. (2021). *"Nature-based solutions" and the biodiversity and climate crises.* Third World Network. Environment & Development Series 21. https://www.twn.my/title/end/pdf/end21.pdf

Statistical Office of the Republic of Serbia – SORS. (2012). *Obrada i održavanje zemljišta* [Cultivation and maintenance of land]. https://www.stat.gov.rs/sr-latn/oblasti/poljoprivreda-sumarstvo-i-ribarstvo/popis-poljoprivrede/popisni-rezultati-nivo-naselja-eksel-tabele/

Statistical Office of the Republic of Serbia – SORS. (2024a). *Area, livestock (LSU), labor force and standard output (SO) by legal status of holding and agricultural size of farm (UAA).* Census of Agriculture 2023. https://data.stat.gov.rs/Home/Result/1300020101?languageCode=en-US. Last updated on: 6/6/2024.

Statistical Office of the Republic of Serbia – SORS. (2024b). *Fertilizers.* Census of Agriculture 2023. https://data.stat.gov.rs/Home/Result/1300021001?languageCode=en-US. Last updated on: 6/20/2024.

Statistical Office of the Republic of Serbia – SORS. (2024c). *Number of farms and areas of different crops and categories by agricultural size of farm (UAA).* Census of Agriculture 2023. https://data.stat.gov.rs/Home/ Result/1300020201?language-Code=en-US. Last updated on: 10/7/2024.

Statistical Office of the Republic of Serbia – SORS. (2024d). *Number of farms and irrigated area by different crops and categories*. Census of Agriculture 2023. https://data.stat.gov.rs/Home/Result/1300020301? languageCode=en-US. Last updated on: 6/14/2024.

Statistical Office of the Republic of Serbia – SORS. (2024e). *Soil conservation.* Census of Agriculture 2023. https://data.stat.gov.rs/Home/Result/1300020902 ?languageCode=en-US. Last updated on: 6/20/2024.

Statistical Office of the Republic of Serbia – SORS. (2025a). *Soil management practice.* Census of Agriculture 2023. https://data.stat.gov.rs/Home/Result/1300020901 ?languageCode=en-US. Last updated on: 2/20/2025.

Statistical Office of the Republic of Serbia – SORS. (2025b). *Strukturne promene u poljoprivredi i njihov uticaj na ekonomski rast u Srbiji* [Structural changes in agriculture and their impact on economic growth in Serbia]. Census of Agriculture 2023. https://www.stat.gov.rs/sr-latn/publikacije/publication/?p=17265&tip=12

The Association of Balkan Eco-Innovation – ABE. (2023). *Izveštaj o barijerama za širu primenu regenerativnih praksi u Srbiji* [Report on barriers to wider application of regenerative practices in Serbia]. https://balkanecoinnovations.org/wp-content/uploads/2024/02/Savez-Reg-Agri-Izvestaj-Barijere.pdf-1.pdf

The Association of Balkan Eco-Innovation – ABE. (2024). *Savez za regenerativnu poljoprivredu Srbije. Beli papir. Ukratko* [The Regenerative Agriculture Alliance of Serbia. White Paper. In Brief]. https://regagrisrbija.rs/ wp-content/uploads/2025/01/RegAgri-Savez-Beli-papir-2024.pdf

The Government of the Republic of Serbia. (2024). National Programme for the Adoption of the Acquis (NPAA) 2024-2027. https://www.mei.gov.rs/upload/documents/nacionalna_dokumenta/npaa/npaa_2024-2027_en.pdf

Ugrenović, V., Saljnikov, E., Pivić, R., Koković, N., Grujić, T., Filipović, V., Oljača, S., Simić, I., Subić, J., & Jeločnik, M. (2022). *Klimatska neutralnost poljoprivrede* [Climate neutrality of agriculture]. MAFWM. https://www.researchgate.net/publication/359203824_ Klimatska_neutralnost_poljoprivrede.

UN. (2015). *Adoption of the Paris Agreement* (FCCC/CP/2015/L.9/Rev.1). UNFCCC.

UN. (2019). *Improved soil carbon, soil health and soil fertility under grassland and cropland as well as integrated systems, including water management.* Koronivia joint work on agriculture. Workshop report (FCCC/SB/2019/2). UNFCCC.

UN. (2025). Message to Parties and Observers. *UN Climate Change Quarterly Update: Q4 2024*. ES/MTP/O/QR4 2024. https://unfccc.int/about-us/reports-highlights/quarterly-updates/un-climate-change-quarterly-update-q4-2024

UNEP. (2024). *Emissions gap report 2024: No more hot air ... please! With a massive gap between rhetoric and reality, countries draft new climate commitments.* UNEP., DOI: 10.59117/20.500.11822/46404

UNFCCC. (2022). *Sharm el-Sheikh joint work on implementation of climate action on agriculture and food security.* Decision 3/CP.27 (FCCC/CP/2022/10/Add.1). UNFCCC.

van der Voort, T. S., Verweij, S., Fujita, Y., & Ros, G. H. (2023). Enabling soil carbon farming: Presentation of a robust, affordable, and scalable method for soil carbon stock assessment. *Agronomy for Sustainable Development*, *43*(1), 22. DOI: 10.1007/s13593-022-00856-7

Vermeulen, S., Bossio, D., Lehmann, J., Luu, P., Paustian, K., Webb, C., Augé, F., Bacudo, I., Baedeker, T., Havemann, T., Jones, C., King, R., Reddy, M., Sunga, I., Von Unger, M., & Warnken, M. (2019). A global agenda for collective action on soil carbon. *Nature Sustainability*, *2*(1), 2–4. DOI: 10.1038/s41893-018-0212-z

Verschuuren, J. (2017). Towards a regulatory design for reducing emissions from agriculture: Lessons from Australia's carbon farming initiative. *Climate Law*, *7*(1), 1–51. DOI: 10.1163/18786561-00701001

Verschuuren, J. (2022). Achieving agricultural greenhouse gas emission reductions in the EU post-2030: What options do we have? *Review of European, Comparative & International Environmental Law*, *31*(2), 246–257. DOI: 10.1111/reel.12448

Vuković Vimić, A., Petrović, N., Weinreich, A., & Pistorius, T. (2021). *Nature-based Solutions for climate change and potential for their implementation in Serbia.* UNDP. https://www.klimatskepromene.rs/wp-content/uploads/2021/10/NBS_CC_SERBIA_English.pdf

Walker, T. W. N., Kaiser, C., Strasser, F., Herbold, C. W., Leblans, N. I. W., Woebken, D., Janssens, I. A., Sigurdsson, B. D., & Richter, A. (2018). Microbial temperature sensitivity and biomass change explain soil carbon loss with warming. *Nature Climate Change*, *8*(10), 885–889. DOI: 10.1038/s41558-018-0259-x

Weltin, M., Zasada, I., Piorr, A., Debolini, M., Geniaux, G., Moreno Perez, O., Scherer, L., Marco, L. T., & Schulp, C. J. E. (2018). Conceptualising fields of action for sustainable intensification – A systematic literature review and application to regional case studies. *Agriculture, Ecosystems & Environment, 257*, 68–80. DOI: 10.1016/j.agee.2018.01.023

Wiese, L., Wollenberg, E., Alcántara-Shivapatham, V., Richards, M., Shelton, S., Esther Hönle, S., Heidecke, C., Madari, B. E., & Chenu, C. (2021). Countries' commitments to soil organic carbon in Nationally Determined Contributions, *Climate Policy, 21*(8), 1005-1019. https://doi.org/. 2021.1969883.DOI: 10.1080/14693062

Wiesmeier, M., Urbanski, L., Hobley, E., Lang, B., von Lützow, M., Marin-Spiotta, E., van Wesemael, B., Rabot, E., Ließ, M., Garcia-Franco, N., Wollschl ger, U., Vogel, H.-J., & K gel-Knabner, I. (2019). Soil organic carbon storage as a key function of soils - a review of drivers and indicators at various scales. *Geoderma, 333*, 149–162. DOI: 10.1016/j.geoderma.2018.07.026

World Bank. (2024).. . *State and Trends of Carbon Pricing, 2024*. Advance online publication. DOI: 10.1596/978-1-4648-2127-1

Yang, J. Q., Zhang, X., Bourg, I. C., & Stone, H. A. (2021). 4D imaging reveals mechanisms of clay-carbon protection and release. *Nature Communications, 12*(1), 622. DOI: 10.1038/s41467-020-20798-6

Živanović Miljković, J., Popović, V., & Gajić, A. (2022). Land take processes and challenges for urban agriculture: A spatial analysis for Novi Sad, Serbia. *Land (Basel), 11*(6), 769. DOI: 10.3390/land11060769

Živanović Miljković, J., Popović, V., & Srnić, D. (2025). Spatial patterns and agricultural land use dynamics – A GIS-based analysis for peri-urban areas of Belgrade and Novi Sad, Serbia. In Sahana, M. (Ed.), *Remote Sensing and GIS in Peri-Urban Research – Perspectives on Global Change, Sustainability and Resilience* (pp. 617–638). Elsevier., DOI: 10.1016/B978-0-443-15832-2.00027-7

ADDITIONAL READING

Fuss, S., Lamb, W. F., Callaghan, M. W., Hilaire, J., Creutzig, F., Amann, T., Beringer, T., Garcia, W. D. O., Hartmann, J., Khanna, T., Luderer, G., Nemet, G. F., Rogelj, J., Smith, P., Vicente, J. L. V., Wilcox, J., Dominguez, M. D. M. Z., & Minx, J. C. (2018). Negative emissions-Part 2: Costs, potentials and side effects. *Environmental Research Letters, 13*(6), 063002. DOI: 10.1088/1748-9326/aabf9f

Griscom, B. W., Adams, J., Ellis, P. W., Houghton, R. A., Lomax, G., Miteva, D. A., Schlesinger, W. H., Shoch, D., Siikamäki, J. V., Smith, P., Woodbury, P., Zganjar, C., Blackman, A., Campari, J., Conant, R. T., Delgado, C., Elias, P., Gopalakrishna, T., Hamsik, M. R., & Fargione, J. (2017). Natural climate solutions. *Proceedings of the National Academy of Sciences of the United States of America, 114*(44), 11645–11650. DOI: 10.1073/pnas.1710465114

Lal, R. (2013). Soil carbon management and climate change. *Carbon Management, 4*(4), 439–462. DOI: 10.4155/cmt.13.31

Lokuge, N., & Anders, S. (2022). Carbon-credit systems in agriculture: A review of literature. *The School of Public Policy Publications*, 15(1), 1-44. DOI: 10.11575/sppp.v15i1.74591

Mattila, T. J., Hagelberg, E., S derlund, S., & Joona, J. (2022). How farmers approach soil carbon sequestration? Lessons learned from 105 carbon-farming plans. *Soil & Tillage Research, 215*, 105204. DOI: 10.1016/j.still.2021.105204

Roe, S., Streck, C., Beach, R., Busch, J., Chapman, M., Daioglou, V., Deppermann, A., Doelman, J., Emmet-Booth, J., Engelmann, J., Fricko, O., Frischmann, C., Funk, J., Grassi, G., Griscom, B., Havlik, P., Hanssen, S., Humpenöder, F., Landholm, D., & Lawrence, D. (2021). Land-based measures to mitigate climate change: Potential and feasibility by country. *Global Change Biology, 27*(23), 6025–6058. DOI: 10.1111/gcb.15873

Rumpel, C., Amiraslani, F., Koutika, L.-S., Smith, P., Whitehead, D., & Wollenberg, E. (2018). Put more carbon in soils to meet Paris climate pledges. *Nature, 564*(7734), 32–34. DOI: 10.1038/d41586-018-07587-4

Sykes, A. J., Macleod, M., Eory, V., Rees, R. M., Payen, F., Myrgiotis, V., Williams, M., Sohi, S., Hillier, J., Moran, D., Manning, D. A. C., Goglio, P., Seghetta, M., Williams, A., Harris, J., Dondini, M., Walton, J., House, J., & Smith, P. (2020). Characterizing the biophysical, economic and social impacts of soil carbon sequestration as a greenhouse gas removal technology. *Global Change Biology, 26*(3), 1085–1108. DOI: 10.1111/gcb.14844

KEY TERMS AND DEFINITIONS

Carbon Farming Business Model: A business model that allows farmers to generate income for climate change mitigation results, while respecting ecological principles favorable to biodiversity and natural capital as a whole.

Carbon Farming: Any practice or process carried out over an activity period of at least five years, related to the management of a terrestrial or coastal environment and resulting in the capture and temporary storage of atmospheric or biogenic carbon in biogenic carbon pools, or in the reduction of soil emissions.

Carbon Offset: A unit of CO2-equivalent emissions that is reduced, avoided, or sequestered to compensate for emissions occurring elsewhere.

Carbon Removal: Anthropogenic activities removing carbon dioxide (CO2) from the atmosphere and durably storing it in geological, terrestrial, or ocean reservoirs, or in products.

Climate Change Mitigation: A human intervention to reduce emissions or enhance the sinks of greenhouse gases.

Mitigation Potential: The quantity of net greenhouse gas emission reductions as the sum of reduced emissions and/or enhanced sinks, which can be achieved by a given mitigation option relative to specified emission baselines.

Nature-Based Solutions: Actions to protect, sustainably manage and restore natural or modified ecosystems that address societal challenges effectively and adaptively, simultaneously providing human well-being and biodiversity benefits.

Soil Emissions Reduction: The reduction of net greenhouse gas emissions from soil carbon pools through carbon farming activities.

Chapter 10
Romanian Rural Entrepreneurship: From Challenges and Opportunities to Sustainable Business Models

Cosmina-Simona Toader
https://orcid.org/0000-0003-1564-8558
University of Life Sciences "King Mihai I" from Timisoara, Romania

ABSTRACT

A complex universe, with a rich history and traditions passed down from one generation to another, with a unique rhythm of life, the Romanian rural environment is a vast space, with a specific cultural, economic and cultural identity, covering 85% of Romania's surface and hosting 9645.9 thousand inhabitants (44.2% of the total population). Beyond the main challenges, as depopulation and aging of the population, the lack of qualified labour, poor infrastructure, difficult access to financing, lack of support, lack of know-how, competition from large companies, rural area hides a significant development potential, which is based on rich natural and cultural resources, authentic traditions and a close connection with nature. In this context, the chapter addresses the Romanian entrepreneurship landscape and a responsible business model, and its aim is to contribute to current empirical research through a real-life experience.

DOI: 10.4018/979-8-3373-2898-0.ch010

INTRODUCTION

Viewed as a dynamic phenomenon with multiple implications, rural entrepreneurship plays a key role in promoting regional development, stimulating job creation and alleviating poverty globally. Rural entrepreneurship is a critical pathway for economic diversification and resilience in areas that rely on primary industries. Globally, rural areas often face unique socio-economic challenges, such as limited access to resources, infrastructure deficits and demographic changes. In response, entrepreneurial initiatives are vital drivers for revitalizing local economies, preserving cultural heritage and promoting sustainable livelihoods. International reports and studies highlight the transformative potential of rural entrepreneurship in building strong and self-sufficient communities, demonstrating its capacity to transform local assets into viable economic opportunities (Barber et al, 2021; Deng et al, 2024; Habersetzer et al, 2020; Mariotti&Sasso, 2024; OECD, 2022).

The European context further underlines the strategic importance of rural development. Through the Common Agricultural Policy (CAP) and various cohesion funds, the European Union actively supports rural areas to address their specific challenges and to develop their potential. EU policies aim to promote balanced territorial development, increase competitiveness and ensure sustainable management of natural resources. By providing financial instruments, technical assistance and strategic frameworks, the EU aims to create an environment conducive to the prosperity of rural businesses, thus contributing to the overall economic and social cohesion of the Union (European Commission, n.d.a, n.d.b, 2024; Stathopoulou et al, 2004).

A country with a significant rural population and a rich agrarian heritage, Romania presents itself as a compelling case study for examining the complexities and opportunities of rural entrepreneurship. The landscape of rural Romania is characterized by a unique blend of traditional practices and evolving modern dynamics. Demographically, Romania's rural areas often face challenges such as population aging and the emigration of young people to urban centers or abroad in search of better economic prospects. Economically, although agriculture remains a predominant activity, a substantial part of agriculture is still at a subsistence or semi-subsistence level, limiting its capacity for large-scale economic growth (Dan et al, 2016).

However, rural areas boast a rich cultural heritage, diverse natural resources, and a strong sense of community, all of which can serve as foundations for innovative entrepreneurial initiatives. The economic well-being of the rural population is linked to the trajectory of national development, making the promotion of rural entrepreneurship a national imperative (Dan&Popescu, 2017; Răzvanţă Puie, 2020).

The historical context further shapes the current entrepreneurial dynamics in rural Romania. The period of collectivization during the communist regime profoundly altered traditional land ownership patterns and suppressed private initiative, leaving behind a legacy of centralized control and limited entrepreneurial experience. The post-1989 transition to a market economy brought land restitution and the re-emergence of private agriculture, but the development of non-agricultural rural businesses was a slow and difficult process (Otiman et al, 2023). Subsequent accession to the European Union opened up new markets and access to substantial financing opportunities, but also introduced increased competition and the need to adapt to EU standards and regulations. Understanding this historical evolution is crucial for understanding the contemporary challenges and opportunities facing Romanian rural entrepreneurs.

This chapter aims to provide a comprehensive and nuanced analysis of Romanian rural entrepreneurship, exploring its multiple dimensions from the perspective of both inherent challenges and emerging opportunities. The main objective is to contribute to a deeper understanding of the entrepreneurial landscape in rural Romania and to identify pathways towards the development of sustainable business models that can promote resilient and prosperous rural communities. Therefore, this chapter aims to address critical questions: What are the specific obstacles that Romanian rural entrepreneurs face in their endeavours? What unique, often untapped opportunities exist in the rural landscape that can be harnessed for sustainable development? And, most importantly, how can sustainable business models be effectively conceptualized, developed, and supported to ensure the long-term prosperity and resilience of rural communities in Romania?

The chapter is systematically organized to provide a coherent and in-depth exploration of Romanian rural entrepreneurship. The study begins by defining rural entrepreneurship and sustainable business models, maps the current landscape of entrepreneurial activities in rural Romania, which includes a historical overview, current state and key sectors, policy and institutional framework, analyses the main challenges faced by rural entrepreneurs and explores the various opportunities available. The last part of the chapter shifts its focus to the development of sustainable business models, presenting a case study as well as strategic recommendations. The chapter concludes with a summary of the main findings and a discussion of their implications for practice and policy.

THEORETICAL FRAMEWORK: RURAL ENTREPRENEURSHIP AND SUSTAINABLE BUSINESS MODELS

Rural Entrepreneurship

In a broad sense, entrepreneurship is often defined as the process of identifying, creating and pursuing opportunities, often involving innovation, risk-taking and mobilizing resources to create economic, social or environmental value.

Applied in rural areas, the concept of entrepreneurship takes on distinct characteristics, giving rise to the notion of rural entrepreneurship. Rural entrepreneurship is not just the presence of businesses in rural areas, but rather a dynamic process that harnesses local resources (natural, cultural, human) to generate new economic activities and foster community development. The characteristics of rural entrepreneurship often include a reliance on indigenous knowledge, a strong integration into the local community, a tendency towards smaller-scale operations and a potential for multiple activities, in which individuals combine traditional agriculture with other diverse activities, such as tourism, crafts or local services (Avramenko&Silver, 2009; Barber et al, 2021).

The typologies of rural entrepreneurship are diverse, reflecting the varied economic structures and resource endowments of rural areas. Agricultural entrepreneurship extends beyond traditional agriculture to include value-added activities such as organic products, specialised crop farming, direct sales to consumers and agri-food processing. Non-agricultural rural entrepreneurship includes a wide range of activities, from agritourism and rural tourism, which capitalise on the natural beauty and cultural heritage of an area, to traditional crafts, small-scale production and various local services that meet the needs of rural residents (Popescu et al, 2023). In addition, social entrepreneurship is gaining importance in rural areas, focusing on addressing social or environmental problems through innovative business models, often with a strong community focus. Relevant theories of rural development, such as endogenous development, emphasise that sustainable growth in rural areas must come from within, using local resources and capacities, with entrepreneurship serving as a key driver of this internal dynamism. Territorial development theories further emphasise the importance of place-based approaches, in which entrepreneurial activities are tailored to the specific assets and needs of a given rural territory (Arias-Vargas et al, 2022; Barber et al, 2021).

Sustainable Business Models

A sustainable business model is defined as a framework that creates value for the business, while also creating value for society and the environment [9]. This framework goes beyond the traditional singular focus on financial profit to integrate environmental and social considerations into a business's core strategy and operations. This holistic approach ensures long-term viability by addressing the interconnectedness of economic, social and ecological systems (Stubbs& Cocklin, 2008).

Various frameworks and approaches underpin the development of sustainable business models, each offering a unique lens through which to integrate sustainability principles:

Circular economy principles. This model fundamentally moves away from the linear "take-make-throw" approach towards a regenerative one. It focuses on reducing waste and pollution, keeping products and materials in use, and regenerating natural systems. In rural contexts, this can translate into businesses that reuse agricultural waste, repair and reuse tools, or create closed-loop systems for water and energy (Ellen MacArthur Foundation, 2019).

Creating shared value. This concept focuses on creating economic value in a way that also creates value for society by addressing its needs and challenges. It involves redesigning products and markets, redefining productivity in the value chain, and building supportive local clusters. For rural entrepreneurs, this could mean developing products that address local health issues, improving agricultural practices to enhance soil health, or creating employment opportunities for disadvantaged groups (Porter& Kramer, 2011).

Stakeholder theory. This theory posits that a business should create value for all stakeholders—including employees, customers, suppliers, communities, and the environment—not just shareholders. Therefore, a sustainable business model considers the interests and impacts of all these groups, fostering long-term relationships and mutual benefits. In rural areas, this often translates into strong community involvement, fair relationships with local suppliers, and transparent communication with all stakeholders (Freeman, 2015).

Cradle-to-cradle design. This approach, an extension of the principles of the circular economy, advocates for the design of products and processes that are not only efficient, but also waste-free and regenerative. Materials are viewed as nutrients that can be recycled endlessly in either biological or technical metabolisms. Although often applied in manufacturing industries, its principles can inspire rural businesses to design products with the end of their life cycle in mind, ensuring that materials can be safely returned to nature or recycled endlessly (Sustainability Guide, n.d.).

These models can be applied in various rural contexts to promote sustainability. For example, agri-food cooperatives can adopt circular economy principles by composting organic waste and using it as fertilizer, or by processing surplus produce to reduce food waste. Ecotourism initiatives can implement shared value by hiring local guides, sourcing food from local farms, and investing a portion of profits in conservation efforts. Renewable energy cooperatives can empower local communities by providing clean energy while generating local economic benefits. Businesses that use local waste streams, such as those that transform agricultural residues into biofuels or building materials, exemplify the regenerative potential of sustainable models. The overall goal is to shift from a purely extractive economic model to one that is regenerative, inclusive and resilient, ensuring that rural enterprises contribute positively to the well-being of both people and the planet.

THE LANDSCAPE OF ROMANIAN ENTREPRENEURSHIP

Historical Overview

To understand the current landscape of Romanian rural entrepreneurship, a brief overview of its historical evolution is necessary, especially the profound transformations experienced during and after the communist era. Before the mid-20th century, Romanian rural society was predominantly agrarian, characterized by a mosaic of small-scale private landholdings and a strong tradition of self-sufficiency (Otiman et al, 2023). Although not officially recognized, entrepreneurial activities were rooted in everyday life, encompassing various forms of agricultural production, local crafts, and small-scale trade within rural communities. This period encouraged a degree of entrepreneurial spirit rooted in necessity and direct involvement in the market, albeit within a largely localized and informal economy.

The communist regime, established after World War II, brought about a radical restructuring of rural life through forced collectivization. Private land ownership was largely abolished, and agricultural production was centralized under state control (Otiman et al, 2023). This systemic change severely suppressed private initiative and dismantled traditional rural economic structures. Entrepreneurship, as a concept, was seen as antithetical to the planned economy, and individual economic agency was significantly reduced. The emphasis shifted from individual enterprise to collective production, leading to a decline in diverse rural economic activities and a homogenization of rural livelihoods. This period left a lasting legacy of centralized decision-making and a diminished culture of individual economic risk-taking in many rural areas.

The post-1989 transition to a market economy initiated a complex and often difficult process of decollectivization and land restitution. Although land was returned to former owners or their heirs, this process often resulted in highly fragmented land tenure, which made large-scale and efficient agricultural production difficult. The reemergence of private agriculture was a significant step, but the development of non-agricultural rural businesses proved to be a slow and more arduous process. Many rural residents, accustomed to the collective system, lacked the necessary entrepreneurial skills, market knowledge, and access to capital to successfully navigate the new economic environment. The early years of transition were marked by economic instability, high unemployment in rural areas, and a significant exodus of the rural population to urban centers or abroad. Romania's subsequent accession to the European Union in 2007 was another crucial moment. EU membership opened up new markets for Romanian products and provided access to substantial structural and cohesion funds, notably through the Common Agricultural Policy (CAP) and the European Agricultural Fund for Rural Development (EAFRD) (Raicov et al, 2021). These funds were designed to modernise agriculture, diversify rural economies and improve living conditions in rural areas (Opria, 2023). While these opportunities were significant, they also introduced increased competition from established EU markets and required adaptation to strict EU standards and regulations (Dan et al, 2017; Grecu et al, 2024). The historical trajectory therefore highlights a rural landscape shaped by periods of traditional entrepreneurship, suppression and a gradual, often difficult, re-emergence of entrepreneurial activity, significantly influenced by broader political and economic changes (Chiru, 2021).

Current State and Key Sectors

In the last three decades, the country has seen a major increase in the number of businesses, reflecting an evolution of 58% more economic entities compared to 2009. If in the early 1990s only a few percent of businesses were found in rural areas, currently 32% of them are found in rural areas. This evolution shows a notable increase in entrepreneurial interest in rural areas, even though urban areas remain the predominant economic center. Rural businesses generate income, but not profits, with a considerable gap between the two environments. Even though the income of urban and rural businesses has grown at a similar pace since 2008, rural areas fail to generate profits as consistently as urban areas. Between 2021 and 2023, in the context of a 60% increase in total income, profits in rural areas advanced by only 39%, compared to a 57% increase in urban areas. This difference highlights the challenges of rural areas in transforming revenues into net profit, highlighting higher operational costs and lower efficiency than in urban areas (European Commission, 2025; Impact Hub Bucharest, 2024; Popescu et al, 2022; Sima, 2022).

Currently, the Romanian rural economy is a mosaic of traditional and emerging entrepreneurial activities, reflecting both its historical roots and ongoing efforts to modernize.

Thus, the sectors that dominate the Romanian countryside are traditional agriculture, agritourism, and rural tourism. Agriculture remains the most prevalent sector, encompassing cereal cultivation (maize, wheat), livestock farming (cattle, sheep, pigs), horticulture (vegetables, fruits), viticulture (wine production), and beekeeping.

Although a substantial part of this activity is still characterized by small-scale farms, often oriented towards subsistence, there is a growing trend toward value-added processing. This includes the production of artisanal cheeses, traditional jams, fruit brandies and high-quality wines, which allow producers to capture a larger share of the value chain and differentiate their products in the market (Deiac&Arion, 2025; Otiman et al, 2023).

By capitalizing on Romania's picturesque landscapes, rich cultural heritage and authentic village life, agritourism and rural tourism have experienced significant growth. This sector mainly involves the development of agritourism guesthouses, offering visitors an immersive experience of rural life, local cuisine and traditional customs. These initiatives often integrate with local agricultural activities, allowing tourists to participate in agricultural work or enjoy culinary experiences directly from the farm. The appeal lies in offering unique and authentic experiences, which contrast with mass tourism (Ciolac et al, 2022).

At the same time, emerging sectors in rural Romania include renewable energy, traditional crafts and artisanal production, local services and retail.

Possessing abundant natural resources, some rural areas of Romania are witnessing the emergence of renewable energy projects, especially photovoltaic and wind power plants, and even biogas and micro-hydropower plants. All of these initiatives represent a significant opportunity for energy independence and local economic development (Rădulescu et al, 2014; Rujescu et al, 2025; Sima, 2022).

The preservation of Romania's rich tradition of crafts, such as wood carving, pottery, weaving and traditional costumes, is increasingly becoming a basis for entrepreneurial activity. These businesses often serve tourists or niche markets, emphasizing authenticity, craftsmanship and cultural heritage (Popescu et al, 2023).

In addition to agriculture and tourism, rural areas also support a wide range of essential local services, including small retail stores, construction services, car repairs and various personal services. These businesses meet the daily needs of the local population and contribute to the comfort and quality of life in rural communities. It should be noted that there are regional variations in entrepreneurial activity in Romania. For example, regions with strong wine traditions (Moldova, Muntenia) present a higher concentration of businesses related to viticulture and wine tourism, while mountainous areas (Maramure , Bucovina) are more inclined towards agritourism and traditional crafts, and lowland regions remain dominated by agriculture (Adamov et al, 2020). Understanding these regional specificities is crucial for adapting support programs and identifying localized opportunities.

Policy and Institutional Framework

The development of rural entrepreneurship in Romania is significantly influenced by a complex interaction between national policies and European Union initiatives. The overall framework is largely shaped by the EU Common Agricultural Policy (CAP) and its rural development pillar, which provides substantial financial and strategic support for the modernisation of agriculture, the diversification of rural economies and the improvement of the quality of life in rural areas (Chiru, 2021).

Romania has developed several National Rural Development Programmes (NRDPs) in line with the EU programming periods, which outline the strategic priorities and specific measures for the allocation of funds from the European Agricultural Fund for Rural Development (EAFRD) (Feher, 2025; Răzvanţă Puie, 2020). Key objectives include increasing the competitiveness of the agri-food sector, promoting the sustainable management of natural resources and encouraging balanced territorial development in rural areas. Specific measures within these programmes often aim at supporting young farmers, investing in physical assets on farms, developing non-agricultural activities in rural areas and supporting local development strategies (European Commission, 2025).

The European Agricultural Fund for Rural Development (EAFRD) is the main EU financial instrument supporting rural development. The EAFRD co-finances a wide range of projects, including those aimed at: modernising and restructuring farms, diversifying rural activities, setting up young farmers, basic services and village renewal.

The LEADER programme (Liaison Entre Actions de Développement de l'Économie Rurale) is a component of the EAFRD that promotes a participatory, bottom-up approach to rural development, empowering local communities to design and implement their own development strategies (Opria et al, 2023). This is done through Local Action Groups (LAGs), which are partnerships between public, private and civil society actors at local level. LAGs develop Local Development Strategies (LDS) and manage the allocation of EAFRD funds to projects that align with these strategies. The LEADER programme is particularly important for encouraging innovation, supporting small-scale projects and promoting local entrepreneurship adapted to specific territorial needs (Staic et al, 2022).

Numerous institutions play a role in the implementation and management of these policies and programmes, such as:

- Ministry of Agriculture and Rural Development (MADR) - the main national authority responsible for agricultural and rural development policies, including the management of EAFRD funds.

- Agency for the Financing of Rural Investments (AFIR) - the paying agency responsible for the management and distribution of EAFRD funds to beneficiaries.
- Local authorities (County Councils, Municipalities, Communes) play a role in co-financing projects, providing local infrastructure and supporting local development initiatives.
- Non-governmental organizations (NGOs) and business associations - provide consultancy, training and advocacy services for rural entrepreneurs. They often act as intermediaries in accessing financing and information.

Even though these policies and programs offer significant opportunities, their effectiveness and accessibility for rural entrepreneurs can be hindered by numerous factors, such as: complex application procedures, bureaucratic obstacles, limited co-financing capacity for small entrepreneurs and challenges in ensuring equitable distribution of funds between different regions and types of beneficiaries. Critical evaluation of these aspects is essential to improve the impact of public support on rural entrepreneurial development (Grecu et al, 2024; Raicov et al, 2021).

Challenges Faced by Romanian Rural Entrepreneurs

Despite their resilience and innovative spirit, Romanian rural entrepreneurs navigate a complex landscape, subject to numerous challenges that can hinder the establishment, growth and sustainability of their businesses. These challenges often stem from a combination of historical legacies, structural deficiencies and socio-economic factors inherent in rural environments (Sima, 2022).

One of the most significant and frequently mentioned challenges for rural entrepreneurs in Romania is the limited access to adequate and affordable finance. This challenge manifests itself in the lack of collateral, limited financial literacy, risk aversion of banks, complex processes for accessing grants, the prevalence of informal financing (Dan et al, 2016; Nastase et al, 2019; Paul, 2020).

A large proportion of rural entrepreneurs, especially those involved in small-scale agriculture or incipient non-agricultural businesses, often do not possess the tangible assets or sufficient collateral required by traditional financial institutions to obtain loans. Land fragmentation and low asset values in rural areas further exacerbate this problem (Rădulescu et al, 2014).

An overwhelming proportion of rural residents have limited financial literacy, making it difficult to understand complex credit products, prepare comprehensive business plans, or navigate the often complicated processes of applying for grants and subsidies. This knowledge gap can discourage potential entrepreneurs from seeking formal financing channels.

Banks also often view rural businesses, especially those in agriculture or emerging sectors, as high-risk investments due to perceived market volatility, dependence on weather conditions, and lack of established business models. This risk aversion translates into stricter lending criteria, higher interest rates, or an outright reluctance to lend to rural businesses.

Although European Union funds offer substantial grant opportunities, application processes are frequently characterized by their complexity, extensive documentation requirements, and long approval times. Small entrepreneurs, who often lack dedicated administrative staff or expertise in writing grant applications, find these procedures daunting and difficult to manage, leading to low absorption rates of available funds (Raicov et al, 2021). In the absence of accessible formal financing, many rural entrepreneurs rely on informal sources, such as personal savings, family loans, or local lenders. While these sources offer flexibility, they are often insufficient for significant investments, limit growth potential, and may come with unfavorable terms. The limited availability of venture capital or angel investment networks in rural areas further restricts options for business expansion or investment in technology and innovation.

Inadequate infrastructure is another challenge for rural entrepreneurs in Romania, significantly affecting their operational efficiency, market reach and overall competitiveness. Disparities in infrastructure development between urban and rural areas are evident and contribute to the isolation of many rural communities (Popescu et al, 2022; Sima, 2022).

The fact that many rural roads are unpaved, poorly maintained or non-existent makes transporting goods and accessing markets difficult, time-consuming and expensive, and this directly affects businesses that rely on the timely delivery of raw materials or the distribution of finished products, such as agricultural producers, artisans or tourism operators. Poor road conditions also discourage potential customers and investors from visiting rural businesses.

Despite progress, reliable and high-speed internet connectivity remains a significant problem in many remote rural areas. This digital divide severely limits the ability of rural entrepreneurs to leverage e-commerce platforms, access online marketplaces, use digital marketing tools, or benefit from online training and information resources (Popescu et al, 2022).

Access to modern and reliable utility services, such as drinking water supply and adequate sanitation systems, in rural areas of Romania is deficient. Businesses, especially those in the food, manufacturing, or hospitality industries, require stable and high-quality utility services for their operations. Disruptions or lack of access to these basic services can lead to increased operational costs, production delays, and a reduced ability to meet quality standards. These infrastructure deficiencies burden rural entrepreneurs because they increase logistical costs, reduce efficiency, limit access to information and markets, and ultimately diminish the attractiveness of rural areas for investment and business development (Pavel et al, 2018).

One of the factors determining entrepreneurial success is the availability of skilled human capital. In many rural areas of Romania, skilled human capital is a significant challenge. Numerous factors contribute to the human capital and skills deficit that can hinder entrepreneurial development: aging population, lack of entrepreneurial education, limited marketing expertise, digital literacy gap (Dan et al, 2016; Grecu et al, 2024; Popescu et al, 2022).

Addressing this human capital and skills gap requires specific interventions, including the development of accessible and tailored vocational training programs, entrepreneurial education initiatives, and digital literacy courses. In addition, strategies to attract and retain skilled young people in rural areas, such as incentives for rural living or support for remote work opportunities, are crucial to fostering a more dynamic entrepreneurial ecosystem.

Even when rural entrepreneurs manage to overcome financial and infrastructure barriers, they often face significant challenges in accessing wider markets and competing effectively with larger, more established businesses. Due to factors such as poor transportation infrastructure, limited marketing knowledge, and a lack of established distribution channels, many rural businesses struggle to reach customers beyond their immediate local communities. This restricts their customer base and limits their growth potential, keeping them confined to niche markets or direct sales at local fairs.

Rural entrepreneurs often struggle to compete with the economies of scale, marketing budgets, and established supply chains of larger urban businesses or imported goods. Consumers, especially in urban areas, may prioritize the convenience and lower prices offered by supermarkets or large retailers, making it difficult for small rural producers to gain market share (Chiru, 2021; Dan et al, 2016).

Accessing larger and more profitable markets (national retail chains, export markets) often requires compliance with strict quality standards, certifications (organic certifications, food safety) and packaging requirements. Rural entrepreneurs may not have the resources, knowledge or technical capacity to meet these requirements, limiting their market opportunities. The cost of obtaining and maintaining such certifications can also be prohibitive for small businesses.

While many rural entrepreneurs possess excellent production skills, a large proportion of them lack expertise in modern marketing, branding and sales strategies. This can result in products that, despite their high quality or unique features, fail to attract sufficient attention or command premium prices in competitive markets. The absence of strong collective branding or regional marketing initiatives further exacerbates this problem.

Romanian rural entrepreneurs frequently face significant bureaucratic and regulatory hurdles that can stifle their initiative and add a considerable burden to their operations. The process of registering a business, obtaining the necessary licenses, and complying with various permits can be complicated and time-consuming. Rural entrepreneurs, who often operate with limited legal or administrative support, may find it difficult to navigate the multitude of requirements, leading to delays or even the abandonment of their businesses.

Businesses in rural areas, particularly those involved in food production, tourism, or environmental activities, are subject to a wide range of regulations, including food safety standards, environmental protection laws, labor laws, and tax regulations. Keeping up with these regulations, understanding their implications, and ensuring compliance can be a significant challenge, especially when regulations are frequently updated or interpreted inconsistently by different authorities (Nastase et al, 2019).

The administrative burden associated with reporting, record-keeping and inspections can be particularly burdensome for small rural businesses. Unlike larger companies, which can afford dedicated administrative or legal departments, rural entrepreneurs often have to manage these tasks themselves, diverting valuable time and resources from core business activities.

Simplifying administrative procedures, providing clear and accessible guidance on regulations and promoting a more transparent and enabling regulatory environment are crucial steps to alleviate the burden on rural entrepreneurs and encourage the development of formal businesses.

Beyond the tangible challenges related to finance, infrastructure and skills, Romanian rural entrepreneurship can also be influenced by less tangible but equally significant factors related to traditional mentalities and a certain resistance to change. These cultural and psychological elements can influence entrepreneurial attitudes, the propensity to take risks and the adoption of innovative practices (Brezuleanu et al, 2013; Matei, 2013). In this sense, a first barrier is represented by the attachment to subsistence agriculture and a family economic model, oriented towards safety and conservation, not towards growth and risk. In many rural communities, success is still measured by stability and predictability, and initiatives that deviate from this pattern can be viewed with skepticism. This perspective is often doubled by a managerial culture described as "poor and fragmented", based more on instinct and relationships than on formal entrepreneurial education. Secondly, resistance to change manifests itself as an inhibiting force. This can stem from the fear of failure, a general distrust of the new, or the anxiety generated by breaking out of routine. In an environment where traditions are strongly rooted, any innovation, whether it is technology, a new business model, or a modern marketing strategy, can be perceived as a threat to the way of life. However, it is important to note that tradition is not exclusively an obstacle. When properly capitalized on, it can become a powerful economic differentiator. Businesses in rural tourism, crafts, or traditional food production demonstrate how cultural heritage can be transformed into a unique competitive advantage, attracting customers precisely through the authenticity it offers. The challenge, therefore, is to find a balance: preserving the valuable essence of tradition, while integrating the innovation and pro-active mentality needed to thrive in today's economy (Damasaru &Craciun, 2016; Sate i commune, n.d.).

In many rural communities, there is a strong adherence to established, often generations-old, ways of farming or conducting small-scale trade. This preference for tradition, while preserving cultural heritage, can sometimes lead to a reluctance to adopt new technologies, modern business practices or innovative approaches that could increase efficiency or open up new markets. The comfort of familiar methods can outweigh the perceived benefits of change.

Entrepreneurship inherently involves risk-taking. However, in rural contexts where economic security may be precarious and safety nets limited, there may be a heightened aversion to financial or operational risks. This may manifest itself as a reluctance to invest in new businesses, expand existing ones or experiment with unproven business models, even if they have significant potential for growth and sustainability. Memories of past economic hardship or uncertainties can further reinforce this cautious approach.

In some rural areas, a robust entrepreneurial culture, characterized by a spirit of innovation, autonomy, and a willingness to pursue new opportunities, may be less developed than in urban centers. This can be partly attributed to historical factors, such as the period of collectivization, which suppressed private initiative and fostered dependence on state-controlled systems. The absence of visible entrepreneurial models or a supportive ecosystem may also contribute to this cultural gap.

Addressing these deeply rooted mindsets requires more than just financial incentives or training programs. Long-term efforts are needed to foster an entrepreneurial culture through education, mentoring, showcasing local success stories, and creating support networks that encourage experimentation and risk-taking in a safe environment.

Starting from the main challenges faced by Romanian entrepreneurs (poor infrastructure, limited market access, low level of digital literacy), it is necessary to discuss the complex interconnections between them, highlighting how these challenges mutually exacerbate each other and contribute to economic and social underdevelopment. These problems reinforce each other, hindering investment, education and innovation. In this sense, an understanding of the causal relationships is essential for formulating effective development strategies, and a visual representation of these interdependencies is crucial to understand the complex dynamics of these challenges (Figure 2).

The interconnections between poor infrastructure, limited market access and digital literacy create a vicious cycle that stunts development. Breaking this vicious circle requires a strategic and integrated approach that simultaneously addresses the multiple facets of the problem: priority investments in physical infrastructure through the modernization and expansion of transport networks, the expansion of digital infrastructure, national digital literacy programs, support for SMEs, better coordination between national, regional and local strategies, and the efficient use of European funds to ensure a coherent approach and maximum impact of investments. A holistic approach to the challenges can allow the transformation of the vicious circle of underdevelopment into a virtuous cycle of economic growth, social inclusion and innovation.

Figure 1. Causal Diagram

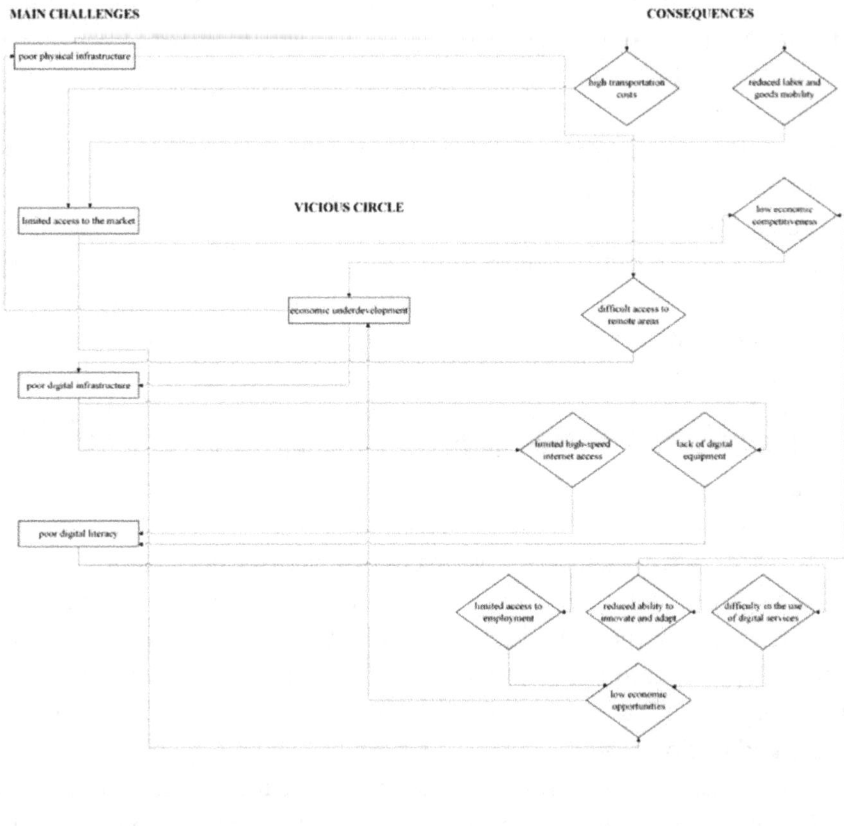

Physical infrastructure, including transport networks, utilities and public buildings, forms the basis of a modern economy. Inadequate or underdeveloped physical infrastructure generates a series of negative consequences, with a direct and indirect impact on market access and, ultimately, on digital literacy. Therefore, a poor transport network (bad roads, lack of highways or efficient connections), significantly increases the transport costs for goods and services, and this directly affects the competitiveness of local products, which become more expensive on domestic and foreign markets. Labor mobility is also limited, making it difficult for people to access jobs and for employers to access a wider pool of talent.

Producers in remote areas face major difficulties in distributing their products, which reduces their opportunities for growth and integration into regional and national value chains.

In Romania, transport infrastructure is still underdeveloped, with visible gaps between east and west. Although essential for the mobility of people and goods, investments in secondary transport infrastructure are often insufficient. At the same time, poor road infrastructure not only slows down transport, but also increases vehicle wear and tear, adding additional costs to businesses and consumers. The limited access to regional and national markets caused by these deficiencies reduces the efficiency of economic activities and discourages productive investments.

Regarding the impact of physical infrastructure on digital literacy, although it does not seem like it, it is still significant. Usually, areas with poor physical infrastructure are also often those with low investment in digital infrastructure. The high costs of implementing fiber optic networks or other connectivity solutions in rural or isolated areas, where roads are difficult to access, discourage service providers. At the same time, the lack of adequate educational infrastructure (modern, properly equipped schools) in these areas limits access to quality education, including digital skills training. Without a conducive learning environment and without physical access to training centers, the development of digital literacy is severely hampered.

Digital infrastructure, which includes access to high-speed internet, mobile communication networks and the availability of digital equipment, is the backbone of the information society. Deficiencies in this area have a profound and direct impact on digital literacy and market access.

Lack of access to high-speed internet, coupled with the unavailability or high cost of digital equipment, are fundamental barriers to the development of digital literacy. Individuals cannot acquire digital skills without access to the necessary tools and resources. This "digital divide" exacerbates social and economic inequalities, creating a class of digitally illiterate citizens unable to fully participate in modern society.

Digital education requires not only access to technology, but also appropriate training. However, without a robust digital infrastructure, efforts to improve digital skills through online courses, educational platforms or open resources are limited. Schools in areas with weak digital infrastructure cannot provide students with the learning experiences needed to develop essential digital skills, thus perpetuating the gap.

A poor digital infrastructure severely limits market access in the digital age. Businesses, especially SMEs, face difficulties in accessing critical market information (prices, trends, competition), in using e-commerce platforms to sell their products or services, or in taking advantage of online banking and other digital financial instruments. This reduces their ability to compete effectively and scale their operations. It also limits opportunities for remote work and access to new technology-based business models that could boost economic growth.

Digital literacy is not just about the ability to use a device, but also about critical thinking, problem solving and understanding the ethical implications of online actions. A low level of digital literacy has significant repercussions on market access and the adaptive capacity of a society.

Thus, individuals with a low level of digital literacy have difficulty navigating the modern labor market, where digital skills are increasingly in demand. They may be excluded from employment opportunities that require the use of technology, from continuing online education or from accessing e-government services. All of this lack of skills limits their participation in the digital economy and reduces their chances of social and economic mobility.

Also, a low level of digital literacy affects the ability of individuals to access information relevant to economic decisions, such as comparing prices, identifying business opportunities or understanding regulations. This makes them more vulnerable to online disinformation and fraud, reducing their trust in and participation in the digital environment.

A population with poor digital literacy is less able to adopt new technologies, innovate and adapt to rapid changes in the economy. This slows down technological progress at national and regional levels, affecting overall competitiveness. In a world of continuous technological evolution, the lack of digital skills is becoming a major obstacle to sustainable development and economic resilience.

Opportunities for Romanian Rural Entrepreneurs

Despite significant challenges, Romanian rural areas possess immense untapped potential and emerging opportunities that, if strategically harnessed, can stimulate sustainable entrepreneurial development. These opportunities are rooted in natural resources, evolving consumer preferences, technological advances, and supportive policy frameworks. Romania is endowed with numerous natural resources that form a considerable basis for a wide range of entrepreneurial activities in rural areas. The sustainable use of these resources presents significant economic potential.

Alongside traditional agriculture, there is a huge potential for practicing organic agriculture, driven by Romania's fertile lands and varied climate and supported by the growing demand for organic products.

Rural entrepreneurs can capitalize on the demand for organic products by establishing direct sales channels, such as farm gate sales, community supported agriculture schemes, and participation in local and regional agricultural markets. These short supply chains ensure freshness and quality and also allow producers to build direct relationships with consumers, promoting trust and loyalty. This model allows producers to capture a higher share of the retail price, improving their profitability compared to selling through intermediaries (Stefan et al, 2021).

Also, the development of niche crops, such as berries, aromatic herbs, truffles or specialized horticultural products, are attractive for small and medium-sized farms because they require small land areas, offer higher yields and can serve specific market segments.

Romania boasts one of the largest forest areas in Europe. Sustainable forestry practices can support not only timber production, but also the development of non-timber forest products, such as wild mushrooms, berries, medicinal plants and honey. Entrepreneurial enterprises can focus on harvesting, processing and marketing these products, ensuring ecological balance and community benefits (Toader et al, 2022a). In addition, the potential for environmentally friendly wood processing and the production of sustainable wood products can add significant value at the local level.

The Romanian rural environment holds considerable potential for renewable energy generation. Agricultural lands offer opportunities for biomass production for heating or electricity generation. The country's rivers and streams can support microhydropower projects, especially in mountainous regions, providing decentralized energy solutions for local communities and businesses. In addition, the increase in solar radiation and wind potential in certain areas can be harnessed for solar and wind energy projects, contributing to energy independence and generating additional income for landowners (Chiciudean et al, 2018; Rujescu et al, 2025).

Another opportunity is the development of local processing units. Instead of selling raw materials at low prices, rural entrepreneurs can set up small-scale processing units for fruits (jams, juices, dried fruits), vegetables (pickles, preserves), milk (cheeses, yogurts), meat (cold cuts, sausages) and cereals (flour, pastries). This adds significant value, creates local jobs and allows producers to capture a higher share of the final product price. At the same time, it supports the development of unique, regionally branded products that attract consumers interested in authenticity and quality (Uliu&Vladu, 2020).

With a rich culinary heritage and a wide range of traditional products, Romania has significant potential for the certification and branding of these products (traditional cheeses, cold cuts, specific fruit varieties, honey, artisanal bread) to highlight their authenticity, quality and regional distinctiveness (Toader et al, 2025). Obtaining geographical indications (GI) or traditional speciality guaranteed (TSG) labels at EU level can provide legal protection, increase market recognition and command premium prices. Branding can differentiate Romanian rural products in both domestic and international markets, attracting consumers looking for unique and high-quality gastronomic experiences (Dicu et al, 2025; Constantin&Popescu, 2025).

Romania's natural beauty, diverse landscapes, and well-preserved cultural heritage offer significant potential for the development of agritourism and rural tourism. This sector offers a powerful avenue for rural entrepreneurs to diversify their incomes, create local jobs, and promote sustainable development by capitalizing on the unique assets of their communities (Adamov et al, 2020). From the Carpathian Mountains, the Danube Delta, medieval towns, painted monasteries, to traditional villages, and vibrant folk traditions, Romania offers tourists seeking alternatives to mass tourism authentic experiences of itinerant tourism, ecotourism, rural tourism, cultural tourism, and religious tourism (Sorea et al, 2023).

The establishment of agritourism guesthouses is a cornerstone of Romanian agritourism. These often family-run businesses offer comfortable accommodations, traditional Romanian cuisine, and an engaging experience of rural life. Culinary tourism, focused on local, organic and traditional foods, is a strong attraction (Toader et al, 2022b). In this sense, entrepreneurs can develop unique culinary experiences, such as cooking classes, wine tastings or farm-to-table dining, showcasing regional specialties and local products.

In addition to relaxation, rural areas can meet the needs of adventure tourism with activities such as hiking, cycling, horse riding and wildlife observation. Cultural tourism can be developed around traditional craft workshops (pottery, weaving, wood carving), folklore festivals and historical sites. These activities not only attract tourists, but also contribute to the preservation of local traditions and provide additional sources of income for artisans and cultural practitioners (Ciolac et al, 2022).

Despite the existing challenges related to internet connectivity in some rural areas, digitalization and the growth of e-commerce present a transformative opportunity for Romanian rural entrepreneurs. Leveraging digital tools can help overcome geographical barriers, expand market coverage, and increase business efficiency (Rădulescu et al, 2014; Sima, 2022).

E-commerce platforms and online marketplaces offer rural businesses direct access to national and international customer bases, bypassing the limitations imposed by poor physical infrastructure and remote locations. Products that could otherwise only be sold locally can reach a much wider audience, including urban consumers in Romania and buyers from abroad interested in authentic Romanian products. This expanded market reach can significantly increase sales volumes and revenues for rural businesses (Butu et al, 2024).

Entrepreneurs can use various online platforms, from dedicated e-commerce websites to broader social media channels for marketing and sales. Social media, in particular, offers a cost-effective way to build brand awareness, engage with customers, showcase products, and tell the story behind their rural businesses. Visual content, such as high-quality photos and videos of production processes or the countryside, can be extremely effective in attracting customers.

To fully harness the potential of digitalization, however, it is important to address the digital literacy gap among rural entrepreneurs. In this regard, training programs focused on practical skills, such as setting up online stores, managing digital payments, using social media for marketing, and understanding online customer behavior, are essential. These programs can enable entrepreneurs to independently manage their online presence and sales channels (Ionitescu et al 2023).

Across Romania, there are already examples of rural businesses successfully using digital tools. These include small producers selling organic products directly to urban consumers through online ordering systems, artisans selling traditional crafts on national and international e-commerce platforms, and agritourism guesthouses using online booking sites and social networks to attract tourists.

European Union funding and support programs are a cornerstone of rural development in Romania, providing substantial financial and technical assistance that can be leveraged by rural entrepreneurs. Although the complexity of EU funding mechanisms can be a barrier, the large volume and diversity of support available make these programs indispensable for promoting rural entrepreneurship in Romania. Effective use requires strong local leadership, capacity building, and the dissemination of specific information to potential beneficiaries (Ciobanu&Vladu, 2024).

Romania's rich and diverse cultural heritage, especially traditional crafts and folk art, is a unique and valuable asset for rural entrepreneurship. The preservation and commercialization of these traditions offers significant economic potential, contributing to both cultural sustainability and local economic development (Ciolac et al, 2022).

Traditional crafts such as pottery (Horezu ceramics), weaving (traditional textiles, carpets), wood carving (Maramure gates, household items) and traditional costumes are not only artistic expressions, but also tangible products with market value. Entrepreneurs can set up workshops and small businesses focused on the production and sale of these authentic items. The demand for handmade products with cultural significance is growing, especially among tourists and collectors, both domestically and internationally. This offers an opportunity to create high-value products that reflect Romanian identity and craftsmanship (Bu et al, 2017; Corpădean, 2011). Success in this area often depends on highlighting the authenticity, heritage and unique story behind each product.

Traditional crafts and cultural events can be seamlessly integrated into tourism offerings. This integration creates a synergistic relationship where tourism supports the preservation of crafts, and crafts enhance the tourist experience.

By strategically investing in and supporting these resource-based opportunities, Romanian rural entrepreneurship can build a resilient and diversified economic base that respects environmental limits and creates sustainable livelihoods.

TOWARDS SUSTAINABLE BUSINESS MODELS IN RURAL ROMANIA

The transition to sustainable business models in rural Romania is an essential step to reduce economic and social gaps compared to the urban environment. In the context where entrepreneurship is seen as a key solution for the development of rural areas, it becomes crucial to explore business models that not only generate profit, but also integrate principles of ecological sustainability and social inclusion. This approach is vital to capitalize on local potential, from tourism and agritourism to crafts and organic production, while ensuring a harmonious and long-term development of communities. Challenges such as limited access to financing and modern infrastructure require innovative and adapted solutions. The case study analyses in depth a responsible business model, focused on sustainability and inclusion, offering a practical perspective on how these concepts can be successfully implemented in the Romanian rural entrepreneurial landscape.

Study Case. Sustainability and Inclusion in Rural Business: A Responsible Business Model

Research Methodology. In carrying out the case study, the following steps were taken: identification of a rural entrepreneur, data collection, data analysis and interpretation, and presentation of findings.

Data collection was carried out using a personal, face-to-face interview. The interview was a semi-structured interview, based on a questionnaire with open questions. The interview took place on March 25, 2025, for 2 hours, and began with the presentation of the purpose of the study and obtaining consent to participate in the interview and record the conversation.

Also, desk research (document analysis) was also used as a data collection method, the data collection sources being a report with financial data, generated by the risco.ro platform, the Development Strategy of the Giarmata commune, the 2021 Population and Housing Census and the TEMPO-online statistical database of the National Institute of Statistics of Romania.

Presenting the context. Giarmata commune is located in the central part of Timiş county, on the terminal forms of the Vingăi Plain, which make the transition between the Lipovei Hills and a low plain, 12 km northeast of Timi oara. Giarmata commune consists of Giarmata residence and Cerneteaz.

From a numerical, ethnic and confessional point of view, the population of the Giarmata locality has had a dynamic course over time. So, if in the period 1796 - 1782 Giarmata hosted 327 families of German colonists, alongside Romanians, until World War II the entire community was made up of ethnic Germans. After 1945, there is a gradual re-establishment of Romanians in Giarmata, simultaneously with the departure of ethnic Germans to Germany. Thus, on January 1, 1995, the population numbered 4,536 inhabitants (2,245 men and 2,291 women), the ethnic composition being as follows: Romanians 94.3%, Hungarians 2%, Germans 1.6%, other nationalities 2.1%.

According to data provided by the National Institute of Statistics of Romania, in 2024, 8,018 people lived in Giarmata (National Institute of Statistics, 2024a). In terms of confessional affiliation, in 2021, the majority of the inhabitants were Orthodox (72.63%), but there were also Pentecostals (7.4%) and Roman Catholics (1.75%). For 15.23% of the population, the religious affiliation is unknown (National Institute of Statistics, 2023). In terms of ethnicity, the majority of the inhabitants are Romanians (83.77%), along with them live Roma (1.59%), Hungarians (0.52%), Germans (0.146%), Ukrainians, Slovaks and Macedonians. For 13.57% of the population, the ethnicity is unknown (National Institute of Statistics, 2023).

From an economic point of view, agriculture has an important share, with agricultural activity being supported by 8 commercial companies with an agricultural and livestock profile. The agricultural area is composed of arable land (5,498 ha), pastures (492.25 ha) and hayfields (140 ha). The cultivated agricultural area of the commune is approximately 5,000 ha, without irrigation systems, only with drainage canals. The arable area is cultivated with wheat, corn, rapeseed, sunflower, soybeans, barley, and barley. The livestock sector is dominated by sheep and cattle breeding (Local Development Strategy of Giarmata Commune).

According to the information found in the Local Development Strategy of Giarmata commune, the share of turnover related to the CAEN codes included in divisions 01 (Agriculture, hunting and related services) and 03 (Fishing and aquaculture) represents approximately 1% of the total turnover recorded at the commune level during the period 2017-2021 (Local Development Strategy of Giarmata Commune; National Institute of Statistics, 2025).

As for the industrial sector, in recent years several renowned multinational companies have opened production points in the commune, contributing significantly to the local budget revenues and creating employment opportunities not only for the commune's residents, but also for the entire area. In this regard, it is worth mentioning that approximately 80% of the turnover of companies registered in the commune comes from industry in the period 2017-2021 (Local Development Strategy of Giarmata Commune).

Trade is carried out through wholesale and retail units, such as grocery stores, restaurants, bakeries, confectioneries, pharmacies, construction materials, etc. Thus, the turnover recorded in the period 2017-2021 by traders carrying out activities according to the CAEN codes included in divisions 45 (Wholesale and retail trade, maintenance and repair of motor vehicles and motorcycles), 46 (Wholesale trade) and 47 (Retail trade) represents approximately 5% of the total turnover recorded at the commune level (Local Development Strategy of Giarmata Commune; National Institute of Statistics, 2025).

Regarding services, economic operators are registered in the commune that carry out activities according to the CAEN codes included in divisions 49 (Land transport and pipeline transport), 72 (Research and development), 80 (Investigation and protection activities) and 82 (Secretarial activities, support services and other service activities provided mainly to businesses) and whose turnover represented approximately 9% of the total turnover recorded at the commune level in the period 2017-2021 (Local Development Strategy of Giarmata Commune; National Institute of Statistics, 2025).

Analyzed from a tourist point of view, the commune does not present any special attractions, and the economic results in the tourism sector are insignificant. The turnover recorded by the 3 economic agents that carry out activities according to the division of the CAEN code 55 (Hotels and other accommodation facilities) was approximately 0.1% in the period 2017-2021 (Local Development Strategy of Giarmata Commune; National Institute of Statistics, 2025).

Due to the commune's location near the city of Timi oara, an important economic center in the western part of Romania, the commune has a high level of population employment, the commune's workforce being employed both in the over 200 economic entities registered in the area and outside the commune. The average number of employees in the commune has remained relatively constant in recent years, from 2,110 employees in 2017 to 2,323 employees in 2021 (Local Development Strategy of Giarmata Commune). A constant evolution is also recorded in the number of unemployed in recent years. In 2024, 19 unemployed people were registered (7 men and 12 women), the share of registered unemployed in the total labor resources being 0.4% (National Institute of Statistics, 2024a; National Institute of Statistics, 2024c).

Business description. Seeds of Kenosis Design is a limited liability company, based in Giarmata commune, Timi county, Romania. The company's business activity is "wholesale of wood and construction materials and sanitary equipment" (CAEN code 4683).

The business, started in 2018 by the Swedish citizen, Samuelsson Erik Andreas, is based on the desire to highlight the natural characteristics of both material resources (wood, leather, resin) and human resources (members of the Roma community), and to transform imperfection into something special.

The business idea emerged from social activities carried out by the business initiator in Cerneteaz, a village belonging to Giarmata commune. If at first the activities aimed at educating children from Roma families, in a short time the problems faced by the entire Roma community were known and these activities were carried out through the Seeds of Kenosis Association, whose mission is the social inclusion of the entire Roma community in Cerneteaz. Therefore, by carefully observing the way of life of Roma families, their skills and aptitudes, the idea of a business in which wood and leather would be processed, and even reinvented by the creativity and skilled hands of Roma people, was shaped. The start of the business was not based on a well-defined business plan and strategy, but on the strong desire to do something useful for the members of the Roma community. In this regard, it is necessary to mention the values promoted by Seeds of Kenosis Design: social inclusion, valorization of cultural identity, valorization of natural elements. The mission of the business is to create a place where every person is seen, heard, encouraged and appreciated.

In the company's workshop, natural elements, mainly wood, along with resin and leather, gain personality through products designed to use and beautify homes, offices and restaurants.

The product portfolio includes household items made of wood (chopping boards, platters, trays), wooden furniture items (bookcases, tables, chairs), leather items (accessories, baskets, bags, wallets, chairs, aprons) and jewelry (earrings, rings, hairpins, pendants, bracelets, brooches, key chains). The business stands out on the market for its unique products. Currently, the products are sold to customers directly at the company's headquarters, through its own website, at fairs, exhibitions and through collaborators (9 stores selling handmade products in Alba-Iulia, Bucharest, Bra ov, Viscri and a chain of bookstores). The distribution of products is carried out through courier companies, and locally it is provided by the entrepreneur.

Products are promoted online (website, social media accounts) and by participating in various events (fairs, exhibitions) where products are exhibited. In many cases, some orders attract other orders. For example, the first order was from a well-known chef in Romania who ordered 2 tables for his own restaurant. His order was followed by an order from a restaurant recognized for the unique culinary experiences offered to customers. In this way, they entered the HORECA field with their products, being recognized for listening to customer requirements and carrying out original projects (for example, embedding a very old wooden cross in a table).

Customers are individuals who want personalized products, which give a special touch to their homes. Some customers come with their own ideas and even materials (for example, wooden elements from old houses that they do not want to give up and to which they give a new utility and appearance).

Also, customers are also legal entities, Kenosis products can be found in restaurants, hotels, offices, medical offices. The business's commitment to sustainable practices is an integral part of the business identity and reflects respect for nature and future generations through: - intelligent valorization of existing resources. Old wood from houses and structures is given a new life, being transformed into unique products with a rich history. This practice contributes to reducing the demand for new wood and to the conservation of forests;

- minimizing waste in a creative way. Every piece of wood is precious, and wood remains are transformed into jewelry, chopping boards and other ingenious objects (wooden cubes with QR codes used in restaurants to consult menus, wooden awards), following a “zero waste” approach;
- reducing waste in the production process. We try to optimize each stage of the production process to minimize the amount of lost material;
- using environmentally friendly packaging. The products are carefully packaged using natural and recyclable materials (cardboard, twine), avoiding plastic and other environmentally harmful materials;
- promoting a circular economy. By reusing and transforming existing materials, the environmental impact is reduced and the life cycle of wood is extended;
- awareness and inspiration. The aim is to inspire customers and other businesses to adopt sustainable practices, showing that beauty and quality can go hand in hand with environmental responsibility.

The financial analysis of Seeds of Kenosis Design reveals a remarkable development from a modest start-up to a consolidated business. According to the latest reports, in 2023, with a team of 6 employees, the company achieved a turnover of 271,144 euros and a net profit of 21,734 euros, with a profit margin of 8% (Seeds of Kenosis Design Report). This development is the culmination of an exponential growth, especially visible after 2019. For a complete picture of the economic trajectory, the detailed evolution of the main financial indicators is presented in table 1.

Table 1. Evolution of main financial indicators of Seeds of Kenosis Design Company (euro)

	2018	2019	2020	2021	2022	2023
Number of employees	2	5	5	4	5	6
Turnover	906	106,712	169,210	208,617	246,520	271,144
Total income	907	121,494	172,714	212,916	249,336	283,560

continued on following page

Table 1. Continued

	2018	2019	2020	2021	2022	2023
Total expenditure	3,549	118,871	107,468	175,882	214,179	259,521
Gross Profit/Loss	-2,642	2,623	65,246	37,034	35,157	24,039
Net Profit/Loss	-2,651	1,419	63,587	35,196	33,056	21,734
Fixed assets	58	-	0	731	12,102	8,497
Current assets	7,896	42,287	120,348	118,156	194,676	250,470
Stocks	1,357	16,410	71,233	58,787	121,204	181,299
Debts	4,775	11,979	25,245	33,340	58,877	55,603
Cash and bank accounts	1,764	13,898	23,869	26,029	14,595	13,567
Capital	-2,608	-1,139	62,470	58,520	92,442	114,413
Social capital	43	42	41	41	41	41
Liabilities	10,562	43,426	57,877	59,367	114,335	144,695
Exchange rate RON / EURO	4.653	4.745	4.837	4.920	4.931	4.918

Source: Report Seeds of Kenosis Design

The analysis of the evolution of the company's main financial indicators, during the period 2018-2023, outlines the profile of a business with remarkable growth and progressive consolidation. Starting from an almost symbolic level in 2018, the company recorded an exponential expansion of turnover, reaching over 270,000 euros in 2023, which demonstrates a strong validation of its business model on the market.

A turning point was the year 2020, which marked a peak in profitability, with a net profit of over 63,000 euros. Although in the following years the profit margin stabilized at a lower level (8% in 2023), this happened in the context of a continuous increase in operating expenses and inventories, suggesting a strategy of reinvestment and capacity expansion. The steady growth of current assets and equity, which became positive and consolidated after 2019, indicates robust financial health and increased independence from debt.

The financial data reflects a successful trajectory, characterized by accelerated growth, structural consolidation and a strategy oriented towards long-term development, transforming a modest initiative into a stable economic player in the rural entrepreneurial landscape.

In addition to the positive development of the main financial indicators, the economic health of the company is also confirmed by an external assessment. In 2023, Seeds of Kenosis Design obtained a normal financial rating of 6.5, indicating low risk and solid stability (Figure 2). This assessment is supported by the level of operational profitability and solvency indicators, which together reflect a comfortable financial position. As can be seen in table 2, the company has the ability to honor its long-term financial obligations, thus strengthening its reputation as a reliable business partner.

Figure 2. Rating of Seeds of Kenosis Design Company

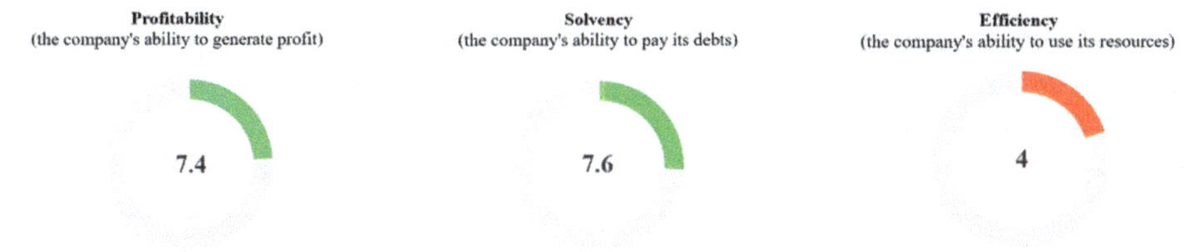

Although the current performance is solid, there is a possibility that in the future the company will face certain operational or financial risks, inherent to any expanding business. This perspective makes it necessary to constantly monitor the financial evolution and, moreover, requires the adoption of pro-active measures. Financial data analysis reveals risks like decreasing profit margins despite revenue growth, rising operational costs, inventory overload, liquidity issues, and manageable debt levels. Limited capital social compared to rapid growth poses external funding risks. Additionally, operational risks from human errors, reputation damage, technological lag, rural resource limitations, seasonality, and access to finance are highlighted.

Seeds of Kenosis Design demonstrates above-average profitability and solvency, with outstanding asset utilization. The main area of concern is inventory turnover efficiency, where there is a significant gap from the average. Addressing this area could unlock additional capital and further improve the company's liquidity and overall performance (Table 2).

Table 2. Evaluation of the main financial indicators

Indicator	Evaluation	2023	Average	Company vs Average
Profitability				
Net profit margin (%)		8	4.8	3.2
Increase in turnover (%)		9.7	9.7	0.0
Return on assets (%)		255.8	38.7	217.1

continued on following page

Table 2. Continued

Indicator	Evaluation	2023	Average	Company vs Average
Capital return (%)		19.8	18.1	0.9
Solvability				
Total debt level (%)		55.8	56.0	-0.2
Debt coverage ratio (%)		15.0	14.0	1.0
Efficiency				
Customer collection period (days)		75	78	-3
Stock rotation period (days)		244	85	159

Source: Report Seeds of Kenosis Design

The company has no outstanding debts, and its value is 366,680 euros.

Seeds of Kenosis Design demonstrates a remarkable growth trajectory and solid financial health, confirmed by a good financial rating, a 0% probability of insolvency and a significant company value. Its performance in terms of profitability and return on assets exceeds the industry average, highlighting efficient resource management and a robust value generation capacity. However, certain aspects that require increased attention are also highlighted, in particular inventory management and maintaining a healthy net profit margin in the context of rapidly increasing expenses. Operational and rural risks, although not critical at present, require a proactive approach. In this regard, cost optimization, inventory management, cash flow consolidation and continuous adaptation to market specifics will allow the company to consolidate its competitive advantage, mitigate vulnerabilities and ensure sustainable and profitable growth in the long term, transforming challenges into development opportunities.

Opportunities. Current trends in interior design highlight an increased preference for sustainability and the integration of natural elements, reflected in the harmony between aesthetics and functionality. In this context, wood remains a central element, both due to its appearance and durability.

Participation in various events dedicated to beauty and jewelry (Romanian Jewelry Week 2024, Beautiful Days Timisoara 2025) opens up new opportunities for development and entry into new markets. Kenosis jewelry is made by a woman from the Roma community who creates as she feels, doing so with great pleasure, although she does not have a "past" in the art of jewelry making.

Business development prospects. Considering the fact that it currently operates in a rented space, because the workshop was destroyed in a fire and the available space is limited, with the return to the old location it is planned to set up a space where people interested in making their own furniture have access to consultation, the necessary tools and equipment.

Along with wood, clay is another fundamental natural material, with a long history of use in various forms, from construction to art and crafts. Given that the two elements can be combined and complement each other, they plan to set up a clay processing department.

They are also thinking about expanding and multiplying the business in other rural areas where socio-economic imbalances are recorded. They want to set up hubs in poor rural communities where various products can be made with the help of locals (jewelry, chopper, etc.). The hubs are designed as a workplace located near the living space. The products made in the hubs will be sold in stores.

Challenges. The main challenges they faced and are currently facing are largely the challenges that most Romanian entrepreneurs face (excessive bureaucracy, legislative instability, unfair competition, poor infrastructure). In some periods they had staff fluctuations, a situation that they managed to manage each time without having major effects on the activity. There are also periods when the number of orders decreases, the fact that the products are personalized does not ensure a constant level of sales as mass production could ensure.

The biggest challenge of the business, however, was a fire that destroyed the workshop (hall) by 80% in 40 minutes. After the fire, only the equipment and piles of burned products remained. It was a moment of balance for the entrepreneur, at which point he thought about closing the business. But just as the entrepreneur, through his business, reached out to those in need, he also received support from the community through physical or financial contributions. There were people who bought shredders that bore the marks of the fire after they had been previously sanded and oiled. They also received numerous orders that were paid in advance and with generous delivery terms. According to the entrepreneur, it was the moment when "they saw the power of the community and the relationships built in the community and realized the sustainability of the business."

Social responsibility. On various occasions or upon request, creative woodworking workshops are organized for children and adults. The results of the work and the effect of working with wood on the participants are miraculous. If at first most of the participants are reserved, shy and do not know what to do with the piece of wood in front of them, after putting into practice the instructions received and holding a new object in their hands, they open up and show delight in their work. Woodworking can be seen as an opportunity to disconnect from technology and reconnect with the self.

By actively participating in charitable sports events (Timotion), Seeds of Kenosis Design supports initiatives aimed at the personal development and social integration of Roma children through educational activities, reaffirming its commitment to the community.

Main findings. The business has a strong identity, it is distinguished by the combination of craftsmanship in woodworking with the creativity of members of the Roma community. This synergy gives rise to unique products with a special charge and personality.

Through the recovery of old wood, the use of remains and environmentally friendly packaging, the business demonstrates a concrete commitment to environmental protection and the principles of the circular economy.

The business contributes to the economic and social development of the Roma community by creating employment opportunities, promoting inclusion and leveraging the skills and abilities of local people.

The business represents a responsible business model, which integrates cultural values, concern for the environment and positive social impact in its operational strategy.

In the context of a growing demand for unique, sustainable products, the business has significant potential for growth and to attract a loyal clientele.

Recommendations. Considering the fact that the business is a social one, efforts aimed at personal development, mental well-being and social interaction can be continued. In this regard, a space dedicated to woodworking and clay workshops can be arranged, accessible to people interested in benefiting from the positive effects of this manual and creative activity (children, people who want to develop practical skills, people looking for a way to express themselves creatively, people who face stress, anxiety, depression, people who want to improve their concentration, etc.).

Regarding the expansion of the business from a geographical point of view, this is a strategic decision that involves careful planning and efficient implementation. Although the benefits of geographical expansion can be multiple (increasing the level of income, profit, business value, strengthening the market position), it is necessary to clearly define the objectives, analyze the market, secure financial resources, identify and manage potential risks associated with the expansion. Failure to pay due attention to these aspects may lead to some "discomforts" (operational problems, financial issues, difficulties in managing human resources, etc.).

The case study of Seeds of Kenosis Design reveals a remarkable success story, demonstrating accelerated growth and solid financial health, confirmed by a good financial rating, a 0% probability of insolvency and a significant company value. This evolution is all the more relevant when analyzed through the lens of the historical and political context of Romanian rural entrepreneurship, where the company managed to transform environmental challenges into a competitive advantage. Its exceptional performances in terms of profitability and return on assets exceed the industry average, highlighting efficient resource management and a robust capacity to generate value, even in the face of pressures on net profit margin and inventory management.

By proactively implementing the proposed recommendations, focused on cost optimization, inventory management, cash flow consolidation and continuous adaptation to market specifics, Seeds of Kenosis Design will not only consolidate its competitive advantage and mitigate the identified vulnerabilities, but will continue to serve as an inspirational model. Its success explicitly demonstrates how entrepreneurial initiatives can contribute to the economic and social development of rural communities in Romania, responding efficiently and innovatively to the dynamics and opportunities offered by this broader context.

Overall, this case study provides a valuable perspective on the challenges and opportunities faced by Romanian rural businesses operating in the current context of globalization and the increasing emphasis on sustainability.

Strategies for Developing Sustainable Business Models

Based on the case study, but also on the findings obtained from the landscape of Romanian entrepreneurship, the table 3 presents key strategies that Romanian rural entrepreneurs can adopt to develop and implement sustainable business models. These strategies emphasize a holistic approach, integrating economic viability with environmental responsibility and social equity.

Table 3. Effective key strategies for Romanian rural entrepreneurs

Key strategy	Implications
Value chain optimization	• *Reduce waste* by implementing practices such as composting organic waste, recycling packaging materials and optimizing production processes. For agricultural businesses, reducing waste can mean using all parts of a crop, an animal or finding innovative uses for by-products. • *Improve efficiency* by investing in energy-efficient equipment, optimizing logistics to reduce emissions from transport and adopting precision farming techniques to minimize water and fertilizer use. • *Increase transparency* by providing consumers with clear information about the origin of products, production methods and environmental impact. This can build trust and differentiate products in the market. • *Shortening supply chains* by prioritizing local input sourcing and direct sales to consumers reduces transport costs and emissions and supports local economies.
Community engagement and social impact	• *Creating local jobs* (e.g. prioritizing employment of local residents, especially youth and marginalized groups, and ensuring fair wages and safe working conditions). • *Supporting local suppliers* by sourcing resources (e.g. raw materials, services) from other local businesses strengthens the regional economy and promotes a collaborative ecosystem. • *Investing in community development* by contributing to local infrastructure, education or social programs (e.g. direct financial contributions, volunteer efforts or partnerships with local NGOs). • *Ensuring fair wages and ethical practices* by complying with labor laws, providing fair compensation and promoting a positive work environment that respects the rights and well-being of employees.
Eco-innovation and green technologies	• *Adopting renewable energy* by installing solar panels, small wind turbines or biomass systems to power operations, thereby reducing dependence on fossil fuels and lowering energy costs. • *Sustainable packaging*. Using biodegradable, recyclable or reusable packaging materials to reduce plastic waste and environmental pollution. • *Water-saving techniques*. Implementing efficient irrigation systems (e.g. drip irrigation), rainwater harvesting and recycling water in processing facilities. • *Organic and regenerative farming methods*. Switching to practices that improve soil health, biodiversity and ecosystem services, such as no-till farming, cover crops and integrated pest management.

continued on following page

Table 3. Continued

Key strategy	Implications
Diversification and niche markets	• Creating unique products/services by developing distinctive products or experiences that capitalize on local resources, traditions, or cultural heritage (e.g. artisanal foods, ecotourism packages, traditional crafts). • Serving specific consumer segments involves targeting consumers who are willing to pay a premium price for organic, fair trade, locally sourced, or environmentally friendly products. This requires effective marketing and branding that communicates the unique value proposition. • Value-added processing by transforming raw agricultural products into higher-value goods (e.g. fruit into jams, milk into specialty cheeses) to increase profitability and reduce post-harvest losses.
Certification and branding	• *Organic certifications.* Obtaining national or EU organic certifications for agricultural products signals compliance with strict environmental standards and opens up access to organic markets. • *Fairtrade labels.* For products involving multiple producers or supply chains, fairtrade certifications ensure ethical sourcing and fair compensation for producers. • *Strong local branding* involves developing a compelling brand identity that communicates the origin, quality and sustainable practices of the business and may include regional branding initiatives that promote a collective identity for products from a specific geographical area.

Strategic implementation of these approaches can lead to building resilient and profitable businesses that contribute significantly to the sustainable development of rural communities and the region at large.

The Role of Collaboration and Partnerships

Collaboration and partnerships are indispensable when it comes to promoting sustainable rural entrepreneurship. Given the often limited resources, geographical dispersion and diverse challenges faced by individual rural enterprises, collective action can unlock synergies, increase competitiveness and facilitate access to markets, knowledge and finance. Collaborations can take various forms, both horizontal (between similar enterprises) and vertical (at different stages of the value chain) and can involve public, private and civil society actors (López et al, 2019; Stanimirov&Stanimirova, 2023).

The horizontal approach involves collaborations between businesses operating at the same level of the value chain and can involve farmer cooperatives, artisan associations. Through cooperatives, farmers can pool their resources for the purchase of raw materials, product processing, marketing, distribution. In this way, farmers have greater bargaining power, their costs are reduced and they can meet greater market demands (Cretu et al, 2023; Dumitrescu et al, 2016). At the same time, cooperatives can facilitate the exchange of knowledge on sustainable agricultural practices. Another example of horizontal collaboration is that of artisan associations, which can collectively promote their products, organize craft fairs, share workshop spaces, and develop common branding. This approach can help them reach wider markets, maintain quality standards, and preserve traditional techniques.

Agritourism networks are another example of a horizontal approach to collaboration in the field of rural entrepreneurship. In this sense, guesthouses and local service providers can form networks to offer complete tourism packages, promote each other and jointly market their region as a tourist destination (Ciolac et al, 2022; Popescu et al, 2023).

The vertical approach involves partnerships between businesses at different stages of the value chain, for example farm-to-fork partnerships or tourism value chains.

Farm-to-fork partnerships involve direct collaborations between rural producers and urban restaurants, hotels or retailers to ensure a steady supply of fresh, local and often organic produce. This provides producers with guaranteed markets and fair prices, while consumers gain access to high-quality, traceable products (Deiac&Arion, 2025).

Tourism value chains involve partnerships between agritourism guesthouses, local food producers, craft workshops and adventure tour operators to create integrated tourism experiences. This enhances the overall attractiveness of the destination and ensures that tourism spending benefits a wider range of local businesses (Foris et al, 2020).

Public-private partnerships can play an important role in addressing systemic challenges in rural areas, such as poor infrastructure and limited market access. In this regard, local authorities can work with private telecommunications companies to expand broadband internet access to remote villages, which is vital for e-commerce and digital literacy. Similarly, public-private partnerships can be established to develop and manage local processing facilities, cold storage facilities or logistics centers that are too expensive for individual entrepreneurs (Popescu, 2019).

Regarding market access, public bodies can collaborate with private sector entities, such as large retailers, export agents, to develop platforms or programs that facilitate access of rural products to the national or international market. This could involve joint marketing campaigns, quality assurance schemes or facilitating participation in trade fairs (Stanciu, 2015).

In promoting a supportive rural entrepreneurial ecosystem, highlighting the roles of local action groups and business incubators is also important. Local action groups are essential in promoting a collaborative environment, as they act as facilitators, bringing together diverse local stakeholders to identify needs, develop strategies and implement projects. Their community-led approach ensures that initiatives are tailored to local contexts and that funding reaches projects at the grassroots. LAGs can also provide crucial networking opportunities, connecting entrepreneurs with potential partners, mentors and resources (Buda&Pop, 2024).

As for business incubators, even though they are more often found in urban areas, they can significantly support emerging rural businesses. These entities offer shared workspaces, mentoring, business development training, access to funding networks, and legal/financial advice (Capatina et al, 2023). Business incubators can help rural entrepreneurs refine their business models, overcome initial obstacles, and scale up their operations. Specialized incubators focused on agribusiness, tourism, or traditional crafts can be particularly effective.

Promoting and actively supporting forms of collaboration and partnership in Romania contributes to building a resilient, interconnected and sustainable rural entrepreneurial ecosystem, thus freeing individual enterprises to thrive in a supportive collective framework.

Policy Recommandations for Fostering Sustainable Rural Entrepreneurship

In order to effectively promote sustainable rural entrepreneurship in Romania, a comprehensive and coordinated policy framework is essential. The policy recommendations are designed based on the identified challenges, aiming to capitalize on existing opportunities and develop a favourable environment in which rural enterprises can thrive sustainably and can be seen in table 4. The recommendations target financial support, infrastructure development, education and training, support for market access, regulatory simplification and the promotion of innovation and research.

Table 4. Recommandations for fostering sustainable rural entrepreneurship

Direction of action	Specific action	Initiative
Financial support	Simplified access to grants and microcredits	Optimizing EU and national grant application processes (Raicov et al, 2021).
		Introducing dedicated microcredit schemes with favorable interest rates and flexible repayment terms, specifically tailored to the needs of rural startups and small businesses (Henegar et al, 2024).
	Specialized funds for sustainable businesses	Creating or expanding dedicated financing lines for businesses that integrate solid social and environmental sustainability criteria (Staic et al, 2022).
	Financing incubators and accelerators	Providing financial support for the establishment and operation of rural business incubators and accelerators that provide mentoring, training and seed funding for promising sustainable rural businesses (Capatina et al, 2023).

continued on following page

Table 4. Continued

Direction of action	Specific action	Initiative
Infrastructure development	Rural road investments	Prioritize and accelerate investments in improving and expanding the rural road network to increase connectivity, reduce transport costs, and facilitate access to markets for rural products (Pavel et al, 2018).
	Utility networks	Continued investment in modernizing and expanding water, sanitation, and energy utility networks in rural communities, which are fundamental to commercial operations and quality of life (Adamov et al, 2020).
Education and training	Personalized entrepreneurial education	Developing and integrating practical entrepreneurial education programs in rural schools and vocational training centers, focusing on business planning, financial management and marketing specific to rural contexts (Grecu et al, 2024).
	Digital skills training	Implementing extensive digital literacy programs for rural residents and entrepreneurs, covering e-commerce platforms, online marketing, and basic IT skills (Butu et al, 2024).
	Professional programs for sustainable practices	Providing specialized vocational training in sustainable agriculture, ecotourism management, preservation of traditional crafts, and renewable energy technologies to strengthen local capacity and expertise (Brezuleanu et al, 2013).
	Mentoring and counseling services	Creating networks of experienced entrepreneurs and business consultants to provide mentoring and advisory services to rural startups, especially in the initial stages of their development (Sălă an et al, 2017).
Market access support	Regional branding and promotion	Supporting the development of strong regional brands for traditional and organic products and promoting them through national and international marketing campaigns (Dicu et al, 2025; Stefan et al, 2021).
	E-commerce platforms and logistics	Facilitate the creation or adoption of user-friendly e-commerce platforms specifically designed for rural producers, and support the development of efficient logistics and distribution networks for rural products.
	Participation in fairs and exhibitions	Providing financial and logistical support to rural entrepreneurs to participate in national and international trade fairs, exhibitions and farmers markets, to expand their market reach and network.
	Public procurement policies	Encourage public institutions to prioritize the procurement of food and other products from local rural enterprises, promoting a stable local market.
Regulatory simplification	Streamlining administrative procedures	Simplifying and digitizing business registration, licensing and compliance procedures for rural businesses, reducing the administrative burden and time required (Dan et al, 2016).
	Clear guidance and support	Providing clear and accessible information and dedicated support services to help rural entrepreneurs navigate the regulatory landscape.

continued on following page

Table 4. Continued

Direction of action	Specific action	Initiative
Promotion of innovation and research	R&D in sustainable practices	Funding research and development initiatives focused on sustainable agricultural practices, resource-efficient technologies and innovative business models relevant to rural areas (Rădulescu et al, 2014).
	Technology transfer	Facilitating the transfer of knowledge and technology from research institutions and universities to rural enterprises, ensuring that entrepreneurs have access to the latest advances (Harpa et al, 2015, Vajda et al, 2025).

Implementing the recommended policies involves a concerted effort from government agencies, local authorities, NGOs and the private sector, but a collaborative approach, adapted to the specific needs and potential of Romania's rural areas, is essential for harnessing the full potential of sustainable rural entrepreneurship.

CONCLUSION

Summary of Key Findings

Exploring Romanian rural entrepreneurship has revealed a landscape shaped by both historical legacies and contemporary dynamics. The main findings are summarized below.

Rural entrepreneurs in Romania continue to face substantial obstacles. These include, but are not limited to, limited access to finance, poor infrastructure, human capital and skills shortages, an aging rural population and youth migration, market access and intense competition from urban enterprises, bureaucratic complexities, and traditional mindsets resistant to change, creating a difficult operating environment for many rural enterprises.

Despite these challenges, Romanian rural areas possess untapped potential. Romania's rich natural resources offer opportunities for high-value agricultural products (organic farming, niche crops), sustainable forestry, and renewable energy generation. Growing domestic and external demand for local and organic products creates fertile ground for direct sales and short supply chains. Romania's unique natural beauty and cultural heritage also provide a solid basis for agritourism and rural tourism development, attracting visitors seeking authentic experiences. Digitalization and the increasing accessibility of e-commerce platforms provide a powerful tool to overcome geographical barriers and expand market reach. Crucially, significant funding and support programs from the European Union provide vital financial and technical assistance. Thus, the preservation and commercialization of Romania's rich cultural heritage and traditional crafts are unique economic and cultural opportunities.

The chapter highlights that sustainable business models are not just an ideal but a practical necessity for long-term rural development. To ensure a prosperous future for the Romanian rural area, sustainable business models are proving to be essential. By adopting sustainable business models, entrepreneurs can contribute to the economic, social and environmental development of rural communities by creating resilient, competitive and responsible businesses. In pursuit of this goal, collaboration between decision-makers, entrepreneurs, local communities and other stakeholders is particularly important, in order to promote and implement sustainable business models. Organic farming, regenerative agriculture, rural tourism, agritourism, crafts, local services and the circular economy are just some of the directions in which sustainable business models can be developed in rural areas. In this sense, it is worth mentioning a few examples of sustainable business models that are suitable for the Romanian rural area:

- the practice of agritourism. By combining agricultural activities with tourism, it offers tourists the opportunity to experience life in the countryside, taste local products and learn about agriculture and local traditions;
- production of renewable energy. By using local resources (solar energy, wind energy, biomass) in the production of electricity or heat, dependence on fossil fuels can be reduced, contributing to environmental protection;
- transition to a circular economy by implementing business models that reduce the amount of waste, use resources efficiently and create added value through recycling and reuse;
- practicing traditional crafts by producing and marketing artisanal products, preserving cultural heritage and offering communities new employment opportunities;
- providing local services by developing businesses that meet the needs of communities (home care services, consulting, transportation, cleaning, event organization, repairs, etc.).

Essentially, Romanian rural entrepreneurship is at a crossroads. Even though significant historical and contemporary challenges persist, the inherent strengths of its natural and cultural resources, together with evolving market demands and available external support, present a compelling case for optimism. The path to a vibrant and resilient rural economy, therefore, lies in strategically promoting sustainable business models, supported by strong collaborative networks and supportive public policies.

Implications for Practice and Policy

The analysis and findings presented in this chapter have implications for both current and aspiring rural entrepreneurs in Romania, as well as for policymakers and support organizations. Translating these insights into concrete strategies is crucial for promoting a dynamic and sustainable rural economy.

As for rural entrepreneurs, they need to realize that traditional approaches are not enough to ensure long-term success. They need to adapt to ongoing market demands, consumer preferences and technological advances. In this regard, they must be willing to innovate in product development, production methods and marketing strategies, in particular by leveraging digital tools and e-commerce.

Also, integrating environmental and social considerations into the business model from the very beginning is not only an ethical choice, but an economic imperative. Businesses that focus on organic production, resource efficiency, waste reduction and fair labor practices are increasingly favored by consumers and can access financing and specialized markets. This strengthens resilience against future environmental and social challenges.

Collaboration and partnerships are issues that entrepreneurs need to consider, as overcoming boundaries and securing resources often require collaboration. Rural entrepreneurs should actively seek and engage in horizontal collaborations (joining or establishing cooperatives, associations with other producers) and vertical partnerships (direct sales to urban markets, collaborations with travel agencies). These networks can provide rural entrepreneurs with access to shared resources, collective marketing power and knowledge exchange.

Another aspect that should not be neglected is continuous learning and skills development. Entrepreneurs should actively pursue training in business management, financial literacy, digital marketing and specific sustainable practices relevant to their sector, as it enhances their ability to manage and grow their businesses effectively. Capitalizing on local resources is another aspect that rural entrepreneurs need to consider. The unique natural and cultural assets of rural Romania represent a competitive advantage. Entrepreneurs should identify and build businesses around these distinctive resources, whether it is high-quality agricultural products, traditional crafts or authentic tourism experiences. Emphasizing authenticity and regional identity can create strong brand differentiation.

As for policymakers and support organizations, they should design and implement financial support mechanisms specifically tailored to the realities of rural businesses. This means simplifying grant application procedures, expanding microcredit schemes and creating dedicated funds for sustainable rural enterprises.

Risk assessment models for rural loans should also be reassessed to better reflect the potential of these businesses, and continued and accelerated investment in rural infrastructure is essential. Investment in infrastructure is essential to facilitate market access, digital transformation and increase the overall attractiveness of rural areas as places to live and do business.

Regarding education and training, there is a need to develop practical, accessible and relevant education and training programmes for rural residents. Through training programs, rural entrepreneurs should develop entrepreneurial skills, digital competencies, and receive specialized vocational training in sustainable agriculture, ecotourism, and traditional crafts. In this regard, mobile training units or online platforms can help reach remote communities.

In order to facilitate market access, but also to promote products, it is necessary to implement policies and programs that actively support rural enterprises in accessing wider markets by promoting regional branding, supporting participation in national and international trade fairs and developing dedicated e-commerce platforms.

Adopting these practical and policy-oriented recommendations can unlock the full potential of its rural areas, turning challenges into opportunities and encouraging a new generation of sustainable rural entrepreneurs who contribute significantly to Romania's economic prosperity, environmental health and social cohesion. The future of rural Romania lies in empowering its inhabitants to build stable, innovative and sustainable businesses that honor its entire heritage while embracing the future.

AKNOWLEDGEMENT

The completion of the study case would not have been possible without the support of Seeds of Kenosis Design. I thank to all the staff Seeds of Kenosis Design for their cooperation and kind support throughout my research period. Deep appreciation and special thanks to Rebeca and Andreas Samuelsson for their time and invaluable support in facilitating this study case, ensuring a productive research experience.

REFERENCES

Adamov, T., Ciolac, R., Iancu, T., Brad, I., Pe , E., Popescu, G., & muleac, L. (2020). Sustainability of Agritourism Activity. Initiatives and Challenges in Romanian Mountain Rural Regions. *Sustainability (Basel)*, *12*(6), 2502. DOI: 10.3390/su12062502

Arias-Vargas, F. J., Ribes-Giner, G., & Garcés-Giraldo, L. F. (2022). Rural entrepreneurship: A historical approach. *Retos Revista de Ciencias de la Administración y Economía*, *12*(23), 45–66. DOI: 10.17163/ret.n23.2022.03

Avramenko, A., & Silver, J. A. K. (2009). Rural entrepreneurship: Expanding the horizons. *International Journal of Entrepreneurship and Innovation Management*, *11*(2), 140. Advance online publication. DOI: 10.1504/IJEIM.2010.030065

Barber, D.III, Harris, M. L., & Jones, J. (2021). An Overview of Rural Entrepreneurship and Future Directions. *Journal of Small Business Strategy*, *31*(4), 1–4. DOI: 10.53703/001c.29468

Brezuleanu, C. O., Brezuleanu, S., & Constantin Iaţco, C. (2013). Development of labour market and entrepreneurial spirit in rural areas. *Environmental Engineering and Management Journal*, (11), 4.

Buda, D., & Pop, A. (2024). Romanian Local Action Groups' (LAGs) Economic Impact: A Solution to a Problem or a Perpetuating Status Quo of a Gimmick? *Transylvanian Review of Administrative Sciences*, *20*(71), 23–43. DOI: 10.24193/tras.71E.2

Buş, R.-M., Lung, M.-S., & Colcer, A.-M. (2017). Traditional crafts and folklore as a means of economic development in the land of Călata. *Territorial Identity and Development Journal*, *2*(1), 64–77. Advance online publication. DOI: 10.23740/TID120175

Butu, M., Dragomir, V., Badan, (Voicila), D.N. (2024) Romania's rural digital transformation and implications for agriculture. *Scientific Papers. Series "Management, Economic Engineering in Agriculture and rural development"*, Vol. *24*(3).

Capatina, A., Cristea, D. S., Micu, A., Micu, A. E., Empoli, G., & Codignola, F. (2023). Exploring causal recipes of startup acceptance into business incubators: A cross-country study. *International Journal of Entrepreneurial Behaviour & Research, 29*(7), 1584–1612. Advance online publication. DOI: 10.1108/IJEBR-06-2022-0527

Chiciudean, G. O., Harun, R., Arion, F. H., Chiciudean, D. I., Oroian, C. F., & Muresan, I. C. (2018). A Critical Approach on Sustainable Renewable Energy Sources in Rural Area: Evidence from North-West Region of Romania. *Energies, 11*(9), 2225. DOI: 10.3390/en11092225

Chiru, G. (2021). The Development of Entrepreneurship in Romanian rural Area. *Acta Universitatis Danubius Oeconomica, 17*(6).

Ciobanu F.B., Vladu M. (2024). The Leader Programme evolution in the European Union and Romania. *Scientific Papers. Series "Management, Economic Engineering in Agriculture and rural development", 24*(1).

Ciolac, R., Iancu, T., Popescu, G., Adamov, T., Feher, A., & Stanciu, S. (2022). Smart Tourist Village—An Entrepreneurial Necessity for Maramures Rural Area. *Sustainability (Basel), 14*(14), 8914. DOI. 10.3390/su14148914

Constantin, D.-L., & Popescu, I.-A. (2025). Traditions and entrepreneurial spirit: The evolving geography of craft brewing in Romania and dynamic interactions with the local development environment. *Applied Geography (Sevenoaks, England), 176*, 103543. Advance online publication. DOI: 10.1016/j.apgeog.2025.103543

Corpădean, I.-R. (2011). Izvoru Crişului - a Handicraft Based Tourist Village. *Journal of Settlements and Spatial Planning, 2*(1).

Cretu, O.R., Tudor, V.C., Lascar, E. (2023). Agricultural cooperative – viable alternative for the economic-social development of small and medium farmers. Case study Călăra i County, Romania. *Scientific Papers. Series "Management, Economic Engineering in Agriculture and rural development", 23*(3).

Damasaru, C., & Crăciun, A. (2016). *Managementul poten ialului antreprenorial în Romania rurală*. Pro Universitaria Publishing House.

Dan, E., Ghi ă (Haque), C.M., & Dona, I. (2016). Rural entrepreneurship in Romania: importance, premises and limitations. *Scientific Papers Series Management, Economic Engineering in Agriculture and Rural Development, 16*(2), Issue 2.

Dan, M.-C., & Popescu, C. (2017). Entrepreneurship in the rural areas of Romania. The impact of the 2007-2013 EU funding programmes. In *Proceedings of the International Conference on Business Excellence, 11*(1). Retrieved from https://sciendo.com/article/10.1515/picbe-2017-0116

Deiac, F., & Arion, F. H. (2025). Analysis of the agricultural sector in the North-West Region of Romania from the point of view of cluster excellence. *Scientific Papers. Series Management, Economic, Engineering in Agriculture and Rural Development*, *25*(1).

Deng, J., Chi, H., & Zhang, T. (2024). Effects of Entrepreneurial Activities on Rural Revitalization: Based on Dissipative Structure Theory. *Agriculture, 14*(9), 1474. DOI: 10.3390/agriculture14091474

Dicu, A. M., Rad, D., Barbu, F., Cuc, L. D., Feher, A., Roman, D., Mazuru, L., Sanda, G., & Pîrvulescu, L. (2025). From Attachment to Action: Consumer Identification and the Sustainable Buying of Rural Brand Products Like "Pită de Pecica". *Sustainability (Basel), 17*(9), 4133. DOI: 10.3390/su17094133

Dumitrescu, C. S., Salasan, C., Mateoc-Sirb, N., & Gavruta, A. (2016). Contribution of local products in developing agricultural systems and local economy - case study. *SGEM 2016, BK 2: Political Sciences, Law, Finance, Economics and Tourism Conference Proceedings*, Vol. IV.

Ellen MacArthur Foundation. (2019). Circular Economy Introduction. Retrieved from https://www.ellenmacarthurfoundation.org/the-circular-economy-in-detail-deep-dive

European Commission. (2024). Study on funding for EU rural areas: final report, Publications Office of the European Union. Retrieved from https://data.europa.eu/doi/10.2762/901111

European Commission. (2025). Factsheet on 2014-2020 Rural Development Programme for Romania. Retrieved from https://agriculture.ec.europa.eu/system/files/2023-11/rdp-factsheet-romania_en_.pdf

European Commission. (n.d.a). Common agricultural policy funds. Retrieved from https://agriculture.ec.europa.eu/common-agricultural-policy/financing-cap/cap-funds_en

European Commission. (n.d.b). The common agricultural policy at a glance. Retrieved from https://agriculture.ec.europa.eu/common-agricultural-policy/cap-overview/cap-glance_en

Feher, A. (2025). *Community funding policies and programs.* Pro Universitaria Publishing House.

Foris, D., Florescu, A., Foris, T., & Barabas, S. (2020). Improving the Management of Tourist Destinations: A New Approach to Strategic Management at the DMO Level by Integrating Lean Techniques. *Sustainability (Basel), 12*(23), 10201. DOI: 10.3390/su122310201

Freeman, R. E. (2015). *Strategic Management: A Stakeholder Approach.* Cambridge University Press.

Grecu, M., Surleanu C.A., Gusan O., Smedescu D.I., Vlad G., Panait R., Tudor V.C. (2024). Analysis of the efficiency of the implementation of financing programs from the European social fund on education in the rural environment in Romania. *Scientific Papers. Series "Management, Economic Engineering in Agriculture and rural development"*, 24(2).

Habersetzer, A., Rataj, M., Eriksson, R. H., & Mayer, H. (2020). Entrepreneurship in rural regions: The role of industry experience and home advantage for newly founded firms. *Regional Studies, 55*(5), 936–950. DOI: 10.1080/00343404.2020.1826038

Harpa, E., Moica, S., & Rus, D. (2015). A predictive model of innovation in rural entrepreneurship. *Procedia Technology*, •••, 19.

Henegar, D., Ilie , G. L., Mure an, I. C., Poru iu, A. R., Arion, I. D., & Arion, F. H. (2024). Customers' Perception of Microfinance Services as a Tool for Rural Development: A Romanian Case Study. *Agriculture, 14*(7), 1087. Advance online publication. DOI: 10.3390/agriculture14071087

Impact Hub Bucharest, Startarium i Datable. (2024). Entrepreneur Profile 2024. Retrieved from file:///C:/Users/Cosmina/Downloads/Profil%20de%20Antreprenor%20 2024.pdf

Ionitescu, S., Popescu, A., Gudanescu, N.L., Cristea A. (2023) Digitalization and agriculture - impact on human resources in the European Union and Romania. *Scientific Papers. Series "Management, Economic Engineering in Agriculture and rural development", 23*(3).

Local Development Strategy of Giarmata Commune. 2021-2027. Retrieved from https://primariagiarmata.ro/strategia-de-dezvoltare/

López, M., Cazorla, A., & Panta, M. P. (2019). Rural Entrepreneurship Strategies: Empirical Experience in the Northern Sub-Plateau of Spain. *Sustainability (Basel), 11*(5), 1243. DOI: 10.3390/su11051243

Mariotti, I., & Sasso, S. (2024). *Revitalizing rural areas through innovation and entrepreneurship: public and private initiatives to train, attract and retain human capital*, Publications Office of the European Union. Retrieved from https://data.europa.eu/doi/10.2760/4727653

Matei, D. (2013). Entrepreneurship in the Romanian Rural Areas. Case Study: Suceava County. *Journal of Settlements and Spatial Planning. 2.*

Nastase, C., Cha ovschi, C., Lucaci, A. (2019). Opportunities and Challenges for a Sustainable Rural Entrepreneurship. *Ovidius University Annals, Economic Sciences Series,* XIX(1).

National Institute of Statistics. (2023). *Population and Housing Census 2021. Resident population by ethnicity, by counties, municipalities, cities, communes.* Retrieved from https://www.recensamantromania.ro/rezultate-rpl-2021/rezultate-definitive-caracteristici-etno-culturale-demografice/

National Institute of Statistics. (2024a). *Population by domicile on January 1 by age and age groups, sexes, counties and localities.* Retrieved from Tempo online – statistical database http://statistici.insse.ro:8077/tempo-online/#/pages/tables/insse-table

National Institute of Statistics. (2024b). *Registered unemployed at the end of the month, by gender, counties and localities.* Retrieved from Tempo online – statistical database http://statistici.insse.ro:8077/tempo-online/#/pages/tables/insse-table

National Institute of Statistics. (2024c). *Share of unemployed people registered at the end of the month in the total labor resources, by gender, counties and localities.* Retrieved from Tempo online – statistical database http://statistici.insse.ro:8077/tempo-online/#/pages/tables/insse-table

National Institute of Statistics. (2025). *Classification of Activities in the National Economy* [PDF Document]. Retrieved from https://insse.ro/cms/files/CAEN/CAEN-Rev.3_structura-completa.pdf

OECD. (2022). Rural entrepreneurship and start-ups. In *Unlocking Rural Innovation.* OECD Publishing., DOI: 10.1787/60d226dd-

Opria, A.-M., Ro u, L., & Ia u, C. (2023). The Economic Impact of the LEADER Program in the Rural Communities of Romania. *Scientific Annals of Economics and Business, 70*(3), 399–420. DOI: 10.47743/saeb-2023-0026

Otiman, P. I., Mateoc-Sîrb, N., Go a, V., Băne , A., Sălă an, C., Feher, A., Raicov, M., & Iucu, Z. (2023). *Where is Romania's agriculture and where it is going?* Romanian Academy Publishing House.

Paul, L. (2020). Rural Development in Romania – A Few Considerations. *Studies in Business and Economics, 15*(2), 165–174. DOI: 10.2478/sbe-2020-0032

Pavel, A., Moldovan, B., Neamtu, B., & Hintea, C. (2018). Are Investments in Basic Infrastructure the Magic Wand to Boost the Local Economy of Rural Communities from Romania? *Sustainability (Basel), 10*(10), 3384. DOI: 10.3390/su10103384

Popescu, A., Tindeche, C., Mărcu ă, A., & Mărcu ă, L. (2022). Rural areas in Romania - discrepancies versus urban areas and European Union. *Scientific Papers. Series Management, Economic, Engineering in Agriculture and Rural Development, 22*(1).

Popescu, C. A., Iancu, T., Popescu, G., Adamov, T., & Ciolac, R. (2023). The Impact of Agritourism Activity on the Rural Environment: Findings from an Authentic Agritourist Area—Bukovina, Romania. *Sustainability (Basel), 15*(13), 10294. DOI: 10.3390/su151310294

Popescu, G. (2019). Prerequisites for Relaunching Economic Growth in Romanian Agriculture by Promoting Associativity. In Popescu, G. (Ed.), *Agrifood Economics and Sustainable Development in Contemporary Society* (pp. 186–209). IGI Global Scientific Publishing., DOI: 10.4018/978-1-5225-5739-5.ch009

Porter, M. E., & Kramer, M. R. (2011). Creating Shared Value. *Harvard Business Review, 89*(1-2).

Rădulescu, E., Marian, L., & Moica, S. (2014). Innovations and Opportunities for Entrepreneurial Rural Developments. *Procedia Economics and Finance, 15*, 1495–1500. Advance online publication. DOI: 10.1016/S2212-5671(14)00616-9

Raicov M., Banes A., Brad I., Feher A. (2021). Absorption of rural development funds. A lesson learned?. *Scientific Papers. Series "Management, Economic Engineering in Agriculture and rural development"*, 21(2).

Răzvanță Puie, F. (2020). The role of European funds in developing and sustaining rural entrepreneurship in Romania. In *Proceedings of the International Conference on Business Excellence, 14*(1), 2020. 134-148. DOI: 10.2478/picbe-2020-0014

Report Seeds of Kenosis Design [PDF document]. Retrieved from RisCo website https://www.risco.ro/date-firma/40006371/euro

Rujescu, C.-I., Feher, A., Toader, C.-S., Sîrbulescu, E. C., Raicov, M., Todor Marković, T., & Kokot, Z. (2025). Rural residential energy behaviour: A trans-generational and cross-country research. *Environmental Research Communications, 7*(7), 075004. Advance online publication. DOI: 10.1088/2515-7620/ade8d9

Sălă an, C., Moisa, S., & Radulov, I. (2017). Impact of advisory and consultancy work over the project-based development choices of a rural territory. *AgroLife Scientific Journal*, *6*(2).

Sate i comune (n.d.). *Tradi ii i obiceiuri: păstrarea culturii rurale.* Retrieved from https://sate-comune.ro/2024/06/02/traditii-si-obiceiuri-pastrarea-culturii-rurale/

Sima, E. (2022). The Romanian Rural Economy Diversification – Realities And Perspectives, *Agricultural Economics and Rural Development*, Institute of Agricultural Economics, *19*(2)

Sorea, D., Defta, M., & Popescu, I. M. (2023). Journeys to Significant Places in Orthodoxy as a Source of Sustainable Local Development in Romania. *Sustainability (Basel)*, *15*(7), 5693. DOI: 10.3390/su15075693

Staic, L.G., Uliu, D.V., Vladu, M. (2022). Analysis of the influence of financing on the sustainable local development of the rural territories, part of the LAGs, through the LEADER method. *Scientific Papers. Series "Management, Economic Engineering in Agriculture and rural development"*, *22*(1).

Stanciu, S. (2015). The Romanian Retail Food Market - Survival or Success for Domestic Companies. *Procedia Economics and Finance*, *23*, 1584–1589. Advance online publication. DOI: 10.1016/S2212-5671(15)00505-5

Stanimirov, E., & Stanimirova, M. (2023). Collaboration and financial sustainability of business in rural areas. *Bulgarian Journal of Agricultural Science*, *29*(Supplement 1), 147–151.

Stathopoulou, S., Psaltopoulos, D., & Skuras, D. (2004). Rural entrepreneurship in Europe: A research framework and agenda. *International Journal of Entrepreneurial Behaviour & Research*, *10*(6), 404–425. DOI: 10.1108/13552550410564725

Stefan, D., Vasile, V., Popa, M. A., Cristea, A., Bunduchi, E., Sigmirean, C., Stefan, A.-B., Comes, C.-A., & Ciucan-Rusu, L. (2021). Trademark potential increase and entrepreneurship rural development: A case study of Southern Transylvania, Romania. *PLoS One*, *16*(1), e0245044. DOI: 10.1371/journal.pone.0245044

Stubbs, W., & Cocklin, C. (2008). Conceptualizing a "Sustainability Business Model". *Organization & Environment*, *21*(2), 103–127. DOI: 10.1177/1086026608318042

Sustainability Guide. (n.d.). Cradle-to-cradle. Retrieved from https://sustainabilityguide.eu/methods/cradle-to-cradle/

Toader, C. S., Brad, I., Feher, A. A., Sîrbu, C. C., & Sîrbulescu, C. (2022a). Aspects regarding the evolution of Romanian businesses related to collection of non-wood forest products from spontaneous flora. *Proceedings of the 5th International Scientific Conference on Water*, Szarvas, Hungary.

Toader, C. S., Feher, A., Orboi, M. D., Crainic, D., & Pîrvulescu, L. (2022b). Local gastronomic business - premise for the development of Romanian gastronomic tourism. *Review on Agriculture and Rural Development, 11*(1-2), 133–138. Advance online publication. DOI: 10.14232/rard.2022.1-2.133-138

Toader, C.S., Feher, A., Rujescu, C. (2025). The culinary heritage of Banat - how is it passed on to future generations? *Agricultura Banatului, 2*(164).

Uliu, D.V. & Vladu M. (2020). Researches regarding the increase and modernization of the meat processing capacities by using the funds offered through the National Rural Development Program in the North West Development Region. *Scientific Papers. Series "Management, Economic Engineering in Agriculture and rural development", 20*(1).

Vajda, B., Drăgan, G., Vajda, L., Gáspár, M.-M., & Bagoly, M. L. (2025). The Role of Entrepreneurial Clusters in Advancing Circular Bioeconomy and Innovation: A Case Study from Romania. *Sustainability (Basel), 17*(9), 3787. DOI: 10.3390/su17093787

KEY TERMS AND DEFINITIONS

Circular economy: a production and consumption model that involves sharing, renting, reusing, repairing, refurbishing and recycling existing materials and products for as long as possible, with the aim of minimizing waste and promoting the sustainable use of natural resources with the aim of keeping products and materials in use, regenerating natural systems and reducing dependence on natural resources.

Economic sustainability: involves practices that aim at the long-term economic development of a company or nation, while managing environmental, social and human resources responsibly, by focusing on ensuring economic prosperity without compromising the ability of future generations to meet their own needs.

Entrepreneurship: the process of creating, developing and managing a new business with the aim of making a profit, by identifying opportunities, assuming financial risks and organising resources to bring new ideas, goods or services to market.

Environmental sustainability: the responsible management of natural resources and the protection of global ecosystems to support the health and well-being of current and future generations, by maintaining an ecological balance and conserving natural resources to ensure their long-term availability.

Rural entrepreneurship: refers to the creation and management of new businesses in rural areas, focusing on using local resources, skills and opportunities to create new income streams and economic diversification.

Shared value creation: a business concept that focuses on creating economic value for a company, while simultaneously creating value for society by addressing its needs and challenges, and that involves identifying and expanding the connections between societal and economic progress, recognizing that the competitiveness of a company and the health of the communities around it are mutually dependent.

Social entrepreneurship: an approach by individuals or organizations to develop, finance and implement solutions to social, cultural or environmental problems. Unlike traditional businesses, the primary mission of social enterprises is to create social impact, although they often operate with a business model to achieve financial sustainability.

Social responsibility: an ethical framework in which individuals and organizations have a civic duty to act for the benefit of society as a whole, and which involves a commitment to avoid causing harm and to contribute positively to the well-being of the community and the environment.

Social sustainability: focuses on identifying and managing the impact of business, both positive and negative, on people and communities, and involves creating sustainable and successful places that promote well-being, by understanding what people need from their communities to thrive.

Stakeholder: any individual, group, or organization that has a personal interest or "stake" in the success or failure of a company, project, or other initiative. Stakeholders may be directly or indirectly affected by the actions, goals, and policies of the organization.

Sustainability: meeting the needs of the present without compromising the ability of future generations to meet their own needs.

Sustainable business model: a framework for how an organization creates, delivers and captures value based on the principles of sustainable development, focusing on generating profit while simultaneously creating value for society, the economy and the environment.

Chapter 11

The Importance of Digital Knowledge for a Successful Entrepreneurial Venture

Nataša Papić-Blagojević
https://orcid.org/0000-0002-1110-3414
Novi Sad School of Business, Serbia

Boris Kuzman
Institute of Agricultural Economics, Belgrade, Serbia

ABSTRACT

The success of a business in today's world depends on acquiring and developing the necessary digital knowledge and skills. More than ever, entrepreneurship relies on advancements in digital technologies, particularly in areas such as digital marketing, the effective use of communication and collaboration tools, financial management applications, and access to online platforms that offer various courses to enhance entrepreneurial skills. According to official data (Eurostat, Micro & small businesses, 2024), the European Union had 32.3 million enterprises in 2022, employing 160.1 million people. Of these, micro and small enterprises accounted for 77.5 million employees, representing almost half of the total workforce in enterprises. Considering the importance of digitalization in modern business, this paper analyzes the Digital Intensity Index (DII), which measures the use of 12 different digital technologies by companies, with a particular focus on small and medium-sized enterprises.

DOI: 10.4018/979-8-3373-2898-0.ch011

INTRODUCTION

The impact of digital technologies on everyday life has become increasingly evident. Over the past decades, the world has encountered numerous challenges that have significantly influenced the social, environmental, and economic foundations of society (Tešin et al., 2024). Digital technologies, manifested through various tools and applications, significantly shape the world we live in today. For this reason, digital transformation is a key priority in the European Union, with the Digital Decade Initiative setting goals to be achieved by 2030 (European Commission, *Europe's Digital Decade*, 2024).

The wave of digitalization has also transformed entrepreneurship, playing a key role in empowering entrepreneurs by offering a diverse range of tools and creating opportunities that were almost unimaginable in the pre-digital era. The importance of developing additional skills for entrepreneurs by acquiring new competencies arises from the expectations of future employers, who recognize their considerable potential for growth (Matić et al., 2022). Therefore, adequate digital competencies are essential not only for entrepreneurs but for all citizens to effectively navigate digitally transformed societies (Burns et al., 2020).

By 2030, the EU (European Union) aims to achieve two key objectives for the digital transformation of businesses: ensuring that over 90% of SMEs (Small and Medium Enterprises) attain at least a basic level of digital intensity and that 75% of EU companies adopt cloud computing services, conduct big data analysis, or utilize artificial intelligence (Eurostat, *Digitalization in Europe*, 2024).

This phenomenon has been widely studied in recent years. For instance, Berger et al. (2021) identify digitalization as the most influential force driving entrepreneurship and innovation today. They argue that digital entrepreneurship and digital innovation emerge from the intersection of digital technologies with traditional entrepreneurial practices, as well as the processes and outcomes of innovation. Furthermore, they assert that both domains are propelled by the transformative impact of digital advancements.

Chatterjee et al. (2022) highlights the crucial role of digitalization in SME entrepreneurship, emphasizing that entrepreneurs' subjective attitudes significantly influence their intention to adopt digital platforms. Based on this premise, the authors conducted a study to examine the impact of age, gender, and education level on entrepreneurs' decisions to integrate digital platforms into their businesses. The findings reveal that factors such as age and gender significantly contribute to the ability to anticipate and adopt digital technology more quickly in daily operations. Plečko et al. (2023) argue that digitalization is gradually transforming business practices; however, the factors that motivate entrepreneurs to adopt digital technologies in sales strategies remain insufficiently explored. Their study investigated the key factors influencing entrepreneurs' adoption of digital technologies in business strategies. Contrary to Chatterjee et al. (2022), the findings indicate that demographic factors such as gender, age, and education do not significantly affect digital adoption. In contrast, entrepreneurs driven by altruistic goals exhibit a strong tendency to integrate digitalization into their sales strategies.

Furthermore, Nambisan (2017) argues that new digital technologies have reshaped the nature of uncertainty inherent in entrepreneurial processes and outcomes, as well as the approaches to managing such uncertainty. In this context, Nambisan explores and defines the concept of digital entrepreneurship. Digital entrepreneurship positively impacts job creation and economic growth as digital entrepreneurs create value by acquiring, processing, and distributing digital information (Sahut et al., 2021). Digital entrepreneurship (Kraus et al., 2019) has become increasingly relevant as technological advancements and infrastructure development create diverse opportunities for entrepreneurs. While society places significant emphasis on new digital business models, relatively little research has explored the opportunities, challenges, and success factors associated with digital entrepreneurship.

Fossen and Sorgner (2021) investigated the relationship between the latest wave of occupational digitalization and entry into various forms of entrepreneurship, including digital entrepreneurship. Their findings indicate that highly skilled employees and those working in ICT (Information and Communication Technology) occupations are more likely to transition into entrepreneurship compared to low-skilled individuals. Ghazi et al. (2022) analyzed the relationship between entrepreneurship and productivity across 27 EU member states using panel data. Recognizing the crucial role of digitalization in the entrepreneurial ecosystem, the model was estimated using the Digital Economy and Society Index (DESI) and its subcomponents as instruments for entrepreneurship. The results indicate a significant positive relationship between entrepreneurship and productivity, as well as a positive correlation between digitalization and entrepreneurship. Given the importance of digitalization and the need for skill enhancement in today's business environment, an analysis was conducted on the level of digital literacy among entrepreneurs over the past decade. This analysis offers insight into entrepreneurs' readiness to utilize digital tools and technologies to enhance their businesses, as well as the challenges they may encounter in the process.

Given the significance of digitalization in entrepreneurship, particularly its impact over the past decade, this study is focused on examining the Digital Intensity Index (DII), which measures the extent to which companies incorporate digital technologies into their operations. In this regard, an analysis of available Eurostat data is conducted, considering the predefined classification of enterprises by size. Special attention is given to the position of small and medium-sized enterprises in EU member states as well as candidate countries, including the Republic of Serbia.

DIGITALIZATION OF SMALL AND MEDIUM ENTREPRISES

Small and medium-sized enterprises represent a fundamental pillar of economic development and serve as key drivers of industry and regional growth. Their significant role in national economies is reflected in their contribution to GDP (Gross Domestic Product) through employment, productivity, and expansion (Viswanathan & Telukdarie, 2021). Despite often being overshadowed by larger corporations, the unique characteristics, agility, and business models of SMEs continue to attract the attention of economic and business experts (Thrassou et al., 2020). The experience of developed countries shows that a successful SME sector is an important developmental factor for efficient economic development, as well as for solving many economic and social issues (Papić-Blagojević & Stankov, 2024; Jovičić Vuković et al., 2020). Representing nine out of every ten enterprises, SMEs generate two-thirds of all jobs but beyond employment, they drive entrepreneurial spirit and innovation, making them essential for enhancing competitiveness and economic growth (European Commission, *User guide to the SME Definition*, 2019).

Over the past two decades, we have witnessed the rapid advancement of information and communication technologies, which has left a profound impact on all sectors of the economy and society, including the position of small and medium-sized enterprises. This influence can be viewed from two perspectives: on the one hand, increased competition from large corporations has potentially threatened their survival, while on the other, ICT development has provided SMEs with access to new tools and markets, enabling them to reach previously inaccessible customers.

However, despite the advantages that ICT technologies bring, small and medium-sized enterprises navigate and overcome the challenges of digitalization in different ways. Not all SMEs can successfully implement digital transformation; the smaller the enterprise, the lower the likelihood of adopting advanced digital practices and the higher the reliance on basic services. Consequently, the level of digitalization largely depends on the specific characteristics of the sector in which the enterprise operates (Organization for Economic Co-operation and Development/OECD, *The Digital Transformation of SMEs*, 2021).

Thus, although SMEs play a significant role in the economy, there is limited knowledge about the factors influencing their digital transformation, as well as the consequences and challenges it entails (Eller et al., 2020). Consequently, it is not possible to reliably determine the extent to which small and medium-sized enterprises have adopted digital technologies to achieve and promote sustainability goals. Digital transformation holds substantial potential for fostering innovation, enhancing sustainability, increasing competitiveness, and adapting products and services to market demands (Raihan, 2024). Therefore, understanding this process is crucial for improving support strategies and advancing SME development in the digital environment.

By analyzing the obstacles encountered by SMEs throughout their development, we can classify them into distinct categories (Telukdarie et al., 2023; Elhusseiny & Crispim, 2022):

- **Technical barriers** – Insufficient ICT infrastructure and a lack of adequately qualified employees and managers.
- **Organizational barriers** – Limited financial resources, weak managerial support, resistance to change, and inadequate infrastructure for research and development.
- **Technological barriers** – Due to a lack of awareness, SMEs tend to be cautious in adopting advanced technologies that enable innovation in production and logistics.
- **Legal barriers** – Restricted collaboration and integration between different organizational levels, along with data privacy concerns.

In this way, by clearly differentiating the barriers faced by small and medium-sized enterprises, it can be concluded that continuous support is necessary to facilitate their overcoming and enhance SME competitiveness in the digital environment.

European Digital Decade and Digital Transformation Targets

In the European Union, the need for comprehensive support for entrepreneurs, particularly in the field of financing, has been widely recognized. In this context, the EU provides financial assistance through local, regional, and national institutions, as well as banks and investment funds. This support includes increased access to financial resources, lower interest rates, and eased application requirements for funding, facilitating business growth and development (Papić-Blagojević & Stankov, 2024). Additionally, financial support is directed towards assisting entrepreneurs in the process of digital transformation. In this regard, the Digital Decade policy programme establishes clear targets and objectives for 2030, providing a roadmap for Europe's digital transformation and technological advancement.

Figure 1. Digital Targets for 2030. Source: Author's adoptation based on European Commission, Europe's Digital Decade: Digital Targets for 2030. https://commission.europa.eu/strategy-and-policy/priorities-2019-2024/europe-fit-digital-age/europes-digital-decade-digital-targets-2030_en

The key objectives of this program (European Commission, *Europe's Digital Decade: Digital Targets for 2030*, 2024) are defined as follows (Figure 1):

1. Achieving a minimum level of digital skills for at least 80% of the population, along with at least 20 million IT specialists, ensuring equal representation of men and women.
2. Driving the digital transformation of enterprises, with 75% of companies utilizing Cloud, AI, or Big Data, while more than 90% of SMEs reaching at least a basic level of digital intensity.
3. Developing secure and sustainable infrastructure by improving connectivity.
4. Enabling the digitalization of public services, ensuring that all key public services are available online, while all citizens have online access to medical records and a digital identification document.

As part of the implementation of these specific targets for 2030, the Digital Intensity Index serves as one of the key performance indicators for measuring progress in digital transformation. The index is calculated based on 12 variables, with each variable assigned a score of 1 point if considered valid.

Between 2019 and 2024, different versions of measurement methodologies for these indicators were defined. A summary of the described indicators, which are evaluated at the enterprise level, is presented in Table 1.

Table 1. Digital Intensity Index (DII) indicator composition

Indicator	Indicator Description
1	Businesses in which more than 50% of employees utilize computers with internet access for work-related activities.
2	The fastest fixed internet connection has a maximum contracted download speed of at least 30 Mb/s.
3	Businesses where e-commerce sales account for at least 1% of total revenue.
4	Businesses in which web sales exceed 1% of total revenue, with B2C transactions accounting for more than 10% of overall online sales.
5	Businesses where more than 20% of employees are provided with portable devices, utilize cloud computing services over the internet, and maintain official ICT security documentation.
6	Businesses ensure employees are informed about ICT security responsibilities, maintain websites with key business details, and invest in advanced or intermediate cloud computing services.
7	Businesses implement at least three ICT security measures, maintain an active website, and engage on two or more social media platforms.
8	Businesses engage on social media, utilize 3D printing, and offer ICT skills training to employees.
9	Businesses leverage social media for multiple purposes, employ ICT specialists, integrate IoT solutions, and conduct data analytics in-house or via external providers.
10	Businesses engage in cross-border e-commerce, utilize industrial or service robots, and implement AI technologies.
11	Businesses utilize ERP software, invest in advanced cloud computing, and enable remote access to emails, documents, and applications for employees.
12	Businesses send automated eInvoices, utilize CRM systems, and conduct remote meetings online.

Source: Authors' adaptation based on Eurostat. (2024). *Digital Intensity Index (DII) composition overview 2015-2024.* https://ec.europa.eu/eurostat/documents/341889/725524/DII+v1+v2+v3+v4+2015-2023.pdf/2d0e55ee-8306-54db-a6e2-29a86583c1fe?t=1703234324067

Note: The table presents a summarized overview of all described indicators for the period from 2015 to 2024.

Based on the presented indicators, a company is considered to have at least a basic level of digital intensity if it utilizes at least four out of the twelve selected variables. Furthermore, businesses are classified into categories with very low, low, high, and very high levels of DII.

These criteria categorize businesses according to their degree of digital intensity, offering valuable insights for policymakers and enterprises to effectively navigate digital transformation.

EU Incentive Strategies for Supporting SME Digitization

The European Union actively promotes the digital transformation of small and medium-sized enterprises through various measures, including financial programs, regulatory policies, and strategic initiatives (Figure 2). These efforts aim to enhance digitalization, strengthen competitiveness, and foster innovation in the SME sector.

Figure 2. European Union Incentive Strategies

Financial programs	Regulatory policies	Strategic initiatives
• Digital Europe Programme • Single Market Programme • Horizon Europe • European Regional Development Fund (ERDF) • InvestEU • Recovery and Resilience Facility	• SME Strategy for a Sustainable and Digital Europe • Digital Services Act (DSA) • Digital Markets Act (DMA) • COSME	• Digital Transformation of SMEs • European Digital Innovation Hubs (EDIHs) • Enterprise Europe Network (EEN)

Source: Authors' adaptation

If we consider financial programs, one of the most significant initiatives is undoubtedly the *Digital Europe Programme* - DIGITAL (European Commission, *The Digital Europe Programme*, 2025), which represents an EU-driven effort to support the digital transformation of businesses, citizens, and public administration during the period 2021–2027. Its goal is the strategic enhancement of digital capacities through investments in key areas, such as supercomputing, artificial intelligence, cybersecurity, advanced digital skills, and the widespread application of digital technologies in the economy and society.

This program provides support to industries, small and medium-sized enterprises, and public institutions, enabling them to adopt advanced technologies and improve their digital capabilities, fostering competitiveness, innovation, and sustainable development. With a budget exceeding €8.1 billion, DIGITAL aims to accelerate the digital transformation of the European economy and society while complementing existing EU funding mechanisms, offering additional support for the adoption of advanced technologies and the strengthening of digital capacities.

The *Single Market Programme* is an EU initiative aimed at financially supporting the strengthening and full functionality of the single market during the 2021–2027 period. This program provides a comprehensive set of measures focused on support, regulatory alignment, and efficient management of the European single market.

Its key objectives include (European Commission, *The Single Market Programme*, 2025):

- Food safety
- Consumer protection
- Enhancing the sustainability of SMEs
- Improving business resilience
- Ensuring the efficient functioning of the single market
- Developing high-quality European statistics
- Applying standardized regulatory frameworks.

Through this approach, the program seeks to strengthen economic stability and competitiveness across Europe, ensuring sustainable conditions for business growth and digital transformation.

For the 2021–2027 period, the *European Regional Development Fund* (ERDF) has been established as a financial support program, providing funding to public and private entities across the EU to reduce economic, social, and geographical disparities. The fund offers financial assistance through national and regional programs, facilitating investments that contribute to the development of Europe and its regions.

During the specified period, funds are directed towards the following areas (European Commission, *European Regional Development Fund, 2025*):

- Enhancing competitiveness and digitalization – Strengthening innovation, supporting SMEs, and improving digital connectivity.
- Sustainable development – Transitioning to a low-carbon economy and increasing resilience to climate challenges.
- Improving infrastructure connectivity – Advancing mobility and transport solutions.
- Social inclusion – Promoting employment, education, skills development, equal access to healthcare, and strengthening the role of culture and sustainable tourism.
- Local and urban development – Supporting initiatives focused on the sustainable growth of cities and communities across the European Union.

The *SME Strategy for a Sustainable and Digital Europe* (Digital Skills & Jobs Platform, *European Initiatives, 2021*) was published in 2020 with the goal of supporting the core principles of the European Green Deal, the Digital Decade, and other EU initiatives aimed at integrating digital and green transitions. Its focus is on building a climate-neutral, resource-efficient, and resilient digital economy, while actively engaging small and medium-sized enterprises across various industrial sectors in Europe.

Actions within the European SME Strategy are structured around three key pillars: (1) strengthening capabilities and support for sustainability and digital transformation; (2) reducing administrative burdens and facilitating market access; and (3) improving financial availability for SMEs. Through the SME Strategy for a Sustainable and Digital Europe, the European Commission has sought to provide support and strengthen SMEs across various sectors—from innovative tech startups to traditional craft industries, helping them better adapt to the digital and sustainable economy.

The *COSME program*, introduced by the European Union for the 2014–2020 period, was designed to support small and medium-sized enterprises by strengthening their competitiveness and reducing unemployment. The program focused on key aspects of SME support, including (Enterprise Europe Network, *COSME – Program for the Competitiveness of SMEs*) facilitating access to financing for small and medium-sized enterprises; encouraging entrepreneurial initiatives and creating a favorable business environment for growth; providing business support and improving market access; strengthening the competitiveness and sustainability of enterprises, with a specific focus on the tourism sector; and enhancing access to the European market, enabling SMEs better integration into the EU single market.

When discussing EU strategic initiatives, one of the most significant is the *European Digital Innovation Hubs* (EDIHs), which provide small and medium-sized enterprises with support in adopting advanced digital tools, enabling them to enhance their business operations. These hubs offer training and skill development in cutting-edge technologies such as artificial intelligence, blockchain, and the Internet of Things (IoT), ensuring that businesses have access to expert knowledge and resources (European Commission, *European Digital Innovation Hubs, 2025*).

Funded through the Digital Europe Programme, the Digital Innovation Hubs initiatives assist companies in building digital capacities and finding a qualified workforce. Additionally, through programs such as Digital Volunteers, enterprises receive support in transitioning to digital business models, enhancing their competitiveness and sustainability in the market (Tregubov, 2024).

Another program developed to support small and medium-sized enterprises is the *Enterprise Europe Network* (EEN), which is considered the world's largest network aimed at expanding into foreign markets. The network operates globally, bringing together experts from various member organizations known for their business support expertise. EEN members include chambers of commerce, regional development agencies, universities, research institutes, and innovation centers. While individual enterprises cannot become direct members, they can access a wide range of services offered by EEN, including advisory support, access to international partners, and opportunities for business development and innovation (European Union, *Enterprise Europe Network*).

Through the combined efforts of various initiatives and strategies introduced by the competent bodies of the European Union, significant support is provided for the development and advancement of small and medium-sized enterprises (SMEs). This support extends beyond digitalization, encompassing substantial financial assistance and the expansion of international networks. Additionally, this approach enhances the significance and appeal of SMEs, while encouraging and empowering young individuals to embark on independent entrepreneurial ventures.

These claims are also supported by official Eurostat data from 2024, which shows that in 2022, the European Union had 32.3 million enterprises, employing a total of 160.1 million people. Among them, micro and small enterprises played a significant role, providing employment for 77.5 million individuals, which accounts for nearly half of the total workforce in the business sector.

METHODOLOGY

To assess the level of digital tool adoption in small and medium-sized enterprises, the Digital Intensity Index was used. This index measures the extent to which companies and organizations implement digital technologies. For SMEs, the DII goes beyond assessing their current digital capabilities—it serves as a key indicator of their growth potential and competitiveness in a rapidly evolving digital economy (Digital 4 Business, 2024). As digital technologies become increasingly integral to all industries, the ability of SMEs to adopt and effectively utilize these tools has a direct impact on their long-term success.

For the purposes of this research, data available on Eurostat has been used, specifically data related to *Digital Intensity by size class of enterprise*. Given that the available data are classified according to company size, specifically into the following categories: up to 10 employees, from 10 to 49 employees, from 50 to 249 employees, and more than 250 employees, and considering that the focus of the research is on small and medium-sized enterprises, the authors have chosen to observe the movement of this index for companies with 10 to 49 employees and those with 50 to 249 employees.

This selection is logical, considering that according to the Organization for Economic Co-operation and Development (OECD, *Enterprises by Business Size*, 2020), SMEs are defined as those with fewer than 250 employees, further subdivided into micro enterprises (fewer than 10 employees), small enterprises (10 to 49 employees), and medium-sized enterprises (50 to 249 employees).

The European Union regulation is even more specific (European Commission, *User guide to the SME Definition*, 2019), stating that micro, small, and medium-sized enterprises are those that employ fewer than 250 people and have an annual turnover not exceeding 50 million euros or an annual balance sheet total not exceeding 43 million euros. In order to qualify as an SME, a company must meet the employee number criterion, but it can fall into this category by meeting either the turnover limit or the balance sheet total, not necessarily both.

In addition to classifying enterprises by size, the available data also categorize them according to the use of digital technologies using the DII index. In this way, companies are ranked based on 12 indicators and divided into those with a very low level (score of 0 to 3), low level (score of 4 to 6), high level (score of 7 to 9), and very high level (score of 10 to 12) of digital technology usage. A company is considered to have a basic level of digital intensity if it scores at least 4.

Based on all of the above, the following analysis presents a comparison of the use of digital technologies among small and medium-sized enterprises in the European Union member states, with a special focus on the relationship between the EU and the Republic of Serbia, as a candidate country for EU accession.

RESULTS

To examine the success of digital transformation in small and medium-sized enterprises in the European Union countries, as well as in the Republic of Serbia as a candidate for EU membership, data available in the Eurostat database for 2022 and 2024 were used (Eurostat, *Digital Intensity by size class of enterprise*, 2025). The analysis separately examines small and medium-sized enterprises according to their level of digital technology adoption, with the aim of gaining a clearer insight into which SMEs demonstrate greater or lesser success by this measure.

Since the data categorize enterprises based on their level of digital intensity, the analysis will first focus on identifying the countries where small enterprises exhibit the lowest levels of digital technology adoption.

Analysis of the DII for SMEs in European Union countries

The analysis of small and medium-sized enterprises based on the Digital Intensity Index provided insight into the situation across the European Union member states. Based on the indicators presented in Table 1, enterprises were categorized as having very low, low, high, or very high DII. All graphical representations in the following sections were adapted by the authors using data available from Eurostat. (*Digital Intensity by size class of enterprise*, 2025).

Figure 3. Small Enterprises with Very Low Digital Intensity Index (DII) in EU Member States

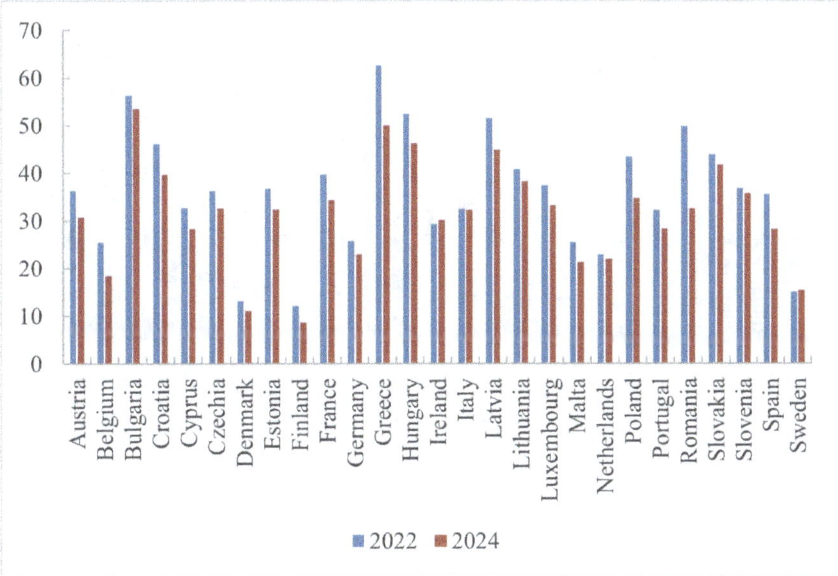

Figure 3 shows the values for small enterprises with a very low Digital Intensity Index (DII). Based on these values, it can be concluded that in 2022 the highest proportion of such enterprises was recorded in Greece (62.56%), Bulgaria (56.33%), and Hungary (52.44%), while, as expected, the lowest share was observed in Sweden (14.99%), Denmark (13.18%), and Finland (12.14%).

In 2024, a downward trend in the percentage of these enterprises is noticeable, with the most significant decrease observed in Greece, where the share dropped by 12.54 percentage points. The lowest proportion of enterprises with a very low DII in 2024 was recorded in Finland, at 8.66%.

It is considered that enterprises scoring between 4 and 6 exhibit a low level of digital intensity (Figure 4). The highest percentage of enterprises with a low level of DII in 2022 was recorded in Ireland (44.77%), Italy (44.39%), and France (43.74%), while the lowest share of such enterprises was in Bulgaria (28.66%), Hungary (27.90%), and Greece (23.26%).

Figure 4. Small Enterprises with Low Digital Intensity Index (DII) in EU Member States

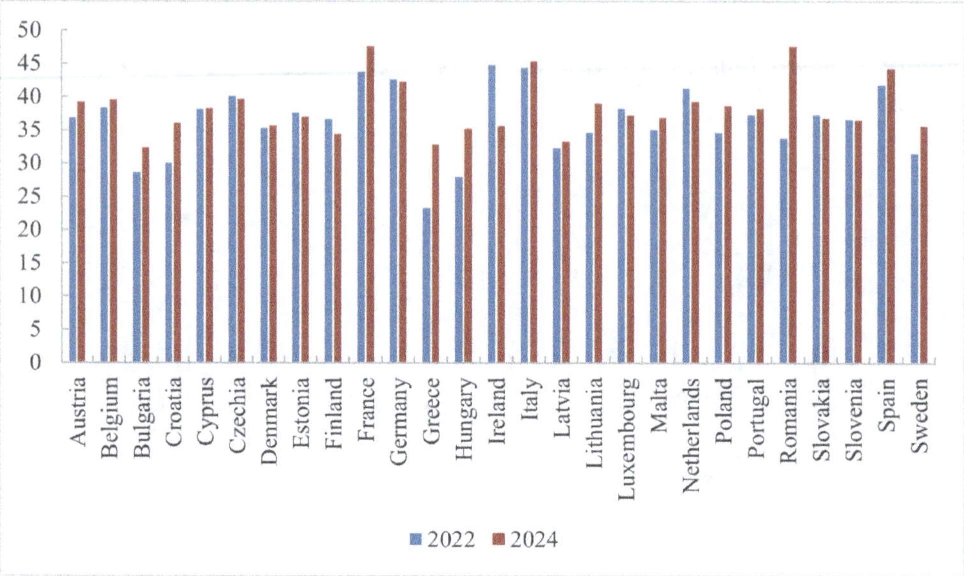

In 2024, the largest share of these enterprises, with nearly the same percentage of 47.56% and 47.55%, was observed in Romania and France, respectively. On the other hand, the lowest numbers remained in Greece and Bulgaria.

When discussing enterprises with a high level of digital technology usage, scoring between 7 and 9 (Figure 5), it can be observed that the largest shares of such enterprises are in Sweden (47%), Finland (44.53%), and Denmark (42.58%).

Figure 5. Small Enterprises with High Digital Intensity Index (DII) in EU Member States

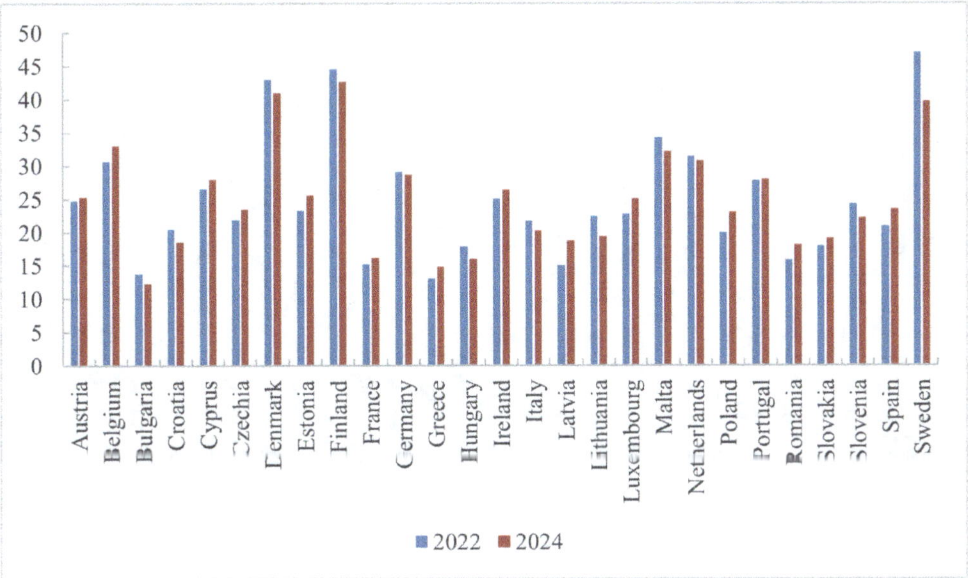

In contrast, the lowest percentage of small enterprises with a high level of digital technology adoption is found in Latvia, Bulgaria, and Greece.

Figure 6. Small Enterprises with Very High Digital Intensity Index (DII) in EU Member States

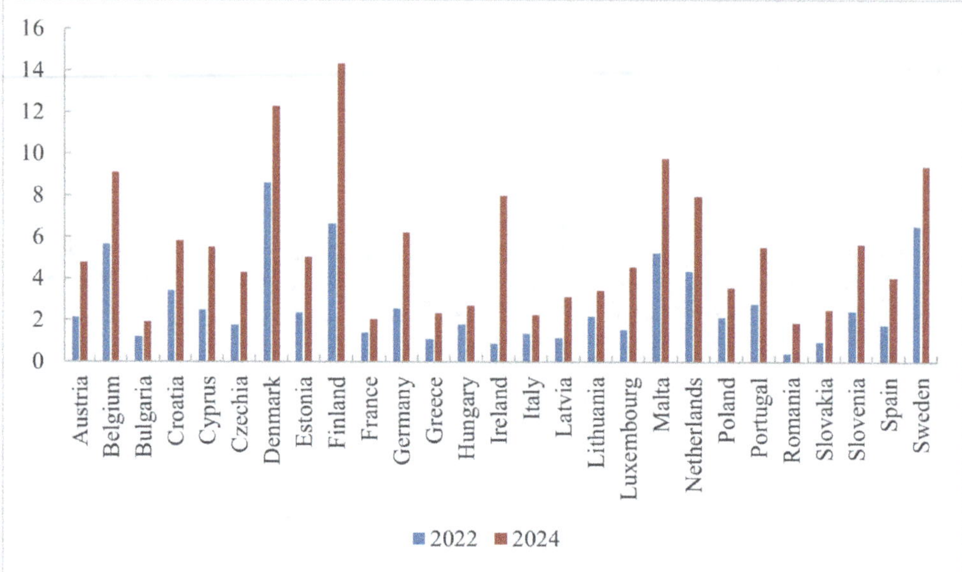

Finally, the largest share of small enterprises with a very high level of digital technology adoption is found in Denmark, Finland, and Sweden, while the smallest shares are in Slovakia, Romania, and Ireland (Figure 6). The number of these enterprises increased in 2024, rising in Denmark from 8.60% to 12.28%, in Finland from 6.64% to 14.33%, in Malta from 5.24% to 9.76%, and in Sweden from 6.53% to 9.39%. At the same time, Ireland, which recorded only 0.88% of enterprises with a very high level of digital technology adoption in 2022, made significant progress by 2024, with the share rising to 7.97%. Romania remains at the bottom, with only 0.41% in 2022 and 1.88% in 2024.

The second part of the analysis focused on examining the use of digital technologies in medium-sized enterprises within the European Union member states, where companies were also categorized according to their very low, low, high, and very high Digital Intensity Index.

Among medium-sized enterprises with 50 to 249 employees (Figure 7), the highest share of enterprises with a very low DII in 2022 was found in Romania (34.67%), Bulgaria (33.67%), and Greece (25.95%), while the lowest percentages were recorded in Sweden (1.99%), Finland (1.53%), and Denmark (1.10%). The situation remained largely unchanged in 2024, with the highest shares still present in Bulgaria, Greece, and Romania; however, Romania saw a significant decrease of 12 percentage points in the share of these enterprises. A similar ranking was observed among the countries with the lowest share of enterprises with a very low DII, with Sweden (2.73%), Denmark (1.61%), and Finland (1.23%) at the bottom of the list.

Figure 7. Medium Enterprises with Very Low Digital Intensity Index (DII) in EU Member States

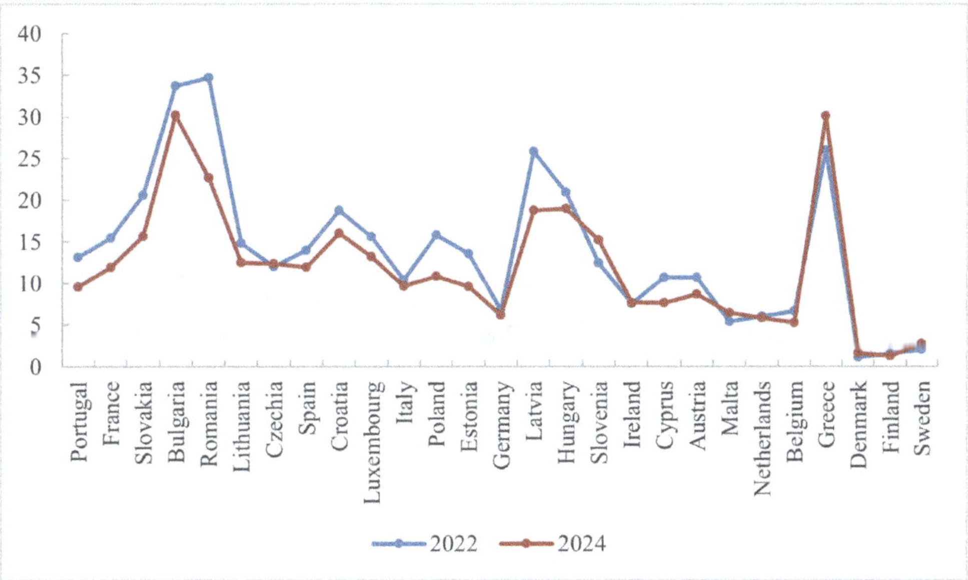

A comparison of small and medium-sized enterprises across EU member states with very low levels of digital technology adoption reveals that Bulgaria and Greece have the largest proportions of these enterprises, whereas Sweden, Denmark, and Finland have the smallest.

Looking at medium-sized enterprises with a low level of digital technology adoption (Figure 8), the highest shares of such enterprises in 2022 were found in France (40.68%), Slovakia (39.63%), and Bulgaria (38.37%), while the lowest shares were in Denmark (17.98%), Finland (17.34%), and Sweden (13.12%).

Figure 8. Medium Enterprises with Low Digital Intensity Index (DII) in EU Member States

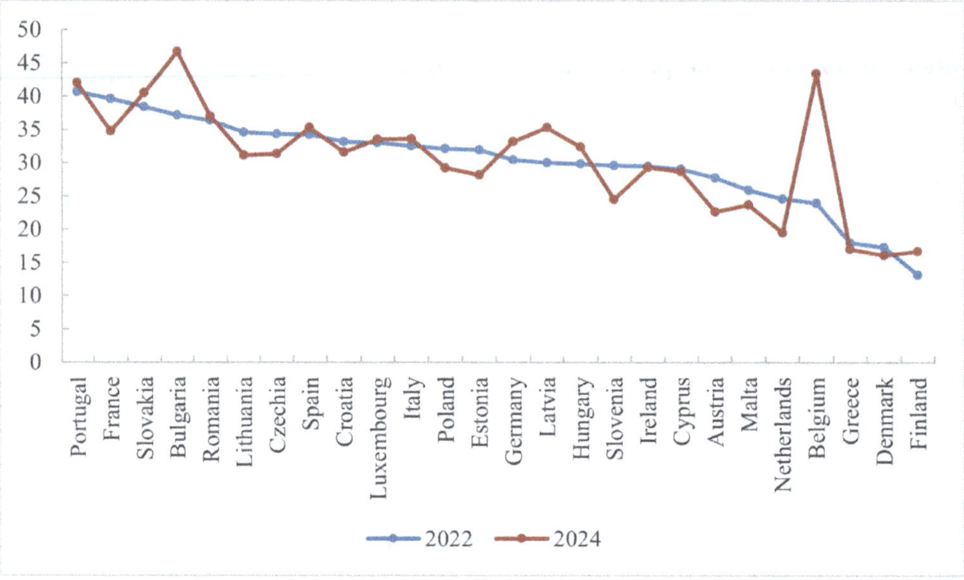

In 2024, the percentage of these enterprises in Romania increased to 46.63%, followed by Greece with 43.43%, and France with 41.99%, indicating a growth in the share of medium-sized enterprises with low digital technology adoption in these EU member states. Denmark, Sweden, and Finland continue to have the smallest proportions of medium-sized enterprises with low digital technology usage.

When comparing the share of small and medium-sized enterprises in EU countries with low levels of the Digital Intensity Index, certain differences among these businesses become noticeable. Specifically, France had the highest number of SMEs in both size categories in 2022 and 2024. Additionally, other countries mentioned in this context include Slovakia and Bulgaria for medium-sized enterprises, while Ireland and Italy are highlighted for small enterprises.

In Figure 9, the trend of digital technology adoption among medium-sized enterprises in certain EU countries is evident. Finland (61.22%), Sweden (59.22%), and the Netherlands (54.75%) had the highest share of such enterprises. By 2024, alongside Sweden and the Netherlands, Ireland also emerged as a country with a significant share of businesses with high Digital Intensity Index (DII) (46.78%).

Figure 9. Medium Enterprises with High Digital Intensity Index (DII) in EU Member States

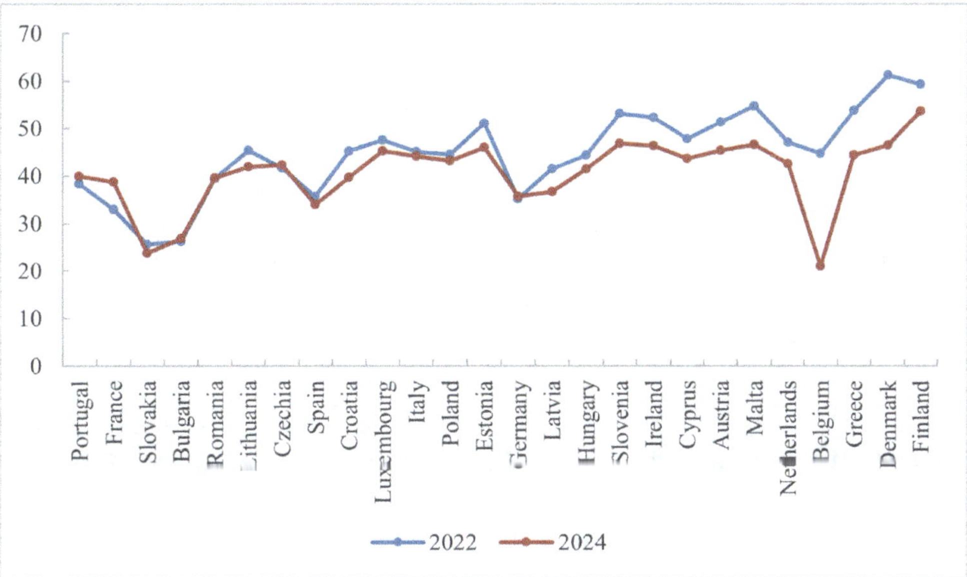

On the other hand, the lowest percentage of such enterprises was recorded in Slovakia, Romania, and Bulgaria in 2022, while in 2024, Greece had the smallest share of these businesses.

When analyzing the differences among countries with a high adoption of digital technologies in small and medium-sized enterprises (SMEs), it is evident that Sweden and Finland have the largest number of SMEs utilizing these technologies. Conversely, Greece and Bulgaria have the fewest SMEs that widely apply modern digital tools.

Finally, Figure 10 tracks the share of medium-sized enterprises with a very high level of adoption of digital technology. The highest presence of these enterprises was recorded in Denmark (27.22%), Sweden (25.68%), and Belgium (21.83%). By 2024, this percentage increased by 10 percentage points in Denmark and 11 percentage points in Belgium.

Figure 10. Medium Enterprises with Very High Digital Intensity Index (DII) in EU Member States

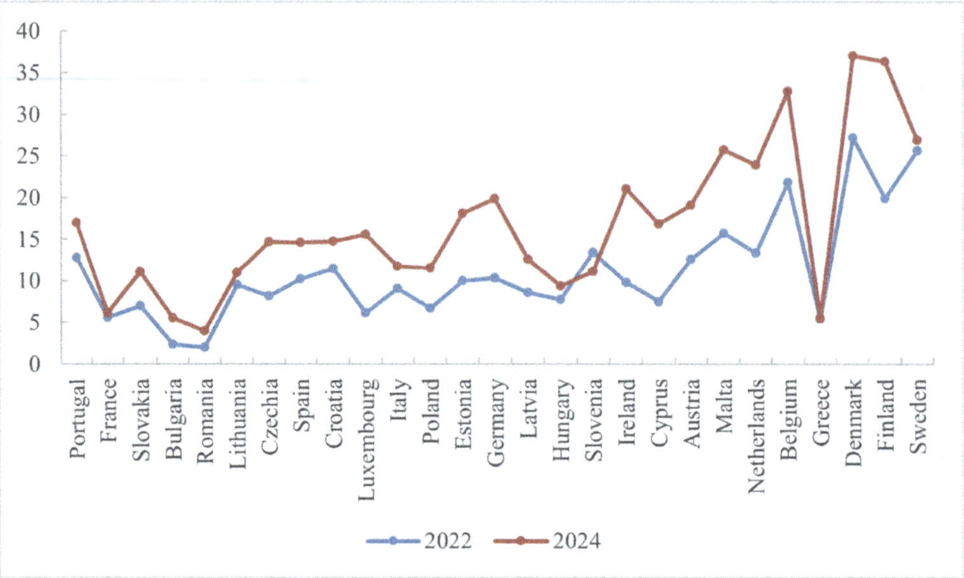

As in the previous part of the analysis, the lowest percentage of these enterprises was recorded in Greece, Bulgaria, and Romania in 2022 and 2024.

When comparing the differences between businesses with exceptionally high digital technology adoption, it is evident that medium-sized enterprises in Denmark and Sweden significantly outnumber small enterprises meeting these criteria. The gap in favor of medium-sized enterprises ranges between 15 to 20 percentage points. On the other hand, Bulgaria and Romania have the lowest share of SMEs with a very high Digital Intensity Index.

Comparative Analysis of the Digital Intensity Index in EU Countries and the Republic of Serbia

Digital transformation has profoundly influenced contemporary social and business dynamics, not only within the European Union member states but also in countries in the process of EU accession. Accordingly, the Government of the Republic of Serbia has acknowledged the strategic significance of the digital economy and digital society as crucial drivers for bolstering regional integration, improving digital resilience, fostering enhanced cross-sector cooperation, and advancing closer convergence with the European Union.

Serbia's primary digitalization initiative, Strategy on Digital Skills Development in the Republic of Serbia for the period 2020 to 2024 (2020), aims to enhance digital literacy and competencies across all societal groups, including vulnerable populations. The strategy focuses on continuously monitoring advancements in information and communication technologies across sectors while aligning educational efforts with the evolving demands of the economy and labor market (European Commission, 2021). Since the Republic of Serbia has the status of a candidate country for European Union membership, the Strategy focuses on the areas defined by the EU's New Skills Agenda. It includes an analysis of the current state of digital competencies in Serbia, an assessment of statistical indicators, as well as forecasts and projections of future sector development, aligned with the demand for digital skills in an appropriate scope.

However, despite the development of strategic documents not only in Serbia but also in other Western Balkan countries (Montenegro, North Macedonia, Bosnia and Herzegovina, and Albania), the adoption of digital technologies among SMEs remains significantly lower than the EU average, with a regional adoption rate of 35% compared to 55% in the EU. In 2021, only 7% of enterprises in the WB region utilized big data, 16% implemented cloud solutions, and 3% adopted artificial intelligence—considerably behind the EU figures of 14%, 34%, and 8%, respectively (Tintor et al., 2022).

Due to the growing influence of the EU market, which is becoming increasingly pronounced (Đerčan et al., *2022*), and in order to better understand the differences in the level of digital technology adoption among small and medium-sized enterprises, the authors conducted a comparison of the Digital Intensity Index between EU member states (overall data) and Serbia for 2022 and 2024.

The analysis was performed separately for small and medium-sized enterprises, considering businesses with very low, low, high, very high, and at least a basic level of digital intensity (minimum score of 4). The graphical representations below have been adjusted based on data available from Eurostat (*Digital Intensity by Size Class of Enterprise*, 2025)

Based on the comparison of small enterprises (Figure 11), it can be observed that in both 2022 and 2024, EU countries had a higher share of enterprises with a *very low* level of Digital Intensity Index (DII). However, according to other criteria, Serbia recorded a higher percentage of small enterprises with a *low* level of digital technology adoption (42.92% in 2022 and 48.30% in 2024). When it comes to a *high* level of DII, Serbia leads by approximately 6% compared to EU small enterprises.

Figure 11. Comparative Analysis of Small Enterprises by Digital Intensity Index (DII) in the EU and the Republic of Serbia

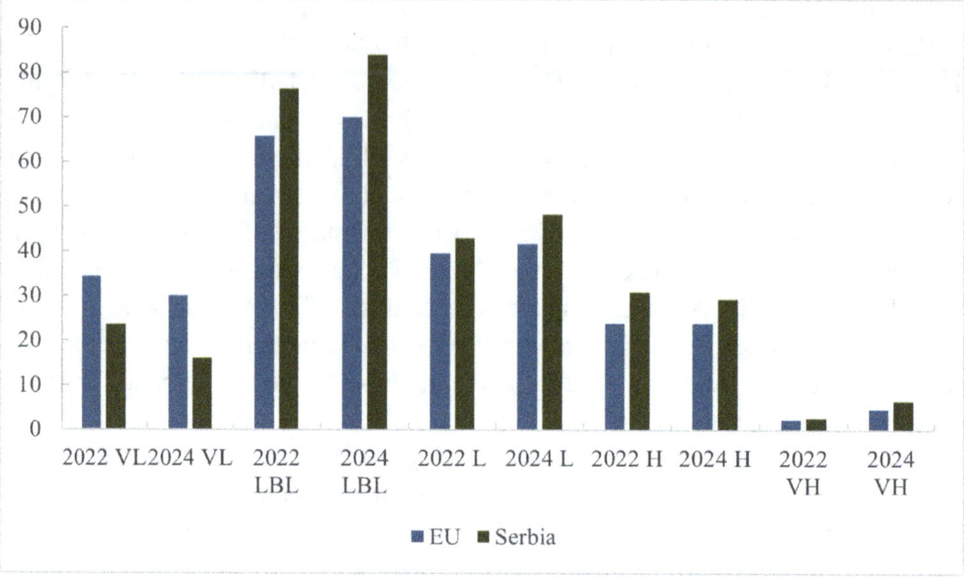

The share of enterprises with a *very high* level of digital intensity appears to be relatively balanced between Serbia and the EU. Furthermore, if we look at small enterprises that demonstrate at least a *basic* use of ICT, the data once again favors Serbia—with 76.39% in 2022 and 83.94% in 2024, compared to 65.79% in the EU in 2022 and 70.07% in 2024.

In the following analysis, a comparison was made between the levels of digital intensity in medium-sized enterprises in EU member states and Serbia, with the results presented in Figure 12.

Figure 12. Comparative Analysis of Medium Enterprises by Digital Intensity Index (DII) in the EU and the Republic of Serbia

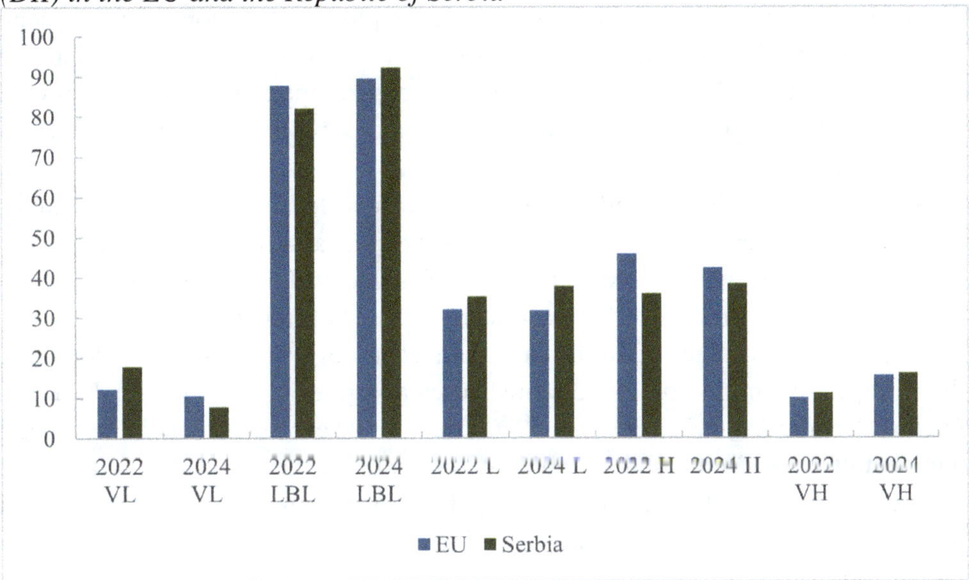

For medium-sized enterprises with a *very low* level of Digital Intensity Index, Serbia had a slightly higher share in 2022, with a positive difference of approximately 5.5 percentage points compared to the EU average. However, by 2024, the share of such enterprises in Serbia had significantly decreased—by 10 percentage points, while the decline in the EU was more modest, at around 1.5 percentage points.

Similar to the trend observed among small enterprises, medium-sized enterprises in Serbia also show a higher share of those with a *low* level of digital technology adoption (35.14% in 2022 and 37.82% in 2024). At the same time, Serbia reports a relatively higher proportion of enterprises with a *very high* DII, indicating progress at both extremes of the digital spectrum.

On the other hand, EU countries lead in the share of enterprises with a *high* level of digital technology use (45.91% in 2022 and 42.22% in 2024) and are on average about 7 percentage points higher than in medium-sized enterprises in Serbia. As with small enterprises, the largest share of medium-sized enterprises in both Serbia and the EU have at least a *basic* level of digital intensity. In Serbia, this share was 82.19% in 2022 and rose to 92.28% in 2024, while in the EU it stood at 87.83% in 2022 and 89.48% in 2024.

CONCLUSION

Today, mastering digital skills is essential for employment, personal development, and success, particularly among young people. Those who continuously improve their digital knowledge gain the opportunity to participate in modern economic flows, establish their own businesses, and gain a competitive edge in increasingly demanding market conditions.

The spectrum of digital skills encompasses various levels: from basic digital literacy, which is essential for all citizens, through technical skills required for specific professional tasks, to advanced IT competencies that enable individuals to engage in specialized jobs and scientific research in the field of information technologies.

Due to the importance of digital skills and technologies for future development, the European Commission has established clear strategic goals within *Europe's Digital Decade: Digital Targets for 2030* initiative. These goals include increasing the level of basic digital skills among at least 80% of the population, advancing the digital transformation of the economy, building secure and sustainable digital infrastructure through improved connectivity, and enabling the comprehensive digitalization of public services.

Recognizing the importance of digital transformation and the strategic goals set for 2030, as well as the pivotal role of small and medium-sized enterprises as a cornerstone of economic development, the authors conducted an analysis of the current state of digital transformation implementation within SMEs across the European Union. Special attention was given to a comparative overview between EU member states and the Republic of Serbia.

Analyzing small and medium-sized enterprises (SMEs) in European Union member states with low levels of digital technology adoption, the highest concentration of such enterprises was observed in Bulgaria and Greece, while their numbers were lowest in Sweden, Denmark, and Finland.

Conversely, in the analysis of enterprises with exceptionally high digital technology adoption, it was noted that Denmark and Sweden have a significantly greater proportion of medium-sized enterprises compared to small ones meeting these criteria, with a difference favoring medium-sized companies ranging between 15 and 20 percentage points. In contrast, Bulgaria and Romania record the lowest shares of both small and medium-sized enterprises with very high levels of digital intensity.

If we compare the available data on small and medium-sized enterprises (SMEs) in the European Union and the Republic of Serbia, Serbia does not appear to be significantly lagging in digital transformation. However, since the analysis relies on aggregated EU data—encompassing both the best- and worst-performing countries in SME digitalization—the presented findings should not be considered fully representative. The level of digitalization among SMEs in Serbia remains below the European average.

ACKNOWLEDGMENT

The paper is a part of research financed by the MSTDI RS, agreed in decision no. 451-03-136/2025-03/200009 from 4.2.2025.

We have no conflict of interest to disclose.

REFERENCES

Berger, E. S., Von Briel, F., Davidsson, P., & Kuckertz, A. (2021). Digital or not–The future of entrepreneurship and innovation: Introduction to the special issue. *Journal of Business Research, 125*, 436–442. DOI: 10.1016/j.jbusres.2019.12.020

Burns, E., Silvennoinen, E., Kopnov, V. A., Shchipanova, D. E., Papić-Blagojević, N., & Tomašević, S. (2020). Supporting the Development of Digitally Competent VET Teachers in Serbia and Russia. *The Education and Science Journal, 22*(9), 174-203, ISSN: 1994-5639, DOI: DOI: 10.17853/1994-5639-2020-9-174-203

Chatterjee, S., Chaudhuri, R., Vrontis, D., & Thrassou, A. (2022). SME entrepreneurship and digitalization–the potentialities and moderating role of demographic factors. *Technological Forecasting and Social Change, 179*, 121648. DOI: 10.1016/j.techfore.2022.121648

Đerčan, B., Bubalo Živković, M., Gatarić, D., Lukić, T., Dragin, A., Kalenjuk Pivarski, B., Lutovac, M., Kuzman, B., Puškarić, A., Banjac, M., Grubor, B., & Simović, O. (2022). Experienced Well-Being in the Rural Areas of the Srem Region (Serbia): Perceptions of the Local Community. *Sustainability (Basel), 14*(1), 248. DOI: 10.3390/su14010248

Digital 4 Business. (2024, September 4). Harnessing the power of digitalisation for European SMEs: The Digital Intensity Index. https://digital4business.eu/digital-intensity-index/

Digital Skills & Jobs Platform. (2021). *European Initiatives.* https://digital-skills-jobs.europa.eu/en/actions/european-initiatives/sme-strategy-sustainable-and-digital-europe

Elhusseiny, H. M., & Crispim, J. (2022). SMEs, Barriers and Opportunities on adopting Industry 4.0: A Review. *Procedia Computer Science, 196*, 864–871. DOI: 10.1016/j.procs.2021.12.086

Eller, R., Alford, P., Kallmünzer, A., & Peters, M. (2020). Antecedents, consequences, and challenges of small and medium-sized enterprise digitalization. *Journal of Business Research, 112*, 119–127. DOI: 10.1016/j.jbusres.2020.03.004

Enterprise Europe Network. (n.d.). COSME—Program za konkurentnost malih i srednjih preduzeća. https://www.een.rs/cosme-program-za-konkurentonost-malih-srednjih-preduzeca/

European Commision. (2025). *The Single Market Programme*. https://commission.europa.eu/funding-tenders/find-funding/eu-funding-programmes/single-market-programme/overview_en

European Commission. (2019). *User guide to the SME Definition*. https://ec.europa.eu/docsroom/documents/42921/attachments/1/translations/en/renditions/native

European Commission. Directorate-General for Employment, Social Affairs and Inclusion & Beker, K. (2021). *Digitalisation and digital transformation in Serbia: implications for persons with disabilities*, Publications Office of the European Union. https://data.europa.eu/doi/10.2767/271459

European Commission. (2025). *European Digital Innovation Hubs*. https://digital-strategy.ec.europa.eu/en/policies/edihs

European Commission. (2025). *European Regional Development Fund*. https://commission.europa.eu/funding-tenders/find-funding/eu-funding-programmes/european-regional-development-fund-erdf_en

European Commission. (2025). *The Digital Europe Programme*. https://digital-strategy.ec.europa.eu/en/activities/digital-programme

European Commission. (n.d.). *Europe's Digital Decade: Digital targets for 2030*. https://commission.europa.eu/strategy-and-policy/priorities-2019-2024/europe-fit-digital-age/europes-digital-decade-digital-targets-2030_en

European Union. (n.d.). *Enterprise Europe Network*. https://een.ec.europa.eu/about-enterprise-europe-network

Eurostat. (2024). *Digital Intensity Index (DII) composition overview 2015-2024*. https://ec.europa.eu/eurostat/documents/341889/725524/DII+v1+v2+v3+v4+2015-2023.pdf/2d0e55ee-8306-54db-a6e2-29a86583c1fe?t=1703234324067

Eurostat. (2024). *Digitalization in Europe – 2024 edition*. https://ec.europa.eu/eurostat/web/interactive-publications/digitalisation-2024

Eurostat. (2024). *Micro & small businesses*. https://ec.europa.eu/eurostat/web/products-eurostat-news/w/ddn-20241025-1

Eurostat. (2025). *Digital Intensity by size class of enterprise*. https://ec.europa.eu/eurostat/databrowser/view/isoc_e_dii__custom_16907592/default/table?lang=en

Fossen, F. M., & Sorgner, A. (2021). Digitalization of work and entry into entrepreneurship. *Journal of Business Research, 125*, 548–563. DOI: 10.1016/j.jbusres.2019.09.019

Jovičić Vuković, A., Jošanov-Vrgović, I., Jovin, S., & Papić-Blagojević, N. (2020). Socio-demographic characteristics and students' entrepreneurial intentions. *Stanovnistvo, 58*(2), 57–75. DOI: 10.2298/STNV200423007J

Kraus, S., Palmer, C., Kailer, N., Kallinger, F. L., & Spitzer, J. (2019). Digital entrepreneurship: A research agenda on new business models for the twenty-first century. *International Journal of Entrepreneurial Behaviour & Research, 25*(2), 353–375.

Matić, R., Gonzales-Serrano, M. H., Damnjanović, J., Maksimović, B., Papić-Blagojević, N., Milošević, I., & Vuković, J. (2022). Professional competencies development of sports science students: the need for more entrepreneurship education. *Management & Marketing. Challenges for the Knowledge Society, 17*(S1), 426-448, ISSN: ISSN: 2069-8887, DOI: . https://sciendo.com/article/10.2478/mmcks-2022-0024DOI: 10.2478/mmcks-2022-0024

Nambisan, S. (2017). Digital entrepreneurship: Toward a digital technology perspective of entrepreneurship. *Entrepreneurship Theory and Practice, 41*(6), 1029–1055. DOI: 10.1111/etap.12254

Organisation for Economic Co-operation and Development. (2021). *The digital transformation of SMEs* (OECD Studies on SMEs and Entrepreneurship). OECD Publishing. DOI: 10.1787/bdb9256a-en

Organisation for Economic Co-operation and Development/OECD. (2020). *Enterprises by business size*. https://www.oecd.org/en/data/indicators/enterprises-by-business-size.html

Papić-Blagojević, N., & Stankov, B. (2024). Analysis of trends in youth unemployment in the European Union: The role and importance of youth entrepreneurship. In Grigoresku, A., & Andrei, J. V. (Eds.), *Entrepreneurship and Development for a Green Resilient Economy* (pp. 181–204). Emerald Publishing Limited., DOI: 10.1108/978-1-83797-088-920241007

Plečko, S., Tominc, P., & Širec, K. (2023). Digitalization in entrepreneurship: Unveiling the motivational and demographic influences towards sustainable digital sales strategies. *Sustainability (Basel), 15*(23), 16150. DOI: 10.3390/su152316150

Raihan, A. (2024). A review of the digitalization of the small and medium enterprises (SMEs) toward sustainability. *Global Sustainability Research, 3*(2), 1–16. DOI: 10.56556/gssr.v3i2.695

Sahut, J. M., Iandoli, L., & Teulon, F. (2021). The age of digital entrepreneurship. *Small Business Economics, 56*(3), 1159–1169. DOI: 10.1007/s11187-019-00260-8

Strategy on Digital Skills Development in the Republic of Serbia for the period 2020 to 2024. (2020). *Official Gazette of the RS*, No. 21/20. https://pravno-informacioni-sistem.rs/eli/rep/sgrs/vlada/strategija/2020/21/2/reg

Telukdarie, A., Dube, T., Matjuta, P., & Philbin, S. (2023). The opportunities and challenges of digitalization for SMEs. *Procedia Computer Science, 217*, 689–698. DOI: 10.1016/j.procs.2022.12.265

Tešin, A., Dragin, A. S., Mijatov Ladičorbić, M., Jovanović, T., Zadel, Z., Surla, T., Košić, K., Amezcua-Ogáyar, J. M., Calahorro-López, A., Kuzman, B., & Stojanović, V. (2024). Quality of Life and Attachments to Rural Settlements: The Basis for Regeneration and Socio-Economic Sustainability. *Land (Basel), 13*(9), 1364. DOI: 10.3390/land13091364

Thrassou, A., Uzunboylu, N., Vrontis, D., & Christofi, M. (2020). Digitalization of SMEs: A Review of Opportunities and Challenges. In Thrassou, A., Vrontis, D., Weber, Y., Shams, S. M. R., & Tsoukatos, E. (Eds.), *The Changing Role of SMEs in Global Business*. Palgrave Studies in Cross-disciplinary Business Research, In Association with EuroMed Academy of Business. Palgrave Macmillan., DOI: 10.1007/978-3-030-45835-5_9

Tintor, V., Jovanović, N., Bocarova, V., & Bugarski, M. (2022). *Western Balkans Digital Economy Society Index - WB DESI 2022 Report*. Regional Cooperation Council.

Tregubov, O. (2024). Digital Transformation of SMEs in the EU: Support, Strategic Initiatives, and Challenges on the Path to Sustainable Development. In *4th International conference on economics, accounting and finance (ICEAF)*. Scientific Center of Innovative Research, Estonia. DOI: 10.36690/ICEAF-2024-33-34

Viswanathan, R., & Telukdarie, A. (2021). A systems dynamics approach to SME digitalization. *Procedia Computer Science, 180*, 816–824. DOI: 10.1016/j.procs.2021.01.331

Chapter 12
Transition Economics and Market Reforms

Natia Surmanidze
https://orcid.org/0000-0003-2116-6571
Ilia State University, Georgia

ABSTRACT

This chapter explores the theoretical bases for transition economics, focusing on market reform models like liberalization, privatization, and stabilization. It compares shock therapy and gradualism and highlights the role that institutional change and governance can play in determining the outcomes for reform efforts. The chapter also discusses criticism against orthodox reform paradigms as well as introducing emerging frameworks that incorporate dimensions of equity, sustainability, and local development.

INTRODUCTION

The collapse of centrally planned economies toward the end of the 20th century constituted a watershed in the shaping of the worldwide economic order, triggering widespread efforts to reform national economies in line with the precepts of market liberalization, property rights, and institutional reform. This evolution, commonly known as "transition economics," became a central theme in debates over economic reform in post-Socialist and post-Soviet countries (surmanidze, 2022). The experience of transition was marked by a multifaceted and variegated path, characterized by inconsistencies in the pace, order, and success of the transitioning processes. Economists and policymakers had lively debates on the best approach to building market capitalism, often pitting against each other the positions of those who rec-

DOI: 10.4018/979-8-3373-2898-0.ch012

ommended fast liberalization and those who supported a gradual, institutionally driven reform strategy (Roland, 2000; Kornai, 1992).

Theoretical foundations for transition economics fall within the extended debates in development economics, focusing on the divergence in theories between institutional and neoclassical perspectives. The paradigm of "shock therapy" supported by economists like Sachs (1994) prioritized the imperative need for rapid liberalization, deregulation, and far-reaching privatization efforts. In contrast, academics like Stiglitz (1999) and Rodrik (2007) have rebuffed these approaches for ignoring the decisive role of institutions, quality in governance, and social solidarity. These differing positions represent a fundamental philosophical disagreement in the balance between the role of the state and market forces in bringing about economic transition. Understanding the dynamics for transition, therefore, requires not just a knowledge of economic policy, but also a sensibility to the institutional and political environments that shape the reform process.

The transition countries have often faced challenges that go far beyond macroeconomic stabilization alone. Accelerating levels of increasing inequality, corruption, illegal markets, and weak legal enforcement have revealed the imperatives and limitations of solely technocratic reform strategies. As North (1990) put it, institutions—the basic rules shaping behavior—play a defining role in ensuring systemic economic success. Not understanding the role of informal institutions, historical legacies, and power relations has created reform fatigue and the need for approaches to more inclusive and enduring development models. In reaction to this reality, the field of transition economics itself has grown by bringing in disciplines from political science, sociology, and legal studies.

The aim in this chapter is to provide a thorough analysis of the theoretical progress and practical applications of market reform in transitional economies. It emphasizes the interaction among liberalization, privatization, and reconstruction of institutions as essential elements in the transition experience. In taking a wider comparative approach to those events in the political economy framework, this chapter aims to explain how different reform approaches have shaped (or hindered) regional development and economic stability. Special focus shall be on the continued relevance of transition theories in resolving current challenges like globalization, digitalization, and efforts for regional integration.

The chapter further examines the tension between universal reform ideas and the specific conditions found in different countries. In spite of international financial institutions exerting pressure for adopting similar policy models in the 1990s and early 2000s, the outcomes differed clearly in different world regions. This difference has been traced to the differences in institutional capacity, starting conditions, political processes, and social resilience (Åslund, 2013; Havrylyshyn, 2020). In a critical reexamination of those debates, the chapter proposes a framework that explains why some countries achieved economic sustainability, but others stagnated or even regressed, even as they followed similar reform trajectories. The approach to this chapter is theoretically and analytically oriented, using concepts from transition economics, institutional theory, and development studies. To provide improved conceptual clarity and nuance in the theoretical debate, the chapter includes specific, targeted country examples as analytical case study illustrations rather than original empirical work. Short treatments of Georgia, Poland, and Kazakhstan will be presented to explain how various reform trajectories relate to and fall within the theoretical frameworks described. The case studies utilize second-level reading material and attempt to translate abstract economic theory into reality-based descriptions.

The transition experience is not limited to economic dimensions, but also has important political and social aspects. The application of reform processes has inherently vital implications for state-building, social capital accumulation, and democratic consolidation processes. This chapter examines, therefore, the role played by political will, elite interests, and foreign actors (the IMF, World Bank, and EU, for example) in determining the scope and content of market reform. It is necessary to understand those determinants in order to design strategic interventions with a view to promoting growth, in keeping with the wider goals of regional stability and long-term development.

In addition, transition economics offers a unique approach to understanding the interaction between emerging and entrenched institutional systems. The legacies of centralized planning, hierarchical organizations, and state monopolies often survived in reform periods, shaping the evolution of emerging systems of governance. Incomplete or lagged dismantling of earlier legacies sometimes resulted in hybrid systems characterized by incomplete liberalization, patronage, and state capture. These findings challenge linear models of modernization and propose a deeper understanding of institutional transformation (Boettke & Coyne, 2009).

This chapter contributes to the current debate on economic models and technological progress by bringing historical changes into connection with current challenges in the field of regional development. Economic difficulties arising from technological upheavals, environmental changes, and changes in geopolitical relations heighten economic problems, making previous reform experiences even more applicable. A study of institutional adaptability, sequences in the processes of reform, and functions performed by a variety of actors can present a basic understanding that is vital in making sound policy in both transition countries at present and in developing nations in the future. In sum, this section positions transition economics as a central area in the study of regional development. By combining multiple theoretical models, case study analyses, and cross-disciplinary approaches, this chapter presents a comprehensive picture of the impacts that market reform imposes on economic outcomes in post-socialist and developing countries, as well as taking into account the implications of the impacts from both historical and modern perspectives. Following sections discuss main reform frameworks, theoretical debates, and institutional arrangements, thus building a basis for a thorough investigation into long-term repercussions of transition processes.

The chapter seeks to provide a comprehensive theoretical analysis of transition economics, focusing on the attributes, motives, and outcomes related to post-socialist market transformation. It seeks to explore the main intellectual constructs—liberalization, privatization, and stabilization—and examine how they have been theoretically established and empirically supported in earlier studies. In essence, the chapter also seeks to emphasize the role played by institutional changes, policy frameworks, and the order of policy application in shaping economic outcomes. By embodying necessary theoretical debates alongside a comprehensive case study scrutiny of selected countries, this chapter heightens the understanding of the role played by transition approaches in determining economic change and the development in the post-communist framework. In addition, the chapter discusses the gains from such experiences with respect to the ongoing cross-border changes, including technological upheaval, globalization, and the search for models that promote inclusive and green growth.

Methodology The chapter is based upon a conceptual and theoretical framework supported by a critical examination of scholarly literature in the following areas: transition economics, institutional economics, and political economy. Rather than involving original empirical studies, the chapter draws on existing scholarly scholarship to clarify the development of reform theories and corresponding reality effects. To add richness to the theoretical discussion, it includes selective case studies in the transition economies in Georgia, Poland, and Kazakhstan. These case studies serve as a form of analytical template that offers contextual knowledge of the application of different reform paradigms and the role played by institutional arrangements in determining effects. Involving references to cases, which are drawn from secondary literature as well as established scholarly studies, the chapter sustains its theoretical as well as interpretive focus at the same time as it increases clarity and relevance through targeted application.

UNDERSTANDING TRANSITION ECONOMICS: CONCEPTS AND CONTEXT

Transition economics as a discipline emerged as a response to the widespread transition from centrally-planned to market-oriented economic systems, a change that took place after the fall of the Soviet Union and the dissolution of socialist regimes in Central and Eastern Europe. It posed a unique challenge: determining the processes by which command economies, with state control and central planning, could be replaced by frameworks built upon private enterprise, market prices, and competitive market institutions. As a niche area within comparative and development economics, transition economics has developed to provide theoretical models and policy suggestions aimed at smoothing the transition (Roland, 2000).

The central assumption in transition economics is that, with proper structuring and policymaker frameworks, markets can maximize resource allocation efficiency and spur long-run economic growth. Early proponents in this area called for rapid liberalization steps, such as dismantling price controls, drastic subsidy reductions, and greater international openness, as starting points towards economic revivals. This approach, commonly described as "shock therapy," assumed that economic actors would quickly adjust to market conditions and that transitory disruptions would ultimately translate to long-run growth (Sachs, 1994). However, the social implications that automatically ensue from fast transitions, e.g., inflation, unemployment, and inequalities, generally did not get adequate attention.

Another perception emerged, focusing on the primacy of institutions and the need for incremental reform. Gradualists believed that markets function in a social and legal order that cannot be created overnight. North (1990) pointed out that institutions—the building blocks that shape interaction in society—are vital for hedging against uncertainty and cooperation. Hence, the reforms need to be done in a manner that lays down credible institutions, like property rights, a fair and impartial system of justice, and a system for regulation, before embarking on broad liberalization efforts. Countries that did not possess such basic institutions found themselves with greater vulnerability to reform reversals.

Privatization is a central element in the field of transition economics. This transformation from a system involving state-owned to privately owned enterprises brought productivity improvements and created incentives for innovation. However, the methods adopted and the speed with which privatization occurred varied tremendously from country to country. In some cases, voucher-based mass privatization aimed to spread ownership to a large number in a relatively brief time, in others, insider privatization transferred ownership interests to enterprise managers and workers. Both methods had a mixed track record, often leading to the centralization of ownership power, asset stripping, or poor corporate governance (Megginson & Netter, 2001). The methods through which privatization occurred created long-term impacts on wealth distribution and institutional trust.

The application of stabilization policy was necessary in the early stages of transition. The widespread problems that characterized such situations included inflation, fiscal imbalances, and external debts, which were characteristic bequests from the command economies. Transition economists often advocated for macroeconomic stabilization through tight monetary policy, fiscal discipline, and currency reform.

These actions, even though they were necessary to restore economic credibility, often had social costs in the form of higher poverty levels and reduced public services. The success of stabilization depended not just on sound macroeconomic management but also on political commitment to withstand transient hardship in order to gain long-term benefits (Fischer & Sahay, 2000). One of the notable features of the transition experience was the difference in performance that was seen in different countries. For example, some Central European countries, such as Poland and the Czech Republic, experienced rapid recovery and obtained successful membership in the EU. On the contrary, some countries, especially those who emerged from the previous Soviet Union, experienced lengthy crises, cases of state capture, and institutional integrity degradation. This heterogeneity led scholars to discard universal models and turn their focus towards studying initial conditions, cultural environments, and geopolitical factors. As suggested by Havrylyshyn (2020), efforts toward reform were primarily driven by subtle economic policy concerns as opposed to the models of political institutions and the personal characteristics of leadership.

The weaknesses of previous transition models soon emerged. It is suggested that economic liberalization, without adequate institutional support, can promote greater inequality, corruption, and oligarchic tendencies. In addition, overdependence on market fundamentalism has surfaced as a main area of susceptibility, as expressed by Stiglitz (1999), who suggests that efficiency and equity both risk being lost in the lack of a proper policy and legal environment. Therefore, the post-Washington Consensus framework highlighted the relevance of good governance, social protection, and inclusive institutions as a necessity for the successful implementation of economic reform.

Transition economics shed light on some important questions about the role of external actors and international institutions. The International Monetary Fund, World Bank, and European Bank for Reconstruction and Development have become actors that supported reform efforts and offered financial aid. However, foreign organizations often neglected the local environments in making generalized policy suggestions. Foreign conditionality sometimes reinforced the reforming processes, but sometimes it evoked opposition, for example, in cases where such reform resulted in social unrest or domestic actors viewed it as being imposed from outside (Pop-Eleches, 2009). The impacts of the experience of transition can be seen within post-socialist countries' institutional frameworks, economic models, and political environments. Despite improvements in almost every field, persistent problems like lack of rule of law, corrupt economic habits, and disparities in some regions remain. To evaluate those persistent problems and develop adequate solutions for challenges like digitalization and transitioning to green economies, it is essential to update the underlying transition economics theories. In summary, transition economics is a powerful analytical tool for understanding changes in economic frameworks, while institutional instability and political risks stand for serious threats. Early models specialized in rapid liberalization and privatization; nonetheless, the case evidence is that the functions performed by institutions, state presence, and social conditions also bear a strong impact, which may be higher in value compared to that initially assigned to them. The following discussion examines the evolution of models, lessons learned from reform, and the implications that those findings offer for prospective developmental trajectories in countries in structural transition.

STAGES OF REFORM: LIBERALIZATION, STABILIZATION, AND INSTITUTIONALIZATION

The move toward market-oriented systems from centrally controlled ones is often described as being in three stages, which are closely related: liberalization, stabilization, and institutionalization. In practice, they might not be sequential, and the success in total is determined by the interaction between economic policy, politics, and society. An understanding of each stage's theoretical basis is a framework for understanding the various routes that countries can take in adopting market-oriented reform (Roland, 2000).

Liberalization means the removal of government regulations controlling prices, production, and trade. In command-structured economies, government officials controlled virtually all aspects of economic activity, including price setting and resource allocation. The main objective of liberalization is to restore market signals and incentives by allowing supply and demand forces to determine prices and quantities produced. This stage typically includes the elimination of price subsidies, deregulation of markets, and liberalization of foreign trade and investment (Fischer & Sahay, 2000). The rationale behind this measure is that markets have a better ability to allocate resources than do centralized bureaucratic systems, leading to higher productivity and a greater choice for consumers.

However, rapid liberalization, especially without adequate supporting institutions, can also bring serious negative short-term effects. In many post-socialist countries, liberalization of prices led to hyperinflation, as hitherto subsidized prices readjusted to market levels. In addition, sudden exposure to international competition left state enterprises unprepared and vulnerable, with far-reaching retrenchment and a fall in manufacturing output (Sachs, 1994). These outcomes are often described as necessary transition costs, yet they also provoked public resentment and political resistance against reform.

The next phase, known as stabilization, focuses on the restoration of macroeconomic balance and the control of inflationary processes. This phase typically requires implementing tighter fiscal and monetary policies, limiting budgetary deficiencies, and keeping currency stable. Stabilization is essential to generate confidence among investors and a system in which market mechanisms can function effectively. In a situation without price stability, liberalization efforts could not deliver long-term growth, as uncertainty and speculation dominate economic decision-making (Campos & Coricelli, 2002).

The implementation of stabilization policy requires a careful balance. On the one hand, tight fiscal responsibility is required to counter the risk of runaway inflation. On the other, overly strict controls may inflate the risk of a relapse into recession and make social hardships worse. Many transition countries implemented stabilization programs supported by the International Monetary Fund (IMF), which often required rapid fiscal consolidation, a reduction in the public sector payroll, and the removal of subsidies. In some cases, the strategies succeeded in restoring macroeconomic stability, yet they resulted in a rise in inequality and poverty in some others (Stiglitz, 1999).

The third step, termed institutionalization, can be the most complex and long-lasting part of the reform process. This phase includes building institutions as well as developing legal, regulatory, and administrative structures necessary for a market economy that can succeed. Key elements include securing property rights, developing financial markets, implementing policies for encouraging fair competition, and establishing an independent judiciary (North, 1990). These institutions create the basic framework necessary for contract enforcement, dispute resolution, and the reduction of transaction costs. Institutional development is not automatically achieved alongside liberalization or stabilization efforts. In fact, a lack of strong institutions has often undermined the success of the early stages of reform. For example, without a transparent legal regime, privatized companies can fall prey to being taken over by oligarchs or insiders, leading to inefficiency and corruption. Similarly, without efficient regulatory institutions, financial markets would be exposed to manipulation and crises (Roland, 2000). Therefore, the institutionalization process must be seen not as a final stage, but as a fundamental component that must progress in parallel with the other reform efforts.

One of the biggest challenges to institutional development is the persistence of informal institutions and behavior that were created in the command economy's era. These informal institutions include patron-client relations, rent-seeking, and resistance to rule-of-law-based governance. Formal institution-building requires not just the enactment of legal systems, but a shift in cultural values and traditions—a quest that is typically confronted by opposition from vested interests (Boettke & Coyne, 2009). Institutional capacity is also weak in those vital sectors that need reform, such as taxation, the courts, and enforcement through regulations.

The sequence of these reform stages has sparked intense debate. One group of researchers contends that liberalization and stabilization processes must come before institutional reform in order to strengthen market incentives and build momentum for change. The writers contend that early liberalization done in the absence of proper institutional arrangements can produce negative results such as corruption, inequality, and economic dualism (Rodrik, 2007). Evidence shows that countries which practiced a carefully sequenced transition, focusing first on institution-building achieved greater sustainable and balanced outcomes.

One of the main conclusions drawn from the study of transition experiences is that reform processes hold both the possibility of reversibility and non-linearity. Countries can be faced with failures in implementing reform processes through political resistance, economic downturns, or changes in geopolitical environments. Specifically, instances where stabilization processes can be hindered by movements that seek a return to former system forms, or that institutional processes can be undermined by poor quality of governance. Therefore, the interaction between the three stages is characterized by dynamic behavior, which calls for a description of the reform path that considers endogenous as well as exogenous variables (Havrylyshyn, 2020). On this basis, the political climate surrounding liberalization, stabilization, and institution building is a starting point for understanding economic transformation. Each phase deals with different reform dimensions; nonetheless, they are interdependent. Successful transitions rely not just on sound economic policies but also on political legitimacy, institutional trust, as well as widespread public support. An awareness that reform processes move in multifaceted and diverse environments is required to promote theoretical understanding, policy design, as well as strategic enactment in post-socialist as well as developing countries.

CASE STUDIES: COMPARATIVE INSIGHTS FROM CENTRAL AND EASTERN EUROPE, THE CAUCASUS, AND CENTRAL ASIA

The transition from centrally planned systems to market-oriented ones evolved in different forms in post-socialist countries. Despite the majority starting off with similar institutional development projects, the outcomes that emerged differed immensely from nation to nation. Central and Eastern Europe (CEE), the Caucasus, and Central Asia provide a worthwhile comparative model in looking at how ordering reform, quality of governance, and external conditions have shaped developmental trajectories. The following analysis discusses specific experiences in order to distill valuable insights from these regions.

Poland is often cited as a prime example of a successful transition. In 1990, the country launched a fast-paced reform program called the Balcerowicz Plan, which rapidly established comprehensive price liberalization, fiscal stabilization, and full privatization. Following a transitional phase with inflation and increasing job loss, Poland stabilized and embarked on a course of economic expansion by 1992 (Sachs, 1994). A decisive factor in Poland's success was a swift establishment of political consensus combined with a firm determination to become a member of the European Union, which served as the outside anchor for institutional reform (Roland, 2000).

Conversely, Romania had a politically divided and cautionary approach to transition. Reforms were initially hampered by delays, and privatization processes were marred by indeterminacy. Romania's reform path was also hampered by weak political institutions, corruption, and resistance from communist elites (EBRD, 1999). Despite the apparent pick-up in momentum in the late 1990s, fueled by EU integration prospects, the early part of the transition was drenched in stagnation and institutional weakening. This is a lesson in how continuity in elites and institutional inertia can constrain reform effectiveness.

The Czech Republic offers an interesting case for comparative examination. It pursued a "voucher privatization" strategy intended to bring about rapid extensive ownership of state property. While this strategy created a broad range of shareholders, it lacked the requisite regulatory and legal framework essential for ensuring effective corporate governance. Thus, many firms were exposed to asset-stripping or opportunism by investment funds (Coffee, 1996). However, the Czech Republic strengthened its regulatory institutions over time and benefited from steadfast political support for reforms in accordance with European Union norms.

Moving eastwards, Georgia is a case in point for profound institutional change following the Rose Revolution in 2003. The newly instituted government undertook quick changes aimed at curbing corruption, liberalization, and the simplification of regulations. Public services experienced modernization, with a rise in the transparency of business registration. These actions brought Georgia international accolades for business-friendliness (World Bank, 2008). Detractors, however, argue that such reform prioritized efficiency over equity and failed to sufficiently tackle poverty and social protection (Papava, 2009). The case in Georgia both highlights the promise and limitations brought by rapid institutional reorganization.

By comparison, Armenia followed a cautious and gradualist reform path. While the nation started trade and price liberalization early, its privatization was slow and lacked transparency. Political instability and the existence of oligarchic institutions were obstacles to institutional reforms. While it witnessed moderate macroeconomic growth, Armenia continued to contend with issues of inequality and lack of judicial independence (ADB, 2017). This example demonstrates how a gradualist approach without governance reform can limit the long-term benefits that are linked to transition. Kazakhstan pursued a mixed model that combined market-based reforms with a strong centralized state. The country pursued price liberalization and privatization policies while keeping strong state control in key sectors like energy. Kazakhstan attracted large amounts of foreign investment, especially in oil and gas sectors, which supported macroeconomic stability. However, the growth of democratic institutions was slow, and economic power increasingly became vested in elite groups (Pomfret, 2006). This case shows how resource abundance can make possible stable transitions, but it can also, at the same time, entrench authoritarianism.

In Uzbekistan, state-guided and -orchestrated reform was the rule. The government had total control over prices and commerce in the 2000s, with a priority given to social stability over liberalization. This strategy improved short-term social stability compared to that seen in other countries, but had the negative effects of economic stagnation, inadequate investment, and limited institutional reform (Spechler, 2000). It is not until recently that Uzbekistan has begun implementing freer market policies under a change in leadership, signaling a belated but perhaps vital transition stage.

Like Kazakhstan, Azerbaijan has invested its oil revenues into nurturing gradual reform. In the early 2000s, the country achieved macroeconomic stability and a large increase in GDP, led largely by the oil sector. However, this growth masked serious challenges in governance, including corruption and lack of observance of the rule of law (EBRD, 2007). Azerbaijan's experience is a demonstration of the limitation that oil-facilitated growth imposes despite institutional inertia.

In Kyrgyzstan, the transition process was marred by political instability and weak institutions. While early reforms included price liberalization and privatization, enforcement was inconsistent. Frequent leadership changes and social unrest undermined investor confidence and led to cycles of reform and reversal (World Bank, 2003). Kyrgyzstan exemplifies the vulnerability of transition economies when political institutions lack legitimacy and continuity.

Turkmenistan and Tajikistan can be described as the most inactive reformers in the region. During the early 2010s, Turkmenistan maintained a command-type economic system, with high subsidies and a low propensity for market-oriented reforms. After a crippling war in the 1990s, Tajikistan faced immense difficulties in establishing basic state functions, much less implementing wide-ranging market reforms (ADB, 2016). These examples highlight the paramount significance of political stability and institutional capacity as the key prerequisites for an effective transition.

Contrasting a comparison of these countries, a review shows that external pressures, whether due to membership in the EU or cooperation with the International Monetary Fund, often had a substantial role in shaping the course of reform. Countries with strong disincentives to align with Western institutions generally practiced more systematic, transparent reform processes (Vachudova, 2005). In countries with weaker external pressures, or resisting them, reform processes developed in an ad-hoc perspective, driven by those interests rather than by development goals.

In addition, political and leadership elites' commitment to reform was also crucial. In Georgia and Poland, reform-minded leaders were able to mobilize public support and implement far-reaching reform efforts. In Uzbekistan and Turkmenistan, elites' opposition to reform resulted in policy gridlock or limited liberalization. This is in line with the argument that economic policy cannot unilaterally control transitional outcomes in the face of a lack of corresponding political and structural changes. In summary, the diverse experiences of Central and Eastern Europe, the Caucasus, and Central Asia provide strong proof that results of transitional processes are determined not exclusively by economic policy but also by political will, institutional structures, and special contextual factors. The individual case studies confirm the notion that there is no single model for successful transitions. Rather, effective reform has to be adaptable, responsive to local conditions, and underpinned by strong systems of governance that ensure long-term sustainable development.

INSTITUTIONAL CHALLENGES AND GOVERNANCE FAILURES

Another important and multifaceted challenge faced by transition economies has been the lack of institutional arrangements necessary for the growth of a functioning market system. In spite of a lot of attention devoted to liberalization and stabilization efforts in the early 1990s, progress in institutional development was not sufficient. This deficiency led to situations in which market mechanisms operated in the absence of adequate legal protection or supervisory control, leading to widespread inefficiencies and corruption (North, 1990; Roland, 2000).

Institutions—both formal (laws, regulations, enforcement agencies) and informal (norms, trust, culture)—form the foundation upon which markets function. In many post-socialist countries, formal institutions inherited from the planned economy were inadequate for a market-based system, while new institutions were often weakly enforced or captured by vested interests. This institutional vacuum hindered contract enforcement, property rights protection, and rule of law, resulting in a low-trust business environment (Kaufmann & Kraay, 2002).

One strong determinant of institutional failure is the capture of the state by economic elites, also known as "state capture." This has been a chronic problem in countries like Russia, Ukraine, and Azerbaijan, wherein powerful individuals or groups dominate policy-making and legislative processes in order to promote personal gains. Hellman, Jones, and Kaufmann (2000) described this situation as a situation wherein the "winners of partial reform" take advantage of institutional vulnerabilities in order to consolidate power and hinder future reform attempts.

One main institutional obstacle has been the politicization in both the judiciaries and the police forces. In several transition countries, the judiciaries had weaknesses in terms of professionalism, independence, and overall performance. These situations undermined the credibility of the legal system and discouraged possible investments. In cases where laws could be arbitrarily read or could be ignored, commercial disputes often went unregulated, with economic actors counting on personal networks or political connections for protection (Frye & Shleifer, 1997). As a result, reforming the judiciaries became one of the toughest and least successful aspects of institutional transition.

Corruption flourished in environments where there was great administrative discretion and a lack of accountability mechanisms. Bribery became a familiar practice in most sectors, such as customs, taxation, and government procurement. Transparency International's Corruption Perceptions Index regularly placed many transition nations as being among the most corrupt during the early stages of their reforms. Corruption not only distorted market signals but also undermined public faith in government and reform policies (Treisman, 2000). Without transparency, policy credibility suffered, hence the loss of enthusiasm for the reform process.

Another area marked by weakness in governance was public administration reform. The transition required the development of new state functions with a focus on regulating competition, supervising compliance, and managing public finance. Despite this, many countries lacked adequate bureaucratic capacity and institutional continuity necessary for the smooth performance of these tasks. Civil service reform was also often shallow, with merit recruitment and performance evaluation being undermined by political and patronage motives (Grindle, 1997). This largely impaired the state's ability to implement reform in a systematic and neutral manner.

Privatization, intended as a cornerstone of transition, often exacerbated institutional weaknesses. In the absence of regulatory frameworks, privatization enabled asset stripping, insider deals, and wealth concentration. In Russia, for example, the loans-for-shares scheme in the mid-1990s transferred valuable state assets to a few politically connected individuals, fueling the rise of oligarchs and public disillusionment (Black, Kraakman, & Tarassova, 2000). Rather than creating a competitive private sector, such outcomes reinforced monopolies and undermined the legitimacy of reform.

Informal institutions effectively filled in the void left by weak formal frameworks. Trust in public institutions was low, and so individuals and companies began to rely even more on personal contacts (blat) and informal deals in order to negotiate the economy. These informal mechanisms enabled the economy to continue in the face of institutional disarray, but they also discouraged formalization, rule compliance, and innovation (Ledeneva, 2006). This double framework of institutionalism created a shadow economy with a lack of transparency and discriminatory sanctions.

Poor enforcement of property rights was another systemic problem. Often, land and business ownership were poorly documented or contested, leading to legal disputes and uncertainty. These situations deterred investment prospects and the ability to engage in long-term strategic planning. Without secure property rights, the incentive for entrepreneurship and productivity was seriously undermined (De Soto, 2000). Additionally, political interference in judicial processes often resulted in the arbitrary withdrawal of property rights, thus undermining investor confidence even more.

Regulators, particularly in sectors like energy, banking, and telecommunications, moved at a slow rate and were often determined by politics. The situation of capture by influential companies led to policy design that favored established players and stifled competition. This lack of stringent regulation allowed for price fixation, delivery inefficiency, and practices that discriminated against some market participants. In addition, it allowed for wealth and power accumulation by a limited group, stifling inclusive economic progress (Djankov et al., 2003).

The second is related to the gap between the enactment of laws and subsequent institutional implementation. Many countries moved very fast in adopting laws and regulations in line with international best practice. These legal frameworks, however, faced enforceability or selective application. The legislative changes, being driven by donor conditions or requirements for joining the European Union, often did not translate into practice in environments with weak mechanisms for enforcement or dysfunctional characteristics (Pistor, Raiser, & Gelfer, 2000). This gap led to a divergence between theoretical underpinnings and application, thus hindering domestic reform processes as well as international integration processes. In the end, institution-building projects initiated by donors sometimes had negative consequences, leading to failures in governance. Outside agencies often promoted one-size-fits-all models of institutional design without attention to particular local conditions. Reforms were assessed largely based on the passage of legislation, as opposed to improvement in implementation or consequent outcomes. Such a technocratic approach was not sufficient to tackle the inherent political and cultural constraints to institutional change (Andrews, 2013). In many cases, institutions existed only in name, with little impact on actual governance or economic effectiveness. In summary, transition experience proves that institutions not only serve as technical organizations but also as ones rooted in political and social contexts. The failures in institutions in the transition period highlight that making economic reform successful requires factors in addition to macroeconomic stability and market liberalization. It is necessary to create competent, legitimate, and accountable institutions that can function effectively in disciplining markets, resolving disputes, and offering public goods. Without those crucial factors, even well-designed reform can fail or produce unintended consequences that deter long-term development.

GLOBALIZATION, EXTERNAL ANCHORS, AND POLICY CONDITIONALITIES

Globalization has had a great impact on the developmental trajectories of transition economies. With a transition from centrally planned to market-based systems, international dealings in trade, finance, and institutions became vital for the economic progress of transition countries. Globalization has a duality in benefits and drawbacks—offering market access, foreign investment flows, and innovative ideas, as well as exposing vulnerable economies to outside shocks and competitive pressures (Rodrik, 1999).

One of the most notable features in globalization, especially in transition economies, is the substantial impact that international financial institutions (IFIs), such as the International Monetary Fund (IMF), the World Bank, and the European Bank for Reconstruction and Development (EBRD), had upon the domestic reform efforts. They not only provided finance, but also technical aid, as well as policy guidelines that guided reform efforts inside countries. Conditionality, a scheme in which the provision of finance is tied to the adoption of policy reform, became a key instrument for achieving transition (Vreeland, 2003).

The International Monetary Fund (IMF) was instrumental in bringing macroeconomic stabilization in the 1990s. Many transition economies that emerged in the post-socialist bloc had faced large fiscal imbalances, inflation, and balance-of-payment crises. The arrangements put in place by the IMF provided finance in times of need subject to the adoption of fiscal contraction, the reduction in subsidies, and monetary contraction. Despite the fact that such arrangements often succeeded in stabilizing macroeconomically, they also exacted social prices, including rising levels of unemployment and rising poverty (Fischer & Sahay, 2000).

The World Bank stressed structural adjustment and institutional reform, approving policies that promote liberalization, privatization, and improvements in the area of governance. It advocated for reform in different sectors such as health care, education, public administration, and the judiciary system. However, critics argue that the uniform models adopted by the Bank ignored post-socialist countries' specific historical and institutional backgrounds. In many cases, reform was implemented in form, not content, leading to ineffective results and a large-scale perception of disillusionment with outside advice (Stiglitz, 2002).

The EU has had a profound influence on the Central and Eastern European region's political and economic environment. Unlike other International Financial Institutions, the EU had a specific driving factor—its membership potential. Accession prospect served as a powerful external catalyst that induced countries to pursue ambitious reform efforts. The EU's conditionality included stringent criteria for democratic rule, respect for the rule of law, sound market functioning, and respect for human rights (Vachudova, 2005). Countries like Poland, Hungary, and the Czech Republic adopted EU-standard oriented reform efforts more systematically and obtained comparatively successful outcomes.

By contrast, countries in the Caucasus and Central Asia, lacking credible prospects for EU accession, were more dependent on IMF and World Bank programs. Without the pull factor of EU integration, reforms in these regions often lacked political momentum and popular legitimacy. For example, while Georgia and Armenia adopted some Western-oriented reforms, others like Uzbekistan and Turkmenistan maintained statist economic models for much longer, prioritizing sovereignty over integration (Hale, 2015). Another important aspect was the role played by trade liberalization and accession to the World Trade Organization (WTO). The transition countries opened up their markets for international business and investment, often with international financial institutions (IFIs) behind them. Seeking membership to the WTO was with a double objective: accessing international markets as well as legal and institutional legitimation. However, the fast rate of trade liberalization uncovered domestic industries being unprepared for greater exposure to competition, leading to cases of deindustrialization and structural joblessness (Hoekman & Kostecki, 2009).

Foreign direct investment (FDI) became a prominent vehicle through which globalization impacted transition economies. Countries that successfully attracted FDI benefited from the spillover of technology, improved managerial skills, and export diversification. Despite this, uneven distribution of FDI among countries—often benefiting those rich in resources or with political stability—amplified development asymmetries. In addition, weak institution-building sometimes allowed foreign investors to appropriate institution-wide gaps, gain economic benefits, and leave without making a long-term commitment (Jensen, 2008).

Policy conditionality has been long-criticized for being inelastic and non-responsive to local conditions. The dominant "one-size-fits-all" approach has assumed that neoliberal reform could be uniformly transferred without regard for specific contextual factors. This assumption did insufficiently account for the role played by starting conditions, historical institutional arrangements, as well as domestic political processes. Countries that undertook reform for international purposes, as opposed to building domestic consensus, often suffered from inadequate ownership and shallow institutionalization (Bird, Hussain, & Joyce, 2004).

Despite such criticism, external anchors played a substantial role in stabilization and coordination in different contexts. They legitimized reformists in home environments, facilitated the provision of funding from outside, and facilitated knowledge exchange. In countries where elites were committed to reform agendas, conditionality helped ensure policy coordination and facilitated strategic long-term planning.

In some cases, it became a mechanism through which elites gained international legitimacy at the expense of meaningful domestic reform (Carothers, 2002).

The financial crisis of 2008 globally laid bare the vulnerabilities in paradigms that emphasize externally-induced reform. Many transition economies, particularly those that relied heavily on foreign capital flows, registered severe contractions in the economy. This resulted in a resurgence of debates on the role played by globalization in development processes. Critics highlighted the need for greater policy space, stronger domestic institutions, and greater control over international capitals (Epstein, 2009).

The rise of China and multipolarity in the globalization context has immensely shaped the international conditions faced by transition economies. Currently, Central Asian and Caucasus countries face the dilemma of upholding their relationship with Western allies while at the same time adjusting to the expanding influence being represented by China and Russia. The changes in geopolitical landscapes brought changes in reform drives, with some governments displaying a bias towards different funding avenues that put less political or regime-oriented conditions (Cooley, 2012). In total, globalization and external anchors both positively and negatively influenced transition economies. As much as they offered vital support and inspiration for reform, they hinged on domestic institutions, leadership, and the ability to tailor external designs to fit domestic conditions. The experience gained through conditionality recognizes the need for international support to be combined with locally tailored strategies, as well as ensuring serious domestic buy-in to reform efforts.

IMPACTS ON REGIONAL DEVELOPMENT AND GROWTH PATTERNS

The transition from the centrally planned to market-oriented systems has led to dramatically different patterns of development in Central and Eastern Europe (CEE), the Caucasus, and Central Asia. As some countries experienced rapid economic progress and successfully integrated with the international market, others faced situations that included stagnation, inequalities, and weaknesses in institutions. In order to understand the different growth patterns, there is a need to examine the ways reform efforts, structural determinants, and international engagements influenced the economic outcomes in the region.

In the Central and Eastern European regions, several countries witnessed fast economic growth after the economic contraction that had happened in the early 1990s. Particularly, from 1995 to 2008, Poland's gross domestic product showed an average growth rate of 4.3 percent per annum, while the Czech Republic and Slovakia had more than 3% annual growth over the same period (World Bank, 2010).

Increased efforts to promote liberalization, strong institutional reforms, and joining the European Union's single market led to improvement in investment, trade, and compliance with regulatory norms.

By contrast, many countries in the post-Soviet space faced a less stable growth path. Russia, for instance, faced a severe economic crisis in the 1990s that led to a loss of over 40% in GDP between the years 1991 and 1998 (IMF, 2000). The nation rebounded in the 2000s, with a growth rate over 6% every year, fueled mostly by oil revenues, but this growth was not accompanied by increases in institutional strength or economic diversification. Thus, this growth was susceptible to commodity prices and external sanctions.

The South Caucasus states—Armenia, Georgia, and Azerbaijan—illustrate varying outcomes in spite of starting under similar conditions. Georgia's liberal market reform has created improved business rankings and reduced corruption, but it is still relatively low in terms of GDP per capita, estimated at approximately $6,200 (current US$) in 2023 (World Bank, 2024). Azerbaijan, meanwhile, enjoyed explosive growth in the oil bonanza between 2005 and 2015, with GDP per capita peaking above $7,800 in 2014; the economy is, however, still largely hydrocarbon dependent, with weak diversification (IMF, 2021).

Within Central Asia, Kazakhstan has shown one of the most significant trends of economic development, with its GDP rising five times between 2000 and 2020. According to the World Bank (2021), Kazakhstan's GDP per capita rose from $1,220 in 2000 to more than $9,000 in 2020, a pattern largely driven by oil exports, state-driven industrialization, and foreign direct investment. However, the growth has not been equally shared in the region, with cities like Almaty and Nur-Sultan having dramatically outpaced rural areas, which still suffer from a lack of infrastructure, education, and employment opportunities.

Regional inequality is one of the defining features of experiences related to transition processes. In many countries, capital cities and some industrialized regions have benefited most from reforms, with peripheral and rural areas significantly lagging behind. In Romania, for instance, Bucharest generates over 25% of the country's GDP, although it is home to only 10% of the population (Eurostat, 2022). Similar tendencies can be seen in Russia, where Moscow and Saint Petersburg account for a considerable proportion of the total economic output, creating issues associated with internal migration and demographic trends.

A key driver of regional imbalances is the uneven distribution of infrastructure and investment resources. Countries that have invested in transport, energy, and digital connectivity have increased both regional cohesion and export competitiveness. For example, the use of EU structural funds by Poland led to its large-scale upgrading of infrastructure, with over €100 billion of investments between 2007 and 2020 (European Commission, 2021). This investment was instrumental in promoting regional convergence, thus reducing the income gap between Poland's eastern and western regions.

Human capital has played a tremendous role in shaping the path of economic progress. Countries that preserved or improved their educational systems enjoyed higher returns in the form of innovation and labor productivity. For example, the Czech Republic and Estonia ranked as top performers in reading and science tests in the 2018 OECD assessments (OECD, 2019). In addition, such countries benefited from a well-educated labor force that attracted foreign investment in manufacturing and the technology sector.

Human labor migration has emerged as a double-edged phenomenon of intra-regional disparity, being both a symptom and a cause. In the transition period, there was a large-scale outflow from less developed countries and regions towards their wealthier counterparts. It was estimated in 2020 that over 5 million Ukrainians, 1.3 million Georgians, and 2.6 million Moldovans worked abroad (IOM, 2020). While remittances supported household spending and macroeconomic stabilization, they also underscored the weakness in domestic labor markets and resulted in a loss of skilled labor in the countries of origin.

Social outcomes also varied extensively by countries and area. In the early 1990s, poverty rates increased significantly in the ex-Soviet region. For example, in Kyrgyzstan, poverty levels stood at a high of 71% in 1993; however, they decreased incrementally to a reading of 20.1% by the year 2021, reflecting improved economic management and international financial institution support (World Bank, 2023). Multidimensional poverty, specifically in the fields of education and health, is, however, a persistent issue in remote and rural Central Asia.

Environmental conditions have increasingly shaped the patterns of regional development. Countries that adopt extractive models of growth—such as Kazakhstan, Azerbaijan, and Turkmenistan—are facing mounting concerns over environmental degradation and vulnerability to climate change. Poor environmental management in the mining and energy industries has led to water shortages, pollution, and public health risks, ultimately affecting the sustainability of regional development (UNDP, 2022).

The rise in the digital economy has brought in new opportunities for local progress. Countries that embraced digitalization can overcome some infrastructural challenges that hindered traditional development in the past. The e-governance system in Estonia and Georgia's systems for electronic business registration improved public services and facilitated a leaner business environment. Disparities in digital accessibility, however, continue, particularly in rural areas and for older age groups, and can worsen long-standing disparities (World Economic Forum, 2020).

Institutional quality is a determinant explanatory factor in shaping outcomes related to regional development. As per the Worldwide Governance Indicators

(World Bank, 2022), countries that have improved regulatory quality and efficient anti-corruption efforts—such as in the cases of Estonia and Slovenia—evidence less growth volatility and less disparity. Countries with weaker institutional environments, as seen in the cases of Tajikistan and Uzbekistan, continue to struggle to achieve inclusive development despite recent reform efforts. The regional disparities have been reinforced by foreign direct investment (FDI) trends. For example, in countries like Slovakia and Hungary, FDI has largely gone to automotive cluster industries, thus promoting regional growth and advancing integration in the value chain with Western Europe. In contrast, some regions in the Caucasus and Central Asia have faced relatively lower levels of investment, mostly in the extractive sectors. This has hindered the development of a diversified economic structure and increased dependence on volatile resource prices (UNCTAD, 2022). In summary, the impact of transition reform on regional development has shown diversity. The reform, globalization, and changes in institutions helped some countries and regions achieve sustainable development, but others became trapped in processes of repeated vulnerability and dependency. Evidence from experience supports the need for tailored interventions that address regional inequalities, promote human development, and upgrade institutional capacity. The transition experience yields the lesson that growth is not enough; instead, fair distribution, sustainability, and governance are essential building blocks for lasting regional progress.

POLICY IMPLICATIONS FOR FUTURE TRANSITIONS

The experiences over the last thirty years in post-socialist environments provide a sound foundation for making future transitions. With young sectors, areas, and institutions confronting the need for structural adjustments due to breakthroughs in technology, climate change, or political shifts, the understanding of the policy conclusions derived from economic transitions becomes increasingly important. The next generation of reformers is challenged to take valuable lessons from both successes and failures of past transitions in order to design strategies that are economically sound, socially fair and politically feasible.

One far-reaching consequence of policy is the need for strategic sequencing of reforms. Early transition policy often focused on rapid liberalization without sufficiently building the necessary institutional foundations. Empirical evidence supports that those countries that implemented market reform together with institutional building—i.e., institutionalizing the rule of law, securing property rights, and building greater capacity to regulate—achieved more long-term growth (North, 1990; Roland, 2000). Subsequent transitions would be best in avoiding rushed liberalization that surpasses the capabilities of institutions.

Another one is that there is a need to develop reform that is sensitive to the context. The generic models that became popular in the 1990s often ignored localities' unique political, cultural, and historical conditions. New reform efforts need to be tailored to fit local capacities and conditions for enforcement, not imposed from outside. Successful reform efforts must be flexible, iterative, and responsive to continually changing constituent, market, and institutional feedback (Andrews, Pritchett, & Woolcock, 2017).

Improvement in institutional capacity cannot be seen as a marginal aspect; instead, it is a core element in reform processes. Institutions that provide for law enforcement, services, and market regulation need to be professionalized, depoliticized, and endowed with adequate funding. This requires not just reform in the legal and institutional systems but investment in human resources, digital systems, and civic education schemes. Public trust in institutions is essential for reform legitimacy and longer-term sustainability (Kaufmann, Kraay, & Zoido-Lobatón, 1999).

The incorporation of governance and anti-corruption measures in all stages of the transition process is key. Poor governance weakens economic performance and undermines public support for reform programs. Instituting mechanisms that ensure transparency in procurement, creating independent audit institutions, and facilitating independent media are imperative in building accountability. Countries with strong anti-corruption institutions, as seen in Estonia and Georgia in the 2000s, have demonstrated that institutional reforms can rapidly improve competitiveness and strengthen investor confidence (World Bank, 2008).

Social protection policies are essential to mitigate the negative effects that come with structural change. The most common criticism of the original transition policy is its failure to put in place adequate social protection, which has led to social disruption and policy fatigue. Any future transition should include special aid for displaced workers, assistance for vulnerable households, and measures for reducing the distributional effects of economic restructuring (Barr, 2001). Countries can introduce conditional cash transfers, retraining, and high-quality education systems to enable the benefits of economic development to be shared fairly.

It is essential for policymakers to realize the importance of both political leadership and elite consensus. The process of implementing reforms requires not just technical expertise but also the willingness to act politically and build coalitions. Leaders must clearly articulate reform goals, manage stakeholders' expectations, and generate broad-based support across social groups and geographic locations. In the case of Poland and the Baltic states, strong leadership in combination with unified reform teams has been instrumental in sustaining reform efforts during adverse moments (Åslund, 2002).

External institutions, such as membership in the European Union or other trade agreements, can provide powerful incentives for reform. These institutions enhance policy compliance, provide access to markets, and grant external legitimacy. It is important, however, that these institutions are supplemented by genuine domestic commitment to reform programs. Conditionalities perceived as externally imposed without local ownership can lead to resistance or nominal compliance. Policymakers would do well to seek congruence between external incentives and national development goals (Vachudova, 2005).

Technologic progress and digitalization present a two-way environment, both challenging and full of opportunity for future transitions. Automation and artificial intelligence threaten the risk of displacement and increasing inequalities, but digital platforms can make governments less corrupt, reduce inequalities, and make services more efficient. Countries that invest in digital skills and digital infrastructure can move forward in their development trajectories and close long-term gaps. It is imperative that the digital reforms occur in a fair and inclusive manner backed by robust data governance systems (World Economic Forum, 2020).

The embedding of environmental sustainability into the core design of economic transition policies is imperative. Climate change and environmental degradation are increasingly central to national security and competitiveness considerations. Transitions going forward must be aligned with international sustainability goals, such as the United Nations SDGs and the Paris Agreement. Policies like green investment, carbon pricing, and renewable energy incentives can support not just economic development but ecological resilience as well (OECD, 2022).

The role and presence of participatory governance and civic society are another essential element. Empirical observation shows that policymaking and monitoring processes that involve citizens are linked with greater chances of success and sustainability. Institutions like participatory budgeting, public hearings, and civic monitoring initiatives help to make the administrative system answerable and promote a civic ethos. In addition, strong civil societies can act as a brake on excessive executive actions, thus ensuring reforms continue to be in the wider public interest (Carothers & Brechenmacher, 2014).

Training and education are essential elements of all transition processes. Economic change demands new knowledge, skills, and mindsets. Policy in the future must stress the value of lifelong learning, vocational training, and entrepreneurial competencies in a bid to equip workers for the constantly changing labor markets. Countries that invest in education not only increase national productivity but also enable the flexibility necessary to steer intricate transitions (Hanushek & Woessmann, 2015).

Another policy implication entails proactive regional disparity management. Regional disparities in development can fuel political fragmentation, cause migration pressures, and lead to social unrest. Targeted regional development programs, investments in infrastructure, and the encouragement of decentralization can promote a more balanced growth path and ensure the benefits of transition are within reach for all citizens. In addition, spatially inclusive planning is key to promoting social cohesion and long-term stability (World Bank, 2009). Finally, future transitions can be guided by flexibility and learning. Policymakers need to approach reform as ongoing processes, not as episodic events. Integration of monitoring, evaluation, and learning into reform efforts is central. Pilots, mechanisms for generating feedback, and evidence-based policymaking can, in turn, maximize effectiveness and responsiveness. Countries that develop a learning state—receptive to testing, adaptation, and innovation—are best able to cope with the uncertainty that is part and parcel of transitions (Rodrik, 2007). In essence, lessons from historical transitions highlight that transformation in the economic sense is not limited to policy, but also includes institutions, inclusivity, and adaptability. Coming transitions must occur in a more complex international environment driven by technologies, environmental risks, and shifts in geographics. It is important for policymakers to see transitions as a comprehensive process that integrates economic efficiency with social equity, institutional resilience, and long-term sustainability.

CONCLUSION

The transition from centrally-planned to market-based systems is one of the greatest and most ambitious changes seen in recent times. The experiences, as they are recorded from Central and Eastern Europe, the Caucasus, and Central Asia, demonstrate both the promise as well as the challenges that may be faced with such a dramatic change. While a few countries in the region had achieved a fair amount of progress in economic performance as well as institutional improvements, others lagged behind due to persistent problems of inequality, poor governance, and weak institutional frameworks.

One major conclusion that can be derived from the transition experience is the central role that institutions must play. Countries that built strong, transparent, and accountable institutional systems in early steps in the transition process found themselves much more likely to realize enduring economic growth and social stability. Countries that focused on liberalization and privatization at the expense of building proper institutional arrangements often found themselves plagued by corruption, state capture, and social unrest. The idea of strong institutions includes administrative ones, as well as regulations and conventions that distribute resources, resolve disputes, and administer justice in societies.

The sequence and pace of reforms were also discovered to be important. Strategies marked by gradualism, and especially when underpinned by long-term strategic planning and institutional preparedness, often outperformed attempts at rapid, disorganized liberalization. Policymakers involved in later transitions must therefore balance the urgency of reform with the need to build consensus, sustain public confidence, and put in place the institutional infrastructure vital for market support. Reforms that are rushed and lack popular support or adequate administrative capacity can lead to fragile progress and social backlash.

The processes of globalization and external stakeholder involvement have had a considerable impact on the outcomes of transition processes. Multilateral funding agencies, financial institutions, and international organizations have provided technical assistance, financial aid, and conditional demands that facilitated the articulation of domestic reform agendas. However, the impact of foreign aid cannot substitute for the need for domestic legitimacy. Externally driven reform, as opposed to reform emerging from a domestic consensus, is supported by inadequate ownership and sustainability. Future transition efforts must make efforts to balance international contributors with reform strategy formulation that is grounded in local contexts.

The social repercussions that come with the transition have also been characterized by stark inequalities. In some cases, the supported reforms have created or sharpened disparities, leading to imbalances in different localities, as well as a weakening of social protection mechanisms. These points highlight the need for equity and inclusiveness to be prime elements in reform processes. Economic progress must be complemented with social policies that protect vulnerable groups, support transitions in labor markets, and ensure equal access to the benefits of progress. Failing to address the above might translate into reform fatigue and, by extension, political instability.

In addition, a profound evolution has taken place in the world order since the early 1990s. Future transitions would be taking place in the space of digital progress, climate change, geopolitical dispersion, and shifting public expectations. These future challenges call for the evolution of flexible and robust policy frameworks that are native to democratic governance, sustainability, and innovation. Modern transition approaches must capture not just the economic logic of markets, but also the ethical and environmental roles that are built into the developmental paradigm in the 21st century. In sum, transition must not be seen as a non-linear, ongoing, and incomplete process; instead, it represents a multifaceted and dynamic evolution that is driven by historical circumstances, institutional arrangements, and multiple stakeholders. The cases described in this chapter demonstrate that successful outcomes depend not just on the choice of policy but also on the approaches, order, and actors through which the transition is implemented. Future transitions need to draw on such key observations in order to craft reform agendas that are inclusive, institutionally rooted, and sensitive to the interconnectedness of a system world.

REFERENCES

ADB. (2016). *Asian Development Outlook*. Asian Development Bank.

ADB. (2017). *Armenia Country Partnership Strategy*. Asian Development Bank.

Andrews, M. (2013). *The limits of institutional reform in development*. Cambridge University Press. DOI: 10.1017/CBO9781139060974

Andrews, M., Pritchett, L., & Woolcock, M. (2017). *Building state capability: Evidence, analysis, action*. Oxford University Press. DOI: 10.1093/acprof:oso/9780198747482.001.0001

Åslund, A. (2002). *Building capitalism: The transformation of the former Soviet bloc*. Cambridge University Press.

Åslund, A. (2013). How Capitalism Was Built: The Transformation of Central and Eastern Europe, Russia, the Caucasus, and Central Asia (2nd ed.). Cambridge University Press.

Barr, N. (2001). *The welfare state as piggy bank: Information, risk, uncertainty, and the role of the state*. Oxford University Press. DOI: 10.1093/0199246599.001.0001

Bird, G., Hussain, M., & Joyce, J. (2004). Many happy returns? Recidivism and the IMF. *Journal of International Money and Finance*, *23*(2), 231–251. DOI: 10.1016/j.jimonfin.2003.12.002

Black, B. S., Kraakman, R., & Tarassova, A. (2000). Russian privatization and corporate governance: What went wrong? *Stanford Law Review*, *52*(6), 1731–1808. DOI: 10.2307/1229501

Boettke, P. J., & Coyne, C. J. (2009). Context matters: Institutions and entrepreneurship. *Foundations and Trends in Entrepreneurship*, *5*(3), 135–209. DOI: 10.1561/0300000018

Campos, N. F., & Coricelli, F. (2002). Growth in transition: What we know, what we don't, and what we should. *Journal of Economic Literature*, *40*(3), 793–836. DOI: 10.1257/jel.40.3.793

Carothers, T. (2002). The end of the transition paradigm. *Journal of Democracy*, *13*(1), 5–21. DOI: 10.1353/jod.2002.0003

Carothers, T., & Brechenmacher, S. (2014). *Accountability, transparency, participation, and inclusion: A new development consensus?* Carnegie Endowment for International Peace.

Coffee, J. C. (1996). Institutional investors in transitional economies: Lessons from the Czech experience. In Frydman, R., Gray, C., & Rapaczynski, A. (Eds.), *Corporate Governance in Central Europe and Russia*. CEU Press. DOI: 10.1515/9789633865606-006

Cooley, A. (2012). *Great games, local rules: The new power contest in Central Asia*. Oxford University Press. DOI: 10.1093/acprof:oso/9780199929825.001.0001

De Soto, H. (2000). *The mystery of capital: Why capitalism triumphs in the West and fails everywhere else*. Basic Books. DOI: 10.37199/t40002609

Djankov, S., La Porta, R., Lopez-de-Silanes, F., & Shleifer, A. (2003). Courts. *The Quarterly Journal of Economics*, *118*(2), 453–517. DOI: 10.1162/003355303321675437

EBRD. (1999). *Transition Report 1999: Ten Years of Transition*. European Bank for Reconstruction and Development.

EBRD. (2007). *Transition Report 2007: People in Transition*. European Bank for Reconstruction and Development.

Epstein, G. (2009). *Beyond capital account liberalization: Enhancing macroeconomic policy autonomy and financial stability*. International Labour Office.

European Commission. (2021). EU Cohesion Policy 2007–2020: Investing in Europe's regions. https://ec.europa.eu

Eurostat. (2022). Regional GDP per capita in the EU. https://ec.europa.eu/eurostat

Fischer, S., & Sahay, R. (2000). The transition economies after ten years. IMF Working Paper, WP/00/30.

Frye, T., & Shleifer, A. (1997). The invisible hand and the grabbing hand. *The American Economic Review*, *87*(2), 354–358.

Grindle, M. S. (1997). *Getting good government: Capacity building in the public sectors of developing countries*. Harvard University Press.

Hale, H. E. (2015). *Patronal politics: Eurasian regime dynamics in comparative perspective*. Cambridge University Press.

Hanushek, E. A., & Woessmann, L. (2015). *The knowledge capital of nations: Education and the economics of growth*. MIT Press. DOI: 10.7551/mitpress/9780262029179.001.0001

Havrylyshyn, O. (2020). *Present at the Transition: An Inside Look at the Role of History, Politics and Personalities in Post-Communist Countries*. Cambridge University Press. DOI: 10.1017/9781108553834

Hellman, J. S., Jones, G., & Kaufmann, D. (2000). Seize the state, seize the day: State capture and influence in transition economies. World Bank Policy Research Working Paper, No. 2444.

Hoekman, B., & Kostecki, M. (2009). *The Political Economy of the World Trading System* (3rd ed.). Oxford University Press. DOI: 10.1093/oso/9780199553761.001.0001

IMF. (2000). Russian Federation: Recent economic developments. International Monetary Fund.

IMF. (2021). Azerbaijan: Staff country report. https://www.imf.org

IOM. (2020). Migration data portal: Eastern Europe and Central Asia. https://migrationdataportal.org

Jensen, N. M. (2008). *Nation-states and the multinational corporation: A political economy of foreign direct investment*. Princeton University Press. DOI: 10.1515/9781400837373

Kaufmann, D., & Kraay, A. (2002). Growth without governance. World Bank Policy Research Working Paper, No. 2928.

Kaufmann, D., Kraay, A., & Zoido-Lobatón, P. (1999). Governance matters. World Bank Policy Research Working Paper, No. 2196.

Kornai, J. (1992). *The Socialist System: The Political Economy of Communism*. Princeton University Press.

Ledeneva, A. V. (2006). *How Russia really works: The informal practices that shaped post-Soviet politics and business*. Cornell University Press.

Megginson, W. L., & Netter, J. M. (2001). From state to market: A survey of empirical studies on privatization. *Journal of Economic Literature*, *39*(2), 321–389. DOI: 10.1257/jel.39.2.321

North, D. C. (1990). *Institutions, institutional change and economic performance*. Cambridge University Press. DOI: 10.1017/CBO9780511808678

OECD. (2019). *PISA 2018 Results* (Vol. I). OECD Publishing.

OECD. (2022). Green Growth and Sustainable Development. https://www.oecd.org/greengrowth

Papava, V. (2009). Anatomical pathology of Georgia's Rose Revolution. *Problems of Economic Transition*, *52*(5), 5–18.

Pistor, K., Raiser, M., & Gelfer, S. (2000). Law and finance in transition economies. *Economics of Transition*, *8*(2), 325–368. DOI: 10.1111/1468-0351.00047

Pomfret, R. (2006). *The Central Asian Economies since Independence*. Princeton University Press. DOI: 10.1515/9780691222509

Pop-Eleches, G. (2009). *From Economic Crisis to Reform: IMF Programs in Latin America and Eastern Europe*. Princeton University Press.

Rodrik, D. (1999). *The new global economy and developing countries: Making openness work. Policy Essay No. 24*. Overseas Development Council. DOI: 10.56021/9781565170278

Rodrik, D. (1999). *The new global economy and developing countries: Making openness work*. Overseas Development Council. DOI: 10.56021/9781565170278

Rodrik, D. (2007). *One economics, many recipes: Globalization, institutions, and economic growth*. Princeton University Press. DOI: 10.1515/9781400829354

Roland, G. (2000). *Transition and economics: Politics, markets, and firms*. MIT Press.

Sachs, J. (1994). *Poland's Jump to the Market Economy*. MIT Press.

Spechler, M. C. (2000). Uzbekistan: The silk road to nowhere? *Contemporary Economic Policy*, *18*(3), 295–303. DOI: 10.1111/j.1465-7287.2000.tb00026.x

Stiglitz, J. E. (1999). Whither reform? Ten years of the transition. *World Bank Annual Conference on Development Economics*.

Stiglitz, J. E. (2002). *Globalization and its discontents*. W.W. Norton & Company.

Surmanidze, N. (2022). Legislative Challenges of Georgian Entrepreneurship and Business Competitiveness. Institutions and Economies, 1-24.

Treisman, D. (2000). The causes of corruption: A cross-national study. *Journal of Public Economics*, *76*(3), 399–457. DOI: 10.1016/S0047-2727(99)00092-4

UNCTAD. (2022). World Investment Report. https://unctad.org

UNDP. (2022). *Central Asia Human Development Report*. United Nations Development Programme.

Vachudova, M. A. (2005). *Europe Undivided: Democracy, Leverage, and Integration After Communism*. Oxford University Press. DOI: 10.1093/0199241198.001.0001

Vreeland, J. R. (2003). *The IMF and Economic Development*. Cambridge University Press. DOI: 10.1017/CBO9780511615726

World Bank. (2003). *Kyrgyz Republic: Enhancing Pro-Poor Growth.* World Bank.

World Bank. (2008). Doing Business 2009: Georgia Profile. https://www.worldbank.org

World Bank. (2008). *Doing Business 2009.* World Bank.

World Bank. (2009). World Development Report: Reshaping Economic Geography. https://www.worldbank.org

World Bank. (2010). Transition: The First Ten Years. https://www.worldbank.org

World Bank. (2021). Kazakhstan Economic Update. https://www.worldbank.org

World Bank. (2022). Worldwide Governance Indicators. https://info.worldbank.org/governance/wgi

World Bank. (2023). Kyrgyz Republic Poverty and Equity Brief. https://www.worldbank.org

World Bank. (2024). Georgia Overview. https://www.worldbank.org

World Economic Forum. (2020). The Global Competitiveness Report 2020. https://www.weforum.org

Chapter 13
A Participatory Vision of the Local Producers Regarding the Future Development of the Specific Activities

Mihai Alexandru Chi ea
https://orcid.org/0000-0001-5294-2604
Institute of Agricultural Economics, Bucharest, Romania

Ioan Sebastian Brumă
Rural Development Research Platform, Romania

Marioara Rusu
Rural Development Research Platform, Romania

Meda Gâlea
Romanian Academy, Ia i, Romania

Diana Elena Creangă
Rural Development Research Platform, Romania

Lorena Florentina Chi ea
Institute of Agricultural Economics, Bucharest, Romania

ABSTRACT

This chapter approaches the theme of rural economy' products from the perspective of local agrifood producers from the North-East development region of Romania, that have participated, throughout the time at the fair for agri-food producers "Ia i in Dishes". The research activities were conducted in two stages based on a questionnaire developed by a joint team of researchers. The second stage of the Delphi exercise, that represents the subject of this chapter, involved 30 local producers that have also participated in the first stage, the main objectives in this case being:

DOI: 10.4018/979-8-3373-2898-0.ch013

to identify the main problems and challenges faced by the respondents, to outline respondents' perception regarding the possible changes determined by a series of factors and to delineate a participatory vision of local producers regarding the marketing events periodically organized in Ia i municipality – from the perspective of: participation' motivation, perceived benefits and the need for the involvement of certain entities/institutions in the process of promoting this type of marketing events.

INTRODUCTION

Without aiming to elaborate an extensive literature review, some important aspects regarding the concept of rural economy and different approaches developed throughout the time, at national and international level, can facilitate a better understanding of the strong relations between the local agrifood producers, the production areas and urban and national economy.

The rural economy, as a distinct branch of the national economy, was outlined in a general acceptance at the beginning of the 19th century, the common element of the different definitions being agriculture, the main activity in the rural areas (Dona, 2015). Thus, the rural space was approached through rural economy, identified in general by agriculture' economy in the absence of a clear conceptual demarcation between the rural and agricultural space (Rusu, 2005). In this context, the rural area is considered a specific way of space' usage, characterized by a relative low density of inhabitants and buildings, dominance of natural landscapes and a predominantly agro-forestry-pastoral economic activity (Gavrilescu & Florian, 2007).

Later, during the middle of the 20th century, the first approaches that suggested that rural economy could be difficult to enclose into a single typology emerged, having in view that it presents a mix of natural environment dependable factors (Kolb & Brunner, 1946). Thereby, the following definitions were elaborated (Auge-Laribe, 1949):

- Rural economy – represents a mix of methodological observations, laws and precepts specific to political economy that apply to activities and producers' life and relations with other professions – highlighting agriculture' role in national economy and international relations;
- Agricultural economy – a branch of the national economy that studies agricultural enterprises, production conditions, relations between its different elements and trades – that lead to economic results.

At the end of the 20th century, the approach of rural economy diversifies into two main levels, the first - as the entire economic activities based on agriculture and the second – through the economic activities taking place in the rural areas (Errington, 1997).

Based on the profound changes experienced by the rural economies during the last decades (development of the peri-urban areas, increase of employment in the service sector and rural-urban mobility, competition with the large retail chains etc), when we approach rural economy we cannot refer only to agricultural activities, but also need to consider other aspects regarding the integration in value added channels, local action groups, non-agricultural economy (Dona, 2015). At regional level, rural economy preserves the characteristics of a system based, in general, on agricultural resources, but to a large extent assumes the aspect of a services economy, driven by demand' structural changes, technological progress and access to production factors (Berthelier & Lipchitz, 2005).

The discussions regarding the rural activities include both agricultural and non-agricultural ones, the increase of the agricultural incomes generating rural demand' growth, supporting the development of new activities and economic exchanges. Nevertheless, in general, the activities of rural households are usually separately evaluated, based on different factors: activity' domain, functions and location (Barret & Reardon, 2000). The incomes obtained within rural economies are grouped in agricultural incomes (from agriculture, animal breeding, employment incomes) and non-agricultural incomes – from non-agricultural sectors, independent activities and transfers (Davis et al, 2007).

Summarizing, from the perspective of economic sciences (Rusu, 2005):

- The development of rural economy has taken place alongside agriculture' progress, using, in general, the labor force freed from the agricultural production to support other economic sectors;
- The specific occupations of rural economy are both traditional but also new ones, emerged along with the ingression of urban civilization, associated with the industrial, services and infrastructure' sectors;
- The rural economy' role concentrates on fulfilling rural' functions – protection of natural resources, sustainable development of agricultural activities in synergy with non-agricultural ones, preserving and capitalizing rural' socio-cultural traditions.

Thereby, it is evident that rural economies will display a functional interdependence with urban and national economy – nowadays the economic and social viability of rural areas depend on the intensity of connections with urban centers, that offer facilities for an attractive living environment, but also the necessary social and educational infrastructure. The interdependence relation manifest itself in both ways, the participation of agricultural producers and other rural areas inhabitants to the development of urban economies being much more intense now compared to the previous decades (Dona, 2015).

In this context, the analysis presented in this chapter aims to contribute to the knowledge base regarding the strong interdependence between rural and urban areas from the perspective of local agri-food producers from the North-East development region of Romania, by addressing important issues related to their specific activities (main problems and challenges, diverse factors that could support/inhibit future development) and to the direct relation with consumers and development of short supply chains, supported by the participation at the "*Ia i in Dishes: Organic, Traditional, Mountain and Artisan Products*" fair.

METHODOLOGICAL ASPECTS

The research activities that constitute the base of this chapter were conducted as a Delphi exercise in two stages, involving local agri-food producers from the North-East development region of Romania. In this context, a short introduction of the Delphi method can support the choice for the methodological approach.

The Delphi method represents one of the most popular forecasting techniques (based on human judgement) that emerged somewhere around the second half on the 20th century. Initially, it was developed for the industrial sector, where the fast technological advancements hindered the achievement of reliable predictions (Horrillo et al, 2016). As, in time, the Delphi method seemed to be a useful tool also for other sectors, it was adapted to various domains including agri-food sector, forestry management, climate/ecological changes and many more. It is considered a method/instrument for reaching consensus, especially for researches that cover a complex theme where experts from a specific area need to be involved (Fefer et al., 2016). As a semi structured, iterative and anonymized survey of a group of participants, the Delphi method is very useful for achieving consensus in case of various and delicate subjects, where other direct interaction methods (like focus groups) would be, likely, inadequate (Mukherjee et al., 2015).

Coming back to the present study, the Delphi exercise was implemented in two stages: in the first one, 34 local producers from the North-East region have participated in this study; the aim of this first stage was to study the structure, location, motivation and potential benefits that could be useful in the individual or collective decision-making process (producers/public authorities). The second stage of the Delphi exercise, that represents the subject of this chapter, involved 30 local producers that have also participated in the first stage, the main objectives in this case being:

- To identify the demographic, educational and occupational characteristics of the local producers that participated at this second stage;
- To identify the main problems and challenges faced by the respondents regarding the operation of their specific activities;
- To outline respondents' perception regarding the possible changes determined by a series of factors (ecological/climate changes, changes at policy level/specific legislation regarding this sector, technological changes, consumers' preferences, sales channels);
- To delineate a participatory vision of local producers regarding the marketing events periodically organized in Ia i municipality – from the perspective of: participation' motivation, perceived benefits and the need for the involvement of certain entities/institutions in the process of promoting this type of marketing events.

The data collection process was based on a questionnaire elaborated by researchers from the Romanian Academy – Ia i branch, the Institute of Agricultural Economics (Bucharest) and the Rural Development Research Platform (Le cani, Ia i county), structured on three main categories of questions:

- Introductive information – regarding the production area, types of products, demographic, and educational characteristics, type of organization, type of certification;
- General information regarding the specific activity – main problems/challenges, potential changes, perception regarding the influence of diverse factors (climate, legislative, technological, consumers' preferences) on the future activities, the need for supplementary skills;
- Information regarding the participation at the fair for agri-food producers - "*Ia i in Dishes: Organic, Traditional, Mountain and Artisan Products*" – history of participations, the main reason for the first participation/ later participations, evaluation of participation' benefits and advertisement of this type of events, the role of different institutions in supporting/promoting these events.

After the questionnaire was finalized during the working meetings between researchers from the three institutions, it was transformed into an electronic version with the help of a specific survey software and applied to the participants (local producers from North-East development region), mainly face to face, but also online. At the end of the data collection process, the information was transferred to a data base in SPSS format for data processing.

RESULTS AND DISCUSSIONS

At the first round of the Delphi exercise 34 local producers from the North-East development region have participated. These participants represented the target group for the second round of the exercise, that took place between 19-21st of July 2024, during the "*Ia i in Dishes: Organic, Traditional, Mountain and Artisan Products*" fair, organized in Ia i municipality. Out of the 34 respondents from the first round, 30 of them have also participated in the second round.

This high rate of participation at the second round of the study ("Producers fairs in the knowledge ecosystems") highlights the grown interest of local producers for the research theme, as well as the evident need to communicate the problems and challenges faced in operating their specific activities.

Introductive Information

The first section of the questionnaire applied to local producers targeted the demographic and educational characteristics of respondents, as well as the main information regarding their specific activities, including location, types of agri-food products sold, organizational form and certification types.

Participants' structure based on the county of origin/production area is dominated by local agri-food producers from Ia i county, followed by Neam , Vaslui and Boto ani counties (Figure 1). Bacău and Suceava counties were each represented in this target group by one local producer.

Figure 1. County of origin/production area

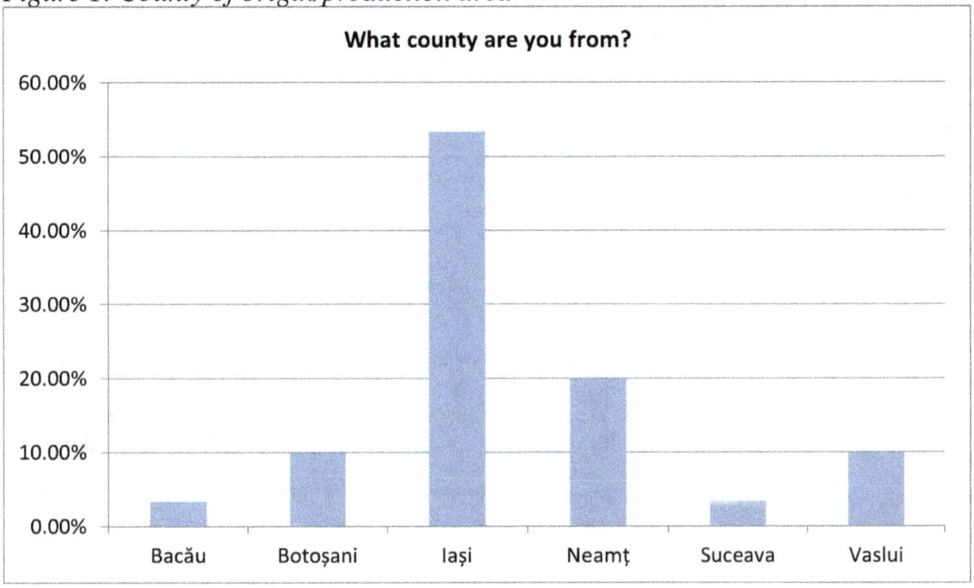

Source: own processing based on Delphi database

As regards the types of products sold by local producers that have participated at this second round of the Delphi exercise, the main categories were the following (Figure 2):

- Vegetables, fruits, juices, can products,
- Bee products,
- Meat / meat-based products (fish, pork, chicken, beef, wild boar and deer),
- Grain mill, bakery, pastry products,
- Cosmetic products,
- Dairy products,
- Alcoholic drinks.

Figure 2. Main types of products sold

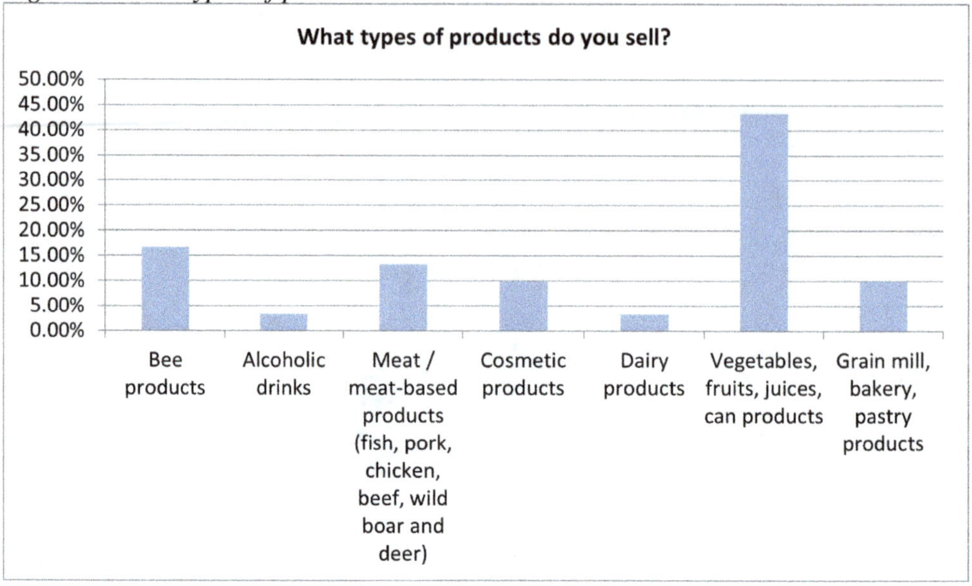

Source: own processing based on Delphi database

Based on the organization form of the entities present at the "Ia i in dishes" fair, most of them represented commercial companies, followed by individual enterprises and certified producers. Only one entity that participated to this study represented the associations sector (Table 1).

Table 1. The organization form of the participant entities

Organization form	Number of entities	% in total
Association	1	3.33%
Individual enterprise	7	23.33%
Certified producer	7	23.33%
Commercial company	15	50.00%

Source: own processing based on Delphi database

Moving one, the next questions from the introductive information section targeted the demographical and educational characteristics of the local producers that represented the target group. The majority of respondents have an age up to 49 years, the largest share in total being the age group below 34 years (Table 2).

Table 2. Demographic characteristics of the participants

Age group	**Number**	**% in total**
Below 34 years	8	26.67%
Between 35 and 39 years	0	0.00%
Between 40 and 44 years	6	20.00%
Between 45 and 49 years	7	23.33%
Between 50 and 54 years	4	13.33%
Between 55 and 59 years	3	10.00%
Between 60 and 64 years	2	6.67%
Over 65 years	0	0.00%
Gender structure	Number	% in total
Male	19	63.33%
Female	11	36.67%

Source: own processing based on Delphi database

As regards the educational profile of the participants, most of them have a higher education level, a significant share being represented by the technical specializations: engineer, agronomist engineer, zootechnician engineer, food industry and biophysics (Figure 3).

Figure 3. What is your profession?

Source: own processing based on Delphi database

Alongside technical specializations, there are also other professions from the educational, juridical, economic, business administration, agriculture, forestry and agri-food domains represented in the target group.

The last question from the first section investigated the type of certification that participants to this study hold (Table 3).

Table 3. What type of certification do you hold?

Certification type	Number	% in total
Ecological	9	30.00%
Mountain product	7	23.33%
Traditional	3	10.00%
Not yet certified/ Does not know	13	43.33%
Total	30	100.00%

Source: own processing based on Delphi database

More than 50% of participants held some type of certification, the “ecological” category ranking first, followed by “mountain product” and “traditional” certification. On the other hand, almost 44% of respondents have declared that they were not certified at the time when the study was conducted.

General Information Regarding the Specific Activity

The second section of the questionnaire applied to local agri-food producers from the North -East development region of Romania focused on the identification of the main problems/challenges, potential changes at the level of the specific activities, perception regarding the influence of climate/ technological/ legislative/ consumers preferences factors on future development and on the supplementary skills that respondents consider that they would need to acquire in order to face these changes.

The first question from this section focused on six major problems that could affect the current activities of the local producers. The respondents were asked to analyze and prioritize these problems based on their specific situation (Table 4). Depending on their options, each major problem was assigned a position from 1 to 6, where 1 represents the most important one. At the end, a final score was calculated for each of the main problems.

Table 4. Producers' perception regarding the main problems that affect the current activity

Problems/Hierarchy	1	2	3	4	5	6	Final score
Bureaucracy	7	7	3	5	5	3	3.9
Increase of prices	6	10	6	4	1	3	4.23
Lack of labor force	7	5	7	7	4	0	4.13
Marketplace	6	4	9	4	5	2	3.87
Climate changes	1	3	1	4	8	13	2.2
Time	3	1	4	6	7	9	2.67

Source: own processing based on Delphi database

As the first option, the most important current problems for the respondents are those related to lack of labor force, bureaucracy, the increase of prices and ensuring the marketplace for their products. The next options (positions from 2 to 6) highlight some motions regarding the hierarchy of the problems, but some of them reach a constant number of votes throughout the ranking exercise. Thus, based on the final score calculated, the hierarchy of the main current problems faced by local producers does not change significantly, the increase of prices, lack of labor force, bureaucracy and enduring the marketplace remaining the most important ones. On the last places in this hierarchy, we find the problem of time (perceived as the volume dedicated by local producers to the specific activity) and the climate changes.

Similar to the first question, participants were asked next to prioritize the main current challenges faced by them in conducting their activities. In this case, the ranking exercise focused on four main challenges, at the end a final score being calculated for each one (Table 5).

Table 5. Participants' perception regarding the main challenges for the current activities

Challenges/ Hierarchy	1	2	3	4	Final score
Specialized labor force	11	8	5	6	2.8
Communication channels with clients	1	9	12	8	2.1
Adaptation to clients' needs	5	4	10	11	2.1
Production sale possibilities	13	9	3	5	3

Source: own processing based on Delphi database

The first option of respondents brought in spotlight the challenges related to the production sale possibilities, followed by the ones linked to the effort of ensuring the needed specialized labor force for the current activities. With a lower number of votes, still, the adaptation to clients' needs foreshadows as a challenge taken into consideration by the local producers who have participated in the study.

It is evident that we cannot say the same about the communication channels with clients, that doesn't outline as an important first option. This situation can be explained by the fact that the majority of respondents have participated to several editions of the "*Ia i in Dishes: Organic, Traditional, Mountain and Artisan Products*" fair and to similar marketing events, by their presence on dedicated on-line platforms (like "Taste of Ia i"), but also by their own on-line marketing efforts/ projects (social media accounts, web pages) – all these allowing them, throughout the time, to develop an extended base of clients and to increase their visibility, at local, regional and national level.

The final score calculated for the main challenges confirms the hierarchy based on the participants' first option, where production sale possibilities and specialized labor force rank firsts.

Having in view the main problems and challenges that local producers have to deal with now, the next question addressed the potential changes regarding the specific activities that these would implement at this time (Table 6).

Table 6. If you were to implement, at this time, some changes in your activity, what would be the most important?

Potential changes in current activity	**Number**	**% in total**
Employing qualified personnel	3	10.00%
Enlargement/development of activity	15	50.00%
A better organization of activity	12	40.00%
Others, please specify....	0	0.00%
Total	30	100.00%

Source: own processing based on Delphi database

From the perspective of some potential changes that they would like to implement in their current activities, the majority of respondents consider the enlargement/ development of activity as the first option taken into account, followed by a better organization of activity. The changes related to the human resources, namely employment of qualified personnel is also an option for 10% of participants to this study.

How local producers perceive their potential contribution in the achievement of some of EU' important objectives related to their activity domain was the aim of the next question from this section (Table 7).

Table 7. To what extent do you consider that your activity can contribute to the achievement of EU's objective related to:? -no. of answers-

Objectives/Evaluation	Not at all	Small extent	Medium	Large extent	Very much	Weighted average
Combating climate changes	2	4	11	7	6	3.37
Development of organic agriculture	1	2	6	12	9	3.87
Development of short supply chains	1	0	8	12	9	3.93
Animal welfare	4	5	8	6	7	3.23
Environmental protection	0	3	6	8	13	4.03

Note: scale from 1 to 5, where 1 represents "Not at all" and 5 – "Very much"
Source: own processing based on Delphi database

Participants' answers highlight a significant level of "ecological identification", on the first place, based on the weighted average, being the objective related to "environmental protection", and on the third place the "development of organic agriculture". Between these, on the second place, the "development of short supply chains" represents an EU's objective to which respondents consider that they are already contributing, based on the specific activities that they are conducting. With some lower values, but still positioned towards an over average contribution there are also the objectives related to climate changes and animal welfare.

In this context it was interesting to investigate if the characteristics of the local producers and their specific activities could determine some differences regarding the perception of their contribution to the achievement of EU's objectives under assessment (Table 8). The characteristics included in the analysis were age, gender, type of organization and type of certification. In case of age, the initial categories were collapsed into three main ones for a better distribution of the participants – under 34 years, between 34-49 years and 50 years and over.

The analysis highlights the following differences based on the characteristics included in data processing:

- Respondents' age: the participants from the 34-49 years category exhibit higher levels as regards their contribution to EU's important objectives, based on the weighted average values – with only one exception (for "animal welfare"), all other values are the highest registered and strongly supporting a personal "ecological identification". These are local producers with an extensive experience in agri-food production, inclined to adapt easier to potential changes at the level of their specific activities. They are followed by the "Under 34 years" category, with slightly lower values, but still supporting their contribution to these objectives. The participants "50 years and over" seem less inclined to positively evaluate their contribution, especially in terms of "animal welfare" and "combating climate changes";

- Respondents' gender: the male participants consider that they have a greater contribution, as compared to female participants; this is especially noticeable when it comes to "animal welfare" and "combating climate changes";

Table 8. To what extent do you consider that your activity can contribute to the achievement of EU's objective related to: ? (contingency table – participants/activity characteristics) -weighted average-

Category	Subcategories	Combating climate changes	Development of organic agriculture	Development of short supply chains	Animal welfare	Environmental protection
Age group	Under 34 years	3.38	3.88	3.88	3.75	4.00
	34-49 years	3.69	4.23	4.08	3.69	4.31
	50 years and over	2.89	3.33	3.78	2.11	3.67
	Total	3.37	3.87	3.93	3.23	4.03
Gender	Masculine	3.68	3.89	3.95	3.53	4.16
	Feminine	2.82	3.82	3.91	2.73	3.82
	Total	3.37	3.87	3.93	3.23	4.03
Organization form	Association	3.00	4.00	4.00	2.00	3.00
	Individual enterprise	3.71	4.57	4.29	3.71	4.43
	Certified producer	3.29	3.71	3.57	3.00	3.57
	Commercial company	3.27	3.60	3.93	3.20	4.13
	Total	3.37	3.87	3.93	3.23	4.03
Type of certification	Ecological	4.00	4.56	4.33	3.67	4.56
	Mountain product	4.00	4.50	4.00	3.50	4.00
	Traditional	2.50	2.83	4.00	2.33	4.17
	Not yet certified/ Does not know	3.23	3.77	3.62	3.31	3.62
	Total	3.37	3.87	3.93	3.23	4.03

Note: scale from 1 to 5, where 1 represents "Not at all" and 5 – "Very much"
Source: own processing based on Delphi database

- Organization form: based on the type of organization that they represent, the participants from "individual enterprise" category registered the highest values for all the EU's objectives, the ones with over 4 points on this scale being "'development of organic agriculture", "environmental protection" and "development of short supply chains". The participants representing "certified producers" and "commercial companies", although recording lower values they are still inclined to positively evaluate their contribution to these objectives;
- Type of certification: there is an evident correlation between the first two types of certification (ecological and mountain product) and a positive evaluation of the contribution to the EU's objectives, both scoring consistently higher compared to the other categories (traditional and not yet certified/ doesn't know).

Moving on, the participants were asked to evaluate the potential influence of some factors (ecological/technological/political/ related to consumers' preferences/ sales channels) on the future development of their activities (Table 9).

Table 9. How do you think the next factors would influence the development of your activity in the future? -no. of answers-

Factors/Evaluation	Strongly negative	Negative	Neutral	Positive	Strongly positive	Weighted average
A. Ecological/climate changes	9	6	10	4	1	2.4
B. Technological changes	1	3	6	9	11	3.87
C. Changes at the level of the policy/Specific legislation supporting the agricultural activities	6	4	9	0	11	3.2
D. Changes at the level of consumers' preferences	1	2	13	6	8	3.6
E. Changes at the level of the sales channels	1	4	9	5	11	3.7

Note: scale from 1 to 5, where 1 represent a "Strongly negative" influence and – "Strongly positive"
Source: own processing based on Delphi database

Respondents' opinions outline a clustering of the A-E factors into two main categories: the first one, grouping the factors that will, most probably, have a positive influence on the activities' future development and the second one, of the factors that could negatively influence the future evolution of the activities.

From the first category, the main factors that according to the participants would support the future development are "technological changes" (development of new production technologies, more efficient), "changes at the level of the sales channels" (appearance of new methods/ sales channels, that could extend the trade area) and "changes at the level of consumers' preferences " (that would support the development of the product range and the enhancement of the relation between producers and consumers). Last but not least, the "changes at the level of the policy/Specific legislation supporting the agricultural activities" could have, to some degree, a positive influence if they are implemented with the aim of supporting the agricultural activities.

On the other side, the factors that will rather have a negative influence of the future development of the activities are those related to "ecological/climate changes" – outlining as a more difficult element to be managed by the participants at this study.

Based on the participants' and activities' characteristics, there are some differences regarding the evaluation of the positive/negative influence of the A-E factors (Table 10). For example, in the case of "ecological/climate changes", generally evaluated as having a rather negative influence of the activities' future development, those that strongly support this scenario are the participants that hold an "ecological certification", represent an "individual enterprise" and are "50 years and over".

Table 10. How do you think the next factors would influence the development of your activity in the future? (contingency table – participants/activity characteristics) -weighted average-

Category	**Factors/ changes**	**Ecological/ climate**	**Technological**	**Policy/ Specific legislation**	**Consumers' preferences**	**Sales channels**
Age group	Under 34 years	2.50	4.38	3.13	3.88	3.75
	34-49 years	2.69	3.38	2.85	3.23	3.38
	50 years and over	1.89	4.11	3.78	3.89	4.11
	Total	2.40	3.87	3.20	3.60	3.70
Gender	Masculine	2.58	3.79	3.32	3.63	3.68
	Feminine	2.09	4.00	3.00	3.55	3.73
	Total	2.40	3.87	3.20	3.60	3.70

continued on following page

Table 10. Continued

Category	Factors/ changes	Ecological/ climate	Technological	Policy/ Specific legislation	Consumers' preferences	Sales channels
Organization form	Association	2.00	4.00	3.00	3.00	3.00
	Individual enterprise	1.86	3.86	2.29	3.14	3.43
	Certified producer	2.71	3.57	4.43	4.00	3.86
	Commercial company	2.53	4.00	3.07	3.67	3.80
	Total	2.40	3.87	3.20	3.60	3.70
Type of certification	Ecological	1.67	4.11	2.00	3.44	3.56
	Mountain product	2.50	4.00	3.00	3.00	4.50
	Traditional	2.17	3.67	3.67	3.83	4.00
	Not yet certified/ Does not know	3.00	3.77	3.85	3.69	3.54
	Total	2.40	3.87	3.20	3.60	3.70

Note: scale from 1 to 5, where 1 represent a "Strongly negative" influence and 5 – a "Strongly positive" one
Source: own processing based on Delphi database

When it comes to the "technological changes", there is an important agreement between participants regarding the positive influence on the future development (the highest value among A-E factors), firstly supported by those "under 34 years" and "50 years on over", those with an "ecological" and "mountain product" certification, female participants and representatives of "associations" and "commercial companies".

The changes at the level of the policy/specific legislation supporting the agricultural activities, although slightly evaluated towards having a positive influence, did receive both negative and positive ratings from the participants. Those that firstly consider these changes to have a positive influence are "certified producers", those who do not have at this moment a type of certification and with a traditional one, from "50 years and over" category. On the other side, a rather negative rating was received from respondents with an "ecological" certification, representing "individual enterprises" and between 34-49 years.

As regards "consumers' preferences" and "sales channels" changes, although there are some pointwise differences based on the selected characteristics, the overall assessment of these factors supports a positive influence on the future development of the specific activities.

Moving on, the next question investigated the participants' perception regarding the possible changes at the level of their activities that the above A-E factors could prompt in the future (Table 11).

Table 11. Taking into account the A-E factors above, please evaluate the following aspects of your activity that could register some changes -no. of answers-

Aspects/Evaluation	Strong disagreement	Disagreement	Neutral	Agreement	Strong agreement	Weighted average
I will have to gain new skills	0	3	5	5	17	4.2
I will need a larger volume of labor force	1	4	7	9	9	3.7
The labor force will have to gain new skills	0	4	6	5	15	4.03
Labor force' wage level will increase	0	2	6	12	10	4
My work volume will increase	2	1	3	11	13	4.07
I will need consultancy services from competent institutions	1	1	6	11	11	4
Collaboration between producers will develop	1	0	5	9	15	4.23
I will have to communicate better with my clients	1	0	5	7	17	4.3

Note: scale from 1 to 5, where 1 represent a "Strong disagreement" and 5 – a "Strong agreement"
Source: own processing based on Delphi database

The main aspect of the current activities, prone to experiencing some changes in the future, that meet an important agreement level relate to the relation between producers and clients (I will have to communicate better with my clients), the relations between producers (Collaboration between producers will develop), the need for the development of producers' professional/educational skills (I will have to gain new skills), the increasing personal involvement in the activities conducted (My work volume will increase), as well as to the need for the labor force' professional development (The labor force will have to gain new skills).

Other aspects that met a significant agreement level highlight the need for support from competent institutions (regarding consultancy services), the expected impact of the new wage level (an estimated increase), but also the probability of a needed larger labor force volume.

Based on the participants' and activities' characteristics, the analysis highlights the following findings (Table 12):

- The need for supplementary skills – for local producers: the highest ratings in support of this aspect are connected with respondents representing associations and individual enterprises, 50 years and older, that hold a mountain product or ecological certification;
- Volume of labor force: there is a significant agreement regarding the need for a larger volume of labor force, but especially in the case of respondents under 34 years, women, representing associations and having a traditional product certification;
- The need for supplementary skills – for labor force: there is an evident need for the development of skills, but particularly in the case of participants of 50 years and over, representing associations and individual enterprises, men, holding a traditional product certification;

Table 12. Taking into account the A-E factors above, please evaluate the following aspects of your activity that could register some changes (contingency table – participants/activity characteristics) -weighted average-

Category	Factors/ changes	My skills	Labor force volume	Labor force skills	Wage level	My work volume	Consultancy services	Producers' collaboration	Communication with clients
Age group	Under 34 years	3.75	4.00	3.88	4.13	4.00	3.63	4.13	4.00
	34-49 years	4.08	3.38	3.92	3.85	4.08	4.15	4.23	4.31
	50 years and over	4.78	3.89	4.33	4.11	4.11	4.11	4.33	4.56
	Total	4.20	3.70	4.03	4.00	4.07	4.00	4.23	4.30
Gender	Masculine	4.26	3.53	4.05	3.89	4.16	3.89	4.21	4.32
	Feminine	4.09	4.00	4.00	4.18	3.91	4.18	4.27	4.27
	Total	4.20	3.70	4.03	4.00	4.07	4.00	4.23	4.30
Organization form	Association	5.00	4.00	5.00	4.00	4.00	4.00	4.00	3.00
	Individual enterprise	4.71	3.57	4.14	4.14	4.71	4.00	4.43	4.43
	Certified producer	3.86	3.43	3.86	3.57	3.43	4.00	3.86	4.14
	Commercial company	4.07	3.87	4.00	4.13	4.07	4.00	4.33	4.40
	Total	4.20	3.70	4.03	4.00	4.07	4.00	4.23	4.30

continued on following page

Table 12. Continued

Category	Factors/ changes	My skills	Labor force volume	Labor force skills	Wage level	My work volume	Consultancy services	Producers' collaboration	Communication with clients
Type of certification	Ecological	4.44	3.33	4.00	3.67	3.78	3.67	4.11	4.00
	Mountain product	4.50	3.50	4.00	4.00	5.00	4.00	4.00	3.50
	Traditional	3.83	4.00	4.17	4.17	4.33	4.00	4.17	4.50
	Not yet certified/ Does not know	4.15	3.85	4.00	4.15	4.00	4.23	4.38	4.54
	Total	4.20	3.70	4.03	4.00	4.07	4.00	4.23	4.30

Note: scale from 1 to 5, where 1 represent a "Strong disagreement" and 5 – a "Strong agreement"
Source: own processing based on Delphi database

- Labor force' wage level: the expected increase of the labor force' wage level in the future is firstly supported by respondents under 34 years and those 50 years and over, women, representing individual enterprises and commercial companies and holding a traditional product certification but also by those not yet certified;
- My work volume: in this case, there is a strong agreement between participants regarding the expected increase of their needed involvement when it comes to the personal work volume in the future, more noticeable in the case of participants of 50 years and over, men, representing individual enterprises and holding a mountain or traditional product certification;
- Need for consultancy services: here also, there is a significant agreement regarding participants' need for specialized help from competent authorities/ institutions, the respondents more inclined to apply to these services being those between 34-49 years, women, who currently are not yet certified;
- Collaboration between producers: with the second highest average among the aspects that could register some changes, the collaboration between local producers is expected to increase in the future, the strongest supporters of this scenario being the participants of 50 years al older, especially women, representing individual enterprises and commercial companies, not holding at this moment a type of certification;
- Communication with clients: out of all investigated aspects above, the communication with clients received the highest rating, highlighting the local producers' need to strengthen the direct relations with the clients – a scenario firstly supported by respondents of 50 years and over, especially men, representing individual enterprises and commercial companies, being not yet certified or holding a traditional product certification.

Following the evident need for the development of local producers' professional and educational skills, the participants were asked to indicated what do they feel they need to learn in order to face the potential changes in the next period of time. Being an open question, they had the possibility of offering multiple answers that later were grouped into six main categories (Table 13).

Table 13. What would be the supplementary skills that you would have to gain in order to face the potential changes determined by the above factors? (A-E)

Supplementary skills – main categories	Number of answers
Commercial skills (marketing, sales, negotiation)	7
Technological skills (production technics and technologies)	8
IT skills (knowledge, on-line visibility, artificial intelligence)	4
Economic skills (business management, financial management)	4
Consumers relation skills (communication, adapting to clients' needs)	6
Other skills -professional/educational (specialized trainings, entrepreneurial development, legislative/juridical knowledge)	11

Source: own processing based on Delphi database

Respondents' opinions regarding the supplementary skills needed are pointing, firstly, to those from the professional/educational category, followed by technological skills, commercial skills and consumers relation skills – especially regarding the communication abilities and adaption to clients' needs. Beside those, other skills referring to the IT domain and business management have also been mentioned by participants as important in order to face the potential future changes.

The last questions from this second section of the questionnaire aimed to capture participants' vision regarding the future development of their activities, taking into account the A-E factors that could determine some changes (Table 14).

Table 14. Taking into account the A-E factors above, how do you think your activity will evolve during the next years?

Participants' vision	Number of answers	% in total
I will probably be forced to give up the current activity	0	0.00%
It will reduce	0	0.00%
It will remain the same	7	23.33%
It will develop	16	53.33%
It will develop significantly	7	23.33%

Source: own processing based on Delphi database

To a large extent, the participants' answers outline a vision towards the development of their activities in the next period of time, even taking into account the A-E factors that could solicit some changes, both from a personal perspective (skills, aptitudes, new knowledge and abilities) and a professional one – the need to adapt their activities to a new set of coordinates of climatic, technological and political nature.

Based on the age of the participants, those more inclined to support the future development scenario are under 34 years, followed by the 34-39 years category (Table 15). The respondents of 50 years and over, to a significant extent, also support the idea that the activities will remain the same in the next period. When it comes to gender, women respondents are more inclined to envisage an expansion of their activities, as compared to men. As regards the organization form, the participants representing certified producers mainly support the balanced scenario, where the activities will remain the same in the future, while those representing commercial companies strongly endorse the development scenario. Last but not least, based on the type of certification, the participants that, firstly, support the idea that their activities will develop in the future are those holding an ecological and traditional certification.

Table 15. Taking into account the A-E factors above, how do you think your activity will evolve during the next years? (contingency table – participants/activity characteristics)

Category	Factors/ % in total category	Give up the current activity	Will reduce	Will remain the same	Will develop	Will develop significantly
Age group	Under 34 years	-	-	-	62.50	37.50
	34-49 years	-	-	23.08	53.85	23.08
	50 years and over	-	-	44.44	44.44	11.11
	Total	-	-	23.33	53.33	23.33
Gender	Masculine	-	-	26.32	47.37	26.32
	Feminine	-	-	18.18	63.64	18.18
	Total	-	-	23.33	53.33	23.33

continued on following page

Table 15. Continued

Category	Factors/ % in total category	Give up the current activity	Will reduce	Will remain the same	Will develop	Will develop significantly
Organization form	Association	-	-	-	100.00	-
	Individual enterprise	-	-	28.57	42.86	28.57
	Certified producer	-	-	71.43	28.57	-
	Commercial company	-	-	-	66.67	33.33
	Total	-	-	23.33	53.33	23.33
Type of certification	Ecological	-	-	11.11	66.67	22.22
	Mountain product	-	-	50.00	50.00	-
	Traditional	-	-		100.00	-
	Not yet certified/Does not know	-	-	38.46	23.08	38.46
	Total	-	-	23.33	53.33	23.33

Source: own processing based on Delphi database

Information Regarding the Participation the Fair for Agri-Food Producers: "Iași in Dishes: Organic, Traditional, Mountain and Artisan Products"

The third and last section of the questionnaire applied to local producers from the North-East development region aimed to investigate the participation history, the motives for the producers' first and subsequent participation at the fair, the main advantages of participation, how the fair was promoted and the need for the involvement of different institutions in the process of supporting this type of events.

The first question from this section approached the respondents' participation history at the "*Ia i in Dishes*" fair (Table 16).

Table 16. At how many editions of the "Ia i in Dishes" fair have you participated?

Number of editions?	Number of answers
1	0
2	0
3	1
4	2
5	3
6	4
7	5
8	5
9	0
10	10

Source: own processing based on Delphi database

Most participants represent a constant presence at the fair, 1/3 of them having participated at all editions so far and 90% to at least five editions.

The next question focused on the main reason for the first participation at the "*Ia i in Dishes*" fair. The participants were asked to rank 5 main reasons, at the end a total score being calculated for each one – where a higher value indicates a greater importance, according to the respondents, for the respective reason (Table 17).

Table 17. When you have participated for the first time at "Ia i in Dishes" fair, what was the main reason?

Reason/Ranking	1	2	3	4	5	Total score
I have heard of this fair from other producers and I thought to participate also	6	2	3	6	13	2.4
I considered it to be a good opportunity to promote my products	15	12	3	0	0	4.4
I wanted to develop a direct relation with clients	5	12	8	2	3	3.47
I considered it to be a good opportunity to increase my sales volume	4	3	13	7	3	2.93
I wanted to engage in an experience exchange with other participants	0	1	3	15	11	1.8

Source: own processing based on Delphi database

As the first option (rank 1), the most important reason for the first participation at the "*Ia i in Dishes*" fair was the opportunity to promote their products, followed by the fact that they have heard of this fair from other producers and thought to participate also, the need to develop a direct relation with clients and the opportunity to increase the sales volume.

The next options (ranks 2-5) highlight a concentration of participants' motivation around the opportunity to promote their products, the wish to develop a direct relation with clients and to increase the sales volume – this being also the final hierarchy based on the calculated total score for each reason.

Moving one, the next question investigated participants' options regarding the main motivation that led to their decision to participate at several editions of the "*Ia i in Dishes*" fair. In this case, the respondents were asked to assign a note from1 to 5, where 1 represents "Do not agree at all" and 5 "I agree completely" (Table 18).

Table 18. What were the main motives behind the decision to participate at several editions of the "Ia i in Dishes" fair?

Motives/Note	1	2	3	4	5	Weighted average
It has become a tradition for me to participate	0	1	4	7	18	4.4
I had satisfactory financial results	0	0	11	8	11	4
I have managed to develop a network of constant clients	0	0	5	9	16	4.37
My activity has become more visible	0	1	5	8	16	4.3
I have learned from other participants' experience and I have developed partnerships	0	7	6	6	11	3.7
I like the feeling of being part of a dynamic community of local producers	0	0	1	6	23	4.73

Note: scale from 1 to 5, where 1 represents "I do not agree at all" and 5 "I agree completely"
Source: own processing based on Delphi database

The motivation behind the participation at several editions of the "*Ia i in Dishes*" fair can, firstly, be found in the occupational identity sphere, namely the feeling of being part of a dynamic community of local producers, followed by aspects related to the personal sphere – the fact that it has become a tradition for respondents. Also, the development of a network of constant clients, the increased activity' visibility and obtaining some satisfactory financial results outline as important reasons for the participants at this study. On the last position, based on the weighted average calculated, the experience exchange and development of partnerships were also considered as one of the reasons for the constant participation at this fair.

Are there any noticeable differences as regards the motives, based on the participants and activities' characteristics? Will investigate this next (Table 19).

Table 19. What were the main motives behind the decision to participate at several editions of the "Ia i in Dishes" fair? (contingency table – participants/activity characteristics)

Category	Motives/ weighted average	Motive 1	Motive 2	Motive 3	Motive 4	Motive 5	Motive 6
Age group	Under 34 years	4.50	4.25	4.63	4.38	3.63	4.75
	34-49 years	4.46	4.00	4.31	4.15	3.77	4.62
	50 years and over	4.22	3.78	4.22	4.44	3.67	4.89
	Total	4.40	4.00	4.37	4.30	3.70	4.73
Gender	Masculine	4.32	3.95	4.21	4.26	3.53	4.74
	Feminine	4.55	4.09	4.64	4.36	4.00	4.73
	Total	4.40	4.00	4.37	4.30	3.70	4.73
Organization form	Association	4.00	4.00	5.00	4.00	4.00	4.00
	Individual enterprise	4.71	4.29	4.57	4.86	4.14	4.86
	Certified producer	4.00	3.57	3.86	4.00	3.00	4.43
	Commercial company	4.47	4.07	4.47	4.20	3.80	4.87
	Total	4.40	4.00	4.37	4.30	3.70	4.73
Type of certification	Ecological	4.56	4.22	4.44	4.22	4.33	4.67
	Mountain product	4.50	4.50	4.50	5.00	4.00	4.50
	Traditional	4.50	3.50	4.33	4.50	3.17	4.83
	Not yet certified/Does not know	4.23	4.00	4.31	4.15	3.46	4.77
	Total	4.40	4.00	4.37	4.30	3.70	4.73

Notes: 1. scale from 1 to 5, where 1 represents "I do not agree at all" and 5 "I agree completely"
2. Motives 1-6 correspond to those listed in table 18 above
Source: own processing based on Delphi database

The fact that the participation at this fair has become a personal tradition is one of the most important motives – strongly supported by respondents, but firstly by those representing individual enterprises, with an ecological certification, under 34 years old, predominantly women. Having satisfactory financial results also outlines as an important reason, in this case the participants that were less inclined to support this being those holding a traditional certification, representing certified producers and being of 50 years and over.

When it comes to developing a network of constant clients, as an important factor for participating at several editions of the fair, young respondents, predominantly women, representing associations and holding a mountain product certification are first to support their choice. Next, increasing the activity' visibility seems to be especially important for the local producers of 50 years and over, women, representing individual enterprises and again, holding a mountain product certification.

The following motive, learning from other participants' experience and developing partnerships, thou slightly leaning towards the agreement part of the scale, has registered the lowest average value, the participants less inclined to support it being those under 34 years old, predominantly men, representing certified producers and holding a traditional certification.

As for the feeling of being part of a dynamic community of local producers there is no doubt that it strongly influenced the decision behind the participation at several editions of the "*Ia i in Dishes*" fair, placing first among all motives, in this case the strongest pillars being the participants of 50 years and older, representing commercial companies and individual enterprises and holding a traditional certification.

Moving one, when it comes to participants' perception regarding the benefits of participating at the events like "*Ia i in Dishes*", there a strong agreement between respondents – an average value of 4.7 on a scale from 1 to 5, where 1 represents "It did not help me at all" and 5 – "It helped me very much". As regards the way that participants consider these events to have been promoted, in this case the average value (4.16) highlights a positive evaluation of the endeavors undertaken to this end (Table 20).

Tabel 20. How much do you consider these events like "Ia i in Dishes" to have been promoted?

Number of answers	Mean
30	4.16

Note: scale from 1 to 5, where 1 represents "Not at all" and 5 – "Very much"
Source: own processing based on Delphi database

The following question focused on the entities/institutions that according to the participants should be involved in the process of promoting the events like "*Ia i in Dishes*" fair. The respondents were asked to assign a note for each one, on a scale from 1 to 5, where 1 represent "Not at all" and 5 – "Very much" (Table 21).

Table 21. How much do you think the next entities should be involved in promoting the evets like "Ia i in Dishes" fair?

Entities/Note	1	2	3	4	5	Weighted average
Local authorities	0	0	2	5	23	4.7
Producers' associations	0	0	0	4	26	4.87
Academic sector – universities, research institutes and centers	0	0	2	3	25	4.77
Consumers' associations	0	0	4	4	22	4.6
Agricultural consultancy	0	1	3	8	18	4.43
Mass media	0	0	0	4	26	4.87
Nongovernmental organizations	0	0	7	5	18	4.37

Note: scale from 1 to 5, where 1 represents "Not at all" and 5 – "Very much"
Source: own processing based on Delphi database

Participants' answers highlight the need for the involvement of all entities/institutions in promoting this type of events, but the main role should go to producers' associations, mass media, academic sector (universities, research institutes and centers) and to local authorities. Alongside these, also consumers' associations and nongovernmental organizations should play an important role in this process according to the respondents.

Based on the participants and activity's characteristics, a higher need for the involvement of these entities in promoting the events like "*Ia i in Dishes*" fair is supported, firstly, by the respondents under 34 years, representing commercial companies and holding an ecological certification (Table 22). As regards gender, the female respondents seem to endorse this scenario to a higher extent as compared to male respondents, when it comes to the academic sector, consumers' associations, agricultural consultancy, mass media and NGOs.

Table 22. How much do you think the next entities should be involved in promoting the evets like "Ia i in Dishes" fair? (contingency table – participants/activity characteristics)

Category	Entities/ weighted average	LA	PA	AS	CA	AC	MM	NGO
Age group	Under 34 years	5.00	5.00	5.00	4.75	4.50	5.00	4.13
	34-49 years	4.69	4.77	4.62	4.62	4.23	4.85	4.38
	50 years and over	4.44	4.89	4.78	4.44	4.67	4.78	4.56
	Total	4.70	4.87	4.77	4.60	4.43	4.87	4.37
Gender	Masculine	4.74	4.89	4.74	4.53	4.37	4.84	4.26
	Feminine	4.64	4.82	4.82	4.73	4.55	4.91	4.55
	Total	4.70	4.87	4.77	4.60	4.43	4.87	4.37
Organization form	Association	4.00	5.00	5.00	4.00	4.00	4.00	4.00
	Individual enterprise	4.86	5.00	4.86	4.86	4.86	5.00	4.86
	Certified producer	4.00	4.43	4.14	4.00	4.00	4.57	4.00
	Commercial company	5.00	5.00	5.00	4.80	4.47	5.00	4.33
	Total	4.70	4.87	4.77	4.60	4.43	4.87	4.37
Type of certification	Ecological	4.89	5.00	5.00	4.89	4.44	4.89	4.67
	Mountain product	4.50	5.00	4.50	4.50	4.50	5.00	4.50
	Traditional	4.83	4.83	4.83	4.33	4.50	4.83	4.33
	Not yet certified/ Does not know	4.54	4.77	4.62	4.54	4.38	4.85	4.15
	Total	4.70	4.87	4.77	4.60	4.43	4.87	4.37

Notes: 1.scale from 1 to 5, where 1 represents "Not at all" and 5 – "Very much"

2. Acronyms represent: LA – local authorities, PA – producers' associations, AS – academic sector, CA- consumers' associations, AC – Agricultural consultancy, MM- mass media, NGO- nongovernmental organizations

Source: own processing based on Delphi database

The last question from this third section dedicated to the events like "*Ia i in Dishes*" fair focused on the respondents' intention to participate at the future editions that will be organized (Tabel 23).

Table 23. How do you evaluate your intention to participate, in the future, at the events like "Ia i in Dishes" fair?

Number of answers	Mean
30	4.83

Notes: scale from 1 to 5, where 1 represents 'I will certainly not participate" and 5 – "I will certainly participate"

Source: own processing based on Delphi database

Respondents' answers outline an important agreement regarding the intention to participate at the future editions of the fair for agri-food producers "*Ia i in Dishes: Organic, Traditional, Mountain and Artisan Products*", highlighting the importance of these events for the agricultural activities that they are conducting.

Finally, besides the above-mentioned sections of the Delphi exercise, a final question addressed the importance of studies such as this one for local producers from the North-East development region of Romania (Table 24).

Table 24. Are studies such as this one important to you?

Answer	Number
Yes	30
No	0

Source: own processing based on Delphi database

Unanimously, the local producers that have participated at this research considered this type of study important to them, highlighting their increased interest for the subject, as well as the need to communicate, in this way, the problems and challenges they are facing in conducting their specific activities.

CONCLUSION

This study that approached the subject of local producers' participation at the events like "*Ia i in Dishes*" focused on the *main problems and challenges* in deployment of the specific activities, the *participatory vision regarding their contribution to some EU's important objectives*, on the *potential changes* determined by a series of diverse factors (climate, technological, legislative, consumers' preferences) as well as on aspects related to their participation, throughout the time, at numerous editions of this fair – from the perspective of participation' history, motivation, perceived benefits, organization and the need for the involvement of different entities in promoting the events of this type.

If we were to outline the main demographical, educational and occupational characteristics of the participants at this study, those would be:

- The majority – people under 49 years of age, with a higher educational level – especially in technical domains (engineer, agronomist engineer, zootechnician engineer, food industry and biophysics);
- Over 50% from Ia i county, representing mainly commercial companies, but also certified producers and individual enterprises and selling vegetables/ fruits/ juices/ can products, bee products, meat / meat-based products (fish, pork, chicken, beef, wild boar and deer), Grain mill, bakery, pastry products and cosmetic products;
- The majority hold some type of certification – ecological, traditional and/or mountain product

As regards the current *main problems and challenges* faced in deployment of their activities, the most important ones, according to respondents, are related to increase of prices, lack of labor force, bureaucracy, production sales possibilities and ensuring the needed specialized labor force. Even in this context, most of them would opt for the activity' development and a better organization, as some of the changes that they would like to implement in the next period.

When in comes to the contribution of their activity to reaching *some EU's important objectives*, the answers outline a high level of "ecological identification" – environmental protection and development of organic agriculture being two of the main objectives that they mainly consider to contribute to, but also to the development of short supply chains.

How would diverse factors (climate, technological, legislative, consumers' preferences, distribution channels) influence the development of the activities in the future? The respondents' opinions outline two categories, the first grouping factor that would likely have a positive impact and the second one, of factors that could negatively influence the future evolution. In the first category, the main factors that, according to participants, would support the development are technological changes, changes at the level of the sales channels and changes at the level of consumers' preferences, while in the second category, with a negative influence, there are the ecological/climate changes.

What changes could these factors determine at the level of the specific activities? The main ones, according to respondents, could occur at the level of the relations between producers and clients (a better communication), between producers (a stronger collaboration), the educational/professional skills of producers (the need to gain new competences, skills) and of the personal involvement in the activities conducted (an increase of the work volume).

So, what are the *supplementary skills* that respondents consider they need to gain in order to face these changes? The answers firstly turn to professional/educational ones, followed by technological skills (production technics and technologies), commercial skills (marketing, sales, negotiation) and consumers relation skills – especially communication abilities and adaption to clients' needs.

What is the *participatory vision* regarding the future of the activities, taking into account the potential changes determined by the diverse factors (climate, technological, legislative, consumers' preferences, distribution channels)? To a large extent, the respondents' options outline a *vision towards the development of their activities* in the next period – over 75% of them considering that their activities will develop or significantly develop in the future.

The *Ia i in Dishes"* fair – participation' history, the motives behind the first/later participations, perceived benefits, promoting the events of this type and the need for involvement of different entities in this process:

- The main reason for being *present for the first time* at "*Ia i in Dishes"* fair? There is an evident concentration of participants' motivation around the opportunity to promote their products, the wish to develop a direct relation with consumers and to increase the sales volume. But what about the ones related to the *participation at several editions*? In this case, these are, firstly, connected to the occupational sphere, namely the feeling of being part of a dynamic community of local producers, followed by aspects related to the personal sphere – the fact that is has become a tradition for them to participate. Also, the development of a network of constant clients, the increase of activity' visibility and obtaining some satisfactory financial results also represent important motives for the participants at this study;
- Local producers' perception regarding *the benefits of participating* at the events like "*Ia i in Dishes"* fair? In this context, there is an important agreement between participants, the mean value of answers being 4.7 (on a scale from 1 to 5, where 1 represent "It did not help me at all" and 5 – "It helped me very much");
- What about the way these events *were promoted*? Participants' options outline a positive evaluation of the effort taken to promote these events, but also leaving some space for improvement –a mean values of 4.16, on a scale from 1 to 5, where 1 represents "Not at all" and 5 – "Very much";
- What entities/ institutions should be involved in the process of *promoting these events*? In this case, there was a significant agreement between participants regarding the need of involvement of all institutions in this process, but

the main role should go to producers' associations, mass media, academic sector (universities, research institutes and centers) and to local authorities;

- Intention of *participating at the future editions* of the "*Ia i in Dishes: Organic, Traditional, Mountain and Artisan Products*" fair? There is a general consensus regarding the intention of participating at the future editions of the " *Ia i in Dishes*" fair, highlighting the importance of these events for the activities that local producers are conducting.

ACKNOWLEDGMENT

This research was carried out within CITIES 2030 Horizon Project – "*Co-creating resIlient and susTaInable food systEms towards FOOD 2030*". This project has received funding from the European Union's Horizon 2020 research and innovation programme under grant agreement No 101000640.

REFERENCES

Auge-Laribe, M. 1949. Bulletin de la Societe francaise d'economie rurale, Vol I, issue 1-2, pp. 31.39

Barret, C. B., & Reardon, T. (2000). *Asset, Activity and Income diversification Amomg African Agriculturalists: Some practical Issues*. Cornell University.

Berthelier, P., & Lipchitz, A. (2005). Quel role joue l'agriculture dans la croissance et le development? *Revue Tiers Monde*, *183*(3), 603–624.

Davis, B., Winters, P., Carlleto, G., Covarrubias, K., Quinones, E., Zezza, A., Stamoulis, K., Bonomi, G., & DiGiuseppe, S. 2007. Rural income generating Activities: A cross country comparison. Washinghton DC, World Bank – FAO. Background paper for the World Development Report 2008

Dona, I. (2015). *Economie rurală*. Editura Economică.

Errington, A. (1997). *Coming home? The emerging Agenda for Rural Development Research in the UK*, Annual Conference of the Agricultural Economics Society Conference, Edinburgh, pp 21-24, March 1997

Fefer, J. P., De-Urioste Stone, S., Daigle, J., & Silka, L. (2016). Using the Delphi technique to identify key elements for effective and sustainable visitor use planning frameworks. *SAGE Open*, *6*(2), 1–16. DOI: 10.1177/2158244016643141

Gavrilescu, D., & Florian, V. (coordonatori). Autori: Alexandri, C., Chi ea, L.F., Chi ea, M.A., Florian, V., Popescu, M., Rusu, M., Toderoiu, F., Tudor, M.M. (2007). *Economia rurală din România*. Editura Terra Nostra, Ia i, ISBN 978-973-8432-76-5

Horrillo, A. M., Mesias, F. J., Elghannam, A., & Gaspar, P. (2016). Is there a future for organic production in high ecological value ecosystems? *Agricultural Systems*, *143*, 114–125. DOI: 10.1016/j.agsy.2015.12.015

Kolb, J. H., & Brunner, E. D. (1946). *A Study of Rural Society*. Houghton Mifflin.

Mukherjeel, N., Hug, J., Sutherland, W. J., McNeil, J., Van Opstal, M., Dahdouh-Guebas, F., & Koedam, N. (2015). The Delphi technique in ecology and biological conservation: Applications and guidelines. *Methods in Ecology and Evolution*, *6*(9), 1097–1109. DOI: 10.1111/2041-210X.12387

Rusu, M. (2005). *Dezvoltare rurală – politici i structuri economice*. Editura Expert.

Compilation of References

Abnett, K. (2025, April 7). EU considering international CO2 credits to meet new climate goal, sources say. *Reuters*. https://www.reuters.com/sustainability/cop/eu-considering-international-co2-credits-meet-new-climate-goal-sources-say-2025-04-07/

Adamov, T., Ciolac, R., Iancu, T., Brad, I., Pe , E., Popescu, G., & muleac, L. (2020). Sustainability of Agritourism Activity. Initiatives and Challenges in Romanian Mountain Rural Regions. *Sustainability (Basel)*, *12*(6), 2502. DOI: 10.3390/su12062502

Adamowicz, M., & Zwolińska-Ligaj, M. (2018). New concepts for rural development in the strategies and policies of the European Union. *Economic and Regional Studies/Studia Ekonomiczne i Regionalne, 11*(3), 7-31.

ADB. (2016). *Asian Development Outlook*. Asian Development Bank.

ADB. (2017). *Armenia Country Partnership Strategy*. Asian Development Bank.

Adewusi, A. O., Chiekezi, N. R., & Eyo-Udo, N. L.Adebunmi Okechukwu AdewusiNjideka Rita ChiekezieNsisong Louis Eyo-Udo. (2022). Cybersecurity threats in agriculture supply chains: A comprehensive review. *World Journal of Advanced Research and Reviews*, *15*(3), 490–500. DOI: 10.30574/wjarr.2022.15.3.0888

Adhikari, L., Komarek, A. M., de Voil, P., & Rodriguez, D. (2023). A framework for the assessment of farm diversification options in broadacre agriculture. *Agricultural Systems*, *210*, 103724. DOI: 10.1016/j.agsy.2023.103724

Ağızan, S., & Bayramoğlu, Z. (2021). Comparative investment analysis of agricultural irrigation systems. *Tekirdag Ziraat Fakültesi Dergisi*, *18*(2), 222–233. DOI: 10.33462/jotaf.745548

Agoraki, K. K., Deirmentzoglou, G. A., Psychalis, M., & Apostolopoulos, S. (2024). Types of Innovation and Sustainable Development: Evidence from Medium-and Large-Sized Firms. [IJITM]. *International Journal on Management of Innovation & Technology*, *21*(02), 1–18. DOI: 10.1142/S0219877024500135

AgriCaptureCO2. (2023). Project plan and deliverables. https://agricaptureco2.eu/project-plan-and-deliverables/

Ahlmeyer, F., & Volgmann, K. (2023). What Can We Expect for the Development of Rural Areas in Europe?—Trends of the Last Decade and Their Opportunities for Rural Regeneration. *Sustainability (Basel)*, *15*(6), 5485. DOI: 10.3390/su15065485

Ahmadzai, H., Tutundjian, S., & Elouafi, I. (2021). Policies for Sustainable Agriculture and Livelihood in Marginal Lands: A Review. *Sustainability (Basel)*, *13*(16), 8692. DOI: 10.3390/su13168692

Ahmed, N., De, D., & Hussain, I. (2018). Internet of Things (IoT) for smart precision agriculture and farming in rural areas. *IEEE Internet of Things Journal*, *5*(6), 4890–4899. DOI: 10.1109/JIOT.2018.2879579

Ahmed, N., & Shakoor, N. (2025). Advancing agriculture through IoT, Big Data, and AI: A review of smart technologies enabling sustainability. *Smart Agricultural Technology*, *10*, 100848. DOI: 10.1016/j.atech.2025.100848

Aiello, G., Giovino, I., Vallone, M., & Catania, P. (2017). A multi objective approach to short food supply chain management. *Chemical Engineering Transactions*, *58*, 313–318. DOI: 10.3303/CET1758053

Aiken, J. D. (2021, April 21). Ag carbon credits. *Cornhusker Economics*. https://agecon.unl.edu/ag-carbon-credits

Ala'F, K., Alqammaz, A., Khasawneh, A., Abualigah, L., Darabkh, K., & Zinonos, Z. (2025). An environmental remote sensing and prediction model for an IoT smart irrigation system based on an enhanced wind-driven optimization algorithm. *Computers & Electrical Engineering*, *122*, 109889. DOI: 10.1016/j.compeleceng.2024.109889

Al-Ababneh, H. A. (2020). Modern trends of digital marketing development in the world. *PalArch's Journal of Archaeology of Egypt/Egyptology, 17*(8): 121-139.

Al-Busaidi, Z. Q. (2008). Qualitative research and its uses in health care. *Sultan Qaboos University Medical Journal*, *8*(1), 11–19. DOI: 10.18295/2075-0528.2688

Alessandrini, M. (2024a). Final reflections—Short Food Supply Chains in the agri-food context: Charting the future agenda. In *Regulating Short Food Supply Chains in the EU* (Vol. 28). Springer., DOI: 10.1007/978-3-031-69390-8_8

Almansour, M., & Akrami, M. (2024). Towards Zero Waste: An In-Depth Analysis of National Policies, Strategies, and Case Studies in Waste Minimisation. *Sustainability (Basel), 16*(22), 10105. DOI: 10.3390/su162210105

Alonso, I. B., & Pozas, B. M. (2024). Following the circular economy in European rural municipalities through the Spanish Urban Agenda. *Ecological Economics, 224*, 108263. DOI: 10.1016/j.ecolecon.2024.108263

Altieri, M. A., & Toledo, V. M. (2011). The agroecological revolution in Latin America: Rescuing nature, ensuring food sovereignty and empowering peasants. *The Journal of Peasant Studies, 38*(3), 587–612. DOI: 10.1080/03066150.2011.582947

Ameen, A., & Raza, S. (2017). Green revolution: A review. *International Journal of Advances in Scientific Research, 3*(12), 129–137. DOI: 10.7439/ijasr.v3i12.4410

Amelung, W., Bossio, D., de Vries, W., Kögel-Knabner, I., Lehmann, J., Amundson, R., Bol, R., Collins, C., Lal, R., Leifeld, J., Minasny, B., Pan, G., Paustian, K., Rumpel, C., Sanderman, J., van Groenigen, J. W., Mooney, S., van Wesemael, B., Wander, M., & Chabbi, A. (2020). Towards a global- scale soil climate mitigation strategy. *Nature Communications, 11*(1), 5427. DOI: 10.1038/s41467-020-18887-7

Anderson, A., McElwee, G., & Vesala, K. (2006). Developing the entrepreneurial skills of farmers: Some myths explored. *International Journal of Entrepreneurial Behaviour & Research, 12*(1).

Anderson, T. R., Hawkins, E., & Jones, P. D. (2016). CO2, the greenhouse effect and global warming: From the pioneering work of Arrhenius and Callendar to today's Earth System Models. *Endeavour, 40*(3), 178–187. DOI: 10.1016/j.endeavour.2016.07.002

Andrews, M. (2013). *The limits of institutional reform in development.* Cambridge University Press. DOI: 10.1017/CBO9781139060974

Andrews, M., Pritchett, L., & Woolcock, M. (2017). *Building state capability: Evidence, analysis, action.* Oxford University Press. DOI: 10.1093/acprof:oso/9780198747482.001.0001

Angelakis, A., Zaccaria, D., Krasilnikoff, J., Salgot, M., Bazza, M., Roccaro, P., Jimenez, B., Kumar, A., Yinghua, W., Baba, A., Harrison, J., Jimenez, A., & Fereres, E. (2020). Irrigation of world agricultural lands: Evolution through the millennia. *Water (Basel), 12*(5), 1285. DOI: 10.3390/w12051285

Antonijević, M., Bradić-Martinović, A., Banović, J., & Ivanović, Đ. (2023). Is There a Relationship Between Country Development and Citizens' Level of Digital Skills?. *Economic Analysis: journal of emerging economies 56*, 57-68, https://doi .org/.DOI: 10.28934/ea.23.56.1

Antonio, A., & Tuffley, D. (2014). The Gender Digital Divide in Developing Countries. *Future Internet*, *6*(4), 673–687. DOI: 10.3390/fi6040673

Aouinait, C., Christen, D., Carlen, C., Mehauden, L., Mora, P., Massar, B., & Frederiks, M. (2022). Motivations and barriers for engagement in short food supply chains: Insights from European focus groups. *International Journal of Food Studies, 11*(SI), a8. DOI: 10.7455/ijfs/11.si.2022.a8

Apostolopoulos, S., Makris, I., Macaulay, B., & Dimitrakopoulos, P. (2024). Private Enterprises and Innovative Interventions in Long-Term Care for Older People: Insights Into Residual Stereotypes of Greek Rural Areas. In *European Conference on Innovation and Entrepreneurship* (pp. 54-61). Academic Conferences International Limited. DOI: 10.34190/ecie.19.1.2402

Apostolopoulos, N., Al-Dajani, H., Holt, D., Jones, P., & Newbery, R. (2018). Entrepreneurship and the sustainable development goals. In *Entrepreneurship and the sustainable development goals* (pp. 1–7). Emerald Publishing Limited. DOI: 10.1108/S2040-724620180000008005

Apostolopoulos, N., Liargovas, P., Stavroyiannis, S., Makris, I., Apostolopoulos, S., Petropoulos, D., & Anastasopoulou, E. (2020b). Sustaining rural areas, rural tourism enterprises and EU development policies: A multi-layer conceptualisation of the obstacles in Greece. *Sustainability (Basel), 12*(18), 7687. DOI: 10.3390/su12187687

Apostolopoulos, N., Ratten, V., Stavroyiannis, S., Makris, I., Apostolopoulos, S., & Liargovas, P. (2020a). Rural health enterprises in the EU context: A systematic literature review and research agenda. *Journal of Enterprising Communities: People and Places in the Global Economy, 14*(4), 563–582. DOI: 10.1108/JEC-04-2020-0070

Arias-Vargas, F. J., Ribes-Giner, G., & Garcés-Giraldo, L. F. (2022). Rural entrepreneurship: A historical approach. *Retos Revista de Ciencias de la Administración y Economía, 12*(23), 45–66. DOI: 10.17163/ret.n23.2022.03

Aronica, M., Cracolici, M. F., Insolda, D., Piacentino, D., & Tosi, S. (2023). A long-term vision for rural areas: A case study of Sicilian farms. *Regional Studies, Regional Science, 10*(1), 640–658. DOI: 10.1080/21681376.2023.2225569

Arru, B., Furesi, R., Madau, F. A., & Pulina, P. (2021). Economic performance of agritourism: An analysis of farms located in a less favoured area in Italy. *Agricultural and Food Economics, 9*(1), 1–21. DOI: 10.1186/s40100-021-00199-z

Arsić, S., Stojanović, A., Milošević, I., & Gajić, M. (2022). Positioning of the Republic of Serbia according to the index of digital economy and society in South-East Europe. *An international serial publication for theory and practice of Management Science*, International May Conference on Strategic Management – IMCSM22, May 28, 2022, Bor, Serbia, 300-309.

Arsić, S., Bulatović, M., Rakin, M., Jeločnik, M., & Subić, J. (2018). Economic and Ecological Profitability of the Use of Whey in Dairy and Food Industry. *Large Animal Review, 24*(3), 99–105.

Åslund, A. (2013). How Capitalism Was Built: The Transformation of Central and Eastern Europe, Russia, the Caucasus, and Central Asia (2nd ed.). Cambridge University Press.

Åslund, A. (2002). *Building capitalism: The transformation of the former Soviet bloc*. Cambridge University Press.

Asmit, B., Simatupang, T. M., Rudito, B., & Novani, S. (2024). Uncovering the building blocks of rural entrepreneurship: A comprehensive framework for mapping the components of rural entrepreneurial ecosystems. *Heliyon, 10*(1), e24139. DOI: 10.1016/j.heliyon.2024.e24139

Aubry, C., & Kebir, L. (2013). Shortening food supply chains: A means for maintaining agriculture close to urban areas? The case of the French metropolitan area of Paris. *Food Policy, 41*, 85–93. DOI: 10.1016/j.foodpol.2013.04.006

Auge-Laribe, M. 1949. Bulletin de la Societe francaise d'economie rurale, Vol I, issue 1-2, pp. 31.39

Avramenko, A., & Silver, J. A. K. (2009). Rural entrepreneurship: Expanding the horizons. *International Journal of Entrepreneurship and Innovation Management, 11*(2), 140. Advance online publication. DOI: 10.1504/IJEIM.2010.030065

Azevedo, D. (2019). Precision agriculture and the smart village concept. In *Smart Villages in the EU and Beyond* (pp. 83–97). Emerald Publishing Limited. DOI: 10.1108/978-1-78769-845-120191007

Bakić, O. (2010). *Marketing u turizmu*. Univerzitet Singidunum.

Balaban, S., Joksimović, M., & Stoiljković, B. (2022). The determinants of growing agri-food export: The case of CEE countries. *Ekonomika Poljoprivrede, 69*(3), 877–886. DOI: 10.5937/ekoPolj2203877B

Balaban, S., Milenkovic, I., & Joksimović, M. (2023). *The euro exchange rate's resistance to the exogenous shock caused by COVID-19*. Strategic Management-International Journal of Strategic Management and Decision Support Systems in Strategic Management.

Banaduc, D., Simic, V., Cianfaglione, K., Barinova, S., Afanasyev, S., Oktener, A., McCall, G., Simic, S., & Curtean Banaduc, A. (2022). Freshwater as a sustainable resource and generator of secondary resources in the 21st century: Stressors, threats, risks, management and protection strategies, and conservation approaches. *International Journal of Environmental Research and Public Health, 19*(24), 16570. DOI: 10.3390/ijerph192416570 PMID: 36554449

Bannor, R. K., Ros-Tonen, M. A., Mensah, P. O., Derkyi, M., & Nassah, V. F. (2021). Entrepreneurial behaviour among non-timber forest product-growing farmers in Ghana: An analysis in support of a reforestation policy. *Forest Policy and Economics, 122*, 102331. DOI: 10.1016/j.forpol.2020.102331

Banu, N., & Fazal, S. (2025). Climate Change, Livelihood Crisis and Resilience: An Introduction. In *Livelihoods and Well-Being in the Era of Climate Change*. Springer., DOI: 10.1007/978-3-031-81132-6_1

Barber, D.III, Harris, M. L., & Jones, J. (2021). An Overview of Rural Entrepreneurship and Future Directions. *Journal of Small Business Strategy, 31*(4), 1–4. DOI: 10.53703/001c.29468

Baron, J., Poff, N., Angermeier, P., Dahm, C., Gleick, P., Hairston, N.Jr, Jackson, R., Johnson, C., Richter, B., & Steinman, A. (2002). Meeting ecological and societal needs for freshwater. *Ecological Applications, 12*(5), 1247–1260. DOI: 10.1890/1051-0761(2002)012[1247:MEASNF]2.0.CO;2

Barot, S., Allard, V., Cantarel, A., Enjalbert, J., Gauffreteau, A., Goldringer, I., Lata, J.-C., Le Roux, X., Niboyet, A., & Porcher, E. (2017). Designing mixtures of varieties for multifunctional agriculture with the help of ecology. A review. *Agronomy for Sustainable Development, 37*(2), 1–20. DOI: 10.1007/s13593-017-0418-x

Barret, C. B., & Reardon, T. (2000). *Asset, Activity and Income diversification Amomg African Agriculturalists: Some practical Issues*. Cornell University.

Barr, N. (2001). *The welfare state as piggy bank: Information, risk, uncertainty, and the role of the state*. Oxford University Press. DOI: 10.1093/0199246599.001.0001

Barry, C. (2012). *Commercialisation des produits agricoles. Un producteur sur cinq vend en circuit court.* Agreste Primeur, 275. http://agreste.agriculture.gouv.fr/IMG/pdf/primeur275.pdf

Bartolini, F., Andreoli, M., & Brunori, G. (2014). Explaining determinants of the on-farm diversification: Empirical evidence from Tuscany region. *Bio-Based and Applied Economics*, *3*(2), 137–157.

Bayir, B., Charles, A., Sekhari, A., & Ouzrout, Y. (2022). Issues and challenges in short food supply chains: A systematic literature review. *Sustainability (Basel)*, *14*(5), 3029. DOI: 10.3390/su14053029

Bazzani, C., & Canavari, M. (2017). Is local a matter of food miles or food traditions? *Italian Journal of Food Science*, *29*(3), 505–517.

Beekwilder, J., Hall, R. D., & de Vos, C. H. R. (2005). Identification and dietary relevance of antioxidants from raspberry. *BioFactors (Oxford, England)*, *23*(4), 197–205. DOI: 10.1002/biof.5520230404

Belletti, G., Brunori, G., Marescotti, A., & Rossi, A. (2003). Multifunctionality and rural development: a multilevel approach.

Benedek, Z., Fertő, I., Galamba Marreiros, C., Aguiar, P. M. D., Pocol, C. B., Čechura, L., Põder, A., Pääso, P., & Bakucs, Z. (2021). Farm diversification as a potential success factor for small-scale farmers constrained by COVID-related lockdown. Contributions from a survey conducted in four European countries during the first wave of COVID-19. *PLoS One*, *16*(5), e0251715. DOI: 10.1371/journal.pone.0251715

Berger, E. S., Von Briel, F., Davidsson, P., & Kuckertz, A. (2021). Digital or not–The future of entrepreneurship and innovation: Introduction to the special issue. *Journal of Business Research*, *125*, 436–442. DOI: 10.1016/j.jbusres.2019.12.020

Berthelier, P., & Lipchitz, A. (2005). Quel role joue l'agriculture dans la croissance et le development? *Revue Tiers Monde*, *183*(3), 603–624.

Berti, G., & Mulligan, C. (2016). Competitiveness of small farms and innovative food supply chains: The role of food hubs in creating sustainable regional and local food systems. *Sustainability (Basel)*, *8*(7), 616. DOI: 10.3390/su8070616

Bessière, J. (1998). Local development and heritage: Traditional food and cuisine as tourist attractions in rural areas. *Sociologia Ruralis*, *38*(1), 21–34. DOI: 10.1111/1467-9523.00061

Bilska, B., Piecek, M., & Kołożyn-Krajewska, D. (2018). Food valorization in sustainable development. *Problems of World Agriculture, 18*(2), 22–28.

Bin, X., & Jiangyong, L. U. (2009). Foreign direct investment, processing trade, and the sophistication of China's exports. *China Economic Review, 20*(3), 425–439. DOI: 10.1016/j.chieco.2009.01.004

Bird, G., Hussain, M., & Joyce, J. (2004). Many happy returns? Recidivism and the IMF. *Journal of International Money and Finance, 23*(2), 231–251. DOI: 10.1016/j.jimonfin.2003.12.002

Black, B. S., Kraakman, R., & Tarassova, A. (2000). Russian privatization and corporate governance: What went wrong? *Stanford Law Review, 52*(6), 1731–1808. DOI: 10.2307/1229501

Blay-Palmer, A., Santini, G., Halliday, J., Malec, R., Carey, J., Keller, L., Ni, J., Taguchi, M., & van Veenhuizen, R. (2021). City region food systems: Building resilience to COVID-19 and other shocks. *Sustainability (Basel), 13*(3), 1325. DOI: 10.3390/su13031325

Bocken, N. M. P., Short, S. W., Rana, P., & Evans, S. (2014). *A literature and practice review to develop sustainable* business *model archetypes. Journal of Cleaner Production, 65*, 42–56. DOI: 10.1016/j.jclepro.2013.11.039

Boettke, P. J., & Coyne, C. J. (2009). Context matters: Institutions and entrepreneurship. *Foundations and Trends in Entrepreneurship, 5*(3), 135–209. DOI: 10.1561/0300000018

Bogdanov, N. (2007). Mala ruralna domaćinstva u Srbiji i ruralna nepoljoprivredna ekonomija, MPŠV RS, UNDP, Beograd.

Bogdanov, N., & Babović, M. (2014). Radna snaga i aktivnosti poljoprivrednih gazdinstava, Republički zavod za statistiku, Beograd.

Bojago, E., & Abrham, Y. (2023). Small-scale irrigation (SSI) farming as a climate-smart agriculture (CSA) practice and its influence on livelihood improvement in Offa District, Southern Ethiopia. *Journal of Agriculture and Food Research, 12*, 100534. DOI: 10.1016/j.jafr.2023.100534

Bonell, F. E., & Vaccaro, I. (2022). Techno-herds and cyborg-shepherds in the age of spectacularized bucolism: What lies behind the postcard. *Journal of Rural Studies, 95*, 40–49. DOI: 10.1016/j.jrurstud.2022.07.025

Borensztein, E., De Gregorio, J., & Lee, J. W. (1998). How does foreign direct investment affect economic growth? *Journal of International Economics*, *45*(1), 115–135. DOI: 10.1016/S0022-1996(97)00033-0

Borowiecki, R., Siuta-Tokarska, B., Maroń, J., Suder, M., Thier, A., & Żmija, K. (2021). Developing digital economy and society in the light of the issue of digital convergence of the markets in the European Union countries. *Energies*, *14*(9), 2717. 7. DOI: 10.3390/en14092717

Borsellino, V., Schimmenti, E., & El Bilali, H. (2020). Agri-food markets towards sustainable patterns. *Sustainability (Basel)*, *12*(6), 2193. DOI: 10.3390/su12062193

Bossio, D. A., Cook-Patton, S. C., Ellis, P. W., Fargione, J., Sanderman, J., Smith, P., Wood, S., Zomer, R. J., von Unger, M., Emmer, I. M., & Griscom, B. W. (2020). The role of soil carbon in natural climate solutions. *Nature Sustainability*, *3*(5), 391–398. DOI: 10.1038/s41893-020-0491-z

Bosworth, G. (2012). Characterising rural businesses–Tales from the paperman. *Journal of Rural Studies*, *28*(4), 499–506. DOI: 10.1016/j.jrurstud.2012.07.002

Botsiou, M., & Dagdilelis, V. (2013). Aspects of incorporation of ICT in the Greek agricultural enterprises: The case of a prefecture. *Procedia Technology*, *8*, 387–396. DOI: 10.1016/j.protcy.2013.11.051

Boyne, S. (2005). New Directions in Rural Tourism Impact Research. In Hall, D., Roberts, L., & Mitchell, M. (Eds.), *New Directions in Rural Tourism* (pp. 19–37). Ashgate Publishing Limited.

Brezuleanu, C. O., Brezuleanu, S., & Constantin Iaţco, C. (2013). Development of labour market and entrepreneurial spirit in rural areas. *Environmental Engineering and Management Journal*, (11), 4.

Brummel, R. F., & Nelson, K. C. (2014). Does multifunctionality matter to US farmers? Farmer motivations and conceptions of multifunctionality in dairy systems. *Journal of Environmental Management*, *146*, 451–462. DOI: 10.1016/j.jenvman.2014.07.034

Brunori, G., Nieto, E., Casares, B., Debruyne, L., Tisenkopfs, T., & Brunori, A. (2021). Experts' recommendations to boost sustainable digitalisation of agriculture, forestry and rural areas by 2040. *Pisa, Italy*.

Brunori, G. (2022). Agriculture and rural areas facing the "twin transition": Principles for a sustainable rural digitalisation. [REA]. *Rivista di Economia Agraria*, *77*(3), 3–14. DOI: 10.36253/rea-13983

Buckley, F., Upton, J., Shalloo, L., & Murphy, M. D. Optimizing the Cooling Schedule of Stored Milk on Dairy Farms to Reduced Costs and Carbon Emissions. Available at *SSRN* 5222087.

Buda, D., & Pop, A. (2024). Romanian Local Action Groups' (LAGs) Economic Impact: A Solution to a Problem or a Perpetuating Status Quo of a Gimmick? *Transylvanian Review of Administrative Sciences*, *20*(71), 23–43. DOI: 10.24193/tras.71E.2

Buhalis, D. (2022). Tourism Management and Marketing in Transformation: Introduction and Editor's Statement. In Buhalis, D. (Ed.), *Encyclopedia of Tourism Management and Marketing*. Edward Elgar Publishing., https://www.elgaronline.com/view/nlm-book/9781800377479/b9781800377486.tourism.management.marketing.xml

Bullvine (2025). AI Slashes Feed Costs $31 Per Cow While Your Competitors Pull Further Ahead: The Data-Driven Revolution Reshaping Dairy's Future. https://www.thebullvine.com/news/ai-slashes-feed-costs-31-per-cow-while-your-competitors-pull-further-ahead-the-data-driven-revolution-reshaping-dairys-future/

Burns, E., Silvennoinen, E., Kopnov, V. A., Shchipanova, D. E., Papić-Blagojević, N., & Tomašević, S. (2020). Supporting the Development of Digitally Competent VET Teachers in Serbia and Russia. *The Education and Science Journal, 22*(9), 174-203, ISSN: 1994-5639, DOI: DOI: 10.17853/1994-5639-2020-9-174-203

Buş, R.-M., Lung, M.-S., & Colcer, A.-M. (2017). Traditional crafts and folklore as a means of economic development in the land of Călata. *Territorial Identity and Development Journal*, *2*(1), 64–77. Advance online publication. DOI: 10.23740/TID120175

Butu, M., Dragomir, V., Badan, (Voicila), D.N. (2024) Romania's rural digital transformation and implications for agriculture. *Scientific Papers. Series "Management, Economic Engineering in Agriculture and rural development"*, Vol. *24*(3).

Butu, A., Brumă, I. S., Tanasă, L., Rodino, S., Dinu Vasiliu, C., Dobo , S., & Butu, M. (2020). The impact of COVID-19 crisis upon the consumer buying behavior of fresh vegetables directly from local producers. Case study: The quarantined area of Suceava County, Romania. *International Journal of Environmental Research and Public Health*, *17*(15), 5485. DOI: 10.3390/ijerph17155485

Cabrera VE. (2025). Artificial intelligence applied to dairy science: insights from the Dairy Brain Initiative. Anim Front. Jan 4;14(6):60-63. DOI: 10.1093/af/vfae040

Cachia, M., & Millward, L. (2011). The telephone medium and semi-structured interviews: A complementary fit. *Qualitative Research in Organizations and Management, 6*(3), 265–277. DOI: 10.1108/17465641111188420

Calvo-Sotomayor, I., Laka, J. P., & Aguado, R. (2019). Workforce Ageing and Labour Productivity in Europe. *Sustainability (Basel), 11*(20), 5851. DOI: 10.3390/su11205851

Campos, N. F., & Coricelli, F. (2002). Growth in transition: What we know, what we don't, and what we should. *Journal of Economic Literature, 40*(3), 793–836. DOI: 10.1257/jel.40.3.793

Canfora, I. (2016). Is the short food supply chain an efficient solution for sustainability in food market? *Agriculture and Agricultural Science Procedia, 8*, 402–407. DOI: 10.1016/j.aaspro.2016.02.036

Cantó Calvo, V. M. (2022). *Development of a circular economy evaluation model for hotels* (Doctoral dissertation, Universitat Politècnica de València).

Cao, X., Yan, M., & Wen, J. (2023). Exploring the level and influencing factors of digital village development in China: Insights and recommendations. *Sustainability (Basel), 15*(13), 10423. DOI: 10.3390/su151310423

Capatina, A., Cristea, D. S., Micu, A., Micu, A. E., Empoli, G., & Codignola, F. (2023). Exploring causal recipes of startup acceptance into business incubators: A cross-country study. *International Journal of Entrepreneurial Behaviour & Research, 29*(7), 1584–1612. Advance online publication. DOI: 10.1108/IJEBR-06-2022-0527

Carayannis, E., Jones, P., Liargovas, P., & Apostolopoulos, N. (2020). Entrepreneurship and the European Union policies after 60 years of common European vision: Regional and spatial perspectives. *Journal of Small Business and Entrepreneurship, 32*(6), 517–522. DOI: 10.1080/08276331.2020.1769883

Cardillo, C., Cimino, O., De Rosa, M., & Francescone, M. (2023). The evolution of multifunctional agriculture in Italy. *Sustainability (Basel), 15*(14), 11403. DOI: 10.3390/su151411403

Carmela Annosi, M., Brunetta, F., Capo, F., & Heideveld, L. (2020). Digitalization in the agri-food industry: The relationship between technology and sustainable development. *Management Decision, 58*(8), 1737–1757. DOI: 10.1108/MD-09-2019-1328

Carothers, T. (2002). The end of the transition paradigm. *Journal of Democracy, 13*(1), 5–21. DOI: 10.1353/jod.2002.0003

Carothers, T., & Brechenmacher, S. (2014). *Accountability, transparency, participation, and inclusion: A new development consensus?* Carnegie Endowment for International Peace.

Carrêlo, I., Almeida, R., Narvarte, L., Martinez Moreno, F., & Carrasco, L. (2020). Comparative analysis of the economic feasibility of five large-power photovoltaic irrigation systems in the Mediterranean region. *Renewable Energy, 145*, 2671–2682. DOI: 10.1016/j.renene.2019.08.030

Chakraborty, S. (2021). *Water: Its properties, distribution, and significance*. Riverine Ecology Volume 1: Eco-functionality of the Physical Environment of Rivers, Springer, Cham, Germany, DOI: 10.1007/978-3-030-53897-2_2

Chang, B. P., Massri, C., Reipurth, M., Petropoulou, E., Hüttl-Maack, V., Gawlik, D., ... & Hieke, S. (2022). Barriers and facilitators of purchasing from short food supply chains: Evidence from consumer focus groups in Germany, Spain, Greece and Hungary. *International Journal of Food Studies, 11*(SI), 208-218. https://doi.org/DOI: 10.7455/ijfs/11.SI.2022.a7

Charatsari, C., Kitsios, F., & Lioutas, E. D. (2020). Short food supply chains: The link between participation and farmers' competencies. *Renewable Agriculture and Food Systems, 35*(6), 643–652. DOI: 10.1017/S1742170519000309

Chartier, O., Salle, E., Kull, M., Miller, D., Nieto, E., Vestergård, L., & Iadecola, F. (2021). *Long-yerm vision of rural areas: contribution from the SHERPA science-society-policy platforms: SHERPA position paper*. SHERPA.

Chase, L. E., & Fortina, R. (2023). Environmental and Economic Responses to Precision Feed Management in Dairy Cattle Diets. *Agriculture, 13*(5), 1032. DOI: 10.3390/agriculture13051032

Chatterjee, S., Chaudhuri, R., Vrontis, D., & Thrassou, A. (2022). SME entrepreneurship and digitalization–the potentialities and moderating role of demographic factors. *Technological Forecasting and Social Change, 179*, 121648. DOI: 10.1016/j.techfore.2022.121648

Cheng, C., Gao, Q., Ju, K., & Ma, Y. (2024). How digital skills affect farmers' agricultural entrepreneurship? An explanation from factor availability. *Journal of Innovation & Knowledge, 9*(2), 100477. DOI: 10.1016/j.jik.2024.100477

Chenu, C., Angers, D. A., Barré, P., Derrien, D., Arrouays, D., & Balesdent, J. (2019). Increasing organic stocks in agricultural soils: Knowledge gaps and potential innovations. *Soil & Tillage Research, 188*, 41–52. DOI: 10.1016/j.still.2018.04.011

Chiciudean, G. O., Harun, R., Arion, F. H., Chiciudean, D. I., Oroian, C. F., & Muresan, I. C. (2018). A Critical Approach on Sustainable Renewable Energy Sources in Rural Area: Evidence from North-West Region of Romania. *Energies, 11*(9), 2225. DOI: 10.3390/en11092225

Chiffoleau, Y., & Dourian, T. (2020). Sustainable food supply chains: Is shortening the answer? A literature review for a research and innovation agenda. *Sustainability (Basel), 12*(23), 9831. DOI: 10.3390/su12239831

Chirico, F., Sirmon, D. G., Sciascia, S., & Mazzola, P. (2011). Resource orchestration in family firms: Investigating how entrepreneurial orientation, generational involvement, and participative strategy affect performance. *Strategic Entrepreneurship Journal, 5*(4), 307–326. DOI: 10.1002/sej.121

Chiru, G. (2021). The Development of Entrepreneurship in Romanian rural Area. *Acta Universitatis Danubius Oeconomica, 17*(6).

Cicea, C., Subić, J., & Cvijanović, D. (2008). Beyond agriculture and rural development: investments, efficiency, econometrics. Institute of Agricultural Economics, Belgrade, Serbia.

Ciobanu F.B., Vladu M. (2024). The Leader Programme evolution in the European Union and Romania. *Scientific Papers. Series "Management, Economic Engineering in Agriculture and rural development", 24*(1).

Ciolac, R., Iancu, T., Popescu, G., Adamov, T., Feher, A., & Stanciu, S. (2022). Smart Tourist Village—An Entrepreneurial Necessity for Maramures Rural Area. *Sustainability (Basel), 14*(14), 8914. DOI: 10.3390/su14148914

Čirič, M., Filipovski, Gj. (1972). Regional'nye počvenno-geografičeskie zakonomernosti v Jugoslavii [Regional pedo-geographical features in Yugoslavia], Počvovedenie, AN SSSR, Moskva, 2, 34–38.

Ciruela-Lorenzo, A. M., Del-Aguila-Obra, A. R., Padilla-Meléndez, A., & Plaza-Angulo, J. J. (2020). Digitalization of agri-cooperatives in the smart agriculture context. proposal of a digital diagnosis tool. *Sustainability (Basel), 12*(4), 1325. DOI: 10.3390/su12041325

Clapp, J. (2021). The problem with growing corporate concentration and power in the global food system. *Nature Food, 2*(6), 404–408. DOI: 10.1038/s43016-021-00297-7

Climate Bonds Initiative. (2024). *Sustainable Debt Market Summary 2024*

Coffee, J. C. (1996). Institutional investors in transitional economies: Lessons from the Czech experience. In Frydman, R., Gray, C., & Rapaczynski, A. (Eds.), *Corporate Governance in Central Europe and Russia.* CEU Press. DOI: 10.1515/9789633865606-006

Constantin, D.-L., & Popescu, I.-A. (2025). Traditions and entrepreneurial spirit: The evolving geography of craft brewing in Romania and dynamic interactions with the local development environment. *Applied Geography (Sevenoaks, England), 176*, 103543. Advance online publication. DOI: 10.1016/j.apgeog.2025.103543

Cooley, A. (2012). *Great games, local rules: The new power contest in Central Asia.* Oxford University Press. DOI: 10.1093/acprof:oso/9780199929825.001.0001

Cooper, T., Pezold, T., Keenleyside, C., Đorđević-Milošević, S., Hart, K., Ivanov, S., Redman, M., & Vidojević, D. (2010). *Developing a National Agri-Environment Programme for Serbia.* IUCN.

Corpădean, I.-R. (2011). Izvoru Crişului - a Handicraft Based Tourist Village. *Journal of Settlements and Spatial Planning, 2*(1).

Cotula, L. (2009). *Land grab or development opportunity?: agricultural investment and international land deals in Africa.* Iied.

Cretu, O.R., Tudor, V.C., Lascar, E. (2023). Agricultural cooperative – viable alternative for the economic-social development of small and medium farmers. Case study Călăra i County, Romania. *Scientific Papers. Series "Management, Economic Engineering in Agriculture and rural development", 23*(3).

Csordás, A., Lengyel, P., & Füzesi, I. (2022). Who prefers regional products? A systematic literature review of consumer characteristics and attitudes in short food supply chains. *Sustainability (Basel), 14*(15), 8990. DOI: 10.3390/su14158990

Cue, R., Doornink, M., George, R., Griffiths, B., Jorgensen, M. W., Rogers, R., Saha, A., Taysom, K., Cabrera, V. E., Wangen, S. R., & Fadul-Pacheco, L. (2021, October 15). Data Governance in the Dairy Industry. *Animals (Basel), 11*(10), 2981. DOI: 10.3390/ani11102981

Cui, X. (2025). The Impact of Digital Transformation on Enterprises—Taking Mengniu Dairy as an Example. Advances in Economics. *Management and Political Sciences, 177*, 181–186. DOI: 10.54254/2754-1169/177/2025.22480

Cvijanović, D. (2016). *Marketing u turizmu*, Univerzitet u Kragujevcu Fakultet za hotelijerstvo i turizam, Vrnjačka Banja.

Cvijanović, D., Ignjatijević, S., & Vapa Tankosić, J. (2017). Raspberry trade as a strategic export potential of the Republic of Serbia. *Competitiveness of Agro-Food and Environmental Economy*, 74–85.

Cvijanović, D., Paraušić, V., & Subić, J. (2014). *Popis poljoprivrede u 2012 – Poljoprivredna gazdinstva prema ekonomskoj veličini i tipu proizvodnje u Republici Srbiji*, Republički zavod za statistiku, Beograd.

Cvijanović, D., Radović, G., & Cvijanović, G. (2016). Resources and the rural tourism development in the Republic of Serbia, *Horizons International Scientific Journal*, Series A, Social Sciences and Humanities, Year X, Volume 20, 41-51. Dostupno na: https://www.uklo.edu.mk/tabs/view/d95527c021a7b5c063ab1e094136937c

Cvijanović, D., Mihailović, B., Čavlin, M., & Čavlin, G. (2015). Impact of marketing consulting on performances of agrarian clusters in Serbia. *Sustainability (Basel)*, *7*(2), 1099–1115. https://doi.org/doi:10.3390/su7021099. DOI: 10.3390/su7021099

Da Costa Miranda, C. N., & Shukla, M. (2025). Blockchain-based smart dairy supply chain: Catching the momentum for digital transformation. *Asian Journal of Management and Commerce*, *6*(1), 502–514. DOI: 10.22271/27084515.2025.v6.i1f.493

Dai, X., Wu, Z., Fan, Y., Li, B., Yang, Z., Nan, B., & Bi, X. (2019). Characteristics and determinants of livelihood diversification of different household types in far Northwestern China. *Sustainability (Basel)*, *12*(1), 64. DOI: 10.3390/su12010064

Dale, A., Tzanetakis, I. E., & Walsh, C. S. (2013). Raspberry. In Badenes, M. L., & Byrne, D. H. (Eds.), *Fruit Breeding* (pp. 233–251). Springer.

Damasaru, C., & Crăciun, A. (2016). *Managementul poten ialului antreprenorial în Romania rurală*. Pro Universitaria Publishing House.

Dan, E., Ghi ă (Haque), C.M., & Dona, I. (2016). Rural entrepreneurship in Romania: importance, premises and limitations. *Scientific Papers Series Management, Economic Engineering in Agriculture and Rural Development, 16*(2), Issue 2.

Dan, M. C., & Popescu, C. (2017). Entrepreneurship in the rural areas of Romania. The impact of the 2007-2013 EU funding programmes. In *Proceedings of the International Conference on Business Excellence* (Vol. 11, No. 1, pp. 1129-1136). DOI: 10.1515/picbe-2017-0116

Dan, M.-C., & Popescu, C. (2017). Entrepreneurship in the rural areas of Romania. The impact of the 2007-2013 EU funding programmes. In *Proceedings of the International Conference on Business Excellence, 11*(1). Retrieved from https://sciendo.com/article/10.1515/picbe-2017-0116

Daniel, E. M., Krupnick, A. S., Heur, Y. H., Blinzler, J. A., Nims, R. W., & Stoner, G. D. (1989). Extraction, stability, and quantitation of ellagic acid in various fruits and nuts. *Journal of Food Composition and Analysis*, *2*(4), 338–349. DOI: 10.1016/0889-1575(89)90005-7

Dašić, D., Ratković, M., Marčetić, A., & Tošić, M. (2023). Promotion on the internet as a function of agribusiness development in Central Serbia. *Ekonomika Poljoprivrede*, *70*(2), 479–491. DOI: 10.59267/ekoPolj2302479D

Daskalopoulou, I., & Petrou, A. (2002). Utilising a farm typology to identify potential adopters of alternative farming activities in Greek agriculture. *Journal of Rural Studies*, *18*(1), 95–103. DOI: 10.1016/S0743-0167(01)00027-4

Davis, B., Winters, P., Carlleto, G., Covarrubias, K., Quinones, E., Zezza, A., Stamoulis, K., Bonomi, G., & DiGiuseppe, S. 2007. Rural income generating Activities: A cross country comparison. Washinghton DC, World Bank – FAO. Background paper for the World Development Report 2008

Dax, T. (1996). Defining rural areas–International comparisons and the OECD indicators1. *Rural Society*, *6*(3), 3–18. DOI: 10.5172/rsj.6.3.3

De Rosa, M., McElwee, G., & Smith, R. (2019). Farm diversification strategies in response to rural policy: A case from rural Italy. *Land Use Policy*, *81*, 291–301. DOI: 10.1016/j.landusepol.2018.11.006

De Soto, H. (2000). *The mystery of capital: Why capitalism triumphs in the West and fails everywhere else*. Basic Books. DOI: 10.37199/t40002609

Deakin, H., & Wakefield, K. (2014). Skype interviewing: Reflections of two PhD researchers. *Qualitative Research*, *14*(5), 603–616. DOI: 10.1177/1468794113488126

Declaration of Nyéléni. (2007). *Declaration of Nyéléni*. https://nyeleni.org/IMG/pdf/DeclNyeleni-en.pdf

Deiac, F., & Arion, F. H. (2025). Analysis of the agricultural sector in the North-West Region of Romania from the point of view of cluster excellence. *Scientific Papers. Series Management, Economic, Engineering in Agriculture and Rural Development*, *25*(1).

Deininger, K. (2011). Challenges posed by the new wave of farmland investment. *The Journal of Peasant Studies*, *38*(2), 217–247. DOI: 10.1080/03066150.2011.559007

DeJonckheere, M., & Vaughn, L. M. (2019). Semistructured interviewing in primary care research: A balance of relationship and rigour. *Family Medicine and Community Health*, *7*(2), e000057. DOI: 10.1136/fmch-2018-000057

Đekić, S., & Vučić, S. (2003). Savremeni ruralni turizam i rekreacija, Zbornik radova, Drugi Forum: *Ruralni turizam i održivi razvoj Balkana*, Kragujevac, 7-9. maj 2003,169-174.

Del Giudice, E., Elia, V., & Tedeschi, A. (2009). The role of water in the living organisms. *Neural Network World, 19*(4), 355–360.

Deng, J., Chi, H., & Zhang, T. (2024). Effects of Entrepreneurial Activities on Rural Revitalization: Based on Dissipative Structure Theory. *Agriculture, 14*(9), 1474. DOI: 10.3390/agriculture14091474

Denzin, N. K., Lincoln, Y.S., (2005). Introduction: The discipline and practice of qualitative research.

Đerčan, B., Bubalo Živković, M., Gatarić, D., Lukić, T., Dragin, A., Kalenjuk Pivarski, B., Lutovac, M., Kuzman, B., Puškarić, A., Banjac, M., Grubor, B., & Simović, O. (2022). Experienced Well Being in the Rural Areas of the Srem Region (Serbia): Perceptions of the Local Community. *Sustainability (Basel), 14*(1), 248. DOI: 10.3390/su14010248

Dias, C. S., Rodrigues, R. G., & Ferreira, J. J. (2019). What's new in the research on agricultural entrepreneurship? *Journal of Rural Studies, 65*, 99–115. DOI: 10.1016/j.jrurstud.2018.11.003

Dicu, A. M., Rad, D., Barbu, F., Cuc, L. D., Feher, A., Roman, D., Mazuru, L., Sanda, G., & Pîrvulescu, L. (2025). From Attachment to Action: Consumer Identification and the Sustainable Buying of Rural Brand Products Like "Pită de Pecica". *Sustainability (Basel), 17*(9), 4133. DOI: 10.3390/su17094133

Digital 4 Business. (2024, September 4). Harnessing the power of digitalisation for European SMEs: The Digital Intensity Index. https://digital4business.eu/digital-intensity-index/

Digital Skills & Jobs Platform. (2021). *European Initiatives.* https://digital-skills-jobs.europa.eu/en/actions/european-initiatives/sme-strategy-sustainable-and-digital-europe

Dinić, J. B. (1997). *Prirodni potencijal Srbije. Ekonomsko-geografska analiza i ocena* [The natural potential of Serbia. Economic-geographical analysis and evaluation]. Univerzitet u Beogradu. Ekonomski fakultet.

Djankov, S., La Porta, R., Lopez-de-Silanes, F., & Shleifer, A. (2003). Courts. *The Quarterly Journal of Economics, 118*(2), 453–517. DOI: 10.1162/003355303321675437

Djorić, Ž. (2020). Digital economy-basic aspects and the case of Serbia. *Economic Outlook/Ekonomski Pogledi, 22*(2), 73-96.

Djuričin, D., & Vuksanović, I. (2016). The future of Serbia and how to survive IT: Catching up and convergence with the EU. *Economics of Enterprise*, *64*(1-2), 15–36. DOI: 10.5937/ekopre1602015D

Dmitrović, V., Petrović, M., & Jakovljević, N. (2024). Smart Agriculture, Data and AI in in the Context of Cobit 2019: Analysis of Potential and Risks. *Western Balkan Journal of Agricultural Economics and Rural Development*, *6*(2), 83–196. DOI: 10.5937/WBJAE2402183D

Dobre, C. A., Stoian, M., Hontus, A. C., Chiurciu, I. A., & Soare, E. (2024). Component of marketing in authentic Romanian rural tourism. *Scientific Papers. Series Management, Economic, Engineering in Agriculture and Rural Development*, *24*(1), 335–340.

Doernberg, A., Piorr, A., Zasada, I., & Adewumi, M. O. (2022). Sustainability assessment of short food supply chains (SFSC): Developing and testing a rapid assessment tool in one African and three European city regions. *Agriculture and Human Values*, *39*(3), 885–904. DOI: 10.1007/s10460-021-10288-w

Dona, I. (2015). *Economie rurală*. Editura Economică.

Drakopoulou-Dodd, S., McDonald, S., McElwee, G., & Smith, R. (2014). A Bourdieuan analysis of qualitative authorship in entrepreneurship scholarship. *Journal of Small Business Management*, *52*(4), 633–654. DOI: 10.1111/jsbm.12125

Dries, L., Germenji, E., Noev, N., & Swinnen, J. F. (2009). Farmers, vertical coordination, and the restructuring of dairy supply chains in Central and Eastern Europe. *World Development*, *37*(11), 1742–1758. DOI: 10.1016/j.worlddev.2008.08.029

Dries, L., Reardon, T., & Swinnen, J. F. (2004). The rapid rise of supermarkets in Central and Eastern Europe: Implications for the agrifood sector and rural development. *Development Policy Review*, *22*(5), 525–556. DOI: 10.1111/j.1467-7679.2004.00264.x

Drobnjaković, M., Stojanović, Ž., & Josipović, S. (2022). Rural areas and rural economy in Serbia. *The Geography of Serbia: Nature, People, Economy*, 289-303. https://DOI: 10.1007/978-3-030-74701-5_22

Dumitrescu, C. S., Salasan, C., Mateoc-Sirb, N., & Gavruta, A. (2016). Contribution of local products in developing agricultural systems and local economy - case study. *SGEM 2016, BK 2: Political Sciences, Law, Finance, Economics and Tourism Conference Proceedings*, Vol. IV.

Dzingirai, M. (2021). The role of entrepreneurship in reducing poverty in agricultural communities. *Journal of enterprising communities. People and Places in the Global Economy*, *15*(5), 665–683.

Eastwood, C. R., Knook, J., Turner, J. A., & Renwick, A. (2023). Policy approaches for enhanced dairy sector innovation – a review of future pathways and policies for effective implementation of digital agriculture. *New Zealand Economic Papers*, *57*(2), 164–171. DOI: 10.1080/00779954.2022.2161935

EBRD. (1999). *Transition Report 1999: Ten Years of Transition*. European Bank for Reconstruction and Development.

EBRD. (2007). *Transition Report 2007: People in Transition*. European Bank for Reconstruction and Development.

EC. (2021). Rural Tourism and the Green Deal: A Path Towards Sustainability. European Commission (EC), Brussels, Belgium.

Egbo, O., Ezeaku, H., Okolo, V., Anisiuba, C., Ibe, G., Okeke, O., & Igwe, P. (2023). Enhancing agricultural and industrial productivity through freshwater withdrawals and management: Implications for the BRICS countries. *Environment, Development and Sustainability*, *25*(4), 3771–3799. DOI: 10.1007/s10668-022-02202-z

El Moll, A. (2023). Water resources and climate change: Regional, national and international perspective. In Prasad, M., & Smol, M. (Eds.), *Sustainable and circular management of resources and waste towards a green deal* (pp. 309–336). Elsevier., DOI: 10.1016/B978-0-323-95278-1.00010-3

Elhusseiny, H. M., & Crispim, J. (2022). SMEs, Barriers and Opportunities on adopting Industry 4.0: A Review. *Procedia Computer Science*, *196*, 864–871. DOI: 10.1016/j.procs.2021.12.086

Ellen MacArthur Foundation. (2013). *Towards the Circular Economy: Economic and business rationale for an accelerated transition*.

Ellen MacArthur Foundation. (2019). Circular Economy Introduction. Retrieved from https://www.ellenmacarthurfoundation.org/the-circular-economy-in-detail-deep-dive

Eller, R., Alford, P., Kallmünzer, A., & Peters, M. (2020). Antecedents, consequences, and challenges of small and medium-sized enterprise digitalization. *Journal of Business Research*, *112*, 119–127. DOI: 10.1016/j.jbusres.2020.03.004

Enterprise Europe Network. (n.d.). COSME—Program za konkurentnost malih i srednjih preduzeća. https://www.een.rs/cosme-program-za-konkurentonost-malih-srednjih-preduzeca/

EP. (2023). Rural tourism. European Parliament (EP), Brussels, Belgium.

Epstein, G. (2009). *Beyond capital account liberalization: Enhancing macroeconomic policy autonomy and financial stability*. International Labour Office.

Erickson, B., & Fausti, S. W. (2021). The role of precision agriculture in food security. *Agronomy Journal, 113*(6), 4455–4462. DOI: 10.1002/agj2.20919

Errington, A. (1997). *Coming home? The emerging Agenda for Rural Development Research in the UK*, Annual Conference of the Agricultural Economics Society Conference, Edinburgh, pp 21-24, March 1997

European Commision. (2025). *The Single Market Programme*. https://commission.europa.eu/funding-tenders/find-funding/eu-funding-programmes/single-market-programme/overview_en

European Commission, (2021). A long-term Vision for the EU's Rural Areas-Towards stronger, connected, resilient and prosperous rural by 2040, SWD (2021) 166 final.

European Commission, DG CLIMA. (2023). *Pricing agricultural emissions and rewarding climate action in the agri-food value chain*. Study. Trinomics. https://doi:.DOI: 10.2834/200

European Commission, DG CLIMA. (2025). *Support to the design of policy options for financial incentives for carbon farming*. Deloitte. .DOI: 10.2834/3087542

European Commission. (2019). *User guide to the SME Definition*. https://ec.europa.eu/docsroom/documents/42921/attachments/1/translations/en/renditions/native

European Commission. (2021). EU Cohesion Policy 2007–2020: Investing in Europe's regions. https://ec.europa.eu

European Commission. (2023). *Digitalisation. Agriculture and Rural Development.* https://agriculture.ec.europa.eu/overview-vision-agriculture-food/digitalisation_en

European Commission. (2023). The update of the nationally determined contribution of the European Union and its member states. https://unfccc.int/sites/default/files/NDC/2023-10/ES-2023-10-17%20EU%20 submission%20NDC%20update.pdf

European Commission. (2024). Study on funding for EU rural areas: final report, Publications Office of the European Union. Retrieved from https://data.europa.eu/doi/10.2762/901111

European Commission. (2025). *European Digital Innovation Hubs*. https://digital-strategy.ec.europa.eu/en/policies/edihs

European Commission. (2025). *European Regional Development Fund*. https://commission.europa.eu/funding-tenders/find-funding/eu-funding-programmes/european-regional-development-fund-erdf_en

European Commission. (2025). Factsheet on 2014-2020 Rural Development Programme for Romania. Retrieved from https://agriculture.ec.europa.eu/system/files/2023-11/rdp-factsheet-romania_en_.pdf

European Commission. (2025). *The Digital Europe Programme*. https://digital-strategy.ec.europa.eu/en/activities/digital-programme

European Commission. (n.d.). *Europe's Digital Decade: Digital targets for 2030*. https://commission.europa.eu/strategy-and-policy/priorities-2019-2024/europe-fit-digital-age/europes-digital-decade-digital-targets-2030_en

European Commission. (n.d.a). Common agricultural policy funds. Retrieved from https://agriculture.ec.europa.eu/common-agricultural-policy/financing-cap/cap-funds_en

European Commission. (n.d.b). The common agricultural policy at a glance. Retrieved from https://agriculture.ec.europa.eu/common-agricultural-policy/cap-overview/cap-glance_en

European Commission. DG CLIMA. (2024). *Incentivizing climate action for a sustainable and competitive agri-food value chain*. Follow-up study presentation. Trinomics, IEEP, Ricardo, and WUR. https://climate.ec.europa.eu/document/download/f76a263a-69b4-4032-a604-e9cf6caa3944_en?filename= policy_crcf_agri-food_ws_ ieep_en.pdf

European Commission. Directorate-General for Employment, Social Affairs and Inclusion & Beker, K. (2021). *Digitalisation and digital transformation in Serbia: implications for persons with disabilities*, Publications Office of the European Union. https://data.europa.eu/doi/10.2767/271459

European Court of Auditors. (2021). *Common Agricultural Policy and climate. Half of EU climate spending but farm emissions are not decreasing*. Special Report. .DOI: 10.2865/285879

European Environment Agency – EEA. (2023). *Land cover and change accounts 2000-2018*. https://www.eea.europa.eu/en/analysis/maps-and-charts/land-cover-and-change-statistics-dashboards. Published 25 Sept 2019, Modified 22 Aug 2023.

European Investment Bank (EIB). (2021). *The EIB Circular Economy Guide: Supporting the circular transition.*

European Union. (n.d.). *Enterprise Europe Network.* https://een.ec.europa.eu/about-enterprise-europe-network

Eurostat. (2022). Regional GDP per capita in the EU. https://ec.europa.eu/eurostat

Eurostat. (2024). *Digital Intensity Index (DII) composition overview 2015-2024.* https://ec.europa.eu/eurostat/documents/341889/725524/DII+v1+v2+v3+v4+2015-2023.pdf/2d0e55ee-8306-54db-a6e2-29a86583c1fe?t=1703234324067

Eurostat. (2024). *Digitalization in Europe – 2024 edition.* https://ec.europa.eu/eurostat/web/interactive-publications/digitalisation-2024

Eurostat. (2024). *Micro & small businesses.* https://ec.europa.eu/eurostat/web/products-eurostat-news/w/ddn-20241025-1

Eurostat. (2025). *Digital Intensity by size class of enterprise.* https://ec.europa.eu/eurostat/databrowser/view/isoc_e_dii__custom_16907592/default/table?lang=en

Evett, S., Colaizzi, P., Lamm, F., O'Shaughnessy, S., Heeren, D., Trout, T., Kranz, W., & Lin, X. (2020). Past, present, and future of irrigation on the US Great Plains. *Transactions of the ASABE, 63*(3), 703–729. DOI: 10.13031/trans.13620

Evola, R. S., Peira, G., Varese, E., Bonadonna, A., & Vesce, E. (2022). Short food supply chains in Europe: Scientific research directions. *Sustainability (Basel), 14*(6), 3602. DOI: 10.3390/su14063602

FAO & ITPS. (2021). *Recarbonizing global soils: A technical manual of recommended management practices. Volume 3: Cropland, Grassland, Integrated systems and farming approaches – Practices overview.* FAO. .DOI: 10.4060/cb6595en

FAO (Food and Agriculture Organization). (2021). The State of Food and Agriculture 2021: Transforming Food Systems for Affordable Healthy Diets. FAO (https://www.fao.org/publications/sofa/2021/en/)

FAO, & INRAE. (2020). *Enabling sustainable food systems: Innovators' handbook.* FAO.

FAO. (2019). *Recarbonization of global soils. A tool to support the implementation of the Koronivia joint work on agriculture.* FAO.

FAO. (2020). *A protocol for measurement, monitoring, reporting and verification of soil organic carbon in agricultural landscapes – GSOC-MRV Protocol.* FAO., DOI: 10.4060/cb0509en

FAO. (2021). *FAOSTAT – Raspberry Production and Export Data*. https://www.fao.org/faostat/en

FAO. (2022a). *Global Soil Organic Carbon Sequestration Potential Map – GSOCseq v.1.1*. Technical report. .DOI: 10.4060/cb9002en

FAO. (2022b). *The State of the World's Forests 2022. Forest pathways for green recovery and building inclusive, resilient and sustainable economies*. FAO., DOI: 10.4060/cb9360en

Fatimah, Y. A., Govindan, K., Murniningsih, R., & Setiawan, A. (2020). Industry 4.0 based sustainable circular economy approach for smart waste management system to achieve sustainable development goals: A case study of Indonesia. *Journal of Cleaner Production*, *269*, 122263. DOI: 10.1016/j.jclepro.2020.122263

Feagan, R. (2007). The place of food: Mapping out the 'local' in local food systems. *Progress in Human Geography*, *31*(1), 23–42. DOI. 10.1177/0309132507073527

Feenstra, G. W. (1997). Local food systems and sustainable communities. *American Journal of Alternative Agriculture*, *12*(1), 28–36. DOI: 10.1017/S0889189300007165

Fefer, J. P., De-Urioste Stone, S., Daigle, J., & Silka, L. (2016). Using the Delphi technique to identify key elements for effective and sustainable visitor use planning frameworks. *SAGE Open*, *6*(2), 1–16. DOI: 10.1177/2158244016643141

Feher, A. (2025). *Community funding policies and programs*. Pro Universitaria Publishing House.

Felici, F. B., & Mazzocchi, G. (2022). Territory matters: A methodology for understanding the role of territorial factors in transforming local food systems. *Land (Basel)*, *11*(7), 1046. DOI: 10.3390/land11071046

Ferguson, H. J., Bowen, J. M., McNicol, L. C., Bell, J., Duthie, C.-A., & Dewhurst, R. J. (2024). The impacts of precision livestock farming tools on the greenhouse gas emissions of an average Scottish dairy farm. *Frontiers in Sustainable Food Systems*, *8*, 1385672. DOI: 10.3389/fsufs.2024.1385672

Ferrari, A., Bacco, M., Gaber, K., Jedlitschka, A., Hess, S., Kaipainen, J., Koltsida, P., Toli, E., & Brunori, G. (2022). Drivers, barriers and impacts of digitalisation in rural areas from the viewpoint of experts. *Information and Software Technology*, *145*, 106816. DOI: 10.1016/j.infsof.2021.106816

Ferrell, O. C. (2021). *Marketing Strategy* (5th ed.). South Western Cengage Learning.

Filatotchev, I., Ireland, R. D., & Stahl, G. K. (2022). Contextualizing management research: An open systems perspective. *Journal of Management Studies, 59*(4), 1036–1056. DOI: 10.1111/joms.12754

Filipovski, Gj. (1974). *Pedologija* [Pedology], (2nd revised edition). Univerzitet "Kiril i Metodij" Skopje.

Fischer, S., & Sahay, R. (2000). The transition economies after ten years. IMF Working Paper, WP/00/30.

Flammer, C. (2021). Corporate green bonds. *Journal of Financial Economics, 142*(2), 499–516. DOI: 10.1016/j.jfineco.2021.01.010

Food and Agriculture Organization of the United Nations - FAO. (2017). *The future of food and agriculture – Trends and challenges,* Retrieved February 02, 2019 from https://www.fao.org/3/i6583e/i6583e.pdf

Food and Agriculture Organization of the United Nations. (2024). Statistical Yearbook 2024: Chapter 2 Production of livestock and livestock commodities. https://openknowledge.fao.org/server/api/core/bitstreams/d784864f-7f28-49d2-903e-6680d09a9d97/content/cd2971en.html#chapter-2_2

Foris, D., Florescu, A., Foris, T., & Barabas, S. (2020). Improving the Management of Tourist Destinations: A New Approach to Strategic Management at the DMO Level by Integrating Lean Techniques. *Sustainability (Basel), 12*(23), 10201. DOI: 10.3390/su122310201

Fossen, F. M., & Sorgner, A. (2021). Digitalization of work and entry into entrepreneurship. *Journal of Business Research, 125*, 548–563. DOI: 10.1016/j.jbusres.2019.09.019

Fossey, E., Harvey, C., McDermott, F., & Davidson, L. (2002). Understanding and evaluating qualitative research. *The Australian and New Zealand Journal of Psychiatry, 36*(6), 717–732. DOI: 10.1046/j.1440-1614.2002.01100.x

Freeman, R. E. (2015). *Strategic Management: A Stakeholder Approach.* Cambridge University Press.

Frye, T., & Shleifer, A. (1997). The invisible hand and the grabbing hand. *The American Economic Review, 87*(2), 354–358.

Furmankiewicz, M., Knieć, W., & Atterton, J. (2015). Rural governance in the new EU member states: The experience of the Polish LEADER+ Pilot Programme (2004–2008). *Governance in transition*, 133-153.

G20 Green Finance Study Group. (2016). *G20 Green Finance Synthesis Report.*

Ganzorig, B., & Nachin, D. (2006). Trends in international investment flows: Foreign direct investment in Mongolia. *Journal of International Logistics and Trade*, *4*(2), 107–120. DOI: 10.24006/jilt.2006.4.2.107

Gargano, G., Licciardo, F., Verrascina, M., & Zanetti, B. (2021). The agroecological approach as a model for multifunctional agriculture and farming towards the European Green Deal 2030—Some evidence from the Italian experience. *Sustainability (Basel)*, *13*(4), 2215. DOI: 10.3390/su13042215

Garlinska, M., Osial, M., Proniewska, K., & Pregowska, A. (2023). The Influence of Emerging Technologies on Distance Education. *Electronics (Basel)*, *12*(7), 1550. DOI: 10.3390/electronics12071550

Gavrilescu, D., & Florian, V. (coordonatori). Autori: Alexandri, C., Chi ea, L.F., Chi ea, M.A., Florian, V., Popescu, M., Rusu, M., Toderoiu, F., Tudor, M.M. (2007). *Economia rurală din România*. Editura Terra Nostra, Ia i, ISBN 978-973-8432-76-5

Gaworski, M., & Kic, P. (2024). Assessment of Production Technologies on Dairy Farms in Terms of Animal Welfare. *Applied Sciences (Basel, Switzerland)*, *14*(14), 6086. DOI: 10.3390/app14146086

Gereffi, G., Humphrey, J., & Sturgeon, T. (2005). The governance of global value chains. *Review of International Political Economy*, *12*(1), 78–104. DOI: 10.1080/09692290500049805

Gillespie, A. H., & Smith, L. E. (2008). Food decision-making framework: Connecting sustainable food systems to health and well-being. *Journal of Hunger & Environmental Nutrition*, *3*(2-3), 328–346. DOI: 10.1080/19320240802244363

Gioia, D. A., Corley, K. G., & Hamilton, A. L. (2013). Seeking qualitative rigor in inductive research: Notes on the Gioia methodology. *Organizational Research Methods*, *16*(1), 15–31. DOI: 10.1177/1094428112452151

Gittins, P., Apostolopoulos, S., Anastasopoulou, E. E., & Apostolopoulos, N. (2025). Responding to Greece's constrained agricultural context: Farm diversification strategies used by family farmers. *Journal of Rural Studies*, *113*, 103522. DOI: 10.1016/j.jrurstud.2024.103522

Gittins, P., & McElwee, G. (2023). Constrained rural entrepreneurship: Upland farmer responses to the socio-political challenges in England's beef and sheep sector. *Journal of Rural Studies*, *104*, 103141. DOI: 10.1016/j.jrurstud.2023.103141

Gleick, P., & Cooley, H. (2021). Freshwater scarcity. *Annual Review of Environment and Resources*, *46*(1), 319–348. DOI: 10.1146/annurev-environ-012220-101319

Glover, D., & Sumberg, J. (2025). Skill and deskilling in an uncertain agricultural world: Introduction to the special issue. *Outlook on Agriculture, 54*(2), 123-132. (Original work published 2025)DOI: 10.1177/00307270251337112

Gontijo, D., Santana, D. R., de Assis Costa, G., Cabrera, V. E., & de Andrade Freitas, E. N. (2025). Dairy GPT: Empowering dairy farmers to interact with numerical databases through natural language conversations. *Smart Agricultural Technology, 12*, 101097. DOI: 10.1016/j.atech.2025.101097

Goodman, D., DuPuis, E. M., & Goodman, M. K. (2012). *Alternative food networks: Knowledge, practice, and politics*. Routledge., DOI: 10.4324/9780203804520

Grecu, M., Surleanu C.A., Gusan O., Smedescu D.I., Vlad G., Panait R., Tudor V.C. (2024). Analysis of the efficiency of the implementation of financing programs from the European social fund on education in the rural environment in Romania. *Scientific Papers. Series "Management, Economic Engineering in Agriculture and rural development"*, 24(2).

Greenaway, D., Sousa, N., & Wakelin, K. (2004). Do domestic firms learn to export from multinationals? *European Journal of Political Economy, 20*(4), 1027–1043. DOI: 10.1016/j.ejpoleco.2003.12.006

Greenberg, Z., Farja, Y., & Gimmon, E. (2018). Embeddedness and growth of small businesses in rural regions. *Journal of Rural Studies, 62*, 174–182. DOI: 10.1016/j.jrurstud.2018.07.016

Grindle, M. S. (1997). *Getting good government: Capacity building in the public sectors of developing countries*. Harvard University Press.

Grujić Vučkovski, B., Paraušić, V., Jovanović Todorović, M., Joksimović, M., & Marina, I. (2022). Analysis of influence of value indicators agricultural production on gross value added in Serbian agriculture. *Custos e Agronegocio, 18*(4), 349–372.

Gusev, A. S., Beznosov, G. A., Ziablitckaia, N. V., Kholmanskikh, M. V., Novopashin, L. A., Denyozhko, L. V., & Sadov, A. A. (2019). An analysis of research areas in precision agriculture. *International Transaction Journal of Engineering Management & Applied Sciences & Technologies, 10*(10), 1–10.

Habersetzer, A., Rataj, M., Eriksson, R. H., & Mayer, H. (2020). Entrepreneurship in rural regions: The role of industry experience and home advantage for newly founded firms. *Regional Studies, 55*(5), 936–950. DOI: 10.1080/00343404.2020.1826038

Hale, H. E. (2015). *Patronal politics: Eurasian regime dynamics in comparative perspective*. Cambridge University Press.

Hans, F., Kuramochi, T., Black, R., Hale, T., & Lang, J. (2022). *Net Zero Stocktake 2022*. NewClimate Institute, Oxford Net Zero, Energy & Climate Intelligence Unit, Data-Driven EnviroLab.

Hanushek, E. A., & Woessmann, L. (2015). *The knowledge capital of nations: Education and the economics of growth*. MIT Press. DOI: 10.7551/mitpress/9780262029179.001.0001

Harpa, E., Moica, S., & Rus, D. (2015). A predictive model of innovation in rural entrepreneurship. *Procedia Technology*, •••, 19.

Hassoun, A., Garcia-Garcia, G., Trollman, H., Jagtap, S., Parra-Lopez, C., Cropotova, J., Bhat, Z. F., Centobelli, P., & Aït-Kaddour, A. (2023). Birth of dairy 4.0: Opportunities and challenges in adoption of fourth industrial revolution technologies in the production of milk and its derivatives. *Current Research in Food Science*, *7*, 100535. DOI: 10.1016/j.crfs.2023.100535

Havrylyshyn, O. (2020). *Present at the Transition: An Inside Look at the Role of History, Politics and Personalities in Post-Communist Countries*. Cambridge University Press. DOI: 10.1017/9781108553834

Hediger, W., & Knickel, K. (2009). Multifunctionality and sustainability of agriculture and rural areas: A welfare economics perspective. *Journal of Environmental Policy and Planning*, *11*(4), 291–313. DOI: 10.1080/15239080903412453

Hellman, J. S., Jones, G., & Kaufmann, D. (2000). Seize the state, seize the day: State capture and influence in transition economies. World Bank Policy Research Working Paper, No. 2444.

Helpman, E. (1984). A simple theory of international trade with multinational corporations. *Journal of Political Economy*, *92*(3), 451–471. DOI: 10.1086/261236

Henegar, D., Ilie , G. L., Mure an, I. C., Poru iu, A. R., Arion, I. D., & Arion, F. H. (2024). Customers' Perception of Microfinance Services as a Tool for Rural Development: A Romanian Case Study. *Agriculture*, *14*(7), 1087. Advance online publication. DOI: 10.3390/agriculture14071087

Henry, B., Dalal, R., Harrison, M. T., & Keating, B. (2023). Creating frameworks to foster soil carbon sequestration. In Rumpel, C. (Ed.), *Understanding and fostering soil carbon sequestration* (pp. 767–808). Burleigh Dodds Science Publishing., DOI: 10.19103/AS.2022.0106.25

Hinrichs, C. C. (2000). Embeddedness and local food systems: Notes on two types of direct agricultural market. *Journal of Rural Studies*, *16*(3), 295–303. DOI: 10.1016/S0743-0167(99)00063-7

Hinrichs, C. C. (2003). The practice and politics of food system localization. *Journal of Rural Studies, 19*(1), 33–45. DOI: 10.1016/S0743-0167(02)00040-2

Hobbs, J. E. (2021). Food supply chain resilience and the COVID-19 pandemic: What have we learned?. *Canadian Journal of Agricultural Economics/Revue canadienne d'agroeconomie, 69*(2), 189-196.

Hoekman, B., & Kostecki, M. (2009). *The Political Economy of the World Trading System* (3rd ed.). Oxford University Press. DOI: 10.1093/oso/9780199553761.001.0001

Holzinger, A., Fister, I., Kaul, H., & Asseng, S. (2024). Human-centered AI in smart farming: Toward agriculture 5.0. *IEEE Access : Practical Innovations, Open Solutions, 12*, 62199–62214. DOI: 10.1109/ACCESS.2024.3395532

Horrillo, A. M., Mesias, F. J., Elghannam, A., & Gaspar, P. (2016). Is there a future for organic production in high ecological value ecosystems? *Agricultural Systems, 143*, 114–125. DOI: 10.1016/j.agsy.2015.12.015

Hrustek, L. (2020). Sustainability driven by agriculture through digital transformation. *Sustainability (Basel), 12*(20), 8596. DOI: 10.3390/su12208596

Huang, J., Tichit, M., Poulot, M., Darly, S., Li, S., Petit, C., & Aubry, C. (2015). Comparative review of multifunctionality and ecosystem services in sustainable agriculture. *Journal of Environmental Management, 149*, 138–147. DOI: 10.1016/j.jenvman.2014.10.020

Hyland, J., Henchion, M. M., Olomo, O., Attard, J., & Gaffey, J. (2024). Sustainable and healthy food consumption in Europe: An analysis of consumer purchase patterns, motivations and barriers towards foods from SFSCs. *British Food Journal, 126*(4), 1429–1455. DOI: 10.1108/BFJ-01-2023-0058

IAE. (2024). *Collected dataset related to investment in fully automated irrigation system*. Internal documentation, Institute of Agricultural Economics, Belgrade, Serbia.

Iakovidou, O., Koutsouris, A., & Partalidou, M. (2002). The development of rural tourism in Greece, through the initiative Leader II: The case of northern and central Chalkidiki. *A Mediterranean Journal of Economics, Agriculture and Environment. New Medit. Journal, 1*(4), 35–38.

Ilbery, B. W. (1991). Farm diversification as an adjustment strategy on the urban fringe of the West Midlands. *Journal of Rural Studies, 7*(3), 207–218. DOI: 10.1016/0743-0167(91)90085-7

Ilbery, B., & Maye, D. (2005). Food supply chains and sustainability: Evidence from specialist food producers in the Scottish/English borders. *Land Use Policy, 22*(4), 331–344. DOI: 10.1016/j.landusepol.2004.06.002

IMF. (2000). Russian Federation: Recent economic developments. International Monetary Fund.

IMF. (2021). Azerbaijan: Staff country report. https://www.imf.org

Impact Hub Bucharest, Startarium i Datable. (2024). Entrepreneur Profile 2024. Retrieved from file:///C:/Users/Cosmina/Downloads/Profil%20de%20Antreprenor%20 2024.pdf

Interreg, I. P. A. Hungary-Serbia. (2024). Climate Smart Soil for ZERO-CARBON farms. https://hungary-serbia.eu/projects/c-farms

IOM. (2020). Migration data portal: Eastern Europe and Central Asia. https://migrationdataportal.org

Ionitescu, S., Popescu, A., Gudanescu, N.L., Cristea A. (2023) Digitalization and agriculture - impact on human resources in the European Union and Romania. *Scientific Papers. Series "Management, Economic Engineering in Agriculture and rural development", 23*(3).

IPCC. (2019). Summary for Policymakers. In Shukla, P.R., Skea, J., Calvo Buendia, E., Masson-Delmotte, V., Pörtner, H.- O., Roberts, D. C., Zhai, P., Slade, R., Connors, S., van Diemen, R., Ferrat, M., Haughey, E., Luz, S., Neogi, S., Pathak, M., Petzold, J., Portugal Pereira, J., Vyas, P., Huntley, E., …Malley, J. (Eds.), *Climate Change and Land: an IPCC special report on climate change, desertification, land degradation, sustainable land management, food security, and greenhouse gas fluxes in terrestrial ecosystems*. IPCC.

IPCC. (2023). Summary for Policymakers. In Lee, H., & Romero, J. (Eds.), *Climate Change 2023: Synthesis Report of the IPCC Sixth Assessment Report (AR6)* (pp. 1–34). IPCC., DOI: 10.59327/IPCC/AR6-9789291691647

ITC – International Trade Centre. (2021). *Trade Map – Serbia Raspberry Export Statistics* https://www.trademap.org/tradestatistics.aspx

Ivona, A. (2021). Sustainability of rural tourism and promotion of local development. *Sustainability (Basel), 13*(16), 8854. DOI: 10.3390/su13168854

Jackson, R., Carpenter, S., Dahm, C., McKnight, D., Naiman, R., Postel, S., & Running, S. (2001). Water in a changing world. *Ecological Applications, 11*(4), 1027–1045. DOI: 10.1890/1051-0761(2001)011[1027:WIACW]2.0.CO;2

Jafari, J., & Xiao, H. (2024), (eds.). Encyclopedia of Tourism. 2nd edition, Springer, Cham, Switzerland, Dostupno na: https://doi.org/ (pristup: 11.05.2025.).DOI: 10.1007/978-3-030-74923-1

Jarosz, L. (2008). The city in the country: Growing alternative food networks in Metropolitan areas. *Journal of Rural Studies*, *24*(3), 231–244. DOI: 10.1016/j.jrurstud.2007.10.002

Jarzębowski, S., Bourlakis, M., & Bezat-Jarzębowska, A. (2020). Short food supply chains (SFSC) as local and sustainable systems. *Sustainability (Basel)*, *12*(11), 4715. DOI: 10.3390/su12114715

Jat, M. L., Chakraborty, D., Ladha, J. K., Parihar, C. M., Datta, A., Mandal, B., Nayak, H. S., Maity, P., Rana, D. S., Chaudhari, S. K., & Gerard, B. (2022). Carbon sequestration potential, challenges, and strategies towards climate action in smallholder agricultural systems of South Asia. *Crop and Environment*, *1*(1), 86–101. DOI: 10.1016/j.crope.2022.03.005

Javadian, G., Dobratz, C., Gupta, A., Gupta, V. K., & Martin, J. A. (2020). Qualitative Research in Entrepreneurship Studies: A State-of-Science. *The Journal of Entrepreneurship*, *29*(2), 223–258. DOI: 10.1177/0971355720930564

Jeločnik, M., & Subić, J. (2021). *Economic effects of the wind-turbine and solar panels application in vegetables' production at the family farms.* In: Atanov, I. (edt.) IX International scientific-practical conference: Innovative aspects of the development service and tourism, Stavropol State Agrarian University, Stavropol, Russian Federation, pp. 61-75.

Jeločnik, M., & Subić, J. (2022). *Irrigation costs management at the family farms.* In: X International scientific-practical conference: Innovative aspects of the development service and tourism. Faculty of Social and Cultural Service and Tourism, Stavropol state agrarian university, Stavropol, Russian Federation, pp. 116-128.

Jeločnik, M., Nastić, L., & Kuzman, B. (2023). *Improving the vegetable growing by the use of new technologies.* In: Andrei, J., Mateoc Sirb, N., Feher, A. (eds.) I International Conference TENDEV 2023 - Challenges and strategies for sustainable development facing the climate change (eds.), Peter Lang GmbH, Berlin, Germany, pp. 123-144.

Jeločnik, M., Puška, A., Nedeljković, M., Božanić, D., & Subić, J. (2024). Possibility of renewable energy solutions usage in rural areas of Western Balkans: Fuzzy-rough approach. *Rural Sustainability Research*, *51*(346), 1–19. DOI: 10.2478/plua-2024-0001

Jeločnik, M., & Subić, J. (2020). Evaluation of economic efficiency of investments in organic production at the family farms. In Platania, (Eds.), *Course for trainers: Organic farming, eco-market and their capitalization through the entrepreneurial initiative* (pp. 261–300). Alexandru Ioan Cuza University.

Jeločnik, M., Subić, J., & Zdravković, A. (2022). Economic effects of investment in irrigation systems implementation at the small family farms. *Ekonomika Poljoprivrede*, *69*(3), 793–817. DOI: 10.5937/ekoPolj2203793J

Jeločnik, M., Subić, J., Zubović, J., & Zdravković, A. (2016). Ekonomski aspekti primene obnovljivih izvora energije u procesu navodnjavanja u povrtarstvu. *Ecologica*, *23*(83), 473–479.

Jeločnik, M., Zubović, J., & Zdravković, A. (2019). Estimating impact of weather factors on wheat yields by using panel model approach: The case of Serbia. *Agricultural Water Management*, *221*, 493–501. DOI: 10.1016/j.agwat.2019.05.015

Jennings, D. L. (1988). *Raspberries and Blackberries: Their Breeding, Diseases and Growth*. Academic Press.

Jensen, N. M. (2008). *Nation-states and the multinational corporation: A political economy of foreign direct investment*. Princeton University Press. DOI: 10.1515/9781400837373

Jervell, A. M. (2011). The family farm as a premise for entrepreneurship. In *The handbook of research on entrepreneurship in agriculture and rural development*. Edward Elgar Publishing. DOI: 10.4337/9780857933249.00009

Jia, F., Shahzadi, G., Bourlakis, M., & John, A. (2024). Promoting resilient and sustainable food systems: A systematic literature review on short food supply chains. *Journal of Cleaner Production*, *435*, 140364. DOI: 10.1016/j.jclepro.2023.140364

Jing, X. (2006). *Rural Tourism and Sustainable Community Development*, International Forum on Rural Tourism, China, September, 4-6, 2006, Final Report World Tourism Organization.

Jobber, D., & Fahy, J. (2022). *Foundations of Marketing*. McGraw-Hill Education (UK) Ltd. (Paperback) ISBN 978-1-5268-4900-7 (eBook): ISBN 978-1-5268-4901-4.

Joksimovic, M., Grujic, B., & Joksimovic, D. (2017). Foreign direct investment and their impact on economic development countries in transition. Progress in Economic Sciences, (4), 239-246.ceedings, 217-221.

Joksimović, M., Grujić, B., & Joksimović, D. (2018). Correlation and regression analysis of the impact of leasing on agricultural production in Republic of Serbia. Economic of agriculture, 65(2), 583-600.

Joksimovic, M., & Stoimenov, S. (2024). The importance of green bonds for the development of the green economy. *Bizinfo (Blace), 15*(1), 107–111. DOI: 10.5937/bizinfo2401107J

Jovičić Vuković, A., Jošanov-Vrgović, I., Jovin, S., & Papić-Blagojević, N. (2020). Socio-demographic characteristics and students' entrepreneurial intentions. *Stanovnistvo, 58*(2), 57–75. DOI: 10.2298/STNV200423007J

Kaewbang, J., Lohanawakul, J., Ketnuam, N., Prapakornmano, K., Khamta, P., Raza, A., Swangchan-Uthai, T., Makararpong, D., & Inchaisri, C. (2024). Smart sensors in Thai dairy reproduction: A case study. *Veterinary World, 17*(6), 1251–1258. DOI: 10.14202/vetworld.2024.1251-1258

Kalanović-Bulatović, B., Dimitrijević, B., Milić, D., & Milovančević, Z. (2015). Organization and costs of repurchasing, transportation, warehousing and storage of raspberry fruit. *Ekonomika Poljoprivrede, 62*(4), 1017–1030. DOI: 10.5937/ekoPolj1504017K

Kallio, H., Pietilä, A. M., Johnson, M., & Kangasniemi, M. (2016). Systematic methodological review: Developing a framework for a qualitative semi-structured interview guide. *Journal of Advanced Nursing, 72*(12), 2954–2965. DOI: 10.1111/jan.13031

Kanniainen, V., & Vesala, T. (2005). Entrepreneurship and labor market institutions. *Economic Modelling, 22*(5), 828–847. DOI: 10.1016/j.econmod.2005.05.002

Karagianni, M., Georgakopoulou, S., & Delitheou, V. (2019). Agrotourism: A lever for rural development based on the cultural reserve of Greece. In *Smart Tourism as a Driver for Culture and Sustainability: Fifth International Conference IACuDiT, Athens 2018* (pp. 193-206). Springer International Publishing. DOI: 10.1007/978-3-030-03910-3_14

Karagiannis, I., & Soldatos, P. (2008). Water desalination cost literature: Review and assessment. *Desalination, 223*(1-3), 448–456. DOI: 10.1016/j.desal.2007.02.071

Kaufmann, D., & Kraay, A. (2002). Growth without governance. World Bank Policy Research Working Paper, No. 2928.

Kaufmann, D., Kraay, A., & Zoido-Lobatón, P. (1999). Governance matters. World Bank Policy Research Working Paper, No. 2196.

Kay, M., Bunning, S., Burke, J., Boerger, V., Bojic, D., Bosc, P., Clark, M., Dale, D., England, M., Hoogeveen, J., Koo Oshima, S., Mejias Moreno, P., Muchoney, D., Nachtergaele, F., Olivera Sanchez, C., Salman, M., Schlingloff, S., Unver, O., Vargas, R., . . . Ziadat, F. (2022). *The state of the world's land and water resources for food and agriculture 2021. Systems at breaking point.* Report, Food and Agriculture Organization of EU (FAO), Rome, Italy, DOI: 10.4060/cb9910en

Kemp, R., & Pearson, P. (2007). *Final report MEI project about measuring eco-innovation.* European Commission.

Khan, S., Mushtaq, S., & Chen, C. (2010). A decision support tool for irrigation infrastructure investments. *Irrigation and Drainage*, *59*(4), 404–418. DOI: 10.1002/ird.501

Kilic, Z. (2020). The importance of water and conscious use of water. *International Journal of Hydrology*, *4*(5), 239–241. DOI: 10.15406/ijh.2020.04.00250

Kirchherr, J., Reike, D., & Hekkert, M. (2017). Conceptualizing the circular economy: An analysis of 114 definitions. *Resources, Conservation and Recycling*, *127*, 221–232. DOI: 10.1016/j.resconrec.2017.09.005

Kiss, K., Koncz, G., Nagy-Demeter, D., Varró, B., Németh, M., & Ruszkai, C. (2019). Survey of consumers responsiveness to small-scale producers marketing in the Northern Hungary Region. [TMP]. *Theory Methodology Practice*, *15*(1), 25–34. DOI: 10.18096/TMP.2019.01.03

Kljajić, N. (2012). *Ekonomska efikasnost investicija u različitim uslovima proizvodnje maline* (Doktorska disertacija, Univerzitet u Novom Sadu, Poljoprivredni fakultet).

Kljajić, N., Paraušić, V., & Kostić, Z. (2024). Economic aspects of digitalization in Serbian agriculture: Perceptions of farm managers. *Ekonomika Poljoprivrede*, *71*(3), 943–956. DOI: 10.59267/ekoPolj2403943K

Kljajić, N., Subić, J., & Sredojević, Z. (2017). Profitability of raspberry production on holdings in the territory of Arilje. *Ekonomika Poljoprivrede*, *64*(1), 57–69. DOI: 10.5937/ekoPolj1701057K

Kneafsey, M., Venn, L., Schmutz, U., Balázs, B., Trenchard, L., Eyden-Wood, T., ... & Blackett, M. (2013). *Short food supply chains and local food systems in the EU. A state of play of their socio-economic characteristics.* JRC Scientific and Policy Reports, European Commission. DOI: 10.2791/88784

Kneafsey, M., Cox, R., Holloway, L., Dowler, E., Venn, L., & Tuomainen, H. (2008). *Reconnecting consumers, producers and food: Exploring alternatives.* Bloomsbury Publishing. DOI: 10.5040/9781350047631

Knickel, K., Renting, H., & Van der Ploeg, J. D. (2004). Multifunctionality in European agriculture. *Sustaining agriculture and the rural economy: Governance, policy and Multifunctionality. Edward Elgar Publishing Inc*, 81-103.

Knierim, A., Kernecker, M., Erdle, K., Kraus, T., Borges, F., & Wurbs, A. (2019). Smart farming technology innovations–Insights and reflections from the German Smart-AKIS hub. *NJAS Wageningen Journal of Life Sciences*, *90*(1), 100314. DOI: 10.1016/j.njas.2019.100314

Kojima, K. (1975). International trade and foreign investment: Substitutes or complements. *Hitotsubashi Journal of Economics*, *16*(1), 1–12.

Kokko, A. (2003). *The economics of foreign direct investment incentives* (No. 3775). CEPR Discussion Papers.

Kolb, J. H., & Brunner, E. D. (1946). *A Study of Rural Society*. Houghton Mifflin.

Komarek, A., De Pinto, A., & Smith, V. (2020). A review of types of risks in agriculture: What we know and what we need to know. *Agricultural Systems*, *178*, 102738. DOI: 10.1016/j.agsy.2019.102738

Kornai, J. (1992). *The Socialist System: The Political Economy of Communism*. Princeton University Press.

Korsgaard, S., Müller, S., & Tanvig, H. W. (2015). Rural entrepreneurship or entrepreneurship in the rural–between place and space. *International Journal of Entrepreneurial Behaviour & Research*, *21*(1), 5–26. DOI: 10.1108/IJEBR-11-2013-0205

Kotler, P., Bowen, J. T., Makens, J. C., & Baloglu, S. (2021). *Marketing for hospitality and tourism* (8th ed.). Pearson Education.

Kotler, P., Bowen, J. T., & Makens, J. T. (2017). *Marketing for Hospitality and Tourism*. Pearson Education.

Kotler, P., & Levy, S. J. (1969). Broadening the concept of marketing. *Journal of Marketing*, *33*(1), 10–15. DOI: 10.1177/002224296903300103 PMID: 12309673

Kraus, S., Palmer, C., Kailer, N., Kallinger, F. L., & Spitzer, J. (2019). Digital entrepreneurship: A research agenda on new business models for the twenty-first century. *International Journal of Entrepreneurial Behaviour & Research*, *25*(2), 353–375.

Kreft, S. F., & Sobel, R. S. (2005). Public policy, entrepreneurship, and economic freedom. *The Cato Journal*, *25*, 595.

Kušen, E. (2007). Kako ugostiti turiste na vlastitom imanju, Institut za turizam, Zagreb.

Kusio, T., & Fiore, M. (2022). Which Stakeholders' Sector Matters in Rural Development? That Is the Problem. *Energies, 15*(2), 454. DOI: 10.3390/en15020454

Kusio, T., Kudełko, J., Borges, A., Delic, A., & Stroila, I. (2022). Are there any differences in rural development challenges within European countries? Social and economic contexts from EU rural leaders. *The International Food and Agribusiness Management Review, 25*(5), 737–756. DOI: 10.22434/IFAMR2021.0147

Lacy, P., & Rutqvist, J. (2015). *Waste to Wealth: The Circular Economy Advantage*. Palgrave Macmillan.

Lage, C. F. A., Marques, T. C., Bruno, D. R., Endres, M. I., Ferreira, F., Pires, A. P. A., Leão, K., & de Lima, F. S. (2024). Farmers' Perceptions on Implementing Automatic Milking Systems in Large USA Dairies: Decision-Making Process, Management Practices, Labor, and Herd Performance. *Animals (Basel), 14*(2), 218. DOI: 10.3390/ani14020218

Lal, R., Smith, P., Jungkunst, H. F., Mitsch, W. J., Lehmann, J., Nair, P. K. R., McBratney, A. B., Sá, J. C. M., Schneider, J., Zinn, Y. L., Skoru-pa, A. L. A., Zhang, H., Minasny, B., Srinivasrao, C., & Ravindranath, N. H. (2018). The carbon sequestration potential of terrestrial ecosystems. *Journal of Soil and Water Conservation, 73*(6), 145A–152A. DOI: 10.2489/jswc.73.6.145A

Lans, T., Van Galen, M. A., Verstegen, J. A. A. M., Biemans, H. J. A., & Mulder, M. (2014). Searching for entrepreneurs among small business ownermanagers in agriculture. *NJAS Wageningen Journal of Life Sciences, 68*(1), 41–51. DOI: 10.1016/j.njas.2013.12.001

Lavrijsen-Kromwijk, L., Demba, S., Müller, U., & Rose, S. (2024). Impact of Automation Level of Dairy Farms in Northern and Central Germany on Dairy Cattle Welfare. *Animals (Basel), 14*(24), 3699. DOI: 10.3390/ani14243699

Ledeneva, A. V. (2006). *How Russia really works: The informal practices that shaped post-Soviet politics and business*. Cornell University Press.

Ledger, M., & Milner, A. (2015). Extreme events in running waters. *Freshwater Biology, 60*(12), 2455–2460. DOI: 10.1111/fwb.12673

Lee, K. S. (2023). Cooking up food memories: A taste of intangible cultural heritage. *Journal of Hospitality and Tourism Management, 54*, 1–9. DOI: 10.1016/j.jhtm.2022.11.005

Lee, M., & Seo, S. (2021). Wearable Wireless Biosensor Technology for Monitoring Cattle: A Review. *Animals (Basel), 11*(10), 2779. DOI: 10.3390/ani11102779

Léon, Y. (2005). Rural development in Europe: A research frontier for agricultural economists. *European Review of Agriculture Economics*, *32*(3), 301–317. DOI: 10.1093/eurrag/jbi012

Lipsey, R. E., & Sjöholm, F. (2005). The impact of inward FDI on host countries: why such different answers?. *Does foreign direct investment promote development*, 23-43.

Liu, D., Li, G., Hu, N., & Ma, Z. (2019). Application of real options on the decision-making of mining investment projects using the system dynamics method. *IEEE Access : Practical Innovations, Open Solutions*, *7*, 46785–46795. DOI: 10.1109/ACCESS.2019.2909128

Liu, Y. L., Chiang, J. T., & Ko, P. F. (2023). The benefits of tourism for rural community development. *Humanities & Social Sciences Communications*, *10*(1), 1–12. DOI: 10.1057/s41599-023-01610-4 PMID: 37016690

Local Development Strategy of Giarmata Commune. 2021-2027. Retrieved from https://primariagiarmata.ro/strategia-de-dezvoltare/

Local Market. (2019). Retrieved December 12, 2021 from https://www.lokalnipazar.rs/o-inicijativi

Lokhorst, C., de Mol, R. M., & Kamphuis, C. (2019). Invited review: Big Data in precision dairy farming. *Animal*, *13*(7), 1519–1528. DOI: 10.1017/S1751731118003439

Lokier, J., Morris, W., & Thomas, D. (2021). Farm shop diversification: Producer motivations and consumer attitudes. *International Journal of Entrepreneurship and Innovation*, *22*(4), 215–228. DOI: 10.1177/1465750320985364

López-i-Gelats, F., Milán, M. J., & Bartolomé, J. (2011). Is farming enough in mountain areas? Farm diversification in the Pyrenees. *Land Use Policy*, *28*(4), 783–791. DOI: 10.1016/j.landusepol.2011.01.005

López, M., Cazorla, A., & Panta, M. P. (2019). Rural Entrepreneurship Strategies: Empirical Experience in the Northern Sub-Plateau of Spain. *Sustainability (Basel)*, *11*(5), 1243. DOI: 10.3390/su11051243

Losch, B. (2004). Debating the multifunctionality of agriculture: From trade negotiations to development policies by the South. *Journal of Agrarian Change*, *4*(3), 336–360. DOI: 10.1111/j.1471-0366.2004.00082.x

Lucas, A., Moruzzo, R., & Granai, G. (2024). Farmers' markets contribution to the resilience of the food systems. *Agricultural and Food Economics*, *12*(1), 50. DOI: 10.1186/s40100-024-00345-3

Lugato, E., Bampa, F., Panagos, P., Montanarella, L., & Jones, A. (2014). Potential carbon sequestration of European arable soils estimated by modelling a comprehensive set of management practices. *Global Change Biology*, *20*(11), 3557–3567. DOI: 10.1111/gcb.12551

Lugato, E., Leip, A., & Jones, A. (2018). Mitigation potential of soil carbon management overestimated by neglecting N2O emissions. *Nature Climate Change*, *8*(3), 219–223. DOI: 10.1038/s41558-018-0087-z

Lund, M. (2012). Multi-stakeholder co-operatives: Engines of innovation for building a healthier local food system and a healthier economy. *Journal of Co-operative Studies*, *45*(1), 32–37.

Luo, W., Dong, Q., & Feng, Y. (2023). Risk prediction model of clinical mastitis in lactating dairy cows based on machine learning algorithms. *Preventive Veterinary Medicine*, *221*, 106059. DOI: 10.1016/j.prevetmed.2023.106059

Lutz, J., Smetschka, B., & Grima, N. (2017). Farmer cooperation as a means for creating local food systems—Potentials and challenges. *Sustainability (Basel)*, *9*(6), 925. DOI: 10.3390/su9060925

Lyson, T. A. (2004). *Civic agriculture: Reconnecting farm, food, and community*. University Press of New England.

Magesa, M., Jonathan, J., & Urassa, J. (2023). Digital Literacy of Smallholder Farmers in Tanzania. *Sustainability (Basel)*, *15*(17), 13149. DOI: 10.3390/su151713149

Majewski, E., Komerska, A., Kwiatkowski, J., Malak-Rawlikowska, A., Wąs, A., Sulewski, P., Gołaś, M., Pogodzińska, K., Lecoeur, J.-L., Tocco, B., Török, Á., Donati, M., & Vittersø, G. (2020). Are short food supply chains more environmentally sustainable than long chains? A life cycle assessment (LCA) of the eco-efficiency of food chains in selected EU countries. *Energies*, *13*(18), 4853. DOI: 10.3390/en13184853

Makris, I. A., Apostolopoulos, S., & Masouras, A. (2025). EU policies and female entrepreneurship in Greek rural areas in relation to digital challenges. In *Real-World Tools and Scenarios for Entrepreneurship Exploration* (pp. 203–222). IGI Global.

Makris, I., Apostolopoulos, S., & Dimitrakopoulos, P. (2024). Analysing supporting mechanisms, cultural shaping and incentives for circular economy: The case of local governments. *Interdisciplinary Environmental Review*, *23*(3), 218–235. DOI: 10.1504/IER.2024.139254

Malak-Rawlikowska, A., Majewski, E., Wąs, A., Borgen, S. O., Csillag, P., Donati, M., Freeman, R., Hoàng, V., Lecoeur, J.-L., Mancini, M. C., Nguyen, A., Saïdi, M., Tocco, B., Török, Á., Veneziani, M., Vittersø, G., & Wavresky, P. (2019). Measuring the economic, environmental, and social sustainability of short food supply chains. *Sustainability (Basel), 11*(15), 4004. DOI: 10.3390/su11154004

Malmqvist, B., & Rundle, S. (2002). Threats to the running water ecosystems of the world. *Environmental Conservation, 29*(2), 134–153. DOI: 10.1017/S0376892902000097

Manasijević, A., Milojković, M., & Mastilo, D. (2019). Digital Village Transformation: A Model for Relativizing Regional Disparities in the Republic of Serbia. *Economics-časopis za inovacijska i ekonomska istraživanja, 7*(2), 125-138. DOI: 10.2478/eoik-2019-0013

Manić, E., & Janković, I. (2019). Održivost u sektoru malinarstva: primer Srbije. *Ekonomski vidici, 24*(1–2), 79–92.

Mantravadi, S., Srai, J. S., & Møller, C. (2023). Application of MES/MOM for Industry 4.0 supply chains: A cross-case analysis. *Computers in Industry, 148*, 103907. DOI: 10.1016/j.compind.2023.103907

Mariotti, I., & Sasso, S. (2024). *Revitalizing rural areas through innovation and entrepreneurship: public and private initiatives to train, attract and retain human capital*, Publications Office of the European Union. Retrieved from https://data.europa.eu/doi/10.2760/4727653

Marković, S., & Ostojić, M. (2012). Četiri decenije seoskog turizma u Moravičkom kraju, Zbornik radova, Prvi stručni skup o ruralnom turizmu i održivom razvoju, Kragujevac, 28-40.

Marsden, T., Banks, J., & Bristow, G. (2000). Food supply chain approaches: Exploring their role in rural development. *Sociologia Ruralis, 40*(4), 424–438. DOI: 10.1111/1467-9523.00158

Martinez, S., Hand, M., Da Pra, M., Pollack, S., Ralston, K., Smith, T., . . . Newman, C. (2010). *Local food systems: Concepts, impacts, and issues* (Report No. ERR-97). U.S. Department of Agriculture, Economic Research Service.

Martinho, V. J. P. D. (2020). Agricultural entrepreneurship in the European Union: Contributions for a sustainable development. *Applied Sciences (Basel, Switzerland), 10*(6), 2080. DOI: 10.3390/app10062080

Masouras, A., Anastasiadou, S., Constantelou, A., & Apostolopoulos, S. (Eds.). (2024). *Real-world Tools and Scenarios for Entrepreneurship Exploration*. IGI Global. DOI: 10.4018/979-8-3693-3100-2

Matei, D. (2013). Entrepreneurship in the Romanian Rural Areas. Case Study: Suceava County. *Journal of Settlements and Spatial Planning. 2.*

Matić, R., Gonzales-Serrano, M. H., Damnjanović, J., Maksimović, B., Papić-Blagojević, N., Milošević, I., & Vuković, J. (2022). Professional competencies development of sports science students: the need for more entrepreneurship education. *Management & Marketing. Challenges for the Knowledge Society, 17*(S1), 426-448, ISSN: ISSN: 2069-8887, DOI: . https://sciendo.com/article/10.2478/mmcks-2022 -0024DOI: 10.2478/mmcks-2022-0024

Mbam, B. N., & Nwibo, S. U. (2013). Entrepreneurship development as a strategy for poverty alleviation among farming households in Igbo-Eze North Local Government Area of Enugu State, Nigeria. *Greener Journal of Agricultural Sciences, 3*(10), 736–742. DOI: 10.15580/GJAS.2013.3.100613883

McDonald, H., Frelih-Larsen, A., Lóránt, A., Duin, L., Pyndt Andersen, S., Costa, G., & Bradley, H. (2021). *Carbon farming. Making agriculture fit for 2030.* European Parliament. Policy Department for Economic, Scientific and Quality of Life Policies. https://www.europarl.europa.eu/supporting-analyses

McElwee, G. (2008). A taxonomy of entrepreneurial farmers. *International Journal of Entrepreneurship and Small Business*, *6*(3), 465–478. DOI: 10.1504/IJESB.2008.019139

McElwee, G., & Smith, R. (2012). Classifying the strategic capability of farmers: A segmentation framework. *International Journal of Entrepreneurial Venturing*, *4*(2), 111–131. DOI: 10.1504/IJEV.2012.046517

McFadden, J.. (2022). The digitalisation of agriculture: A literature review and emerging policy issues. In *OECD Food, Agriculture and Fisheries Papers, No. 176.* OECD Publishing., DOI: 10.1787/285cc27d-

Mcintosh, R. W., & Goeldner, S. R. (1984). *Tourism – Phnciples, Practices*, Philosophies, John Wiley and Sons, New York.

Meert, H., Van Huylenbroeck, G., Vernimmen, T., Bourgeois, M., & van Hecke, E. (2005). Farm household survival strategies and diversification on marginal farms. *Journal of Rural Studies*, *21*(1), 81–97. DOI: 10.1016/j.jrurstud.2004.08.007

Meeus, J. H. (1993). The transformation of agricultural landscapes in Western Europe. *The Science of the Total Environment, 129*(1-2), 171–190. DOI: 10.1016/0048-9697(93)90169-7

Megginson, W. L., & Netter, J. M. (2001). From state to market: A survey of empirical studies on privatization. *Journal of Economic Literature, 39*(2), 321–389. DOI: 10.1257/jel.39.2.321

Merli, R., Preziosi, M., & Acampora, A. (2018). How do scholars approach the circular economy? A systematic literature review. *Journal of Cleaner Production, 178*, 703–722. DOI: 10.1016/j.jclepro.2017.12.112

Mesić, Ž., Petljak, K., Borović, D., & Tomić, M. (2020). Segmentation of local food consumers based on altruistic motives and perceived purchasing barriers: A Croatian study. *Ekonomska Istrazivanja, 34*(1), 221–242. DOI: 10.1080/1331677X.2020.1782243

Meuwissen, M. P., Feindt, P. H., Spiegel, A., Termeer, C. J., Mathijs, E., De Mey, Y., & Reidsma, P. (2019). A framework to assess the resilience of farming systems. *Agricultural Systems, 176*, 102656. DOI: 10.1016/j.agsy.2019.102656

Meyerding, S. G. H., Trajer, N., & Lehberger, M. (2019). What is local food? The case of consumer preferences for local food labeling of tomatoes in Germany. *Journal of Cleaner Production, 207*, 30–43. DOI: 10.1016/j.jclepro.2018.09.224

Michalcewicz-Kaniowska, M., & Zajdel, M. (2019). Rural development in European Union policy. *Economic science for rural development, 50*, 140-146.

Michel-Villarreal, R., Vilalta-Perdomo, E. L., Canavari, M., & Hingley, M. (2021). Resilience and digitalization in short food supply chains: A case study approach. *Sustainability (Basel), 13*(11), 5913. DOI: 10.3390/su13115913

Mihailović, B., Birmančević, B., & Obradović, M. (2014). The selection factors of consultants in Serbian agro-sector. *Ekonomika Poljoprivrede, 61*(1), 149–162. DOI: 10.5937/ekoPolj1401149M

Mihailović, B., & Popović, V. (2021). Digital marketing of agri-food products in support of rural tourism during the Covid pandemic. In *Tourism International Scientific Conference Vrnjačka Banja-TISC,* Vol. 6, No. 1, 111-126. DOI: 10.52370/TISC21111BM

Mihailović, B., & Radić Jean, I. (2019). Resources and potential of agri-food products with added value in Braničevo-Podunavlje region. *Ekonomika Poljoprivrede, 66*(3), 669–680. DOI: 10.5937/ekoPolj1903669M

Mihailović, B., Simonović, Z., & Brzaković, T. (2018). Strategic planning of sustainable development of agriculture of Lajkovac Municipality. *Ekonomika Poljoprivrede, 65*(2), 465–884. DOI: 10.5937/ekoPolj1802475M

Milestad, R., Dedieu, B., Darnhofer, I., & Bellon, S. (2012). Farms and farmers facing change: The adaptive approach. In Darnhofer, I., Gibbon, D., & Dedieu, B. (Eds.), *Farming Systems Research into the 21st Century: The new Dynamic* (pp. 365–385). Springer. DOI: 10.1007/978-94-007-4503-2_16

Miletić, D., Vojvodić, A., & Vojvodić, M. (2017). The basic characteristics of the information technology sector in Serbia. *SEER: Journal for Labour and Social Affairs in Eastern Europe*, 5-20.

Milić, D., Sredojević, Z., & Lukač-Bulatović, M. (2017). Sustainability organizational-economic model of value chain organic raspberry. *Journal on Processing and Energy in Agriculture, 21*(3), 163–167. DOI: 10.5937/JPEA1703163M

Milisavljević, M. (1996). *Marketing*, Savremena administracija, Beograd.

Ministry of Environmental Protection – MEP. (2022). *Nationally determined contribution (NDC) of the Republic of Serbia for the 2021–2030.* https://unfccc.int/sites/default/files/NDC/2022-08/NDC%20Final_ Serbia%20english. pdf

Ministry of Environmental Protection – MEP. (2024a). The third national communication of the Republic of Serbia to the UNFCC. https://unfccc.int/sites/default/files/resource/3NC_Serbia.pdf

Ministry of Environmental Protection – MEP. (2024b). *Nacrt Akcionog plana Strategije zaštite životne sredine za 2024-2028* [Draft Environmental Protection Strategy Action Plan for 2024-2028]. https://www.ekologija.gov.rs/informacije-od-javnog-znacaja/javne-rasprave

Ministry of Finance of the Republic of Serbia. *Database on Raspberry Export.* Available at: https://www.carina.rs/

Mishra, R. (2023). Fresh water availability and its global challenge. *British Journal of Multidisciplinary and Advanced Studies, 4*(3), 1–78. DOI: 10.37745/bjmas.2022.0208

Mitchell, M., & Hall, D. (2005). Rural Tourism as Sustainable Business: Key Themes and Issues. In Hall, D., Kirkpatrick, I., & Mitchell, M. (Eds.), *Rural Tourism and Sustainable Business* (pp. 1–15). Channel View Publications. DOI: 10.2307/jj.27195513.6

Mogues, T., Fan, S., & Benin, S. (2015). Public investments in and for agriculture. *European Journal of Development Research, 27*(3), 337–352. DOI: 10.1057/ejdr.2015.40

Moinet, G. Y. K., Hijbeek, R., van Vuuren, D. P., & Giller, K. E. (2023). Carbon for soils, not soils for carbon. *Global Change Biology, 29*(9), 2384–2398. DOI: 10.1111/gcb.16570

Mondal, P., & Basu, M. (2009). Adoption of precision agriculture technologies in India and in some developing countries: Scope, present status and strategies. *Progress in Natural Science, 19*(6), 659–666. DOI: 10.1016/j.pnsc.2008.07.020

Monteleone, S., Moraes, E., Tondato de Faria, B., Aquino, P.Junior, Maia, R., Neto, A. T., & Toscano, A. (2020). Exploring the adoption of precision agriculture for irrigation in the context of agriculture 4.0: The key role of internet of things. *Sensors (Basel), 20*(24), 7091. DOI: 10.3390/s20247091 PMID: 33322252

Montenegro Hernandez, J. (2024). Blockchain Applications in the Food Industry: A Systematic Literature Review. *International Journal of Applied Research in Business and Management, 5*(2). Advance online publication. DOI: 10.51137/ijarbm.2024.5.2.23

Moragues-Faus, A., & Morgan, K. (2015). Reframing the foodscape: The emergent world of urban food policy. *Environment and Planning A. Environment & Planning A, 47*(7), 1558–1573. DOI: 10.1177/0308518X15595754

Morgan, S. L., Marsden, T., Miele, M., & Morley, A. (2010). Agricultural multifunctionality and farmers' entrepreneurial skills: A study of Tuscan and Welsh farmers. *Journal of Rural Studies, 26*(2), 116–129. DOI: 10.1016/j.jrurstud.2009.09.002

Moser, A., & Korstjens, I. (2018). Series: Practical guidance to qualitative research. Part 3: Sampling, data collection and analysis. *The European Journal of General Practice, 24*(1), 9–18. DOI: 10.1080/13814788.2017.1375091

Muhi, B. (2009). *Primena marketinga u seoskom turizmu Vojvodine*, Univerzitet Educons, Fakultet poslovne ekonomije, Sremska Kamenica.

Mukherjeel, N., Hug, J., Sutherland, W. J., McNeil, J., Van Opstal, M., Dahdouh-Guebas, F., & Koedam, N. (2015). The Delphi technique in ecology and biological conservation: Applications and guidelines. *Methods in Ecology and Evolution, 6*(9), 1097–1109. DOI: 10.1111/2041-210X.12387

Mulibana, L., & Tshikovhi, N. (2024). Rural Entrepreneurship and Innovation in BRICS Economies: Secondary Evidence from Rural Areas in South Africa. *Sustainability (Basel), 16*(6), 2408. DOI: 10.3390/su16062408

Mullen, W., McGinn, J., Lean, M. E. J., MacLean, M. R., Gardner, P., Duthie, G. G., & Crozier, A. (2002). Ellagitannins, flavonoids, and other phenolics in red raspberries and their contribution to antioxidant capacity and vasorelaxation properties. *Journal of Agricultural and Food Chemistry, 50*(18), 5191–5196. DOI: 10.1021/jf020140n

Mundler, P. (2022). The role of proximity in food systems. In *Handbook on the Geographies of Proximity* (pp. 368–381). Edward Elgar Publishing. DOI: 10.4337/9781786434784.00027

Mundler, P., & Laughrea, S. (2016). The contributions of short food supply chains to territorial development: A study of three Quebec territories. *Journal of Rural Studies, 45*, 218–229. DOI: 10.1016/j.jrurstud.2016.04.001

Musik, C., & Bogner, A. (2019). Book title: Digitalization & society: A sociology of technology perspective on current trends in data, digital security and the Internet. *Osterreichische Zeitschrift fur Soziologie, 44*(S1), 1–14. DOI: 10.1007/s11614-019-00344-5

Naftel, H. (2022). *Understanding the Barriers to Carbon Farming on Private Lands*. All Graduate Plan B and other Reports. 1677. https://digitalcommons.usu.edu/gradreports/1677

Nambisan, S. (2017). Digital entrepreneurship: Toward a digital technology perspective of entrepreneurship. *Entrepreneurship Theory and Practice, 41*(6), 1029–1055. DOI: 10.1111/etap.12254

Naorem, A., Jayaraman, S., Dang, Y., Dalal, R., Sinha, N., Rao, C., & Patra, A. (2023). Soil constraints in an arid environment: Challenges, prospects, and implications. *Agronomy (Basel), 13*(1), 220. DOI: 10.3390/agronomy13010220

Nastase, C., Cha ovschi, C., Lucaci, A. (2019). Opportunities and Challenges for a Sustainable Rural Entrepreneurship. *Ovidius University Annals, Economic Sciences Series,* XIX(1).

Nasution, M., Rahmad, D., & Rusyanto, R. (2018). Financial and Economic Analysis Irrigation Area Development Bajayu–Serdang Bedagai. *SPECTA Journal of Technology, 2*(1), 53–62. DOI: 10.35718/specta.v2i1.95

National Institute of Statistics. (2023). *Population and Housing Census 2021. Resident population by ethnicity, by counties, municipalities, cities, communes.* Retrieved from https://www.recensamantromania.ro/rezultate-rpl-2021/rezultate-definitive-caracteristici-etno-culturale-demografice/

National Institute of Statistics. (2024a). *Population by domicile on January 1 by age and age groups, sexes, counties and localities.* Retrieved from Tempo online – statistical database http://statistici.insse.ro:8077/tempo-online/#/pages/tables/insse-table

National Institute of Statistics. (2024b). *Registered unemployed at the end of the month, by gender, counties and localities.* Retrieved from Tempo online – statistical database http://statistici.insse.ro:8077/tempo-online/#/pages/tables/insse-table

National Institute of Statistics. (2024c). *Share of unemployed people registered at the end of the month in the total labor resources, by gender, counties and localities.* Retrieved from Tempo online – statistical database http://statistici.insse.ro:8077/tempo-online/#/pages/tables/insse-table

National Institute of Statistics. (2025). *Classification of Activities in the National Economy* [PDF Document]. Retrieved from https://insse.ro/cms/files/CAEN/CAEN-Rev.3_structura-completa.pdf

Neculai-Valeanu, A.-S., Sanduleanu, C., Amaritii, G., & Bruma, I. S. (2025b). Precision livestock farming and its role for assuring a sustainable cattle management – A study case on connected cow. *Scientific Papers. Series Management, Economic Engineering in Agriculture and Rural Development, 25*(1), 689–696. ISSN 2284-7995.

Neculai-Valeanu, A.-S., Sanduleanu, C., & Porosnicu, I. (2025a). From tradition to precision: Leveraging digital tools to improve cattle health and welfare. *Frontiers in Veterinary Science, 12*, 1549512. Advance online publication. DOI: 10.3389/fvets.2025.1549512

Nedilska, L., & Oleniuk, D. (2020). Agribusiness digitalization: Trends and funding sources. *Scientific Horizons*, *6*(91), 26–32. DOI: 10.33249/2663-2144-2020-91-6-26-32

Neergaard, H., & Ulhøi, J. P. (Eds.). (2007). *Handbook of qualitative research methods in entrepreneurship.* Edward Elgar Publishing. DOI: 10.4337/9781847204387

Neethirajan, S. (2025). Safeguarding digital livestock farming: A comprehensive cybersecurity roadmap for dairy and poultry industries. *Frontiers in Big Data, 8*, 1556157. Advance online publication. DOI: 10.3389/fdata.2025.1556157

Nejašmić, P., & Barišić, P. (2021). Analiza situacije digitalnog marketinga ruralnog turizma u Republici Hrvatskoj. In: *Prema sigurnijoj socijalnoj budućnosti. Istraživanje o socijalnim uslugama u Belom Manastiru,* 1-27.

Njegovan, Z., & Pejanović, R. (2009). Ruralna regionalizacija AP Vojvodine, Monografija, Univerzitet u Novom Sadu, Poljoprivredni fakultet, Departman za ekonomiku poljoprivrede i sociologiju sela, Novi Sad.

North, D. C. (1990). *Institutions, institutional change and economic performance*. Cambridge University Press. DOI: 10.1017/CBO9780511808678

OECD. (2011). *Fostering Innovation for Green Growth*.

OECD. (2019). *PISA 2018 Results* (Vol. I). OECD Publishing.

OECD. (2020). *Developing Sustainable Finance Definitions and Taxonomies*.

OECD. (2022). Green Growth and Sustainable Development. https://www.oecd.org/greengrowth

OECD. (2022). Rural entrepreneurship and start-ups. In *Unlocking Rural Innovation*. OECD Publishing., DOI: 10.1787/60d226dd-

OECD. (2023). *Towards Orderly Green Transition: Investment Requirements and Managing Risks to Capital Flows*

OECD. (2025). *Agricultural Outlook 2025-2034*. https://www.oecd.org/en/publications/oecd-fao-agricultural-outlook-2025-2034_601276cd-en.html

Okafor, N. (2011). *Environmental Microbiology of Aquatic and Waste Systems*. Springer., DOI: 10.1007/978-94-007-1460-1

Oltean, R. C., & Arion, F. H. (2023). The European rural development vision in Romanian context, 72-75

Onozaka, Y., Nurse, G., & McFadden, D. T. (2010). Local food consumers: How motivations and perceptions translate to buying behavior. *Choices*, *25*(1), 1–15. DOI: 10.22004/ag.econ.93822

Opria, A.-M., Ro u, L., & Ia u, C. (2023). The Economic Impact of the LEADER Program in the Rural Communities of Romania. *Scientific Annals of Economics and Business*, *70*(3), 399–420. DOI: 10.47743/saeb-2023-0026

Organisation for Economic Co-operation and Development. (2021). *The digital transformation of SMEs* (OECD Studies on SMEs and Entrepreneurship). OECD Publishing. DOI: 10.1787/bdb9256a-en

Organisation for Economic Co-operation and Development/OECD. (2020). *Enterprises by business size*. https://www.oecd.org/en/data/indicators/enterprises-by-business-size.html

Osman, K. (2013). *Soils: Principles, properties and management*. Springer., DOI: 10.1007/978-94-007-5663-2

Otiman, P. I., Mateoc-Sîrb, N., Go a, V., Băne , A., Sălă an, C., Feher, A., Raicov, M., & Iucu, Z. (2023). *Where is Romania's agriculture and where it is going?* Romanian Academy Publishing House.

Palma, O., Plà-Aragonés, L. M., Mac Cawley, A., & Albornoz, V. M. (2025). AI and Data Analytics in the Dairy Farms: A Scoping Review. *Animals (Basel), 15*(9), 1291. DOI: 10.3390/ani15091291

Pandey, N., Kamboj, N., Sharma, A., & Kumar, A. (2022). An overview of recent advancements in the irrigation, fertilization, and technological revolutions of agriculture. In Bahukhandi, K., Kamboj, N., & Kamboj, V. (Eds.), *Environmental Pollution and Natural Resource Management* (pp. 167–184). Springer., DOI: 10.1007/978-3-031-05335-1_11

Pantić, M., & Čolić, N. (2023). Digital participation framework for mountain areas in Serbia. *Transylvanian Review of Administrative Sciences, 19*(68), 78–95. DOI: 10.24193/tras.68E.5

Pan, Y., Zhang, S., & Zhang, M. (2024). The impact of entrepreneurship of farmers on agriculture and rural economic growth: Innovation-driven perspective. *Innovation and Green Development, 3*(1), 100093. DOI: 10.1016/j.igd.2023.100093

Panyik, E. (2015). Rural tourism governance: Determinants of policy-makers' support for tourism development. *Tourism Planning & Development, 12*(1), 48–72. DOI: 10.1080/21568316.2014.960603

Paoletti, J., & Shortridge, J. (2020). Improved representation of uncertainty in farm-level financial cost-benefit analyses of supplemental irrigation in humid regions. *Agricultural Water Management, 239*, 106245. DOI: 10.1016/j.agwat.2020.106245

Papava, V. (2009). Anatomical pathology of Georgia's Rose Revolution. *Problems of Economic Transition, 52*(5), 5–18.

Papić-Blagojević, N., & Stankov, B. (2024). Analysis of trends in youth unemployment in the European Union: The role and importance of youth entrepreneurship. In Grigoresku, A., & Andrei, J. V. (Eds.), *Entrepreneurship and Development for a Green Resilient Economy* (pp. 181–204). Emerald Publishing Limited., DOI: 10.1108/978-1-83797-088-920241007

Patel, B., & Chavda, K. (2013). Rural entrepreneurship in India: Challenge and problems. *International Journal of Advance Research in Computer Science and Management Studies, 1*(2).

Patel, R. (2009). Food sovereignty. *The Journal of Peasant Studies, 36*(3), 663–706. DOI: 10.1080/03066150903143079

Pathak, M., Slade, R., Shukla, P. R., Skea, J., Pichs-Madruga, R., & Ürge-Vorsatz, D. (2022). Technical Summary. In *Climate Change 2022: Mitigation of Climate Change. Contribution of WG III to the IPCC Sixth Assessment Report (AR6)*. Cambridge University Press., DOI: 10.1017/9781009157926.002

Patton, M. Q. (1990). *Qualitative evaluation and research methods*. SAGE Publications, inc.

Paul, C., Bartkowski, B., D nmez, C., Donc, A., Mayerd, S., Steffens, M., Weigl, S., Wiesmeierd, M., Wolfg, A., & Helming, K. (2023). Carbon farming: Are soil carbon certificates a suitable tool for climate change mitigation? *Journal of Environmental Management, 330*, 117142. https://doi.org/. 2022.117142.DOI: 10.1016/j.jenvman

Paul, L. (2020). Rural Development in Romania – A Few Considerations. *Studies in Business and Economics, 15*(2), 165–174. DOI: 10.2478/sbe-2020-0032

Paunović, I., Apostolopoulos, S., Miljković, I. B., & Stojanović, M. (2024). Sustainable rural healthcare entrepreneurship: A case study of Serbia. *Sustainability (Basel), 16*(3), 1143. DOI: 10.3390/su16031143

Paustian, K., Larson, E., Kent, J., Marx, E., & Swan, A. (2019). Soil C Sequestration as a Biological Negative Emission Strategy. *Frontiers in Climate*, *1*, 8. DOI: 10.3389/fclim.2019.00008

Pavel, A., Moldovan, B., Neamtu, B., & Hintea, C. (2018). Are Investments in Basic Infrastructure the Magic Wand to Boost the Local Economy of Rural Communities from Romania? *Sustainability (Basel), 10*(10), 3384. DOI: 10.3390/su10103384

Pavlović, V., Knežević, G., Joksimović, M., & Joksimović, D. (2019). Fraud detection in financial statements applying Benford's law with Monte Carlo simulation. *Acta Oeconomica, 69*(2), 217–239. DOI: 10.1556/032.2019.69.2.4

Pāvulēns, E., & Vilka, L. (2024). Digitalisation in the provision of social services: Rural counties perspective. In *SHS Web of Conferences* (Vol. 184, p. 05002). EDP Sciences.

Paxton, A. (1994). *The food miles report: The dangers of long-distance food transport*. SAFE Alliance.

Pejanović, R. (2013). Ogledi iz agrarne i ruralne ekonomije, Monografija, Univerzitet u Novom Sadu, Poljoprivredni fakultet, Departman za ekonomiku poljoprivrede i sociologiju sela, Novi Sad.

Peng, J., Liu, Z., Liu, Y., Hu, X., & Wang, A. (2015). Multifunctionality assessment of urban agriculture in Beijing City, China. *The Science of the Total Environment, 537*, 343–351. DOI: 10.1016/j.scitotenv.2015.07.136

Petropoulou, E., Benos, T., Theodorakopoulou, I., Iliopoulos, C., Castellini, A., Xhakollari, V., ... & Petruzzella, D. (2022). Understanding social innovation in short food supply chains: An exploratory analysis. *International Journal of Food Studies, 11*(SI), a5. DOI: 10.7455/ijfs/11.si.2022.a5

Petrović, M., Marina, I., & Jeločnik, M. (2024). The significance and role of using innovative technologies in modern agricultural production. [JRISS]. *Journal of Research and Innovation for Sustainable Society, 6*(2), 289–303. DOI: 10.33727/JRISS.2024.2.32:289-303

Phillip, D., & Ndirpaya, Y. D. (2020). Digitalization in Agriculture. *Food and Nutrition-A Case Study of Nigeria. FARA Research Report, 5*(10), 66.

Phillipson, J., Tiwasing, P., Gorton, M., Maioli, S., Newbery, R., & Turner, R. (2019). Shining a spotlight on small rural businesses: How does their performance compare with urban? *Journal of Rural Studies, 68*, 230–239. DOI: 10.1016/j.jrurstud.2018.09.017

Pinstrup Andersen, P., & Hazell, P. (1985). The impact of the Green Revolution and prospects for the future. *Food Reviews International, 1*(1), 1–25. DOI: 10.1080/87559128509540765

Pistor, K., Raiser, M., & Gelfer, S. (2000). Law and finance in transition economies. *Economics of Transition, 8*(2), 325–368. DOI: 10.1111/1468-0351.00047

Plečko, S., Tominc, P., & Širec, K. (2023). Digitalization in entrepreneurship: Unveiling the motivational and demographic influences towards sustainable digital sales strategies. *Sustainability (Basel), 15*(23), 16150. DOI: 10.3390/su152316150

Poeplau, C., & Dechow, R. (2023). The legacy of one hundred years of climate change for organic carbon stocks in global agricultural topsoils. *Scientific Reports, 13*(1), 7483. DOI: 10.1038/s41598-023-34753-0

Poggensee, K., & Poggensee, J. (2021). Static investment calculation methods. In *Investment Valuation and Appraisal: Theory and Practice* (pp. 31–84). Springer., DOI: 10.1007/978-3-030-62440-8_2

Polas, M. R. H., Raju, V., Muhibbullah, M., & Tabash, M. I. (2022). Rural women characteristics and sustainable entrepreneurial intention: A road to economic growth in Bangladesh. *Journal of Enterprising Communities: People and Places in the Global Economy, 16*(3), 421–449. DOI: 10.1108/JEC-10-2020-0183

Pomfret, R. (2006). *The Central Asian Economies since Independence*. Princeton University Press. DOI: 10.1515/9780691222509

Poojari, M., Hanumanthappa, H., Prasad, C. D., Jathanna, H. M., Ksheerasagar, A. R., Shetty, P., Shanmugam, B. K., & Vasudev, H. (2024). Computational modelling for the manufacturing of solar-powered multifunctional agricultural robot. [IJIDeM]. *International Journal on Interactive Design and Manufacturing*, *18*(8), 5725–5736. DOI: 10.1007/s12008-023-01291-y

Pop-Eleches, G. (2009). *From Economic Crisis to Reform: IMF Programs in Latin America and Eastern Europe*. Princeton University Press.

Popescu, A., Tindeche, C., Mărcu ă, A., & Mărcu ă, L. (2022). Rural areas in Romania - discrepancies versus urban areas and European Union. *Scientific Papers. Series Management, Economic, Engineering in Agriculture and Rural Development*, *22*(1).

Popescu, C. A., Iancu, T., Popescu, G., Adamov, T., & Ciolac, R. (2023). The Impact of Agritourism Activity on the Rural Environment: Findings from an Authentic Agritourist Area—Bukovina, Romania. *Sustainability (Basel)*, *15*(13), 10294. DOI: 10.3390/su151310294

Popescu, G. (2019). Prerequisites for Relaunching Economic Growth in Romanian Agriculture by Promoting Associativity. In Popescu, G. (Ed.), *Agrifood Economics and Sustainable Development in Contemporary Society* (pp. 186–209). IGI Global Scientific Publishing., DOI: 10.4018/978-1-5225-5739-5.ch009

Popescu, G., Popescu, C. A., Iancu, T., Brad, I., Pe , E., Adamov, T., & Ciolac, R. (2022). Sustainability through rural tourism in Moieciu area-development analysis and future proposals. *Sustainability (Basel)*, *14*(7), 4221. DOI: 10.3390/su14074221

Popović, V., Katić, B., & Živanović-Miljković, J. (2010). Rural development network and territorial competitiveness. *Economics of Agriculture, 57*(Special nu), 111-120.

Popović, V. Ž., Kalanović, B., & Živković, V. R. (2003). Malina u proizvodnji i izvozu poljoprivrede Srbije. *Ekonomika Poljoprivrede*, *50*(3), 267–275.

Popović, V., Katić, B., & Savić, M. (2011). Rural development in Serbia and the local communities. *Economics of Agriculture*, *58*(1), 33–44.

Popović, V., & Mihailović, B. (2023). Women Entrepreneurship in multifunctional agriculture for rural revival in Serbia. In *Sustainable growth and global social development in competitive economies* (pp. 225–247). IGI Global. DOI: 10.4018/978-1-6684-8810-2.ch012

Popović, V., Mihailović, B., & Simonović, Z. (2018). Modern Food Retail and Unfair Trading Practices. *Ekonomika Poljoprivrede*, *65*(4), 1499–1512. DOI: 10.5937/ekoPolj1804499P

Popović, V., & Mijajlović, N. (2014). Climate change and sustainable development in agriculture and forestry. In *Sustainable practices: Concepts, methodologies, tools, and applications* (pp. 18–48). IGI Global. DOI: 10.4018/978-1-4666-4852-4.ch002

Popović, V., Miljković, J. Ž., Subić, J., Jean-Vasile, A., Adrian, N., & Nicolăescu, E. (2015). Sustainable Land Management in Mining Areas in Serbia and Romania. *Sustainability (Basel)*, *7*(9), 11857–11877. DOI: 10.3390/su70911857

Popović, V., Sarić, R., & Jovanović, M. (2012). Sustainability of agriculture in Danube basin area. *Economics of Agriculture*, *59*(1), 73–87.

Popp, D., Hafner, T., & Johnstone, N. (2020). Environmental policy and innovation: A decade of research. *International Review of Environmental and Resource Economics*, *14*(3-4), 265–337. DOI: 10.1561/101.00000111

Porter, M. E. (2008). The five competitive forces that shape strategy. *Harvard Business Review*, *86*(1), 78.

Porter, M. E., & Kramer, M. R. (2011). Creating Shared Value. *Harvard Business Review*, *89*(1-2).

Potter, C., & Tilzey, M. (2005). Agricultural policy discourses in the European post-Fordist transition: Neoliberalism, neomercantilism and multifunctionality. *Progress in Human Geography*, *29*(5), 581–600. DOI: 10.1191/0309132505ph569oa

Project "Internet of Food and Farm 2020", EU, 2021. Retrieved May 03, 2025 from https://cordis.europa.eu/project/id/731884

Rađenović, Ž., Janjić, I., Talić, M., Đokić, M., Rađenović, T., Boskov, T., & Krstić, B. (2025). Digital mapping of business performance indicators of agricultural holdings in Serbia. *Ekonomika Poljoprivrede*, *72*(1), 225–240. DOI: 10.59267/ekoPolj2501225R

Radić, V., Radić, N., & Cogoljević, V. (2022). New technologies as a driver of change in the agricultural sector. *Ekonomika Poljoprivrede*, *69*(1), 147–162. DOI: 10.5937/ekoPolj2201147R

Radosavljević, K. (2008). Market chain of fruit production in Serbia – Case study of raspberry and sour cherry. *Economic Annals*, *177*(177), 103–121. DOI: 10.2298/EKA0877103R

Radosavljević, K. (2016). Enhancing agri-competitiveness – A cost-benefit analysis of raspberry production on a family farm. *The Economics of Enterprise*, *7–8*(7-8), 492–498. DOI: 10.5937/ekopre1608492R

Radosavljević, K. (2024). The path of the Republic of Serbia into the global raspberry marketing channel. *The Economics of Enterprise*, *7–8*(7-8), 379–386. DOI: 10.5937/EKOPRE2408379R

Radovanović, J., Radosavljević, K., & Pătârlăgeanu Simona, R. (2024). Analysis of the role of FDI in the economic growth and environmental protection with particular reference to certain economic sectors in Serbia. *International Review, Faculty of Business Economics and Entrepreneurship, 3–4/2024*, 22–32.

Radović, G. & Pejanović, R. (2019). Importance of Promotion in Specialized Media for the Development of Rural Tourism in Serbia, *Media dialogues,* Vol. 12, No. 3, 97-108.

Radović, G. (2015). Modaliteti finansiranja ruralnog turizma u Republici Srbiji, Doktorska disertacija, Univerzitet u Novom Sadu, Poljoprivredni fakultet, Departman za ekonomiku poljoprivrede i sociologiju sela, Novi Sad.

Radović, G. (2016a). Sources of finance for rural tourism in the Republic of Serbia, *Economics of Agriculture, 63*(3), 1053-1065. ISSN 0352-3462. COBISS.SR-ID 27671. UDC: 338.48-44(1-22)(497.11). https://bsaae.bg.ac.rs/images/Ekonomika%20kompletna/2016/EP%203%202016lq.pdf

Radović, G. (2016b). Razvoj ruralnog turizma u Sloveniji - moguće smernice Srbiji, *HiT Menadžment – Menadžment u hotelijerstvu i turizmu, 4* (2/2016), 103-111.

Radović, G. (2017). *Experience of foreign countries in rural tourism development - lessons for Serbia,* In: Cvijanović, D. et al. (Eds), 2nd International Scientific Conference "Tourism in Function of Development of the Republic of Serbia – Tourism Product as a Factor of Competitiveness of the Serbian Economy and Experiences of other Countries", University of Kragujevac, Faculty of Hotel Management and Tourism, Vrnjačka Banja, Serbia, June 1-3, 2017, Thematic Proceedings II, 429-443. http://www.tisc.rs/proceedings/index.php/hitmc/article/view/112/109

Radović, G. (2020b). Underdevelopment of rural tourism in Serbia: Causes, consequences and possible directions of development, *Economics of Agriculture, 67*(4), 1337-1352. ISSN 0352-3462. COBISS.SR-ID 27671. https://doi:DOI: 10.5937/ekoPolj2004337R

Radović, G., Drãcea, R. M., Vuković, P., & Zejak, D. (2024). *Financing of Rural Tourism in Romania, Serbia and Montenegro in the Period of Integration into the European Union,* In: Proceedings of the 18th International Conference on Business Excellence Smart Solutions for a Sustainable Future (ICBE 2024), 21-23 March 2024, Bucharest, Romania, 2664-2684. https://sciendo.com/article/10.2478/picbe-2024-0223

Radović, G., Košić, K., & Demirović, D. (2018). Financing as a key factor of the Strategy of sustainable rural tourism development in the Republic of Serbia, *Economics of Agriculture, 65*(1), 413-426. ISSN 0352-3462. COBISS.SR-ID 27671. . www.ea.bg.ac.rs/index.php/EA/issue/view/1/Volume%2065%20Issue%20%601%20 2018DOI: 10.5937/ekoPolj1801413R

Radović, G., Subić, J., & Pejanović, V. (2024). Analysis of implementation of the IPARD II program in Serbia. *Economics of agriculture, 71*(3), 1017-1031. DOI: 10.59267/ekoPolj24031017R

Radović, G. (2013). Problemi razvoja ruralnog turizma u Republici Srbiji. *Agroekonomika, Br., 59-60*, 114–123.

Radović, G., Pejanović, R., & Njegovan, Z. (2012). Značaj i uloga integrisanog ruralnog turističkog proizvoda u Republici Srbiji, *Ekonomski vidici - tematski broj: Privredni preobražaj Srbije – mogućnosti i ograničenja*, God. XVII. *Broj, 4*, 577–591.

Radović, G., Petrović, D. M., Demirović-Bajrami, D., Radovanović, M., & Vuković, N. (2020a). Can Proper Funding Enhance Sustainable Tourism in Rural Settings? Evidence from a Developing Country, *Sustainability, 12*(18), 7797, 1-16. COBISS. *SR-ID, 64033033*. Advance online publication. DOI: 10.3390/su12187797

Radović, G., Popović, V., & Grujić-Vučkovski, B. (2024). Incentives for Credit Support of Agriculture in the Republic of Serbia [WBJAERD]. *Western Balkan Journal of Agricultural Economics and Rural Development*, *6*(1), 65–75. DOI: 10.5937/WBJAE2401065R

Rădulescu, E., Marian, L., & Moica, S. (2014). Innovations and Opportunities for Entrepreneurial Rural Developments. *Procedia Economics and Finance, 15,* 1495–1500. Advance online publication. DOI: 10.1016/S2212-5671(14)00616-9

Ragkos, A., Koutsou, S., Theodoridis, A., Manousidis, T., & Lagka, V. (2018). Labor management strategies in facing the economic crisis. Evidence from Greek livestock farms. *New Medit, 17*(1), 59–72. DOI: 10.30682/nm1801f

Raicov M., Banes A., Brad I., Feher A. (2021). Absorption of rural development funds. A lesson learned?. *Scientific Papers. Series "Management, Economic Engineering in Agriculture and rural development"*, 21(2).

Raihan, A. (2024). A review of the digitalization of the small and medium enterprises (SMEs) toward sustainability. *Global Sustainability Research, 3*(2), 1–16. DOI: 10.56556/gssr.v3i2.695

Rakić, T., & Hanžek, M. (2022). Promocija ruralnih turističkih destinacija: analiza službene web stranice za Hrvatsku kao turističku destinaciju. In: *2nd International Scientific and Professional Conference for the Development of Rural Tourism: Sustainable and responsible development of the rural area,* 116-133.

RARIS. (2012). Vodič za ruralni turizam, Regionalna agencija za razvoj Istočne Srbije, Dostupno na: http://www.raris.rs (pristup: 14.05.2025.)

Răzvanţă Puie, F. (2020). The role of European funds in developing and sustaining rural entrepreneurship in Romania. In *Proceedings of the International Conference on Business Excellence, 14*(1), 2020. 134-148. DOI: 10.2478/picbe-2020-0014

Reardon, T., & Timmer, C. P. (2014). Five inter-linked transformations in the Asian agrifood economy: Food security implications. *Global Food Security, 3*(2), 108–117. DOI: 10.1016/j.gfs.2014.02.001

Refai, D., Elkafrawi, N., & Gittins, P. (2024). Creating a sustainable ripple in rural entrepreneurship–the case of Deserttulip in resource-constrained rural Jordan. *International Journal of Entrepreneurial Behaviour & Research, 30*(1), 180–199. DOI: 10.1108/IJEBR-02-2023-0168

Refai, D., & McElwee, G. (2023). Refugee subentrepreneurship: The emergence of a liquid cage. *Work, Employment and Society, 37*(4), 1032–1051. DOI: 10.1177/09500170211062817

Regional Cooperation Council – RCC. (2021). Action Plan for the Implementation of the Sofia Declaration on the Green Agenda for the Western Balkans 2021-2030. https://www.rcc.int/pubs/183/action-plan-for-the-implementation-of-the-sofia-declaration-on-the-green-agenda-for-the-western-balkans-2021-2030

Reich, B. J., Beck, J. T., & Price, J. (2018). Food as ideology: Measurement and validation of locavorism. *The Journal of Consumer Research, 45*(4), 849–868. DOI: 10.1093/jcr/ucy027

Renkema, M., & Hilletofth, P. (2022). Intermediate short food supply chains: A systematic review. *British Food Journal, 124*(13), 541–558. DOI: 10.1108/BFJ-06-2022-0463

Rennings, K. (2000). Redefining innovation—Eco-innovation research and the contribution from ecological economics. *Ecological Economics, 32*(2), 319–332. DOI: 10.1016/S0921-8009(99)00112-3

Renting, H., Marsden, T. K., & Banks, J. (2003). Understanding alternative food networks: Exploring the role of short food supply chains in rural development. *Environment & Planning A, 35*(3), 393–411. DOI: 10.1068/a3510

Renting, H., Rossing, W. A., Groot, J. C., Van der Ploeg, J. D., Laurent, C., Perraud, D., Stobbelaar, D. J., & Van Ittersum, M. K. (2009). Exploring multifunctional agriculture. A review of conceptual approaches and prospects for an integrative transitional framework. *Journal of Environmental Management, 90*, S112–S123. DOI: 10.1016/j.jenvman.2008.11.014

Renting, H., Schermer, M., & Rossi, A. (2012). Building food democracy: Exploring civic food networks and newly emerging forms of food citizenship. *International Journal of Sociology of Agriculture and Food, 19*(3), 289–307.

Report Seeds of Kenosis Design [PDF document]. Retrieved from RisCo website https://www.risco.ro/date-firma/40006371/euro

Republic Statistical Office (RZS). (2020). *Statistical Yearbook of the Republic of Serbia*. Belgrade, Serbia: Republic Statistical Office.

Rhouma, A., El Jeitany, J., Mohtar, R., & Gil, J. M. (2024). Trends in the Water–Energy–Food Nexus Research. *Sustainability (Basel), 16*(3), 1162. DOI: 10.3390/su16031162

Ribeiro, M., & Marques, C. (2002). Rural tourism and the development of less favoured areas—Between rhetoric and practice. *International Journal of Tourism Research, 4*(3), 211–220. DOI: 10.1002/jtr.377

Richter, A., Waidelich, L., Kölmel, B., Bulander, R., Glaser, P., Proske, M., & Brügmann, S. (2019). Digitalisation and Future Challenges in Rural Areas: An Open Innovation based Research. In *ICETE (1)*, 153-159.

Robert, P. C. (2002). Precision agriculture: a challenge for crop nutrition management. In *Progress in Plant Nutrition: Plenary Lectures of the XIV International Plant Nutrition Colloquium: Food security and sustainability of agro-ecosystems through basic and applied research* (pp. 143-149). Springer Netherlands. DOI: 10.1007/978-94-017-2789-1_11

Roberts, E., Beel, D., Philip, L., & Townsend, L. (2017). Rural resilience in a digital society. *Journal of Rural Studies, 54*, 355–359. DOI: 10.1016/j.jrurstud.2017.06.010

Roberts, L., & Hall, D. (2003). *Rural tourism and Recreation: Principles to Practise*. CABI Publishing.

Rockström, J., Falkenmark, M., Karlberg, L., Hoff, H., Rost, S., & Gerten, D. (2009). Future water availability for global food production: The potential of green water for increasing resilience to global change. *Water Resources Research*, *45*(7), 1–16. DOI: 10.1029/2007WR006767

Rodrik, D. (1999). *The new global economy and developing countries: Making openness work. Policy Essay No. 24*. Overseas Development Council. DOI: 10.56021/9781565170278

Rodrik, D. (2007). *One economics, many recipes: Globalization, institutions, and economic growth*. Princeton University Press. DOI: 10.1515/9781400829354

Roland, G. (2000). *Transition and economics: Politics, markets, and firms*. MIT Press.

Romstad, E. (2002). Policies for promoting public goods in agriculture. Paper presented at the 10th EAAE Congress in Zaragoza, Spain, 28-31

Ronzhin, A., Figurek, A., Surovtsev, V., & Dibirova, K. (2025). Digital Transformation and Precision Farming as Catalysts of Rural Development. *Land (Basel)*, *14*(7), 1464. DOI: 10.3390/land14071464

Rose, S., Khatri-Chhetri, A., Stier, M., Wiese-Rozanova, L., Dittmer, K. M., Shelton, S., & Wollenberg, E. (2022). *Ambition for SOC sequestration in the new and updated NDCs: 2020-2022. Analysis of agricultural sub-sectors in national climate change strategies*. CCAFS Info Note. https://cgspace.cgiar.org/server/api/core/bitstreams/056fa862-9e65-4a0f-b72f-bc13eb83212c/content

Ruchay, V. K., Guo, H., & Pezzuolo, A. (2024). On-barn cattle facial recognition using deep transfer learning and data augmentation. *Computers and Electronics in Agriculture*, *225*, 109306. DOI: 10.1016/j.compag.2024.109306

Rujescu, C.-I., Feher, A., Toader, C.-S., Sîrbulescu, E. C., Raicov, M., Todor Marković, T., & Kokot, Z. (2025). Rural residential energy behaviour: A trans-generational and cross-country research. *Environmental Research Communications*, *7*(7), 075004. Advance online publication. DOI: 10.1088/2515-7620/ade8d9

Rumpel, C., Amiraslani, F., Chenu, C., Garcia Cardenas, M., Kaonga, M., Koutika, L.-S., Ladha, J., Madari, B., Shirato, Y., Smith, P., Soudi, B., Soussana, J.-F., Whitehead, D., & Wollenberg, E. (2020). The 4p1000 initiative: Opportunities, limitations and challenges for implementing soil organic carbon sequestration as a sustainable development strategy. *Ambio*, *49*(1), 350–360. DOI: 10.1007/s13280-019-01165-2

Rusu, M. (2005). *Dezvoltare rurală – politici i structuri economice*. Editura Expert.

Sachs, J. (1994). *Poland's Jump to the Market Economy*. MIT Press.

Sachs, J., & Reid, W. (2006). Investments toward sustainable development. *Science, 312*(5776), 1002–1002. DOI: 10.1126/science.1124822 PMID: 16709769

Sage, C. (2014). The transition movement and food sovereignty: From local resilience to global engagement in food system transformation. *Journal of Consumer Culture, 14*(2), 254–275. DOI: 10.1177/1469540514526281

Sahut, J. M., Iandoli, L., & Teulon, F. (2021). The age of digital entrepreneurship. *Small Business Economics, 56*(3), 1159–1169. DOI: 10.1007/s11187-019-00260-8

Saiz Rubio, V., & Rovira Mas, F. (2020). From smart farming towards agriculture 5.0: A review on crop data management. *Agronomy (Basel), 10*(2), 207. DOI: 10.3390/agronomy10020207

Sălă an, C., Moisa, S., & Radulov, I. (2017). Impact of advisory and consultancy work over the project-based development choices of a rural territory. *AgroLife Scientific Journal, 6*(2).

Salemink, K., Strijker, D., & Bosworth, G. (2017). Rural development in the digital age: A systematic literature review on unequal ICT availability, adoption, and use in rural areas. *Journal of Rural Studies, 54*, 360–371. DOI: 10.1016/j.jrurstud.2015.09.001

Samsudin, N., Zakaria, T., Osman, J., Ramdan, M. R., Khalid, I. K. M., Mohamad, N., & Sastraredja, S. (2024). The Digitalization Technology for Sustainable Rural Entrepreneurship: A Structured Review. *Journal of Advanced Research in Applied Sciences and Engineering Technology, 42*(1), 14–30. DOI: 10.37934/araset.42.1.1430

Sanderman, J., Hengl, T., & Fiske, G. J. (2017). Soil carbon debt of 12,000 years of human land use. *Proceedings of the National Academy of Sciences of the United States of America, 114*(36), 9575–9580. DOI: 10.1073/pnas.1706103114

Sanz-Cañada, J., Sánchez-Hernández, J. L., & López-García, D. (2023). Reflecting on the concept of local agroecological food systems. *Land (Basel), 12*(6), 1147. DOI: 10.3390/land12061147

Sate i comune (n.d.). *Tradi ii i obiceiuri: păstrarea culturii rurale.* Retrieved from https://sate-comune.ro/2024/06/02/traditii-si-obiceiuri-pastrarea-culturii-rurale/

Saxena, S. (2012). Problems Faced By Rural Entrepreneurs and Remedies to Solve. *Journal of Business and Management, 3*(1), 23–29.

Scaramuzzi, S., Gabellini, S., Belletti, G., & Marescotti, A. (2021). Agrobiodiversity-oriented food systems between public policies and private action: A socio-ecological model for sustainable territorial development. *Sustainability (Basel), 13*(21), 12192. DOI: 10.3390/su132112192

Schanbacher, W. D. (2010). *The politics of food: The global conflict between food security and food sovereignty*. Praeger. DOI: 10.5040/9798400698576

Schuett, L. (2024). Permanence and liability: Legal considerations on the integration of carbon dioxide removal into the EU emissions trading system. *Transnational Environmental Law, 13*(1), 87–110. DOI: 10.1017/S2047102524000013

Seelan, S. K., Laguette, S., Casady, G. M., & Seielstad, G. A. (2003). Remote sensing applications for precision agriculture: A learning community approach. *Remote Sensing of Environment, 88*(1-2), 157–169. DOI: 10.1016/j.rse.2003.04.007

Senić, R. & Senić, V. (2016): *Marketing menadžment u turizmu*, Univerzitet u Kragujevcu, Fakultet za hotelijerstvo i turizam, Vrnjačka Banja.

Serbian Environmental Protection Agency – SEPA. (2024). *Report on the state of the environment in the Republic of Serbia 2023*. https://sepa.gov.rs/wp-content/uploads/2025/02/ZivotnaSredina2023.pdf

Seuneke, P., Lans, T., & Wiskerke, J. S. (2013). Moving beyond entrepreneurial skills: Key factors driving entrepreneurial learning in multifunctional agriculture. *Journal of Rural Studies, 32*, 208–219. DOI: 10.1016/j.jrurstud.2013.06.001

Shafi, U., Mumtaz, R., García-Nieto, J., Hassan, S. A., Zaidi, S. A. R., & Iqbal, N. (2019). Precision agriculture techniques and practices: From considerations to applications. *Sensors (Basel), 19*(17), 3796. DOI: 10.3390/s19173796

Sharma, A., Goar, V., Kuri, M., & Chowdhary, C. L. (2023). Supply chain management using blockchain security enhancement. In V. Goar, M. Kuri, R. Kumar, & T. Senjyu (Eds.), *Advances in Information Communication Technology and Computing* (Lecture Notes in Networks and Systems, Vol. 628, pp. 221–233). Springer, Singapore. DOI: 10.1007/978-981-19-9888-1_15

Sharma, V., & Irmak, S. (2020). Economic comparisons of variable rate irrigation and fertigation with fixed (uniform) rate irrigation and fertigation and pre-plant fertilizer management for maize in three soils. *Agricultural Water Management, 240*, 106307. DOI: 10.1016/j.agwat.2020.106307

Shine, P., Upton, J., Sefeedpari, P., & Murphy, M. D. (2020). Energy Consumption on Dairy Farms: A Review of Monitoring, Prediction Modelling, and Analyses. *Energies, 13*(5), 1288. DOI: 10.3390/en13051288

Shockley, J., & Snell, W. (2021, April 29). Carbon markets 101. *Economic and Policy Update, 21*(4), 1-3. https://agecon.ca.uky.edu/files/carbon_markets_101.pdf

Silva, A., Silva, B., Souza, C., Azevedo, B., Bassoi, L., Vasconcelos, D., Bonfi, G., Juarez, J., dos Santos, A., & Carneiro, F. (2020). Irrigation in the age of agriculture 4.0: Management, monitoring and precision. *Revista Ciência Agronômica, 51*(5), e20207695. DOI: 10.5935/1806-6690.20200090

Sima, E. (2022). The Romanian Rural Economy Diversification – Realities And Perspectives, *Agricultural Economics and Rural Development*, Institute of Agricultural Economics, *19*(2)

Sima, V., Gheorghe, I., Subić, J., & Nancu, D. (2020). Influences of the industry 4.0 revolution on the human capital development and consumer behavior: A systematic review. *Sustainability (Basel), 12*(10), 4035. DOI: 10.3390/su12104035

Simić, I. (2025, May 18). *Organska proizvodnja u Srbiji na tek 0,85 odsto površina, uglavnom se izvozi* [Organic production in Serbia is only 0.85 percent of the area, mostly exported]. N1 News. https://n1info.rs/biznis/organski-proizvodi-izvoz-srbija/

Sims, R. (2009). Food, place and authenticity: Local food and the sustainable tourism experience. *Journal of Sustainable Tourism, 17*(3), 321–336. DOI: 10.1080/09669580802359293

Singh, D., & Sobti, R. (2022). Long-range real-time monitoring strategy for Precision Irrigation in urban and rural farming in society 5.0. *Computers & Industrial Engineering, 167*, 107997. DOI: 10.1016/j.cie.2022.107997

Sisto. R., Lopolito, A, van Vliet, M. 2018. Stakeholder participation in planning rural development strategies: Land Use Policy 7- 442-450.

Sivini, S., & Vitale, A. (2023). Multifunctional and Agroecological Agriculture as Pathways of Generational Renewal in Italian Rural Areas. *Sustainability (Basel), 15*(7), 5990. DOI: 10.3390/su15075990

Slavin, J. L. (2005). Dietary fiber and body weight. *Nutrition (Burbank, Los Angeles County, Calif.), 21*(3), 411–418. DOI: 10.1016/j.nut.2004.08.018

Smit, A. B. (2004). Changing external conditions require high levels of entrepreneurship in agriculture. In *XV International Symposium on Horticultural Economics and Management 655* (pp. 167-173). DOI: 10.17660/ActaHortic.2004.655.21

Smith, B., Lawrence, G., & Richards, C. (2020). Consumption, identity and local food: A symbolic interactionist perspective. *Sociologia Ruralis, 60*(3), 646–665. DOI: 10.1111/soru.12290

Sojka, R., Bjorneberg, D., & Entry, J. (2002). *Irrigation: An historical perspective.* In: Lal R. (edt.) Encyclopedia of soil science, pp. 745-749, CRC Press Boca Raton, USA.

Song, B., Robinson, G. M., & Bardsley, D. K. (2020). Measuring multifunctional agricultural landscapes. *Land (Basel)*, *9*(8), 260. DOI: 10.3390/land9080260

Sonnino, R., & Marsden, T. (2006). Beyond the divide: Rethinking relationships between alternative and conventional food networks in Europe. *Journal of Economic Geography*, *6*(2), 181–199. DOI: 10.1093/jeg/lbi006

Sorea, D., Defta, M., & Popescu, I. M. (2023). Journeys to Significant Places in Orthodoxy as a Source of Sustainable Local Development in Romania. *Sustainability (Basel)*, *15*(7), 5693. DOI: 10.3390/su15075693

SORS. (2024). *Census of Agriculture 2023*. SORS, Belgrade, Serbia, retrieved at: Brosura KON 16 april.cdr (stat.gov.rs)

Sott, M. K., Furstenau, L. B., Kipper, L. M., Giraldo, F. D., Lopez-Robles, J. R., Cobo, M. J., Zahid, A., Abbasi, Q. H., & Imran, M. A. (2020). Precision techniques and agriculture 4.0 technologies to promote sustainability in the coffee sector: State of the art, challenges and future trends. *IEEE Access : Practical Innovations, Open Solutions*, *8*, 149854–149867. DOI: 10.1109/ACCESS.2020.3016325

Spechler, M. C. (2000). Uzbekistan: The silk road to nowhere? *Contemporary Economic Policy*, *18*(3), 295–303. DOI: 10.1111/j.1465-7287.2000.tb00026.x

Sredojević, Z., Kljajić, N., & Popović, N. (2013). *Investing in raspberry as an opportunity of sustainable development of rural areas of western Serbia. Buletinul Revista categoria B+ CNCSIS, Seria Stiinte Economice, Petrol-Gaze din Ploiesti, 1/201, II.* LXV.

Srivastava, R., Verma, H., Mohanty, S., & Pattnaik, S. (2003). Investment decision model for drip irrigation system. *Irrigation Science*, *22*(2), 79–85. DOI: 10.1007/s00271-003-0072-8

Stabinsky, D. (2021). *"Nature-based solutions" and the biodiversity and climate crises*. Third World Network. Environment & Development Series 21. https://www.twn.my/title/end/pdf/end21.pdf

Staic, L.G., Uliu, D.V., Vladu, M. (2022). Analysis of the influence of financing on the sustainable local development of the rural territories, part of the LAGs, through the LEADER method. *Scientific Papers. Series "Management, Economic Engineering in Agriculture and rural development"*, *22*(1).

Stamenović, A. P. (2024). The concept of smart rural development on the example of the municipality of Petrovac na Mlavi. In *Proceedings The First International Conference FUTURE-BME 2024 (Forging the Future: Pioneering Approaches in Business, Management and* Economics Engineering to Overcome Emerging Global Challenges), 279-285.

Stanciu, S. (2015). The Romanian Retail Food Market - Survival or Success for Domestic Companies. *Procedia Economics and Finance*, *23*, 1584–1589. Advance online publication. DOI: 10.1016/S2212-5671(15)00505-5

Stanimirov, E., & Stanimirova, M. (2023). Collaboration and financial sustainability of business in rural areas. *Bulgarian Journal of Agricultural Science*, *29*(Supplement 1), 147–151.

State Audit Institution – SAI. (2023). *Audit and Performance Audit Report: The Impact of Regional Development on Demographic Trends in the Republic of Serbia – Parallel Performance Audit*. Presentation.

Stathopoulou, S., Psaltopoulos, D., & Skuras, D. (2004). Rural entrepreneurship in Europe: A research framework and agenda. *International Journal of Entrepreneurial Behaviour & Research*, *10*(6), 404–425. DOI: 10.1108/13552550410564725

Statistical Office of the Republic of Serbia – SORS. (2012). *Obrada i održavanje zemljišta* [Cultivation and maintenance of land]. https://www.stat.gov.rs/sr-latn/oblasti/poljoprivreda-sumarstvo-i-ribarstvo/popis-poljoprivrede/popisni-rezultati-nivo-naselja-eksel-tabele/

Statistical Office of the Republic of Serbia – SORS. (2024a). *Area, livestock (LSU), labor force and standard output (SO) by legal status of holding and agricultural size of farm (UAA)*. Census of Agriculture 2023. https://data.stat.gov.rs/Home/Result/1300020101?languageCode=en-US. Last updated on: 6/6/2024.

Statistical Office of the Republic of Serbia – SORS. (2024b). *Fertilizers*. Census of Agriculture 2023. https://data.stat.gov.rs/Home/Result/1300021001?languageCode=en-US. Last updated on: 6/20/2024.

Statistical Office of the Republic of Serbia – SORS. (2024c). *Number of farms and areas of different crops and categories by agricultural size of farm (UAA)*. Census of Agriculture 2023. https://data.stat.gov.rs/Home/ Result/1300020201?language-Code=en-US. Last updated on: 10/7/2024.

Statistical Office of the Republic of Serbia – SORS. (2024d). *Number of farms and irrigated area by different crops and categories*. Census of Agriculture 2023. https://data.stat.gov.rs/Home/Result/1300020301? languageCode=en-US. Last updated on: 6/14/2024.

Statistical Office of the Republic of Serbia – SORS. (2024e*). Soil conservation.* Census of Agriculture 2023. https://data.stat.gov.rs/Home/Result/1300020902 ?languageCode=en-US. Last updated on: 6/20/2024.

Statistical Office of the Republic of Serbia – SORS. (2025a). *Soil management practice*. Census of Agriculture 2023. https://data.stat.gov.rs/Home/Result/1300020901 ?languageCode=en-US. Last updated on: 2/20/2025.

Statistical Office of the Republic of Serbia – SORS. (2025b). *Strukturne promene u poljoprivredi i njihov uticaj na ekonomski rast u Srbiji* [Structural changes in agriculture and their impact on economic growth in Serbia]. Census of Agriculture 2023. https://www.stat.gov.rs/sr-latn/publikacije/publication/?p=17265&tip=12

Stefan, D., Vasile, V., Popa, M. A., Cristea, A., Bunduchi, E., Sigmirean, C., Stefan, A.-B., Comes, C.-A., & Ciucan-Rusu, L. (2021). Trademark potential increase and entrepreneurship rural development: A case study of Southern Transylvania, Romania. *PLoS One*, *16*(1), e0245044. DOI: 10.1371/journal.pone.0245044

Štetić, S., Cvijanović, D., & Šimičević, D. (2014). Posebni oblici turizma Dunavskog regiona, Monografija, Institut za ekonomiku poljoprivrede, Beograd.

Stiglitz, J. E. (1999). Whither reform? Ten years of the transition. *World Bank Annual Conference on Development Economics*.

Stiglitz, J. E. (2002). *Globalization and its discontents*. W.W. Norton & Company.

Stiglitz, J., & Greenwald, B. (2014). *Creating a learning society: A new approach to growth, development, and social progress*. Columbia University Press., DOI: 10.7312/stig15214

STIPS – Agricultural Market Information System of Serbia. (2010). *Izveštaj o izvozu voća* [*Report on fruit exports*]. Ministry of Agriculture, Forestry and Water Management of the Republic of Serbia.

Stojanova, S., Cvar, N., Verhovnik, J., Božić, N., Trilar, J., Kos, A., & Stojmenova Duh, E. (2022). Rural digital innovation hubs as a paradigm for sustainable business models in europe's rural areas. *Sustainability (Basel)*, *14*(21), 14620. DOI: 10.3390/su142114620

Stojanović, M., Gligorijević, J., Grubor, M., Popović, M., Ćorić, B., Zarev, D., & Šmelcerović, M. (2024). the potential of digital marketing in the promotion of organic agricultural products. *Ekonomika Poljoprivrede, 71*(4), 1237–1251. DOI: 10.59267/ekoPolj24041237S

Strategy on Digital Skills Development in the Republic of Serbia for the period 2020 to 2024. (2020). *Official Gazette of the RS*, No. 21/20. https://pravno-informacioni-sistem.rs/eli/rep/sgrs/vlada/strategija/2020/21/2/reg

Stubbs, W., & Cocklin, C. (2008). Conceptualizing a "Sustainability Business Model". *Organization & Environment, 21*(2), 103–127. DOI: 10.1177/1086026608318042

Subić, J. (2010). *Specificities of investment process in agriculture (Specifičnosti procesa investiranja u poljoprivredi).* Institute of Agricultural Economics, Beograd, Serbia.

Subić, J., Jeločnik, M., & Petrović, M. (2025). *Economic assessment of investments in rural infrastructure in hilly-mountain areas.* In: Subic et al. (eds.) V International Scientific Conference "Sustainable agriculture and rural development". Institute of Agricultural Economics, Belgrade, Serbia, pp. 301-316.

Subic, J., Kljajic, N., & Jelocnik, M. (2017b). *Renewable energy and irrigation in the function of sustainable development of agriculture: Economic aspects (Obnovljivi izvori energije i navodnjavanje u funkciji održivog razvoja poljoprivrede: Ekonomski aspekti).* Institute of Agricultural Economics, Belgrade, Serbia.

Subić, J., Vasiljević, Z., Rodić, A. (2024). *Razvoj inovativnih rešenja u oblasti pametnog korišćenja zemljišta u poljoprivredi u cilju smanjenja emisije gasova u atmosferu sa efektom staklene bašte primenom obnovljivih izvora energije i naprednih informacionih tehnologija – Ocena ekonomske efektivnosti investicije.* Interna dokumentacija, Institut za ekonomiku poljoprivrede (IEP), Beograd, Srbija.

Subic, J., & Jelocnik, M. (2013). Economic and environmental aspects of controlled vegetable production within the region of Danube basin. In Andrei, J., Turek, A., Subic, J., & Dusmanescu, D. (Eds.), *Sustainable Technologies, Policies, and Constraints in the Green Economy* (pp. 39–62). IGI Global., DOI: 10.4018/978-1-4666-4098-6.ch003

Subić, J., Jeločnik, M., & Potrebić, V. (2021). Economic justification of innovative subsurface capillary irrigation system appliance in vegetable production in protected areas (Ekonomska opravdanost primene inovativnog podpovršinskog kapilarnog navodnjavanja u plasteničkoj proizvodnji povrća). In *Kljajic, N. (edt.) Techno and agro-economic analysis toward pros and cons of wider application of innovative way of subsurface capillary irrigation in the sector of agriculture (Tehno i agro-ekonomska analiza prednosti i nedostataka šire primene inovativnog načina podpovršinskog kapilarnog navodnjavanja u poljoprivrednom sektoru), Institute of agricultural economics* (pp. 117–144). Serbia.

Subić, J., Jovanović, M., Despotović, Ž., & Jeločnik, M. (2017a). Possibilities of Applying Robotic Systems and Smart Sensor Networks in Integrated Agricultural Apple Production. In *Advances in Robot Design and Intelligent Control* (pp. 269–281). Springer., DOI: 10.1007/978-3-319-49058-8_30

Subić, J., & Kuzman, B. (2016). Guide and model for business plan development at the farms (Uputstvo i model za izradu biznis plana na poljoprivrednim gazdinstvima). In Subic, (Eds.), *Advancement of financial knowledge and recording at farms in the Republic of Serbia (Unapređenje finansijskih znanja i evidencije na poljoprivrednim gazdinstvima u Republici Srbiji), Institute of Agricultural Economics*. Serbia.

Subić, J., Nastić, L., & Potrebić, V. (2013). Economic effects of the thermal water use in vegetable production on the territory of Central Danube Region. *Economics of Agriculture*, *60*(4), 745–757.

Surmanidze, N. (2022). Legislative Challenges of Georgian Entrepreneurship and Business Competitiveness. Institutions and Economies, 1-24.

Sustainability Guide. (n.d.). Cradle-to-cradle. Retrieved from https://sustainabilityguide.eu/methods/cradle-to-cradle/

Tagarakis, A. C., van Evert, F., Kempenaar, C., Ljubicic, N., Milic, D., Crnojevic-Bengin, V., & Crnojevic, V. (2018). Opportunities for precision agriculture in Serbia. In *Proceedings of the 14th International Conference on Precision Agriculture,* Montreal, QC, Canada (Vol. 24), 1-12.

Tanasă, L. (2024). Implications of Short Food Supply Chains in the Local Agri-Food System of the North-East Development Region, *Annals of the Academy of Romanian Scientists - Series on Agri-culture, Silviculture and Veterinary Medicine Sciences*, Vol. 13, No. 2/2024, ISSN 2344-2085, pp. 5-19, 2024, https://aos.ro/wp-content/anale/AVol13Nr2Art.1.pdf

Tanasă, L. (2024). In Clujeană, P. U. (Ed.), *Sisteme agroalimentare locale i lan uri scurte de aprovizionare func ionale din jude ul Bacău, în Rezilien ă i sustenabilitate în sistemele rurale, coord.: Ioan Sebastian Brumă i Diana Elena Creangă* (pp. 227–262)., http://www.editura.ubbcluj.ro/bd/ebooks/pdf/4469.pdf

Tangorra, F. M., Buoio, E., Calcante, A., Bassi, A., & Costa, A. (2024). Internet of Things (IoT): Sensors Application in Dairy Cattle Farming. *Animals (Basel), 14*(21), 3071. DOI: 10.3390/ani14213071

Telukdarie, A., Dube, T., Matjuta, P., & Philbin, S. (2023). The opportunities and challenges of digitalization for SMEs. *Procedia Computer Science, 217*, 689–698. DOI: 10.1016/j.procs.2022.12.265

Tešin, A., Dragin, A. S., Mijatov Ladičorbić, M., Jovanović, T., Zadel, Z., Surla, T., Košić, K., Amezcua-Ogáyar, J. M., Calahorro-López, A., Kuzman, B., & Stojanović, V. (2024). Quality of Life and Attachments to Rural Settlements: The Basis for Regeneration and Socio-Economic Sustainability. *Land (Basel), 13*(9), 1364. DOI: 10.3390/land13091364

The Association of Balkan Eco-Innovation – ABE. (2023). *Izveštaj o barijerama za širu primenu regenerativnih praksi u Srbiji* [Report on barriers to wider application of regenerative practices in Serbia]. https://balkanecoinnovations.org/wp-content/uploads/2024/02/Savez-Reg-Agri-Izvestaj-Barijere.pdf-1.pdf

The Association of Balkan Eco-Innovation – ABE. (2024). *Savez za regenerativnu poljoprivredu Srbije. Beli papir. Ukratko* [The Regenerative Agriculture Alliance of Serbia. White Paper. In Brief]. https://regagrisrbija.rs/ wp-content/uploads/2025/01/RegAgri-Savez-Beli-papir-2024.pdf

The Government of the Republic of Serbia. (2024). National Programme for the Adoption of the Acquis (NPAA) 2024-2027. https://www.mei.gov.rs/upload/documents/nacionalna_dokumenta/npaa/npaa_2024-2027_en.pdf

Thrassou, A., Uzunboylu, N., Vrontis, D., & Christofi, M. (2020). Digitalization of SMEs: A Review of Opportunities and Challenges. In Thrassou, A., Vrontis, D., Weber, Y., Shams, S. M. R., & Tsoukatos, E. (Eds.), *The Changing Role of SMEs in Global Business*. Palgrave Studies in Cross-disciplinary Business Research, In Association with EuroMed Academy of Business. Palgrave Macmillan., DOI: 10.1007/978-3-030-45835-5_9

Tintor, V., Jovanović, N., Bocarova, V., & Bugarski, M. (2022). *Western Balkans Digital Economy Society Index - WB DESI 2022 Report*. Regional Cooperation Council.

Toader, C.S., Feher, A., Rujescu, C. (2025). The culinary heritage of Banat - how is it passed on to future generations? *Agricultura Banatului, 2*(164).

Toader, C. S., Brad, I., Feher, A. A., Sîrbu, C. C., & Sîrbulescu, C. (2022a). Aspects regarding the evolution of Romanian businesses related to collection of non-wood forest products from spontaneous flora. *Proceedings of the 5th International Scientific Conference on Water*, Szarvas, Hungary.

Toader, C. S., Feher, A., Orboi, M. D., Crainic, D., & Pîrvulescu, L. (2022b). Local gastronomic business - premise for the development of Romanian gastronomic tourism. *Review on Agriculture and Rural Development, 11*(1-2), 133–138. Advance online publication. DOI: 10.14232/rard.2022.1-2.133-138

Todorović, M., & Štetić, S. (2009). Ruralni turizam, Univerzitet u Beogradu, Geografski fakultet, Beograd.

Tohidyan Far, S., & Rezaei-Moghaddam, K. (2019). Multifunctional agriculture: An approach for entrepreneurship development of agricultural sector. *Journal of Global Entrepreneurship Research, 9*(1), 1–23. DOI: 10.1186/s40497-019-0148-4

Tomashuk, I., Koliadenko, S., & Burdiak, M. (2025). The impact of digital innovations on the development of agricultural business. *Baltic Journal of Economic Studies, 11*(1), 361–375. DOI: 10.30525/2256-0742/2025-11-1-361-375

Toth, A., Nagy, L., Kennedy, R., Bohus, B., Abonyi, J., & Ruppert, T. (2023). The human-centric Industry 5.0 collaboration architecture. *MethodsX, 11*, 102260. DOI: 10.1016/j.mex.2023.102260 PMID: 37388166

Tregear, A. (2011). Progressing knowledge in alternative and local food networks: Critical reflections and a research agenda. *Journal of Rural Studies, 27*(4), 419–430. DOI: 10.1016/j.jrurstud.2011.06.003

Tregubov, O. (2024). Digital Transformation of SMEs in the EU: Support, Strategic Initiatives, and Challenges on the Path to Sustainable Development. In *4th International conference on economics, accounting and finance* (*ICEAF*). Scientific Center of Innovative Research, Estonia. DOI: 10.36690/ICEAF-2024-33-34

Treisman, D. (2000). The causes of corruption: A cross-national study. *Journal of Public Economics, 76*(3), 399–457. DOI: 10.1016/S0047-2727(99)00092-4

Trendov, N. M., Varas, S., & Zeng, M. (2019). *Digital technologies in agriculture and rural areas: Status report*. Food and Agriculture Organization of the United Nations., https://www.fao.org/3/ca4985en/ca4985en.pdf

Tuli, F. (2010). The basis of distinction between quantitative and qualitative in social science: Reflection on ontological, epistemological and methodological perspectives. *Ethiopian Journal of Education and Sciences*, *6*(1), 97–108.

Ugrenović, V., Saljnikov, E., Pivić, R., Koković, N., Grujić, T., Filipović, V., Oljača, S., Simić, I., Subić, J., & Jeločnik, M. (2022). *Klimatska neutralnost poljoprivrede* [Climate neutrality of agriculture]. MAFWM. https://www.researchgate.net/publication/359203824_ Klimatska_neutralnost_poljoprivrede.

Uliu, D.V. & Vladu M. (2020). Researches regarding the increase and modernization of the meat processing capacities by using the funds offered through the National Rural Development Program in the North West Development Region. *Scientific Papers. Series "Management, Economic Engineering in Agriculture and rural development"*, *20*(1).

UN. (2015). *Adoption of the Paris Agreement* (FCCC/CP/2015/L.9/Rev.1). UNFCCC.

UN. (2019). *Improved soil carbon, soil health and soil fertility under grassland and cropland as well as integrated systems, including water management.* Koronivia joint work on agriculture. Workshop report (FCCC/SB/2019/2). UNFCCC.

UN. (2025). Message to Parties and Observers. *UN Climate Change Quarterly Update: Q4 2024*. ES/MTP/O/QR4 2024. https://unfccc.int/about-us/reports-highlights/quarterly-updates/un-climate-change-quarterly-update-q4-2024

UNCTAD. (2022). World Investment Report. https://unctad.org

UNDP. (2022). *Central Asia Human Development Report.* United Nations Development Programme.

UNEP. (2016). *Definitions and Concepts: Background Note for G20 Green Finance Study Group.*

UNEP. (2024). *Emissions gap report 2024: No more hot air ... please! With a massive gap between rhetoric and reality, countries draft new climate commitments.* UNEP., DOI: 10.59117/20.500.11822/46404

UNFCCC. (2022). *Sharm el-Sheikh joint work on implementation of climate action on agriculture and food security.* Decision 3/CP.27 (FCCC/CP/2022/10/Add.1). UNFCCC.

UNIDO. (2020). *Short food supply chains for promoting local food on local markets.* United Nations Industrial Development Organization.

Unković, S., & Zečević, B. (2011). Ekonomika turizma, Univerzitet u Beogradu, Ekonomski fakultet, Centar za izdavačku delatnost, Beograd.

USDA – U.S. Department of Agriculture. (2022). *FoodData Central: Raspberries, raw*. https://fdc.nal.usda.gov/

Vachudova, M. A. (2005). *Europe Undivided: Democracy, Leverage, and Integration After Communism*. Oxford University Press. DOI: 10.1093/0199241198.001.0001

Vahdanjoo, M., Grøn Sørensen, C., & Nørremark, M. (2025). Digital transformation of the agri-food system. *Current Opinion in Food Science*, *63*, 101287. Advance online publication. DOI: 10.1016/j.cofs.2025.101287

Vajda, B., Drăgan, G., Vajda, L., Gáspár, M.-M., & Bagoly, M. L. (2025). The Role of Entrepreneurial Clusters in Advancing Circular Bioeconomy and Innovation: A Case Study from Romania. *Sustainability (Basel)*, *17*(9), 3787. DOI: 10.3390/su17093787

Valipour, M., Krasilnikof, J., Yannopoulos, S., Kumar, R., Deng, J., Roccaro, P., Mays, L., Grismer, M., & Angelakis, A. (2020). The evolution of agricultural drainage from the earliest times to the present. *Sustainability (Basel)*, *12*(1), 416. DOI: 10.3390/su12010416

Van Burg, E., Cornelissen, J., Stam, W., Jack, S., (2020). Advancing Qualitative Entrepreneurship Research: Leveraging Methodological Plurality for Achieving Scholarly Impact.

Van der Ploeg, J. D., & Roep, D. (2003). Multifunctionality and rural development: the actual situation in Europe. *Multifunctional agriculture: a new paradigm for European agriculture and rural development, 3*, 37-54.

Van der Ploeg, J. D. (2020). From biomedical to politico-economic crisis: The food system in times of Covid-19. *The Journal of Peasant Studies*, *47*(5), 944–972. DOI: 10.1080/03066150.2020.1794843

van der Voort, T. S., Verweij, S., Fujita, Y., & Ros, G. H. (2023). Enabling soil carbon farming: Presentation of a robust, affordable, and scalable method for soil carbon stock assessment. *Agronomy for Sustainable Development*, *43*(1), 22. DOI: 10.1007/s13593-022-00856-7

Vapa Tankosić, J., Ignjatijević, S., Lekić, N., Kljajić, N., Ivaniš, M., Andžić, S., & Ristić, D. (2023). The role of environmental attitudes and risk for adoption in respect to the farmers' participation in the agri-environmental practices. *Agriculture*, *13*(12), 2248. DOI: 10.3390/agriculture13122248

Vásáry, V., Biró, S., Kis, M., & Varga, E. (2021). Long-Term Vision For Rural Areas. *Multidiszciplináris kihívások, sokszínű válaszok-Gazdálkodás-és Szervezéstudományi folyóirat*, (1), 51-77.

Vásáry, V., & Szabolcs, B. (2020). Long-term vision of rural areas in Hungary, focusing on foresights. *Rural Areas and Development*, *17*, 90–104.

Vasilevska, Lj. (2009). Ruralni turizam u okviru multifunkcionalne poljoprivrede – mogućnosti i ograničenja, Zbornik radova, *Prva regionalna turistička konferencija: Regionalna saradnja u razvoju turizma*, Privredna komora Beograd, Beograd, 35-46.

Vermeulen, S., Bossio, D., Lehmann, J., Luu, P., Paustian, K., Webb, C., Augé, F., Bacudo, I., Baedeker, T., Havemann, T., Jones, C., King, R., Reddy, M., Sunga, I., Von Unger, M., & Warnken, M. (2019). A global agenda for collective action on soil carbon. *Nature Sustainability*, *2*(1), 2–4. DOI: 10.1038/s41893-018-0212-z

Verschuuren, J. (2017). Towards a regulatory design for reducing emissions from agriculture: Lessons from Australia's carbon farming initiative. *Climate Law*, *7*(1), 1–51. DOI: 10.1163/18786561-00701001

Verschuuren, J. (2022). Achieving agricultural greenhouse gas emission reductions in the EU post-2030: What options do we have? *Review of European, Comparative & International Environmental Law*, *31*(2), 246–257. DOI: 10.1111/reel.12448

Vesala, H. T., & Vesala, K. M. (2010). Entrepreneurs and producers: Identities of Finnish farmers in 2001 and 2006. *Journal of Rural Studies*, *26*(1), 21–30. DOI: 10.1016/j.jrurstud.2009.06.001

Vik, J., & McElwee, G. (2011). Diversification and the entrepreneurial motivations of farmers in Norway. *Journal of Small Business Management*, *49*(3), 390–410. DOI: 10.1111/j.1540-627X.2011.00327.x

Viswanathan, R., & Telukdarie, A. (2021). A systems dynamics approach to SME digitalization. *Procedia Computer Science*, *180*, 816–824. DOI: 10.1016/j.procs.2021.01.331

Vittersø, G., Torjusen, H., Laitala, K., Tocco, B., Biasini, B., Csillag, P., & de Labarre, M. D. (2019). Short food supply chains and their contributions to sustainability: Participants' views and perceptions from 12 European cases. *Sustainability (Basel)*, *11*(17), 4800. DOI: 10.3390/su11174800

Vlaicu, P. A., Gras, M. A., Untea, A. E., Lefter, N. A., & Rotar, M. C. (2024). Advancing livestock technology: Intelligent systemization for enhanced productivity, welfare, and sustainability. *AgriEngineering*, *6*(2), 1479–1496. DOI: 10.3390/agriengineering6020084

Volanen, R. (2000). For Harmony of functions: On governance of multifunctionality and its scientific support–the point of view of the ecological function. In *Seminar "Science and Governance: CAP and Multifunctionality of Agriculture within the European Research Area* (pp. 23-24).

Vreeland, J. R. (2003). *The IMF and Economic Development*. Cambridge University Press. DOI: 10.1017/CBO9780511615726

Vuković Vimić, A., Petrović, N., Weinreich, A., & Pistorius, T. (2021). *Nature-based Solutions for climate change and potential for their implementation in Serbia*. UNDP. https://www.klimatskepromene.rs/wp-content/uploads/2021/10/NBS_CC_SERBIA_English.pdf

Vuković, P. (2019). Informaciono-komunikacione tehnologije kao pretpostavka uspešnog razvoja ruralnog turizma u Republici Srbiji. Journal: *Zbornik Matice srpske za drustvene nauke*, 169 (1). pp 109-123, ISSN 0352-5732.

Vuković, P. (2019). Konkurentnost ruralnih turističkih destinacija u području Donjeg Podunavlja u Republici Srbiji, Monografija, Institut za ekonomiku poljoprivrede, Beograd.

Vuković, P., Čavlin, G., & Čavlin, M. (2015). Complementarity in the development of rural tourism with the development of thermal baths, spa and welness tourism. Journal: *Ekonomika poljoprivrede/Economic of Agriculture*, No.1, Vol. 62. pp.259-270.

Vuković, P., Andrei, J. V., Kljajic, N., & Arsic, S. (2024). Vasile, Jean A., Kljajić, N. and Arsić, S. (2024). Possibilities for active tourist holidays in rural areas in the region of AP Vojvodina, Serbia. *Journal of Tourism Management Research, 11*(1), 98–110. DOI: 10.18488/31.v11i1.3780

Walker, T. W. N., Kaiser, C., Strasser, F., Herbold, C. W., Leblans, N. I. W., Woebken, D., Janssens, I. A., Sigurdsson, B. D., & Richter, A. (2018). Microbial temperature sensitivity and biomass change explain soil carbon loss with warming. *Nature Climate Change*, *8*(10), 885–889. DOI: 10.1038/s41558-018-0259-x

Wang, H., & Lu, X. (2025). A Comparative Study on the Promoting Effects of Different Tourism Development Models on Rural Revitalization: Case Studies from Two Typical Villages in China. *Sustainability (Basel)*, *17*(2), 714. DOI: 10.3390/su17020714

Welter, F., Baker, T., Audretsch, D. B., & Gartner, W. B. (2017). Everyday entrepreneurship-a call for entrepreneurship research to embrace entrepreneurial diversity. *Entrepreneurship Theory and Practice*, *41*(3), 311–321. DOI: 10.1111/etap.12258

Weltin, M., Zasada, I., Piorr, A., Debolini, M., Geniaux, G., Moreno Perez, O., Scherer, L., Marco, L. T., & Schulp, C. J. E. (2018). Conceptualising fields of action for sustainable intensification – A systematic literature review and application to regional case studies. *Agriculture, Ecosystems & Environment, 257*, 68–80. DOI: 10.1016/j.agee.2018.01.023

Whitt, C. (2022). From flooded fields to a vanished lake: The politics of broken water cycles in the Bolivian Altiplano. *Geoforum, 131*, 243–251. DOI: 10.1016/j.geoforum.2018.03.009

Wiese, L., Wollenberg, E., Alcántara-Shivapatham, V., Richards, M., Shelton, S., Esther Hönle, S., Heidecke, C., Madari, B. E., & Chenu, C. (2021). Countries' commitments to soil organic carbon in Nationally Determined Contributions, *Climate Policy, 21*(8), 1005-1019. https://doi.org/. 2021.1969883.DOI: 10.1080/14693062

Wiesmeier, M., Urbanski, L., Hobley, E., Lang, B., von Lützow, M., Marin-Spiotta, E., van Wesemael, B., Rabot, E., Ließ, M., Garcia-Franco, N., Wollschl ger, U., Vogel, H.-J., & K gel-Knabner, I. (2019). Soil organic carbon storage as a key function of soils - a review of drivers and indicators at various scales. *Geoderma, 333*, 149–162. DOI: 10.1016/j.geoderma.2018.07.026

Wilson, G. A. (2001). From productivism to post-productivism… and back again? Exploring the (un) changed natural and mental landscapes of European agriculture. *Transactions of the Institute of British Geographers, 26*(1), 77–102. DOI: 10.1111/1475-5661.00007

Woodward, G., Bonada, N., Brown, L., Death, R., Durance, I., Gray, C., Hladyz, S., Ledger, M., Milner, A., Ormerod, S., Thompson, R., Pawar, S. (2016). The effects of climatic fluctuations and extreme events on running water ecosystems. *Philosophical Transactions of the Royal Society B: Biological Sciences*, 371(1694):20150274, DOI: 10.1098/rstb.2015.0274

World Bank. (2003). *Kyrgyz Republic: Enhancing Pro-Poor Growth*. World Bank.

World Bank. (2008). *Doing Business 2009*. World Bank.

World Bank. (2008). Doing Business 2009: Georgia Profile. https://www.worldbank.org

World Bank. (2009). World Development Report: Reshaping Economic Geography. https://www.worldbank.org

World Bank. (2010). Transition: The First Ten Years. https://www.worldbank.org

World Bank. (2021). *Digital agriculture: Tools, policies and perspectives*. World Bank., DOI: 10.1596/978-1-4648-1658-4

World Bank. (2021). Kazakhstan Economic Update. https://www.worldbank.org

World Bank. (2022). Worldwide Governance Indicators. https://info.worldbank.org/governance/wgi

World Bank. (2023). Kyrgyz Republic Poverty and Equity Brief. https://www.worldbank.org

World Bank. (2024). Georgia Overview. https://www.worldbank.org

World Bank. (2024).. . *State and Trends of Carbon Pricing, 2024*. Advance online publication. DOI: 10.1596/978-1-4648-2127-1

World Economic Forum. (2020). The Global Competitiveness Report 2020. https://www.weforum.org

Wróblewska, W., Pawlak, J., & Paszko, D. (2019). Economic aspects in the raspberry production on the example of farms from Poland, Serbia and Ukraine. *Journal of Horticultural Research*, *27*(2), 71–80. DOI: 10.2478/johr-2019-0019

Wronka-Pośpiech, M., & Twaróg, S. (2024). Social enterprises and short food supply chains: Insights from exploratory case studies. *Scientific Papers of Silesian University of Technology. Organization & Management/Zeszyty Naukowe Politechniki Slaskiej. Seria Organizacji i Zarzadzanie, (212)*. https://managementpapers.polsl.pl/wp-content/uploads/2025/02/212-Wronka-Po%C5%9Bpiech-Twar%C3%B3g.pdf

Wu, A., Liu, Y., & Song, D. (2021). The Impact of Regional Entrepreneurial Ecosystem on Farmers' Performance and Efficiency-Empirical Evidence from Zhejiang Province. *Agricultural Technology Economy*, (1), 12.

Wu, J. (2024). Digitizing Agriculture: Strategic Insights into Traditional Challenges and Modern Management Solutions. Advances in Economics. *Management and Political Sciences*, *121*(1), 215–219. DOI: 10.54254/2754-1169/121/20242631

Yang, J. Q., Zhang, X., Bourg, I. C., & Stone, H. A. (2021). 4D imaging reveals mechanisms of clay-carbon protection and release. *Nature Communications*, *12*(1), 622. DOI: 10.1038/s41467-020-20798-6

Ye, S., & Tiong, R. (2000). NPV-at-risk method in infrastructure project investment evaluation. *Journal of Construction Engineering and Management*, *126*(3), 227–233. DOI: 10.1061/(ASCE)0733-9364(2000)126:3(227)

Yin, R. K. (1994). Discovering the future of the case study. Method in evaluation research. *Evaluation Practice*, *15*(3), 283–290.

You, L., Xie, H., Wood Sichra, U., Guo, Z., & Wang, L. (2014). Irrigation potential and investment return in Kenya. *Food Policy*, *47*, 34–45. DOI: 10.1016/j.foodpol.2014.04.006

Yuan, Y., & Sun, Y. (2024). Practices, Challenges, and Future of Digital Transformation in Smallholder Agriculture: Insights from a Literature Review. *Agriculture*, *14*(12), 2193. DOI: 10.3390/agriculture14122193

Zaninović, V., & Skender, P. (2025). *[Placeholder for forthcoming work]*.

Zarić, V. (2025). *Struktura, ekonomska snaga i marketing proizvoda poljoprivrednih gazdinstva u Srbiji*, Republički zavod za statistiku, Beograd. Dostupno na: https://publikacije.stat.gov.rs/G2025/Pdf/G202512005.pdf

Zatrochova, M., & Katrencik, I. (2023). Investment evaluation methods for business performance. In Kryvinska, N., Greguš, M., & Fedushko, S. (Eds.), *Developments in Information and Knowledge Management Systems for Business Applications: Studies in Systems, Decision and Control* (pp. 211–244). Springer., DOI: 10.1007/978-3-031-27506-7_9

Zdravković, M., Grekulović, V., Štrbac, N., Zdravković, B., Gorgievski, M., Marković, M., & Marković, M. (2024). Malina i kupina gajene u Srbiji sa aspekta Zelene agende [Raspberries and blackberries grown in Serbia from the perspective of the Green Agenda]. *Ecologica*, *31*(114), 137–143. DOI: 10.18485/ecologica.2024.31.114.3

Zeithaml, V. A., Bitner, M. J., & Gremler, D. D. (2018). *Services marketing: Integrating customer focus across the firm*. McGraw-Hill.

Zepeda, L., & Li, J. (2006). Who buys local food? *Journal of Food Distribution Research*, *37*(3), 1–11.

Zhang, , BYang, , YBi, , J. (2011). Tracking the implementation of green credit policy in China: Top-down perspective and bottom-up reform. *Journal of environmental management, 92*(4), 1321-1327.

Zhang, K. H., & Song, S. (2001). Promoting exports: The role of inward FDI in China. *China Economic Review*, *11*(4), 385–396. DOI: 10.1016/S1043-951X(01)00033-5

Zhang, Q. (2016). *Precision agriculture technology for crop farming*. Taylor & Francis.

Zhang, X., & Yu, X. (2021). Short supply chain participation, and agrochemicals' use intensity and efficiency: Evidence from vegetable farms in China. *China Agricultural Economic Review*, *13*(4), 721–735. DOI: 10.1108/CAER-05-2020-0108

Zhan, J., & Santos Paulino, A. (2021). Investing in the Sustainable Development Goals: Mobilization, channeling, and impact. *Journal of International Business Policy*, *4*(1), 166–184. DOI: 10.1057/s42214-020-00093-3

Zhuravlova, T. (2019). BANK LENDING OF AGRICULTURAL ENTERPRISES. *Інвестиції: практика та досвід*, (23), 35-41.

Ziolkowska, J. (2015). Is desalination affordable? Regional cost and price analysis. *Water Resources Management*, *29*(5), 1385–1397. DOI: 10.1007/s11269-014-0901-y

Živanović Miljković, J., Popović, V., & Gajić, A. (2022). Land take processes and challenges for urban agriculture: A spatial analysis for Novi Sad, Serbia. *Land (Basel)*, *11*(6), 769. DOI: 10.3390/land11060769

Živanović Miljković, J., Popović, V., & Srnić, D. (2025). Spatial patterns and agricultural land use dynamics – A GIS-based analysis for peri-urban areas of Belgrade and Novi Sad, Serbia. In Sahana, M. (Ed.), *Remote Sensing and GIS in Peri-Urban Research – Perspectives on Global Change, Sustainability and Resilience* (pp. 617–638). Elsevier., DOI: 10.1016/B978-0-443-15832-2.00027-7

Živkov, D., Joksimović, M., & Balaban, S. (2021). Measuring parametric and semiparametric downside risks of selected agricultural commodities.

Živkov, D., Balaban, S., & Joksimović, M. (2022). Making a Markowitz portfolio with agricultural commodity futures. *Zemedelská Ekonomika*, *68*(6), 219–229. DOI: 10.17221/78/2022-AGRICECON

Zubović, J., Jeločnik, M., Zdravković, A., Subić, J., & Radovanović, S. (2018). Using spatial and seasonal panel model to determine impact of climatic factors on maize yields in Serbia. *Romanian Biotechnological Letters*, *23*(2), 13383–13393.

About the Contributors

Andrei Jean Vasile is full professor at Petroleum-Gas University of Ploiesti, Department of Business Administration and Ph.D mentor in economics at Bucharest University of Economic Studies, Romania. He is co-founder and scientific coordinator of the Research Network on Resources Economics and Bioeconomy. Andrei Jean-Vasile holds a Ph.D. in Economics from the National Institute of Economics Research – Romanian Academy of Sciences. He has earned a BA degree in Administrative Sciences (2005) and in Banks and Finances (2007) from the Petroleum-Gas University of Ploiesti. He has an MA degree in Economics, Administrative and Business Management (2007) earned at the same university. Jean Andrei is also Associate Editor of Economics of Agriculture (Serbia), scientific reviewer and committee member for numerous international conferences. He is member of scientific organizations: The Balkan Scientific Association of Agrarian Economists, Serbia (2008), DAAAM Vienna and Information Resources Management Association (2011). Issues like: agricultural economics and rural development, energy and resource economics and business economics are among his research and scientific interests.

Brumă Ioan Sebastian graduated the Faculty of Agriculture at the University of Agronomic Sciences and Veterinary Medicine in Bucharest and he is PhD in Agronomy since 2012, within the Doctoral School of the University of Agricultural Sciences and Veterinary Medicine "Ion Ionescu de la Brad" in Iasi. Since 2018 he is a scientific researcher grade II at the Institute of Economic and Social Research "Gh. Zane" of the Romanian Academy - Ia i Branch, where he has been working since 2004. His main academic background is in agronomy, with a special interest in organic agriculture, sustainable rural development, agricultural economics, rural entrepreneurship, rural economics, short food supply chains, urban food systems, consumer behavior and knowledge transfer. Research results have been disseminated through participation in over 100 national and international scientific conferences as well as the publication of over 130 studies and articles, as author or co-author. Since 2019 he is founding member and President of the Rural Development Research Platform Association.

Jonel Subic, Ph.D., Assistant Professor, and Principal Research Fellow had defended doctoral thesis under the title Determination of economic effectiveness of investments in agriculture (South Banat – FR Yugoslavia) in November 2003 at the Faculty of Management, Bucharest Academy of Economic Sciences, Romania. Since November 2004, he has been full-time employed in the Institute of Agricultural Economics Belgrade, Serbia within the sector for scientific-research work. Since January 2015 he worked as director of IAE. He is mainly oriented to agro-economy and economy, with special accent to the economic effectiveness of investments, strategic planning of local communities. He is author/co-author at over 200 bibliographic units with national and international importance. He is also a member of following professional associations: Balkan Environment Association (B.EN.A.); European Association of Agrarian Economists (E.A.A.E.); Serbian Association of Agrarian Economists (SAAE); Balkan Scientific Association of Agrarian Economists (BSAAE). Among editorial activities next can be pointed out: corresponding editor of the Journals International Journal of Sustainable Economies Management and Scientific Papers Series - Management, Economic Engineering in Agriculture and Rural Development; member of the scientific board of the Journal BULLETIN - Economic Sciences Series; member of supervisory committee of the Journals Economy - Management Series and Transition; associate editor of the Journal Economics of Agriculture; member of editorial board of the Journal Ekonomika.

Dumitru Nancu is an experienced professional with expertise in top management, corporate governance, finance, banking, public administration, and academia. He has built a distinguished career in the financial and public sectors while contributing significantly to economic development, digital transformation, and education. Dumitru Nancu has contributed to numerous articles and studies on economics, sustainability, and digital convergence.

Mile Vasic obtained his MA and PhD in the field of Human Resources Management. He has acted as a Dean of Faculty of Technical Sciences, Dean of Faculty of Economics and Management, Vice-Rector of PIM University and Vice-Rector and Rector of Slobomir P University. He was a guest lecture in Greece, Romania, Slovenia, Serbia, and the United Kingdom. Besides academic work, his passion is the implementation of scientific knowledge and skills in practice. He has been consulting and providing in-company training worldwide and most important clients were Coca-Cola, Renault, BH Mont Trade Srl., Johnson & Johnson, McDonald's, OMV. Between 2015 and 2018 professor Vasic served as an Ambassador Extraordinary and Plenipotentiary of Bosnia and Herzegovina to Romania. Dr. Mile Vasic is currently President of European Marketing and Management Association (EUMMAS).

***

Sotiris Apostolopoulos is a Lecturer in Entrepreneurship and Development at the University of Neapolis (Paphos, Cyprus). He also acts as Coordinator of the Undergraduate Programs in Business Administration & Digital Business of the Department of Economics and Business for the same University. He holds a PhD degree from the School of Management of University of the Peloponnese and two Master's degrees (MSc) in Healthcare Administration and in Finance as well. He specialises in rural entrepreneurship, European policies and the socio-economic development of the rural areas with emphasis on private and social health enterprises. His research interests focus on local development, European policies, private and social enterprises as well as on innovation. He has many years' experience working in the management of private companies. He served as Head of Communication and Public Relations of the Marketing Department of the Rehabilitation & Recovery Center "Diaplasis" in Greece and Chief Operating Officer (COO) at the largest regional private hospital "City Hospital" of the Peloponnese Region. His research articles have been published in major scientific journals by publishers such as Wiley, Emerald, MDPI, while he has participated in studies that were included and published as book chapters in edited volumes (IGI Global, Eburon, etc.). In parallel, he has taken part through research work in international and European conferences on Economics, Entrepreneurship and Innovation held in Greece, Cyprus, UK, Switzerland, Italy, Spain, Portugal and Montenegro. He has experience in submitting and implementing proposals related to European programmes. Recently, the World Health Organization included in its official database two research papers of Sotiris (co-author), concerning the rural health enterprises during the Covid-19 pandemic.

Diana-Elena Creangă is a business consultant, researcher and project manager. She is specialized in rural development. With a PhD focused on the role of clusters in rural economies, she has coordinated several projects with non-reimbursable funding. Diana has extensive experience in managing entrepreneurial programs. Through the projects she has carried out, she is dedicated to promoting entrepreneurship in rural communities. In her research activity, she carries out a sustained activity in publishing articles in peer-reviewed journals.

Biljana Grujic Vuckovski graduated 2010 on the Faculty of Agriculture, University of Belgrade. Doctoral thesis degree 2017 at the Faculty of Business Studies, Megatrend University (John Naisbitt University), and gained title a Ph.D. of Economic Sciences. She is employed in the Tamiš Research and Development Institute Pančevo, Serbia from 2024 on possition Senior Research Associate. The main area of research is rural policy, sustainable agriculture, rural development, and rural economy.

Marijana Joksimović is a Full-Time Professor at Alfa BK University and a Senior Scientific Associate at the Institute for Agricultural Economics in Belgrade. Born in 1980 in Čačak, Serbia, she completed her undergraduate and master's studies in financial services management at the Faculty of Utility Business in Novi Sad, and earned her PhD from the Faculty of Business Studies at Megatrend University in 2010. Her academic career began in 2006 as an assistant, progressing through roles at both the Faculty of Utility Business and Megatrend University, where she was promoted to Associate Professor in 2015. She later joined Alfa BK University, where she has served as Vice-Dean, University Quality Committee Secretary, and Rector (2021–2022), and currently serves as Director of International Cooperation. Prof. Joksimović was elected Scientific Associate in 2016 at the Faculty of Economics, University of Priština, and promoted to Senior Scientific Associate in 2023. Her research focuses on international economics and international finance. She teaches Banking, Financial Risk Management, and International Business Finance. She has published over 110 scientific and professional papers, five books, and three monographs. In addition to her academic roles, she is a reviewer for SSCI- and Scopus-listed journals and serves on the editorial boards of Megatrend Review, Ecologika, and Audit, where she is also Finance Editor. She was a visiting professor at Franklin University from SAD in 2014/15 and visiting professor at Adratic University from Monte Negro in 2022/2023.

Nataša Ž. Kljajić was born on August 24, 1975, in Serbia. She graduated from the Faculty of Agriculture, University of Belgrade in 2000, earned her master's degree in 2007, and obtained her Ph.D. in Agricultural Sciences in 2012 at the University of Novi Sad, focusing on the economic efficiency of raspberry production investments. Since 2006, she has been employed at the Institute of Agricultural Economics in Belgrade, where she is a Senior Research Associate and member of both the Management Board and Scientific Council. She has participated in national and international projects on sustainable agriculture and raspberry production, including a key project on rural development within the Danube Region. As an author or co-author, she has published over 80 scientific and professional works.

She is a member of several professional associations in the fields of agroeconomics, soil science, and environmental protection.

Branko Mihailović was born on October 19, 1978, in Smederevska Palanka, Republic of Serbia. He graduated from the Faculty of Economics, Marketing Department, in Belgrade, on April 23, 2002. He completed his master's studies with the thesis titled "The Role of Consulting in Enterprise Restructuring in Transition" on March 6, 2006, at the Faculty of Economics, Management Department, in Belgrade. His doctoral dissertation, titled "Development of Consulting Services in Serbia and Their Impact on the Performance of Enterprises in the Agribusiness Sector," was successfully defended on January 26, 2010, at the Faculty of Business Economics in Valjevo. From 2002 to 2005, he was employed at the Institute for Market Research (IZIT), Belgrade, within the Center for Marketing Research and Consulting. Since April 15, 2006, he has been employed at the Institute of Agricultural Economics in Belgrade, in the sector for scientific research. He is a Scientific Advisor in the field of Economic Sciences and a Full Professor in the narrower scientific field of Economics and Finance.

Andra-Sabina Neculai-Valeanu is a researcher (PhD, Vet Med) in animal science & agri-digital innovation. Passionate about One Health, sustainability, and promoting gender equity by empowering women in science & youth in STEM.

Nataša Papić-Blagojević has been a professor of applied studies in undergraduate and master's programs at the Department of Quantitative Analysis and Business Informatics at the Novi Sad School of Business, Republic of Serbia, since 2005. She has extensive experience as a coordinator and researcher on both national and international projects. Her research output includes more than 90 scientific papers published in journals, monographs, and presented at national and international conferences. She is the author or co-author of several books, including Quantitative Methods, Financial and Actuarial Mathematics, Financial Mathematics and Tariff Calculation in Life Insurance, as well as publications such as EU Handbook, How Well Do We Know Each Other?, and EU for Youth – Challenges and Opportunities.

Vesna Popović is PhD in Economics and works as Principal Research Fellow at the Institute of Agricultural Economics (IAE), Belgrade, Serbia. She deals with issues related to agricultural trade and trade policy, sustainable agriculture and rural development, and land use policy and planning.

Katica Radosavljević was born on July 16, 1975, in Gothenburg, Sweden. Since 2000, she has been employed at the Faculty of Economics, University of Belgrade. As of January 2024, she holds the position of Senior Research Associate at the Institute of Agricultural Economics. She successfully defended her doctoral dissertation titled The strategy of marketing channel development in agribusiness of the Republic of Serbia. As an author or co-author, she has contributed to more than 70 bibliographic entries. She has been actively involved as a principal investigator or researcher in numerous projects of both scientific and professional significance. She is a member of the Scientific Society of Economists of Serbia and serves on the editorial board of the journal Acadlore Mecha: Opportunities and Challenges in Sustainability.

Gordana Radović has published more than 100 scientific, review and research papers. She has a self-published monograph called *Agricultural Financing in the Republic of Serbia in 2014*, as a monograph of national importance, which is the result of her years' long research in the field of agricultural financing in the Republic of Serbia. She has a self-published monograph called *Agricultural Insurance in the Republic of Serbia in 2024*, as a monograph of national importance, which is the result of her years' long research in the field of agricultural insurance in the Republic of Serbia.

Natia Surmanidze is an Associate Professor and researcher with a focus on political economy and institutional development. She holds a PhD in Economics, with her dissertation focusing on the issue of institutional reforms in transition economies. Her research mainly focuses on market liberalization, governance, and economic transformation in post-socialist environments. Dr. Surmanidze has contributed immensely to academic literature, publishing several peer-reviewed articles related to liberalization and reform processes in developing economies.

Cosmina-Simona Toader is currently lecturer at Faculty of Management and Rural Tourism from University of Life Sciences “King Mihai I” from Timisoara, Romania, author of 2 works guides dedicated to students (Project Management. Applications. Case studies. Tests; Project Planning...from idea to project), 1 course for students (Project Management), author and co-author of over 150 articles published in the volumes of national and international scientific events in the field of management, project management, agricultural business management and tourism. She currently teaches Engineering and Project Management, Agricultural Business Management, Business Management, Business Entrepreneurship, Tourism Products.

Predrag Vuković is senior research associate. Graduated 2003 on the Faculty of Economics, University of Belgrade. Postgraduate specialist studies finished 2006 and Master's thesis degree 2008. Doctoral thesis 2016 degreed at the Faculty of Economics, University of Kragujevac. He has been working in the Institute of Agricultural Economics, Belgrade since 2004. He has been actively engaging as a member of the research team on projects of the Ministry of Education, Science and Technological Development of the Republic of Serbia. He has also been engaged in numerous projects of the Institute of Agricultural Economics, as well as the development of a numerous of development strategies of cities, municipalities and local communities as a member of research teams and manager of project teams. In doctoral thesis, master thesis, specialist thesis and numerous scientific articles published in national and international professional journals, presented at scientific conferences of national and international importance, he dealing with the issues of tourism marketing, management of tourist destinations, rural tourism, rural development and agriculture issues of economics. He is member of scie

Jelena Živanović Miljković is a spatial and urban planner. She holds a PhD in Spatial Planning (University of Belgrade, Serbia) and works as a Senior Research Fellow at the Institute of Architecture and Urban & Spatial Planning of Serbia (IAUS). Her expertise includes spatial and urban planning, land use, zoning regulation, and spatial analyses. Main research fields include land use, land policy, land rights, agricultural land, urban and peri-urban development. She participated in five national and international scientific projects and published over 50 scientific papers in relevant scientific publications.

Index

A

B

C

D

N

P

R

S

www.ingramcontent.com/pod-product-compliance
Lightning Source LLC
LaVergne TN
LVHW061528290926
849162LV00004B/709